The
BOOKER T. WASHINGTON
Papers

The
BOOKER T. WASHINGTON
Papers

VOLUME 11

1911–12

Louis R. Harlan
and
Raymond W. Smock

EDITORS

Geraldine McTigue

ASSISTANT EDITOR

University of Illinois Press
URBANA · CHICAGO · LONDON

The Booker T. Washington *Papers*
is supported by
The National Endowment for the Humanities
The National Historical Publications and Records Commission
The University of Maryland

© 1981 BY THE BOARD OF TRUSTEES OF THE UNIVERSITY OF ILLINOIS
MANUFACTURED IN THE UNITED STATES OF AMERICA

Library of Congress Cataloging in Publication Data

Washington, Booker Taliaferro, 1856–1915.
   The Booker T. Washington papers.

   Vol. 11   edited by L. R. Harlan and R. W. Smock
Geraldine McTigue, assistant editor.
   Includes bibliographies.
   CONTENTS: v. 1. The autobiographical writings.
—v. 2.   1860–89.–[etc.]—v. 11, 1911–12.
   1. Washington, Booker T., 1856–1915.
   2. Afro-Americans—History—1863–1877—Sources.
   3. Afro-Americans—History—1877–1964—Sources.
   4. Afro-Americans—Correspondence. I. Harlan,
Louis R.   II.   Smock, Raymond W.
   E185.97.W274   301.45'19'6073024   75–186345
   ISBN 0-252-00887-1 (v. 11)

To the Faculty of
Tuskegee Institute, 1881–1915

CONTENTS

vii

Contents

CONTENTS

xiii

Contents

Contents

INTRODUCTION

In the years covered by this volume, Booker T. Washington personally and his Tuskegee Machine suffered systemic shocks from which they only partially recovered. The volume begins with the Ulrich incident. It ends during the presidential campaign of 1912, when Washington's personal liking for Theodore Roosevelt was in conflict with his loyalty to the Republican party and to William Howard Taft, the party nominee.

On the night of March 18, 1911, a white man named Henry Albert Ulrich brutally beat Washington with a cane and brought about his arrest on the charge of molesting Ulrich's wife and peeking through the keyhole in the vestibule of his apartment in a West Side district of uncertain reputation in New York City. Washington said he was in the neighborhood in search of the auditor of Tuskegee Institute, and when the police found out who Washington was they released him and charged Ulrich with assault. Many aspects of this incident are inexplicable, and after a long-delayed trial the assailant was acquitted by the split decision of a three-judge court.

During the wave of sympathy for Washington that followed news of the assault, Oswald Garrison Villard tried to bring about a rapprochement between the Tuskegean and the National Association for the Advancement of Colored People. Washington was willing to exchange delegates between the NAACP and the National Negro Business League, but when Washington's black enemies in the NAACP supported a resolution of sympathy but blocked an expression of faith in Washington's innocence in the Ulrich incident, the efforts at accord broke down.

In February of 1911 Washington purchased a house on Long Island that became his summer headquarters. It was well that he did so, for the hotel where he generally stayed during his frequent trips to New York refused him accommodations after the Ulrich incident, on the ground that the swarm of reporters disrupted the work of the hotel and gave it a notoriety it did not want. Washington got little rest at his summer home, however, for he brought with him an entourage of secretaries and stenographers to keep up with his heavy correspondence and to prepare a number of articles.

Washington was busy in these years with the promotion of many enterprises of the Tuskegee Machine. He continued to lead the Jeanes Foundation in the improvement of teaching in the black rural schools, continued to select the small industrial schools to receive contributions from Jacob Schiff, and began a close collaboration with Julius Rosenwald, who became a trustee of Tuskegee Institute in 1912. He advised the Census Bureau on the gathering and classification of racial data. He encouraged and secured financial support for the efforts of the all-black town of Mound Bayou, Mississippi, and spoke at the dedication of its cottonseed-oil mill in November 1912. He secured the appointment of the black Boston lawyer William H. Lewis to the highest federal post held by a black man prior to the New Deal, as assistant attorney general in the Taft administration. Continuing the educational speaking tours of previous years, he traveled through Texas in 1911 and Florida in 1912.

Washington also broadened his interests to include other continents. He organized the International Conference of the Friends of Africa in the spring of 1912, attracting to it missionaries and spokesmen of the black people of western and southern Africa. In 1910 he toured England and the continent of Europe in order to study conditions of life among the working classes of London, Liverpool, the Sicilian sulphur mines, the Warsaw ghetto, and various places in the Austro-Hungarian Empire. His observations led to a book, *The Man Farthest Down,* published the following year. While Washington's main interest was the working class in Europe, he also took the opportunity to dine with the king and queen of Denmark.

In 1911 Washington published *My Larger Education.* The autobiographical parts of this volume have been reproduced in the first volume of *The Booker T. Washington Papers.* The sociologist Robert E. Park was the principal author of *The Man Farthest Down* (1912), and it was Park who held the copyright. Included in this volume of the

Booker T. Washington Papers are parts of *The Man Farthest Down* that appeared in article form.

Washington's political role as presidential adviser had steadily declined all through the Taft administration, both because of disfranchisement and because Taft had no genuine sympathy with black political aspirations. The presidential campaign of 1912 posed a special dilemma for Washington. One of the candidates, Roosevelt, was a long-time patron of Washington and a member of the Tuskegee Institute board of trustees. Taft, on the other hand, was a fellow trustee of the Jeanes Foundation and a symbol of regular Republicanism. The evidence shows that Washington himself supported Taft, despite his political neglect of blacks and removal of many black officeholders, because of party loyalty.

The editors appreciate the help in the preparation of this volume given by Handy Bruce Fant, Sara D. Jackson, Richard Sheldon, and the staff of the Division of Manuscripts of the Library of Congress. Sadie M. Harlan has saved us from many errors and omissions. Linda Waskey and Susan M. Valenza helped with the typing and proofreading.

We are grateful to the National Endowment for the Humanities, the National Historical Publications and Records Commission, and the University of Maryland for their support of this project.

SYMBOLS AND ABBREVIATIONS

Sᴛᴀɴᴅᴀʀᴅ ᴀʙʙʀᴇᴠɪᴀᴛɪᴏɴs for dates, months, and states are used by the editors only in footnotes and endnotes; textual abbreviations are reproduced as found.

DOCUMENT SYMBOLS

1. A — autograph; written in author's hand
   H — handwritten by other than signator
   P — printed
   T — typed

2. C — postcard
   D — document
   E — endorsement
   L — letter
   M — manuscript
   W — wire (telegram)

3. c — carbon
   d — draft
   f — fragment
   p — letterpress
   t — transcript or copy made at much later date

4. I — initialed by author
   r — representation; signed or initialed in author's name
   S — signed by author

Among the more common endnote abbreviations are: ALS — autograph letter, signed by author; TLpI — typed letter, letterpress copy, initialed by author.

REPOSITORY SYMBOLS

Symbols used for repositories are the standard ones used in *Symbols of American Libraries in the National Union Catalog of the Library of Congress,* 10th ed. (Washington, D.C., 1969).

A-Ar	Alabama Department of Archives and History, Montgomery, Ala.
ATT	Tuskegee Institute, Tuskegee, Ala.
DCU	Catholic University of America, Washington, D.C.
DHU	Howard University, Washington, D.C.
DLC	Library of Congress, Washington, D.C.
MH	Harvard University, Cambridge, Mass.
MU	University of Massachusetts, Amherst
NNC	Columbia University, NYC
NcD	Duke University, Durham, N.C.

OTHER ABBREVIATIONS

BTW	Booker T. Washington
Con.	Container
NNBL	National Negro Business League
RG	Record Group
Ser.	Series

Documents, 1911–12

From Emmett Jay Scott

Tuskegee Ala [Mar.] 20 1911

Garland Penn calls me from Atlanta on telephone early this morning to say that sensational article of column in length appears in Constitution this morning respecting yourself   have requested him to telegraph character of article to you, and to urge that you see officials of associated press and have these harmful statements corrected in afternoon editions today and in tomorrow mornings papers. Shall do everything possible at this end to counteract effects. Shall send out dispatch today from here expressing confidence of teachers and officers if you think well of it   please instruct me fully.

E. J. S.

HWIr   Con. 607   BTW Papers   DLC.

Emmett Jay Scott to Nathan Hunt

Tuskegee Ala   3/20 1911

Telegraphed you this morning that Montclair friend[1] is here despite strongest kind of pressure from all parts of Country neither he nor I have replied to any telegraphic messages.

Emmett J Scott

HWSr   Con. 606   BTW Papers   DLC.

¹ Daniel Cranford Smith.

Emmett Jay Scott to Nathan Hunt

Tuskegee Ala   3/20 1911

Your telegram recd   unable to understand from it what Copies of letter you wish. Please telegraph me definitely today to Fearing so he can be advised by friends   will meet you at Drew Wednesday.

E J S

HWIr   Con. 606   BTW Papers   DLC.

3

Nathan Hunt to Charles H. Fearing

New York   Mch 20 [1911]

What I want was copies of letters written me by Scott since I left there
— if he did not bring them let matter go   you need not answer any
paper Telegrams.

N H

AWIr   Con. 606   BTW Papers   DLC.

From Henry E. Baker[1]

Washington, D.C., March 20 [1911]

My dear Mr. Washington — I was greatly shocked to read this morning of the outrageous assault upon you last night in New York City,
and I write to offer you my sincere sympathy. To be sure you will be
sustained by the strongest public sentiment and sympathy in every effort you make to bring your assailant[2] to swift and ample justice. Yours
very truly,

Henry E. Baker

ALS   Con. 434   BTW Papers   DLC.

[1] Henry E. Baker was an examiner in the U.S. Patent Office in Washington.
He had been in 1898 the treasurer of Manassas Industrial School.

[2] Henry Albert Ulrich, the assailant, a carpenter by trade, was proprietor of
the West Side Dog Exchange. He had left his wife and two daughters in Orange,
N.J., to live at 11½ West Sixty-third Street, New York City, with Laura Page
Alvarez and her daughter. He had been accused earlier in the year of stealing a
prize Pomeranian, but had been acquitted. Ulrich was a stocky, powerful man in
his forties, about five feet, seven inches tall. After his acquittal on the assault
charge in November 1911, he was imprisoned in Orange County jail for refusal
to pay for child support. BTW described Ulrich as "a 'ward heeler' for one of the
political captains in that part of the city," whose "political influence" secured
Ulrich's acquittal. (BTW to F. K. Collins, Aug. 21, 1912, Con. 451, BTW Papers,
DLC.) The most detailed treatment of the assault is Willard B. Gatewood, "Booker
T. Washington and the Ulrich Affair," *Phylon,* 30 (Fall 1969), 286–302.

From Roscoe Conkling Bruce

Washington, D.C. March 20, 1911

My dear Dr. Washington: I make haste to send you the enclosed clippings from the Washington Post and the Washington Herald. This is certainly a classical instance of how the maudlin talk about the Negro for political purposes has affected the minds of some white people in various sections of the country making them commit acts of the grossest cruelty and injustice. But my purpose in writing to you is to urge upon you the importance of having some person like Seth Low give out to the press a statement of the facts in the case. *I would also earnestly urge that this man Ulrich be punished to fullest extent of the law.* I write hastily but I feel very deeply of this subject.

Believe me, Ever your obedient servant,

Roscoe C. Bruce

TLS   Con. 434   BTW Papers   DLC.

From Francis H. Hill[1]

Tuskegee Institute, Ala., March 20th. 1911

My Dear Doctor Washington: I was simply horror struck when I learned of the dastardly assault made upon you.

The very thought of you, our Leader and Faithful Principal lying in a distant city bruised and bleeding fills me with a grief inexpressible.

Rather, a hundred times and more, would I have received those fearful blows upon my body and saved you than to have you stricken down in so violent a manner.

God is good. The cause of His servants He will plead. You are His servant. He will care for you. God bless and keep you. Sincerely and Fraternally yours,

F. H. Hill

TLS   BTW Papers   ATT.

[1] Francis H. Hill was a teacher in the Phelps Hall Bible Training School of Tuskegee Institute from 1909 to 1913.

From J. Douglas Wetmore

New York City   March 20th, 1911

Dear Mr. Washington: I cannot tell you how shocked and grieved I was when I saw by this morning's paper an account of the cowardly assault made upon you last night, and I was very sorry that our relations of late had not been such that would have justified my immediately going to you and offering what advice and assistance I might be able to give under the circumstances. I have had at least twenty people speak to me about the occurrence to-day and regardless of race they have expressed themselves as believing entirely your version of the matter, and also expressed their sympathy for you.

In that street and in that particular block there are a great many dissolute men and women, and in my opinion there is no other block in the City of New York where colored men are worse hated and more liable to assault than 66th Street between Columbus Avenue and Central Park West. On the corner of Columbus Avenue and 66th St. there is a saloon and restaurant known as "Healy's" and it is notorious as a rendezvous of Negro haters, and a great many colored men have been assaulted and beaten up in or near said saloon. It was only a few weeks ago, certainly not more than a month, that a well known musical entertainer was brutally assaulted at this place. There are a great many women living in this neighborhood known as "street walkers" a considerable number of whom have what is commonly called "lovers" whom they support, and of course quite a number of this low type of men are colored, the result of which is most of the white men in that neighborhood (nearly all of whom are of the common, ordinary type) detest colored men and especially when they are well dressed, and whenever the opportunity offers itself on any kind of a pretext whatever, they proceed to assault any well appearing colored man who is caught in that vicinity, and they probably justify their actions in the belief that said colored man must certainly belong to the type known as "lovers." I realize as fully as you must that this occurrence may do you untold injury with white Southerners on account of the lie told by the wife of the man who assaulted you, so I think you ought to leave no stone unturned in trying to show to the world the true facts concerning the neighborhood and the class of people living there, and

I also think you ought to have a thorough and rigid investigation made as to the character of the man who assaulted you and of the woman who claims to be his wife, for unless you can prove that they are both unworthy of belief, and that blind, unreasoning race prejudice was the cause of this unfair and unjust attack upon you physically, and upon your character, you and the race will suffer untold injury as the result of last night's occurrence.

It is only by the exercise of great selfcontrol that I have been able to keep away from your hotel to-day, as I wanted so much to tell you the things I have just written, but I feared my motives might have been misunderstood so would not call but decided to take a chance and write you anyhow. If I can be of any assistance to you in any way whatever, you have only to command me. Please understand that I am not seeking employment as an attorney, but offering my services to a man for whom I have the highest respect and the kindliest feeling, said services to be rendered gratis.

When I think of the pleasant hours we have spent together and the friendship that once existed between us, and then think that differences of opinion as to public affairs had so far estranged us, that when you were in trouble last night you did not telephone me, and that after I found out about your trouble I did not feel at liberty to call on you, I cannot but think how foolish after all, men are to allow differences of opinions to keep them from being good friends otherwise.

With best wishes for your speedy recovery, and for the best outcome for you of this whole unfortunate affair, I am, Very sincerely yours,

J. Douglas Wetmore

TLS BTW Papers ATT.

George Livingston Peabody[1] to Seth Low

New York, 20 March, 1911

My dear Seth: I was a witness of the case in which Mr. Washington was a victim last night *after the arrival* of the policeman. There was only a small group of people, and I had an opportunity of talking with the chief assailant. I am entirely convinced of the integrity of his belief that he was chasing a marauder: he was very much in earnest — an earnestness which, under the circumstances, I do not believe he could have simulated. On the other hand Mr. Washington, (whom I did not recognize) presented a picture of dignity and reserve force in spite of his excitement and his bleeding face. I left the scene sorely puzzled; and I want to say to you that I have no doubt that it is all the result of a very unfortunate mistake. I do not know the aggressor. I never saw him before, and shall never see him again, and I feel that the whole affair is very deplorable. But I do not believe that he was doing anything beyond what he thought the protection of his rights justified. I am taking my daughter to Lakewood for a week to-morrow; other-wise I should be glad to call upon you. Yours sincerely,

George L. Peabody

TLSr Copy Seth Low Papers NNC.

[1] George Livingston Peabody (1850–1914), a prominent physician in New York City, had been a classmate of Seth Low at Columbia College.

Augustus W. Abbott to Edward Thomas Devine

Orange, N.J. March 20, 1911

My dear Dr. Devine: This Society is interested in the family of a man named Henry Adam [Albert] Ulrich. His wife, Mrs. Mary J. Ulrich, resides at No. 224 High St., Orange, N.J. with her two children: Estelle, born July 8th, 1901, and Dorothy H., born May 10th, 1909.

On Feb. 21, 1911, at our request Mrs. Ulrich appeared against her husband in the Domestic Relations Court, New York City, at which time she made a charge against her husband for desertion and non-support, as a result of which she informs us that the Magistrate ordered Mr. Ulrich to pay $5. per week for her support and also to pay the rent of $23. per month. He is sending his wife $5. per week by postal money order, but he is paying no attention to the matter of the rent. We have written him twice with regard to this matter, but have received no response.

Mr. Ulrich is a carpenter by trade and is also proprietor of the

West Side Dog Exchange, No. 779 — 11th Avenue, near 54th St., New York City, and his wife reports to us that she has every reason to believe her husband is making lots of money, and is living with another woman at No. 11½ West 63rd St., N.Y.C. This woman's maiden name is reported to us as being Laura Page and she was married to a Spaniard named Alvarez, by whom she has one daughter, Dolores, about ten years old. Mrs. Alvarez is said not be living with her own husband at this time.

Our object in calling your attention to this matter is because of the fact that today newspaper articles have appeared with regard to an assault upon Dr. Booker T. Washington and this man Ulrich is said to be the one who committed the assault, on which I understand a hearing took place in the West Side Police Court today. The newspaper articles state emphatically that Mr. Ulrich's wife and daughter were in court, but Mrs. Ulrich was at our office this afternoon with regard to these newspaper stories to ask what action could be taken against her husband for living with this [wo]man and having her and her daughter pass off as his wife and child. Surely there must be some law in New York prohibiting this kind of living and we shall be glad if you will advise us as to what we should say to Mrs. Ulrich and advise her as to what action she could bring against her husband for living with Mrs. Alvarez as man and wife.

We are writing Dr. Washington by this mail, informing him of our knowledge of Mr. Ulrich and perhaps you might be able to take this matter up with him personally, as we see by the paper that he is at The Armstrong Association, No. 39 East 42nd Street, N.Y.C. (Phone number, Murray Hill 1786). Something really ought to be done we think to bring such a man as this to justice and we only regret that because of the fact that he is living out of the State of New Jersey we cannot reach him here.

We shall appreciate your kindness if you will let us hear from you about this matter at an early date. Yours very truly,

A. W. Abbott

TLSr Copy   Seth Low Papers   NNC.   Written on stationery of the Children's Aid and Protective Society of the Oranges, of which Augustus W. Abbott was agent.

To Booker Taliaferro Washington, Jr.

[New York City] March 21, 1911

Trial held this afternoon. Defendant afraid to go to trial and waived examination which means practical guilt. Whole thing lasted about three minutes. Judges, lawyers and everybody else most kind.

B. T. W.

TWcIr Con. 446 BTW Papers DLC. Addressed to BTW, Jr., at Fisk University.

From William Howard Taft

[Washington, D.C.] March 21, 1911

My dear Doctor Washington: I am greatly distressed at your misfortune and I hasten to write you of my sympathy, my hope that you will soon recover from the wounds inflicted by insane suspicion or viciousness, and of my confidence in you, in your integrity and morality of character, and in your highest usefulness to your race and to all the people of this country.

It would be a nation's loss if this untoward incident in any way impaired your great power for good in the solution of one of the most difficult problems before us.

I want you to know that your friends are standing by you in every trial and that I am proud to subscribe myself as one,

WM. H. TAFT

TLSr Copy William Howard Taft Papers DLC. Docketed: "Sent in the President's handwriting." The letter was widely reprinted in the newspapers.

Nathan Hunt to Charles H. Fearing

New York   Mch 21 [1911]

If Montclair[1] not left Tuskegee ask him leave on next train for here

Stopping Payton's House thirteen West one thirty first St   Telephone
me soon as reaching here   Telegraph answer.

N H

AWIr Con. 606 BTW Papers DLC.

¹ Daniel Cranford Smith.

Charles H. Fearing to Daniel Cranford Smith

[Tuskegee, Ala.] March 21, 1911

N. H. requests you go direct to Payton's, thirteen West One Hundred
Thirty first Street   Telephone N. H. as soon as you get there.

F.

TWpIr Con. 55 BTW Papers DLC. Addressed to Smith on a Southern
Railway train en route at Greensboro, N.C.

From Philip J. Allston¹

Boston, Mass., March 21st, 1911

Dear Dr. Washington: Reading yesterday and today of the unfortunate
and sad accident to you — I am writing, both as the President of our
League, and one interested in you, to extend my sympathy and best
wishes that nothing may seriously develop from the contact with the
club.

Mrs. Albert Ulrich² when she says you called her in these terms:
"Hello, sweetheart!" tells the story of what a plain citizen like myself
would be up against in such a case.

When I note the interest of the honorable men back of you, like
Mr. Andrew Carnegie, Mr. W. J. Schieffelin, Mr. G. F. Peabody, and

11

Hon. Seth Low, I quite understand that the intelligent citizens of this country and abroad will see what we have to contend against, and I thank our Heavenly Father that we have such friends, and that they are with you.

No one man in these United States would or could be placed in your position to serve us better at this time as yourself and we thank God for the Mother that gave you to us.

Mrs. Allston and my boys, as well as myself, join in best wishes for your hasty recovery to your normal condition. Yours sincerely,

Philip J Allston

TLS Con. 434 BTW Papers DLC. Written on stationery of the Boston Negro Business League No. 1.

[1] Philip J. Allston (b. 1860) was a manufacturing druggist in Boston who served as president of the Boston NNBL. He was also a director of the Suffolk Investment Association, and president of the Cosmopolitan Equal Rights Association.

[2] Actually Laura Page Alvarez.

From Edgar Starr Barney[1]

New York   March 21, 1911

Dear Dr. Washington, The Instructors of the Hebrew Technical Institute have read with indignation of the assault upon you and beg to extend to you their heartfelt sympathy.

We recall with pleasant memories your visit to our Institute and your inspiring address to the students, which together with the similarity to our own of the noble work in which you are engaged, makes our feeling doubly strong against the outrage upon a visitor to our city from a distant state.

Trusting that soon you may be restored to vigor and assuring you that you will stand all the higher in the minds of the right thinking people of this city; and hoping, too, that we may again entertain you at our school, believe us, Sincerely your friends

Edgar S. Barney

ALS Con. 434 BTW Papers DLC.

[1] Edgar Starr Barney (1861–1938) was principal of Hebrew Technical Institute for more than fifty years. He was also auditor of the Hudson River Day Line for many years beginning in 1889.

From Risden Tyler Bennett[1]

Wadesboro N C. March 21 1911

Hon. Booker Washington, I wish you to know how keenly gentlemen South resent the murderous assault upon you.

Tis a regretable incident   I am Sir   Your admirer

Risden T Bennett
Ex Congressman

ALS   Con. 434   BTW Papers   DLC.

[1] Risden Tyler Bennett (1840–1913), a lawyer in Wadesboro, N.C., was a Democratic member of the U.S. House of Representatives from 1883 to 1887.

From F. Cornelius Caffey[1]

Montgomery, Ala., 3–21 1911

My dear Dr. Washington, I am greatly distressed at your misfortune and hasten to write you of my sympathy.

When you return South I will be very glad to give you a few private lessons in the "manly art of *self* defense" and wrestling, which will greatly aid you in an emergency of this kind while going alone all over this country.

You can become proficient in the art and always be in condition to take care of yourself when you are run into by such a brute as this man Ulrich.

I will be glad to be of any service to you when you call on me. Yours very truly

F C Caffey

ALS   Con. 434   BTW Papers   DLC.

[1] F. Cornelius Caffey, a Montgomery physician, surgeon, and athletic instructor.

From Melvin Jack Chisum

Hare Valley, Va. Mch 21st, 1911

Dear Dr Washington: Accept my and my wife's sincerest sympathy. We have only been able to get the Baltimore papers thus far and they contain a miserably garbled report, but we know there is a horrible mistake some where made.

In any event, we know you have been pounced upon by some malicious brute and are being terribly misrepresented by the Southern Press.

Yours always faithfully and yours to command (any where any minute)

Chisum

ALS Con. 434 BTW Papers DLC. Written on stationery of the Brickhouse Banking Co., of which Chisum was president.

From Edgar B. Haymond

New York March 21, 1911

Dear Sir: A white Virginian, who has spent most of his life in Bedford County, desires to express to you his sympathy, his condolence and entire confidence of your innocence.

As the horrible thing was predestined, each of us is glad it did not happen south of the Potomac. Truly yours,

Edgar B. Haymond

ALS Con. 434 BTW Papers DLC.

From William Ashley Sunday[1]

Lima Ohio   Mar 21 1911

Your explanation regarding the unfortunate affair of Sunday night is believed and accepted by your hosts of friends throughout the west. We have unbounded confidence in your innocence and have no faith in reports to the contrary. I gave public expression to this sentiment before six thousand people assembled in religious meeting tonight.

W A Sunday

TWSr   BTW Papers   ATT.

[1] William Ashley (Billy) Sunday (1862–1935), a former professional baseball player (1883–90), became an evangelist in the 1890s and was ordained as a Presbyterian minister in 1903.

Alfred B. Cruikshank[1] to Seth Low

New York, N.Y., Mar. 21, 1911

Dear Sir: I am glad to see that you have actively taken up the task of vindicating Dr. Washington from the preposterous charges made against him by the Ulrichs. For the sake of the cause which Dr. Washington represents, we are all interested in having these stories put down as false and malicious.

I see by the newspapers that Ulrich now says that Dr. Washington assaulted him in the first place without provocation. I also gather that Ulrich made no charge of this kind on Sunday night at the police station at the time the parties appeared before the police lieutenant. Had Dr. Washington assaulted Ulrich, as he now claims, he would undoubtedly have made that assault the basis of his original complaint, instead of the absurd complaint of peeping through a keyhole. It is perfectly clear to my mind that this last story of an assault upon Ulrich is an afterthought; in other words, a downright lie, gotten up in an attempt to justify his own atrocious assault. The mere fact that Ulrich has changed his story in this essential particular is convincing, and in any investigation to be made, due emphasis should be laid on this part of the case. Yours sincerely,

Alfred B Cruikshank

TLS   Seth Low Papers   NNC.

¹ Alfred B. Cruikshank, a New York lawyer, held memberships in the Democratic, Manhattan, and Single Tax clubs.

To William Howard Taft

New York, March 22, 1911

Your autograph letter received. You do not know how I appreciate your thoughtfulness and your generosity of feeling. I shall never forget your kindness. The whole matter is coming out all right as court proceedings yesterday will show. The persons falsely accusing me have already become ashamed of themselves and have fled the town it is reported.

[Booker T. Washington]

TW Copy   Con. 435   BTW Papers   DLC.   The version in the William Howard Taft Papers, DLC, contains several minor differences of wording and syntax.

A News Item in the Washington *Herald*

[New York City] Mar. 22, 1911

BOOKER T. IS CONFUSED
REGARDING ENCOUNTER

NEGRO EDUCATOR DENIES IN COURT HE EVER DRANK
CHARGE AGAINST ASSAILANT REDUCED

New York, March 21 — "Do you think the suit will now be dropped?" was asked of Booker T. Washington to-night after he had arrived at the Manhattan Hotel subsequent to his appearance in court as prosecuting witness against Henry Ulrich, who, with others unnamed, beat him seriously, after Mrs. Ulrich alleged he had accosted her with "Hello, sweetheart."

"Some one told me," answered Mr. Washington, head of the greatest negro school in the world, "that it looked like a confession of guilt to agree to having the charge against my assailant reduced from felonious assault to simple assault, and the bail from $1,500 to $500, but I have not yet consulted my lawyer upon further procedure."

There had been received a dispatch from Greenville, Ala., announcing a popular subscription there to defray Ulrich's expenses in continuing the case, so Mr. Washington, his head still swathed tightly in bandages, was asked who had come to his side in his distress.

"Andrew Carnegie called this morning; Jacob Schiff, Paul Warburg, Felix Warburg, Seth Low, president of the board of trustees of Tuskegee Institute, George McAneny, one of the trustees of the Anna T. Jeanes fund for educating negroes in the South; W. J. Schieffelin, of the Armstrong Association, came to-day, also ex-Gov. P. B. S. Pinchback, who was governor of Louisiana, (Yes, I think he was originally a Northerner), came to-day."

His table was piled high with letters and telegrams of sympathy and confidence.

Concerning what happened in the police station, Mr. Washington said that perhaps he might have said there was a telegram or letter from Mr. Smith, he was so confused. But he was positive that while he was in the neighborhood he neither recognized nor spoke to man, woman, or child. He couldn't swear that no women passed him in the hall. Later he recalled the fact that some woman with a dog, or possibly two women, had passed him on the street.

"As to my drinking," volunteered Mr. Washington, "I had not touched a drop. I never get drunk. I have never been drunk in my life. Any man who looks at me ought to know that I'm not a drinking man."

The negro educator was not certain whether or not he had ever been in the neighborhood of West Sixty-third street before. His impression was that he had not. He refused to say anything about the whereabouts of Daniel C. Smith until Mr. Smith himself comes forward with a statement explaining about the address. He is confident that Mr. Smith will do that within a few days.

Washington *Herald,* Mar. 22, 1911, 1.

Emmett Jay Scott to Charles H. Fearing

New York 3-22-11

Am filing newspaper dispatch to be delivered tomorrow morning   use no other statement   See that programs for concert friday night are printed for chapel   Chestnut[1] has copy   Keep all New York news-papers evening & morning from library   hold for my return.

E. J. Scott

HWSr   Con. 606   BTW Papers   DLC.

[1] Edwin J. Chesnutt.

From Mary E. B. Bourke

New York, N.Y. March 22nd. 1911

Esteemed, And most highly appreciated Friend: Please allow me to extend my heart felt sympathy to you in this most cruel and unjust assault.

My heart went out to you when I read Monday morning's Herald, most anxiously have I awaited news of you each day, hoping for your speedy recovery.

You do not know who thus address[es] you. But *I* know you and I am praying for you.

And while you have letters and telegrams from distinguished ones from all over the country — Please accept these words of sympathy from just a simple Orphan girl, but proud of an *Honest* heart, trying to live in the *Pure* paths of life.

I am Yours in sincere sympathy,

Mary E. B. Bourke

Native home, Savannah, Ga.

ALS   Con. 417   BTW Papers   DLC.

From Charles Waddell Chesnutt

Cleveland, March 22, 1911

My dear Dr. Washington: I wish to express my regret at the misadventure you suffered the other day in New York, and my sympathy with you in the personal suffering and disagreeable publicity attending it. You might of course have avoided some of the latter by not giving the man in charge,[1] but it was the only thing to do — you owed it both to yourself and those you represent. Assuming your assailant to have been honestly mistaken, he was not mistaken in your race, and that after all, was the real reason for the assault — I can't imagine his treating a well-dressed white man in such cavalier fashion. There are too many white men only too willing to thump a Negro with any possible excuse, and they ought to be taught that a Negro cannot be judged or treated by any different standard from that applied to other men. If your affair can help impress that upon the public mind, it may be worth the annoyance to you. I have more than once heard you say that if you were to be born over, and had your choice of races, you would select that of an American Negro. You have now had the opportunity of suffering physically for your faith — the blood of the martyrs is the seed of the church.

I enclose a cutting from today's Cleveland Leader[2] which expresses, I think the opinion of all who know you. I hope you will make a quick recovery from your wounds, that they will be followed by no disagreeable consequences, and that your assailant may get his just deserts. Cordially yours,

Chas. W. Chesnutt

ALS BTW Papers ATT.

[1] Thus in original. Chesnutt seems to be referring to the fact that BTW could have avoided some publicity by not charging his assailant.

[2] The attached clipping from the Cleveland *Leader,* Mar. 22, 1911, stated that the attack was "a mistake in every sense," and that there was "not the slightest ground for any censure" of BTW.

From John Campbell Dancy

Washington, D.C. Mch. 22. 1911

My dear Dr. Washington: My tardiness in writing is an exhibition of no want of friendly interest. Indeed I have been out of sorts and aroused as I have not been for years on account of the ruffianly attack on you by a demon crazed by race antipathy and race malevolence. I rejoice that the whole country is aroused in sympathy for you. We who know you best and most fondly realize how completely you will be vindicated. I personally know that your character is an open book, and that the tongue of slander is hushed absolutely whenever and wherever your name is mentioned. Indeed you have one of the cleanest records of any man in this country. I know you do not need my help but if you should my services to the limit are at your disposal. Yours always sincerely

Jno. C. Dancy

ALS Con. 434 BTW Papers DLC.

From John H. Day[1]

New Haven, Ct. Mar. 22nd 11

My Dear Dr. Washington, It is hinted in the newspapers that you are to drop the case against Ulrich. This must not be done even if you have to sacrafice a little dignity by appearing against him. The dignity of the whole race in the North is at stake. You must produce Mr Smith and there must be some semblance between the correct address of his New York relatives you were looking for and the address you actually went to Sunday night.

And please remember that in the south, you would have not been allowed to explain anything in a court of record but the woman's word would have been taken and you would have been lynched. No colored person in New Haven believes you guilty and all realize that repeated visits to the house by a white man under similar circumstances would not have been noticed by Ulrich; therefore it is up to you to make an example whereby a colored man may look up any body's address without having his brains knocked out.

It may cost you some dignity to prosecute this man but it will cost us more dignity if you dont prosecute him.

We know that the best element of white people understand the situation but the trouble lies with the ignorance of the lower masses.

Failure to prosecute will lose for you the esteem and respect of your colored friends and gain nothing you haven't got already.

I hope you will see the matter in this light. Very truly

John H. Day

ALS Con. 434 BTW Papers DLC.

[1] John H. Day was listed in the New Haven city directory as a tailor.

From Jesse H. Harris[1]

Boston, Mass., March 22nd 1911

My dear Sir: I write to express my sympathy for you in your trying misfortune. I had feared that owing to your possible weakened condition Physically from possible over work the assault might cause you much suffering; I trust however this fear is entirely groundless.

But may I make this one suggestion in this connection. You know as I do and perhaps better — that the experience you have had men of our race have in New York altogether too frequently — but because we are Negroes, and poor, we have to submit. And I think with your prestige — and your means — you due all of us a service if you will use every means at your command to make this ruffian and all other such white men in New York realize that, there are times even when a Negro's head is not made for their ever ready club. I hope you will not permit any lawyer's selfishness as personal advertizement of their ability, or any other cause to prevent you from making an example of this white brute.

It is a duty you owe us, and you are in the position to maintain it. Respectfully Yours,

J. H. Harris

ALS Con. 434 BTW Papers DLC.

[1] Jesse H. Harris, a resident of Boston, was born in Washington, D.C., in 1864. He was a graduate of Hampton Institute (1888) and president of the Hampton Alumni Association. In 1915 Harris was active in campaigning against the film *Birth of a Nation,* and urged both BTW and W. E. B. Du Bois to make a unified stand against it. (See Jesse H. Harris to BTW, May 3, 1915, below, vol. 13.)

From Andrew B. Humphrey

New York   March, 22, 1911

My dear Sir: I wish to congratulate you upon holding your assailant for trial *before a Court of Justice.*

Your case is only one of too frequent occurrence in recent years and illustrates that *awful curse* of growing *race prejudice.*

I still believe that you will some day come to agree with me that "it will take more than a Bank Account to counteract this *deadly poison!*"

I would gladly offer assistance in your prosecution of this case to the full limit, only I am assured by stronger men that "no necessary aid will be lacking!"

I wish some organization could be built up with sufficient strength and means to prosecute similar cases, where the victims are so hopeless and *pathetically* helpless against mob violence, lawbreakers and "gangs" of "individual toughs!"

Should the attack upon you result in the creation of such an organization, backed by large resources and strong public sentiment, your experiences and sufferings, will not have been in vain!

Wishing you speedy recovery. Very truly yours

A. B. Humphrey

ALS   Con. 434   BTW Papers   DLC.

From Adam Clayton Powell

New York, March 22nd, 1911

My dear Dr. Washington: Knowing that your nervous system was in no condition Monday to read letters or even telegrams, I 'phoned Mr. Fred R. Moore, our mutual friend, to convey to you my heartfelt sympathy. I now wish to further express my absolute and unshaken confidence in your sterling character and to hereby pledge to you my support in your future efforts as a leader and race builder. While the outrageous experience of Sunday night must be unspeakably embarrassing to you, in my humble opinion it will serve to unite the race as no other single occurrence since the Emancipation. I am   Sincerely and sympathetically yours,

A. Clayton Powell

P.S. — If you care to use this note in any way, you are at liberty to do so. Yours,

A. C. P.

TLS   Con. 435   BTW Papers   DLC.

From Oswald Garrison Villard

New York   March 22, 1911

Dear Dr. Washington: The Staff has again taken up carefully the question of capitalizing the word negro, in connection with your letter of March 4th. It feels such deep sympathy with you in your recent trying experience that it finds it all the harder not to waive its own decision and say "Yes, we will oblige Dr. Washington." But our judgment is against it for the same reasons that actuated us when you took the matter up with me once before during the life of Mr. Wendell Phillips Garrison.[1] Cordially yours,

Oswald Garrison Villard

TLS   Con. 55   BTW Papers   DLC.   A copy is in the Oswald Garrison Villard Papers, MH.

[1] Wendell Phillips Garrison (1840–1907) was literary editor of *The Nation* from 1865 to 1906.

Margaret James Murray Washington
to Lugenia D. Burns Hope[1]

Tuskegee Inst. March 22, 1911

My dear Mrs. Hope: I want to thank you for your telegram which came yesterday morning, and I also want to say that *Fate* seems to be against both you and me so far as our getting together is concerned, however it will not always be thus I am sure.

It seems almost impossible to realize how a man so utterly incapable of harming any one as Mr. Washington is could be attacked in this way, but we never know how to understand or interpret a thing of this kind, but [it] comes to us and we must simply bear it.

Aside from the notoriety of it [it] will go but to strengthen the great cause which both your husband and mine are working out.

Mr. Washington dislikes any sort of publicity, and I feel very sorry for him, for the notoriety which a thing like this gives. But every man and woman for all that must pay for his success in many terrible ways.

You have already heard from Mrs. Hall,[2] and know that she plans to come by Atlanta when she leaves here. It has been a great comfort to have her here during these past few days.

Please remember me to Prof. Hope, and believe me to be, Yours sincerely, and remember that I shall see you as soon as I can.

Margaret J. Washington

HLS Photocopy BTW Papers ATT.

[1] Lugenia D. Burns Hope, born in St. Louis, was a social worker in Chicago when she married John Hope in 1897. She continued her social work in the Atlanta black district near Atlanta Baptist College and helped found in 1908 the Neighborhood Union, a pioneering private social service and family assistance agency that spread to other sections of Atlanta.

[2] Mrs. George C. Hall visited Tuskegee Institute on March 14–17 with several other Chicago women. She was guest of honor at several social occasions. (*Tuskegee Student*, 23 [Mar. 17, 1911], 1; [Mar. 25, 1911], 2.)

Seth Low to George Livingston Peabody

[New York City] March 22nd, 1911

Dear Dr. Peabody: I was very much interested by your letter of March 20th. In the interest of justice, I read it over the telephone to the District Attorney, without giving your name. Of course a man may act in perfect good faith without being justified in making such an assault as was made on Dr. Washington. On the other hand, if you have seen the statement made by Dr. Washington, which was printed in the afternoon papers of yesterday, you will observe that he ends by saying: "I think, to do him justice, that the man who struck me made the mistake of thinking that perhaps I was a burglar."

You may also have noticed that the woman who has been figuring in the case as the wife of the assailant is not in fact his wife. In other words, I think the character of those who have attacked Dr. Washington through the papers, in connection with this incident, will not bear investigation. The whole matter is, as you say, most deplorable, but I am hoping that it is now practically ended, and that it will not have done permanent injury to a great man and a good cause. Thank you for writing to me. Yours sincerely,

[Seth Low]

TLc   Seth Low Papers   NNC.

William Howard Taft to Andrew Carnegie

The White House   Washington. March 22, 1911

My dear Mr. Carnegie: I have yours of March 18th. We will take up the matter as soon as Knox returns.

I am full of sorrow over the outrageous attack on Booker Washington. I have written him a letter on the subject. I am glad to see that you have stood by him. Now is the time when he needs us.[1] Sincerely yours,

Wm H Taft

TLS   Andrew Carnegie Papers   DLC.

1 Carnegie replied reassuringly on Mar. 25, 1911, about BTW's health: "I find him in much better condition than expected; voice full and eyes clear, and able to attend court that afternoon, but he has escaped by miracle. He is a noble soul and is to pass into history as having accomplisht a great work, at once the Moses and the Joshua of his people." (Andrew Carnegie Papers, DLC.)

Henry Lewis Stimson[1] to William Howard Taft

[New York City] Mch 22/11

My dear Mr President   Please accept my congratulations upon what under the circumstances was a noble letter from you to Booker Washington. It was one which only a man with a heart as well as a head could write. It will do an immense service. Already timid & gossip loving gentlemen in New York were shaking their heads and saying he "would have to resign," he was "ruined at the South," and the like. Your letter puts a stop at once to all such talk and opens the way for the assault to prove a blessing in disguise, as it awakens sympathy for Washington and his cause.

Your kind and prompt utterance was an act of which any man might well be proud.

I am   Very cordially yours

Henry L. Stimson

ALS   William Howard Taft Papers   DLC.

1 Henry Lewis Stimson (1867–1950) was U.S. Secretary of War from 1911 to 1913. He later served as governor general of the Philippine Islands (1927–29), Secretary of State (1929–33), and again as Secretary of War from 1940 to 1945.

An Account of the Assault on Washington

New York [ca. Mar. 22, 1911]

DR. WASHINGTON BADLY INJURED

MALICIOUSLY ASSAULTED BY INFURIATED
WHITE MAN IN NEW YORK

TAKEN TO FLOWER HOSPITAL

HEAD OF THE FAMOUS TUSKEGEE (ALA.)
INSTITUTE, A MAN OF INTERNATIONAL
REPUTATION, WHO HAS BEEN HONORED
BY KINGS AND PRESIDENTS, ROUGHLY
HANDLED BY BRUTE FORCE

By N. Barnett Dodson

New York — The assault on Dr. Booker T. Washington on Sunday evening, March 19, by one Henry A. Ulrich, at or in the neighborhood of 11½ West Sixty-third street, this city, was one of the most brutal, unprovoked and malicious attacks upon a human being imaginable. According to Dr. Washington's own statement, he arrived in New York on Saturday and put up at the Hotel Manhattan, where he usually stops when in this city.

On Sunday afternoon he spoke at the Mount Olivet Baptist church and later at the Church of the Pilgrims, in Brooklyn. Returning to his room in the hotel, he changed his clothing and about 9 o'clock went in search of the auditor of the Tuskegee Institute, who he understood from a letter which he received from Mr. Emmett J. Scott, his private secretary, was stopping with friends at 11½ West Sixty-third street.

Upon arriving at the above number Dr. Washington scanned the names on the bells leading to the different floors for the name of the person mentioned in Mr. Scott's letter, with whom the auditor of Tuskegee was stopping. Finding what he thought was the right name, he rang the bell, but got no response. Thinking that the occupants were possibly at church, he returned to the street and walked up and down the block for some time. He went back the second time, but did not succeed in getting an answer to his ring. To convince himself of the name of the person and the number of the house he went back the third time.

27

It was on this third visit that the said Henry Ulrich made the attack upon him, saying that Mrs. Ulrich had stated to him that a colored man in the vestibule had accosted her as she entered, calling her "sweetheart." This statement Dr. Washington emphatically denies. He says that he spoke to neither man, woman nor child either on his way to or at 11½ West Sixty-third street. Dr. Washington also denies the charge that he had been drinking. The noted educator said he wanted to make two things very clear to the public — first, that he had not drunk anything all day Sunday, and, second, that he did not nod, motion or bow to any one that night, nor had he ever been drunk in his life.

Dr. Washington and Ulrich were arrested by a policeman after the former had been badly beaten. They were taken to the station house, where a charge of felonious assault was made against Ulrich, whom the magistrate held for a further hearing and examination in court Monday afternoon. But when the case was called in the West Side court Monday afternoon Wilford H. Smith, attorney for Dr. Washington, presented to Magistrate Cornell of that court a signed statement from the attending physician to the effect that Dr. Washington was too ill to appear, whereupon Justice Cornell set 2 o'clock Tuesday afternoon for a hearing, holding Ulrich in $1,500 bail. Dr. Washington's right ear was badly torn, his face bruised and his head cut so severely that sixteen stitches were required to close the wound. He was attended at the Flower hospital.

The fact that Dr. Washington was unable to appear in court on Monday to press his charge against Ulrich started many wild rumors as to the possibility of his appearing at all against his assailant. The public was becoming alarmed, and sentiment in Dr. Washington's favor ripened thick and fast. Some satisfaction, however, was had by the following official statement given out by Seth Low, president of the board of trustees of Tuskegee Institute:

PRESIDENT SETH LOW'S STATEMENT

As president of the board of trustees of the Tuskegee Institute I was shocked to read this morning of the assault that had been made upon Dr. Washington last night.

The facts are these: Dr. Washington reached New York on Saturday morning from Michigan. Yesterday morning he spoke at the Mount Olivet Baptist church and in the afternoon at the Church of the Pilgrims, Brooklyn. In the evening about 9 o'clock he started out to find Mr. Smith, a certified public accountant, who is auditor of the Tuskegee Institute, a white gentleman, whom he expected to find staying with friends at 11½ West Sixty-third street. This is an apartment house of the type occupied by different families on different floors, whose names appear with bells on an index below.

When Dr. Washington first reached the house he entered the vestibule and could get no reply to the bell he rang, and so he moved up and down the street and around the neighboring block where the New theater stands and returned to the house twice, each time entering the vestibule, but not the house.

On his third visit he entered the vestibule and was leaning over to try to find the name he was looking for when suddenly a man rushed in from the street and began to assault him. He defended himself and got out into the street, when a second man with a stick struck him.

Then he tried to escape, when both he and the first one of his assailants were taken to the station house by a policeman who met them. From the time Dr. Washington left the hotel until he was assaulted he spoke to nobody, neither man nor woman.

The trustees of the Tuskegee Institute have absolute confidence in Dr. Washington, and they will give him whatever support and aid he needs.

To assure inquirers that Dr. Washington would surely appear in court Tuesday afternoon Counselor Wilford H. Smith gave out the statement that his client wished a thorough investigation of the most unfortunate affair and would push his case to the limit of the law against his assailant. By 1 o'clock Tuesday the courtroom was crowded with spectators, both white and colored, who had come to witness what is considered to be an all important case. Mrs. Ulrich, who accuses Dr. Washington of calling her "sweetheart," walked to the court, while Dr. Washington came in an automobile, accompanied by his counsel, Borough President McAneny, D. Macon Webster, ex-Governor P. B. S. Pinchback and other distinguished men.

When the case was called counsel for Ulrich entered a plea of not guilty. Magistrate Cornell then told the lawyer that he would hold his client in $500 bond for special sessions. No time was given as to when the case would come up in that court. Disappointed at not seeing and hearing argument by counsel on either side, the crowd left the courtroom in disgust. One white man was so badly affected by the disposal of the case that he immediately fainted on reaching the sidewalk.

Wilford H. Smith, counsel for Dr. Washington, is a lawyer of known ability and has no fears as to the outcome of his client's case. As a pleader and proctor in admiralty he is admitted to have few equals. As a race man he is not of the kind to easily give up a fight for justice according to law. He is well fortified with facts and witnesses to support Dr. Washington's statement as to why he went to 11½ West Sixty-third street on the evening of March 19.

Dr. Washington has received thousands of messages, letters, telegrams, notes and personal calls from friends all over the United States expressing their sympathy for and confidence in him. He was greatly pleased Tuesday morning when he received the following personal letter from President Taft. . . .[1]

PD Con. 435 BTW Papers DLC. This is a printed press release, the weekly Afro-American page of the American Press Association edited by N. Barnett Dodson.

[1] See Taft to BTW, Mar. 21, 1911, above.

From Graduates of Tuskegee Institute

Normal, Ala., March 23, 1911

Dear Sir: We, the graduates of Tuskegee, were grieved to hear of the regrettable accident which caused you so much personal injury and we take this method of extending to you our deepest sympathy and wish for you a speedy recovery. To this end we pledge our support in any way that we may be of service to you.

Praying the blessings of the Lord upon you, we are, Faithfully yours,

> Robert L. Campbell
> Harvey Jones[1]
> Mansfield T. Gardner[2]
> L. A. Van Hoose[3]
> Christopher T. Evans[4]
> Carrie L. Anderson[5]
> Melona S. Byrd[6]
> Walter S. Buchanan, '99
> Elizabeth B. Cooke[7]
> Jno. H. Pinkard, '99[8]

TLS Con. 434 BTW Papers DLC. On stationery of the State Agricultural and Mechanical College for Negroes, Normal, Ala. Addressed "To our beloved Principal."

[1] Harvey Jones of Dresden, Tenn., graduated in 1910.

[2] Mansfield Tyler Gardner of Selma, Ala., graduated in 1910.

[3] Luther Alexander Van Hoose graduated from Tuskegee Institute in 1897 and became an instructor of blacksmithing at Snow Hill (Ala.) Industrial Institute.

[4] Christopher T. Evans of Ware Neck, Va., graduated in 1909.

[5] Carrie Lee Anderson of Montgomery, Ala., graduated in 1910.

[6] Melona Samuel Byrd, of Troy, Ala., graduated in 1910.

[7] Elizabeth Beatrice Cooke of Eatonville, Fla., according to the Tuskegee catalog, left the school as a junior during the 1904–5 school term.

[8] John Henry Pinkard, after graduation in 1899, attended Berea College.

A News Item in the Washington *Post*

Washington, D.C., Mar. 23, 1911

BEATEN AS KIDNAPPER

DR. WASHINGTON MISTAKEN FOR ANOTHER, LAWYER SAYS

MR. TAFT UPHOLDS EDUCATOR

WRITES TO VICTIM OF ASSAULT IN NEW YORK ASSURING HIM OF HIS CONTINUED CONFIDENCE AND FRIENDSHIP — DEVELOPMENTS LEAD TO PLAN TO SEEK INDICTMENT OF ASSAILANT

Special to The Washington Post. New York, March 22. — Booker T. Washington's lawyer, Wilford H. Smith, said today that he had discovered what he called the real motive for the assault on Dr. Washington in front of 11½ West Sixty-third street on last Sunday night. He declared that Mrs. Albert Ulrich, the woman who says Dr. Washington spoke to her, mistook him for a negro who had tried to steal her 10-year-old daughter two or three weeks ago. She told her husband, so Lawyer Smith says, and the beating followed.

The lawyer also asserted that on the strength of new evidence he will ask District Attorney Whitman[1] to try to have Ulrich indicted for felonious assault. He said two or three witnesses would swear that Dr. Washington did not enter the apartment house beyond the vestibule, and therefore could not have attempted to peep into anybody's flat, and that at least one witness will tell about the beating, as she saw it from an upper window of the same house.

Felonious assault was the original charge against Ulrich that Dr. Washington made in the police station after his West Sixty-third street experience. When the case came up in the West Side court on Tuesday the felony charge was changed to one of simple assault, and Ulrich was freed on $500 bail.

BASIS FOR "KIDNAPPING"

The kidnapping story, as Dr. Washington's attorney gets it, runs this way: Mrs. Ulrich's little girl is Dolores Alvarez. She is the daughter of Mrs. Ulrich's former husband, a man of Spanish birth and of the name of Alvarez, from whom she is separated.

Alvarez, so the story goes, had threatened to take his child away from Mrs. Ulrich. Two or three weeks ago, Lawyer Smith says, Alvarez appeared with a negro at her door and said he was going to take Dolores away. The mother locked herself in with the child. She told Ulrich about the attempted "kidnapping," and both of them were on guard against another demonstration. Then Dr. Washington happened along looking for Daniel C. Smith, the Tuskegee auditor. In the dim light of the vestibule Mrs. Ulrich thought him the negro of the previous encounter, according to the theory of Dr. Washington's lawyer.

Dr. Washington today gave out the following letter from President Taft. . . .[2]

Dr. Washington was feeling much better today. Among his visitors were Bishop Greer[3] and former Gov. Horace White.[4]

Washington *Post,* Mar. 23, 1911, 4.

[1] Charles Seymour Whitman (1868–1947), a former New York corporation counsel and member of the board of city magistrates, was district attorney of New York City from 1910 to 1914 and governor of New York from 1915 to 1918. In 1919 he returned to the practice of law, and served a term as president of the American Bar Association (1926–27).

[2] The letter from President Taft of Mar. 21, 1911, above, was inserted here.

[3] David Hummell Greer (1844–1919) was Episcopal bishop of New York.

[4] Horace White (1865–1943), the lieutenant governor of New York (1909–10), served as governor (Oct. 6, 1910–Jan. 1, 1911) upon the resignation of Governor Charles Evans Hughes.

A Resolution of the Washington Annual Conference of the Methodist Episcopal Church

[Lynchburg, Va., ca. Mar. 23, 1911]

BOOKER WASHINGTON RESOLUTION

Whereas the country has been shocked by the account of a cowardly attack upon the person of Dr. Booker T. Washington, the foremost leader of our race in this country, and whereas the perpetrator of that deed, of which this distinguished man has been the victim is now endeavoring to add insult to injury by the implication of improper conduct, wherefore, resolved, that this Washington Annual Conference of the M.E. Church now in session in Lynchburg, hereby record its implicit confidence in his moral integrity, his Christian character and his high sense of honor, and further that he invites a full, thorough and open investigation of the incident, in order that there shall not remain the smallest doubt in the minds of the general public as to his complete vindication of what we believe to be a snare laid to catch his feet.

Signed   Ernest Lyon
J. W. E. Bowen
N. M. Carroll[1]
E. P. Moon
S. H. Norwood[2]
H. J. Naylor[3]
I. G. Penn
D. W. Shaw

TD Copy Con. 435 BTW Papers DLC. Enclosed in Ernest Lyon to BTW, Mar. 23, 1911.

[1] N. M. Carroll was pastor of the Centennial M.E. Church in Baltimore.

[2] Sylvester H. Norwood, a graduate in theology from Howard University in 1888, was pastor of churches in Martinsburg, W.Va., and Baltimore.

[3] Possibly McHenry Jeremiah Naylor, a graduate in theology from Howard University in 1892, pastor of an M.E. church in Baltimore.

An Editorial in the Lynchburg *News*

[Lynchburg, Va., Mar. 23, 1911]

Anything likely to seriously impair Booker Washington's usefulness as a conservative influence among negroes or destroy the confidence in his character which has previously been entertained by the white race, North and South, would furnish cause for genuine and profound regret. And thus we think the press of the country should be ready to defend the man against what appear palpably unjust and damaging charges reflecting upon the honesty of his purpose, or the decency of his conduct. But this doesn't mean that newspapers should be on the alert to white-wash the man simply because he has performed valuable service in the past. Nor do we believe that Washington's prominence should serve as a cloak to prevent a thorough investigation of the causes of any serious scandal-ladened difficulty into whose meshes he may have become entangled. A square deal is in order, therefore, with reference to the affair of last Sunday night — a deal that will show no preferential consideration for either Booker Washington or the white man who assaulted him. And to speak frankly we do not think such a deal has been had. Washington is charged with offensive deportment that merits thorough inquiry. But he is spared a trial. The warrant is arbitrarily dismissed and men of national prominence begin to give out statements tending to vindicate the suspected man. More than this, after a consultation between Washington's friends and the attorney for Mr. Ulrich, Washington's assailant, the charges upon which the white man was arrested are essentially modified at the negro's initiative — and the hearing goes over. Why the modification? If Washington's first account of the matter was true, there should have been no modification. Has anything occurred to change the negro educator's original impressions? Does he shrink from a rigid, thorough court investigation? These questions undoubtedly present themselves when considering the curious circumstances transpiring since the arrests in the case were made. The News was at first strongly disposed to think that Washington was merely the victim of an unfortunate combination of circumstances in this case. Nor do we now disavow that conclusion. But we must confess that Washington has been badly advised in evidently being willing to hush this matter up, and the New York authorities have been so obviously unfair to Ulrich and his wife as to give ground for a suspicion, which would not have sprung up if square deal methods had been promptly employed. As it is, we greatly fear that Washington has lost ground in the good opinion of a great many people, as result of the occurrence. And it's a pity.

Lynchburg *News,* Mar. 23, 1911, Clipping Con. 435 BTW Papers DLC. Enclosed in Ernest Lyon to BTW, Mar. 23, 1911.

A. W. Gray[1] to William Howard Taft

Kansas City, Mo., March 23rd 1911

Dear Sir: I read in our papers of today a purported letter from your honor, to Dr. Booker T. Washington regarding his recent trouble in the Ulrich matter, and we have discussed this letter at length, and we cannot believe that you have written it, and that you would take the trouble to volunteer such a letter to this Negro, and put yourself before the people of this part of our country in so unfavorable light, and I will consider it quite a favor to be informed as to the truth of this letter, a copy of which I enclose, published in the Kansas City Post and in the Kansas City Star.

All white people that I have heard express their feelings in the matter of your attitude toward the Negro, do not think that any good will come from too much friendship being shown to this race, and I am very sure that this letter whether written by you or not, as published in our papers here will lose thousands of Republican votes in Missouri, to my great regret. Very truly yours,

A. W. Gray

TLS William Howard Taft Papers DLC.

[1] A lawyer in Kansas City, Mo.

A Memorandum by Emmett Jay Scott

[New York City, Mar. 23, 1911]

IN DIGEST

American & Times say you intend to press charge. Both publish Taft letter. Times & Tribune refer to the kidnapping *charge*. In American *Moore*[1] indicates that he will throw some "bombshells" if his client is attacked much more — says he has many affidavits & *letters*. American quotes you directly of saying that your attorney is now ready to spring another charge against *Ulrich*. Herald & Times & others refer to the fine reception given you at Drew last night: & of how well you spoke.

Taken as a whole — everything is wholly favorable.

AD   Con. 435   BTW Papers   DLC.

[1] James I. Moore, originally from Texas, defended Henry A. Ulrich.

To John Milton Putnam Metcalf[1]

[New York City] March 24, 1911

Tell son am getting on well. Whole matter fast clearing up. Injustice of assault and remarks made about me being made manifest. Am intending to go home soon. Many friends have been most kind.

Booker T. Washington

TWcSr   Con. 430   BTW Papers   DLC.

[1] John Milton Putnam Metcalf (b. 1864) was president of Talladega College beginning in 1908. He was a graduate of Oberlin College (1885) and Union Theological Seminary (1888). He taught at Oberlin Theological Seminary (1890–93) before moving to Talladega, where he was a professor and dean before becoming president.

Edward Morse Shepard to Seth Low

Washington   Friday, 24th Mch. 1911

Dear Mr. Low, I ought, perhaps, before this to have written you that no message came to me or to my office from Mr. Washington. I assumed that he was content with the arrangements he had made and did not, therefore, feel at liberty to make the offer of professional service which you suggested. I earnestly hope and trust that the circumstances of the case will be so presented upon sworn examination and cross-examination as to prevent malice, or a dislike of the signal service he is rendering humanity, from inducing any distrust of him. Always faithfully yours,

Edward M. Shepard

I am writing Dr. Washington a note of personal sympathy.

ALS   Seth Low Papers   NNC.

Charles William Anderson
to William Howard Taft

New York, N.Y., March 24, 1911

Mr. President: Mr. Henry Clews[1] and myself were with Doctor Washington when your splendid letter reached him, and it was, therefore, my privilege to be among the first to learn of its kind and loyal tenor. After hearing it read, I felt like shouting out that old Hebrew ejaculatory superlative, so dear to the old-time men and women of my race — glory hallelujah!! Nothing could have been finer.

I at once phoned to Mr. Moore, the editor of the New York Age, and reminded him of the prediction made by me last Summer to the effect that he would be compelled to acknowledge that President Taft was the best friend the negroes have ever had in the Presidential chair, before many months passed over his head. It gave me peculiar pleasure to be able to read your letter to Moore, for, in my judgment, no one is ever quite so happy as a prophet who lives to see his prophecies ful-

37

filled. Moore very frankly admitted that the policy of his paper toward you had been wrong in the past, and promised to turn over a new leaf and from now on to lead a clean life, editorially. Whether or not he will keep this promise, I am not quite prepared to say, for to expect loyalty and settled political convictions from him, is to look for grapes from thorns and figs from thistles. I am delighted to inform you, however, that the negroes of this State, with exceptions too slight to be noticed, regard Doctor Washington as the trusted bearer of their standard, and they will never cease to love the President who was great enough to stand by their race — for the Doctor's misfortune was a blow to the entire race — in the hour of its great need.

Hoping I may secure your pardon for the intrusion of this letter, I am, Yours very respectfully,

Charles W. Anderson

TLS   William Howard Taft Papers   DLC.

¹ Henry Clews (1834–1923), the New York banker and stockbroker.

A News Item from the *Tuskegee Student*

Tuskegee, Alabama, March 25, 1911

PRINCIPAL WASHINGTON ASSAULTED IN NEW YORK

Principal Washington was maliciously assaulted in New York City last Sunday night, by a thug who pretended to believe that he mistook him for a burglar. The whole unfortunate affair has been most trying, but the many expressions of confidence and goodwill, which have been received, testify as to the undiminished regards of the best people of the country.

Letters and telegrams have been received from all parts of the country here at Tuskegee and by Principal Washington in New York City. New York papers mention among those who called at his room to offer sympathy and other expressions of goodwill such important individuals as Andrew Carnegie; Henry Clews; the New York banker, Jacob H. Schiff; Felix Warburg; Seth Low, President of the Board of Trustees of Tuskegee Institute; George McAneny, President of the

Borough of Manhattan; James Creelman, the famous correspondent; Mr. Lawrence F. Abbott and Dr. Hamilton W. Mabie of The Outlook Magazine; Robert Underwood Johnson, Editor of The Century Magazine; Dr. H. B. Frissell, Principal of Hampton Institute, Hampton, Va., A. S. Frissell,[1] President Fifth Avenue Bank; Charles W. Anderson, Collector of Internal Revenue for the Second District of New York; Fred R. Moore, Editor of The New York Age; and former Governor P. B. S. Pinchback.

Mr. Low issued the following statement on Monday:

"As president of the board of trustees of the Tuskegee Institute, I was shocked to read this morning of the assault that had been made upon Dr. Washington last night.

"The facts are: Dr. Washington reached New York on Saturday morning from Michigan. Yesterday morning he spoke at the Mt. Olivet Baptist Church and in the afternoon at the Church of the Pilgrims, Brooklyn. In the evening about 9 o'clock he started out to find Mr. Smith, a certified public accountant, who is auditor of the Tuskegee Institute, a white man whom he expected to find staying with friends at No. 11½ West Sixty-third Street. This is an apartment house of the type occupied by different families on different floors whose names appear with bells on an index below.

"When Dr. Washington first reached the house, he entered the vestibule and could get no reply to the bell he rang and so he moved up and down the street and around the neighboring block where the New Theatre stands and returned to the house twice, each time entering the vestibule but not the house.

"On his third visit he entered the vestibule and was leaning over to try to find the name he was looking for when suddenly a man rushed in from the street and began to assault him. He defended himself and got out into the street when a second man with a stick struck him. Then he tried to escape, when both he and the first one of his assailants were taken to the station house by a policeman who met them. From the time Dr. Washington left the hotel until the time of the assault he spoke to no one, neither man nor woman. The trustees of the Tuskegee Institute have absolute confidence in Dr. Washington and they will give to him whatever support and aid he needs."

· · · ·[2]

Tuskegee Student, 23 (Mar. 25, 1911), 1.

1 Algernon Sydney Frissell (1845–1932), the brother of Hollis B. Frissell, was president of the Fifth Avenue Bank beginning in 1885.

2 The article also included the letter from William Howard Taft, Mar. 21, 1911, above.

To Wilford H. Smith

Philadelphia, Pa. March 26, 1911

Dear Mr. Smith: I hope you will keep me daily informed of conditions, as you know I shall be very nervous about how matters are going.

My present feeling is that you had better treat old man Benton[1] rather generously, and for that reason I enclose $10 additional. He has been rather helpful to us and may be more helpful, and I should by all means keep him in good humor. If this is not enough let me know. At any rate, if you think it wise, you can use your judgment as to promising him more. It may be that you can use him to great advantage in getting the parties to sign the statement that we have discussed. At any rate, I should keep near him and keep him in good humor. It may be that you will need his daughters to testify, and that is another reason why he should be kept in good humor. I think he is a well meaning old man, but of course wants pay.

My present feeling is if we can get a full, strong statement of denial and acknowledgement of wrong and asking for forgiveness signed by both this man and his wife and then have the matter called up in court with the understanding that there is to be a suspended judgment or something of that kind, it might answer our purpose, but I should like to know at the very earliest possible moment by telegram if necessary, what the result of Judge McAdoo's[2] effort is.

One other thing. I think you know Dr. Park, the gentleman who helps me in my literary work. He is an old newspaper man, besides he is a firm true friend. Do you think you could use him to any advantage in having him nose around through the district of 63d Street and get pretty well acquainted with this man and his wife as well as their friends and find out just what their state of mind and intentions are. Much would depend, it seems to me, on this as to how they would act. If you need Dr. Park I think I could have him come to New York at once. He is now in Tuskegee. I suggest him rather than a detective agency. The Burns detective agency has offered me their services without any charge, but you cannot ever tell what a detective will do, he may string the thing out in order to get money and involve you in trouble, and I distrust most of them.

Do not be afraid to use the telegraph freely, signing only "W. S.," sending your telegrams to Mr. Scott instead of to me.

There is this element in the case which we and our friends have got to consider, and this element I wish you would talk over with Dr. Schieffelin. Even though we may convict Ulrich and send him to jail or the penitentiary, if the woman goes on making statements that I accosted her or if they both make the statement that I was intoxicated or peeping through the windows, the sending of Ulrich to the prison does not alter very much public opinion so far as my character is concerned. Yours very truly,

[Booker T. Washington]

TLc BTW Papers ATT.

¹ B. H. Benton, a writer, lived in the building where the assault occurred with his two daughters, ages eighteen and nineteen, who were members of the Rob Roy theatrical company playing at the theater a few doors away. He testified in court on Mar. 21, 1911, that his daughters saw a black man as they passed through the vestibule, but that he had not spoken to them. (New York *World*, Mar. 21, 1911, 2.) According to the testimony of detective Chester A. Hagan, at the time of the arrest of BTW the patrolman said he did not think BTW was a burglar. "Then some one said he might have been after those two girls who went in the house, whereupon Ulrich said, 'Oh, that's so-and-so's daughters. I wonder if I ought to change the charge to that.'" (Undated clipping, ca. Nov. 6, 1911, Con. 1059, BTW Papers, DLC.)

² William McAdoo (1853–1930), formerly a member of the New Jersey state legislature, practiced law in New York City beginning in 1904. He served as New York police commissioner, and, beginning in 1910, was chief city magistrate.

To John Stephens Durham

[New York City] 3/27/11

Please see or telephone Dr. Talcott Williams tonight and explain what great injustice his paper has done me in publishing the interview which

I am informed appears in it this morning.[1] I said nothing of my assailant being justified in attacking me, and stated most emphatically case would not be dropped. It is a cruel injustice.

Booker T. Washington

HWSr Con. 52 BTW Papers DLC. Written in E. J. Scott's hand.

[1] The Philadelphia *Press* reported an interview of BTW while in Philadelphia to deliver an address at the Broad Street Theater, quoting Washington as saying: "I understand that Mr. Ulrich has a daughter and that recently several attempts had been made to kidnap her. The man was constantly on the watch, suspecting another attempt, and in these circumstances I can readily believe he would have attacked any man, black or white, as he did me." (Philadelphia *Press,* Mar. 27, 1911, 1.) The headline was: "WASHINGTON MAY DROP ASSAULT CASE/ Colored Leader Intimates That His Alleged New York Assailant Was Excusable." The story was widely circulated in other newspapers.

From Seth Low

New York   March 27th, 1911

My dear Mr. Washington: Since parting with you on Saturday morning I have had a chance to talk with Mr. McKelway, with Edgar Gardner Murphy and with Mr. Oswald Villard. They all think that such a statement as has been suggested, if entirely adequate in substance might well be accepted in lieu of a trial. If my suggestion could be carried out, that in addition to the statement the party might plead guilty with the understanding that sentence would be suspended, I feel sure that substantially everyone would be entirely satisfied. I need scarcely point out to you, however, that everything turns upon the adequacy of the signed statement. Perhaps you can let me see a copy of what is proposed before giving it your final approval, if your own inquiries and reflection lead you to the same conclusion.

Mr. Villard thinks that if Mr. Scott could make a statement to the effect that he had sent you such a letter as you spoke of, and if Mr. Smith, the auditor, would also make a statement to the effect that he sometimes did stay in the house you were seeking, or in the neighborhood, that the effect of such statements would be useful. I submit this suggestion for your consideration.

I hope to hear that your strength is returning to you rapidly. Yours very truly,

Seth Low

TLS   Con. 435   BTW Papers   DLC.

From Seth Low

New York   March 27th, 1911

Dear Mr. Washington: Since writing the other letter enclosed in this envelope I have been talking over the telephone with Edgar Gardner Murphy. He thinks that before writing for publication it is important for him to know whether the "Montgomery Advertiser" has taken an unfriendly attitude or not. If it should have done so, he feels that it is exceedingly important that he should be perfectly equipped for a newspaper controversy. To this end he wants to know whether you were taken to the hospital to have your wounds sewed up at your own suggestion, or at the suggestion of the lieutenant of police. He also thinks it highly important that Mr. Smith, the auditor, should make some statement which will corroborate your expectation of finding him in that locality at that time.

In the matter of the declaration which I discussed with him, he reminds me that many will say if such a declaration be accepted, that these people have been bought off. Probably that is so. This makes it seem to me quite important that one factor in any such settlement should be the plea of guilty with a suspension of sentence, as I suggested when I saw you.

Please let me know what I can say to Mr. Murphy as to the hospital question and as to Mr. Smith. Perhaps the best way would be for you to write to Mr. Murphy direct; and, if you do, I shall be much obliged if you will send a copy of the letter to me. Yours very truly,

Seth Low

TLS   Con. 435   BTW Papers   DLC.

From Charles H. Searcy[1]

Cedar Rapids, Ia. Mar. 27, 1911

My Dear Dr. Washington: With humble Greetings

Underneath the bandage — he smiles.

"Smile
A While,
And while you
Smile
Another Smiles;
And soon there's
Miles and Miles
Of Smiles,
And life's worth
While
Because you
Smile."

Charles Searcy

ALS   Con. 435   BTW Papers   DLC.

[1] Charles H. Searcy was reported in a city directory in 1900 as a black janitor at the Masonic Temple.

Seth Low to Edward Morse Shepard

[New York City] March 27th, 1911

My dear Mr. Shepard: Yours of March 24th from Washington came safely to hand. I dictated a letter to you the other day before receiving this, thanking you for your good offices and explaining to you why you had not been called upon. I hope you have received that letter, but my stenographer is unwell today and I am not sure whether it has gone forward or not. I therefore explain in substance the situation.

Mr. Washington told me of your kind offer to his counsel, Mr. Wilford H. Smith, the colored man. Mr. Smith expressed his great appreciation of it and said he would confer with you in case of need. Later it developed that the District Attorney was giving his personal attention to the matter in such a way that it did not seem to be necessary to trouble you. Mr. Arthur Train[1] also kindly offered his services but it was not necessary even to avail of these.

Dr. Washington and the entire Board of Trustees are deeply grateful to you for your willingness to serve Dr. Washington in this emergency if the occasion had demanded it.

The Doctor has now returned to Tuskegee. He was rapidly recovering from his physical injury and I am inclined to think that the danger of serious harm to his influence has been safely passed. Happily the character of those who attacked and accused him is such that their charges do not carry very great weight. Personally I have entire confidence in Dr. Washington's rectitude and I am sure that his action upon the evening when he was assaulted was absolutely free from criticism. I know that he had received from me a letter which would naturally make him wish to see the auditor, and I have no doubt that his explanation of his visit is exact and truthful.

With renewed thanks, Yours sincerely,

[Seth Low]

TLc Seth Low Papers NNC.

[1] Arthur Train (1875–1945) was a lawyer, novelist, and playwright. He was assistant district attorney of New York County from 1901 to 1908 and again in 1914–15. He served as a special deputy attorney general in 1910, prosecuting political corruption cases in Queens County. His writing career spanned almost forty years, and he produced many novels and plays in which the central theme was the practice of law.

To William Henry Lewis

Tuskegee, Alabama, March 28, 1911

Confidential.

Have long telegram from Villard urging me to send him telegram that can be read at their Boston meeting this week indicating willingness to co-operate and get together. What kind of answer do you think ought to send. Will make it plain in my reply that request comes from him. Telegraph answer my expense.

B. T. W.

TWIr   Con. 428   BTW   Papers   DLC.   Editorial   insertions   in   E.   J.   Scott's hand.

To Charles William Anderson

[Tuskegee, Ala.] March 28, 1911

Personal:

My dear Mr. Anderson: There is no need for my trying to find words with which to thank you for the fine, wise and unselfish service which you rendered me during my trying days in New York last week. I shall not try to put my thanks in words, but in the future I shall try to express them more in deeds than in words.

I have just sent our friend Moore a long telegram urging him to stop fighting people and to pursue the course of reconciliation, especially in view of the fact that practically every one of our enemies excepting Du Bois has had his heart softened and I think we can pursue a wise conciliatory course just now especially in view of the fact that Villard wants my help and we will leave Du Bois standing high and dry on a desert island.

From every quarter in New York I got the impression that Moore is unconsciously making enemies for all of us. This last of course is strictly confidential.

You will be glad to know that the South has stood by me magnificently. I had a Pinkerton man with me on the train all the way, and he said that the only remark he heard made against me by any of the people on the train was made by a man from Boston. This illustrates the remark I have often heard you make. Yours very truly,

Booker T. Washington

TLpS   Con. 52   BTW   Papers   DLC.

To James Calvin Hemphill

Tuskegee Institute, Alabama   March 28, 1911

Personal and Confidential

My dear Sir: I have just reached home, and feel it my first duty to write and thank you from the bottom of my heart for the magnificent and generous editorial which you published soon after the dastardly assault upon me in New York.[1] I feel quite sure that your editorial together with the President's letter had the effect of making people stop and think before passing judgment. I suppose you already know that your editorial was published in the principal New York papers.

I shall never forget you and never cease to thank you for coming to my aid at such a critical time.

There is not the slightest basis for any statement that I have ever accosted or insulted a woman, black or white, either in the North or in the South. That was to me the most hurtful part of the whole experience.

I realize fully that this is no time for jest, but during all the time that I was in New York and passing through the most excruciating and disagreeable experiences, I had in mind a story that I had recently heard concerning a colored man who had moved from Georgia into Ohio. His case represents my own feeling. There occurred a lynching in this Ohio town to which this colored man had recently moved, and he at once began to pack up his things and get ready to move back to Georgia. The white people asked him why he was going back to Georgia. He told them that he did not like to live in the Ohio town because of the recent lynching. The reply on the part of the white people was that the colored people were also lynched in Georgia. The colored man replied, "Yes, I knows that, but if I'se lynched in Georgia I'll be lynched by my friends and not by strangers." That old man's story represents my feeling especially in view of the fact that the white people in the little town of Tuskegee where I have spent practically all of my mature years, have simply poured out their hearts to me during this recent trouble in ways that I cannot describe. They have been more than kind.

Sometime when I see you I shall hope to let you know personally how deeply grateful I am to you.

Major Moton and Dr. Frissell have kept me informed of all your deep and helpful interest in the Hampton Institute. Yours very truly,

Booker T. Washington

TLS   Hemphill Family Papers   NcD.

¹ "Booker Washington's Bad Luck" was the title of the editorial in the Richmond *Times-Dispatch*, Mar. 21, 1911, 4. "Booker Washington will be more inclined than ever to stay among 'my own people' down South after his experiences in New York Sunday night," commented the editorial. It accepted BTW's account of the incident: "We don't believe he insulted anybody, that he made any improper remark to any woman at the scene of Sunday night's affair, and if he were 'down in old Alabam' he would be able to prove his good character by his white neighbors, who respect him for his work and without attacking him for his color. It is different, however, up North, and especially in New York."

From Charles William Anderson

New York, N.Y., March 28, 1911

My dear Doctor: Enclosed please find copy of President Taft's reply to my letter of the 24th instant, thanking him for his loyalty in standing by you.¹

Also please find clippings from yesterday's daily papers here relative to the Bethel Church meeting on Sunday. The meeting was a great success. I talked brass tacks to each speaker before the opening of the meeting, and cautioned them against any intemperance of language. They all promised to remember my admonition and stick to their knitting. I was a little fearful of James L. Curtis² and Chief Lee,³ and, therefore, did not put them on to speak until the newspaper men had left the church. It was well that I took this precaution for Curtis delivered a harangue, and said that he for one was there to denounce. He also said that he was in favor of denouncing the attack in the severest terms, as it was not a question which concerned you alone, but concerned every other colored man in the city, for the reason that if you were not safe, no other man is safe, etc., etc., ad infinitum. He then went on to praise Trotter, whom he styled his friend, for his generous attitude toward the whole affair. It was sickening. Chief Lee asked the meeting to appoint a committee to call on the Mayor to have the Policeman promoted who made the arrest. He praised this officer as a hero, and said he ought to be promoted for his fairness to you. Thank Heaven all of the reporters had gone before these two speeches were made. Bishop Derrick, Rev. W. H. Brooks, Ransom, Dr. York Russell[4] and Rev. Powell all made excellent speeches full of good sense and caution. Powell made the best speech of them all. I think he is going to turn out "all wool and a yard wide."

In my opening address I not only praised the President for his manly stand, but I praised all the other leading men, including Mr. Carnegie and Mr. Low, who had stood up, and I had a word of approval for the fairness of the press of this city. Of course, I did not regard the attitude of the press as being impartial, but I thought I would hand it a little commendation in order to secure a favorable report of a meeting, which was full of explosive possibilities. My little tub to the whale seems to have served its purpose with the reporters, for they all made nice reports of the meeting.

Your telegram reached me at 2:30 this morning, after all the morning papers had gone to the press. I have transmitted it to Mr. Smith, who will handle the matter today. I knew the interview was fictitious as soon as I read it in the World on yesterday. I am sure you will be pleased with the results of the Bethel meeting. In my judgment, it has done much real good. The brethren rose to their feet and cheered lustily when President Taft's name was mentioned. He has builded wiser than he knew, in taking that brave and loyal stand.

Trusting you are very well, and hoping to hear from you in the near future, I remain, Yours faithfully,

Charles

TLS Con. 52 BTW Papers DLC. No newspaper clippings found with letter.

[1] Taft wrote to Anderson, Mar. 25, 1911, that it was a privilege to speak in behalf of BTW, adding: "It is when a fellow is in trouble that he needs his friends." (Con. 52, BTW Papers, DLC.)

[2] James L. Curtis (1870–1917), a black lawyer and Democratic politician, was born in Raleigh, N.C. A graduate of Lincoln University (1889) and Northwestern University Law School (1894), he practiced law in Columbus, Ohio (1894–99), Minneapolis (1899–1906), and New York City (1906–15). He was active in support of Woodrow Wilson as a member of the United Colored Democracy of New York City, and Wilson appointed him minister to Liberia in 1915. Curtis died in office on the African coast.

[3] Edward E. Lee.

[4] York Russell, a New York physician, graduated from Howard University Medical School in 1898.

From Theodore Roosevelt

San Francisco   March 28th 1911

My dear Dr. Washington: I have been equally concerned and indignant at the account of the assault upon you. I earnestly hope that you
will press the charge. Apparently, whatever may have been the previous
character of the man who attacked you, the assault itself was utterly
wanton; and I hope your case will be pressed and a verdict obtained.
Then you can do as you think best about getting the sentence reduced.
Faithfully yours,

Theodore Roosevelt

TLS Con. 438 BTW Papers DLC.

From Gilchrist Stewart

New York, March 28, 1911

My dear Dr. Washington; I trust you will not consider it presumptuous
but will consider it in the same spirit that actuates this letter, i.e. a
desire to acquaint you with average public sentiment upon the outrageous attack accorded you in this city. I am somewhat diffident
about writing this letter, but merely do it because of the friendship
that has existed between us for a number of years. I would not do it
were it otherwise, but it has seemed to me that you should be apprised
of just how the public regarded the various ramifications of the attack
made upon you; particularly for the matters involved in your prosecution of Mr. Ulrich, and what you should lay stress upon in the legal
procedures therein involved.

First. No one believes very much the statement of Mrs. Ulrich.[1]

Second. Public opinion, as I have sized it up, and when I say public
opinion, I mean the average fellow I meet, like my students at Law
School, in the contracting business, the average politician, etc., does
not seem to exactly understand your reasons for being in that locality
at that number. They seem to think that there was some particular
and special motive of a character not explained to the public, i.e. there
is an indefinite assumption that a laxity of morals was involved in

looking for something or somebody. Unfortunately the first statement of a telegram, then a letter and the attorney holding out that the letter would be produced at trial, and then the subsequent statement, that the letter was destroyed, have all given rise to some doubt upon which a thousand interpretations have been stretched.

Now I merely write this confidentially so that you may have an idea of what you should lay most emphasis upon at the trial. The biggest and best men of the city do not countenance the charge or the matter at all. I am merely telling you what the lowly and the humble of public opinion, such as the fellow I meet at the Law School and the average man as I run across him in the contracting business feels.

It is needless for me to say to you, that I am with you in this matter as in all others, while as you know I am out of all "movements," it has been a great source of pleasure for me to interject myself into the situation sufficiently to assure certain white friends of the race, such as, Villard, Milholland, Walling, and others, that you were perfectly innocent in the matter. In this connection, I might say, that I believe that my advice in not antagonizing the so called new movement would be productive of good results. I particularly deprecated the attack on Walling. I thought it both unwise and unjust and think that if several of your friends would move with discretion and precision in reference to such movements, that the cause of the race would be better off.

These few observations that I have deemed it my duty to write to you, I hope you will deem confidential and I merely do so because of my friendship to you. Milholland, Villard and Walling, Miss Ovington, et al. are with you in this matter in despite of the efforts of a number of people to try and convince them that there was an ulterior motive in your being around 63rd Street. Yours sincerely,

Gilchrist Stewart

P.S. While out of "movements" and others things generally, yet I am just staying sufficiently into the game to come back when I get ready.

TLS Con. 435 BTW Papers DLC. Written on stationery of the Manhattan House Cleaning & Renovating Bureau, of which Stewart was general manager.

[1] Actually Laura Page Alvarez.

From Ralph Waldo Tyler

Washington D C   March 28 1911

My opinion of an answer is to-wit. Willing to cooperate with any conservatively correct movement whose aim is advancement they have nothing to offer for your cooperation and you have nothing to lose by cooperation that surrender[s] nothing.

R W Tyler

HWSr   Con. 443   BTW Papers   DLC.

To Seth Low

Tuskegee Ala   March 29. 1911

When I telegraphed Mr Murphy I was in Doubt as to the attitude of southern Newspapers since reaching here and looking into situation fully I find that the attitude of southern Newspapers is so entirely friendly that I do not think it necessary to do anything in the direction mentioned in My Message to Mr Murphy the whole south has stood by me during this trying season in a way that Makes me love it More than ever. Please telephone this to Mr Murphy.

Booker T. Washington

TWSr   Seth Low Papers   NNC.

From Charles William Anderson

New York   Mch 29/1911

Fear it would be unwise to decline Villard proposition   let refusal to cooperate come from other side if it comes at all   Would word telegram cautiously but with ring of sincerety.[1]

Chas W Anderson

HWSr   Con. 52   BTW Papers   DLC.

[1] In a letter of the same date Anderson wrote: "For us to decline the olive branch would be to expose us to the charge of being narrow, and it would give the scoundrels on the other side an excuse for wielding the dirty weapons, which they know so well how to use." (Con. 52, BTW Papers, DLC.)

From William Henry Lewis

Washington, D.C. March 29th [1911]

Suggest following telegram: Knowing your life-long interest and activities in behalf of my race, I gladly welcome any suggestions coming from you looking toward a friendly co-operation of all the workers for the general advancement of the colored people. It seems to me that while we necessarily work along different lines, we may still work together in perfect harmony and sympathy and mutual understanding. It would be a happy day for my race and country, if we could unite all our forces.

William H. Lewis

TWSr   Con. 428   BTW Papers   DLC.

From Robert Russa Moton

Richmond Va   3-29-11

I should by all means send Villard guarded telegram expressing willingness to co-operate.

R. R. Moton

HWSr   Con. 54   BTW Papers   DLC.

From Samuel Laing Williams

Chicago Ills 3-29-11

They evidently need your influence let offer of compromise come from them your program is rooted in public opinion important that you be free to follow your course where there is common ground make the most of it

S. Laing Williams

HWSr Con. 446 BTW Papers DLC.

Charles Fletcher Dole to Seth Low

Jamaica Plain Massachusetts March 29, 1911

My dear Mr. Low With regard to Mr. Washington's most unfortunate occurrence in New York, what can we say in answer to the question that people ask; "Where was Mr. Smith, the auditor, when Mr. W. was trying to find him in the wrong place?" Could you kindly give me a clew about this?

I enclose a clipping from the Boston *Transcript*. How does such a thing get started & into circulation? It all seems a chapter of fatalities. Yours with high respect

Charles F. Dole

ALS Seth Low Papers NNC. No enclosure found with letter.

To Oswald Garrison Villard

[Tuskegee, Ala.] March 30, 1911

Your telegram of March twenty ninth received. Confirming the conversation we had in New York I would state that your lifelong interest and activities in behalf of my race urge me to repeat that I shall be glad to work in friendly cooperation with all the workers for the general advancement of the colored people especially in constructive directions.

It seems to me that while we necessarily may in the future as in the past work along different lines we still may work together in harmony, sympathy and mutual understanding. I am convinced that the time has come when all interested in the welfare of the Negro people should lay aside personal differences and personal bickerings and anything and everything that smacks of selfishness and keep in mind only rendering the service which will best promote and protect the whole race in all of its larger interests. In the last analysis I am sure that we all agree on more points than we disagree on. Further than this, the experience through which I have been passing convinces me that deep down in the heart of all of us there is a feeling of oneness and sympathy and unity. I am sure that all of my friends everywhere will happily cooperate with you in the directions I have mentioned. If your organization now in session can see its way clear to appoint two or more fraternal delegates to attend the next meeting of the National Business League I feel quite sure that our organization will reciprocate in kind.[1] It will be a happy day for my race when all of the forces and organizations while still remaining individually separate can sympathetically and heartily cooperate and work together for its larger good.

Booker T. Washington

TWpSr Con. 55 BTW Papers DLC.

[1] Villard replied after the NAACP annual meeting had passed a perfunctory resolution of regret regarding the Ulrich incident: "It seemed wisest to me not to make a point of fraternal delegates, and I certainly hope that your organization will send three to our next meeting, as one of the next steps towards co-operation. Our people feel that as we have taken this first move it is your move next." (Apr. 10, 1911, Oswald Garrison Villard Papers, MH.)

An Article in *The Independent*

[March 30, 1911]

DURHAM, NORTH CAROLINA, A CITY OF NEGRO ENTERPRISES

For a number of years I have made what I have called "Educational Pilgrimages" thru various Southern States, including Arkansas, Oklahoma, Mississippi, South Carolina, Tennessee, Virginia, Delaware and North Carolina. These tours have been undertaken for the purpose of seeing for myself something of the progress being made by the Negro people of these various States, the actual relations existing between the races, and also for the purpose of saying whatever I can to help cement friendly relations between the races. Both races in the South suffer at the hands of public opinion, because the outside world hears of its disgrace, its crimes, its mobs and lynchings. But it does not hear very much about the many evidences of racial friendship and good will which exist in the majority of the communities of the South. I do not believe that one can find another section of the globe where two races which are dissimilar in many respects dwell in so large numbers where they get on better in all the affairs of life than they do in our Southern States.

The last of these trips was made thru the State of North Carolina during the fall of 1910. I was unusually impressed with the general prosperity of the colored people in the rural villages and smaller towns. Farms, truck farms, well-kept grocery stores, thriving drug stores, insurance houses, and beautiful tho modest homes greeted me continually. Again and again I exprest to the Negro business men in charge of my trip that here were in many ways the most encouraging signs of Negro development that I had seen. But again and again, as often as I said this there would come back from several members of the party the answer, "Wait till you get to Durham."

Now, Durham is one of the large cities of North Carolina, and knowing from my early experiences something of the superficial and hand-to-mouth living of the average city Negro, I became more and more curious to see what Durham had in store for me.

Arriving there about four o'clock on a bright afternoon in October, I found every preparation that was necessary to sweep me from my feet with the conviction that sure enough this was the city of cities to look for prosperity of the Negroes and the greatest amount of friendly feeling between the two races of the South. In one town on my way I had actual roses strewn in my path, but here, if all I saw and heard was genuine, were the real roses that I had been seeking now for more than thirty years. Well, and not foolishly, dressed colored people, colored people representing all manner of business, from the small store to the thriving, thorogoing business enterprise, colored people seated in one and two horse carriages with rubber tires, stood eager to welcome me. Still I was not convinced. I had more than once seen members of my race who paid their last dollar for display, not having enough left to purchase a good meal or even to buy fuel to cook with. But I was assured that these people owned all they claimed to own and that I would be shorn of all my doubt before many hours had passed, and I confess that two hours of driving and visiting more than robbed me of all my skepticism.

In addition to many prosperous doctors, lawyers, preachers and men of other professions, I found some of the most flourishing drug stores, grocery and dry good stores I had ever seen anywhere among Negroes. I found here the largest Negro insurance company in the world,[1] with assets amounting to $100,000, owning its building, a large three-story structure, and being operated with nothing but Negro clerks and agents. Here is located the Durham Textile and the Whitted Wood Working Company, manufacturers of doors, window frames, mantels and all kinds of building materials. Here, too, is the Union Iron Works Company, a Negro company which manufactures general foundry products, turning out plows, plow castings, laundry heaters, grates and castings for domestic purposes, and it was refreshing to learn that in this enterprise as in others that I shall mention there was no evidence of the color line drawn on the part of the purchaser. Each groceryman, each textile manufacturer, each tailor, in fact, all the Negro tradesmen and business men numbered many white customers among their most substantial purchasers.

I began by this time to believe that Durham was a city of Negro enterprises, and, quite convinced now, I was ready to go home, but they wanted to show me one more successful Negro plant. This was the plant known as the Durham Textile Mill, the only hosiery mill in the world entirely owned and operated by Negroes. Regularly incorporated, they operate eighteen knitting machines of the latest pattern, working regularly twelve women and two men and turning out seventy-five dozen pairs of hose each day. The goods so far are standing the test in the market, being equal in every way to other hose of the same price. They are sold mainly by white salesmen, who travel mostly in North Carolina, New York, Indiana, Georgia, South Carolina and Alabama, and again, so far as I have heard, there has been no man to raise the color question when he put on a pair of these hose made by Negroes.

Aside from these flourishing enterprises Durham had many individuals, such as tradesmen and contractors, who were shining examples of what a colored man may become when he is proficient and industrious. I found that Payton A. Smith, a general contractor, had put up some of the largest buildings in the city, that P. W. Dawkins, Jr.,[2] who had learned the carpenter's trade at Hampton, and Norman C. Dadd were not only never out of work, but kept jobs always waiting for them.

It was exceedingly interesting, too, to find here two individuals owning and operating brickyards. Colored people for years and years have been operating brickyards for other people and it was highly encouraging to meet here two men who had grasped the American principle of things, that of advancing from common laborer to owner and operator. With a business amounting to $16,000 per year, R. E. Clegg, manufacturer of all kinds of brick, turns out per season about two million brick. But the pioneer in brick making in Durham is R. B. Fitzgerald.[3] Beginning thirty years ago, Mr. Fitzgerald has supplied the material for many of the largest brick structures in the city. I cannot refrain from emphasizing once more the absence of color discrimination in a work of this sort. This case in particular warrants it, as Fitzgerald owes his success almost entirely to Southern white men. One man in particular, Mr. Blackwell,[4] the great tobacco manufacturer, said to him, "Fitzgerald, get all the Negroes and mules you can and make brick. I will take all that you can make." Fitzgerald followed the instruction and today he not only turns out 30,000 brick a day from his $17,000 plant, but owns besides 100 acres of land within the city limits and has $50,000 worth of real estate.

A Negro bank is no longer a novelty, there being more than fifty in America at the present time, but the one at Durham, in addition to carrying resources of $400,000 and deposits of $20,000, is an instance of what the white Southerner often does to help Negroes. When this bank was opened, the cashier and teller of the leading white bank came over and without charge, helped the colored bankers open and close their books.

With all this prosperity, with flourishing insurance companies, a bank, brickmasons and men in the professions, it was not remarkable that this class of persons should own beautiful homes. It was more of a question of overdoing than not doing enough in their furnishings. And so while I was now ready to believe anything about the prosperity of Durham Negroes, I was curious to see if wealth had driven the people into extravagance. Far from it. With electric lights, steam heat and baths and all the modern equipments, these residences presented a modesty of taste that was more than gratifying. No baubles, no tinsel of furnishing that often represent the abuse of wealth, but conservative and tasteful furniture I found everywhere. Wealthy Negroes like Dr. A. A. Moore,[5] C. C. Spaulding and John Merrick could have fitted up their homes to dazzle the eye and evoke the envy of both white and black, but instead they have rather set a standard of good taste and good judgment to all who know them.

I must here call especial attention to Mr. John Merrick, recognized as the leading Negro of Durham. Mr. Merrick began as a poor man, borrowing money from General Julian S. Carr,[6] a leading white man, to begin his first business. During all the years he has lived in Durham, he has continually expended time and money to promote the interests of colored people, aiding them in securing homes and in establishing organizations of protection. In 1883 he founded the Royal Knights of King David and in 1898 he founded the North Carolina Mutual and Provident Association. He aided in establishing a hospital here for Negroes, is a trustee of the bank, a steward in the St. Joseph A.M.E. Church and president of the Christian Endeavor League. In addition to this he is the largest Negro owner of residence property in the city, collecting per month rents amounting to $550. That all this draws no envy from the white people is illustrated by the fact that a few months ago at the marriage of his daughter more than three hundred of the best white people were present, bringing with them costly presents for the bride.

But with all this prosperity, some doubt still assailed me. The exceptional man is everywhere and among all races. He has always been in evidence among the people of my race. In slavery days one Negro could gain his freedom and himself become a slave owner while his own brethren remained in bondage. These Durham men of whom I am talking had had their opportunities. They had been to college, to medical schools, to dental schools, to schools in the North, enjoying everywhere contact with the best minds and spirits that the nation possessed. It was not so much wonder after all that, given a fair chance, they could create and develop enterprises and enjoy the blessings of life.

But what of the poor man, the unlettered man, the man against whom because of age or adverse circumstances, the door of training had been tightly closed? What was he doing and how was he living? This was my last question put to the city of Durham. If it could answer me this satisfactorily I would yield; because I knew that in this query lay the crux of the whole race situation in the South; for it is with this class that the white people of the South have to deal, and upon the conduct of this class that the real estimate of my race is generally formed.

It is written that we have the poor always with us and it was this poor that I wished to see. I drove through their section of the city, observing closely their homes inside and out, their yards, their fences, their window curtains, their furniture, and I own that in many cases I almost doubted my eyes. The one time hovel and the shack with rags sticking in the windows and fences rotting away, with little gulleys washed in the yards and half clad children standing in front of the door were all gone. I saw no dead dogs or cats or dead fowl in the streets as I sometimes see in our larger Southern cities and I sniffed no feverish odors from dens and dives. Neat cottages stood where in many cities still stands the tubercular shack, and well cared for children in clean yards, many of which were adorned with flower beds, everywhere greeted me. There were windows with clean curtains and clean shades and substantial furniture devoid of the cheap shimmer of the installment house.

Surely I felt there must be something at the bottom of all this and I set myself to inquire what was the secret of this general healthy appearance. Of course, the wealthy doctors, the prosperous school teachers and well-to-do ministers were no longer a mystery or a surprise. If the so-called poor were thus situated the professional man, I well knew, was bound to flourish like the proverbial bay tree.

As this was the class that came most in contact with the white people I asked what was the general spirit existing between the two races. Of all the Southern cities I have visited, I found here the sanest attitude of the white people toward the black. Disabused long ago of the "social equality" bugbear, the white people, and the best ones too, never feared to go among the Negroes at their gatherings and never feared to aid them in securing an education or any kind of improvement. I have already stated that the wealthiest and best thought of Negro in Durham began his business career upon a loan of money from General Julian S. Carr. Perhaps a still stronger instance is that of the Duke family, the famous tobacco manufacturers. The members of this family have always given generously to support the colored schools and churches of the town, and Mr. Washington Duke during his lifetime took such interest in and attended so regularly the African Methodist Episcopal Church, that the colored people counted him as one of their own members. This is a glowing example of what I mean by a sane attitude toward the colored people. If the white people thruout the South, indeed if the employers everywhere, would encourage the Negroes by their presence and personal interest in their undertakings, there would be day by day fewer complaints of the dissolute Negro laborer and the trifling Negro servant. Nobody, white or black, has ever argued that Mr. Washington Duke was in any way contaminated by his contact with the African Methodist Episcopal Church; rather the Negroes are inclined to vie with the whites in doing his memory honor and reverence.

Another example of the substantial encouragement the white people of Durham give the Negroes is found in the attempt last summer to found in the city a Negro Chautauqua. When the colored people showed that they were really in earnest, Dr. James E. Shepard, founder of the school, laid his plans before the white people, who immediately took steps to aid him, the Merchants' Association and B. L. Duke[7] donating to the institution twenty-five acres of land valued approximately at $7,000.

The white people here further show their fine spirit by holding open everywhere the door of opportunity to the Negro. Ignoring color or race, they demand only efficiency. I never saw in a city of this size so many prosperous carpenters, brick masons, blacksmiths, wheelwrights, cotton mill operators and tobacco factory workers among Negroes.

In the larger white mills and the like the Negroes in several instances are the only ones employed. The hook and ladder company of the fire department is manned entirely by black men, showing not only a liberality of spirit, but a recognition that courage can lodge in the breast of a black man as well as in that of a white man. I have referred to the hosiery mill owned and operated solely by Negroes; there is one here also owned by a white man, but operated exclusively by colored men. The proprietor is Gen. Julian S. Carr, to whom I have already referred. General Carr employs 150 women and a few men, and it argues the generous spirit typical here that he was willing to admit a rival Negro mill right here in his neighborhood, many of whose workmen had received their training from him.

But the company that has done most for the Negro, both in employment and in general help, is the W. Duke, Sons & Company,[8] branch of the American Tobacco Company. This company employs more colored laborers than any other firm in the city, keeping steadily at work 1,548 Negro men and women, at an average of 93 cents per day, or paying out $1,400 per day or $440,000 a year to colored people. And it is highly to the credit of the colored people that thru all the changes in the system and in the introduction of new and complex machinery they have been able to hold their positions and give increasing satisfaction to their employers.

Indeed this satisfaction has been so genuine that the American Tobacco Company has for some time been pursuing the policy for its colored employees, which, if adopted by many of our large corporations thruout the country would spare the nation many strikes, lockouts, bloodshed and the suppression of general prosperity. This company has established an employees' bounty, which upon the death of the employee, is paid to the latter's family. The company donates in cash to the person who has been before designated by the employee a sum of money equal to the wages paid to the deceased during the last year of his life; not exceeding, however, in any case, the sum of $500. Tho recently inaugurated this scheme has already allowed to be paid out more than $3,000 to the beneficiaries of the colored employees. In addition to this the company takes cognizance of its employees' health, seeing, no doubt, that better health conditions insure a constantly higher grade of service. The Lincoln Hospital here, a place for the sick colored people and for the training of colored nurses, received its grounds and building, valued all told at $75,000, from Mr. Washington Duke, the founder of the Duke Tobacco Company, and it is in co-operation with this hospital that the firm is now taking active interest in the improvement of the home life of its employees by securing a visiting nurse to work in the Negro section of the city. That thruout all the Negro efforts in Durham these companies have been willing to entrust their money and donations of buildings and grounds to the hands of colored men shows how thoroly established is the confidence of the white men in the honor and efficiency of the Negro doctor, the Negro school teacher and the Negro minister.

Nothing in all this appealed to me more than the information that the white people everywhere encouraged the Negroes to buy and own property. Surely nothing binds a man to the general welfare of a community more than to tie up his interest there in a piece of property, no matter what kind it may be. That so large a proportion own their homes, that the most of those renting rented from Negro landlords, that the southern part of Durham was inhabited almost entirely by colored people, and that Negro possessions in the city amounted to one million dollars, was the key that unlocked for me much of the mystery of prosperity and good feeling between the two races. Two or three far-sighted white men had encouraged some few struggling Negroes to invest in a piece of property. The influence spread itself until out of men whose spirit was comparatively indifferent to their surroundings have been molded loyal, patriotic, law-abiding black citizens.

I found as a result of an interview with several of the white men of the town that the good opinion of the colored men was growing more and more general. Mr. W. T. Bost, the city editor of the Durham *Herald,* spoke in the highest terms of the general thriftiness of the colored people. Mr. Bost, as it happened, had lived in a number of other cities in the State and it was his experience that the Negroes at Durham were more law-abiding than in any other city in which he had lived. There was also less vagrancy here than in any other city. And indeed this might well be, for at the very moment of this interview, Mr. J. F. Freeland, chief of police, was making an active canvass among the colored ministers and others of influence to assist him in a movement to improve further the condition of the lower class of colored people. But to continue with Mr. Bost, the city editor said that it made no difference in Durham when it came to business. "Fitzgerald," he continued, "makes better brick than any other man in town; therefore the people buy Fitzgerald's brick. The Whitted Graded School makes the best furniture in town and so it is always in demand at a good price."

Major W. A. Guthrie,[9] one of the leading lawyers of the city, stated that there was a better feeling between the races than in any other city in the State. "Conditions here," he declared, "are pleasing to both races. The whites have learned that it pays the town to have educated ministers and teachers and such colored business men as John Merrick." Major Guthrie, it may be said here, was for a number of years chairman of the City School Board. Some thirty years ago, on the day that, as chairman of the board, he selected the spot on which to erect the Whitted Graded School, a race riot was taking place in a nearby town. Major Guthrie said to the other members of the board, "I think it is better to buy land and build a schoolhouse for the Negroes than to shoot them down." Thirty years of experience has proved that he was correct.

The Independent, 70 (Mar. 30, 1911), 642-50.

[1] The North Carolina Mutual Life Insurance Co.

[2] Pinckney William Dawkins, Jr.

[3] Richard Burton Fitzgerald, born in New Castle County, Del., of a prosperous free black family, moved south in 1869 and settled in Durham, where he was a leading brick manufacturer, owner of real estate, and president of the first black bank in the city. (Murray, *Proud Shoes,* 55–57, 267.)

[4] William T. Blackwell (b. 1839), partner of Julian S. Carr in tobacco manufacturing.

[5] Probably Aaron McDuffie Moore (b. 1863), Durham's first black physician and a founder of the North Carolina Mutual Life Insurance Co. (Weare, *Black Business in the New South,* 52–56.)

[6] Julian Shakespeare Carr (1845–1924), a former Confederate general, was president of the Bull Durham Tobacco Co. He also owned a hosiery mill in Durham that was operated entirely by blacks.

[7] Brodie L. Duke, eldest son of Washington Duke, established his own tobacco business and also had cotton mill and railroad investments.

[8] Washington Duke (b. 1820) and his sons established a tobacco business in Durham after returning from the Civil War. It merged with other firms to form the American Tobacco Co. in 1890.

[9] William A. Guthrie, a Durham lawyer and a Republican, joined the Populist party in 1894, and in 1896 both the Republicans and Populists nominated him for governor. (Edmonds, *The Negro and Fusion Politics,* 150.)

To William Howard Taft

Tuskegee Institute, Alabama [ca. Mar. 31, 1911][1]

My dear Mr. President: I sent you a telegram from New York expressing my deep thanks for the magnificent and generous service which you rendered me at a trying and critical hour. But I must send you a word in addition in my own very poor hand writing. I shall never cease to thank you for what you have done and shall always try to prove myself worthy of your confidence.

Of course the most trying part of the experience was to be charged with a *base falsehood* which affected my character. My friends however have stood by me finely and more friends have come to light that than I ever knew that I had.

The Southern white people I am glad to say have stood by me finely.

To you Mr. President just now my heart is too full of gratitude for utterance. I shall try to tell you all when I see you. Yours very sincerely

Booker T. Washington

ALS   William Howard Taft Papers   DLC.

[1] Taft received this letter on Apr. 1, 1911, and replied: "I am delighted if my letter helped you." (Apr. 1, 1911, William Howard Taft Papers, DLC.)

From Charles William Anderson

New York, N.Y., March 31, 1911

(Personal)

My dear Doctor: I thought you might be interested to know that I have purposely been walking and talking with all sorts and conditions of people this week, and have only found two men who did not talk "straight." One of these is a man with a grievance, and the other is a well-known Ishmaelite, whose hand is against everybody. I must have talked with five hundred people during the week, so I think you will agree that this is a splendid result. I am gratified more than words can express. I agree with you, that it is a good time to freeze out that little Georgia fellow.[1]

As for your words of appreciation of my activities, I beg to say that when you stop to consider all that I owe to you, all that you have been to me, and all that you have done for me, I think you will conclude that if I had not rolled up my sleeves, I would have shown myself to be beneath contempt. If there is any gratitude in the human heart, or any loyalty in man, it would suggest that my place was at your side at a time when you were the victim of a cruel mistake. Thank God, your life of service and the kindness of your heart toward all those who are unfortunate or distressed, has placed you where no man or mistake can seriously harm you. The American people know a man when they see him, and like Doctor Powell, I never was so proud of being an American before. I never was so proud of President Taft before. In speaking of the uses of adversity, Shakespeare compares them to the toad which "yet wears the precious jewel in its head." So with this misfortune. It has cleared the atmosphere, and taught us all just where to look for sympathy in a day of trial, and it has taught us too to expect to find loyal friends in the most unexpected places, and to look for cowards here and there where we expected to find a brave soul. I did not mean to preach when I started this letter. I merely meant to assure you that whatever I have been, or may be able to do for you, will never repay you for the support, friendship and guidance you have freely given to me for years. Yours truly,

Charles W. Anderson

TLS   Con. 52   BTW Papers   DLC.

[1]W. E. B. Du Bois.

From Daniel Cranford Smith

New York   March 31. 1911

Personal

My dear Mr. Washington: Your letter of the 29th inst. recd. this A.M. I had Mr. B.[1] wire Mr. Hunt that I should do as you wished, but that it would be necessary for me to do some work here first.

When the President[2] of the three Mining Companies for which I am Auditor, learned, through the papers of my presence in New York, he insisted upon my doing some work here, before going to Michigan. For three years past I have had the audits of the New York accounts of these Companies, made by assistants, owing to the pressure of work which has kept me busy elsewhere. Mr. Todd wished me to supervise this work personally this year. It will take me about two weeks longer.

I dont expect to communicate with any of our people here during that time.

As for my expenses, of course, the trip home and thence to Michigan costs forty or fifty dollars more than the direct trip from the South, and involves a couple of extra days traveling. I dont, however, expect to be paid for this.

In the matter of my compensation for my time last week, I can only say that I dont want any thing extra. I should have given it to Tuskegee any way. The Inst. is the only loser, as the folks there will have to work out the matters I was engaged upon with out my help, for the present.

In this connection I may as well tell you what has been on my mind for some time. Namely that the Inst. does not engage (and pay for) enough of my time. You have doubtless thought this yourself, as Mr. Gibson told me that he had an idea that you thought I should spend more time at Tuskegee.

The facts are these. When I made my contract with Mr. Baldwin in 1898, it was specified that I should visit the School twice per year, three weeks to the visit. It was assumed that the time I devoted to the work while away was equivalent to two weeks more. My compensation was based on a fee for eight weeks per year. Nothing has since been said about the time. Beginning with 1901, I have devoted to the work from three to four months each year (this School year I worked for the School in New York and at the School almost four months) and have visited the School as high as four times in one year, as I did in 1910.

I asked for extra compensation only once, in connection with Mr. Haroldson's[3] visit. I have given this extra time freely and for nothing, because there was work for me to do, and of my interest in it. The time I thus lost from my other work cost me $25 per day in loss of fees which I could have earned elsewhere, if I had chosen to do so. It occurs to me, on reflecting upon it, that services given at a money sacrifice, are not appreciated, and that perhaps, in the future in justice to the growing demands upon my income (as my children grow older and their college careers have to be provided for) that I should ask for compensation for all the time I devote to Tuskegee, proportionate to what I receive elsewhere, or else cut down the time to what I contracted to give and for which I am paid.[4]

67

In explanation of why I have given this extra time I may add that I am more interested in the work at Tuskegee than in any other work I do. I enjoy the time I spend there more and it is more profitable to me, in my own intellectual and spiritual development, than any other period of the year. The work there is where my heart is, the very same as is true of you. (This I once told you.) I am working out my ideas there and doing work of social value, especially in training my clerks and student clerks. I am working out original ideas in teaching. This interest is where my main compensation lies, this and the good it does me individually.

When I left Tuskegee last week I had intended to remain two weeks longer. I had more to do, it seemed than ever before. I was giving this work for nothing. Even if I had stayed two weeks longer I should not have finished the work I had underway. Not only the work on the Supply System, the Cost Accounting, the System of Charges, but also reports and improvements in the Farm Accounting, the General Stores and instructions on making inventories (This last being something your brother asked me to do).

In view of the fact I was giving this time freely and for nothing, you can see how little I regard the time lost last week, from my other affairs. I dont expect or wish any compensation for it. It is sufficient for me for you to know that I desire and try to be helpful to you in the large Social and Educational work you are doing, not only for the Negroes, but also for the whole of humanity. I am content simply for you to know this. Yours very sincerely

Daniel Cranford Smith

ALS   Con. 55   BTW Papers   DLC.

[1] Presumably Robert Charles Bedford.

[2] Presumably Albert May Todd (1850–1931), a chemist, manufacturer, and political reformer of Kalamazoo, Mich. He was active in many organizations devoted to direct democracy and public ownership of utilities.

[3] William Wallace Haralson.

[4] BTW replied in regard to Smith's compensation: "We shall hope to work out something that will be wholly agreeable to you." (Apr. 4, 1911, Con. 55, BTW Papers, DLC.)

From Oswald Garrison Villard

Boston, Mass., March 31, 1911

I am glad to tell you that the National Association For The Advancement Of Colored People at its meeting today passed the following resolution:

Resolved that we put on record our profound regret at the recent assault on Dr. Booker T. Washington in New York City in which the Association finds renewed evidence of race discrimination and increased necessity for the awakening of the public conscience.[1]

Oswald Garrison Villard

TWSr Copy   Con. 55   BTW Papers   DLC.

[1] The NAACP decided not to support a stronger resolution expressing confidence in BTW's version of the Ulrich incident. For additional details on the debate among the NAACP officers, see Kellogg, *NAACP*, 80–83.

Seth Low to Charles Fletcher Dole

[New York City] March 31st, 1911

My dear Dr. Dole; I have your letter of the 29th. I saw Dr. Washington on the morning after the assault, while he was still dazed from the blows which he had received. His explanation of his errand in West 63rd Street the evening before was precisely what it has always been, and to me is entirely satisfactory. I had written him a letter a few days before, suggesting, among other things, certain changes in the farm accounting. This letter reached Tuskegee after Dr. Washington had left for the North. It was forwarded to him by his Secretary, Mr. Scott, and it awakened in him, very naturally, the desire to confer with Mr. Smith, the auditor of the School. When Dr. Washington reached New York, he received a letter from his Secretary, Mr. Scott, saying that he thought Mr. Smith would be finished at Tuskegee and might be in New York by the time Dr. Washington arrived, and that, if he were, he would possibly be staying with relatives, whose name and address he gave. This letter Dr. Washington did not keep, but he acted upon the information it contained as to Mr. Smith's possible presence in New York, and went to the street and number, as he recalled them, in the hope of finding Mr. Smith, but without any appointment with him. As [a] matter of fact, I believe that Mr. Smith had not left Tuskegee when Dr. Washington was trying to find him in New York, but that of course Dr. Washington did not know. His explanation is natural, consistent and worthy of belief. I may observe, in passing, that Dr. Washington is much too intelligent a man to give an explanation which could so easily be disproved if the truthfulness of his story depended upon Mr. Smith's presence in New York at that moment, unless he had absolutely known that Mr. Smith were there. I suppose you appreciate that Mr. Smith's home is in Montclair, New Jersey, and that he goes to Tuskegee from time to time, and has been in Tuskegee for the last few weeks in connection with his work as Auditor of the School. So far as I know, Dr. Washington has never wavered in any particular in connection with this explanation, which he subsequently embodied in his public statement, which I suppose you saw. I believe that he is entitled, by reason of his character, to have his statement in this respect accepted, without evidence, as unquestioningly as the same statement would be received from you or myself.

Now, as to the attack upon him. I hand you herewith copy of a letter received from my class-mate, Dr. George L. Peabody, the morning after the assault, which will reveal to you the impression made at the time upon a physician and a highly intelligent man. It is clear that Ulrich gave the impression, at the moment, of being desperately in earnest. This condition of mind is explicable upon the state of facts, which I first learned from Mr. Schieffelin, that an attempt had recently been made to kidnap the daughter of the woman who passed for Ulrich's wife, and that Ulrich supposed that Washington's movements up and down the street between his different calls at the house indicated a purpose to renew the attempt.

If you ask why Ulrich and the woman who passed as his wife did not give this explanation at the outset, the answer I think is easy. It has transpired that the real Mrs. Ulrich lives in New Jersey, and that Ulrich is paying alimony to her. The woman who passed as Mrs. Ulrich in the many interviews about Washington, was not his wife at all. It seems to me clear that both of them, (i.e. this woman and

Ulrich) had a motive for not revealing, at the moment, the true state of facts; and for giving a plausible but untrue explanation for the attack upon Dr. Washington. The real fact appears to have been, that the husband of the woman who claimed to be Ulrich's wife had attempted to kidnap his daughter without the mother's consent. This at least is what Mr. Schieffelin tells me; and, if this be so, the motive for the attack upon Dr. Washington, or any one else acting similarly in the neighborhood, is clearly revealed.

The statements made about Dr. Washington's condition and conduct on the evening of the attack by Ulrich and the woman who first figured as his wife, are entirely unworthy of belief; for these people have shown themselves to be untrustworthy, and their word is not to be accepted against the word of an honorable man like Booker T. Washington.

If Dr. Washington said in Philadelphia what is indicated in the article from the "Transcript," it shows, I think, that he has given entire credence to the story that the Ulrichs were in fear of another kidnapping attempt. Dr. Washington also knows what my friend, Dr. Peabody, wrote to me, for I read him the letter. Whether it was wise to say just what he is reported to have said is another question, but I am not disposed to accept too literally a newspaper abbreviation of his utterances.

I think you will be glad to know that I received from him yesterday from Tuskegee by telegraph a Day Letter, in which he says that, since his return, he finds that the attitude of the Southern newspapers is entirely friendly. He says: "The whole South has stood by me during this trying season in a way that makes me love it more than ever." Yours sincerely,

[Seth Low]

TLc Seth Low Papers NNC.

An Announcement of a Conference
at Tuskegee Institute

[Tuskegee, Ala., ca. March 1911]

INTERNATIONAL CONFERENCE ON THE NEGRO

WEDNESDAY, THURSDAY AND FRIDAY
APRIL 17, 18 AND 19, 1912

For some years past I have had in mind to invite here from different parts of the world — from Europe, Africa, the West Indies and North and South America — persons who are actively interested, or directly engaged as missionaries, or otherwise, in the work that is going on in Africa and elsewhere for the education and upbuilding of Negro peoples.

For this purpose it has been determined to hold at Tuskegee Institute, Alabama, Wednesday, Thursday and Friday, April 17, 18 and 19, 1912, a little more than a year from this time, an International Conference on the Negro. Such a Conference as this will offer the opportunity for those engaged in any kind of service in Africa, or the countries above mentioned, to become more intimately acquainted with the work and the problems of Africa and these other countries. Such a meeting will be valuable and helpful, also, in so far as it will give opportunity for a general interchange of ideas in organizing and systematizing the work of education of the native peoples in Africa and elsewhere and the preparation of teachers for that work. Wider knowledge of the work that each is doing should open means of co-operation that do not now exist.

The object of calling this Conference at Tuskegee Institute is to afford an opportunity for studying the methods employed in helping the Negro people of the United States, with a view of deciding to what extent Tuskegee and Hampton methods may be applied to conditions in these countries, as well as to conditions in Africa.

It is hoped that numbers of people representing the different governments interested in Africa and the West Indies, as well as representatives from the United States, and the countries of South America, will decide to attend this Conference. Especially is it urged that missionary and other workers in these various countries be present and take an active part in the deliberations of the Conference.

It is desirable, in any case, to have any suggestions as to what might be done to make the work of the Conference more helpful to all concerned. The names of persons who would like to be present, with whom you are acquainted, will be appreciated, and through you they are invited to be present and take part in the deliberations of the Conference.

Those who come to Tuskegee properly accredited will be welcomed and entertained as guests of the institution and will be under no expense during their stay here.

> Booker T. Washington, *Principal,*
> Tuskegee Normal and Industrial Institute,
> Tuskegee Institute, Alabama

PDSr   Con. 917   BTW Papers   DLC.

To John Robert E. Lee

[Tuskegee, Ala.] April 1, 1911

Mr. Lee: I wish you would arrange so that from time to time all of the students in the higher classes can visit the poultry yard. I very much fear that many of our students come here and go away without really seeing much of the work of the school. I fear that we have students on the grounds who do not know as much about what is going on as some of our visitors. Of course they might get information which they might work into their composition writing. Just now it is especially interesting and valuable for the students to go to the poultry yard. I only mention this as one example.

B. T. W.

TLpI   Con. 606   BTW Papers   DLC.

A News Item in the New York *Times*

New York, April 2, 1911

LONG ISLAND HOME FOR DR. WASHINGTON

FAMOUS NEGRO EDUCATOR BUYS AN ESTATE IN ONE OF THE MOST ARISTOCRATIC SECTIONS

WHO HIS NEIGHBORS WILL BE

THE PROPERTY PASSES INTO HIS POSSESSION AFTER A SERIES OF TRANSFERS OF TITLE

Dr. Booker T. Washington will spend his Summers hereafter, it is expected, in one of the finest sections of Long Island — a neighborhood where many wealthy New Yorkers have large estates. He has just purchased the J. Cornell Brown property overlooking Long Island Sound at Fort Salonga, in the Town of Huntington. The sale to Dr. Washington was made through William J. Fallon of Manhattan after several transfers of the property. First it was bought by Judson Snyder of Northport, L.I., then transferred to Benjamin Cozart[1] of Manhattan, and by him, in turn, to the famous negro educator.

The property consists of two and one-half acres, with 250 feet of shore front on the Sound. The land is on a knoll and commands a fine view of the Sound and surrounding country, including Smithtown Bay and Crane Neck Point. On the property is a new twelve-room house. The price that Dr. Washington paid for the place is not known.

For near neighbors Dr. Washington will have Francis B. Swayne, a prominent Manhattan lawyer; Miss Farman, a niece of the late Bishop Potter; Dr. Killette, a New York physician; C. O. Wetmore, and H. D. Tremain. Adjoining is a piece of property owned by Willard N. Baylis, another prominent lawyer. Not far away is a tract formerly owned by the late Duchess of Marlborough and maintained as her American home. There she resided during a certain part of each year in order to retain her property rights in America.

Dr. Washington's purchase is also near the famous Indian Head Farm, owned for many years by Mr. and Mrs. H. C. Brown. This farm was well known for the extensive horse breeding that was carried on on it.

It was at first thought that Dr. Washington contemplated the erection of an institution similar to Tuskegee Institute on his newly acquired Long Island tract, but it is not now thought that he will carry out such a project, as it is not large enough for an institution of any size. It is said that he will make the place his Summer home.

New York *Times,* Apr. 2, 1911, 6.

[1] Frederick Cozart, according to the letter from Daniel M. Gerard to BTW, Feb. 16, 1911. (Con. 423, BTW Papers, DLC.)

To Seth Low

Tuskegee Institute, Alabama   April 3, 1911

Dear Mr. Low: I find that I shall have to catch up with my delayed and belated correspondence with you by sections, but I have everything before me and in due time everything will be answered.

When I got home, I found that the reaction was greater than I supposed it would be. The shock to my system and the following excitement was so great that when I reached home, I found myself in rather a collapsed condition. Plenty of sleep, however, and regular work are bringing me around all right and I shall be myself within a few days and I shall be writing you fully regarding all matters covered by your correspondence.

Just now, I am writing regarding your letter of March 8th which covers the matter of employment of Mr. Bedford, together with his salary. Mr. Bedford's case is one that has given me considerable concern for some time. I am deeply interested in it, but I hardly know what to recommend. Speaking confidentially, Mr. Bedford is a thoroughly good man. He does valuable work in visiting our graduates, getting hold of those who are inclined to be discouraged and encouraging them. He also straightens out a good many little tangles in communities where he goes, aside from collecting sums of money in the North. His weak point, however, is that you cannot depend absolutely upon his judgment regarding the condition of a school or the work of one of our graduates, for the reason that he always is inclined to see and report the bright side, leaving the unpleasant things, but nevertheless, his great work is that of an inspirer. His salary constitutes

75

one of those elements in our budget which makes the cost per capita for teaching here larger than it is at the average institution and of course this lays us open somewhat to criticism. If we could in some way get his salary off the regular list, so that it would not enter into the per capita cost of teaching, it would be a good thing, but just now, I confess I do not see any way of doing this, unless we could find some individual who would agree to be responsible for his salary. I ought to add, also, that Mr. Bedford has great ability in getting among Southern white people and helping them to co-operate with Northern white people and with colored people in school work.

Enclosed, I return Mr. Ward's[1] letter. Yours very truly,

Booker T. Washington

TLS   Seth Low Papers   NNC.   A press copy is in Con. 54, BTW Papers, DLC.

[1] Possibly William Hayes Ward.

From William Jay Gaynor[1]

City of New York   Apl. 3, 1911

Dear Dr. Washington: I am very glad to receive your kind letter. I took an interest in the matter because I know how easy it is with the corrupt press that we have in this city to do innocent men great injury. Sincerely yours,

W. J. Gaynor

TLS   Con. 434   BTW Papers   DLC.

[1] William Jay Gaynor (1849–1913), former judge of the New York Supreme Court (1893–1909), resigned from the bench and was elected mayor of New York City (1909–13).

From George Washington Carver

[Tuskegee, Ala.] April 3 — '11

Mr. B. T. Washington, I think you will be interested in some work my classes are doing in working up some possibillities of the native clays of Macon County. It shews how they may be used for interior and exterior decoration instead of paints and whitewash.

I am sure no one realizes what a wealth we have in these clays. I am very anxious for you to see them   they are upstairs in the Class Room at Dorothy Hall. Very truly

G. W. Carver

ALS   Con. 617   BTW Papers   DLC.

From Charles Young

Fort Sam Houston, Texas, April 3, 1911

Dear Doctor Washington: There are many times I think of you and feel that I should write you. But you are busy and so am I, each in his own way. And these ways end at the same goal, that of doing something for our own people, for the benefit finally of our country and its welfare, which we all wish for.

This letter is to relieve any anxiety you may have had or may now entertain relative to the behavior of our troops (9th Cavalry), here in San Antonio.

The conduct of the soldiers has been exemplary, notwithstanding any reports of newspapers, relative to their disregard of the jim-crow laws or to drunken brawling.

Of these there has been none. Their white soldier friends on two occasions removed the signs in the cars, under the protest of the negro soldiers not to do so. There has been no "riding down of white people or flourishing of revolvers."

Both officers and men have been on their metal [mettle] to prevent any trouble. And have succeeded admirably.

These lies you read in the newspapers are simply echoes of Brownsville, no more.

The Negro soldier knows that the reason for which he is, is to uphold the laws and to fight for the country. He and his officers realize with you, all that the permission to soldier means to the colored people in general. When this permission is taken away, our people must sink to a lower caste, far lower than even slavery ever entailed, I fear, so far as its moral effects are concerned.

Speak to the President and to our friends who have faith in us and our ideals, and tell them what I have assured you of in all truth and honesty.

Hoping it is always well with you and praying a Divine Providence to spare you to us and the country for many years to come, Always your sincere,

Chas. Young
Captain, 9th U.S. Cavalry

TLS   Con. 446   BTW Papers   DLC.

To Robert Heberton Terrell

[Tuskegee, Ala.] April 4, 1911

My dear Judge Terrell: In New York a few days ago some one said that you had planned to take "The Development of the Jews" for your commencement subject.[1] I am rather inclined to advise against this. This fact is that the majority of white people who come here for commencement are composed of Jews. Taking for granted that what you said would be in their favor, still I think it would place them in a rather embarrassing position to have the commencement oration based upon them.

You will have to bear in mind that your audience will be composed, for the most part, practically of hard working farmers, men and women of our race, together with a sprinkling of colored people from near by cities, and a sprinkling of white people from the country and near by cities. The lower down the fodder is put, the more of it the animals will get, and digest and enjoy it. Yours very truly,

Booker T. Washington

TLpS   Con. 443   BTW Papers   DLC.

[1] Terrell replied that he had no intention of talking on a subject about which he knew "absolutely nothing." (Apr. 7, 1911, Con. 443, BTW Papers, DLC.) His address on May 28 was on "Negro Schools — a Retrospect." (*Tuskegee Student,* 23 [June 3, 1911], 2–3.)

To Gilbert Thomas Stephenson[1]

[Tuskegee, Ala.] April 4, 1911

My dear Sir   I am greatly obliged to you for sending me a copy of your valuable book, "Race Distinctions in American Law." This is, so far as I know, the first complete and authentic account of this matter which has yet been made. I think everyone who is interested in the subject will feel under obligations to you for the thoroughness with which the work has been performed.

I notice that on Page 352 you refer to a recent case in New York where an award made to a Negro porter for false imprisonment was reduced by a higher court. Was not that the case in which Judge Dugro[2] was concerned? My impression was that the higher courts had to reverse the decision of the lower courts in that case.

I notice that in speaking of the division of the public school fund you state that "it is commonly agreed that the Negro has had and is now getting much more than his share of the public school fund." I am sorry that in regard to this statement you did not quote from the paper of Charles L. Coon read before the Twelfth Annual Conference For Education in the South at Atlanta in 1909. So far as I know Mr. Coon is the only man who has made any systematic attempt to find out what the Negro is actually paying for his own education.

I was greatly interested in the distinction you draw between race discrimination and race distinctions. I heartily agree with your own conclusions on that subject. The real difficulty is that, as a rule, race distinctions have too frequently, as you suggest, found their place in law in order to give legal sanction to race discrimination. When the law is administered in that spirit the white man has usually suffered in my opinion more than the black man.

I thank you sincerely again for your kindness in permitting me to see this book which is, it seems to me, a very real and important contribution to the subject. I am, Very truly yours,

Booker T. Washington

TLpS   Con. 440   BTW Papers   DLC.

¹ Gilbert Thomas Stephenson (1884–1972), a Winston-Salem lawyer, graduated from Harvard Law School in 1910. He was the author of many books on trusts and wills and an officer of the Wachovia Bank and Trust Co.

² Philip Henry Dugro (1855–1920) was an associate justice of the New York Supreme Court from 1896 to 1920.

To Thomas Fowell Buxton

[Tuskegee, Ala.] April 5, 1911

My dear Sir Fowell Buxton: I have your kind letter of recent date¹ regarding the a[ttack?] upon me in New York and I assure you that I apprecia[te] your kind thought of me more than I can express.

The whole matter, however, [is] resulting in bringing to our c[ause?] more friends than we ever had. I believe that great good is go[ing] to come out of it in the long run.

You will be interested to know that the Southern white people, as well as the black and white people throughout the country, have stood by me during this trying experience. Yours very truly,

Booker T. Washington

HLpS Con. 446 BTW Papers DLC. Several words incomplete along right margin of press copy.

¹ Buxton to BTW, Mar. 23, 1911, Con. 446, BTW Papers, DLC.

From George Washington Carver

[Tuskegee, Ala.] April 5 — '11

Mr. B. T. Washington, The Peanut luncheon, given in your honor today, was worked up in my class of Senior girls.

The dishes served were only a few of the many which, the Class & myself hope to verify and publish in bulletin form. The bulletin will take up the history, botany, insects, growing, feeding and the adaptability of the county for its production, similar to the Bull. on sweet potatoes.

I am also preparing to get out a bulletin on the Possibillities of the native clays in Macon Co. Very truly

G. W. Carver

ALS   Con. 617   BTW Papers   DLC.

From Charles William Anderson

New York, N.Y., April 5, 1911

Confidential

My dear Doctor: I think I ought to tell you that my reference to the President at the Bethel Church meeting and the splendid manner in which it was received by the crowd and reported by the newspapers, was not made for the purpose of strengthening myself with the President. I felt that his act was brave, and deserving of all possible commendation, but between ourselves, I never dreamed that the "brethren" would applaud my reference to it so rapturously. It was an agreeable surprise. I wanted the President to know that his generous action was regarded by our folks, as generosity is always regarded by men who are themselves not altogether ungenerous. I am saying this because I fear that some people will say to you that I took the occasion by the hand to throw kisses at the President in order to help myself. I know that such a thought would never enter your mind, but there are persons in the world quite narrow enough to take this view of the case, especially because of the handsome way the newspapers handled it. My preliminary reference to the fair and impartial way the newspapers had treated you in their columns, was not wasted on the reporters. It was meant to be "a tub to the whale," and it was. I do not know that I have ever come upon such satisfactory press reports of a negro mass meeting, and yet that meeting had in it many elements of danger. One mistake in its management, or one too ardent expression from any speaker, would have brought the papers out next morning in red ink. Moore made a little slip, but the papers did not notice it. Before reading the resolutions, he could not resist the temptation to make a few remarks, and during the course of them, he stated that as he and Smith and myself had been phoned for by you on the night of the incident, and had remained by your side ever since, he felt that

81

he ought to give way to some of the other speakers. I stepped up and kicked him on the foot. After the meeting, I explained that as I was chairman of the meeting, and he presented the resolutions, and Smith was sitting by my side, the newspapers might look upon the movement as one engineered by the Doctor's three close friends, rather than a spontaneous uprising of the colored people in his favor, and I warned him that when a man has resolutions to read, it is always best to read them and sit down. Happily, the newspapers took no notice of his bad break.

Again I wish to report that sentiment hereabouts is all that could be desired. I am mixing freely with all classes and conditions of people, and while I never mention the incident myself (because I feel that the best way to treat such incidents is to allow them to be forgotten) I find that most every man with whom I talk is all right on it. This is indeed gratifying.

If you can arrange to do so, I hope you will accept the invitation to that republican club banquet on the 25th. You will find yourself surrounded by Supreme Court Judges and the leading republicans of this city. The president of the club is a deputy collector under me, so you can be assured of a star place on the program and of the very best possible treatment. I am anxious to have you accept all these prominent invitations, for as you know, I hold that "the brother" is always right on any given proposition when the white folks are right, and vice versa.

And now to be thoroughly selfish, I want to tell you that I had the Commissioner of Internal Revenue[1] at my office on last Thursday, at which time I gave a little luncheon to the Internal Revenue Officers' Association, which is composed of the Collectors, Chief Deputies, Revenue Agents and U.S. District Attorneys, in this district. Mr. Cabell took me aside and told me that he regarded me as the all around best Collector in the service, and the best authority on the corporation tax law, of any man he had yet met. He informed me that he had said this to the Secretary of the Treasury and to the President. The compliment was so stunning that outside of yourself and my own wife, I would not dare to repeat it to any one. It would expose me to the charge of having a swelled head. Now that I have sent it to you, I am half ashamed of myself. But I think you will admit that I do not ordinarily blow my own horn. I have six engagements to speak this month already, and mean to accept every one that presents itself. If our friends monopolize the public speaking, we need not fear the influence of that little group of crocheteers in Vesey Street. At the same time, I am treating the Vesey Street crowd with precautionary respect. I have laid in a very large supply of olive branches. I am confident it is the thing to do just now. This talk sounds strange, coming from me, who has always been a fighter, but I think you could readily understand it if you could know just how large a place you occupy in my old heart. Yours truly,

Charles W. Anderson

TLS   Con. 52   BTW Papers   DLC.

¹ Royal Eubank Cabell (1878–1950), U.S. commissioner of internal revenue from 1909 to 1913. After 1913 he resumed law practice in Richmond, Va.

Oswald Garrison Villard to Robert Russa Moton

New York. April 5, 1911

My dear Major Moton: I thank you sincerely for your kind letter of April 3rd, and take pleasure in sending you herewith a complete copy of my address in Boston. I am very much gratified that it has appealed to you.

You will have noticed that the Association passed a resolution of sympathy with Dr. Washington, which we hope marks the beginning of friendly relations with him and the National Negro Business League. It is certainly time that Dr. Washington called off his papers like the Age that have been so villainous in their attacks upon us. This is no time for the colored people to be divided; they should present a solid front to the enemy. With best wishes, Very truly yours,

Oswald Garrison Villard

TLSr Copy   Con. 55   BTW Papers   DLC.

To William Pancoast Clyde, Jr.

[Tuskegee, Ala.] April 6, 1911

Dear Mr. Clyde: Writing you on the presumption that I will not be able to see you in person for a conference this year and that Mr. Williams will, and also on the presumption that the work at Hilton Head is to continue, which I very much hope will be done, I find:

1st — We shall need to carry the work up to this period next year, including the amount of money I now have in hand $[*blank*].

2nd — In addition to this, it will help the whole movement there further if we could have a gin on the island for the people. It is very inconvenient for them to take their cotton off of the island to be ginned, and I think this element of the situation discourages some of the best farmers.

3rd — We ought also to consider the matter of a landing place. The difficulty of landing discourages a great many good people.

4th — We ought to add during the coming year two more houses at a cost of $[*blank*].

5th — We ought to allow something, say $[*blank*] for fences.

Mr. Williams, of course, will explain in detail all the matters that I am referring to in brief. Yours very truly,

Booker T. Washington

I have not attempted to fill out the blanks, indicating the amount of money suggested because Mr. Williams can do this in person when he sees you.

Enclosed I send you copy of a letter recently received from Powell,[1] of Hilton Head.

B. T. W.

TLpS   Con. 444   BTW Papers   DLC.

[1] Stephen Taylor Powell, a graduate of Tuskegee Institute in 1903, went to Hilton Head Island about 1906 to supervise a land-purchase program for tenants, sponsored by William P. Clyde.

To Francis James Grimké
and Archibald Henry Grimké

Tuskegee Institute, Alabama   April 6, 1911

Dear Friends: Your kind letter was received while I was in New York, and it came in the midst of hundreds of other communications so that I could not give it the individual attention which I desired.

Now that I am back in Tuskegee again, I am utilizing the first opportunity that I can command to let both of you know how deeply I appreciate your thought of me. As outrageous as the whole affair was, I cannot believe but that in the providence of God good in some way at some time will come out of it. Of course the hardest part of the whole outrage was the conspiracy to make it appear that I addressed indecent words to a woman, something I never did in my life, but that charge was so preposterous and outrageous that I think it is fast taking care of itself by reason of the real character of the parties who attacked me being brought to the surface.

Nevertheless, I must repeat my thanks to both of you for your letter which I appreciate most heartily. Yours very truly,

Booker T. Washington

TLS   Archibald Henry Grimké Papers   DHU.

To Oswald Garrison Villard

Tuskegee Institute, Alabama   April 6, 1911

Dear Mr. Villard: The following is an extract from a chapter in my forthcoming book, "My Larger Education, or Chapters From My Experience." I meant to have submitted it to you for your criticism several weeks ago, but I have been so interfered with that I did not. I shall be very glad to have you state frankly what you think about it, and submit any changes that you think I should make:

"In this connection I might name another individual who represents another and entirely different type of man, with whom I have frequently come in contact during my travels through Northern states.

I refer to Mr. Oswald Garrison Villard, editor of the New York Evening Post. Mr. Villard is not a practical business man and his interest in the education and progress of the Negro is of a very different kind from that of Mr. Rogers; at least he approached the matter of the Negro from a very different point of view.

"Mr. Villard is the grandson of William Lloyd Garrison, the abolitionist. He is a literary man and an idealist, and he cherishes all the intense zeal for the rights of the Negro which his grandfather before him displayed. He is anxious and determined that the Negro shall have every right and every opportunity that any other race of people has in this country. He is the outspoken opponent of every institution and every individual who seeks to limit in any way the freedom of any man or class of men anywhere. He has not only continued in the same way and by much the same methods that his grandfather used, to fight the battles for human liberty, but he has interested himself personally in the work of helping and building up some of the smaller and struggling Negro schools in the South. He is trustee of at least two of such institutions and takes an active part in the direction and control of their work. He has recently been active and, in fact, largely responsible for the organization of the National Association for the Advancement of the Colored People, a sort of national vigilance committee, which will watch over and guard the rights and interests of the race, and seek through the courts, through legislature and through other public and private means, to redress the wrongs from which the race now suffers in different parts of the country.

"Perhaps, I ought to add, in fairness that, while I sympathize fully with Mr. Villard's purposes, I have frequently differed with him as to the methods he has used to accomplish them. In such cases he has not hesitated to criticize me both publicly in his newspaper and privately in conversation. Nevertheless during all this time, I have always felt that I retained his friendship and good will. I do not think there has ever been a time when I went to him with a request of any kind for myself personally or in order to obtain his help in any way for the work in which I was engaged, that he has not shown himself willing and anxious to do everything in his power to assist me. While I have not always been able to follow his suggestions, or agree with him as to the methods I should pursue I have nevertheless, I think, profited by his criticism and have always felt and appreciated the bracing effect, upon public sentiment, of his vigorous and uncompromising spirit. I have learned also, from Mr. Villard, the lesson that persons who have a common purpose may still maintain helpful, friendly relations, even if they do differ as to details and choose to travel to the common goal by different roads." Yours very truly,

Booker T. Washington

TLS   Oswald Garrison Villard Papers   MH.   A press copy is in Con. 55, BTW Papers, DLC.

Emmett Jay Scott to Wilford H. Smith

[Tuskegee, Ala.] April 6th, 1911

Dear Friend: We telegraphed you last night as follows: "Do not clinch matters with C.[1] until you receive letter or telegram which leaves here tomorrow (meaning Thursday.) He could be skirmishing while waiting for letter."

What we had in mind was this:

1. Our friend here is most anxious that nothing be done which will put him in the position of buying anybody off. This would be permanently hurtful. Matters as they now stand are in reasonably good shape, and you certainly would not help matters if you let it appear that Mr. W. was paying out money for the sole purpose of bringing about a retraction. This does not mean, however, that it would not be proper for him to pay out money for reasonable expenses in connection with anyone's getting at the whole truth.

2. Then there is another danger to be guarded against: If U. is approached in the direction of having both himself and the woman make a retraction, would there not be danger of it going out to the public and their making capital out of the fact that he had been approached?

3. Or, again: If he and the woman did retract, might they not be led afterwards to state that they had been paid or influenced to do so? Of course, in regard to the latter charge, perhaps all the damage has been done that can be done, in that they have already stated that all kinds of influence has been brought to bear upon them.

4. Again: Mr. W. must not be put in the position where people

87

will feel that they can blackmail him from time to time by various trumped up charges, and attempt to get money from him for silence or other service. Of course, Mr. W. takes it for granted that you will arrange with C. for a reasonable charge for his services.

5. As we see it here a straight out retraction on the part of the woman and a straight out statement from the man to the effect that he is now convinced that he was mistaken in the object for which he thought Mr. W. was at the house and in regard to his actions will accomplish all that we can get accomplished.

6. You know, of course, that there [is] a disposition among people doing such work as C. proposes to do to string matters out and to make one thing lap on to another so as never to make an end to the thing. Of course, you will keep all these things in mind. You know him far better than I, but I am simply taking the precaution of mentioning them.

Of course, the whole situation is a delicate one, and we will have to leave it to your judgment. But Mr. W. is particularly anxious that no action be taken that cannot stand on all fours and which he cannot justify to his friends, if necessary. Yours very truly,

E J S

TLpI   Con. 435   BTW Papers   DLC.

[1]Possibly James Crowe. See BTW to Crowe, Feb. 3, 1912, below.

A Statement on the Bible[1]

[Tuskegee, Ala., Apr. 6, 1911]

WHAT THE BIBLE HAS BEEN TO ME

There is no portion of the people of this country, I venture to say, among whom the Bible is more familiar or more often read than is true of the Negro people. It was the first book I became acquainted with and is today the book I know best of all. What is true in my case is true, I am sure, in the case of the majority of my race. It is very seldom that a Negro ever gets up to speak in public that he does not show in his speech or in the turn of his phrases a familiarity with the language of the Bible.

The reason is simple. For two hundred years the Bible was the only book the Negro people knew. In the old slavery days the man or the woman who was able to read a little from the Good Book was looked upon with a sort of reverence by the rest of the slaves. The greatest ambition of the older slaves when they gained their freedom was to get enough knowledge before they died to be able to read their Bibles for themselves.

Somehow, in their simple way, the slaves got to understand the lessons which the Bible taught and took great comfort in its teachings. Many passages, which spoke to them of hope and freedom, seemed especially addressed to them.

Indeed it seems to me today that much that is in the Bible is addressed peculiarly to the members of my race. I do not see how it is possible for a people who are at the top — people who have succeeded, who have no difficult and perplexing problems to face — can understand the Bible in the way that it is understood by a people who are at the bottom, struggling upward.

What I have said will, perhaps, suggest what the Bible has been to me.

TMp   Con. 430   BTW Papers   DLC.

[1] BTW prepared the statement for David Miller, editor of the *United Presbyterian,* for a special number celebrating the 300th anniversary of the King James Version of the Bible. (BTW to Miller, Apr. 6, 1911, Con. 430, BTW Papers, DLC.)

To John Henry Washington

[Tuskegee, Ala.] April 8, 1911

Mr. J. H. Washington: I find that things on the farm, so far as the time of quitting is concerned, is in a deplorable condition; that both students and hired men quit in the morning and in the afternoon about any time they want to regardless of bell or whistle signals.

I am satisfied that this condition has gone on for so long a time that it is very largely the cause of a tremendous loss on the farm. This is one of the kind of things that in the future I want you to give your immediate attention to. In doing so, I advise that you do not spend your time and strength in arguing with Mr. Bridgeforth, but put the facts either before me, or to Mr. Logan, in my absence, and we will deal with Mr. Bridgeforth. The present conditions, however, must be stopped.

In your own way, I want you to keep an eye on this constantly in the future.

Booker T. Washington

TLpS   Con. 608   BTW Papers   DLC.

To Charles William Anderson

[Tuskegee, Ala.] April 8, 1911

My dear Mr. Anderson: I have read with sincere interest your letter of April 5th. No one could have handled the situation better than you did at Old Bethel Church two Sundays ago.

First of all, I am glad that you made such a fine reference to the President. I am sure it will please him immensely, and more than that, he was quite deserving of all that you said in praise of him for the prompt and thoroughgoing manner with which he hastened to put himself on record in connection with the outrageous assault upon me. The fruit of what you had to say was apparent in the newspaper reports the next morning. I thank you again and again for handling the matter in so satisfactory a way.

I am very glad to have your report as to the sentiment about New York. What you have written is just exactly what I wished to know.

I note that you have been "entertaining" the Commissioner of Internal Revenue. The whole thing is most interesting to me, and when I see you I want to talk over some details of this luncheon with you. It was certainly a fine and generous thing in Mr. Cabell to speak to you as he did. His assurance that you are the best all round collector in the service and the best authority on corporation tax law must have made you feel that after all your hard work and your fine service to the government are being properly appraised and appreciated.

I am glad that you are accepting all the invitations which are reaching you to speak. Yours very truly,

Booker T. Washington

TLpS   Con. 52   BTW Papers   DLC.

To Seth Low

Tuskegee Institute, Alabama   April 9, 1911

My dear Mr. Low: Enclosed I send you two personal letters which explain themselves.

As I wrote you several days ago, I have been trying since my return home to catch up with the flood of correspondence which has poured in upon me from every part of the country as the result of my New York experience.

I have delayed answering your two letters of March 27th until I could calmly review the whole situation. I did not realize until I came into the calm and quiet air of Tuskegee how much I was dazed and physically and mentally upset by the assault and subsequent publicity and agitation. After reaching home it took me a long while to get physical and mental command of myself.

Before writing you I have wanted to give careful consideration to all suggestions and advice which I have received as well as the newspaper reports. One of the perplexing elements has been that often advice I have received from one source has been directly contrary to that which I have received from others. This has become all the more perplexing because different kinds of advice has come from equally staunch friends. This has caused me to realize my own responsibility as I never felt it before and to reflect upon the many interests outside of my own which are likely to be affected by what I do or say.

I ought to say that personally, I abhor and detest such publicity as a court trial of any kind brings to the surface. Until recently, I was never in court before either as a complainant or defendant. Nor do I personally have any desire to prosecute Ulrich. I feel that nothing would be gained either for myself or for the interests of the school if I were to let myself appear as cherishing a vindictive spirit towards him. The only thing that deters me from dropping the case is the fact of the statement of the woman who posed as his wife. If there were some way of disposing finally and forever of the statement without going to court, I should feel that is the best way of getting rid of the whole matter.

I confess, too, that it is a strange and uncomfortable position for me to find myself in — the position of prosecuting anyone, but as I look at it now, I see no way of disposing of the charges against me except by going forward with the trial. In the meantime, I believe the best thing for me and for everyone else is to think about the whole matter as little as possible. I want to go on with my work, and try to forget for the time being at least, the whole thing. In fact, I find this absolutely necessary for my physical and mental well being.

I wish I were able to express to you and to all my friends how profoundly grateful I am for the sympathy and confidence shown me in this time of trouble. I want to assure you also that I am more resolved than ever to be worthy of your trust and good will. The words of cheer and confidence which have poured in upon me from all parts of the country and from Europe have touched me deeply.

I have been so dazed by what happened that I have scarcely been able to work or think, and I feel that it is absolutely necessary for me to think about this matter as little as possible.

My lawyer hopes that by the time the trial comes up he will be able to have evidence that will throw a different light on the matter, and I am leaving it very largely in his hands. Yours very truly,

Booker T. Washington

TLS   Seth Low Papers   NNC.   A draft dated Apr. 8, 1911, is in Con. 435, BTW Papers, DLC.

To William S. Hawk[1]

Tuskegee Institute, Alabama   April 9, 1911

Personal and Confidential.

Dear Mr. Hawk: I am writing to say to you in this letter what I wished to say to you in person before I left the hotel two or three weeks ago.

First: I want to be absolutely frank with you in saying that I am heartily sorry because of the notoriety brought to the hotel. I am all the more sorry because of the kind treatment I have always received at the hands of everyone at the hotel.

My main object in writing this letter, however, is to say, above everything else, that it is a matter of importance to me in carrying on my work in connection with the school to be permitted to stop at your hotel. There are conveniences for work there which I could not get at other places. Second, the character of the people with whom I have to come into contact is such that they feel that a place like your hotel is a good place for them to meet me.

I think you and your associates will agree with me that I always avoid making myself unnecessarily conspicuous about the hotel, and especially do I avoid having people call to see me who will attract especial attention or whose presence is objectionable. I think that your associates will agree that this was true up until the time of this recent unfortunate episode. In fact, it has been a real help to me in every direction to be a guest at your hotel.

In the next place, while I do not mean to go to the hotel in the immediate future, certainly not until the newspaper men have been weaned from going there for a little while, I should not like to be compelled to stop at any other hotel in the near future because hurtful comment would be made upon the fact that I had been forced to change hotels. What I do mean to do for the present, if I have occasion to be in New York for some time, is to stop at some private residence so as to be out of the way of the newspaper people. But I should like to be permitted to use my discretion and judgment in the future as to when and upon what occasions I would stop at the hotel, as in the past I think you could trust me not to embarrass you.

Thinking perhaps that you would not care to write upon this subject as frankly as you would care to talk, I have asked my friend, Mr. John S. Durham to hand you this letter in person, and if you desire to give it to him, you can let him have your reply.

Permit me to thank you again and again for all your kindnesses to me. Yours very truly,

Booker T. Washington

P.S. Of course, I realize fully that no first class hotel likes to have the reputation of being the headquarters of any special kind of people.

TLS Con. 434 BTW Papers DLC.

¹ William S. Hawk was president and director of the Hawk and Wetherbee Co., proprietors of the Hotel Manhattan in New York City.

To Robert Russa Moton

[Tuskegee, Ala.] April 10, 1911

My dear Major Moton: I thank you very much for sending me a copy of Mr. Villard's letter to you. It is in fine spirit. I too was very much interested in Mr. Villard's Boston address. Mr. Villard, however, makes the mistake of thinking that I have more influence over colored papers than I actually have, for example: in regard to the New York Age the only influence that I can exert is in a personal and friendly way. I do not own a single dollar's worth of financial interest in the paper. Sometimes Mr. Moore takes my advice and sometimes he does not. I think, however, it would serve a very good purpose if you would write Mr. Moore yourself, telling him that he ought to assume a more friendly spirit toward the Association for the Advancement of Colored People. I have spoken to him in the same direction, and my words backed up by yours would help immensely.

Mr. Moore is a good fellow but when he once makes up his mind to go in a certain direction, it is pretty hard to turn him.

I agree with Mr. Villard's statement to the effect that now is the time for us to get together, stick together and work together, and this sentiment I have found almost unanimously among all classes of colored people.

Thank you so much for letting me see Major Hemphill's letter. I had one from him a day or so ago.

It has been very beautiful and touching to see how the white people in Tuskegee and Macon County have stood right behind me in this recent New York trouble. They have simply overwhelmed me with evidences of kindness and good will. Yours very truly,

Booker T. Washington

TLpS Con. 55 BTW Papers DLC. A copy is in the W. E. B. Du Bois Papers, MU.

To Charles Oscar Hearon[1]

[Tuskegee, Ala.] April 10, 1911

Personal and Confidential.

Dear Sir: A friend of mine living in South Carolina has sent me a copy of your recent editorial bearing upon myself.

I wish to say that I am not writing for the sake of asking you to publish anything from me, but I am simply writing you in order that you may not personally be misinformed. I realize how utterly impossible it is for any man whose name is in any degree before the public not to be misrepresented.

In the first place, I have lived in the Town of Tuskegee and Macon County, Alabama for 28 years, and I think that there is no white man of any standing in the town or county who would say that my life has in any degree changed during these 28 years. During the whole time that I have carried on this work, I have found it necessary to devote my time almost equally between the North and the South.

In regard to the exaggerations which have been put before the public by sensational newspapers regarding the house on Long Island, I might say that for more than 15 years I have spent about two months during each summer at some point in the North. I have found it necessary to do this in the carrying on of my work in connection with this school. For five years I have lived in the Town of Huntington, the same town where I have secured a house for the coming summer.

The house referred to in the dispatches is out in the country, a mile from any other residence. It is a small, inexpensive house, about half the size of the one I live in in the Town of Tuskegee. I am sure that the nearest white neighbor is at least a mile away. In Tuskegee, the richest white man in Macon County lives only a quarter of a mile from my house. There has never been any question raised regarding social equality in connection with this Southern gentleman near whom I live.

If I could carry out my personal wishes, nine tenths of my time would be spent in the South, both in winter and in summer, because there is no spot on earth that I love better than I do the Town of Tuskegee.

But my main purpose in writing you is to say that I understand fully the conditions that surround my race in the South and in this country, and that no gifts on earth could lead me to misunderstand them or to get an exaggerated idea of my own importance or to change in any degree the character and tone of my life work.

During the recent unpleasant experiences through which I have passed in New York, nothing has been of greater encouragement to me than the way that the best white people in Alabama have stood back of me. As an indication of what my Southern white neighbors think of me, I enclose copy of letter which they, of their own accord sent to me some days ago. This letter is signed by practically every white man of standing in my community.[2]

As I said before, I am not writing you for publication, but because of your broad and generous views on the Negro question, I thought I ought to make this explanation.

My friend, Richard Carroll, has often spoken to you [me?] concerning you. Yours truly,

Booker T. Washington

TLpS Con. 425 BTW Papers DLC.

[1] Charles Oscar Hearon (b. 1887) was editor of the Spartanburg (S.C.) *Herald* and president of the Spartanburg Journal Co.

[2] Enclosed was a copy of D. E. Kelley, W. C. Hurt, and fourteen other prominent Tuskegee whites to BTW, Mar. 23, 1911. They expressed their "utmost confidence in the truthfulness of your statements in connection with the assault made upon you."

From Lelon P. Botsford

East Hampton, L.I. Apr. 10, 1911

Dear Mr Washington, Enclosed find the certificate for which you asked which is a simple statement of the facts as I found them. The charge for such a statement is ten dollars, the regular charge among the interns in the hospital.

I have written Dr. Reid[1] telling him that you desire a statement from him. You will doubtless receive it soon. Hoping that this is satisfactory, I remain, Yours truly

Lelon P. Botsford

[*Enclosure*]

Flower Hospital, Apr. 8, 1911

This is to certify that at no time during my attendance upon Booker T. Washington, was he intoxicated nor did he show any symptoms of alcoholism in any manner.

Lelon P. Botsford, M.D.

ALS   Con. 434   BTW Papers   DLC.

¹ John J. Reid, Jr., was the ambulance surgeon at Flower Hospital who attended BTW after he was assaulted.

To Hans Petersen¹

[Tuskegee, Ala.] April 11, 1911

My dear Sir: Your letter of April 5th is received.²

You will find in the April number of the World's Work an article in which I discuss to some extent the needs of Negro education in the South. You will see from that article that the Negro people in different parts of the South are already doing something to improve their schools. They are raising money to build schoolhouses and to lengthen school terms. They are also building a considerable number of private schools which are doing public school work.

I believe that the best way in which the federal government can assist in the building up of an adequate school system for Negroes in the South would be to encourage the efforts that are now being made by the Negroes themselves. For example, I should think it would be possible for the federal government to cooperate with such an organization as the Jeanes Fund Board. A general law could be passed that wherever private individuals were taxing themselves for the improvement of schools, they could receive a certain amount of aid from the government. This aid could take several different forms. It might take the form of a direct subsidy, or it might take the form of supervision of the work that is now being done. In that case, the commissioner of education or the department of education at Washington might do a work similar to the demonstration farm work which is now carried on under the Department of Agriculture. I believe that some plan of this kind is already being considered by Congress.

I am sending you herewith a pamphlet which will give you some idea of what the Negroes are now doing for the public schools in different parts of the South. Yours very truly,

Booker T. Washington

TLpSr Con. 437 BTW Papers DLC. Signature initialed by Charles H. Fearing.

[1] Possibly the Hans Petersen listed in the Chicago city directories as an editor, although Petersen wrote to BTW on the stationery of Butler Brothers, wholesalers of general merchandise.

[2] Petersen had asked for BTW's opinion on federal aid to southern states for the education of the Negro, for use in a debate on the question in a Chicago church. (Apr. 5, 1911, Con. 437, BTW Papers, DLC.)

From John J. Reid, Jr.

Flower Hospital New York, April 11, 1911

Dear Dr. Washington: I trust that by this time you have fully recovered from the mishap which befell you last month. Being the Ambulance Surgeon on the night of that sad occurrence, I have since been interested in your case and hoped that the injuries you received would not remain as a hindrance to your noble work. As I had to leave the hospital the following morning I was unable to ascertain the full extent of your injuries from Dr. Botsford.

Being honored on such an occasion by you, I was fairly bewildered at first and hope that if you found any lack of courtesy, that you will accept my apologies for the same.[1] I would deem it a great favor to hear from you at whatever time that is at your disposal. Sincerely yours,

John J. Reid, Jr.

TLSr Copy Con. 435 BTW Papers DLC.

[1] BTW replied that he felt no lack of courtesy in his treatment while at the Flower Hospital, and thanked the staff for their kindness to him. (BTW to Reid, Apr. 12, 1911, Con. 435, BTW Papers, DLC.)

From Oswald Garrison Villard

New York   April 11, 1911

Dear Dr. Washington: I have your letter of April 6th and I must say that I am quite overcome by the passage you propose to put into your new book in regard to me; I am sure that I do not deserve all these generous words. At first thought it seemed to me that it would be wrong to make even a single suggestion, but I have decided on the whole to call your attention to one or two things. I think it would be rather unkind to say that I am not a practical business man since I am the head of the Evening Post business and have been director of its business affairs for the past ten years. Again, I founded and built up the Dobbs Ferry Hospital from a small institution to one of considerable size, and I think that my practical business experience has been demonstrated at Manassas and in the raising of the Baldwin Fund for you, in my thirteen years of service on the Board of Trustees of the City Club and in other practical associations. I was also formerly director in banks and trust companies and other business enterprises, and still am of some, but most of these Boards I quitted voluntarily in order to save every possible moment for my work for the colored people. I have also gotten out of the Dobbs Ferry Hospital work, which I founded and carried on for many years, in fact ever since I left college, in order that every spare moment may be given to the colored people that is not called for by my profession. If you would change that phrase to simply, "Mr. Villard is primarily not a business man," I think you will hit it about right. Again, I should appreciate it very much if you would mention in this sketch the fact that I planned the Baldwin memorial fund and was the moving spirit in raising it, adding it, $150,000 to your endowment. Again, you might care to add that I am not only a Trustee of Manassas, but President of the Board of Directors. Finally, I think that the first two sentences in the second paragraph beginning — "Perhaps I ought to add in fairness" and ending in "conversation" might give a false impression in their present juxtaposition. It might, for instance, lead people to think that you and I would talk the thing out in private and if you did not agree with me I then pounded you in the Evening Post. That, of course, I have never done; I would therefore suggest a phrase something like this for the second sentence: "Sometimes he has criticized me publicly in his news-paper and privately in his conversation."

Again let me assure you that I am most deeply gratified by the statement as a whole. Sincerely yours,

Oswald Garrison Villard

P.S. As Mr. Rollo Ogden is *the editor,* I should be glad if you would speak of me as *an* editor. It would save me from embarrassment.

O. G. V.

TLS   Con. 444   BTW Papers   DLC.   Postscript in Villard's hand.

Charles Fletcher Dole to Seth Low

Jamaica Plain, Mass. Apr. 11, 1911[1]

My dear Mr. Low   Thank you for your kind note. I wish that it an-swered the questions, which I trust in due time will be all answered. Here is the unfortunate aspect of the whole sorrowful occurrence, namely, that the story of explanation is so full of fatuities, almost sug-gesting temporary aberration of mind.

First, is the strange thing that Dr. Washington should be seeking Mr. Smith in the North at all, inasmuch as he was still at last accounts in Tuskegee, and could not have meditated a visit to New York so early? Why should Mr. Scott have written that Mr. Smith was coming North, when he was not coming?

Then, about the letter, giving an address in New York City where "possibly" Mr. Smith might be. Why only "possibly," or why at all, since Mr. Smith's home is just over the river at Montclair? Why should he not have been at his own home? How should this letter, the key-pin to the whole business, have been lost or destroyed, before the im-portant address had been looked up? A man of affairs does not destroy such a letter, so as to be quite at a loss whether he has the right address?

Again, the place & street number seem to have been almost *obvi-ously* not Mr. Smith's kind? One of Mr. Washington's Negro friends here in Boston said that he had got into "a bad neighborhood." Why then should he have persisted so up to 10 p.m., in hanging about the place?

What extreme importance anyway in finding Mr. Smith, a guest in a stranger's house (so far as Mr. Washington was concerned), so late on a Sunday night?

Moreover, in these days of telephones, before a late call at a stranger's house, upon the bare possibility of finding Mr. Smith, why should he not have used the telephone, & found once for all whether Mr. S. was there? Would not Mr. Smith's type of friends have had a telephone?

Again, the story says that Dr. W. did not fairly enter the house to look up the names, till his *third* visit. But how could he have even rang the bell; so as to know that no one was at home, without consulting the names at first? This is what everyone has to do. Neither do I see what there could have been at all alarming to Ulrich in the fact that some one had come man-fashion two or three times to ring at another familys door? Not even a kidnapper comes to do his work at a time when the man of the house is at home and then rings some ones' else bell.

I think it would be something fatuous, again, if Dr. Washington on the whole exculpated his assailant as having done a "manly" thing, under the circumstances? Why, Ulrich did not even take ordinary care to find out what rightful business the stranger in the common hall of an apartment house might have. Shall a man go free, & even be almost praised, who strikes at random from behind a man bending over the plates and names of his fellow tenants! As for Ulrich's own door, there could have been no reason at all why Dr. W. should have been near it. The Ulrich side of the story is crazy enough! Indeed, with Dr. W. walking around the square two or three times, as any man walks who is going about his business, I hardly see any occasion for the Ulrich woman taking any special notice of him? Mr. W. would presumably have taken due care not to seem to be following the woman into the vestibule! And now, I see that the man has simply pleaded "not guilty," & no one appeared to "call down" in the interest of the public generally, and of the colored race in particular, a man who has risked the killing of a very valuable life, all because of an insane fit of needless suspicion or jealousy! Not that I like to see Ulrich or anyone punished, but if we give costly warnings to any class of dangerous men, I think the lesson ought to be a very serious one, in the case of a man who assails other tenants' visitors in the vestibule of an apartment house, without the slightest real ground, and without waiting to know who the other man was!

Perhaps all this seems foolish, in view of much more intimate knowledge which you possess. But it must be, I suspect, in other minds besides mine. And I simply cannot rest at ease while these questions arise. Of course, the grand volume of Booker Washington's services and character keeps my face to the front, and binds me to trust him. But for his sake, I think the story of that night should be more satisfactorily related, Mr. Smith should be accounted for, and Mr. Ulrich should be very solemnly given his lesson for the sake of the host of innocent people who need to be defended from his ilk, and quite as much for the sake of a crowd of hot-brained people, who think the motives of their own fears and passions are excuse enough for any act of violence. Yours with high respect

Charles F. Dole

ALS   Seth Low Papers   NNC.

¹ Not mailed until Apr. 25. See Dole to Low, Apr. 25, 1911, below.

From Seth Low

[New York City] April 13th, 1911

Confidential.

Dear Mr. Washington; I have received your letter of April 9th, and note carefully what you say. My attention has been called recently to an item appearing [in] the "Philadelphia Press," either as an alleged interview or the report of a speech by you, in which you are said to have exonerated Ulrich, and to have justified him in attacking you, on the ground that he thought you were a kidnapper. This report is causing a good deal of trouble, and I am therefore writing to ask whether the report is accurate, and whether you said anything when in Philadelphia on your way home that could be twisted into such a statement.¹ It is important that I should be fully informed, and, if the alleged interview or speech is without basis, it may be, even now, worth while for you to disavow it. I take it for granted that you will have seen it. An item, summarizing it, was sent to me from Boston, which unfortunately I destroyed, but I have not seen the original publication in the Philadelphia Press. If you have not, please telegraph and I will have it sent to you.

I also feel constrained to advise you not to stop again at the Hotel Manhattan. Mr. Hawk has never acknowledged my letter, and I think there are elements there that are no longer friendly to receiving you as a guest. If you could find some respectable colored family with whom you could arrange to stay when you are in New York, I think the Institute could very properly pay a suitable sum to justify them in reserving rooms for your accommodation as you might need them. I learn that some of your enemies of your own race criticize you for inconsistency in stopping at a hotel like the Manhattan. It is a small spirit, and it may not be worth while to give heed to it; but I suggest the matter for your consideration, in the light of things that have come to me since your trouble. I am sure you will not misunderstand the entirely friendly and sympathetic spirit in which I call the matter to your attention. I am very sure that your decision, whatever it is, will be wise when you have considered the question in the light of what I have just written. Yours very truly,

[Seth Low]

TLc Seth Low Papers NNC.

[1] BTW denied that he had said anything that exonerated Ulrich. (See BTW to John Stephens Durham, Mar. 27, 1911, above.)

From an Admirer

Washington, D.C., April 15, 1911

My dear Mr. Washington: I hate hypocrisy! I had occasion to enter the office of Judge Terrell a few days ago and noticed that he has removed your picture from his wall. On inquiry as to why, he simply shrugged his shoulders and winked.

I consider this a serious matter just at this juncture and an evidence of base ingratitude on his part, for all the City know that he and his wife have risen to high positions, not on merit, but on your favor.

An Admirer

TL Con. 415 BTW Papers DLC. Docketed in E. J. Scott's hand: "I am having this investigated!"

To Charles William Anderson

Whitinsville, Mass. April 16, 1911

Dear Mr. Anderson: One other thing that I meant to have asked you yesterday to do is this.

I wish in some way you would not only find out who is the backer of the District Attorney, but also in your own way get into close personal touch with him something in the same way that you are with the other officials. It might be that you could get a great deal of information regarding him from your friend in the District Attorney's office; but the best thing would be for you to get a close personal hold upon him without bringing up my case at all. Yours very truly,

[Booker T. Washington]

TLc   Con. 52   BTW Papers   DLC.

To Seth Low

Parker House, Boston, Mass. April 16, 1911

My dear Mr. Low: I shall hear from Mr. Taylor before long in reference to Mr. Madison Cooper's suggestion regarding the cold storage.

I have come to Boston and New England to fill some speaking engagements in the interest of the school of long standing. I did not have time to see you when I passed through New York, but hope to see you before I return South.

I had a short interview with my lawyer in New York as I came through, and he had recently seen the Assistant District Attorney who, it seems, has been placed in charge of the case.[1] He said that this attorney was rather emphatic in saying two things. First, that for the present that all agitation and discussion of the subject cease. Second, that at the proper time, either before or at the trial, that he has it in his power to make Ulrich make a statement either in court or out of court to the effect that he had no justification in assaulting me, and also to make him acknowledge that the woman's statement regarding me was false. Whether this meant that he would get the woman herself to say so or not, I do not quite understand. I think, too, as I recall the conversation, that the Assistant District Attorney said that he could arrange for Ulrich to plead guilty with a suspended sentence, but of the latter assertion my recollection may not be correct. But at any rate I am quite sure that my lawyer said that the Assistant Attorney said that he had Ulrich within his power and could make him do what we desired. Just what he bases such a strong assertion on I am not informed.

My lawyer also stated that this attorney was emphatic in suggesting that the whole matter for the present be left to him and that he would bring it out all right. Of course, if the Assistant District Attorney can do what he suggests, it seems that it would be in the line of your own suggestion made to me in a former letter.

Let me add that I can never forget your own deep interest and personal kindness to me during this trying ordeal. I feel now that I know you better and am closer to you than ever before.

Now, regarding the matter of having some one with me constantly when I am going about. Others have spoken to me about taking this precaution. I am trying now to do this to some extent, but at the same time I have not perfected a plan and am trying as best I can to think out a practical working plan to carry the suggestion into effect. I can now realize how easy it would be for any one not only to assault me, but to entrap me into a scheme to be greatly to my damage. Yours very truly,

Booker T. Washington

TLS Seth Low Papers NNC. A carbon is in Con. 54, BTW Papers, DLC.

[1] James E. Smith was the assistant district attorney who prosecuted Henry A. Ulrich.

An Item in the New York *Times*

[New York City, Apr. 16, 1911]

WANTS DR. WASHINGTON'S LAND

WEALTHY RESIDENTS OFFER HIM A PROFIT ON HIS LONG ISLAND PURCHASE

Wealthy residents of the section near which Booker T. Washington recently bought a fine tract of land at Fort Salonga, near Northport,

L.I., with a frontage on the Sound, have formed a syndicate and are trying to buy the property from Dr. Washington. Already $1,500 more than he paid for the property has been offered to him. It has not been learned whether or not he will sell.

It is said that there was no objection when it was learned that the negro educator had bought land upon which to build himself a Summer home, but when the rumor spread that he intended to add enough land to his holdings to erect an institution similar to Tuskegee for the education of negroes there was considerable dissatisfaction. Dr. Washington bought the J. Cornell Brown property.

It is understood that if Dr. Washington should decide to accept the syndicate's offer he will immediately be offered another tract of land on the Sound not far from his present holdings. There he would have among his neighbors Clinton L. Rossiter,[1] John Thatcher, Eversley Childs,[2] and other wealthy men.

New York *Times,* Apr. 16, 1911, 1.

[1] Clinton Lawrence Rossiter (d. 1925) was a banker, former president of the Brooklyn Rapid Transit Co., and officer of several corporations such as Underwood Typewriter Co., Corning Light and Power Co., and Long Island Loan and Trust Co.

[2] Eversley Childs (1867–1953) was co-founder of the Bon Ami Co.

Peter Jefferson Smith, Jr., to Emmett Jay Scott

New York   April 18 — 11

My dear Emmett: I am sorry I did not have time to finish my talk with you this morning. I want to be sure that you understand my position in this matter, so I am going to take the pains to write you.

After leaving you I had another short talk with the Dr. and tried very hard to impress him with the importance of quietly dropping that suit. My specific reason for it is: That nothing can possibly be gained by it.

The colored and white people of the country have signified their unbounded confidence in his integrity, his wounds have all healed, the man has no money, and every body believes it was a mistake, so what is the use of stirring up the stink anew. The sane and constant friends of the Dr's do not want to subject the Dr. to the humiliation that he is likely to be subjected to by the rigid cross examination that is more than likely to be pursued by the counsel for the defense. I suggested to the Dr. that the best thing for him to do when questioned about his intentions in the matter to say "The matter is entirely in the hands of my counsel" and allow it to rest there, having instructed counsel to allow it to die of its own accord. Trotter is anxious for a trial, and I told the Dr. if Trotter were anxious for him to be received in to the heavenly land I should seriously doubt the wisdom of striving to get there. I have noticed that all of the Trotter element are crying trial trial trial and for what; that they may get as they hope something new for the purpose of making enemies for the Dr. I know as you do that the Dr. feels this thing deeply, his fine noble nature could not do other than feel it deeply. I would as I know he would, give the world had it not happened, and now that it has happened, the wounds all healed, and the thing quieted down, what in the name of our blessed Lord is the use of stirring it all up again. Let me urge upon you, than whom no man stands closer, to see to it that it is quietly dropped. The Dr. assured me that he believes in my sincerity as a friend and I think I may add devotee. I hope you also believe in my sincerity. I would not do one single thing wittingly to in any way do him the least bit of harm.

I also spoke to you about what people are saying about the Dr's. association. A man has a right to choose his own company, that is the ordinary man has, but a man who stands at the head of a great people such as does Dr. Washington, and who is almost daily becoming more and more the acknowledged head, can not afford to be indifferent to their wishes as to his association.

I am deeply solicitous for the Dr's health and hope you will make him save himself. It will be sad indeed for him to break completely down and when he is a few years older, and should enjoy what he has worked so hard to obtain, find himself a physical wreck. I think he has grown older since the assault, and I think he worries too. I feel so sorry for him, for tho. he never indicated any special pride, he could not but have it. I know him Emmett like a book and I know that he is as sensitive as a woman about his moral status. I have taken the pains to write you at some length, because I want to be sure that you fully understand my position. I feel tho. that in some things he has not done all for me that I would have done for him were I in his place.

I am free to tell you that I feel if he had put the matter of a position for me up to the President as I would have for him, not as a gratuity, but for real service rendered, I would have landed. Very sincerely yours,

P. J. Smith

TLS Con. 441 BTW Papers DLC. Written on stationery of the Guanajuato–New York Gold Mining Co., with offices in Harlem, of which Smith was general agent.

To Theodore Roosevelt

Parker House, Boston. April 19, 1911

My dear Col. Roosevelt: I thank you very much for the letter which you wrote me from San Francisco. I have not answered it earlier because I wanted to wait until you got back home again.

In view of your own experiences with sensational newspaper misrepresentations, I am sure that you will sympathize with me in having to undergo the many and awful falsehoods which the sensational papers sent into all parts of the country. For example, the dispatch which was cooked up in Philadelphia and sent out from there representing me as saying that Ulrich was justified in assaulting me and that I intended to drop the prosecution was without the slightest foundation and truth.

However, I do not mean just now to burden you with details except to say that the very course which your letter advises we are now trying to follow.

One result of this attack has been to let me know how many warm friends I had all over the country, many more than I had any idea I possessed, and the friendship exhibited as a result of this has been just as warmly shown in the South as elsewhere.

I shall hope to see you sometime in the near future. Yours very truly,

Booker T. Washington

TLS Theodore Roosevelt Papers DLC. A draft in Con. 438, BTW Papers, DLC, does not contain the last two paragraphs.

To Oswald Garrison Villard

Parker House, Boston. April 19, 1911

My dear Mr. Villard: I thank you very much for both of your letters. I meant to have sent you a letter and thought I had done so, thanking the Association for the Advancement of Colored People for the fine resolution which they passed regarding myself. I regret that my word of thanks has not reached you before. It was a most generous act on the part of the Association, and I shall never fail to appreciate it. This resolution, as you say, has been widely used in both white and colored papers, and has accomplished much good.

I shall be very glad to see that the suggestion regarding the appointment of three fraternal delegates from the Business League to attend the next meeting of your Association is carried into effect.

A short time ago I had a talk with Mr. Moorfield Storey,[1] and told him that we are planning to get all the forces to work together. This I am sure can be done. I have had talks recently with several important colored people and white people in the same direction, and all agree with my policy.

Mr. Schieffelin told me a few evenings ago that he would be willing to serve on your educational committee.

Confidentially I want to say that I have had several frank talks with the editor of the New York Age and have gotten friends to talk with him, and I think you will find in the near future that he will modify the tone of his paper regarding your organization. Insofar as I can, I am going to get other colored papers to pursue the same course.

I am glad that you are pleased with what I am to say in my new book regarding yourself. I shall be very glad to make the modifications which your letter suggests. Yours very truly,

[Booker T. Washington]

TLc Con. 55 BTW Papers DLC.

[1] Moorfield Storey (1845–1929), a lawyer and activist in many liberal causes, was president of the Anti-Imperialist League beginning in 1905 and a founder and first president of the NAACP from 1910 to 1915.

To Robert Ezra Park

Parker House, Boston. April 19th, 1911

Dear Dr. Park: I received the chapter which you have sent me and have read it carefully. It is very, very good. I made one or two unimportant changes.

I have just sent you the following telegram: Mr. Villard wants certain changes made in chapter from my experiences regarding himself. Please write or telegraph Mr. Walter H. Page in my name asking him to return the chapter to Tuskegee so that you can make the changes. I am sending Mr. Villard's letter today.

Enclosed I send you Mr. Villard's letter. I am very anxious that these changes be made. I think you might modify to some extent the suggestion regarding the time and money which he gives to colored enterprises. You might make considerable of the Baldwin Memorial. Yours very truly,

[Booker T. Washington]

TLc   Con. 54   BTW Papers   DLC.

To Seth Low

Parker House, Boston, Mass. Apr. 19, 1911

Dear Mr. Low: I thought you might like to see the enclosed letter from Mr. Eastman.

I may of course, in this matter be a poor judge, but ever since the unfortunate occurrence in New York I have been watching and gauging public sentiment among the class of people who have always stood by and supported the school both with money and through sympathy. I have been careful to note their correspondence as well as their donations, and especially have I been careful to see what effect the occurrence has had on my reception in places where I have spoken and in the matter of invitations to speak at public functions, and so far as my own experience and observation are concerned I think I can safely say that I have not noted a single sign of any change of feeling. In addition, I can add that I seem to be received more warmly even than in the past at public meetings, and the invitations to speak on important public occasions have nearly doubled within the last month. I do not see that there has been any change whatever for the worse in our contributions.

I understand that Mr. Vardaman is making a good deal of the matter in his political campaign in Mississippi, but this does not trouble me over-much because Mr. Vardaman has been abusing me for six or seven years in most of his political speeches. When I was making a tour through Mississippi some years ago, both through his newspaper and in public speeches he made a specialty of abusing me both while I was in the state and before I got into the state, but I could not discern that it had any bad effect on the masses of white people in that state. The people there I think have become accustomed to his tirades, and those who are not amused are disgusted.

I have been equally careful to try to gauge public sentiment in the South among the class of white people who have always stood by and supported me, and so far I can not discover what I consider any permanent bad results. Yours very truly,

Booker T. Washington

TLS   Seth Low Papers   NNC.

From Benjamin Jefferson Davis

Atlanta, Ga. April 21, 1911

PERSONAL AND CONFIDENTIAL

My dear Mr. Washington: You have other friends who love you besides Fred Moore, Roscoe Simmons, who was kicked out of the K. of P.'s for larceny, and J. C. Asbury, a self-confessed grafter, who have and are doing more for you and your work out of loyalty to principle than these dependencies can or will do for pay. These friends resent and look with askance upon your actions in surrounding yourself with the knockers who do most to blacken their characters. In spite of your denial, a large majority of the people in this country hold you responsible for the policy of the New York Age. In fact, they believe you own the paper and are largely responsible for its continued attacks upon the Grand United Order of Odd Fellows and other race enterprises. As often as you are in the North, you are surrounded to the exclusion of everybody else, with this little coterie of character villifiers, and immediately after your meeting them, a fresh attack is made on your friends.

Personally, I care nothing for the attacks of the yellow sheet, but it is humiliating to me to have my friends tell me that Booker Washington's paper could not continue to attack me without his acquiescence if not consent. It is well understood in this country that you control this trio of libellers, and that they would immediately cease their abuse if you were to tell them to hush. You well know that we are your friends, that we are able to take care of ourselves, that we ask neither quarter nor favor, but we do not like to have you placed in the light of fighting us by your fool friends. The more these parasites fight us, the stronger we grow in the hearts of the people. But you owe it to us and to the public to make a statement.

I know you are a wise man, but men never get too great to defend the truth. If you do not disavow the Age's policy, in the end you will find that the work you are giving your life for will suffer. I do not want you hurt. My love for you personally and the work for which you stand, alone, prompts me to write you this note. When you were attacked in N. Y., had it been in my power, I would have gladly suffered the personal injury than have you misunderstood or misjudged one moment. I so expressed myself to friends. Sincerely,

B. J. Davis

TLS Con. 421 BTW Papers DLC.

To Lelon P. Botsford

Boston, Mass. April 22, 1911

Dear Dr. Botsford: Replying to your kind letter of recent date enclosing certificate; I am glad to enclose my check to you for ten dollars. I thank you for what you have written.

In some way I have mislaid Dr. Reid's letter, and I fear the certificate also. Will you be kind enough to ask him to write me again and send me another certificate and I [shall] see that a check is sent him. Yours very truly,

[Booker T. Washington]

TLc Con. 434 BTW Papers DLC.

To Charles Stewart

Boston, Mass. April 22, 1911

Personal and Confidential

My dear Mr. Stewart: I have seen your letter in the Baltimore Afro-American regarding the president of Fisk University. I have also seen copies of the correspondence which has passed between you and President Gates.

Sometime when I can see you, which I hope will be in the near future, I want to have a frank talk with you regarding President Gates. I wish to assure you that despite whatever impression you may have gotten of him during your recent visit there, at heart President Gates is all right. He is one of the finest, broadest characters that I know, and no man is more deeply and unselfishly interested in the uplift of our race than he is. I know what I am talking about, and when I can see you and give you the facts I am sure that you will come around to my opinion.[1]

I want you to go to Fisk University again. I want you to meet and know President Gates as he really is, because he is one of the great big characters who is really interested in lifting us up. I want you to write a different letter after you have been differently impressed. I am sure you will do this. Yours very truly,

[Booker T. Washington]

TLc Con. 440 BTW Papers DLC.

[1] Stewart replied on Apr. 27, 1911, that perhaps he had the wrong impression of Gates, which he was "perfectly willing to correct." (Con. 440, BTW Papers, DLC.)

Emmett Jay Scott to Frederick Randolph Moore

[Tuskegee, Ala.] April 25, 1911

Dear Mr. Moore: I have your letter of April 11th at Tuskegee on my return to the school. It discusses somewhat at length the matter you mentioned in person.

Your letter states, if I properly understand it, that you have negotiated a fictitious sale of The Age so as to get around the two judgments which have been taken against The New York Age. You mention that "one has to be up to the tricks to keep from getting caught." While, of course, I am perfectly willing for The Age to preserve itself and come into its own eventually, I wish to be perfectly frank in saying that I am not disposed to see melt by the wayside the $3500 worth of stock which I have in the paper.

I have done too much work for The Age for which I have received not one single cent of money to willingly sit by and see it vanish in the air. I am sure you appreciate my feeling and disposition in the matter and I hope you will write me quite frankly as to just where I stand now and where I am to stand in the future.

I am keeping a carbon copy of this letter so that we may be able to get together in reaching a decision.

I was very glad of the chance we had for a little chat at the depot as I was leaving New York last Thursday afternoon.

I return herewith Fortune's letter. Yours very truly,

Emmett J. Scott

TLpS   Con. 441   BTW Papers   DLC.

From John J. Reid, Jr.

Flower Hospital   New York, April 25 1911

Dear Dr Washington: I have enclosed a certificate which I hope will be of value to you. It has been customary to charge a fee of $10.00 for such, but this I will leave to your own discretion. Hoping that it will be my pleasure to meet you again some time but not as under the previous condition I am   Sincerely yours,

John J Reid

[*Enclosure*]

This is to certify that I being the Ambulance Surgeon on the night of Sunday March 19 inst. had Mr Booker T. Washington as a patient, and after examining his wounds, I further carefully observed his actions speech and any odors which might suggest alcohol. But as a result I am prepared to say that I could a[s]certain nothing which would pertain to alcoholism; I found only the true and courteous character in him, that a man of his rank and ability would exhibit.

John J. Reid

ALS   Con. 435   BTW Papers   DLC.

Charles Fletcher Dole to Seth Low

Jamaica Plain, Mass. April 25, 1911

My dear Mr. Low   I held the enclosed letter[1] for a while, being doubtful of my own judgment. But Saturday at Mr. Washington's request I met him at the Parker House in Boston, & had a talk with him. I am now inclined to follow my first thought & to send you my letter. I talked very frankly with Mr. W. but it seemed to me that he was evasive rather than straightforward. Of course, he pleaded the advice of the lawyers not to talk about details, e.g. the Scott letter &c. But it puzzles me why an innocent man, who has good ground on which to stand, should decline himself or be advised by any true friends to decline, to tell his story just as it was. This is the course which lawyers ask dubious characters to take. But I am shy of the lawyers & their roundabout methods.

But my chief point is that Mr. W. does not *seem* to see the importance of going to the root of this affair for the *sake of his people*. If he can be brutally beaten at the risk of his life in New York, and the assault be treated lightly, why should not negroes be lynched in Alabama, & let off on the ground that their assailants suspected them of evil intent?

Forgive me then if I am stupid & mistaken in telling you frankly how the lawyers' policy of silence seems to strike me.

I have today the report upon the Tuskegee farm which is interesting & important, & I hope will prove very useful. It had seemed to me that large economies were called for in that department! Yours respectfully

Charles F. Dole

ALS   Seth Low Papers   NNC.

¹ See Dole to Low, Apr. 11, 1911, above.

From Robert Ezra Park

Tuskegee Institute, Ala. April 26, 1911

My dear Mr Washington: Your letter of April 23 referring to the way in which my name should appear in the final publication of "The Man Farthest Down," has just been received and while the matter is fresh in my mind I want to outline in a general way what I think about the matter.

It seems to me the best thing to do would be to put my name on the book as joint author. In case that is done a statement could be made in the preface or in the introduction as to what my part in the book was. In case that is done I should not like to be represented as a professional writer who had helped you to put together the book. Rather I should like it to appear that I had been working at Tuskegee, interested in the school as others who are employed here. I would not want to [be] represented as engaged in any philanthropic or "unselfish" work. I should like the real fact stated that I was interested in you and in the work you are doing; that we had traveled about and gotten the same ideas; and it was because I understood you and we understood each other; were interested in the same things that the book came to be written.

I think the matter can be presented in some such way as to add to the interest of the book rather than take away from it. I think the matter can be so presented that it will appear that whatever I have added to the book has really been yours as well as mine. In that way it can not be said that you hired an outsider to write the book as I fear they are likely to say otherwise.

I do not know as I have made myself very clear but if what I have said suggests anything to you I wish you would dictate something on which I can work.

You understand that it is not a desire to have you do justice to me, but to put me in a position where I can talk about the book with some freedom and where I can continue to do the work I have been doing more comfortably. If people understand that whatever I write or may have written in the past is written by one who shares in, believes in and is capable of interpreting what you think and mean that will be a great deal more satisfactory all around than it will if they believe my part in the book is that of mere hired man.

As a matter of fact if the situation were not as I have stated I would never have been willing to do the work that I have done. I am very truly

Robert E. Park

TLS   Con. 54   BTW Papers   DLC.

To Seth Low

En Route, Washington, D.C. April 27 — 1911

Dear Mr. Low: Matters seem to be clearing up a little. I had a talk with my lawyer just before starting South today, and he tells me that Ulrich's lawyer came to him voluntarily this morning and stated in effect that he was getting rather tired with bothering with the case, because Ulrich had not paid him and that Ulrich's friends had made promises to contribute and these promises had not been kept. One person, it seems, promised to give $150.00 to help Ulrich but withdrew the offer after he found that the woman was not Ulrich's wife. It seems from what the lawyer stated, that what money has come into his hands has been spent in trying to manufacture false testimony to the effect that I was under the influence of liquor on the night I was assaulted, and because of my being under the influence of liquor I acted in a way to justify the assault.

Ulrich's lawyer also stated that parties had made affidavit to the effect that I had been seen at various times under the influence of liquor, but these affidavits are evidently so false and show signs of being manufactured, that he would be ashamed to submit them to a court.

Our attorney left U's attorney with the understanding that he is to have a frank talk with his clients and see our attorney later.

Of course it is very important that this conversation not go further than our Trustees, as Mr. Smith is anxious to treat U's attorney in an honorable way.

After the two lawyers have had another conference, I think we will be in position to know what will be the next best statement.

It is a matter of the deepest regret to me that the time and thought of men like yourself and others that should be given to the greater cause, should be taken up with matters regarding myself. Yours very truly,

Booker T. Washington

HLS Seth Low Papers NNC. A typed copy dated Apr. 28, 1911, is in Con. 54, BTW Papers, DLC.

William Calvin Chase to Emmett Jay Scott

Washington, D.C. April 28, 1911

My dear Emmett: I have arrived to a point where I need financial assistance with my paper, and I want you to ask Dr. Washington on his return the importance of this request. My friend Ralph W. Tyler agreed to donate to me Twenty ($20.) dollars per month, and up to March he has contributed to the paper Forty ($40.) Dollars. Of course you know this paper has been serving Dr. Washington which he no doubt appreciates. You know what it costs to run a Negro newspaper. I am not asking Dr. Washington to pay me for defending him or his cause, I would do so anyway, but I do ask him to assist me so I may continue. I am back, or rather I am indebted to my printer to the amount of Four hundred ($400.00) dollars and he has made a demand on me to settle. I must have help at once. Kindly inform Dr. Washington, and let me hear from you by return mail. I am enclosing you a letter from the company to enable you to see. Please return it

to me. This is confidential and I hope that you will be able [to] reach
Dr. Washington, at once. Sincerely yours,

W. Calvin Chase

TLS Con. 419 BTW Papers DLC.

To Paul Drennan Cravath

[Tuskegee, Ala.] April 29, 1911

Dear Mr. Cravath: After leaving your office, I learned on what seemed
to be good authority that Ulrich is at work in an effort to secure manufactured and perjured testimony to the effect that on the night that
he assaulted me I was intoxicated and my actions by reason of the
intoxication constituted his justification for assaulting me.

I think that such a statement as we discussed ought to contain acknowledgement from him that I was not intoxicated. I have certif-
icates from both of the doctors who attended me on the night I was
assaulted that there was no sign of intoxication.

Mr. Wilford H. Smith, my personal attorney, will call to see you
soon. Yours very truly,

Booker T. Washington

The statement also ought to have, it seems to me, something to the
effect that he has not been paid any money for making the retraction.

B. T. W.

TLpS Con. 434 BTW Papers DLC.

To Charles Dewey Hilles

Tuskegee Institute, Alabama May 1, 1911

Personal and Confidential.
My dear Mr. Hilles: It is probable that some colored people, headed
by Jesse Lawson of Washington, will attempt to see the President

within the next few days regarding the plans for the celebration of the Fiftieth Anniversary of the Freedom of the Negro.

I hope the President will not commit himself in this regard before I can have a chance to have a conference with him, or you.

In order to refresh the memories of yourself and the President regarding this matter, I enclose to you paragraphs from the President's messages during the two last Congresses. These paragraphs were put in at my suggestion.

I think it possible that Mr. Lawson's people and myself can work together harmoniously, but I think it would be mixing matters just a little if the President were to commit himself to Mr. Lawson before I have had time to see him or communicate with him. Yours very truly,

Booker T. Washington

TLS William Howard Taft Papers DLC. A press copy is in Con. 53, BTW Papers, DLC.

To George Ruffin Bridgeforth

Tuskegee Institute, Alabama May 1st, 1911

Mr. Bridgeforth: Enclosed I send you a copy of the report made by the committee which was appointed to investigate the whole matter of the use and disposition of the manure. You will find that according to this report that you are not complying in any large degree with the orders which were given you.

Failure to respect the orders of the school in a matter like this strikes at the foundation of our success. It is impossible for us to succeed as a school, or for any department to succeed where the head fails to recognize and respect authority.

I should not speak so frankly and plainly in this matter if this were the first case. In this special instance I not only had several of our best teachers spend a lot of time in getting up the data and in investigating the matter, but you will remember that Mr. Logan, Mr. J. H. Washington and others together with yourself spent a lot of time considering the report, and we finally got in shape an order which you said was satisfactory and the order was duly issued. Now you can imagine what a surprise and disappointment to me it is to find that after all we have done it seems to count for little.

No person can successfully manage a great department until he learns the fundamental lesson of obedience, or respect for orders.

I very much hope that you will begin at once to carry out the order in every detail and continue to carry it out unless permission is given from the office for changes to be made.

Booker T. Washington

TLS   Con. 608   BTW Papers   DLC.

To E. H. Gamlin[1]

Tuskegee Institute, Alabama   May 1, 1911

Mr. Gamlin: You will agree with me, I think, when I say that at least a half dozen times within the past few years, we have warned you and urged you to close up your store on the Sabbath. I have both written you and spoken to you personally regarding it. For some reason you have refused to carry out the policy of the school in this regard.

We have tried in every way to build up a clean and law abiding Sabbath keeping community and I am glad to say that we have interested the people engaged in business in Greenwood in co-operating with us.

In every way possible we have tried to assist and encourage you in building up your business, but notwithstanding this you pursue a policy which is in direct opposition to the wishes of the school authorities. It is a matter of constant remark and criticism in the community that you pay no regard to the school's wishes in this matter, and no regard to the sanctity of the Sabbath.

I have reliable information to the effect that on yesterday that there were at one time in your store as many as twenty people most of them students and other people connected with the school engaged in purchasing, and that buying and selling was kept up all day last Sunday as it has been for a good many Sundays in the past.

You can't expect others to be more interested in your business than you are yourself, and therefore it is my opinion that the school will be justified in view of your disregard of our wishes about closing on the Sabbath, to forbid in the future all students from entering your place of business either during the week or on the Sabbath.

[Booker T. Washington]

TL Copy   Con. 612   BTW Papers   DLC.

¹ E. H. Gamlin ran a grocery and dry-goods store, with an adjoining cafe, in a building owned by BTW near the Tuskegee campus. He often advertised in the *Tuskegee Student.*

To Morris S. Walton¹

[Tuskegee, Ala.] May 1, 1911

Mr. Walton: Your name has been handed me as being among the teachers who were at Mr. Gamlin's store yesterday purchasing goods or by your presence or purchase encouraging him to break the Sabbath and to go against the policy of the school, which seeks to prevent merchandising in the community on the Sabbath day.

I am sure that the mere calling of your attention to this matter will be all that is necessary.

Booker T. Washington

TLpS   Con. 606   BTW Papers   DLC.

¹ Instructor of history and geography at Tuskegee Institute from 1910 to 1912.

To Benjamin Jefferson Davis

[Tuskegee, Ala.] May 2, 1911

Personal and Confidential

My dear Mr. Davis: I have been away from home for some days and on my return I find your letter which I appreciate very much.

I have not been able to get to the point of answering your letter before today.

Let me repeat that which I have already expressed to you that you do not know how much I appreciate and value the service which you have rendered me especially during recent weeks. I shall never forget it.

In regard to the New York Age, I can only repeat that which I have stated before. This sentence I attach on separate sheet and you may quote in any way you please.

It is true that I am on terms of friendship with Mr. Moore and other editors much in the same way that I am on terms of friendship with you and wherever I can and think it proper in certain directions, I try to exert influence over them. Some times in the case of Mr. Moore he follows my advice and some times he does not. I ought to say that my general policy is that wherever I get an opportunity I try to dissuade all of our editors from the policy of personal journalism. Readers are not interested in a personal spat between individuals. Such journalism is not dignified nor helpful. I have told Mr. Moore this as plainly as I could and there are occasions when I think he has been influenced by my opinion.

Speaking very confidentially, I happen to know that a certain party in Atlanta sent Mr. Moore an account of something about your being indicted for using improperly a seal or something of that kind, and I urged Mr. Moore on no account to give any attention to such an allegation against you.

I do not know what I can do or say further than I have done or said. You know there are people who are never convinced when they want to believe the wrong thing.

There are people who stated just as strongly when Mr. Fortune was in charge of The Age that I owned it as they do now since Mr. Moore is in possession of the property. In some way I wish that it were possible for all of our forces to get together and to work together and stop bickering and fighting. We could accomplish a great deal more by pulling together than by pulling apart. In the last analysis there are more points upon which we agree than upon which we disagree and I believe that there is a basis of common work and uniting action for all who want to do the right thing. The race is in too critical a condition for our forces to remain divided when they can be united.

I should be glad to hear from you on any or all of the points which I have raised in this letter.

Let me add in closing that I cannot be responsible for the utterances of the New York Age. While, as I said, in the future I shall try to do as I have in the past, get the paper to give a broad generous attitude rather than a personal and narrow one as to the Odd Fellows. It is really amusing as to the influence that people credit me with having over that organization. I really know practically nothing about secret societies. I am a member of only one and know so little about that that for the life of me I do not think I can ever get into any more. I am not trying to control the Odd Fellows nor any element in the Odd Fellows, and I am sure that you know as well as anybody else that it would be practically impossible for me to carry on the work of this institution involving the securing of the expenditure of $265,000.00 every year and give attention to all the other outside matters that people credit me with being connected with. Yours very truly,

Booker T. Washington

[*Enclosure*]
Extract from letter written by Booker T. Washington to Benjamin J. Davis, Editor of The Atlanta Independent.

"I do not own directly or indirectly, or control directly or indirectly a single dollar's worth of the property of the New York Age; neither do I own or control a single dollar's worth of stock in any publication in this country. I ought to make an exception of the four or five publications sent out from the Tuskegee Institute."

Booker T. Washington

TLpS Con. 421 BTW Papers DLC.

To Charles William Anderson

[Tuskegee, Ala.] May 2, 1911

Personal
My dear Mr. Anderson: The enclosed copy of a letter is from a plain clothes man,[1] who was largely instrumental in saving my life on the night I was attacked in New York. In case the matter had come to trial, he was ready and anxious to give the facts showing that the woman's statement was entirely an after-thought and entirely trumped up.

I am very anxious that in some way his services can be rewarded.

Just now, however, I do not care to make a written request in this direction. I am wondering, however, if in your own way you cannot bring about his promotion. At any rate, I wonder if you will not send for Mr. Hagan and have a talk with him and perhaps he can suggest some measure by which you can serve him. I would rather my name not figure in the matter just as little as possible, if at all. You will have to bear in mind in dealing with the case that there was a uniformed officer present at the same time and if this officer gets the idea that the other fellow is being rewarded and he is being neglected it may make him hostile. Yours very truly,

B. T. W.

TLpI   Con. 52   BTW Papers   DLC.   No enclosure found.

[1] Chester A. Hagan, a New York City detective.

From Anson Phelps Stokes, Jr.[1]

New Haven, Conn., May 2, 1911

Dear Dr. Washington: You probably know that the will of my Aunt, Miss Caroline Phelps Stokes, leaves a considerable sum of money to be used for educational purposes, partially for negro education. I should be glad to have you suggest to me the method which you would like to have considered by which five or ten thousand dollars could be used to the special advantage of negro education of the type that you are now doing at Tuskegee. I am getting similar expressions of opinion from other people in whose judgment I have confidence. Sincerely yours,

Anson Phelps Stokes

TLS   Con. 440   BTW Papers   DLC.

[1] Anson Phelps Stokes, Jr. (1874–1958), son of the New York merchant and financier, was an Episcopal clergyman, secretary of Yale University (1899–1921), and a trustee of the Phelps-Stokes Fund, formed in 1911. In 1924 he became canon of Washington Cathedral. He served on the Tuskegee Institute board of trustees after BTW's death, and in 1929 he was a trustee of the Booker T. Washington Agricultural and Industrial Institute in Liberia.

To Monroe Nathan Work

Tuskegee Institute, Alabama   May 3, 1911

Mr. Work: I am sending you Chapter 16, under the title, "The Women who work in Europe," and I want you to see if you can make two or three changes which I have in mind. Perhaps you might indicate the changes in lead pencil.

1 — On the first page I do not want to emphasize the fact so prominently of my lunching in a restaurant with white women.

2 — I think Dr. Park in writing this chapter took for granted too much that readers would make the comparison in their own mind between the condition of the colored women in America and the white women who work in Europe. I think in three or four places this comparison ought to be communicated a little more prominently.

3 — In speaking of courts dealing with the class of women who come before the court in London — for example: I think it should be stated that in the South the women guilty of the same kind of offences would be punished much more severely.

4 — Toward the latter part, there is a little too much indication of my criticizing adversely the suffragist movement in Europe and perhaps in this country. I hardly want to get into just now that kind of hornet's nest.

B. T. W.

TLI   Con. 614   BTW Papers   DLC.

Emmett Jay Scott to William Calvin Chase

[Tuskegee, Ala.] May 4, 1911

Dear Mr. Chase: It has not been possible to give your letter attention until today.

I telegraphed our friend, Cobb, to see that Fifty Dollars account advertising was handed you at once. Of course my telegram to him was marked "confidential" and nothing will be mentioned regarding same. Sincerely,

E. J. Scott

You are well I hope! I thought it wise to telegraph so as to get the money in your hands promptly. Sorry can do no better now.

This is on our advertising a/c. E. J. S.

TLpS Con. 419 BTW Papers DLC. Postscript in Scott's hand.

To Charles William Anderson

[Tuskegee, Ala.] May 5, 1911

Personal and Confidential

Dear Mr. Anderson: I have just sent a telegram to the parties in charge of the Unitarian Club dinner asking that you be invited. I hope that this can be done. The dinner takes place at the Hotel Manhattan at seven on the 10th.

One other thing. Now that matters have somewhat quieted down, is it not possible for you to get a statement from the Police Department covering the following points:

First, that the portion of the city in which I was on the night of the attack was a decent portion, and that the house, 11½, is a decent house. Mr. Moore says this is what the Police Sergeant told him.

I wonder if you could not get this in some official shape through the Mayor's secretary. Yours very truly,

Booker T. Washington

TLpS Con. 52 BTW Papers DLC.

To Wood, Harmon and Company

[Tuskegee, Ala.] May 5, 1911

Dear Sirs: Some years ago, as you will recall, I bought from you a lot in Rugby Park. At the time there seemed to be some objection on the part of some of the members of your board to selling to a colored man, but that objection it seems was overcome in my case.

I want to be perfectly frank in dealing with you in regard to the property and do not wish to embarrass you. I wish to dispose of the property, and have an offer from a colored man in New York City for it. I have not said, however, that I would accept the figure which he names. I send you a copy of his letter, of course with the understanding that he is not to know that I have sent you this letter.

Before going further with the matter, I want to ask if it will embarrass or injure your property to dispose of the lot to a colored person. Yours truly,

Booker T. Washington

TLpS   Con. 446   BTW Papers   DLC.

From Charles William Anderson

New York, N.Y. May 5, 1911

(Personal)

My dear Doctor: Yours of the 2nd instant at hand. I will take up Mr. Hagan's case at once and do all in my power to land him. The new Deputy Police Commissioner is an old friend of mine. His name is George Dougherty,[1] and was for many years the Superintendent of the Pinkerton Detective Agency. Mayor Gaynor appointed him this week to succeed Mr. Flynn,[2] and he will be in charge of the Detective Bureau. I hope, through him, to be able to land our man. I shall spare no effort to pull this off, and of course, keep your name out of it. I appreciate the advisability of caution in this matter.

In a letter of yesterday, I called your attention to Roscoe's cheap editorial sneer in the Age of this week. In talking to Walton[3] last Sunday, I said Roscoe must have been an idiot to have published the "hold-up" story when he knew, from my own lips, that I had used all of my ingenuity to keep it out of the daily papers, on your account. Walton evidently passed the word along to Roscoe, and as a result this dirty little paragraph. The New York Age is evidently not edited in the house of my friends, for if it were, the hold-up story would not have appeared to begin with, and then there would have been no reason for my using the unpleasant, but thoroughly descriptive term of idiot, when referring to the stripling who writes its editorials. It's hard to fight enemies in front and in the rear at the same time. Yours very truly,

Charles W. Anderson

TLS   Con. 52   BTW Papers   DLC.

[1] George S. Dougherty (1865–1931) worked for Pinkerton's National Detective Agency from 1888 to 1911 in New York City, where he was famous for his exploits. He served from 1911 to 1914 as deputy police commissioner and chief of detectives of New York City. After 1914 he was a partner in Dougherty's Detective Bureau and Mercantile Police. He introduced the fingerprint system of identification in New York City, and was the author of books and articles on detective work.

[2] William James Flynn (1867–1928) had organized the detective bureau of the New York City police in 1910–11, after many years in the U.S. Secret Service. He returned to the Secret Service as its chief from 1912 to 1917.

[3] Lester A. Walton, born in St. Louis about 1881, married Fred R. Moore's daughter Gladys. He was managing editor of the New York *Age* from 1907 to 1915, and a special contributor to the New York *World*.

To Anson Phelps Stokes, Jr.

[Tuskegee, Ala.] May 6, 1911

My dear Mr. Stokes: Replying to your letter of May 2d asking my opinion concerning the use of Five or Ten Thousand Dollars from the estate of Miss Caroline Phelps Stokes, I would reply as follows:

Very few people outside of the South know how much money the colored people themselves are spending for education. The most of this money is raised and spent through the various religious denominations, especially Baptist and Methodist. For example, I find in the whole South that there are about 140 schools and colleges of various kinds being supported by the colored people and almost wholly by the colored people themselves. Now many of these schools are miserable affairs both in physical equipment and in instruction. A few are good, but notwithstanding the poor work that many of them are doing, they are going to exist, going to live from year to year, because they have the churches back of them.

For a number of years, I have contended that one way in which a comparatively small sum of money could be used to accomplish the greater amount of good would be to get hold of these institutions and gradually teach them how to do first class, sensible work. If a person of tact and ability is selected, this individual could go to one of these schools and spend, say, a week or two showing them, in the first place, how to clean up the premises, what cleanliness and order mean, and above all, how to make out a course of study that would actually mean something to the people in the community where the school exists.

You speak in your letter about helping the schools that are doing the same type of work as Tuskegee. Now many of these denominational schools, perhaps most of them, are trying to do the same type of work, but are failing simply because they do not know how. In a word, if two or three people who thoroughly understand Hampton and Tuskegee methods could be employed under proper supervision to go among these denominational schools, they could help them to do from 25 to 50% more good without any additional cost, except the expenses of the agent or agents employed to do the supervising work. I should say that persons could be gotten for about $100.00 per month.

I wrote an article for the Outlook,[1] some years ago, touching on this subject and I am taking the liberty of sending you a copy of it. If you would kindly return it when you are through, I should be glad. The title is "Educational Engineers." In this article, I have spoken a good deal about the small rural schools. What I have in mind in this letter is the larger schools.[2] Yours very truly,

Booker T. Washington

TLpS   Con. 440   BTW Papers   DLC.

[1] BTW, "Educational Engineers," *Outlook*, 95 (June 4, 1910), 266–67.
[2] For further correspondence on the subject of aid to black denominational and private schools, see Anson Phelps Stokes, Jr., to BTW, May 10, 1911, and BTW to Stokes, May 15, 1911, Con. 440, BTW Papers, DLC.

To Charles Dewey Hilles

Tuskegee Institute, Alabama   May 6, 1911

Personal.

My dear Mr. Hilles: I fear I did not make myself very clear in the letter which I wrote you some days ago regarding the celebration of the Fiftieth Anniversary of the Freedom of the Colored people.

If Jesse Lawson or any other group of colored people attempt to see the President on this subject, I very much wish you might see your way clear to suggest to them, since I was instrumental in getting the President to make a recommendation in his Message to Congress, that it might be well for them to consult with me before seeing the President, with a view of getting us to work together in harmony. That would have its proper effect. Yours very truly,

Booker T. Washington

TLS   William Howard Taft Papers   DLC.   A press copy is in Con. 53, BTW Papers, DLC.

An Article in *Outlook*

May 6, 1911

THE MAN FARTHEST DOWN

The Trustees of the Tuskegee Normal and Industrial Institute very kindly arranged for me to spend a number of weeks in Europe last summer taking a rest. Now, I have never learned to rest in the ordinary sense of that term, and have always found my greatest rest and recreation in change of work and scenery. The action of the Trustees in this matter, however, gave me a chance to do something which I had long wanted to do. I had been anxious to get into that portion of the world where the human family is farthest down, to see for myself how the "man farthest down" was living and what was being done to improve his condition, and how this condition compared with that of the average black man in the United States, and to see how the methods being employed in raising him up compared with the methods employed in raising up the black man in America. It is not a satisfaction to me to describe poverty and misery except as a means to an end. If any one who reads the articles which I have written suggests that I saw the worst and am trying to describe the worst instead of the best, I would state frankly that I went to Europe with the deliberate purpose of seeing and describing the worst and not the best.

Another reason that made me anxious to make this trip was that much emphasis is now being placed upon the importance of getting

European immigrants into the Southern States to replace the Negro as a laborer, and I wanted to see to what extent these people would be likely to come into the South and adapt themselves to Southern conditions and become competitors by the side of the Negro. Perhaps the strongest reason, however, for my wanting to make these observations was the service which I thought I could render to my own race in this country. There are not a few Negroes who sometimes become discouraged and feel that their condition and prospects are worse than those of any other group of human beings. I wanted to see groups of people who are much worse off than the Negro, and, through detailing their condition, place such facts before the Negro in America as would make him feel and see that, instead of being the worst off, his condition and prospects are much better than those of millions of people who are in the same relative stage of civilization.

I saw the life of the poorer classes in the East End of London and in several other of the great cities of Europe; the life of farm laborers in Austria, Hungary, and Sicily; visited the salt mines in Poland and the sulphur mines in Sicily; examined the life of a Russian village; near Copenhagen studied the wonderful development of agricultural organization in Denmark; and saw much else that was of value to my purpose.

I ought to state also that I could not have covered the ground or have made the observations that I did without the assistance of Dr. Robert E. Park, of Boston, who has been assisting me for a number of years in my work at Tuskegee Institute. Dr. Park is a graduate of one of the German universities and has the advantage of an acquaintance with several European languages, and has lived and traveled in much of the territory that we covered. He preceded me to Europe by several weeks, making a preliminary survey of the route we intended to take, and afterwards accompanied me upon my whole journey.

B. T. W.

THE MAN AT THE BOTTOM IN LONDON

The Carmania, the ship in which I had sailed, disembarked its passengers late Saturday at Fishguard, off the coast of Wales. The special train which sped us on to London reached the city early Sunday morning, August 28.

As I drove from the railway station in the gray of the early morning my attention was attracted by a strange, shapeless, and disreputable figure which slunk out of the shadow of a building and moved slowly and dejectedly down the silent and empty street. In that quarter of the city, and in comparison with the solid respectability and comfort represented by the houses around him, the figure of this man seemed grotesquely wretched. In fact, he struck me as the most lonely object I had ever laid my eyes on. I watched him down the street as far as I could see. He did not turn to the left or to the right, but moved slowly on, his head bent toward the ground, apparently looking for something he did not hope to find. In the course of my journey across Europe I saw much poverty, but I do not think I saw anything quite so hopeless and wretched.

I had not been long in London before I learned that this man was a type. It is said that there are ten thousand of these homeless and houseless men and women in East London alone. They are, however, not confined to any part of the city. They may be found in the fashionable West End, lounging on the benches of St. James's Park, as well as in the East End, where the masses of the laboring people live. The Salvation Army has erected shelters for them in many of the poorer parts of the city, where, for anything from two to eight cents, they may get a room for the night, and sometimes a piece of bread and a bowl of soup. Thousands of them are not able to compass the small sum necessary to obtain even this minimum of food and comfort. These are the outcasts and the rejected, the human waste of a great city. They represent the man at the bottom in London.

Later, in the course of my wanderings about the city, I met many of these hopeless and broken men. I saw them sitting, on sunshiny days, not only men but women also, crumpled up on benches or stretched out on the grass of the parks. I discovered them on rainy nights, crouching in doorways or huddled away in dark corners where an arch or a wall protected them from the cold. I met them in the early morning hours, before the city was awake, creeping along the Strand and digging with their hands in the garbage-boxes; and again, late at night, on the Thames Embankment, where hundreds of them sleep — when the night watchman permits — on the benches or stretched out on the stone pavements. After a time I learned to distinguish the same type under the disguise of those street venders who stand on street corners and sell collar-buttons, matches, and other trifles, stretching out their hands in a pitiful sort of supplication to passers-by to buy their wares.

Whenever I found an opportunity to do so, I talked with some of these outcasts. Gradually, partly from themselves and partly from others, I learned something of their histories. I found that it was usually drink that had been the immediate cause of their downfall. But there were always other and deeper causes. Most of them, it seemed to me, had simply been borne down by the temptations and the fierce competition of life in a great city. There comes a time when trade is dull; men who had been accustomed to spend much money begin to spend less, and there is no work to be had. At these times it is "the less efficient, the less energetic, the less strong, the less young, the less regular, the less temperate, or the less docile" who are crowded out. In this way these men have lost their hold and sunk to the bottom.

I remember meeting one of these men late at night wandering along the Thames Embankment. In the course of my conversation with him I asked him, among other things, if he voted, and, if so, to what political party he belonged.

He looked at me in amazement, and then he said he had never voted in his life. It was his expression rather than his words that impressed me. This expression told me how out of touch he was with the world about him. He had, in fact, as I learned, no family, no home, friends, trade; he belonged to no society; he had, so far as I could learn, no views on life. In the very midst of this great city he was as solitary as a hermit.

A few weeks later, in a little village in Galicia, I asked the same question of a Polish peasant. "Oh, yes," he eagerly replied; "every one votes here now."

Sixty years ago most of the peasants in this village to which I have referred were serfs, and it was not until two years ago that the Government gave them all the right to vote. Nevertheless, at the present time the people in this village are represented by one of their own number in the Imperial Parliament at Vienna. I stopped on my way through the village at the little store kept by this man. I found two young girls tending the store, his daughters, but the representative himself was not at home.

I do not know why I should mention this circumstance here, except that I was impressed by the contrast in the reply of these two men, the one coming from a peasant in Poland and the other from an Englishman in London.

It is generally said that the Negro represents in America the man farthest down. In going to Europe I had in mind to compare the masses of the Negro people of the South with the masses in Europe in something like the same stage of civilization. It would not be difficult to compare the Negro in the South with the Polish peasant, for example, because the masses of the Poles are, like the masses of the Negroes, an agricultural people.

I know no class among the Negroes in America, however, with whom I could compare the man at the bottom in England. Whatever one may say of the Negro in America, he is not, as a rule, a beggar. It is very rarely that any one sees a black hand stretched out for alms. One does see, to be sure, too many idle and loafing Negroes standing on the street corners around the railway stations in the South; but the Negro is not, as a rule, a degenerate. If he is at the bottom in America, it is not because he has gone backward and sunk down, but because he has never risen.

Another thing in regard to the Negro: although he is frequently poor, he is never without hope and a certain joy in living. No hardship he has yet encountered, either in slavery or in freedom, has robbed the Negro of the desire to live. The race constantly grew and increased in slavery, and it has considerably more than doubled in freedom. There are some people among the members of my race who complain about the hardships which the Negro suffers, but none of them yet, so far as I know, has ever recommended "race suicide" as a solution of the race problem.

I mention this because I found just the contrary to be the case in England. I do not think that anything I saw or heard while I was in England gave me a more poignant impression of the hardships of the laboring man in England than the discovery that one of the most widely read weekly papers in England, under the caption of "The White Slaves of Morality," was making a public campaign in favor of reducing the size of the families among the working classes.

The articles I refer to, which were written by a woman, were a protest, on the one hand, against the clergy, because they taught that it would be immoral for women to refuse to have children, and, on the other hand, against the physicians who withheld from these women the knowledge by which they might be able to limit the size of their families. These articles were followed from week to week by letters purporting to come from working men and women telling of the heartbreaking struggle they were making to support their children on the wages they were able to earn.

What made these articles the more startling was the fact that, at the very time when they were proposing to the English laborer what ex-President Roosevelt has defined as "race suicide," thousands of immigrants from the south of Europe were pouring into London every year to take the places left vacant by the recession of the native Anglo-Saxon.

On my previous visit to England I had been struck by what seemed to me the cold and formal character of the English newspapers. It seemed to me that they were wholly lacking in human interest. Upon my last visit my opinion in regard to the London newspapers was considerably altered. A careful study of the daily newspaper, I found, will repay any one who wants to get an insight into actual conditions in England.

I had not been in London more than a day or two, for example, when my attention was attracted to the following item in one of the morning papers:

STARVING FAMILY
CORONER'S APPEAL TO THE PUBLIC FOR AID

Telling of a terrible case of starvation in the Stoke Newington Coroner's Court, Dr. Wynn Westcott, the coroner, asked the press to bring a deserving case before the notice of the charitable public.

He said that he had held an inquest upon a three-weeks-old baby which had died of starvation. Its father had had no regular work for three years, and only a little casual work in that time. There was so little money that the mother, Mrs. Attewell, of White Hart Street, Stoke Newington, was half starved too. She had only had a crust of bread to sustain her on the day her child died, although she had done nine and a half hours' washing to assist the home.

The home was perfectly clean, although practically destitute of furniture. It was a most deserving case.

After reading this item I began studying the papers more closely, and I was surprised at the frequency with which items of this kind occurred. I learned that the local Government Board, which is represented in the English Cabinet by Mr. John Burns,[1] has issued since 1871 an annual report, or return, as it is called, of the cases in which, upon formal investigation by a coroner's jury, it appears that the persons came to their death in London as a result of starvation. I obtained a copy of the return for 1908, in which are included the statistics on starvation not merely for London but for the rest of England and Wales.

The forms issued to coroners were explicit. They provided that the return should include only cases in which the jury find that death is brought about by starvation or privation due to destitution. Cases in which death was caused by cold, starvation, exposure, etc., unconnected with destitution, are not entered in this return. Of the 125 cases of starvation reported, 52 occurred in London. In 11 cases death was described as due to starvation in conjunction with some other cause; that is to say, disease, drink, exposure, or self-neglect. In 80 of the 125 cases no application was made for poor relief, or application was made only when the deceased had been in a dying condition.

A few days after I had succeeded in getting this report my attention was attracted one morning by the heading of a newspaper article: "How the Poor Die." The article was an account of the finding of the body of an unknown woman in a cellar in the basement of a house not very far from where I was stopping.

"It appears," the article said, "that during the earlier part of the morning the tenant of the building observed a woman sleeping in the cellar, but no particular notice was taken of this because of the fact that strangers frequently utilized the cellar for such purposes. Mr. Oliver, one of the occupants of the building, had occasion to go downstairs, and saw the woman. She was crouched in a corner and her head was lying back. The police were called in and the services of Dr. Barton were requisitioned. . . . Although the cause of death will not be known until a post-mortem examination of the body has been made, death, it is thought, was due to starvation. The woman was about six feet in height, between forty and fifty years of age, and was in a very emaciated condition and clad in very scanty attire."

Not infrequently, when in my public speeches I have made some reference to the condition of the Negro in the South, certain members of my own race in the North have objected because, they said, I did not paint conditions in the South black enough. During my stay in England I had the unusual experience of being criticised in the London newspapers for the same reason, this time by an American white man. At the very moment that this man attacked me because in my public interviews I emphasized the opportunities rather than the wrongs of the Negro in the South I had in my possession the document to which

I have referred, which gives the official history of fifty-two persons, one for every week in the year, who had died in the city of London alone for want of food.

I have never denied that the Negro in the South frequently meets with wrong and injustice; but he does not starve. I do not think a single case was ever heard of, in the South, where a Negro died from want of food. In fact, unless because of sickness or some other reason he has been unable to work, it is comparatively rare to find a Negro in an almshouse.

It has not been my purpose in anything I have written to pass judgment upon the people or the conditions that I have found in the countries which I have visited. Criticism is an ungrateful task at best, and one for which I am not well fitted. Neither shall I attempt to offer any suggestions as to how conditions may be improved; in fact, I am convinced from what I learned that the people on the ground understand conditions much better than I possibly could, and in a later article I hope to tell something of the great work that has been done in England and elsewhere to raise the level of life and comfort among the people who are at the bottom in the countries which I visited. What I am anxious to do here is to emphasize some of the advantages which it seems the members of my own race, and particularly those living in the Southern States, have at the present time. It is not difficult to discover the disadvantages under which the Negroes in the South labor. Every traveler who passes through the South sees the conditions existing, and frequently returns to write books about them. There is danger, however, that the opportunities to which I have referred will be overlooked or not fully appreciated by the members of my race until it is too late.

One direction in which the Negro in the South has an advantage is in the matter of labor. One of the most pitiful things I saw in London, Liverpool, and other English cities were the groups of idle men standing about on the street corners, especially around the bar-rooms, because they were not able to get work.

One day as I was going along one of the main avenues of the city I noticed an unusually large crowd standing in front of a street organ which was drawn up at the side of the pavement. Pausing to see what there was about this organ that attracted so much attention and interest, I found that the man who owned this instrument was using it as an advertisement. He was advertising his poverty.

All over the front of the organ were plastered papers and documents of various kinds. On one side there was a list of advertisements cut from the "Want" columns of the daily newspapers. Attached to this was a statement that these were some of the places that the man had visited the day before in search of work, which he was not able to find. On the other side of the organ were attached six or seven pawn tickets, with the statement that "these are some of the articles which my dear wife pawned to get food for our children." This was followed by a pitiful appeal for help. The pathetic thing about it was that the only persons who stopped to look at these exhibits besides myself were a group of hungry and disreputable-looking men who were evidently in just as great want as the man who ground the organ. I watched those men. After reading the signs they would look inquiringly at the other members of the group and then relapse into the same stolid silence which I had noticed so many times in the forlorn figures that filled the benches of the parks.

It seemed to me that they both pitied and admired the man who had conceived this novel way of advertising his misfortune. I have noticed these same people in other cases where it seemed to me they looked with something like envy upon a beggar who was blind or lame or had some other interesting misfortune which enabled him to win the sympathy of the public.

Of course the persons that I have attempted to describe here and in other portions of this article do not represent the laboring classes. They represent the man at the bottom, but it is the man at the bottom who lives by begging or casual labor. It shows how bitter is the struggle for existence among the laboring class higher up, from which the class below is constantly recruited.

While I was in London I received letters from a great many persons of all classes and conditions. One of these was from a colored man who was born and raised in the South and was anxious to get back home. I am tempted to quote some passages of his letter here, because they will illustrate how conditions impressed a colored man from the South who got closer to actual conditions than I was able to. He had been living, he said, in London for fourteen months without work.

"I have tried to apply for work," he continued. "They said they want Englishmen. It seems to me that all Britain are against the Negro race. Some say, 'Go back to your own country,' knowing if I had the means I would fly to-morrow."

Perhaps I would do better to quote some passages from his letter verbatim. He says:

> I cannot get a passage; to be alone in London without any help or funds, like a pin in a haystack, nothing but sorrow and distress. Hearing Mr. B. T. Washington were in London I appeal to him in the name of God Almighty if he can possibly help me with a ticket to get across, because the lady that was kind enough to give me a shelter is without fund herself; being a Christian woman she gave me food for what she can afford. At night I have to sleep in a house with a widow which has two children which has to make her living by chopping wood, whom some day, does not earn enough to buy a loaf of bread for her children. The winter is coming on and I like to get home to shuck corn or to get to Maryland for a oyster draggin. It is a long time since I had watermelon pig's feet and corn. Say, Mr. Washington, if you ever knew what a man in a hole is I guess I am in a hole and the cover over. I can see the pork chops and the corn bread and the hot biscuits calling me to come over and get some and many a time I have tried but failed. I can't reach them; the great Atlantic Ocean stop me and I remain YOUR OBEDIENT SERVANT.

This letter from which I have given a few extracts is but one of many which I received during my stay in London, not only from colored but from white Americans who had come to England to better their condition or seek their fortune.

These letters served still further to impress me with the fact that the masses of my own people in the South do not fully appreciate the advantages which they have in living in a country where there is a constant demand for labor of all kinds.

If I were asked what I believed would be the greatest boon that could be conferred upon the English laborer, I should say that it would be for him to have the same opportunities for constant and steady work that the Negro now has in the South. If I were asked what would be the next greatest benefit that could be conferred upon the English laborer, I should say that it would be to have schools in which every class could learn to do some one thing well — to have, in other words, the benefit of the kind of industrial education that we are seeking, in some measure, to give to the Negro at the present time in the Southern States.

Outlook, 98 (May 6, 1911), 21–26.

1 John Burns (1858–1943), a Socialist and labor leader, was a member of Parliament (1892–1918) and a cabinet member as president of the local government board (1905–14).

To Sumner Alexander Furniss

Tuskegee, Ala., May 8, 1911

Personal and Confidential: Am informed from Washington Vernon slated to succeed your brother.[1] You should bestir yourself. You can easily secure his Western record. Speak with Mr. New.

W.

TWpIr   Con. 422   BTW Papers   DLC.

[1] Henry Watson Furniss, a black physician and diplomat, was born in Brooklyn in 1868. His father, who had been well educated in Massachusetts, moved during Reconstruction to Mississippi, where he was secretary of state and president of Alcorn College. Going to Indianapolis, W. H. Furniss became a postal clerk but managed to send his sons through Howard University and its medical school. Henry Furniss practiced medicine briefly at Freedmen's Hospital and in Indianapolis. He was consul at Bahia, Brazil, from 1898 to 1905, and minister to Haiti 1905–13. In 1904 he married a German woman in London. After his tour in Haiti he settled in Hartford, Conn.

To Jesse Lawson

[Tuskegee, Ala.] May 8, 1911

Personal.

My dear Mr. Lawson: I have your letter of May 2d.[1]

I do not care to unduly prolong the discussion. If you will read carefully the outline as proposed by the Executive Committee of the National Negro Business League, you will find that it is not an iron-clad suggestion, but one that is flexible and one which will permit you and your organization to go ahead and carry out its plans. We had all this in mind when we made this outline. I hope that you will keep in mind the good to be accomplished, rather than the mere technicality as to the date. That means too little.

There are two things that can be accomplished by a celebration. One is the encouragement of our own people, and secondly, letting the world see what we have accomplished. Now if we will keep these two central thoughts in mind, the mere technicality covering the date means but little.

Our committee discussed fully the matter of having the celebration in September but everyone, who is in touch with the business world, knows that September is the very worst month in the year in which to succeed in doing anything. It is the month when a lot of people, the most important people, have not returned from their summer vacations, and besides, those that have returned, are unsettled and have not effected their plans for the year's work. For example, in Washington, in September, as you know, practically no important public officials are in Washington in September and would not be. What you are proposing to do, if I understand it, would be merely local, so far as Washington is concerned, and it is merely a question, it seems to me, whether we shall all agree upon the one date and have a National Celebration in which all of us can join, or whether by reason of a mere technicality, there shall be some kind of division. It is not likely that the Business League will change the date that it has suggested. We would have gladly recommended September, but for the reasons that I have stated.

If the Celebration is carried out according to the plans of the League, while each community would have its own local celebration, the occasion would be national in scope and national in its being observed.

We might as well face facts. It is impossible to get together in Washington or anywhere else any large sum of money to be used in financing an enterprise of national character. You could not raise, for example, among the colored people in Washington for such an enterprise $2,000 in cash from now until the time for the Celebration and I would guarantee to say that you could not raise from all the colored people in the United States $5,000 in cash for this purpose from now until the Celebration. I have been through the experience of raising money from colored people and know something of what it means. While it is impossible to raise large sums of money from colored people for national objects, when the responsibility is placed upon each local community, they do raise considerable sums of money and will do it in this case. I do not think there is one chance in a thousand of our getting any money from Congress. Mr. Heflin is chairman of the Liberal Arts Committee in the House and you know about how much chance there is of getting money from a committee of which he is Chairman. Yours very truly,

Booker T. Washington

TLpS Con. 428 BTW Papers DLC.

[1] Writing on letterhead of the National Emancipation Commemorative Society in Washington, D.C., of which he was president, Lawson insisted that the celebration should be held on Sept. 22, 1912, instead of the NNBL recommendation of the third week of October 1913. He also opposed the idea of merely local celebrations of such an important occasion. (May 2, 1911, Con. 428, BTW Papers, DLC.) Lawson defiantly insisted on the national celebration in subsequent correspondence. (See Lawson to BTW, May 11 and 13, 1911, Con. 428, BTW Papers, DLC.)

Emmett Jay Scott to Hightower T. Kealing

[Tuskegee, Ala.] May 8, 1911

Personal and Confidential.

Dear Mr. Kealing: It is probably outside of your province, but I am writing to put the following matter before you:

You may remember that we talked when you were here about the man[1] whom you have succeeded as President of Western University. It is stated that he is being considered for the ministership to Haiti. From whom could his record be secured, that is, the record about which we talked when you were here? Who is there in that section who would be disposed to stand up in an emergency?

If you will let me hear from you by return mail, the favor will be greatly appreciated.

Of course, I am writing under the seal of confidence. Yours very truly,

E. J. S.

TLpI Con. 427 BTW Papers DLC.

[1] William Tecumseh Vernon.

To Charles Dewey Hilles

Tuskegee Institute, Alabama [May 9, 1911]

Personal and Confidential.

My dear Mr. Hilles: I am writing you, but this letter is not in any sense official and I hope you will consider it entirely personal.

The case about which I am writing has been before the Attorney General and the President a good deal and they are well acquainted with the facts. I ought to say in the beginning Mr. W. S. Harlan of Lockhart, Alabama, was sentenced, some few months ago to the penitentiary for peonage. I ought to say frankly that Mr. Harlan's case, in the opinion of his best friends, was very much injured by the unwise actions of his attorneys.

Mr. Harlan, I happen to know personally, is a man of high standing and no man in Alabama has treated the colored workman better than he has. I need not go over the history of the case, as the President and Attorney-General will do that.

My special point in writing you just now is to get your personal opinion in this direction: Mr. Harlan has been in the penitentiary now over four months. His time will expire the last of June, in the ordinary course of things. In addition to serving this sentence, he will have to pay a fine of $5,000. His financial condition has been misrepresented I am convinced. He has been receiving a salary of $5,000 a year from the Saw Mill Company, but has had to expend practically his whole fortune in fighting the case. He comes out of the penitentiary almost penniless.

Do you think it wise for me and other of his friends to make an appeal to the President to have this fine remitted? Mr. Harlan, of course, has undergone intense suffering because of his being in prison, and as I have said, has lost practically his entire fortune.

I would be the last to justify peonage, but I do think that Mr. Harlan has certainly suffered enough. As I have said, I do not care at present for you to go before the President with this case, but let me know what action, if any, you think his friends had better take in order to secure the remission of the fine.

I shall treat your answer wholly confidential. Yours very truly,

Booker T. Washington

TLS William Howard Taft Papers DLC. A press copy is in Con. 424, BTW Papers, DLC. The undated letter is filed under date of May 9 in the Taft Papers, and docketed as acknowledged on May 11.

From Sumner Alexander Furniss

Indianapolis. May 10th, 1911

Dear Doctor Washington, I received both of your telegrams Tuesday morning. The afternoon paper on Monday published the statement from Washington that my brother had resigned and that Vernon was slated as his successor. Not knowing anything other than the information I had thus received, I immediately became "busy."

Mr. New was up in Michigan fishing, but I was successful in getting in touch with him and received assurances that he would do all that he could. The organization here (both factions) have taken the matter up and I am sure if anything can be done to head off the matter, they will do all that they can. I very much fear, however, that little can be done at this time. I have today understood from pretty good authority that Vernon had been settled upon and that the appointment would be made on July 1st. A fight in the interest of the present incumbent at this time will probably hasten the appointment of Vernon, unless the fight is sufficiently strong to stop the thing altogether. I feel just as you do about Vernon and really do not see how the President could appoint him.

I shall be pleased to receive any suggestions that you may care to make and I desire to assure you of my appreciation of the kindly interest you have taken in my brother and I feel sure that he will be equally appreciative of it. Anything that you can do will be appreciated.

With kindest regards, I am   Very truly yours,

S. A. Furniss

TLS   Con. 422   BTW Papers   DLC.

From Wood, Harmon and Company

New York, May 10, 1911

Dear Sir; We have your very kind favor of the 5th instant with enclosure of letter from a prospective purchaser of your Rugby property. We wish to thank you for your very kind consideration.

Legally, we could not prevent your disposing of your lots to a colored man, nor will we make any effort, or in any way interfere with your selling to a colored man if you desire to do so. It is true there is an objection on our part to the sale of our properties to colored people. This objection is not formed through any prejudice against the colored man, the objection being purely a business one. We would to-day willingly sell to colored people if we believed it would not interfere with the sale to other parties.

Your letter is kind and frank, and we believe it our duty to be equally frank with you. You have asked if it would embarrass us or injure our property if you were to dispose of your lots to a colored person, and our answer is yes. If your prospective purchaser were to visit us to-day for the purpose of buying property in Rugby or in any other sub-division controlled by us, we would not sell to him (for business reasons only) and we believe the effect is just the same if you sell to him. More than one half million dollars have been expended by our customers for homes in Rugby, and we are quite sure they would not approve of our sanctioning the sale of your property to a colored man, particularly, if he was contemplating building on same.

In conclusion will say we believe you should get a better price than $1200 for the lots, and hope when sale is finally consummated by you, it will not be to a colored man, though, as stated above, we will not interfere in any way with the sale of these lots to a colored person if you desire to sell to him. Very truly yours,

WOOD, HARMON & COMPANY,
By L. Keever

TLS Con. 446 BTW Papers DLC.

An Article in *Outlook*

May 13, 1911

LIFE AND LABOR ON THE CONTINENT

One clear, cold morning, about the first of September, I took a train at Bonar Bridge, in the north of Scotland, southward bound. There was a cold wind blowing, and Bonar Bridge is about the latitude, as I learned from looking at my atlas, of northern Labrador — farther north, in fact, than I had ever in my lifetime dreamed of going.

I spent the next four or five hours looking out of a car window across the bleak, brown moors, studying the flocks of sheep and the little thatch-roofed cottages clinging to the lonesome hillsides.

Three days later I was in the beautiful mountain region below Dresden, on my way to Prague, the capital of Bohemia. In many ways conditions in the farming regions of Bohemia are quite as primitive as they are among the crofters of northern Scotland. There are, for example, a larger number of small farmers owning their own land in Bohemia than there are in Scotland, but the Scottish crofter, although he remains a tenant on a small estate, has, at the present time, a more secure position on the soil than the man who rents his land in Bohemia. In other respects the Scotch Highlanders, whose country I had just left, and the Czechs, whose country I was just entering, are, I should say, about as different as one could well imagine.

Among other things I noticed that the farming people in this part of the world do not live apart, scattered about in the open country, as they do in Scotland, and as is the case everywhere in America. On the contrary, the Bohemian farmers live huddled together in little villages, in the center of the surrounding fields, from which they go out to their work in the morning and to which they return in the evening.

These different manners of settling on the soil are one of the marks by which the people in the north of Europe are distinguished from those in the south. The northern people settle in widely scattered homesteads, while the southern people invariably herd together in little villages, and each individual becomes, to a great extent, dependent upon the community and loses himself in the life about him. This accounts, in large measure, for the difference in character of the northern and southern people. In the north the people are more independent; in the south they are more social. The northern people have more initiative; they are natural pioneers. The southern people are more docile, and get on better under the restraints and restrictions of city life. It is said, also, that this explains why it is that the people who are now coming to America from the south of Europe, although most of them come from the land, do not go out into the country districts in America, but prefer to live in the cities, or, as seems to be the case with the Italians, colonize the suburbs of the great cities.

Another thing that interested me was the sight of women working on the land. I had not gone far on my way south from Berlin before my attention was attracted by the number of women in the fields. As I proceeded southward, the number of these women laborers steadily increased until they equaled and even outnumbered the men. One of these I had an opportunity to see close at hand; she was coarsely clad, barefoot, and carried a rake over her shoulder. I had seen pictures of something like that before, but never the real thing.

Outside of Italy I have rarely seen men going barefoot either in the country or in the city, but in southern Europe it seems to be the custom among the working women, and I took it as an indication of the lower position which women occupy among the people of southern Europe as compared with the position that they occupy in America. I saw many barefoot women later in the course of my journey, both in the field and elsewhere. I confess, however, I was surprised to meet in Vienna, Austria, as I did on several occasions while I was there, women walking barefoot on the pavements in one of the most fashionable streets of the city. One day, in speaking to a native Austrian, I expressed my surprise at what I had seen. "Oh, well," he replied, "they are Slovaks."

How vividly this reminded me of a parallel remark with which I was familiar, "Oh, well, they are Negroes!"

It was the tone of this reply that caught my attention. It emphasized what I soon discovered to be another distinguishing feature of life in southern Europe. Everywhere I went in Austria and Hungary I found the people divided according to the race to which they belonged. There was one race at the top, another at the bottom, and then there were perhaps two or three other races which occupied positions relatively higher or lower in between. In most cases it was some section of the Slavic race, of which there are some five or six different branches in the Austrian Empire, which was at the bottom.

Several times, in my efforts to find out something about these so-called "inferior people," I made inquiries about them among their more successful neighbors. In almost every case, no matter what race it happened to be to which I referred, I received the same answer. I was told that they were lazy and would not work; that they had no initiative; that they were immoral and not fitted to govern themselves. At the same time, I found them doing nearly all the really hard, disagreeable, and ill-paid labor that was being done. Usually I found, also, that, with fewer opportunities than the people around them, they were making progress.

I was frequently surprised at the bitterness between the races. I have heard people talk more violently, but I do not think I have heard any one say anything worse in regard to the Negro than some of the statements that are made by members of one race in Austria in regard to members of some other.

I reached the city of Prague late at night, and awoke next morning in a world that was utterly new to me. It was not that Prague looked so different from other European cities I had seen, but the language sounded more strange than anything else I had ever heard. I do not pretend to understand German, yet it seemed to me that there was something familiar and friendly about that language as compared with Czech.

The Czechs are but one of the seventeen races of Austria-Hungary, each one of which, with the exception of the Jews, who are an exception to everything, is seeking to preserve its own language, and, if possible, compel all its neighbors to learn it. Preserving its own language is not difficult in the country districts, where each race lives apart in its own village and maintains its own peculiar customs and traditions. It is more difficult in the large cities, like Vienna and Budapest, where the different nationalities come in intimate contact with each other and with the larger European world.

There is a region in northeastern Hungary where in the course of a day's ride one may pass through, one after another, villages inhabited by as many as five different races — Ruthenians, Jews, Rumanians, Hungarians, and Germans. A racial map of the dual Empire shows districts in which the bulk of the inhabitants are of one race, dotted with villages in which the fragments of other races still survive, some of them, like the Turks, so few in number that they are not separately counted as part of the population. Under these circumstances travel in this part of the world is made interesting but not easy.

Fortunately, I had letters of introduction to Dr. Albert W. Clark, head of the Austrian branch of the American Board of Missions at Prague, and he introduced me to some of his native assistants who spoke English, and kindly assisted me in finding what I most desired to see of the city and the people. Through him I had an opportunity to get inside of some of the tenements in which European people live, and to see some of the working people in their homes. I did not have an opportunity to explore the parts of the city in which the very poor people live; in fact, I was told that there was nothing in Prague that corresponds to the slums of our English and American cities. There is much poverty, but it is poverty of a self-respecting sort — not of those who have been defeated and gone under, but of those who have never got up.

I found the average Bohemian workman living in two rooms and working for wages considerably less than the same kind of labor would have brought in England, and very much less than the same kind of labor would have brought in America. There is, however, very little use in comparing the wages that men earn unless you are able to compare all the surrounding conditions.

During my stay in Prague I had an opportunity to see something close at hand of the life of the farming population. Under the guidance of one of Dr. Clark's assistants, I drove out one day to a little village where there were a number of people who had come under the influence of the American Mission in Prague, and where I was assured I should find a welcome.

It was not, perhaps, the best place to get an idea of what is most characteristic in Bohemian country life. I had hoped to see something of the local customs of the country people, but, though it was a holiday when I made my visit, I did not see a single peasant costume.

There are still many places in Bohemia, I understand, where the people take pride in wearing the national costumes, and there are still many parts of the Austrian Empire where relics of the older civilization linger. Indeed, I heard of places where, it is said, the peasants are still paying the old feudal dues; in other places the old unfree condition of the peasants is still continued in the form of peonage, as it may still be sometimes found in our Southern States. In this case the peasants have got themselves into debt for land. They are not allowed to work off this debt, and this serves as a pretense for keeping them bound to the soil. But education and the growth of manufacturing industries have banished the traces of the older civilization from the greater part of Bohemia.

In the village which I visited, as in most of the farming villages in this part of the world, the houses of the farmers stand in a row quite close together on either side of the street. In the rear are the quarters of the servants, the storehouses and the stables, the pig-sty and the cow-stalls, all closely connected, so that it was often a little uncertain to me where the quarters for the servants left off and those for the animals began. In fact, in some places no very definite distinction was made.

One of the most interesting places that I visited during my stay in this village was a dairy farm which was conducted by a Jew. He was evidently one of those of the lower or middle class — a type one hears much of in Europe — who, with very little knowledge or skill in the actual work of agriculture, have succeeded by their superior business skill in getting possession of the land, and reducing the peasant to a position not much better than that of a serf. This man not only kept a dairy farm, but he operated two or three brick-yards besides, and had other extensive business interests in the village. Although he was a man of wealth and intelligence, he had his dwelling in the midst of a compound around which were grouped houses for his laborers, cow-stalls, a wheelwright and blacksmith shop, places for pigs, chickens, and dogs, the whole in a condition of indescribable disorder and filth.

The greater part of the work on the farm seemed to be done by women, most of whom were barefooted or wore wooden shoes. I do not think I had seen any one wearing wooden shoes before since the days of slavery. They had remained in my mind as the symbol of poverty and degradation; but they are worn everywhere in country districts in Europe. In fact, I remember in one instance, when I visited an agricultural school, finding one of the teachers working in the garden wearing wooden shoes. The people who worked on this farm all lived, as far as I could see, in one little ill-smelling and filthy room. There was no sign in the homes which I visited of those household industries for which Hungarian peasants are noted, and which should help to brighten and make comfortable the simplest home.

I believe there are few plantations in our Southern States where, even in the small one-room cabins, one would not find the colored people living in more real comfort and more cleanliness than was the case here. Even in the poorest Negro cabins in the South I have found evidences that the floor was sometimes scrubbed, and usually there was a white counterpane on the bed or some evidence of an effort to be tidy.

Prague is one of the most ancient cities in Europe. A thing that impressed me with the antiquity of the town was the fact that before the beginning of the Christian era there was a Jewish quarter in this city. Prague is also one of the most modern cities in Europe. Within a comparatively few years large manufacturing plants have multiplied throughout the country. Bohemia makes, among other things, fezzes, and sells them to Turkey; raises beans, and ships them to Boston.

What is most interesting is the fact that this progress has been, to a very large extent, made possible through the education of the masses of the people. The Bohemians are to-day among the best educated people in Europe. For example, among the immigrants who come from Europe to America, 24.2 per cent over fourteen years of age are unable to read and write. In the case of the German immigrant not more than 5.8 per cent are unable to read or write. In the case of the Bohemians this percentage is only 3 per cent. There is only one class of immigrants among whom the percentage of illiteracy is lower. Among the Danish immigrants it is 0.8 per cent.

There is no part of the Austrian Empire where education is more generally diffused or where the schools are so well adapted to the actual needs of the people. In addition to the ordinary primary schools and the gymnasia (which correspond to our high school) there are several higher institutes of technology which prepare students for industry and commerce. Besides these State schools, there are a large number of industrial schools that are maintained by cities or by private associations. Some of these are located in the small towns and are closely connected with the local industries. Sometimes they are organized by the members of the different trades and crafts as a supplement to the apprentice system. For example, in a town where the inhabitants are engaged in the clay industry, there will be found schools which give practical courses in the making of vases and crockery. In some of the larger towns commercial and industrial instruction is given in "continuation schools." In these schools girls who have learned needlework in the elementary schools will be taught sewing, dressmaking, and embroidery and lace work. There are also courses in which boys are prepared to work in the sugar-making, brewing, watchmaking, and other manufacturing industries.

In the two institutes of technology in Prague, one of which is for Bohemians and the other for Germans, courses are given which prepare students to be engineers, chemists, machinists, architects, bookkeepers, etc. In connection with these courses there are also special departments where students are prepared to be master workmen in such trades as brick-laying, carpentry, cabinet-making, and stone masonry.

There is much in the life and history of the Bohemian people that is especially interesting to a race or a people, like the Negro, that is itself struggling up to a higher and freer level of life and civilization.

Up to 1848 the masses of the Bohemian people were held in a condition of serfdom. Until 1867 they were not allowed to emigrate from the country, and were thus held, as are the Russian peasants to-day, to a certain degree, prisoners in their own country. Most of the land was in the hands of the nobility, who were the descendants of foreigners who came into the country when it was conquered, a century or more before. Even to-day, five families own eight per cent of all the land in the kingdom, and one-tenth of the population own thirty-six per cent of the area of the country. The Emperor and the Catholic Church are also large landowners.

One of the effects of this new education and the new life that has come with it has been to make the land held in larger estates less productive than that which is divided into smaller holdings and cultivated by the men who own it.

It was interesting to me to learn that the Bohemians in their own country suffer from some of the same disadvantages as the Negro in the South. For example, the educational fund is divided between the races — the Germans and the Czechs — just as the money for education is divided in the South between the whites and the blacks, but, as is true in the South, it is not divided equally between the races.

For example, in the city of Prague there is one gymnasium (school) to every 62,000 Czech inhabitants, while the Germans have one gymnasium for every 6,700 inhabitants. Of what are called the real-schools, in which the education is more practical than that of the gymnasia, there is one for every 62,000 Bohemian inhabitants, while the Germans have one for every 10,000 inhabitants. For a number of years past, although the Bohemians represent seventy per cent of the population, they have received only a little more than one-half of the money appropriated for secondary education, both in the gymnasia and the real-schools. The salaries of teachers in the elementary schools range from $155 to $400 per year; in the schools in which the German language is taught, however, teachers receive an added bonus for their services.

To overcome their disadvantages in this direction the Czechs have supplemented the work of the public schools by industrial schools, which are maintained by the contributions of the people in the same way that the Negroes in many parts of the South have supplemented the work of the public schools in order to increase the terms of the school year and to introduce industrial training of various sorts.

More than this, the masses of the people in Bohemia are limited and restricted in all their movements in ways of which no one in America who has not passed through the hands of the immigration inspectors at Ellis Island has any comprehension. For example, the people of Austria have had for a number of years freedom of conscience, and, in theory at least, every one is allowed to worship according to his own inclination and convictions. Nevertheless, it seems to be as much a crime in Austria to say anything that could be construed as disrespectful to the Catholic Church as it would be to insult the name of the Emperor. I heard a story of a woman who ran a small store in which she was using copies of a Catholic newspaper with which to wrap up articles which she had sold to her customers. She was warned by the police that if she continued to use this paper for that purpose she would be liable to arrest. Afterwards packages were found in her store which were wrapped in this paper; she was arrested and the case was carried to the highest court, but the sentence which had been imposed upon her stood, and she was compelled to serve a term in prison as punishment for this offense. It was only with the greatest difficulty, Dr. Clark informed me, that he succeeded in getting permission from the Government to establish a branch of the Young Men's Christian Association in Prague.

I myself had some experience of these restrictions when I spoke before an audience composed largely of young Bohemian workmen in the rooms of this same Young Men's Christian Association. In order that I might be permitted to make this address it was necessary to announce the subject to the officers of the Government three days before I arrived in the city, and at the meeting I had the unusual experience of having my words taken down by a Government official who was present to see that I did not say anything that would disturb the public peace.

Not knowing what else I could say to this audience that would interest them, I told briefly the story of my own life and of the work that we are trying to do for our students at Tuskegee. I told them also that the institution (Hampton Institute) in which I had gained my education had been established by the same American Board of Missions which was responsible for the existence of the Young Men's Christian Association in Bohemia.

In order that my hearers might understand what I said, it was necessary for the secretary of the Association, a Bohemian who spoke very good English, to translate my words sentence by sentence. In spite of these difficulties, I do not think I ever spoke to an audience of laboring people who were more intelligent or more appreciative. It was a great pleasure and satisfaction to me to be able to speak to this audience. I felt, as I think they did, that we had something in common which others, perhaps, could not entirely understand, because each of us belonged to a race which, however different in other respects, was the same in this, that it was struggling upward.

Outlook, 98 (May 13, 1911), 75–80.

From Robert Russa Moton

Hampton, Virginia   May 13, 1911

Very Personal.

My dear Dr. Washington: I have wanted to talk with you about a number of things for a month or so but it looks as if fates are against us. I wanted to see you very much before the New York incident and have naturally wanted to see you since. I was sorry not to have seen you in New York this week as I was in town the very day you were and I always stop at Dr. Charles Roberts[1] on 53d Street. He has a telephone and we could have met easily that day.

I am planning to go to the Race Congress in London this summer. I thought it advisable for some one of us to be present and I am absolutely sure now it will be a good thing for some one to be there or perhaps more than one. I mean some one with our ideas and notions of education and conditions in the South. Dr. Frissell had thought of going. He thinks now that I had better go. I tried to see Mr. Villard in New York but did not. One thing I am sure of that however sanguine Mr. Villard may feel there is a determined effort to do all they can to weaken your influence in this country and abroad. I have information directly from the meeting held in New York night before last or rather a reception to Dr. W. H. Sheppard under the auspices of Miss Ovington in which Milholland, Du Bois and Miss Milholland of course discussed plans by which they could "down" Booker Washington. Dr. Sheppard who took breakfast with me yesterday morning at my invitation gave me the whole story. He, of course, being entirely ignorant of the feeling. I will not go further into details but I shall take up the matter with vigor. I am convinced that Dr. Du Bois, Milholland and Miss Ovington will do everything they can in London this summer to undo the good that you did last year. I have made up my mind that I will go any how now. I wish there were a half dozen or more going. I think we better move together and I hope you will use me in any way you can. In the meantime I hope to see you very soon. Yours sincerely,

R. R. Moton

TLS   Con. 430   BTW Papers   DLC.

¹ Charles H. Roberts, a black dentist in New York City and the brother of the physician Eugene P. Roberts.

To Wilford H. Smith

[Tuskegee, Ala.] May 15, 1911

Confidential

Dear Mr. Smith: One or two things I have in mind to write you about:

First, I hope you have your mind planned upon definite facts that you can use in connection with the charges which we may have to allege against Ulrich. I mean in reference to dog stealing and in reference to his improper living. If called upon we ought to be able to put definite charges in those two respects.

If you need to have it done, I can put you in touch with a good friend of mine in Orange who knows about Ulrich's wife and who can help with her if necessary.

One other thing: When you and Mr. Cravath talk with the Assistant District Attorney,¹ you ought to be careful not to permit him to go so far in threatening Ulrich that he could not hold up a little if necessary. I think you understand what I mean but it might not be necessary to mention this phase of the case to him. Yours very truly,

Booker T. Washington

TLSr Copy   Con. 435   BTW Papers   DLC.

¹ James E. Smith.

To Susan Helen Porter

[Tuskegee, Ala.] May 15, 1911

Miss Porter: I am very anxious that in some way on Commencement Sunday the girls present a brighter appearance. Try to arrange for them to get plenty of sleep if you can.

I wish you also to place student monitors among the girls in different parts of the audience to see that they are kept awake. You could use 12 or 15 teachers or monitors to advantage. Heretofore, when the Commencement sermon has been preached, too many of the girls have been asleep.

Booker T. Washington

TLpS   Con. 616   BTW Papers   DLC.

To Charles Dewey Hilles

Tuskegee Institute, Alabama   May 16, 1911

My dear Mr. Hilles: Some few months ago, the President very kindly used the following sentence in a letter to me: "I am not only glad to permit the use of my name, but shall be pleased to make a personal contribution to the Endowment Fund."

As we are about to close our financial year, and we are also making a strenuous effort to put as much into the Endowment as we can before the year closes, I am wondering if the President would not like to send us a check at this time. I am suggesting this not only because of the good the money will do, but because of the larger influence of his contribution.

Will you also let the President know how greatly his endorsement of my appeal for endowment has helped to bring in money? Yours very truly,

Booker T. Washington

TLS   William Howard Taft Papers   DLC. Docketed: "Draw a check for $100   W H T."

To R. H. Trammell[1]

[Tuskegee, Ala.] May 16, 1911

Confidential.

My dear Sir: I wrote you a letter day before yesterday, but in some way, the letter was lost before it left my office, hence my delay in writing.

I have had a frank letter from the President's Secretary, who has had a conference with the Attorney General on the subject about which I wrote. Both the Attorney General and the President's Secretary, Mr. Hilles are very emphatic in their advice not to take up the matter at present, at least with the President. They both say that to approach the President on this subject now will hurt rather than help, that the President's reducing the time to six months has done a great deal and all that he ought to be asked to do at present. I might say to you, confidentially, that the Attorney General has gotten the idea that the company will pay the fine. Just on what he bases this, I do not know.

If I can serve you or Mr. Harlan in the future, please be kind enough to call upon me. Yours very truly,

Booker T. Washington

TLpS   Con. 442   BTW Papers   DLC.

1 A doctor in Lockhart, Ala.

To William Howard Taft

[Tuskegee, Ala.] May 16, 1911

Personal.

My dear President Taft: In considering a person for the Federal Judgeship in South Carolina, I very much hope that you will look into the record of Senator Mayfield[1] of Denmark, S.C.

I do not, of course, know what his qualifications are as a Judge, but I do know that he is a high-toned, clean, unselfish and liberal Southern white man. I have known him several years. Largely through his influence and that of his mother, one of the largest and best Negro schools of the South has been built up at his home.[2] This school was founded by some of our graduates and now is perhaps the most promising school in South Carolina. From the first, Senator Mayfield has stood loyally back of the colored teachers and has fathered the school in every way possible.

He is a lawyer of high standing. While he is a democrat in politics, I know few men anywhere in the South who are more highly respected and honored by all classes than is true of Senator Mayfield.

I am writing this letter wholly without the knowledge or consent of Senator Mayfield.[3] Yours very truly,

Booker T. Washington

TLpS Con. 55 BTW Papers DLC.

[1] Stanwix Greenville Mayfield (b. 1861), a lawyer and Alabama state senator from Barnwell County (1892–97). When Bamberg County was established in 1897, Mayfield was elected to the senate in that county, serving until 1904.

[2] Voorhees Normal and Industrial School.

[3] On the same date BTW sent a copy of his endorsement to Mayfield. (Con. 430, BTW Papers, DLC.)

To Seth Low

Tuskegee Institute, Alabama May 16, 1911

Dear Mr. Low: I think you will be glad to know that Mr. Paul D. Cravath has, of his own accord without any charge whatever, consented to advise with and work with my personal attorney in all matters in reference to the Ulrich case.

Mr. Cravath is the son, as perhaps you know, of the former President of Fisk University. Mr. Cravath has shown deep interest in the matter. I had a conference with him and my personal attorney while in New York recently and both are working as fast as they think it safe in the direction that we have discussed, and they think that they can succeed in a reasonable time.

I simply write in order that you may be kept informed. Yours very truly,

Booker T. Washington

TLS Seth Low Papers NNC.

From Chester A. Hagan

New York   May 18, 1911

My Dear Sir; Your letter of May 2, 1911 was received by me with pleasure; In that letter you informed me that you wrote to a friend of yours in New York, who would doubtless send for me in a few days to talk matters over. Up to the present time I have not heard from your friend; and I thought It possible that perhaps the letter you sent him may have gone astray, and he did not receive it.

I hope this matter does not annoy you; as I fully understand that a man of your importance and your position has a good deal to tend to; and I thought it possible that my writing to you may annoy you, or that you would think I was taking too much liberty. Hoping that you will do as you think best I Remain   Yours Very Truly

Chester A Hagan

P.S. I would again like to suggest that if you took this matter up with Wm J Gaynor — Mayor he certainly would comply with your request.

C A H

ALS   Con. 425   BTW Papers   DLC.

Extracts From an Address before the
Young Men's Christian Association in Chicago

[Chicago, May 18, 1911]

THE MESSAGE OF THE YOUNG MEN'S
CHRISTIAN ASSOCIATION TO THE
MANHOOD OF AMERICA

Our whole country is greatly indebted to the city of Chicago. Indebted to you of the white race; indebted to you of the colored race. We are indebted to you of the white race for the magnificent example of generosity which you have set. It is generosity not bounded by racial or color line. We are indebted to you of the colored race — of my own race — for the magnificent example and guidance in generosity which you have set for the rest of the members of our race throughout this country.[1] Sometimes when one belongs to a disadvantaged race he has an advantage. One of the advantages of a disadvantaged race consists in the fact that when a disadvantaged race does not come in contact with the members of what is described as a superior race, that it gets in contact with the best of that race. So the Negro in America is fortunate in the South, and in the North, especially in Chicago, as exemplified here tonight, in having the privilege of coming in contact with the strongest and best souls of the white race. The little fellows, the weaklings, are always afraid to come in contact with an unpopular race or with an unpopular cause. It is so in the South, it is so in the North. The people in the South who are closest to the Negro, who are his best friends, are that class of Southern white people who stand so high in their business life, in their social life, that they are not afraid to let the world know that they have an interest in a weak race.

And what is true of the South is equally true of the North and other parts of our country. My race, as I have often said, has disadvantages as races are measured. We constitute a new race in this country just about 45 years of age, and sometimes a new race, like anything else new, has advantages over an older race. We have the advantage of having our future before us, rather than behind us.

If you ask me why with such zeal and energy they seized the opportunity of giving their services and their money in planting a Y.M.C.A. building and organization in this city, I answer it was because they never had the chance to do it before. They said, for the first time in the history of our race, in a great metropolitan city in the North, we have a chance to show the world what we can do in this new movement. So, my friends, they set an example that has made us all proud of the colored man in Chicago. I have always been proud of my race, proud that I am a black man, wouldn't be any other kind of man if I could; wouldn't exchange places with the whitest man on earth. And I was never more proud of my race than since they have done what they did in Chicago. Never more proud than I am tonight when I see this body of strong, superior, clear-minded, clean young men sitting around this banquet table tonight. My friends, such men as you see here tonight are worth saving, worth making part of the perpetual institutions of this country. In a large degree the city population, so far as it concerns my race in Chicago, is composed of people who come here from the Southern States. It is necessary for the people of Chicago to help the sons of colored men to adjust themselves to their new environment. When they come from the Southern States they come in contact with a climate that is strange. They come into a community where the housing conditions are different to that which they have experienced in their own home, where the industrial surroundings are different. Their whole life is transformed. My friends, you must be a little patient with the black man.

This Y.M.C.A. building branch for our people will come first in my opinion in helping the Negro young man of Chicago in finding himself, to articulate himself in its civilization, than any other movement that has been started in the city of Chicago. It has for its object not only the saving of the Negro soul, but the saving of the Negro's body. Now there has never been much question about saving his soul, but the trouble comes in regard to his body down here on this earth and the question of his body gives a lot of trouble, and you not only propose saving his soul, which is of first importance to them, but you mean to save his body through this organization by helping him to put himself in that relationship to life where he can earn enough money to keep his body saved. I take it, with the Negro young man as it is with some white men in Chicago, it is a pretty hard thing to make a Christian of a hungry man. And in proportion as you establish this institution with its soul saving appliances, body saving appliances, with its outfit to make the Negro stronger and more efficient industrially, you save him from every point of view.

You must remember that in most of the large cities of the North where any large number of my race exist, that the young colored men touch the white man only at the white man's weakest point, and many go downward instead of upward on account of imitating that unfortunate experience, but in proportion as you have such an organization as you are putting on foot, you will help to strengthen the black man and will bring him in contact with the stronger side of the white man in the city of Chicago.

The question is sometimes raised as to why a race as large in numbers as my race is in Chicago and other large centers of population, why it is that they have to invite and receive help from any other race in establishing Y.M.C.A. buildings and other philanthropic enterprises. When that question is asked, it must be remembered that during a period of 45 years of freedom, it has had to build its own church houses, has had to sustain its ministers — we had no church houses handed down to us by former generations, we inherited no church houses since we became a free people — within 45 years we have erected 35,000 church buildings and in 90% of cases the money with which to erect these buildings has come out of our own pockets, and while doing this, in a very large degree, we have sustained our own ministers. We have 34,000 Sunday schools that we have organized and that we have sustained. We have 210,000 Negro teachers in the Sunday schools and we have nearly 2,000,000 Negro children in these Sunday schools. We have been building ourselves in large religious movements, hence we have not had time nor the money, in a very large degree, to help as we should have done and hope to do in the future, in extending a helping hand to such organizations as that represented here tonight. But you must remember that but for the work of the Negro church you might not have collected this money you have collected in the city of Chicago from the colored people, because if there is any one institution that teaches the Negro to give money, it is the Negro church, and without the education that the race has received through these churches in giving money, they never would have given in the city of Chicago or anywhere else what they have given towards this enterprise. This movement here in Chicago, more than any other single agency, has helped my race to find itself, to realize its own power, to appreciate its own strength, and it has brought the best colored people and the best white people in touch with each other. The bad colored people and the bad white people always get together. The time has come when the best colored people and the best white people should get together and know each other, and, Mr. Rosenwald, if you had not done anything else through this movement than to give the white people of Chicago a chance to know the kind of colored people they have in Chicago, your investment would be a paying one. It is so often true that races, like individuals, stand far off from each other, are afraid of each other, imagining and thinking the worst things about each other, because they have never shaken hands — have never felt the touch of each other. So you will find the case of my race to be that if you help us and seek the opportunity of knowing and touching the black man in Chicago, you will find you have among them many undiscovered diamonds which you can use in the civic and religious betterment of the City of Chicago and it always helps, in my opinion, for one man to undertake the task of reaching another man who is down

— the farther down the fellow is or the race is, the more unpopular the race is, the deeper down we have to reach in order to touch that race, the more we ourselves are strengthened in our hearts and in our minds when we come in contact with that man or race.

From the reports that come from Philadelphia, Atlanta and Washington, you will realize that we are making progress in the solution of all of our problems in the South. Now, Chicago has given itself a great reputation. Sometimes it is easier to get a reputation than it is to sustain it. We have looked to you in the past and we are going to look to you in the future and we are going to see if you continue to lead the procession and set a high example for the whole country in this fine effort. And let me add, another result of this movement rests in the fact that people now are beginning to praise the Negro. A race, like an individual, deserves censure, deserves chastisement, but like a school boy, a race can be helped by praise as well as by chastisement, and sometimes you can make a very good thing out of a very indifferent thing, and you can make a good race out of a seemingly indifferent race.

In dealing with races we often gain a great deal by praising races as well as blaming them and you can often get the best out of the colored people of Chicago by praising them and by holding up their virtues as well as their vices.

In the last analysis, the black man in this country has some quality and backbone. You can't make him go away and you just as well find out his virtues and cultivate those virtues and make him a good, reliable, safe element in your citizenship. The greatest pleasure in my life is discovering men among my people, discovering virtues where I thought there was none, in discovering worth where I thought there was no worth. In the fundamental elements of citizenship the Negro in America is more like a white man than any other race. We understand your ideas of civilization; we use your ideas of civilization more clearly than any other race, and you know we are the only race with a dark skin that has ever been able to look the white man in the eye and live for any length of time. Every other dark skinned race that has tried that experiment has gone or is going.

Now, we dress like you do, we don't dress like some of these other fellows that come to this country; we speak the same language, we do not hold onto a foreign tongue; profess the same form of religion that you do and, my friends, best of all, and more fundamental than all, deep down in his heart the Negro understands and loves the genius of American institutions, he has an American patriotism and he is ready, willing and anxious to die in defense of his country and flag or his country's honor. We are American citizens and the degree of recognition, and the degree of encouragement which, through this institution, you have given my race in Chicago and throughout this country, will help us to be stronger, more useful and more helpful citizens throughout this broad land than we have ever been in the past. God help you and God bless you all for what you have done and for what you are going to do.

Official Bulletin of the Young Men's Christian Association of Chicago, 8 (June 1911), 20–23.

[1] In another extracted version of the address in typescript, BTW spoke of $67,000 raised by blacks and $25,000 contributed by Julius Rosenwald toward the black Y.M.C.A. building in Chicago. (Con. 957, BTW Papers, DLC.)

To Julius Rosenwald

[Tuskegee, Ala.] May 23, 1911

Personal

My dear Mr. Rosenwald: First, I want to thank you most heartily for the very great and helpful kindness which you showed me during my stay in Chicago.[1] I appreciate it all more than I can express, and I repeat that sometime in the near future I hope you will come to Tuskegee. I want you to see our work and hear our students sing.

I am going to be very frank with you and mention two other matters. I realize that you may not be interested in either one, and in that case I shall not misunderstand you.

First: I am making a desperate effort to end our school year without any debt. In order to do so, however, I shall have to raise between now and June 10 about $24,000. We always try to pursue the policy of not going into debt, of not carrying an obligation over from one year to the other. This year we have extraordinary and unforseen expenses which makes it a desperate task to end without a debt. To be still more frank, I have about exhausted every resource to get money to reduce the amount to the point where it now is.

The second thing is this: We need very much here, and have done so for a long while, a Y.M.C.A. building or a headquarters for our religious and moral work. Ours is the largest Y.M.C.A. I think you will find in the South, having a membership of about 450. Our students go to all parts of the country and become leaders in Y.M.C.A. work, and in helping us toward a building you would be helping a wide section of our country. Such a building as we need would cost $35,000. We could not use to advantage a building costing more than the amount named.

I am glad to say that our students, in small penny collections extending through a period of several years, have raised toward this building $1,166.70.

I think you will find that many of the leading spirits in promoting the Y.M.C.A. movement in Chicago were Tuskegee graduates. The Tuskegee Club in Chicago is among the leading forces for decency in that city.

In case you should [view] the proposition of the Y.M.C.A. building favorably, I very much fear that it would not be possible for us in the near future to meet any condition because we have already drained our friends financially almost to the last cent.

I am not asking you to help us in both these directions, but thought you might be interested to help in one. But I repeat, if you do not help in either direction I will understand it will be from no lack of interest in our work. Yours very truly,

Booker T. Washington

TLpS   Con. 438   BTW Papers   DLC.

[1] At a luncheon in BTW's honor on May 18 at the Blackstone Hotel, Rosenwald introduced him with fulsome praise to twenty-six leading business and professional men of Chicago. (*Tuskegee Student,* 23 [June 17, 1911], 1.)

To Robert Russa Moton

[Tuskegee, Ala.] May 23, 1911

My dear Major Moton: Thank you for your kind letter of May 13th. I would have answered it more promptly, but when your letter came, I was just starting for Chicago, where I delivered a series of addresses.

I am glad you are going to the Racial Congr[ess] in London. I think it well for some level headed people to be present. Dr. C. T. Walker of Augusta [Ga.], has been thinking of going and we have been trying to encourage him to do so. Just what his final decision [is] I do not remember. I hope you will not be disappoin[ted in] the Race Congress. My friends in London write me tha[t] the whole thing is going to be a disappointment. The[y,] however, may be mistaken. The Anti-Slavery Society which usually takes the lead in anything affecting races is having no part in this Congress. If you desire me to do so, I shall be very glad to send you personal letters of introduction to several of my English friends.

What you say regarding the conversation between Milholland, Du Bois and Miss Ovington is very interesting, but not surprising. I do hope, however, that you will seek the very first opportunity at your command to see Mr. Villard and let him know exactly what you have heard. Mr. Villard is being deceived somewhat by these people, but he is gradually getting his eyes open, I think. It is very generous of you to look after my interests in so fine a way. I appreciate it most highly.

I am sorry that I did not know you were in New York. I shall keep in mind your address when I am there again.

When are you planning to go to London? Could you not spend a little while with me at Northport before going? Yours very truly,

Booker T. Washington

TLpS Con. 54 BTW Papers DLC. Bracketed words were obliterated in first page of press copy.

To the Editor of the Omaha *World Herald*

[Tuskegee, Ala.] May 24, 1911

My dear Sir: There appears in the World-Herald of Saturday, May 13, a news article with the headline, "TUSKEGEE STUDENT SENT TO PRISON. LUTHER GIBSON, COLORED, SENTENCED TO THREE YEARS FOR BREAKING AND ENTERING. WANTS TO MAKE A GOOD RECORD IN PRISON AND BE CREDIT TO BOOKER WASHINGTON."

Now, as a matter of fact, Gibson is not a graduate of the Industrial

Department of this institution, nor of the Academic Department, nor is there any record shown that he was ever a student at Tuskegee Institute.

I send this statement to you because I am sure that you do not wish to do us any injustice, and because I think you ought to know just exactly what the facts are in this case. Yours truly,

Booker T. Washington

TLpS   Con. 437   BTW Papers   DLC.

To Margaret James Murray Washington

[Tuskegee, Ala.] May 24, 1911

Mrs. Washington: Last year it was evident that there was a lack of preparation and planning for the serving of the white people from a distance in Dorothy Hall. People who were there tell me that there was no ice water for them until the latter part of the meal, that the preparations generally were not thoroughly looked after.

This whole matter should be thoroughly planned and anticipated to the minutest detail. The tables ought to present a model appearance both in the setting and in the decoration with flowers and the providing of ice water as well as food. There is no reason why the tables might not be set tonight so that everything would be in good shape tomorrow.

It was also evident last year that there was a lack of help. All this should be anticipated this year.

Booker T. Washington

TLpS   Con. 613   BTW Papers   DLC.

To Sanford Henry Lee[1]

[Tuskegee, Ala.] May 24, 1911

Dear Mr. Lee: I have signed a recommendation for you that has been presented to me by the Pullman Car Company. I confess, however, that I am very sorry and somewhat disappointed to see you entering such a line of work. You have no business to become a Pullman Car porter; you were not educated for that purpose.

Now, you will make the same explanation that most of the Pullman Car porters do, that is, you are not going into the service to stay but simply to make money. Nine-tenths of them do the same thing, but I notice when they once go in, they remain. You would help yourself vastly more by coming into the South and starting some kind of business, or taking some kind of profession or going into school work.

I hope you will think about this. Yours very truly,

Booker T. Washington

TLpS   Con. 428   BTW Papers   DLC.

[1] Sanford Henry Lee, of Brockton, Ala., graduated from Tuskegee Institute in 1904.

To Charles William Anderson

[Tuskegee, Ala.] May 24, 1911

Personal

My dear Mr. Anderson: Two things I am writing you about. First, I see by a paper that our friend Moore was hissed at a minister's meeting. Whether or not this report is true I do not know, but I do know that Moore is very unfortunate in his manner of speaking to ministers. There is nothing whatever gained in insulting these men on every possible occasion. While of course they deserve chastisement in many cases, still you cannot always help a man by making him mad or insulting him every time you appear before him.

Second. The main thing about what I want to write is this. I think in one direction we had better not deceive ourselves. Milholland I am sure is making a desperate effort to get President Taft to recognize Du Bois in some way. He has been in Washington three or four times recently and has had Du Bois at the White House once. I hear Milholland is pushing Du Bois for the Haytian Mission. In case Vernon should be defeated and Du Bois get this place, it would be charged up against New York. Aside from that consideration, of course there are others more serious. If you were to take this matter up with the President, or I were to take it up with him, it would be misunderstood. Perhaps you could work it in this way: Explain the whole situation to Mr. Loeb and get him to write a frank letter to the President or to Mr. Hilles telling him about Du Bois' and Milholland's opposition to the President that is constant and personal. It would be one of the worst things the President could do to recognize a man like Du Bois. In the first place, Du Bois has no strong following, and in the second place, if Du Bois and Milholland are recognized because of their bitter opposition to the President in the hope of placating them, it will be putting a premium on opposition in the future and every little white man and Negro will feel that the way to get recognition is to oppose the President in the way Milholland and Du Bois have been doing.

Enclosed I send you a cartoon which appeared in Du Bois's magazine a few months ago. This cartoon itself ought to settle Du Bois forever in the mind of President Taft.[1]

Of course I am writing largely on supposition, but I do not believe I am wrong in making the statement that Milholland is doing everything he can to bring about this man's recognition. Yours very truly,

Booker T. Washington

TLpS Con. 415 BTW Papers DLC.

[1] *Crisis*, 1 (April 1911), 31, contained a cartoon of President Taft, dressed as a chef, giving the black officeholder William H. Lewis a taste from the "political pot stew" with a long-handled spoon that reached across the color line, while white federal officeholders dipped freely into the pot labeled "white help only." The caption read: "Mr. Lewis gets his!"

From Wilford H. Smith

New York, May 25th, 1911

Dear Dr. Washington: I had a conference with Mr. Cravath to-day. He has seen Assistant Dist. Attorney Smith, and found him in full possession of all the facts concerning Ulrich's record.

Mr. Cravath has suggested that District Attorney Smith have Ulrich and his lawyer appear in court and make a statement embodying substantially all the facts contained in the prepared statement which Mr. Scott left with me, and have him acknowledge that it was a case of mistaken identity, and confess that there was absolutely no reason whatever for his assault upon you. After Ulrich makes this confession, I am to state, as your attorney, that since Ulrich has made an apology and retraction in open court, that you have no desire for revenge, and will consent to the charge being withdrawn. Dist. Attorney Smith feels that he can carry out his arrangement, but suggests that nothing be done until next month when the judges will be changed in that court, and the matter can be taken up and disposed of to better advantage.

Please let me know at once whether or not you approve this course and if you do not write Mr. Cravath suggesting the manner in which you prefer the case to be disposed of. If you do approve of it, Dist. Attorney Smith is to inform me what time next month he will take the case up, and I will communicate with you before it is called, and we can then agree upon a form of statement to be given the newspapers. Very truly yours,

Wilford H. Smith

TLS   Con. 435   BTW Papers   DLC.

To Lawrence Fraser Abbott

[Tuskegee, Ala.] May 27, 1911

Personal

My dear Dr. Abbott: I call your attention to the recent decision of the Supreme Court of Alabama, which results in the removal of a sheriff from his office for permitting a colored man charged with rape to be lynched. The words of the Supreme Court in this case, it seems to me, [are] fine. Nothing could be better or braver.

You will be glad to know that our new Governor, Emmet O'Neal,[1] is responsible for the pushing of this case, and the removal of the sheriff.[2] Yours very truly,

Booker T. Washington

TLpS   Con. 50   BTW Papers   DLC.

1 Emmet O'Neal (1853–1922), governor of Alabama from 1911 to 1915.

2 BTW sent an identical letter on the same day to William Hayes Ward, editor of *The Independent*. (Con. 446, BTW Papers, DLC.) Both *Outlook* and *The Independent* published editorials praising the decision of the Alabama Supreme Court in ordering the removal of Sheriff P. W. Jinwright of Bullock County. The court said: "The sheriff who defends his prisoner from violence is defending the constitution of his state, and perchance the lives, the liberty, and the happiness of his own family." (*The Independent*, 70 [June 8, 1911], 1284–85; see also *Outlook*, 98 [June 17, 1911], 317–18.)

To Robert Curtis Ogden

[Tuskegee, Ala.] May 27, 1911

My dear Mr. Ogden: By this mail I am sending you a marked copy of the Montgomery Advertiser[1] containing an account of our commencement exercises day before yesterday.

It was the opinion of all who were here that it was the most satisfactory and helpful exercise of the kind we have ever held. We had present at least eight thousand people, white and colored. We had by far the largest number of prominent white people present from Alabama, Georgia and other Southern states we have ever had. A half dozen of the most prominent schools in the South sent representatives here to witness our closing exercises in order that they might introduce the same methods at their own schools. A white school in Georgia sent six of their teachers.[2]

Notwithstanding we had eight thousand people on our grounds during the day, the Sheriff of the county told me he did not make a single arrest during the day, nor did he see a single intoxicated person, that there was no disorder whatever. Yours very truly,

Booker T. Washington

TLpS Con. 54 BTW Papers DLC. An identical letter was sent to Theodore Roosevelt, May 27, 1911, Con. 438, BTW Papers, DLC.

1 May 26, 1911, 6.
2 The Berry School of Rome, Ga.

To Charles William Anderson

[Tuskegee, Ala.] May 29, 1911

Confidential.

Lewis's confirmation in grave danger. Something will have to be done pretty soon or confirmation will be indefinitely delayed or he will be defeated. Will you not write strong letter and get others to do so if you can to Senator O'Gorman[1] urging him to see that favorable action is taken in Lewis's case.

B. T. W.

TWpIr Con. 428 BTW Papers DLC.

[1] James Aloysius O'Gorman (1860–1943), a Democrat, was a justice of the New York Supreme Court (1900–1911) and U.S. senator (1911–17).

To Charles Dewey Hilles

[Tuskegee, Ala.] May 29, 1911

Personal

It seems there is grave danger that Lewis's confirmation may fail or be indefinitely delayed. It will be great calamity from many points of view should he not be confirmed. Many of us are very hopeful that everything will be done to see he is confirmed. He himself is feeling considerably discouraged.[1] I am wondering if you could have talk with him.

Booker T. Washington

TWpSr Con. 428 BTW Papers DLC.

[1] See William H. Lewis to BTW, May 25, 1911, Con. 428, BTW Papers, DLC.

To William Edwin Chilton[1]

[Tuskegee, Ala.] May 29, 1911

Personal

My dear Sir: I hope you will excuse me for taking a minute of your time. My only excuse for doing so is that I remember you very well when I used to be a school teacher near Malden in Kanawha County. I have watched your progress and success from that time until now, and I am just as proud of everything in the way of recognition that comes to you as anybody possibly can be.

I want to ask your favorable consideration of a matter that is interesting our race just now. William H. Lewis, of Massachusetts, as you perhaps know, has been nominated by the President for the position of Assistant Attorney General of the United States. There seems to be some hesitation and delay about his confirmation.

I am writing to say that I have known Mr. Lewis for a number of years, and that he is a man not only of ability but of discretion, modesty and common sense. He is not a man who would make a fool of himself in that position.

Anything that you can consistently do to further his interest, I very much hope you will do. I am sure that our colored friends in West Virginia will appreciate any interest that you may take in this direction. Yours very truly,

Booker T. Washington

TLpS   Con. 419   BTW Papers   DLC.

1 William Edwin Chilton (1858–1939), a Charleston, W.Va., newspaper publisher and lawyer, served as a Democrat in the U.S. Senate from 1911 to 1917.

From George Washington Carver

[Tuskegee, Ala.] May 29, 1911

Mr. B. T. Washington: I am pleased to see the interest you are taking in the development of the possibilities of our Macon County clays. I will guarantee that you will not be ashamed of the results when they are worked out. This work takes time and careful study — finding an objective and meeting it. I am pleased to say that everyone so far has been met and overcome.

I cannot say how cheaply it can be manufactured and put upon the market, as I have given no attention to that feature of it, but am devoting all my time to working out and illustrating its possibilities both physical and chemical. As soon as my laboratory is ready I will show you some of the chemical possibilities; they will greatly surprise you.

When I began this work I had in mind primarily the rural school-teacher and farmer — how easily, effectively, and inexpensively the former might beautify his schoolhouse inside and outside, his fences, etc., and the latter his dwelling-house, barns, fences, outbuildings, etc. We ought to save ourselves several hundred dollars a year by the use of these native kalsomines. It is my plan this summer to take the summer teachers and actually fit up a room with it. It is also my purpose when finished to get up a little pamphlet, which will serve as a guide for the farmers and others who are unacquainted with its use. I have only worked up about one-fourth of it; so, therefore, when completed, it will be four times as large as it is now.

Mr. Merritt[1] is right when he says it is marvelous. It is, and I am ready, not only to prove it, but to sustain it.

Two white gentlemen from West Point, Ga., examined it and said, "My! what a blessing to the whole South!" They invited me to stop off at West Point sometime in passing through, as they think they have some of the same kind.

Our Mr. Chas. Evans[2] and Mr. Bruce[3] say it can be easily used here.

If I can get my laboratory and the time in which to do it, I can have an exhibit ready for the state and various fairs that will be the biggest drawing card put on exhibition in recent years. When I can get it perfected I will then give more attention to the practical and commercial side — I will stain some furniture, kalsomine some rooms, whitewash some fences, etc., and teach them how to use it.

The paints and stains you saw on exhibition during commencement were made about eight years ago, so you can get somewhat of an idea of its great durability. There are a number of other beautiful colors in the county that I have not had time to collect.

I am further confident that you will find that this one thing will abundantly pay for the establishment of your research laboratory. Yours very truly,

Geo. W. Carver

P.S. A young man from Washington Ga. says they use it pretty generally on the inside of their houses there, they call it white mud.

G. W. C.

TLS Con. 615 BTW Papers DLC. Postscript in Carver's hand.

[1] Henry Paul Merritt, born in Barbour County, Ala., in 1873, established a law practice in Tuskegee in 1896. He served in the state senate (1907–11) and in the state house of representatives for many years beginning in 1911.

[2] Charles H. Evans taught carpentry at Tuskegee Institute.

[3] E. J. Bruce taught house and sign painting at Tuskegee Institute.

From Charles William Anderson

New York, N.Y. May 29, 1911

(Personal) Private

My dear Doctor: The Hagan matter has been interfered with by the recent change of Police Commissioners in this city. As you know, Commissioner Cropsey[1] was forced out, and Captain Rhinelander Waldo[2] was appointed. You may recall that I introduced you to Waldo one day in Nassau Street. He was then Fire Commissioner. He is a good friend of mine, but is, as his name would suggest, an aristocrat, and a great stickler for merit promotions without allowing any other influence to affect them. I will, however, approach him on his gentle side in the very near future, and see if I cannot bring about the desired result.

Concerning the matter mentioned in yours of the 24th instant, I beg to say that I took it up with Mr. Loeb on Saturday and he promised to write "our friend"[3] at Washington at once and tell him all about the man[4] Milholland is pushing. I have secured several samples of the literature put out by the colored democrats last Fall, which was written by "the Atlanta man." All of it criticises, and much of it abuses, President Taft. This ought to prevent his landing. Rest assured that I will leave no stone unturned. Yours very truly,

Charles W. Anderson

TLS Con. 52 BTW Papers DLC.

[1] James Church Cropsey, New York City commissioner of police in 1910–11, was later justice of the New York Supreme Court (1916–30). He died in 1937.

[2] Rhinelander Waldo (1877–1927) was New York City fire commissioner (1910–11) and police commissioner (1911–16). He was responsible for several important innovations in New York police practices, including fingerprinting and the traffic squad.

[3] William Howard Taft.

[4] W. E. B. Du Bois.

From Robert Heberton Terrell

Memphis, Tennessee. June 2, 1911

My dear Doctor Washington: I beg to thank you again for all of the courtesies which you and Mrs. Washington were good enough to show me on my visit to Tuskegee. I am more and more impressed as I think of all that I saw and heard at your wonderful school. And when I go North next week I shall begin to tell the folks in that section in stronger terms than I have before used about the remarkable progress of the colored people of the South. The great business activity of these folks here in Memphis has surprised me beyond measure. In comparison with them the Northern colored man is asleep. The colored man above Mason and Dixon's line has privileges while his brother down here has property, and I believe that the property owner is bound to get all of his rights finally.

I am remaining here to address the business men on Saturday night. I have not much to tell them but I am sure that I shall learn a great deal from them.

My kindest regards for Mrs. Washington and Davidson. Faithfully yours,

Robt. H. Terrell

ALS   Con. 443   BTW Papers   DLC.

An Account of a Tour of Macon County, Alabama

Tuskegee, Alabama, June 3, 1911

On Sunday, May 28th, Principal Booker T. Washington made a trip through the Southwestern part of the county. In addition to the large number of instructors of Tuskegee Institute who accompanied him there were in the party Judge Robert H. Terrell of Washington, D.C., the Hon. Whitefield McKinlay, Collector of Customs, Washington, D.C., Lord Eustace Percy of the British Embassy of Washington; Mr. W. T. B. Williams, Agent for the Anna T. Jeanes Fund and the Slater Board; Dr. Thomas Jesse Jones of the United States Census

Bureau and Mr. George L. Knox, editor and owner of the Indianapolis Freeman.

The first stop was made at the residence of Mr. Lott Ellington. His house, yard and garden were inspected and many favorable comments were passed upon their appearance. The next stop was at Fort Hull where Mr. Morgan Russell, one of the largest white planters of the County had prepared a barbecue breakfast. After partaking of the breakfast the party repaired to the church where a short meeting was held. Mr. Russell in introducing Principal Washington said that one of the greatest needs of the colored people was to have confidence in each other. Principal Washington on behalf of the party thanked Mr. Russell for his kindness to the party and advised the farmers to heed Mr. Russell's advice. The party then set out for Mt. Andrew community.

Just before reaching there a mounted committee met the party. A unique part of this committee was four boys mounted on oxen which were saddled and bridled. The Mt. Andrew community presented a very fine appearance. The farms of the Johnson Brothers were especially good. They own three hundred acres of land, have a store, a gin and good dwelling houses. In the Mt. Andrew community church was an excellent exhibit of the Farmers' Improvement Club which consisted of vegetables, fruits and meat. According to a report that was read, the colored people in this community own over two hundred head of livestock. There were over thirty whitewashed and painted houses here. In the course of his remarks Dr. Washington said that people could not go through a community like this without being encouraged. "Here in Macon County you have good land that will grow abundant crops. You have here a good citizenship and there is every opportunity for you to make this a heaven upon earth. Therefore get land and cultivate your land."

From here the party proceeded to Liberty Hill where a brief stop was made, the exhibits examined and short talks given. In this community the colored people own between twelve hundred and fifteen hundred acres of land. Mt. Pisgah was the next stop. Here a large crowd headed by the Farmers' Improvement Club was waiting. In the schoolhouse was an excellent exhibit of turnips, beets, cabbage, peas, potatoes, hams, canned blackberries, roasting ears and sewing. A. R. Griffin, a former student of Tuskegee and one of the leading farmers of this community introduced Principal Washington. He said that the colored people in this community own over four hundred head of live stock and about two thousand acres of land.

Principal Washington here urged the people to get hold of land and keep it, to do better farming, and grow something besides cotton. He said that they should not depend on the other fellow and should not go to town every first Saturday to draw from the merchants. They had an opportunity to draw from the soil every day corn, peas, beans, hogs, etc. More time he said should be given the wife to work around the house and to raise vegetables. The husbands were told to take their wives into their confidence. If this was done they would get along better and accumulate more. He especially stressed the importance of having conveniences at home, to make the home comfortable, so that the children would not be driven away.

The party now set out for the next stop, Hardaway. All along the road were seen whitewashed houses and well kept premises. A number of excellent demonstration plots were inspected. At Damascus church in Hardaway a crowd of about two thousand people were waiting. Here was found one of the best schoolhouses and churches in the county. After a number of plantation melodies had been sung Dr. Washington and Judge Terrell spoke to the people at considerable length. Principal Washington after commenting upon the fact that Damascus was a Biblical name told the people that they had better soil than was found in the Holy Land where the original Damascus was situated. He complimented the people upon their excellent church and school, their clean fields and whitewashed houses.

The next stop was at Sambo community. Here we found the best farms seen anywhere in the county. Especially worthy of note were the farms of the Henry brothers and J. M. Seals. Altogether the colored people in this community own about eight hundred acres of land. The Sambo school contains a bed room, a kitchen, a dining room and a recitation room.

Sambo was the farthest point on the trip and here the return home was begun. Stops were made at Egypt, Sweet Gum, the Russell Plantation and St. Mark. At all of these places the exhibits of the people were inspected and their work commended. All in all this was the longest and in many ways one of the most interesting trips Principal Washington has made.

Tuskegee Student, 23 (June 3, 1911), 1, 2.

An Article in *Outlook*

June 3, 1911

RACES AND POLITICS

In Prague, the capital of Bohemia, I came in contact for the first time with the advance guard, if I may use the expression, of a new race, the Slavs. I say a new race, because, although the Slavic peoples claim an antiquity as great as that of any other race in Europe, the masses of the race seem just now emerging from a condition of life more primitive than that of almost any other people in Europe.

Many little things, not only what I saw with my own eyes, but what I heard from others, gave me the impression, as I traveled southward, that I was entering into a country where the masses of the people lived a simpler and more primitive existence than any I had seen elsewhere in Europe. I remember, for one thing, that I was one day startled to see, in the neighborhood of the mining regions of Bohemia, a half-dozen women engaged in loading a coal barge — shoveling the coal into wheelbarrows and wheeling them along a narrow plank from the coal wharf to the ship alongside.

I was impressed, again, by the fact that several of the peoples of the Austrian Empire — the Moravians and Ruthenians are an illustration — still preserve their old tribal names. Certain other of these peoples still keep not only the tribal names, but many of the old tribal customs. Among most of the Slavic peoples, for example, custom still gives to the marriage ceremony the character of barter and sale. In fact, I found that in one of the large provincial towns in eastern Hungary the old "matrimonial fairs" are still kept up. On a certain day in each year hundreds of marriageable young women are brought down to this fair by their parents, where they may be seen seated on their trunks and surrounded by the cattle they expect to have for a dowry. Naturally young men come from all the surrounding country to attend this fair, and usually a lawyer sits out under a tree near by prepared to draw up the marriage contract. In some cases as many as forty marriages are arranged in this way in a single day.

Divided into petty kingdoms or provinces, each speaking a separate language, living for the most part in the country districts, and held in some sort of political and economic subjection, sometimes by the descendants of foreign conquerors, and sometimes, as in the case of the

Poles, by the nobility of their own race, the masses of the Slavic peoples in southern Europe have lived for centuries out of touch with the life of cities, and to a large extent out of touch with the world. Compared, therefore, with the peoples of western Europe, who are living in the centers of modern life and progress, the Slavic peoples are just now on the horizon.

In the course of my travels through Austria and Hungary I think I met, at one time or another, representatives of nearly every branch of the Slavic race in the Empire. In Bohemia I became acquainted, as I have said, with the most progressive portion of the race, the Czechs. In Galicia I saw something of the life of the Polish people, both in the towns and in the country districts. Again, in Budapest and Vienna I learned something of the condition of the laboring and peasant classes, among whom the Slavic peoples are usually in the majority. At Fiume, the port of Hungary from which forty thousand emigrants sail every year for the United States, I met and talked with Dalmatians, Croatians, Slovenes, Ruthenians, and Serbs — representatives, in fact, of almost every race in Hungary. In the plains of central Hungary, and again in eastern Prussia, I saw gangs of wandering laborers, made up of men and women who come to this part of the country from the Slavic countries farther south and east to take part in the harvest on the great estates.

During this time I became acquainted to some extent also with representatives of almost every type of civilization, high and low, among the peoples of southern Europe, from the Dalmatian herdsmen, who lead a rude and semi-barbarous existence on the high, barren mountains along the coast of the Adriatic, to the thrifty and energetic artisans of Bohemia and the talented Polish nobility, who are said to be among the most intellectual people in Europe.

I did not, among these classes I have mentioned, see the most primitive people of the Slavic race, nor the type of the man of that race farthest down. In fact, I have heard that in the mountain regions of southern Galicia there are people who make their homes in holes in the ground or herd together in little huts built of mud. I did not see, either, as I should like to have seen, the life of those Slavic people in southwestern Hungary who still hold their lands in common and live together in patriarchal communities, several families beneath one roof, under the rule of a "house father" and a "house mother," who are elected annually to govern the community.

What little I did see of the life of the different branches of the race gave me the impression, however, of a people of great possibilities, who, coming late into the possession of modern ideas and modern methods, were everywhere advancing, in some places rapidly and in others more slowly, but always making progress.

One thing that has hindered the advancement of the Slavs has been the difference in the languages spoken by the different branches of the race. So great an obstacle is this difference of language that some years ago, when a congress of all the Slavic peoples was held at Prague, the representatives of the different branches of the race, having no common tongue, were compelled to speak to each other in the one language that they all professed to hate, namely, German.

Another thing that has hindered the progress of the Slavs has been the inherited jealousies and the memories they cherish of ancient injuries they have inflicted on one another in times past. In general, it seems to be true of the races of Austria-Hungary that each race or branch of the race hates and despises every other, and this hatred is the more bitter the more closely they are associated. For example, there is a long-standing feud between the Polish peasants and the Polish nobility. This division is so great that the Polish peasants have frequently sided against the Polish nobility in the contests of the latter with the central government of Austria. However, this sentiment of caste which separates the two classes of the Polish people is nothing compared with the contempt with which every Pole, whether he be peasant or noble, feels for every Ruthenian, a people with whom the Pole is very closely related by blood, and with whom he has long been in close political association. On the other hand, the Ruthenian in Galicia looks upon the Pole, just as the Czech in Bohemia looks upon his German neighbor, as his bitterest enemy. The two peoples refuse to intermingle socially; they rarely intermarry; in many cases they maintain separate schools, and are represented separately in the Imperial Parliament, each race electing its own representatives. But all are united in hating and despising the Jew, who, although he claims for himself no separate part of the Empire, and has no language to distinguish himself from the other races about him, still clings as tenaciously as any other portion of the population to his own racial traditions and customs.

The Slavic peoples, otherwise divided by language and tradition, are also divided by religion. People speaking the same language, and sharing in other respects the same traditions, are frequently just as widely separated by differences of religion as they could be by differences of race. For example, among the southern Slavs the majority of the Slovenes and the Croatians are Roman Catholics, others are Protestants. On the other hand, the majority of the Serbs, their close neighbors, are members of the Greek Orthodox Church, while others are Mohammedans. So wide is the division between the Roman Catholic and the Orthodox Slavs that in some cases members of the Eastern and Western branches of the Church belonging to the same nationality wear a different costume in order to emphasize the differences of religion that might otherwise be forgotten or overlooked.

In Galicia there are not only the Roman and Orthodox branches of the Church, but there are also three or four other minor branches. One of these, the Uniates, which is a compromise between the two and is intended to be a sort of link between the Eastern and Western Churches, is now, it is said, just as distinct from both as any of the other branches of the Church. In this region, which has been the battleground of all the religions in Europe, religious distinctions play a much more important role than they do elsewhere, because the masses of the people have not yet forgotten the bitterness and the harshness of the early struggles of the sects. The result is that religious differences seem to have intensified rather than to have softened the racial animosities.

In spite of the divisions and rivalries which exist, there seems to be growing up, under the influence of the struggle against the other and dominant races in the Empire, and as a result of the political agitations to which this struggle has given rise, a sense of common purpose and interest in the different branches of the Slavic race; a sort of racial consciousness, as it is sometimes called, which seems to be one of the conditions without which a race that is down is not able to get the ambition and the courage to rise.

It is the presence of this great Slav race in western Europe, groping its way forward under the conditions and difficulties which I have described, that constitutes, as well as I am able to define it, the race problem of southern Europe.

In many respects the situation of the Slavs in the Austro-Hungarian Empire and in southern Europe generally is more like that of the

Negroes in the Southern States than is true of any other class or race in Europe. For one thing, the vast majority of that race are, like the Negroes, an agricultural people. For centuries they have lived and worked on the soil, where they have been the servants of the great landowners, looked down upon by the educated and higher classes as "an inferior race." Although they were not distinguished from the dominant classes, as the Negro was, by the color of their skin, they were distinguished by the language they spoke, and this difference in language seems to have been, as far as mutual understanding and sympathy are concerned, a greater bar than the fact of color has been in the case of the white man and the black man in the South.

Up to a comparatively few years ago an educated Slav did not ordinarily speak, at least in public, the language of the masses of the people. Dr. Clark, the head of the Austrian Mission of the American Board in Prague, told me that as recently as thirty years ago an edu-cated Czech did not care to speak his own language on the streets of Prague. At that time the German language was still the language of the educated classes, and all the learning of Europe was, to a very large extent, a closed book to the people who did not speak and read that language.

To-day conditions have so changed, Dr. Clark tells me, that the people in certain quarters of Prague scowl at any one who speaks Ger-man on the street.

"When we go to visit an official of the Government," said Dr. Clark, "we usually inquire, first of all, which language this particular official prefers to speak, German or Czech. It is wise to do this because most of the officials, particularly if they represent the central government of Vienna, speak German, but a Czech who is loyal to his race will not speak the hated German unless he has to do so."

Dr. Clark told me, as illustrating the fanaticism of the Bohemian people in this matter of language, that his little girls, who had been educated in German schools and preferred to speak that language among themselves, had more than once been hooted at, and even stoned, by young Bohemians in the part of the town where he lives, because they spoke a language which the masses of the people had been brought up to hate.

Another way in which the situation of the Slavic people resembles, to a certain extent, that of the masses of the Negroes in the Southern

States, is in the matter of their political relations to the dominant races. Both in Austria and in Hungary all the races are supposed to have the same political privileges, and, in the case of Austria at least, the Government seems to have made a real effort to secure equal rights to all. Here, again, racial and traditional prejudices, as well as the wide differences in wealth and culture of the different peoples, have kept the political power in Austria proper in the hands of the Germans, and in Hungary in the hands of the Magyars.

What makes the situation more difficult for the dominant races in these two countries is the fact that the so-called inferior peoples are increasing more rapidly than the other races in numbers, and the Germans and Magyars are every year becoming a smaller minority in the midst of the populations which they are attempting to control. The result has been that the Empire seems to the one who looks on from the outside a seething mass of discontent, with nothing but the fear of being swallowed up by some of their more powerful neighbors to hold the nationalities together.

There is one respect in which the situation of the Negro in America is entirely different from the various nationalities of Austria and Hungary. The Negro is not compelled to get his education through the medium of a language that is foreign to the other people by whom he is surrounded. The black man in the South speaks the same tongue and professes the same religion as the white people. He is not seeking to set up any separate nationality for himself nor to create any interest for himself which is separate from or antagonistic to the interest of the other people of the United States. The Negro is not seeking to dominate politically, at the expense of the white population, any part of the country which he inhabits. Although he has suffered wrongs and injustices, he has not become embittered or fanatical. Competition with the white race about him has given the Negro an ambition to succeed and made him feel pride in the successes he has already achieved; but he is just as proud to be an American citizen as he is to be a Negro. He cherishes no ambitions that are opposed to the interests of the white people, but is anxious to prove himself a help rather than a hindrance to the success and prosperity of the other race.

I doubt whether there are many people in our Southern States who have considered how much more difficult the situation in the Southern States would be if the masses of the black people spoke a language different from the white people around them, and particularly if, at the same time, they cherished political and social ambitions that were antagonistic to the interests of the white man.

On the other hand, I doubt whether the Negro people realize the advantage which they have in speaking one of the great world languages, the language, in fact, that is more largely used than any other by the people who are most advanced in science, in the arts, and in all that makes the world better. English is not only a great world language, it is the language of a people and a race among whom the highest are neither afraid nor ashamed to reach down and lift up the lowest, and help them in their efforts to reach a higher and a better life.

In the south of Europe conditions are quite different. The languages spoken there, so far from helping to bring people together, are the very means by which the peoples are kept apart. Furthermore, the masses of the people of Austria speak languages which, until a hundred years ago, had almost no written literature. Up to the beginning of the last century the educated people of Hungary spoke and wrote in Latin, and down to the middle of the century Latin was still the language of the Court. Until 1848 there were almost no schools in the Czech language in Bohemia. Up to that time there were almost no newspapers, magazines, or books printed in the language spoken by the masses of the people.

It has been said that the written or literary languages of the Slavic people have been, with one or two exceptions, almost created during the past hundred years. In fact, some of the Slavs, although they have a rich oral literature, still have, I have been told, no written language of their own.

A great change has been brought about in this respect in recent years. At the present time, of the 5,000 periodicals printed in Austria-Hungary, about 2,000 are printed in German, 938 in Magyar, 582 in Czech, and the remaining 1,480 are in some five or six other languages. The Magyar language is now taught in all the schools of Hungary, whether some other language is taught at the same time or not. Outside of Hungary, in Austria proper, there are some 8,000 exclusively German schools, 5,578 Czech, and 6,632 schools in which are taught other Slav dialects, not to speak of the 645 schools in which Italian is taught, the 162 schools in which Rumanian is taught, and the 5 in which Magyar is taught.

To an outsider it seems as if the purpose of these schools must be to perpetuate the existing confusion and racial animosities in the Empire. On the other side, it must be remembered that it has been an enormous advantage to the masses of the people to be able to read the language which they habitually speak. In fact, the multiplication of these different written languages, and of schools in which they are taught, seems to have been the only way of opening to the masses of the people the learning which had been before that time locked up in languages which they sometimes learned to read but rarely spoke.

As I have considered the complications and difficulties, both political and economic, which not merely Austria but Europe has to face as a consequence of the different languages spoken by the different races, I have asked myself what would probably happen in our Southern States if, as some people have suggested, large numbers of these foreign peoples were induced to settle there. I greatly fear that if these people should come in large numbers and settle in colonies outside of the cities, where they would have comparatively few educational advantages and where they would be better able and more disposed to preserve their native customs and languages, we might have a racial problem in the South more difficult and more dangerous than that which is caused by the presence of the Negro. Whatever else one may say of the Negro, he is, in everything except his color, more like the Southern white man, more willing and able to absorb the ideas and the culture of the white man and adapt himself to existing conditions, than is true of any other race which is now coming into this country.

Perhaps my attempt to compare racial conditions in southern Europe with racial conditions in the Southern United States will seem to some persons a trifle strange and out of place because in the one case the races concerned are both white, while in the other case one is white and one is black. Nevertheless, I am convinced that a careful study of conditions as they exist in southern Europe will throw a great deal of light upon the situation of the races in our Southern States. More than that, strange and irrational as racial conflicts often seem, whether in Europe or in America, I suspect that at bottom they are merely the efforts of groups of people to readjust their relations under changing conditions. In short, they grow out of the efforts of the people who are at the bottom to lift themselves to a higher stage of existence.

If that be so, it seems to me there need be no fear, under a free government where every man is given opportunity to get an education, where every man is encouraged to develop in himself and bring to the service of the community the best that is in him, that racial difficulties should not finally be adjusted, and white man and black man live, each helping rather than hindering the other.

Outlook, 98 (June 3, 1911), 260–64.

From Robert Ezra Park

Wollaston, Mass   June 3, 1911

My dear Mr Washington: I am sending you enclosed the tenth chapter of The Man Farthest Down. I have been working on it, writing and rewriting it, for about three weeks. I do not know that I have got it yet in very decent shape.

I did not like the chapter on The Women who Work in Europe and am sure that if I had taken a little more time I could have greatly improved it. I have made several verbal changes in the proof which I wish you would look over when you are in New York. I am sending the proof there today.

When this stuff gets cold on me it goes very slow but I guess I can move things along better from now on.

I shall hope to see you in Boston in a few days. After all the criticisms of the English paper struck me as quite natural and just.

If the book escapes with nothing harsher than the criticisms already made I shall feel that a great deal has been achieved.

I should like, however, to see all these criticisms because I think that when I rewrite the introductory chapters I can state the matter in such a way as to partially meet them. Very truly

Robert E Park

TLS   Con. 54   BTW Papers   DLC.

From Henry Watson Furniss

Port Au Prince, Haiti. June 3, 1911

Confidential

My dear Dr. Washington: Your confidential letter of the 16th ultimo to hand, and I was pleased at the contents thereof. This is the first mail to the States since its receipt.

The letter from Secretary Knox stated the matter so plainly and so kindly that I could not take it up. I accepted it as a consummated fact, gracefully bowed to the inevitable, and commenced to arrange my personal affairs to relinquish charge here at the time set.

Personally I have sought no influence nor have I made request of anyone to urge my retention. However, I have heard that the large American interests which are just entering here as a result of my assistance, have been urging my retention. This is but natural. Nevertheless, it has been without consulting me.

Whatever the outcome I shall not be "sore." I am of your opinion; that is, if I am to be replaced I would prefer to be succeeded by someone of ability and merit. I shall be pleased to assist you in whatever plan you may have. If there is political necessity to give recognition to another, why can it not be one of our friends like Lewis, Scott, Napier, Courtney, Bruce, etc.?

Personally I am very intimate with the present administration in Haiti and for that reason have accomplished so much. President Simon[1] has particularly expressed his regrets that I am to be supplanted; yet, with all that I have jealously guarded American interests and could receive no greater praise than the commendation given by the Department for the "able and conscientious manner" in which I have performed my duty.

I thank you very much for your interest in me and am in entire accord with you. Very sincerely yours,

H. W. Furniss

TLS Con. 422 BTW Papers DLC.

[1] Antoine Simon, a general who led a successful insurrection in 1908, was president of Haiti from 1908 to 1911. Simon was overthrown by Cincinnatus Leconte and fled to Jamaica, where he died in 1912.

From Chester A. Hagan

N. Y. City [ca. June 3, 1911]

Dear Sir: Received your letter this P.M. but I am very sorry to say that up to the present time I have heard nothing relative to me being made a detective.

If you will be so kind, to send a letter to Mayor Wm. J Gaynor of N. Y. City, explaining the matter to him the way you did to Commissioner "Cropsey" and requesting him to make me a first grade Detective I am positive he will do so.

It is a very easy matter to get assigned to do Detective work if you have some one to speak for you; and if you will do this for me, I can assure you that I will appreciate it; Hoping that you will do this for me; and, I am sure you will, as you assured me you would do anything you could for me; I will be glad to pay you back any way I can. You spoke to me asking me to make a statement.

When this case is over I have found out I can do this; and if at anytime you care to have [me] go to your institution and explain to the students the true side of affair I will gladly do so.

Thanking you in advance I Remain   Respectfully

Chester A. Hagan

ALS   Con. 434   BTW Papers   DLC.

From Ralph Waldo Tyler

Washington, June 4, 1911

Dear Doctor: Your wire regarding Lewis' confirmation at hand. Lewis is becoming very much discouraged, and he cannot be blamed. His name is still in the hands of the sub-committee composed of Senators Root, Sutherland[1] and Bacon. The latter is opposed to his confirmation, but our understanding is that Senator Root is trying to bring him around in order to have the committee make a unanimous report. We understand that Senator Rayner,[2] of Maryland, a negro-hater, and who is chairman of the Senate Committee on Indian depredation claims, is also opposed to the confirmation. They cannot spring that old chestnut, "senatorial courtesy," which they used against Crum for the reason that both of Lewis' senators are for him. It seems to be the opinion, that is among us, that if they were really, and cordially for him, they would push the confirmation through. I think the game is to starve him out, by holding up the confirmation, and letting congress adjourn on him. The Republicans have a clear majority in the senate, and if they favor Lewis, I cannot see why Sutherland and Root don't make a report favorable, and let Bacon make a minority report, if he desires, and then let the name go before the Senate in executive session and make a party issue of it. It is particularly hard on Lewis for the reason that he has no means, and must maintain his family in Cambridge and himself here with no salary coming in. I wrote Charley and he had his club pass resolutions requesting Senator Root to use his influence to have the confirmation brought about. Lewis is now busy with some of his old college chums, getting them to write letters. I think it would be a good thing for you to write Senator Root in the matter.

We here have done what we could. I, through Hilles, got the President to take it up with Root, and others, urging early confirmation. Senator Crane assured Lewis that there was no doubt but what he would be confirmed, but when? is what is agitating Lewis and the rest of us. It seems to me that if confirmation does not come this week we had better fire up the colored people in the country as was done in the Crum case. Back of the delay is only one thing — color, but it does seem tough that a Republican senate should be held at bay by Democrats in this case.

I suggest that you write, or wire Senator Root a strong appeal for early action.

I will take up your presence at Wilberforce with the dailies at Columbus, Dayton and Cincinnati, and try to secure the proper notice before and after. Very truly

R. W. Tyler

TLS Con. 443 BTW Papers DLC.

[1] George Sutherland (1862–1942), a Republican, was a U.S. senator from Utah (1905–17). From 1922 to 1938 he was a justice of the U.S. Supreme Court, where he generally voted with the conservative majority against New Deal legislation.

² Isidor Rayner (1850–1912), a Democrat, was U.S. senator from Maryland (1905–12) after many years in politics as a state legislator, congressman, and state attorney general.

From Charles William Anderson

New York, N.Y., June 5, 1911

Private & confidential

My dear Dr: Immediately on receipt of your letter about Du Bois I called on Mr. Loeb and urged him to write at once and tell "our friend" all about this man's antecedents. Mr. L. then asked me if I still desired Hayti, and I answered that I could not now consider if for fear my place would go astray, but would be inclined to do so, if Mr. Moore could succeed me. He said that would be a very happy arrangement, in his judgment, and if it could be brought about, would insure the support of the Age. He wrote a strong letter against Du Bois, calling attention to the fact that he had opposed the President when he was a candidate, and is still criticising him with unrepentant hostility. He advised Mr. Hilles that a glance at Du Bois' paper would convince the President that nothing ought to be done for him, and ended his letter by suggesting that the arrangement with respect to Moore and myself would bring the Age into line. Saturday I called on Mr. Loeb, and he, in strictest confidence, and under pledge of secrecy, read me Mr. Hilles' reply. In the first place, it stated that Hayti had been preempted, and stated that the President would not consider Moore for *any place whatsoever*. It went on to say that in view of the fact that the paper was controlled by B. T. W., and Moore was his right-hand man, the President could not understand how it was that this paper had kept up its war on the Administration, notwithstanding Cottrill, Lewis, McKinlay, Napier and Pinchback had been appointed, and Tyler and Anderson had been retained, and in view of the splendid stand taken by the President in support of B. T. W. when he met with his misfortune, the President regarded the Age's attitude as inexplicable. This may not be the exact wording of the letter, but it is very close to it. Mr. Loeb said it was his opinion that the letter was written by the President and not by Mr. Hilles. He then read me his answer to this letter, which was to the effect that the Age had opposed the last Administration (Roosevelt's), as persistently as it had this one, and that it was his understanding that it was Milholland and not yourself, that really controlled the paper.

During our conversation Mr. L. said that your opponents had been calling on "our friend" in great numbers and reminding him that he was placing the friends of a man who controlled a newspaper that was persistently criticising and misrepresenting the President and his Administration. He stated further that whenever "our friend" would say that you did not control the paper, these people would invariably say "of course he disclaims it, but everybody knows that he does control it, and most people believe that he does own this paper and that Moore would not dare make war on the Administration unless it had his sanction." I got two very distinct impressions from this interview, one was, that nothing large or small will be done for Moore, and the other was that "our friend" believes that the Age's attitude is winked at by you, and that his determination to appoint Vernon was a sort of service of notice on you, that if this paper does not mend its ways, some appointments will be made from the *other group*. From what Mr. L. says, the other fellows are running to the White House very frequently.

I thought it also significant that although Mr. L. devoted a large part of his first letter to the hostility of Du Bois toward the administration, nothing whatever was said about Du Bois in the answer. The answer was devoted to showing what had been done for your friends both in appointments and retentions, and what was not being done by your friends in the way of supporting the administration. I noticed also that "the Judge" was not included among your friends who were appointed or retained.

As soon as you reach here, I would suggest that you find something to talk over with Mr. L., and during your talk it may be that he will show you this communication. Please be careful however, not to disclose the fact that I passed the information along to you, as he pledged me to secrecy. At the same time I am confident he will put you in possession of all of the aforegoing, if you will drop in on him when you are next in town. Yours very truly,

C. W. A.

P.S. This was dictated to a novice here in the office as a matter of precaution — hence the mistakes.

C. A.

P.P.S. I forgot to say that Mr. Loeb said that he thought you ought to get control of the Age and change its policy. He seemed to think it should support the President & ought to be in new hands. He inquired about your nephew & asked if he was one of the editors. I answered that Simmons was not your nephew, but a distant relative of Mrs W's.

C

TLI   Con. 5   BTW Papers   DLC.

To William F. McGinnis[1]

[Tuskegee, Ala.] June 7, 1911

My dear Sir: In writing you, a few days ago, I meant to have added to my letter that, personally, I have no prejudice whatever against the Catholic Church, or individual members of that church.

We have here at this institution nearly one hundred Catholic students. Aside from that, a number of our teachers are Catholics. We make no difference whatever. Yours very truly,

Booker T. Washington

TLpS   Con. 429   BTW Papers   DLC.

[1] William F. McGinnis (1867–1932), a Catholic clergyman, was pastor of St. Brigid's Church in Westbury, N.Y., from 1904 to 1922. He was president of the International Catholic Truth Association and editor-in-chief of *Truth* magazine.

From Elihu Root

Washington   June 7, 1911

My dear Mr. Washington: I think Lewis's nomination will go through all right, although there is a good deal of opposition and inevitable delay. I have been authorized by the Judiciary Committee of the Senate to report it favorably, which I shall do at the next executive session. I don't think it can be beaten.

With kind regards, I am, Very sincerely yours,

Elihu Root

TLS Con. 428 BTW Papers DLC.

From Edward Ulysses Anderson Brooks[1]

Auburn, N.Y. June 7, 1911

My Dear Mr. Washington: We are trying to raise a fund for the purpose of caring for Mrs. Harriet Tubman Davis,[2] the Moses of her people, who has entered the Harriet Tubman Home which she founded here in this city. She is so feeble she requires the constant attendance of a trained nurse, whom the Home is maintaining at a cost of $10.00 per week.

I felt that you and Mrs. Washington would be interested in the matter and so I write to ask you to make a donation toward the maintenance of Aunt Harriet. She sits up for a while each day, but can not walk alone. She is nearly 100 years old. For the last three months she has been an invalid unable to help herself. She entered the Home on May 19th and has shown much improvement since. It is the desire of the Home management to give her every attention and comfort possible in these her last days. Hoping to hear from you at your convenience I remain   Yours Respectfully,

E. U. A. Brooks

TLS Con. 444 BTW Papers DLC. On stationery of the Harriet Tubman Home for Aged and Indigent Colored People.

[1] Edward Ulysses Anderson Brooks (b. 1872) graduated from Cornell in 1892 and practiced law in Elmira, N.Y., before beginning a career as a minister in the 1890s. He graduated from Auburn Theological Seminary in 1911, and beginning in 1913 was pastor of the A.M.E. Zion Church at Saratoga Springs, N.Y. Brooks was a trustee and general superintendent of the Harriet Tubman Home for Aged and Indigent Colored People in Auburn, N.Y.

[2] Harriet Tubman (ca. 1821–1913), born in slavery on the Eastern Shore of Maryland, escaped from bondage in 1849 and began a remarkable career as an abolitionist and "conductor" on the Underground Railroad, helping more than

300 slaves to freedom. In 1857 she rescued her own parents and settled them in Auburn, N.Y. During the Civil War she worked as a cook, nurse, and laundress for the Union Army and acted as a guide and spy behind Confederate lines. In her home in Auburn she supported a number of old persons. The home continued to operate for several years after her death in 1913.

To James Hardy Dillard

[Tuskegee, Ala.] June 8, 1911

Dear Dr. Dillard: Thank you many times for remembering me with a copy of the New Orleans Picayune, of June 5th,[1] and copy of The States. I shall read your address I know with interest and also with profit. I am glad to get hold of anything you send.

I suppose you already know that there are certain kinds of white people in the North and certain kinds of colored people also who do not like to hear any one say that the Negro is making progress. We run upon strange things some times in our experiences.

It used to be the Southern white man who pretended that the Negro was not making progress. Some of our own people and some of the rank Abolitionists are loudest in their claims that the Negro is not making progress. Yours very truly,

Booker T. Washington

TLpS Con. 50 BTW Papers DLC.

[1] The New Orleans *Picayune,* June 5, 1911, 6, reported an address by Dillard before an audience of religious workers and educators at the Central Congregational Church in New Orleans. Dillard said that in his travels for the Slater and Jeanes funds he had seen education and religion uplifting the black people. He concluded: "Better homes are being acquired, farms are being purchased, and the race is engaging in business pursuits; therefore I take an optimistic view of the situation."

To Frederick Randolph Moore

[Tuskegee, Ala.] June 8, 1911

Dear Mr. Moore: I notice that the publishers of The Crisis claim, on what seems to be good authority, that they print 12,000 copies every month. This indicates that The Age will have to get to hustling in order to maintain its influence and predominance. Yours very truly,

Booker T. Washington

TLpS   Con. 54   BTW Papers   DLC.

To Samuel Edward Courtney

[Tuskegee, Ala.] June 9, 1911

Personal:

Dear Dr. Courtney: I have your letter of June 5th and am glad that you are keeping such close line on the Lewis matter.

I have been writing letters to all of the important Senators and have had some very favorable responses. The favorable report upon his name seems a forecast of his early confirmation.

I hope to talk with you regarding the Haitian matter soon. It is my impression that it is the purpose of the Administration to appoint a dark representative of the race to this position. Yours very truly,

Booker T. Washington

TLpS   Con. 419   BTW Papers   DLC.

To Charles William Anderson

[Tuskegee, Ala.] June 9, 1911

Dear Mr. Anderson: Your kind letter has been received, and I have read it with care. I thank you for the information which it contains.

Well, it looks as if Vernon has been practically shelved for the present at least. Now, unless you yourself want the Haitian ministership, and unless there is a good chance of your getting it, I should think all of us ought to do what we can to keep Furniss there. This, I think, is the easiest way to keep out of getting into a difficult position. But, of course, if you want it, I shall do everything in my power to help you get it.

It is rather a strange coincidence that I received information from parties in Washington by almost the same mail to the effect that certain friends up there were blaming you for the policy of the Age, referring to the fact, as I understood it, that one of the owners of the Age was in constant touch with you and employed in your office, and that you and Moore were quite friendly. Putting what has come to me from Washington with what has come to you from Washington, I am convinced that some mischief maker is loose and busy in Washington and has been misrepresenting conditions in New York and doing both you and me an injustice.

Of course, I know all the weaknesses of our friend Moore — how vain and bullheaded he is in certain directions and at certain times. Still, I have watched in recent months with a good deal of care the editorial utterances of the paper, and unless something has escaped me, the editorials have been in support of the President and his policies. That is, I mean to say, for example, that since you and Mr. Scott went to Beverly and had an understanding that resulted in the appointment of several of our good friends, and since the President has fulfilled his promises so magnificently, it seems that Moore has kept good faith in his editorials.

From time to time, I think various foolish and unnecessary news items have gotten into the paper that might have given a bad impression, however.

The fact is, I do not think that either the President or Mr. Hilles ever sees or reads the Age. The result is that the little clique in Washington give them the impression constantly that the Age is against the Administration, and they succeed to some extent in making the administration believe that those whom the President is trying to please are not loyal to him so far as the Age is concerned.

I wish you would say to Mr. Loeb in your own way and at your own time that which I have repeated over and over again — that I do not own directly or indirectly nor control directly nor indirectly a single dollar's worth in the New York Age or in any other Negro newspaper in America. From time to time, I am able to advise Moore, and sometimes he takes my advice and just as often he does not.

This, I think, has also been true of yourself.

I am going to Washington within a short time, and shall see both

Mr. Hilles and the President and set them right with a straight talk so far as you and myself are concerned in our relations to the New York Age. I feel sure I can do this.

In the meantime, whenever you get an opportunity, I hope you will do the same thing that I am going to do, and that is, advise Moore that his utterances through the Age have an influence in either hurting or helping his friends, and that he ought to be careful as to what he says.

In view of what the President has done to please both you and me, we would be the basest ingrates if we did not in every way stand by him, and that is the policy I mean to pursue. When I see Mr. Hilles and the President, I shall tell them of the many things which I know that you have done to anybody knowing anything about it.

I shall certainly follow your advice to get into contact with Loeb at the very earliest moment possible.

I think it would be well for you to advise Moore to send the President, Mr. Loeb and Mr. Hilles marked copies of the Age from time to time, so that they can see for themselves what the attitude of the paper is toward the Administration.

I see by a recent dispatch that Vernon has been disposed of. This makes the puzzle all the greater regarding Haiti. Perhaps the President has decided to leave Furniss where he is. Yours truly,

Booker T. Washington

P.S. Since thinking this matter over, I am puzzled as to how to bring this subject up with the President and with Mr. Hilles, without breaking a confidence, that is, without involving Mr. Loeb or yourself, or the party in Washington who informed me. Please advise me on that point.

I suppose you understand that the position which Vernon has been given is the assistant superintendency connected with the Black Indians. You know there are a lot of those Indians out there who are blacker than Vernon.

B. T. W.

TLpS   Con. 5   BTW Papers   DLC.

An Article in *Outlook*

June 10, 1911

Naples and the Land of the Emigrant

I had crossed Europe from north to south before I got my first glimpse of an emigrant bound for America. On the way from Vienna to Naples I stopped at midnight at Rome, and in the interval between trains I spent an hour in wandering about in the soft southern air — such air as I had not found anywhere since I left my home in Alabama.

In returning to the station my curiosity was aroused, as I was passing in the shadow of the building, by what seemed to me a large vacant room near the main entrance to the station. As I attempted to enter this room I stumbled over the figure of a man lying on the stone floor. Looking farther, I saw something like forty or fifty persons, men as well as women, lying on the floor, their faces turned toward the wall, asleep.

The room itself was apparently bare and empty of all furniture. There was neither a bench nor a table, so far as I could see, in any part of the room. It seemed that, without any expectation of doing so, I had wandered into the room reserved for emigrants, and come accidentally upon one of the sights I most wanted to see in Italy, namely, a party of emigrants bound for America.

As near as I could learn, these people were, for the most part, peasants, who had come in from the surrounding country, carrying what little property they possessed on their backs or tied up in little bundles in their arms, and were awaiting the arrival of the train that was to take them to the port from which they could take ship for America.

I confess it struck me as rather pathetic that, in this splendid new and modern railway station, in which the foreign traveler and the native Italian of the upper classes were provided with every convenience and luxury, so little thought had been given to the comfort of these humble travelers, who represent the people in Italy who pay proportionately most of the taxes and who, by their patient industry and thrift, have contributed more than any other class to such progress as Italy has made in recent years.

Later on I had an opportunity to pass through the country from which perhaps the majority of these emigrants had come. I traveled through a long stretch of country where one sees only now and then a lonesome shepherd or a wretched hut with one low room and a cow-stall. I also visited some of the little villages which one sees clinging to the barren hilltops, to escape the poisonous mists of the plains below. There I saw the peasants in their homes and learned something of the way in which the lowly people in the rural districts have been neglected and oppressed. After that I was able to understand that it was no special hardship that these emigrants suffered at Rome. Perhaps many of them had never before slept in a place as clean and sanitary as the room the railway provided them.

Early the next morning, as my train was approaching Naples, my attention was attracted by the large number of women I saw at work in the fields. It was not merely the number of women but the heavy wrought-iron hoes, of a crude and primitive manufacture, with which these women worked that aroused my interest. These hoes were much like the heavy tools I had seen the slaves use on the plantations before the Civil War. With these heavy instruments some of the women seemed to be hacking the soil, apparently preparing it for cultivation; others were merely leaning wearily upon their tools, as if they were over-tired with the exertion. This seemed quite possible to me, because the Italian women are slighter and not as robust as the women I had seen at work in the fields in Austria.

I inquired why it was that I saw so many women in the fields in this part of the country, for I had understood that Italian women, as a rule, did not go so frequently into field work as the women do in Austria and Hungary. I learned that it was because so many of the men, who formerly did this work, had emigrated to America. As a matter of fact, three-fourths of the emigration from Italy to America comes from Sicily and the other southern provinces. There are villages in lower Italy which have been practically deserted. There are others in which no one but women and old men are left behind, and the whole population is more than half supported by the earnings of Italian laborers in America. There are cities within twenty miles of Naples which have lost within ten years two-thirds of their inhabitants. In fact, there is one little village not far from the city of which it is said that the entire male population is in America.

Ten days later, coming north from Sicily, I passed through the farming country south of Naples from which large numbers of emigrants go every year to the United States. It is a sad and desolate region. Earthquakes, malaria, antiquated methods of farming, and the general neglect of the agricultural population have all contributed to the miseries of the people. The land itself — at least such portion of it as I saw — looks old, worn-out, and decrepit; and the general air of desolation is emphasized when, as happened in my case, one comes suddenly, in the midst of the desolate landscape, upon some magnificent and lonely ruin, representing the ancient civilization that flourished here two thousand years ago.

Statistics which have been recently collected, after an elaborate investigation, by the Italian Government, show that, in a general way, the extent of emigration from southern Italy is in direct ratio to the neglect of the agricultural classes. Where the wages are smallest and the conditions hardest, there emigration has reached the highest mark. In other words, it is precisely from those parts of Italy where there are the greatest poverty, crime, and ignorance that the largest number of emigrants from Italy go out to America, and, I might add, the smallest number return. Of the 511,935 emigrants who came to North and South America from Italy in 1906, 380,615 came from Sicily and the southern provinces.

One of the most interesting experiences I had while in Europe was in observing the number of different classes and races there are in Europe who look down upon, and take a hopeless view of, certain of their neighbors because they regard them as inferior. For example, one of the first things I learned in Italy was that the people in northern Italy look down upon the people of southern Italy as an inferior race. I heard and read many times while I was in Italy stories and anecdotes illustrating the childishness, the superstition, and the ignorance of the peasant people and the lower classes generally in southern Italy. In fact, nothing that I have known or heard about the superstition of the Negro people in America compares with what I heard about the superstition of the Italian peasants. What surprised me more was to learn that statistics gathered by the Italian Government indicate that in southern Italy, contrary to the experience of every other country, the agricultural laborers are physically inferior to every other class of the population. The people in the rural districts are shorter of stature and in a poorer condition generally than they are in the cities.

For all these reasons I was the more anxious to learn for myself what these people were like. I wanted to find out precisely in what this inferiority of the southern Italian consisted, because I knew that these people were very largely descended from the ancient Greeks, who, by reputation at least, were the most gifted people the world has ever known.

The city of Naples offers some advantages for studying the southern population, since it is the port at which the stream of emigration from the small towns and farming districts of the interior reaches the sea. The exportation of laborers to America is one of the chief businesses of that city. It was at Naples, then, that I gained my earliest first-hand knowledge and acquaintance of the Italians of the south.

I think the thing that impressed me most about Naples was the contrast between the splendor of its natural surroundings, the elegance and solidity of its buildings, and the dirt, disorder, and squalor in which the masses of the people live. It was early morning when I arrived in the city for the first time. The sun, which was just rising over the black mass of Vesuvius, flooded the whole city and the surrounding country with the most enchanting light. In this soft light the gray and white masses of the city buildings, piled against the projecting hillside to the right and stretching away along the curving shores to the left, made a picture which I shall never forget.

Some of this sunshine seemed to have got into the veins of the people, too, for I never saw anywhere so much sparkle and color, so much life and movement, as I did among the people who throng the narrow streets of Naples. I never heard before so many curious human noises or saw such vivid and expressive gestures. On the other hand, I never saw anywhere before so many beggars, so many barefooted men, so many people waiting at the station and around the streets to pick up a casual job. It seemed to me that there were at least six porters to every passenger who got off the train, and these porters were evidently well organized, for I had the experience of seeing myself and my effects calmly parceled out among half a dozen of them, every one of whom demanded, of course, a separate fee for his services.

My experience in Europe leads me to conclude that the number of casual laborers, hucksters, vagabonds, and hunters of odd jobs one meets in a city is a pretty good index of the condition of the masses of the people. By this measure I think that I should have been able to say at the outset that there was in Naples a larger class living in the dirt, degradation, and ignorance at the bottom of society than in any other city I visited in Europe. I make this statement even though cities like Catania and Palermo, in Sicily, which are surrounded by an agricultural population just as wretched, are little, if any, better than Naples in this respect.

Very few persons who go to Naples merely as sightseers ever get acquainted, I suspect, with the actual conditions of the people. Most travelers who see Naples are carried away by the glamour of the sunshine, the color, and the vivacity of the Italian temperament. For that reason, they do not see the hard struggle for existence which goes on in the narrow streets of the city, or, if they do, they look upon the shifts and devices to which this light-hearted people are driven in order to live as merely part of the picturesqueness of the southern life and people.

I have been more than once through the slums and poorer quarters of the colored people of New Orleans, Atlanta, Philadelphia, and New York, and my personal observation convinces me that the colored population of these cities is in every way many per cent better off than the corresponding classes in Naples and the other Italian cities I have named. As far as the actual hardships they have to endure or the opportunities open to them, the condition of the Negro in these cities does not compare, in my opinion, with that of the masses of the Italians in these southern Italian cities.

There is this difference also: the majority of the Negroes in the large cities of the South and North in the United States are from the country. They have been accustomed to range and wander in a country where life was loose and simple and existence hardly a problem. They have not been accustomed to either the comforts or the hardships of complex city life. In the case of the Italians life in the crowded, narrow streets, and the unsanitary intimacy and confusion in which men, goats, and cattle here mingle, have become the fixed habit of centuries.

It is not an unusual thing, for instance, to find a cow or a mule living in close proximity, if not in the same room, with the rest of the family, and, in spite of the skill and artistic taste which show themselves everywhere in the construction and decoration of the buildings, the dirt and disorder in which the people live in these buildings are beyond description. Frequently in passing through the streets of these southern cities one meets a herd of goats wandering placidly along over the stone pavements, nibbling here and there in the gutters or holding up in front of a house to be milked.

Even where the city government has made the effort to widen and improve the streets, let in air and sunlight, and maintain sanitary con-

ditions, the masses of the people have not yet learned to make use
of these conveniences. I recall, in passing along one of these streets,
in the center of the city, which had been recently laid out with broad
stone sidewalks and built up with handsome three and four story stone
buildings, seeing a man and a cow standing on the sidewalk at the
corner of the street. It seemed to me that the natural thing would
have been to let the cow stand in the street and not obstruct the sidewalk. But these people evidently look upon the cow as having the same
rights as other members of the population. While the man who owned
the cow was engaged in milking, a group of women from the neighboring tenements stood about with their pitchers and gossiped, awaiting their turn at the cow.

This method of distributing milk, namely, by driving the animal to
the front door and milking while you wait, has some advantages. It
makes it unnecessary to sterilize the milk, and adulteration becomes
impracticable. The disadvantage is that, in order to make this method
of milk delivery possible, the cow and the goats must become city
dwellers and live in the same narrow streets with the rest of the population. Whatever may be true of the goat, however, I am sure that
the cow is not naturally adapted to city life, and where, as is true in
many instances, whole families are forced to crowd into one or two
rooms, the cow-stall is likely to be still more crowded. Under these
conditions I am sure that the average cow is going to be neither healthy
nor happy.

For my purposes it is convenient to divide the life of Naples into
three classes. There is the life of the main avenues or boulevards, where
one sees all that is charming in Neapolitan life. The buildings are handsome, streets are filled with carriages, sidewalks are crowded with
handsomely dressed people. Occasionally one sees a barefooted beggar
asleep on the marble steps of some public building. Sometimes one
sees, as I did, a woman toiling up the long street side by side with a
donkey pulling a cart. There are a good many beggars, but even they
are cheerful, and they hold out their hands to you with a roguish
twinkle in their eyes that somehow charms the pennies out of your
pocket.

Then there is the life of the narrower streets, which stretch out in
an intricate network all over the older part of the city. Many of these
streets contain the homes as well as the workshops of the artisan class.
Others are filled with the petty traffic of hucksters and small trades-

men. In one street you may find a long row of push-carts, with fish and vegetables, or strings of cheap meat dangling from cords, surrounded by a crowd, chaffering and gesticulating — Neapolitan bargain-hunters. In another street you will find, intermingled with the little shops, skilled artisans with their benches pushed half into the street, at work at their various tasks. Here you will see a woodcarver at his open doorway, busily engaged in carving out an elegant bit of furniture, while in the back of the shop his wife is likely to be engaged in getting the midday meal. A little farther along you may meet a goldsmith, a worker in iron or in copper. One is making a piece of jewelry, the other is mending a kettle. In these streets one sees, in fact, all the old handicrafts carried on in much the same manner and apparently with the same skill that they were carried on three hundred years ago.

Finally, there are the narrower, darker, dirtier streets which are not picturesque and into which no ordinary traveler ventures. This seldom-visited region was, however, the one in which I was particularly interested, for I had come to Naples to see the people and to see the worst.

In the neighborhood of the hotel where I stayed there was a narrow, winding street which led by a stone staircase from the main thoroughfare up the projecting hillside to one of those dark and obscure alleyways for which Naples, in spite of the improvements which have been made in recent years, is still noted. Near the foot of the stairs there was a bakery, and not far away was the office of the State Lottery. The little street to which I refer is chiefly inhabited by fishermen and casual laborers, who belong to the poorest classes of the city. They are the patrons also of the lottery and the bakery, for there is no part of Naples that is so poor that it does not support the luxury of a lottery; and, I might add, there are few places of business that are carried on in a filthier manner than these bakeries of the poorer classes.

I was passing this place late in the afternoon, when I was surprised to see a huckster — I think he was a fish vender — draw up his wagon at the foot of this stone staircase and begin unhitching his mule. I looked on with some curiosity, because I could not, for the life of me, make out where he was going to put that animal after he had unhitched him. Presently the mule, having been freed from the wagon, turned of his own motion and began clambering up the staircase. I was so interested that I followed.

A little way up the hill the staircase turned into a dark and dirty alleyway, which, however, was crowded with people. Most of them were sitting in their doorways or in the street; some were knitting, some were cooking over little charcoal braziers which were placed out in the street. One family had the table spread in the middle of the road and had just sat down very contentedly to their evening meal. The street was strewn with old bottles, dirty papers, and all manner of trash; at the same time it was filled with sprawling babies and with chickens, not to mention goats and other household appurtenances. The mule, however, was evidently familiar with the situation, and made his way along the street, without creating any surprise or disturbance, to his own home.

I visited several other streets during my stay in Naples which were, if possible, in a worse condition than the one I have described. In a city where every one lives in the streets more than half the time, and where all the intimate business of life is carried on with a frankness and candor of which we in America have no conception, there is little difficulty in seeing how people live. I saw, for example, several cases in which the whole family, to the number of six or seven, lived in a single room, on a dirt floor, without a single window. More than that, this one room, which was in the basement of a large tenement-house, was not as large as the average one-room Negro cabin in the South. In one of these one-room homes I visited there was a blacksmith shop in one part of the room, while the family ate and slept in the other part. The room was so small that I took the trouble to measure it, and found it 8 x 13 feet in size.

Many of these homes of the poorer classes are nothing better than dark and damp cellars. More than once I found in these dark holes sick children and invalid men and women living in a room in which no ray of light entered except through the open door. Sometimes there would be a little candle burning in front of a crucifix beside the bed of the invalid, but this flickering taper, lighting up some pale, wan face, only emphasized the dreary surroundings. It was a constant source of surprise to me that under such conditions these people could be so cheerful, friendly, and apparently contented.

I made some inquiry as to what sort of amusements they had. I found that one of the principal forms of amusement of this class of people is gambling. What seems stranger still, this vice is in Italy a Government monopoly. The State, through its control of the lottery, adds to the other revenue which it extracts from the people not less than five million dollars a year, and this sum comes, for the most part, from the very poorest part of the population.

There are, it seems, something like 1,700 or 1,800 offices scattered through the several large cities of Italy where the people may buy lottery tickets. It seemed to me that the majority of these offices must be in Naples, for in going about the city I saw them almost everywhere, particularly in the poorer quarters.

These lottery offices were so interesting that I determined to visit one myself and learn how the game was played. It seems that there is a drawing every Saturday. Any one may bet whatever amount he chooses that a number somewhere between one and ninety will turn up in the drawing. Five numbers are drawn. If you win, the lottery pays ten to one. You may also bet that any two of the five numbers drawn will turn up in succession. In that case, the bank pays the winner something like fifty to one. You may also bet that three out of five will turn up, and in case you win the bank pays 250 times the amount you bet. Of course the odds are very much against the player, and it is estimated that the State gets about fifty per cent of all the money that is paid in. The art of the game consists, according to popular super-stition, in picking a lucky number. In order to pick a lucky number, however, one must go to a fortune-teller and have one's dreams inter-preted, or one must pick a number according to some striking event, for it is supposed that every event of any importance suggests some lucky number. Of course all this makes the game more interesting and com-plicated, but it is, after all, a very expensive form of amusement for poor people.

From all that I can learn, public sentiment in Italy is rapidly being aroused to the evils which cling to the present system of dealing with the agricultural laborer and the poorer classes. But Italy has not done well by her lower classes in the past. She has oppressed them with heavy taxes; has maintained a land system that has worn out the soil at the same time that it has impoverished the laborer; has left the agricultural laborers in ignorance; has failed to protect them from the rapacity of the large landowners; and has finally driven them to seek their fortunes in a foreign land.

In return, these emigrants have repaid their native country by vastly increasing her foreign commerce, by pouring back into Italy the earn-ings they have made abroad, by themselves returning with new ideas and new ambitions and entering into the work of building up the country.

These returned emigrants have brought back to the mother country improved farming machinery, new methods of labor, and new capital. Italian emigrants abroad not only contribute to their mother country a sum estimated at between five and six million dollars annually, but Italian emigration has awakened Italy to the value of her laboring classes, and in doing this has laid the foundation for the prosperity of the whole country. In fact, Italy is another illustration that the condition of the man at the bottom affects the life of every class above him. It is to the class lowest down that Italy largely owes what prosperity she has as yet attained.

Outlook, 98 (June 10, 1911), 295–300.

A Report of the Health Department
at Tuskegee Institute
by John Andrew Kenney

Tuskegee Institute, Ala. June 10, 1911

Mr. B. T. Washington: The sanitary conditions of the school are improving from year to year, with a consequent improvement in the health of the people. Just now with the excessive heat and drought prevailing, we have only nine patients in the hospital, and two of these are from a distance.

In our school community I know of only two or three cases of minor illness. Several special features are responsible for this condition. First, the old open wells with buckets and chains of four or five years ago, gave place to cement tops, and terra cotta curbing, with pumps, and now these are superseded by artesian wells with a good supply of pure sparkling water. Where sewage ran on top of the ground, exposed to flies etc, it is now carried in deeply laid pipes. The grounds are kept in much better condition, streets are sprinkled and swept, also sinks and garbage cans are cared for daily, garbage frequently removed to a safe distance, and the receptacles disinfected. More buildings are screened against flies, and more forces are at work for sanitary improvements than ever before. The good work so nobly begun should be pushed. More sewers should be laid, and the trunk line extended. The present method of hauling the sewage is inadequate. A sewage disposal plant is necessary. While awaiting the installation of such a plant, the present main sewer should be extended, as the present dumping place is entirely too near.

More flush closets should be installed, so as to do away entirely with the earth closets. They are a constant menace to health.

The increase in our population with consequent congestion, common decency, and the health of our people cry out for the abolishment of these relics of past ages.

Our water system should be extended as rapidly as possible throughout the community. More money should be spent on the improvement, care and keeping of our grounds. If necessary the force should be increased, so as to better care for drains, ditches and swamps, and more rapidly and effectively remove all rubbish and waste.

I regard the flies as the most serious menace to our health at present — far more so than mosquitoes. We are trying to enlist the aid of every individual in our fight against them. Their numerous presence means that our surroundings are not clean. Flies breed in filth. We must spend more time in keeping our premises free from rubbish and accumulations. To help us in this fight, the stables and barns should be removed to a longer distance from our dining rooms, dwellings and dormitories.

HOSPITAL

The good influence of our hospital is extending. During the year aside from the treatment of patients from the school and surrounding communities, we have had several to come to us from Fort Davis, Hardaway, Millers Ferry, Auburn, and Opelika, Ala. Two from La Grange, Ga., four from Denmark, S.C., and one from Savannah, Ga.

We have treated in our hospital 1503 ward patients. Of these five were typhoid fever (Last summer and fall) 22 Tuberculosis, 107 Malaria and 12 pneumonia. Among those we had nine deaths as follows: 1 from Epilepsy, 1 Scalded, 1 Extra Uterine Pregnancy, 3 Pneumonia, 2 Tubercular Peritonitis, and 1 Fibroid tumor; of these, only four were students. The others were outsiders, and two of these were patients under treatment of other physicians. During this time we have operated upon 87 patients, of whom in our own service we have lost only one and she was brought to us from Auburn, Ala., in a desperate condition, and we operated only as a last resort; explaining to the husband at the time that there was little hope. There were two deaths from operations as mentioned above, of the number treated, of patients in the service of other physicians.

It may be of interest to you to know that the large majority of these operations were done with our own hospital force — one interne, and nurses. In a few cases we have called in outside assistance. 16 of these were distinctly major operations for different conditions. The others varying in degree.

In our out-patient and dispensary department we have given 3157 treatments & dressings to patients. By far the greatest number of these were small emergencies and dressings, which gave our nurses excellent opportunities in the care and dressing of injuries, wounds, etc.

NURSE TRAINING SCHOOL

Our Nurse Training School is growing. We have yearly a greater demand for admissions to our school than we can accommodate. This year we have enrolled 41 with an average attendance of 30. At the May Commencement we graduated 12 — 10 females, and 2 males. The average educational standard of the class was fairly good. There being five graduates of Normal Schools, and none below the rank of the B. Middle class in our Academic department. This, compared with the records of most of the training schools will give us a fair standard as to the educational preparation of our graduates.

The demand for graduate nurses is greater than the supply. At the present rate of training colored young women in nursing, it will be many years before the field is even well covered, to say nothing of being overstocked.

The call for our pupil nurses has been greater this year than ever. At one time we had out on private duty nine. They have been employed quite largely in our school community and in the town of Tuskegee; also at Enterprise, Union Springs, and Auburn, Ala., La Grange, Ga., and Cincinnati, Ohio, where one spent 50 days, on a very delicate case, with entire satisfaction to family and physicians. In every instance good reports have come in concerning the work of these young women. Several have brought in with them letters testifying to their good service, and in some instances the persons served have written us letters of commendation concerning the work of our girls.

In nine months they have brought into the hospital nearly $600.00.

It is quite apparent that with more room and better facilities, we could do more in the training of nurses, and treatment of patients. Hundreds of our people throughout this section are in need of such treatment as we can give, and can't get it because of no facilities. Our hospital has already with our limited space been the means of helping a great many, both charity and paying patients.

With our location and opportunity, we should furnish the centre for nurse training and hospital treatment, of colored people for the South. We are attempting more and more by various means to reach the people around us, with the influence of our hospital and nurse training school. This I am sure that we have done to a great extent.

Before the end of another year, we hope to have well on the way, a much needed and well equipped modern hospital, which will facilitate our work, and make it more effective. Very truly,

John A. Kenney

TLS   Con. 429   BTW Papers   DLC.

A Codicil to Washington's Will

[Tuskegee, Ala.] June 13, 1911

I, BOOKER T. WASHINGTON, do hereby make, declare and publish this Codicil number one (1) to my last will and testament, to-wit:

CODICIL NUMBER ONE.

A. I give and devise to my said wife, MARGARET J. WASHINGTON, my summer house and the tract of land on which it is located in the town of Huntington, near Northport, Long Island, New York, to have and to use during the term of her natural life, remainder over after her death to my children, PORTIA WASHINGTON PITTMAN, BOOKER T. WASHINGTON, and ERNEST D. WASHINGTON, equally in fee simple.

B. In the event of the death of my said wife, before or after my death, or of her resignation before the provisions of my will are fully executed, I will that my brother, JOHN H. WASHINGTON, my faithful and true friend, WARREN LOGAN, and my faithful and true friend and secretary, EMMETT J. SCOTT, all of Tuskegee, Alabama, or either two if one should refuse to act, should resign or die, be, and they hereby are, appointed and constituted the executors and trustees under my will and this codicil thereto to carry out and execute the provisions thereof; and they, or such two of them, shall be, as such executors and trustees, invested with all the powers and authority, including powers and duties requiring the exercise of judgment and discretion, which are given to my said wife, except that in making division or distribution among my said children, they shall not divide or distribute in property at valuation fixed by themselves: but they may make division and distribution or advancements to my said three children in property at valuations agreed upon in writing by the three children.

C. If, in the opinion of the executrix, or of the executors, as the case may be, the interests of the estate would best be served by keeping the whole or any part of the estate intact before making any distribution for a period of three years, my executrix, or, as the case may be, my executors, has, or have, authority to keep the estate or any portion of it intact for that period after my death.

D. If any one of the persons whom this will is intended to benefit shall resist its probate, or petition to break or set it aside, or enter a contest, or in any way cause unnecessary expense to the executrix or executors, all costs and all expenses incurred thereby, including all attorneys' fees and all counsel fees, are to be deducted from the amount or property which said person to be benefitted would otherwise have received under my will.

IN TESTIMONY WHEREOF, I have hereunto set my hand and seal in the presence of the witnesses whose names as such appear subscribed below, who sign their names hereto as witnesses in my presence and in the presence of each other on this the   day of *June 13,* 1911.

Booker T. Washington (L.S.)

Attesting Witnesses
Chas H. Gibson
J. B. Ramsey
J. H. Palmer

State of Alabama
Macon County
} I, M. B. Abercrombie, Judge of Probate, in and for the county and state aforesaid, hereby certify that the above and foregoing instrument in writing was duly proved and admitted to

Probate in this Court as the last Will and Testament and codicil of *Booker T. Washington,* deceased, and recorded, together with the Proof, in Book *18* of Wills and Appraisements record *18* on the *220 et seq.* page thereof.   This the *22* day of *Nov 1915*

> *M B Abercrombie*
> Judge of Probate.

TDS   Office of Judge of Probate, Macon County, Ala. This was the codicil to the will dated May 25, 1909, above, 10:112–16.

To Charles Dean Washington[1]

[Tuskegee, Ala.] June 13, 1911

Charles D. Washington: I think it must be clear to you now that you made a mistake in permitting yourself to go out into the country Saturday night and be among those who consumed a keg of beer. This within itself was against the policy and wishes of the school, but one of the most hurtful elements in the whole matter consisted in the fact that teachers so far forget themselves as to take a student with them and place themselves on equality with the student both in the drinking and in general association.

This was not only an injustice to the student but an injustice to the whole teaching body.

I very much hope that this note will be all that is necessary to make it certain that no such conduct on your part will take place in the future.

In addition to what I have already stated, it is reported that you are often at Doggett's place of business and there is a strong suspicion and report in the community that you and a few others drink while there. If there is any truth in this report, I hope in the future there will be no such conduct going on in the community.

Booker T. Washington

P.S. I think you are especially blameable because all the evidence shows that you were the most active person, if not the leader in connection with the whole affair.

B. T. W.

TLpS   Con. 617   BTW Papers   DLC.

[1] After his graduation from Tuskegee Institute in 1906, BTW's nephew Charles Dean Washington attended Leonard Medical School of Shaw University, graduating in 1910. He returned to Tuskegee, but BTW advised him to leave town and start over elsewhere. (BTW to C. D. Washington, Aug. 14, 1910, Con. 596, BTW Papers, DLC.) In the summer of 1911 he moved to Decatur, Ala., studying for the Georgia medical examination under Dr. Willis E. Sterrs. BTW described him to Sterrs as "a bright fellow, but he is a little inclined to waste his time and to be a little wild and careless." (June 13, 1911, Con. 440, BTW Papers, DLC.) Sterrs reported his young protegé out too late at night and not serious about his work. (Sterrs to BTW, July 24, 1911, and C. D. Washington to BTW, July 27, 1911, Con. 439, BTW Papers, DLC.) In 1912 C. D. Washington continued his studies at Meharry Medical College. (C. D. Washington to BTW, Nov. 19, 1912, Con. 467, BTW Papers, DLC.)

To J. I. Doggett

[Tuskegee, Ala.] June 13, 1911

Mr. Doggett: I repeat what I said to you Sunday, that your action in connection with the drinking of the beer in the country Saturday night is against the policy of the school.

While we have no direct control over you, you do live in the community and I feel that you are interested in seeing that we have a good, clean, law-abiding community. Further than this, it is reported that you are in the habit of having certain people assemble at your shop for the purpose of drinking. If this is true, I very much hope you will see that t[he] habit is broken up. The school cannot countenance anything but what is right and clean in this community, and I hope th[at] there will be no further cause for me to make complaint regarding this matter.

Booker T. Washington

TLpS   Con. 610   BTW Papers   DLC.

From William Henry Lewis

Washington D C   6/14–11

Confirmed   many thanks   am very happy.

W. H. Lewis

HWSr   Con. 428   BTW Papers   DLC.

From William Edwin Chilton

United States Senate [ca. June 14, 1911]

My dear Sir: I presume that you have heard of the confirmation by the Senate of your friend Lewis.

We can not tell tales out of school, but your interest in the matter was very potential and I congratulate you. Very Truly Yours,

W. E. Chilton

ALS   Con. 428   BTW Papers   DLC.

Extracts from an Address at Wilberforce University[1]

Xenia, [Ohio] June 15 [1911]

We must remember that the forces of nature draw no color line. Sunshine and rain are as helpful to the black hand that tills and owns the soil as the white hand that tills and owns the soil. The history of the civilization of the world teaches that the people who own the soil are the people that are going to grow in independence, grow in education, grow in moral and religious strength.

There are millions of acres of land in the South that can be purchased for cotton raising, for trucking, for dairying and for fruit growing. There are millions of acres from which coal and iron can be gotten, from which lumber can be manufactured. All these are possibilities within the reach of the humblest black man in America.

I know of no one influence, no one element that would add more to the independence and the progress of the 9,000,000 of negroes in the South than for us to have within the next 20 years 100,000 to 200,000 more intelligent, successful, independent farmers scattered throughout this country; and these farmers should not be composed of the ignorant element of our race, but should be composed of the educated element of our race.

Our vision need not be limited to owning and cultivating the soil. There are great opportunities in the direction of manufacturing. Within the past 20 years the cotton manufacturing center of the country has moved from New England into North Carolina and South Carolina. It is not necessary for the negro to confine himself to the mere matter of cotton raising. He can advocate cotton manufacture in some form.

Great Consumer of Cotton Goods

The negro, both in this and other countries, is a great consumer of cotton goods. On a small scale, at least, he can become a manufacturer of cotton goods. Here is another field for the energetic, capable, pushing, educated colored man. Heretofore, in too large a degree, our educated men have felt that they must either teach or preach, and not enter the fields of commerce.

The South is full of the best lumber suited for the manufacture of all kinds of furniture. The lumber, in its use, is as free to the colored man as to the white man. We are great consumers of household furniture. Why should not our educated men begin to manufacture furniture? If we could manufacture one-tenth of the household furniture that we, as a race, consume, we would give employment to thousands of our men and women and add immensely to our wealth, improvement and usefulness.

If we do not want to go into either agriculture or manufacturing there is a vast field open for the educated colored man in the direction of merchandising. With such a field open as we have in the direction of commerce in the South, there is no reason why any intelligent, energetic and educated colored man need go about looking for a job. He can create a job for himself, and when one creates one's own job he gets into a position of power and independence, and is not dependent upon the whims of political parties or color prejudice. There are places in the South for 5000 additional dry goods stores and there are colored people enough to support these dry goods stores.

No Prejudice in Business

In the South the negro merchant is not dependent upon the trade of his own race alone, but throughout the South, while there is prejudice in other directions, in business the negro has little prejudice to contend with along this line. Not only the colored man trades at the colored man's dry goods store, but the best white people are not afraid to patronize a first-class dry goods store, and the same thing is true of other business enterprises owned and controlled by colored people.

There are openings in the South for at least 8000 additional grocery stores, for 3500 additional drug stores. There are openings in the South for 2000 shoe stores, 2000 millinery stores and there are communities in the South where 2000 additional negro banks can be opened and supported. Further than this, there are places in the South where at least 75 self-governing, self-supporting and self-directing towns or cities may be established where the colored people can have their own mayor, their own board of alderman, their own self-government from every point of view. In the last analysis, local self-government is the most precious kind of self-government.

If none of these openings suit the ambition of our educated colored men and women, there is another field that is ripe for the harvest, that of education. There are a million and a half negro children of school age who do not enter any school in the South and there are hundreds of thousands of others who are in school only three months out of the 12 months. We need 30,000 additional school houses built in the South, and we need, at least, 20,000 additional negro school teachers.

Still Further Openings

But if the vision of the educated colored man cannot be realized in any of the callings to which I have referred there are still further openings in the South. I refer to the opportunities in professional directions. There are individual locations in the South for at least 2500 additional doctors and 2000 additional pharmacists, 2000 additional dentists and 1000 veterinary surgeons.

In the line of religious activities I want the young colored men and women to see the vision aside from the opportunities to preach the gospel. Wherever in any community there are 2500 or more colored people they are capable of supporting a Y.M.C.A. building. There are 56 cities in the country, at least, where Y.M.C.A. buildings could be established and supported.

We must not become discouraged by racial relations. True, we have prejudice to contend with in the South as elsewhere. The color line is often unjustly drawn throughout the country. We have to endure injustice, we have to contend with injustice, but instead of letting prejudice discourage us, we should use it as a spur to urge us on to higher effort, to renewed enterprise. All races that have achieved success have come up through ownership of the soil, through cultivating the soil, through manufacture, through merchandise, through making themselves strong in education and in moral and religious directions, and lastly, they have come up through fighting prejudice. Out of the fight they have gained a strength and an experience that they would not have gotten except for racial prejudice. When we are inclined to grow despondent or discouraged, let us compare the present with the past, let us compare the meager and circumscribed opportunities which surrounded a man like Bishop Daniel A. Payne with these we enjoy in America.

PRAISES PRESIDENT TAFT

Who, in this audience, would have thought that within less than 50 years after our race became free that the time would come when we would have a president of the United States who was strong and brave, and wise enough to appoint a colored man to the position of assistant attorney general of the United States; who would have thought that within so short a period of time we would have produced a colored man who in education and refinement and culture was capable of filling such a position, and yet we have found within less than 50 years in President William Howard Taft a president who was capable of making the appointment and in the person of William Henry Lewis we have found the colored man capable of filling the position. When such occurrences take place within so short a period, who will dare be so shortsighted and faithless as to grow discouraged? Truly we are living in an era when old men shall dream dreams and young men shall see visions.

Columbus *Ohio State Journal,* June 16, 1911, 3.

1 The occasion was the centenary of Bishop Daniel A. Payne and the Wilberforce commencement exercises. The same extract, with the word *Negro* capitalized, appeared in the *Tuskegee Student,* 23 (July 1, 1911), 1, 2.

To Emmet O'Neal

Tuskegee Institute, Alabama   June 17, 1911

Dear Sir: Rev. A. F. Owens, one of our instructors, will deliver to your mansion some peaches and butter produced on our farm by student labor. I very much hope that you and Mrs. O'Neal will accept these samples with our compliments.

I have been talking the matter over with Representative Merritt and sometime in the future, when you are not so busy, we shall hope to have you visit our school.

It was my privilege to know your father[1] when he was Governor and I remember his many acts of kindness both to me as an individual and to our race. Yours very truly,

Booker T. Washington

TLS   Official Governors' Papers   A-Ar.

1 Edward Asbury O'Neal.

An Article in *Outlook*

June 17, 1911

CHILD LABOR AND THE SULPHUR MINES

There is one street in Catania, Sicily, which seems to be given over to the trade and industry of the poorer people of the city. It is not mentioned in the guide-books, and there is perhaps no reason why it should be. Nevertheless, there are a great many interesting things to be seen in that street — strange, quaint, homely things — that give a stranger intimate glimpses into the life of the people.

For example, on a street corner, tucked away in one of those snug spaces in which one sometimes finds a crowded fruit-stand, I discovered, one day, a macaroni factory. Within a space perhaps three feet wide and ten or twelve feet in length one man and a boy conducted the whole business of the sale as well as the manufacture of macaroni from the raw grain to the completed article of trade. The process, as it was carried on in this narrow space, was necessarily a simple one. There was a bag of flour, a box in which to mix the paste, and a press by which this paste was forced through holes that converted it into hollow tubes. Afterwards these hollow tubes were laid out on a cloth frame which, because there was no room inside, had been set up in the street. After leaving this cloth frame the macaroni was hung up on little wooden forms for inspection and for sale.

One of the most curious and interesting places on the street was an apothecary's shop in which the apothecary manufactured all his own drugs, and acted at the same time as the poor man's physician or medical adviser. This man had never studied pharmacy in a college. His knowledge of drugs consisted entirely of the traditions and trade secrets which had come down to him from his predecessor in the business. His shop was filled with sweet-smelling herbs, gathered for him by the peasants, and from these he brewed his medicines. The skeleton of a fish hung over the counter from which medicines were dispensed, and the shelves behind were filled with many curious and musty bottles.

The apothecary himself was a very serious person, with a high, pale forehead and the absorbed air of a man who feels the weight of the knowledge he carries around with him. All these things, especially the smell of the herbs, were quite awe-inspiring, and undoubtedly contributed something to the effectiveness of the medicines.

It is a very busy street in which the apothecary, the macaroni manufacturer, and the others are located. In fact, it seems as if work never stopped there, for it is full of little shops where men sit in their doorways or at the open windows until late at night, working steadily at their various trades, making the things they sell, and stopping only now and then to sell the things they make. The whole region is a hive of industry, for it is the neighborhood where the artisans live, those skilled workmen who make everything by hand that, in our part of the world, we have long since learned to make by machine. In fact, in this street it is possible to get a very good picture, I suspect, of the way in which trade and industry were carried on in other parts of Europe before the age of steam.

About nine o'clock Saturday night — the night upon which I arrived in Catania — I was walking down one of the side streets in this part of the city, when my attention was attracted to a man, sitting in his doorway, working by the light of a little smoky lamp. He was engaged in some delicate sort of iron work, and, as near as I could make out, he seemed to be a tool-maker.

What particularly attracted my attention was a little girl, certainly not more than seven years of age, who was busily engaged in polishing and sharpening the stamps he used. I stopped for a moment and watched this man and child, working steadily, silently, at this late hour of the night. I could but marvel at the patience and the skill the child showed at her work. It was the first time in my life that I had seen such a very little child at work, although I saw many others in the days that followed.

I have often heard it said that people who are born under the soft southern skies are habitually indolent, and never learn to work there, as they do in more northern latitudes. This is certainly not true of Sicily, for, so far as my experience goes, there is no other country in Europe where incessant labor is so largely the lot of the masses of the people. Certainly there is no other country where so much of the labor of all kinds, the skilled labor of the artisan as well as the rough labor of digging and carrying on the streets and in the mines, is performed by children, especially boys.

There is a law against Sunday labor in Catania, but the next morning, as I passed through this same quarter of the city, I found the majority of the people still busily at work. I stopped to watch a man who was making mandolins. This man lived in one room, which was at the same time a workshop, kitchen, and bedroom. There was a great heap of mattresses piled high upon the bed in one corner. A little charcoal brazier, on which the cooking for the family was performed, stood upon the work-bench. The ceiling was hung with finished instruments, and the pavement in front of the house was piled with others in various stages of completion. This room was occupied by a family of five, all of whom, with the exception of the wife and mother, were engaged, each in their different ways, in the work of manufacturing mandolins.

All the skilled work (the setting of the decorations and the polishing of the frames) was performed by the boys, but a little girl who was standing near seemed to be making herself handy as a helper in the work of the others.

In this treeless country, where there is almost no wood of any kind to be had, the most useful building material, after stone and plaster, seems to be tile. Not only the roofs but the floors of most of the buildings are made of this material, and its manufacture is consequently one of the principal minor industries of the country. One day, while I was wandering about in the outskirts of Catania, I ran across a plant where two men and three little boys were at work mixing the clay, forming it into octagonal shapes, and piling it out in the sun to dry. The two men were at work in the shade of a large open shed, but I could not make out what they were doing. As nearly as I could see, almost all of the actual work was performed by the children, who ranged, I should say, from eight to twelve years of age. The work of carrying the heavy clay, and piling it up in the sun after it had been formed into tiles, was done by the younger children.

I am certain that if I had not seen them with my own eyes I would never have believed that such very little children could carry such heavy loads, or that they could work so systematically and steadily as they were compelled to do in order to keep pace with the rapid movements of the older boy, who was molding the tiles from the soft clay. The older boy could not have been, as I have said, more than twelve years of age, but he worked with all the skill and the rapidity of an experienced piece-worker driven at the top of his speed. I was so filled with pity and at the same time with admiration for this boy that, as I was unable to speak to him, I ventured to offer him a small coin in token of my appreciation of the skill with which he worked. So intent was he on his task, however, that he would not stop his work even to pick up the money I proffered him, but simply thanked me and nodded his head for me to place it on the bench beside him.

These instances of skilled labor among children are by no means exceptional. At another time I remember stopping to look at a little boy who, it seemed to me, could not be more than eight or nine years of age, working side by side with a man, evidently his father, together with several other men, all of them engaged in building a boat. The boy I speak of was engaged in finishing off with a plane the hardwood rail of the sides of the boat, and as I watched him at his task I was again compelled to wonder at the ease and skill with which these little fellows use their tools.

All these things, as I have said, gave me an idea of the manner in which the trades were carried on before the extensive use of machinery had brought the factory system into existence. It showed me also the easy way in which, in those days, the industrial education of children was carried on. When the work in the handicrafts was performed in the house, or in a shop adjoining the house, it was an easy thing for the father to hand down to the son the trade he himself had practiced. Under the conditions in which trades are carried on in Sicily to-day children are literally born to the trade which their fathers practice. In these homes, where the shop and the home are crowded together in one or two rooms, children see their fathers and mothers at work from the time they are born. As soon as they are able to handle a tool of any kind the boys, at any rate, and frequently the girls also, are set to work helping their parents. As the father, in his turn, has probably inherited the accumulated traditions and skill of generations that preceded him in the same trade, his children are able to get from him, in the easiest and most natural way, an industrial education such as no other kind of school can give.

Whatever may be the disadvantages of the people of Sicily in other respects, they have an advantage over the Negro in learning the skilled trades, the value of which it is difficult to estimate. Everywhere one sees the evidences of this skill with the hand, not only in the public buildings, but in some of the common objects of daily use. I have already referred to the way in which the ordinary little two-wheeled carts, which take the place of the ordinary farmer's wagon in this country, are decorated. I have seen in Catania men at work practically hewing these carts out of the log. I do not know to what extent the frame of the wagon is hewn out in this way, but, at any rate, the spokes are. Every detail is worked out with the greatest possible skill, even to the point of carving little figures or faces at the ends of the beams that make the frames. Likewise the harness of the donkeys that draw these carts is an elaborate and picturesque affair which must require a vast amount of patience and skill to make. The point I wish particularly to emphasize here is that all this skill in the handicrafts, which has become traditional in a people, is the best kind of preparation for every kind of higher education. In this respect the Italian, like the Japanese and Chinese, as well as every other race which has had centuries of training in the handicrafts, has an advantage over the Negro that can only be overcome when the masses of the Negro people have secured a training of the hand and a skill in the crafts that correspond to those of other races.

Not only are children, especially boys, employed at a very early age in all the trades I have mentioned, but young boys from fourteen to sixteen perform, as I have said, in the mines and elsewhere an incredible amount of the crude, rough work of the community.

I remember, one day in Palermo, seeing, for the first time in my life, boys, who were certainly not more than fourteen years of age, engaged in carrying on their backs earth from a cellar that was being excavated for a building. Men did the work of digging, but the mere drudgery of carrying the earth from the bottom of the excavation to the surface was performed by these boys. It was not simply the fact that mere children were engaged in this heavy work that impressed me. It was the slow, dragging steps, the fixed and unalterable expression of weariness that showed in every line of their bodies. Later I learned to recognize this as the habitual manner and expression of the *carusi,* which is the name that the Italians give to those boys who are employed in the sulphur mines to carry the crude ore up from the mines where it is dug and to load it in the cars by which it is conveyed to the surface.

The work in a sulphur mine is organized in many respects, I learned, like that of a coal mine. The actual work of digging the sulphur is performed by the miner, who is paid by the amount of crude ore he succeeds in getting out. He, in his turn, has a man or a boy, sometimes two or three of them, to assist him in getting the ore out of the mine to the smelter, where it is melted and refined. As I myself had had some experience as a boy in work similar to this in the mines of West Virginia, I was interested in learning all I could in regard to these boys and the conditions under which they worked.

In the case of boys employed for this work, the Sicilians have a custom of binding out their children to the miner, or *picconiero,* as he is called. Such a boy is then called, in the language of the country, a *caruso.* As a matter of fact, a *picconiero* who buys a boy from his parents to employ him as a *caruso* actually purchases a slave. The manner in which the purchase is made is as follows: In Sicily, where the masses of the people are so wretchedly poor in everything else, they are nevertheless especially rich in children, and, as often happens, the family that has the largest number of mouths to fill has the least to put in them. It is from these families that the *carusi* are recruited. The father who turns his child over to a miner receives in return a sum of money in the form of a loan. The sum usually amounts to from eight to thirty dollars, according to the age of the boy, his strength and general usefulness. With the payment of this sum the child is turned over absolutely to his master. From this slavery there is no hope of freedom, because neither the parents nor the child will ever have sufficient money to repay the original loan.

Strange and terrible stories are told about the way in which these boy slaves have been treated by their masters. Before coming to Sicily I had met and talked with persons who described to me the processions of half-naked boys, their bodies bowed under the heavy weight of the loads they carried, groaning and cursing as they made their way up out of the hot and sulphurous holes in the earth, as they carried the ore from the mine to the smelter. All that I had heard elsewhere was confirmed later by the details furnished by official reports and special studies of conditions in the mining regions, made at different times and by different persons. In these reports I learned that the mines had been in the past the refuge of a debased and criminal population, whose vices made the bleak, sulphur-smitten region where the mines are located as much like hell as it looks.

The cruelties to which the child slaves have been subjected, as related by those who have studied them, are as bad as anything that was ever reported of the cruelties of Negro slavery. These boy slaves were frequently beaten and pinched, in order to wring from their over-burdened bodies the last drop of strength they had in them. When beatings did not suffice, it was the custom to singe the calves of their legs with lanterns to put them again on their feet. If they sought to escape from this slavery in flight, they were captured and beaten, sometimes even killed.

As they climbed out of the hot and poisonous atmosphere of the mines their bodies, naked to the waist and dripping with sweat, were chilled by the cold draughts in the corridors leading out of the mines, and this sudden transition was the frequent cause of pneumonia and tuberculosis.

In former years children of six and seven years of age were employed at these crushing and terrible tasks. Under the heavy burdens (averaging about forty pounds) they were compelled to carry, they often became deformed, and the number of cases of curvature of the spine and deformations of the bones of the chest reported was very large. More than that, these children were frequently made the victims of the lust and unnatural vices of their masters. It is not surprising, therefore, that they early gained the appearance of gray old men, and that it has become a common saying that a *caruso* rarely reaches the age of twenty-five.

It was with something of all this in my mind that I set out from Palermo a little before daylight one morning in September to visit the mines at Campo Franco, on the southern side of the island, in the neighborhood of Girgenti. My misgivings were considerably increased when, upon reaching the railway station to take the train, I found that the guide and interpreter who had been employed the night before to accompany us on the trip had not made his appearance. We waited until all the porters at the station and the guards on the train were fairly in a fever of excitement in their well-meant efforts to get us and our baggage on the train. Then, at the last moment, with the feeling that we were taking a desperate chance, we scrambled aboard and started off into a wild unknown, which no guide-book had charted and, so far as I knew, no tourist had ever visited.

The train carried us for some distance along the fertile plain between the sea and the hills. It was just possible to make out in the twilight of the early morning the dim outlines of the little towns we passed. At length, just as we were able to catch the first gleams of the morning sun along the crests of the mountains, the railway turned abruptly southward and the train plunged into a wide valley between the brown and barren hills.

At Rocca Palomba we left the main line of the railway, which turns eastward from there in the direction of Catania, and continued our journey with the somewhat ruder comforts of an accommodation train. From this point on the way grew rougher, the country wilder, and the only companions of our journey were the rude country folk, with an occasional sprinkling of miners. At the little town of Lercara we entered the zone of the sulphur mines. From now on at nearly every station we passed I saw great masses of the bright yellow substance, piled in cars, waiting to be carried down to the port of Girgenti for shipment to all parts of the world, and particularly to the United States, which is still the largest market for this Sicilian gold.

The nearer the train approached our destination, the more uncomfortable I grew about the prospect that was before us. I felt very sure that I should be able to reach Campo Franco and perhaps see something of the mines, but whether I should ever be able to get out again and what would become of me if I were compelled to seek shelter in some of the unpromising places I saw along the way was very uncertain.

Fortunately, Dr. Robert E. Park, of Boston, who was traveling with me, and who accompanied me on nearly all of my excursions of this kind, was with me on this trip. Dr. Park had a pretty thorough mastery of the German language, and could speak a little French, but no Italian. He had, however, an Italian grammar in his satchel, and when we finally found ourselves at sea, in a region where neither English, German, nor French was of any help to us, he took that grammar from his satchel and set to work to learn enough Italian between Palermo and Campo Franco to be able to make at least our most urgent wants known. For four hours he devoted himself industriously to the study of that beautiful and necessary language. It was a desperate case, and I think I am safe in saying that Dr. Park studied grammar more industriously during those four hours than he ever did before in his life. At any rate, by the time the train had crossed the rocky crest of the mountains which divide the north and south sides of Sicily, and before we disembarked at the lonesome little station of Campo Franco, he could speak enough Italian, mixed with German, French, and English, to make himself understood. Perhaps another reason for Dr. Park's success was the fact that the Italians understand the sign language pretty well.

The mines at Campo Franco are on the slope of the mountain, just above the railway station. A mile or more across the great empty valley, high up on the slope of the opposite mountain, is the village from which the mines get their name, a little cluster of low stone and cement buildings, clinging to the mountain-side as if they were in imminent danger of slipping into the valley below.

A few hundred yards above the station great banks of refuse had been dumped into the valley, and a place leveled off on the side of the mountain, where the furnaces and smelters were located. There were great rows of kilns, like great pots, half buried in the earth, in which the ore is melted and then run off into forms where it is cooled and allowed to harden.

I confess that I had been very dubious as to the way that we were likely to be received at the mines, seeing that we did not know the customs nor the people, and had very scant supply of Italian in which to make known our wants. The manager, however, who proved to be a very polite and dignified man, could speak a little French and some English. He seemed to take a real pleasure in showing us about the works. He explained the methods by which the sulphur was extracted, insisted upon our drinking a glass of wine, and was even kind enough to loan me a horse and guide, when I expressed a desire to rent one of the passing donkeys to convey me to some of the more inaccessible places, farther up the mountain, where I could see the miners had burrowed into the earth in search of sulphur. On the vast slope of the mountain and at a distance they looked like ants running in and out of little holes in the earth.

It was at the mouth of one of these entrances to the mines that I got my first definite notion of what sulphur miners look like — those unfortunate creatures who wear out their lives amid the poisonous fumes and the furnace heat of these underground hells. There was a rumble of a car, and presently a man, almost stark naked, stepped out of the dark passageway. He was worn, haggard, and gray, and his skin had a peculiar grayish-white tinge. He spoke in a husky whisper, but I do not know whether that is one of the characteristic effects of the work in the mines or not. I was told that, in addition to other dangers, the sulphur has a bad effect upon the lungs. It was explained to me that the sulphur dust gets into the lungs and clogs them up, and that is what accounts for the groans of the *carusi*, so frequently spoken of, when they are tugging up the steep and winding passageways with the heavy burdens of crude ore on their backs.

It had been many years since I had been in a mine, but as I entered the dark, damp gallery and felt the sudden underground chill, the memories of my early experiences all came back to me. As we got farther into the mine, however, the air seemed to grow warmer. Suddenly a door at the side of the gallery opened; a blast of hot air, like that from a furnace, burst out into the corridor, and another of those half-naked men, dripping with perspiration, stepped out.

We passed at intervals along the main corridor a number of these doors, which, as I discovered, led down into parts of the mine where the men were at work. It seemed incredible to me that any one could live and work in such heat, but I had come there to see what a sulphur mine was like, so I determined to try the experiment.

The side passage which I entered was, in fact, little more than a burrow, twisting and winding its way, but going constantly deeper and deeper into the dark depths of the earth. I had known what it was to work deep down under the earth, but I never before so thoroughly realized what it meant to be in the bowels of the earth, as I did while I was groping my way through the dark and winding passages of this sulphur mine.

It is down at the bottom of these holes, and in this steaming atmosphere, that the miners work. They loosen the ore from the walls of the seams in which it is found, and then it is carried up out of these holes in sacks by the *carusi*.

In the mine which I visited the work of getting the ore to the surface was performed in a modern and comparatively humane way. It was simply necessary to carry the ore from the different points where it is mined to the car, by which it is then transported to the smelter. In those mines, however, where the work is still carried on in the old, traditional fashion, which has been in vogue as far back as any one can remember, all the ore is carried on the backs of boys. In cases where the mine descended to the depth of two, three, or four hundred feet the task of carrying these loads of ore to the surface is simply heartbreaking. I can well understand that persons who have seen conditions at the worst should speak of the children who have been condemned to this slavery as the most unhappy creatures on earth.

From all that I can learn, however, the conditions have changed for the better in recent years. In 1902 a law was passed which forbade the employment of children under thirteen years in underground work, and to this was added, a little later, a provision which forbade, after 1905, the employment of children under fifteen in the mines.

So far as I am able to say, this provision was carried out in the mine I visited, for I did not see anywhere inside the mine children at work. I saw a number of the poor little creatures at work in the dumps outside the mine, however. They were carrying refuse ore in bags on their backs, throwing it on screens, and then loading the finer particles back into the cars. Once having seen these gangs of boys at work, I could never mistake their slow, dragging movements and the expression of dull despair upon their faces.

It is said that the employment of boys in the sulphur mines is decreasing. According to law, the employment of children under fifteen years of age has been forbidden since 1905. As is well known, however, in Italy as in America it is much easier to make laws than to enforce them. This is especially true in Sicily. The only figures which I have been able to obtain upon the subject show that from 1880 to 1898 there was an enormous increase in the number of children employed in and about the mines. In 1880 there were 2,419 children under fifteen years working there, among whom were eight girls. Of this number 88 were seven and 163 were eight years of age, while twelve per cent of the whole number were under nine years of age. In 1898, however, the number of children under fifteen years of age was 7,032, of whom 5,232 were at work inside the mines. At this time the Government had already attempted to put some restrictions on the employment of children in the mines, but the age limit had not been fixed as high as fifteen years.

The sulphur mines are located on the southern slopes of the mountains that cross Sicily from east to west. About ten miles below Campo Franco the two branches of the railway, one running directly south from Rocca Palomba, and the other running southwest from Caltanisetta, come together a few miles above Girgenti. On the slopes of the broad valleys through which these two branches of the railway run are located nearly all the sulphur mines in Sicily. From these mines, which furnish something like seventy per cent of the world's supply of sulphur, a constant stream of this yellow ore flows down to the sea at the port of Girgenti.

After leaving Campo Franco I traveled through this whole region. In many places the mountain slopes are fairly honeycombed with holes, where the miners in years past have dug their way into the mountain in search of the precious yellow mineral. For many miles in every direction the vegetation has been blasted by the poisonous smoke and vapors from the smelters, and the whole country has a blotched and scrofulous appearance which is depressing to look upon, particularly when one considers the amount of misery and the number of human lives it has cost to create this condition. I have never in my life seen any place that seemed to come so near meeting the description of the "abomination of desolation" referred to in the Bible. There is even a certain grandeur in the desolation of this country which looks as if the curse of God rested upon it.

I am not prepared just now to say to what extent I believe in a physical hell in the next world, but a sulphur mine in Sicily is about the nearest thing to a hell that is conceivable in my opinion. In the mine to which I went I found the heat, the sulphur, and the people; with these three elements there seemed nothing lacking to constitute a hell.

As I have already said, however, there are indications that in the sulphur mines, as elsewhere in Sicily, the situation of the man farthest down is improving. I pray God that it is so, for I could not picture an existence more miserable than the slow torture of this crushing labor in the hot and poisonous air of these sulphur mines.

Let me say also that I came away from the sulphur mines and from Sicily with a very much better opinion of the people than when I entered. I went to Italy with the notion that the Sicilians were a race of brigands, a sullen and irritable people who were disposed at any moment to be swept off their feet by violent and murderous passions. I came away with the feeling that, whatever might be the faults of the masses of the people, they were, at the very least, more sinned against than sinning, and that they deserve the sympathy rather than the condemnation of the world.

The truth is that, as far as my personal experience goes, I was never treated more kindly in my whole life than I was the day when, coming as a stranger, without an introduction of any kind, I ventured to visit the region which has the reputation of being the most wicked, and is certainly the most unfortunate, in Europe. I mean the region around and north of Girgenti, which is the seat at once of the sulphur mines and the Mafia.

If any one had told me before I went to Sicily that I would be willing to intrust my life to Sicilians away down in the darkness of a sulphur mine, I should have believed that such a person had lost his mind. I had read and heard so much of murders, of the Mafia in Sicily, that for a long time I had had a horror of the name of Sicilians; but when I came in contact with them, before I knew it, I found myself trusting them absolutely to such an extent that I willingly followed them into the bowels of the earth; into a hot, narrow, dark sulphur mine where, without a moment's warning, they might have demanded my life or held me, if they cared to, for a ransom. Nothing of this kind occurred; on the other hand, I repeat, every Sicilian with whom I came in contact in the sulphur mine treated me in the most kindly manner, and I came away from their country having the highest respect for them.

I did not meet while I was there a single person, from the superintendent to the lowest laborer at the mines, who did not seem, not only willing, but even anxious, to assist me to see and learn everything I wanted to know. What is more, Campo Franco was the only place in Europe where I met men who refused to accept money for a service rendered me.

Outlook, 98 (June 17, 1911), 342–49.

From Emmet O'Neal

Montgomery June 19th, 1911

My dear Sir: The peaches and butter delivered by Rev. A. F. Owens, one of your instructors, were duly received, and on behalf of myself and wife I wish to tender you my sincere thanks for your kind consideration. In flavor and quality the peaches and butter could not be excelled.

It will give me great pleasure, some time in the future when my official duties are not so exacting, to visit your school. I am deeply interested in the great work you are doing, and it will be both a duty and a pleasure to make a personal inspection of your institution.

I recall that my father always spoke of you in the very highest terms, and I sincerely trust that I can, as the present Governor of the State, aid you in your work. Very truly yours,

Emmet O'Neal

TLS Con. 431 BTW Papers DLC.

From Henry Watson Furniss

Port-au-Prince, Haiti. June 19, 1911

Personal and Confidential.

My dear Dr. Washington: Under date of the 16th instant I received a telegram from the Department of State informing me that, in view of important questions now pending between the United States and

Haiti, and the increase of American interests here, the President had decided to withhold his acceptance of my resignation and desired me to retain my post until the end of the present administration.

I replied by thanking both the President and the Department for this expression of confidence and said that the President's desire would be acquiesced in.

As to the reasons causing the President to change his mind you are probably better informed than I am. Personally I exerted no influence whatever in my behalf. I understand, though, that practically all the American interests in Haiti used their influence to prevent a change and that numerous others either fought a change or fought the one intended to supplant me which practically amounted to the same thing.

My brother informs me that you were very active in my support for which I thank you very much. I hope I shall always merit your support and esteem and feel highly complimented in having it.

Now that I am to continue to be our representative in Haiti, I again extend to you and yours an invitation to be my guest. Present conditions in Haiti make it more necessary that a man of your prominence should be thoroughly acquainted with the country than was the case when I first extended you an invitation.

Mrs. Furniss joins me in sending kind regards to Mrs. Washington and in wishing you both good health and prosperity. Sincerely yours,

H. W. Furniss

TLS Con. 422 BTW Papers DLC.

To Susan Helen Porter

Fort Salonga, N.Y. June 26th, 1911

Dear Miss Porter: We shall have to be increasingly careful at Tuskegee to get rid of every student who is not promising. We must be patient with the students, give them time to overcome their faults and defects, but after exercising patience with them and they do not respond we must get rid of them at once. We cannot afford to carry dead weight upon our rolls when there are so many worthy students wanting to enter. I am afraid that in the past we have carried too much of such material too long. Yours very truly,

[Booker T. Washington]

TLc   Con. 616   BTW Papers   DLC.

An Article in *World's Work*

June 1911

How Denmark Has Taught Itself Prosperity and Happiness

The Rural High Schools Which Have Made Over a Nation

On the railway train, between Copenhagen, Denmark, and Hamburg, Germany, I fell into conversation with an English traveler who had been in many parts of the world and who, like myself, was returning from a visit of observation and study in Denmark. We exchanged travelers' experiences with each other. I found that he had had opportunity to study conditions in that country a great deal more thoroughly than was true in my case and he gave me much information that I was glad to have about the condition of agriculture and the life of the people.

In return I told him something of the places I had visited before going to Denmark and of the way I had attempted to dig down, here and there in different parts of Europe, beneath the crust and see what was going on in the lower strata of social life. I said to him, finally, that, after all I had seen, I had come to the conclusion that the happiest country in Europe, perhaps the happiest country in the world, is Denmark. Then I asked him if he knew any part of the world where the people seemed to come so near to solving all their problems as in Denmark.

He seemed a little startled and a little amused at that way of putting the matter but, after considering the question, he confessed that he had never visited any other part of the world that seemed to be in a more generally healthy and wholesome condition than this same little country which we were just leaving behind us.

Denmark is not rich in the sense that England and the United States are rich. I do not know what the statisticians say about the matter, but I suppose that in Denmark there are few if any such great fortunes as one finds in England, in the United States, and in many parts of Europe. In fact, there is hardly room enough in this little land for a multi-millionaire to move about in, as it is less than one-third the size of the state of Alabama, although it has one-third more population.

Denmark is an agricultural country. About two-fifths of the whole population are engaged in some form or other of agriculture. The farms in Denmark have been wonderfully prosperous in recent years. I doubt, however, whether as much money has been made or can be made in Denmark as has been made on the farms in the best agricultural districts in America. The soil is not particularly rich. A large section of the country is, or has been until recent years, made up of barren heath like that in northern Scotland. Within the past few years, as a result of one of the most remarkable pieces of agricultural engineering that has ever been attempted, large tracts of this waste have been made over into fruitful farm land.

In spite of disadvantages, however, the country has greatly prospered for a number of years past. People have been coming from all over the world to study Danish agriculture and they have gone away marvelling at the results. I am not going to try to tell in detail what these results were or in what manner they have been obtained. I will merely say that it seems to be generally conceded that, both in the methods of culture and in the marketing of the crops, Denmark has gone farther and made greater progress than any other part of the world. Furthermore, there is no country, I am certain, not even the United States or Canada, where the average farmer stands so high or exercises so large an influence upon political and social life as he does in Denmark at the present time.

"What's back of the Danish farmer?" I said to my English friend. "What is it that has made agriculture in this country?"

"It's the Danish schools," he replied.

I had asked the same question before and received various replies, but they all wound up with a reference to the schools, particularly the country high schools. I had heard much of them in America; I heard of them again in England; for 90 per cent. of Denmark's agricultural exports goes to England.

It was not, however, until I reached Denmark, saw the schools themselves, and talked with some of the teachers — not, in fact, until after I had left Denmark and had an opportunity to look into and study their history and organization, that I began to comprehend the part that the rural high schools were playing in the life of the masses of the Danish people, and to understand the manner in which they had influenced and helped to build up the agriculture of the country.

There are two things about these rural high schools that were of peculiar interest to me. First, they have had their origin in a movement to help the common people, and to lift the level of the masses, particularly in the rural district; second, they have succeeded. I venture to say that in no part of the world is the general average intelligence of the farming class higher than it is in Denmark. I was impressed in my visits to the homes of some of the small farmers by the number of papers and magazines to be found in their homes.

In recent years there has sprung up in many parts of Europe, a movement to improve the condition of the working masses through education. Wherever any effort has been made on a large scale to improve agriculture, it has almost invariably taken the form of a school of some sort or other. For example, in Hungary, the state has organized technical education in agriculture on a grand scale. Nowhere in Europe, I learned, has there been such far reaching effort to improve agriculture through experimental and research stations, agricultural colleges, high schools, and common schools. There is this difference, however; Hungary has tried to improve agriculture by starting at the top, creating a body of teachers and experts who are expected in turn to influence and direct the classes below them. Denmark has begun at the bottom.

One of the principal aims of the Hungarian Government, as appears from a report by the Minister of Agriculture, was "to adapt the education to the needs of the different classes and take care, at the same time, that these different classes did not learn too much, did not learn anything that would unfit them for their station in life."

I notice, for example, that it was necessary to close the agricultural school at Debreczen, which was conducted in connection with an agricultural college at the same place, because, as the report of the

Minister of Agriculture states, "the pupils of this school, being in daily contact with the first year pupils of the college, attempted to imitate their ways, wanted more than was necessary for their social position and at the same time aimed at a position they were unable to maintain."

All this is in striking contrast to the spirit and method of the Danish rural high school, which started among the poorest farming class, and has grown, year by year, until it has drawn within its influence nearly all the classes in the rural community. In this school it happens that the daughters of the peasant and of the nobleman sometimes sit together on the same bench, and that the sons of the landlord and of the tenant frequently work and study side by side, sharing the personal friendship of their teacher and not infrequently the hospitality of his home.

The most striking thing about the rural high school in Denmark is that it is neither a technical nor an industrial school and, although it was created primarily for the peasant people, the subject of agriculture is almost never mentioned at least not with the purpose of giving practical or technical education in that subject.

It may seem strange that, in a school for farmers, nothing should be said about agriculture, and I confess that it took some time for me to see the connection between this sort of school and Denmark's agricultural prosperity. It seemed to me, as I am sure it will seem to most other persons, that the simplest and most direct way to apply education to agriculture was to teach agriculture in the schools.

The real difference between the Hungarian and the Danish methods of dealing with this problem is, however, in the spirit rather than in the form. In Hungary the purpose of the schools seems to be to give each individual such training as it is believed will fit him for the particular occupation which his station in life assigns him, and no more. The government decides. In other words, education is founded on a system of caste. If the man below learns in school to look to the man in station above him, if he begins to dream and hope for something better than the life to which he has been accustomed — then, a social and political principle is violated, and, as the Commissioner of Agriculture says, "the Government is not deterred from issuing energetic orders."

Of course, the natural result of such measures is to increase the discontent. Just as soon as any class of people feel that privileges granted to others are denied to them, immediately these privileges — whether they be the opportunities for education, or anything else — assume in the eyes of the people to whom they are denied, a new importance and value.

The result of this policy is seen in emigration statistics. I doubt, from what I have been able to learn, whether all the efforts made by the Hungarian Government in the way of agricultural instruction have done very much to allay the discontent among the masses of the farming population. Thousands of these Hungarian peasants every year still prefer to try their fortune in America, and the steady exodus of the farming population continues.

The rural high school in Denmark has pursued just the opposite policy. It has steadily sought to stimulate the ambitions and the intellectual life of the peasant people. Instead, however, of compelling the ambitious farmer's boy, who wants to know something about the world, to go to America, to the ordinary college, or to the city, the schools have brought the learning of the colleges and the advantages of the city to the country.

The most interesting and remarkable thing about these high schools is the success that they have had in presenting every subject that an educated man should know about in such a form as will make it intelligible and interesting to country boys and girls who have only had, perhaps, the rudiments of a common school education.

The teachers in these country high schools are genuine scholars. They have to be, for the reason that the greater part of their teaching is in the form of lectures without text books of any kind, and their success depends upon the skill with which they can present their subjects. In order to awaken interest and enthusiasm, they have to go to the sources for their knowledge.

Most of the teachers whom I met could speak two or three languages. I was surprised at the knowledge which everyone I met in Denmark, from the King and Queen to the peasants, displayed in American affairs, and the interest they showed in the progress of the Negro and the work we have been doing at Tuskegee. As an illustration of the wide interests which occupy the teachers in these rural schools, I found one of them engaged in translating Prof. William James's book on Pragmatism into the Danish language.

I have heard it said repeatedly since I was in Denmark that the

Danish people as a whole were better educated and better informed than any other people in Europe. Statistics seem to bear out this statement; for, according to the immigration figures of 1900, although 24.2 per cent. of all persons over fourteen years of age coming into the United States as immigrants, could neither read nor write, only .8 per cent. of the immigrants from Scandinavia were illiterate. Of the Germans, among whom I had always supposed education was more widely diffused than elsewhere in Europe, 5.8 per cent. were illiterate.

Before I go further, perhaps, I ought to give some idea of what these rural high schools look like. One of the most famous of them is situated about an hour's ride from Copenhagen, near the little city of Roskilde. It stands on a piece of rolling ground, overlooking a bay, where the little fisher vessels and small seafaring craft are able to come far inland, almost to the centre of the island. All around are wide stretches of rich farm land, dotted here and there with little country villages.

There is, as I remember, one large building with a wing at either end. In one of these wings, the head master of the school lives, and in the other is a gymnasium. In between are the school rooms where the lectures are held. Everything about the school is arranged in a neat and orderly manner — simple, clean, and sweet — and I was especially impressed by the wholesome, homelike atmosphere of the place. Teachers and pupils eat together at the same table and meet together in a social way in the evening. Teachers and students are thus not merely friends, they are in a certain sense, comrades.

In the school at Roskilde there are usually about one hundred and fifty students. During the winter term of five months, the young men are in school; in the summer the young women take their turn. Pupils pay for board and lodging twenty crowns, a little more than five dollars a month, and for tuition, twenty crowns the first month, fifteen the second, ten the third, five the fourth, and nothing the fifth. These figures are themselves an indication of the thrift as well as the simplicity with which these schools are conducted. Twenty years ago, when they were first started, I was told the pupils used to sleep together, in a great sleeping room on straw mattresses and eat with wooden spoons out of a common dish, just as the peasant people did at that time. This reminds me that just about this same time, at Tuskegee, pupils were having similar hardships. For one thing, I recall that, in those days, the food for the whole school was cooked in one large iron kettle and that sometimes we had to skip a meal because there wasn't anything to put in the kettle. Since that time, conditions have changed, not only in the rural high schools of Denmark, but among the country people. At the present day, if not every peasant cottage, at least every coöperative dairy has its shower-bath. The small farmer, who, a few years ago looked upon every innovation with mistrust, is likely now to have his own telephone — for Denmark has more telephones to the number of the population than does any other country in Europe — and every country village has its gymnasium and its assembly hall for public lectures.

I have before me, on my desk, a school plan showing the manner in which the day is disposed of. School begins at eight o'clock in the morning and ends at seven o'clock in the evening, with two hours' rest at noon. Two-thirds of the time of the school is devoted to instruction in the Danish mother-tongue and in history. The rest is given to arithmetic, geography, and the natural sciences.

It is peculiar to these schools that most of the instruction is given in the form of lectures. There are no examinations and few recitations. Not only the natural sciences, but even the higher mathematics are taught historically, by lectures. The purpose is not to give the student training in the use of these sciences, but to give him a general insight into the manner in which different problems have arisen and of the way in which the solution of them has widened and increased our knowledge of the world.

In the Danish rural high school, emphasis is put upon the folk songs, upon Danish history and the old Northern mythology. The purpose is to emphasize, in opposition to the Latin and Greek teaching of the colleges, the value of the history and the culture of the Scandinavian people, and, incidentally, to instill into the minds of the pupils the patriotic conviction that they have a place and mission of their own among the people of the world.

There are several striking things about this system of rural high schools, of which there are now 120 in Denmark. The first thing about them that impressed me was the circumstances in which they had their origin. In the beginning the rural high schools were a private undertaking, as indeed they are still, although they get a certain amount of support from the State. The whole scheme was worked out by a few courageous individuals, who were sometimes opposed, but frequently assisted by the Government. The point which I wish to emphasize is that they did not spring into existence all at once, but that they grew up slowly and are still growing. It took long years of struggles to formulate and popularize the plans and methods which are now in use in these schools. In this work the leading figure was a Lutheran bishop, Nicolai Frederik Severen Grundvig,[1] who is often referred to as the Luther of Denmark. The rural school movement grew out of a nonsectarian religious movement and was, in fact, an attempt to revive the spiritual life of the masses of the people.

Rural high schools were established as early as 1844, but it was not until twenty years later, when Denmark, as a result of her disastrous war with Prussia, had lost one-third of her richest territory, that the rural high school movement began to gain ground. It was at that time, when affairs were at their lowest ebb in Denmark, that Grundvig began preaching to the Danish people the gospel that what had been lost without, must be regained within; and that what had been lost in battle must be gained in peaceful development of the national resources.

Bishop Grundvig saw that the greatest national resources of Denmark, as it is of any country, was its common people. The schools he started and the methods of education he planned were adapted to the needs of the masses. They were an attempt to popularize learning, put it in simple language, rob it of its mystery and make it the common property of the common people.

Another thing peculiar about these schools is that they were not for children, but for older students. Eighty per cent. of the students in the rural high schools are from eighteen to twenty-five years of age; 12 per cent. are more than twenty-five years of age and only 8 per cent. are under eighteen. These schools, are, in fact, farmers' colleges. They presuppose the education of the common school. The farmer's son and the farmer's daughter, before they enter the rural high school, have had their training in the public schools and have had practical schooling in the work of the farm and the home. At just about the age when a boy or a girl begins to think about leaving home and of striking out in the world for himself; just at the age when there comes, if ever, to a youth the desire to know something about the larger world and about all the mysteries and secrets that are buried away in books or handed down as traditions in the schools — just at this time the boys and girls are sent away to spend two seasons or more in a rural high school. As a rule they go, not to the school in their neighborhood, but to some other part of the country. There they make the acquaintance of other young men and women who, like themselves, have come directly from the farms, and this intercourse and acquaintance helps to give them a sense of common interest and to build up what the socialists call a "class consciousness." All of this experience becomes important a little later in the building up of the coöperative societies, coöperative dairies, coöperative slaughter houses, societies for the production and sale of eggs, for cattle raising and for other purposes.

The present organization of agriculture in Denmark is indirectly but still very largely due to the influence of the rural school.

The rural high school came into existence, as I have said, as the result of a religious rather than of a merely social or economic movement. Different in methods and in outward form as these high schools are from the industrial schools for the Negro in America, they have this in common, that they are non-sectarian, but in the broadest deepest sense of that word, religious. They seek, not merely to broaden the minds, but to raise and strengthen the moral life of masses of the people. This peculiar character of the Danish rural high school was defined to me in one word by a gentleman I met in Denmark. He called them "inspirational."

It is said of Grundvig that he was one of those who did not look for salvation merely in political freedom. In spite of this fact, the rural high schools have had a large influence upon politics in Denmark. It is due to them, although they have carefully abstained from any kind of political agitation, that Denmark, under the influence of its "Peasant Ministry," has become the most democratic country in Europe. It is certainly a striking illustration of the result of this education that what, a comparatively few years ago, was the lowest and the most oppressed class in Denmark, namely the small farmer, has become the controlling power in the State, as seems to be the case at the present time.

I have gone to some length to describe the plans and general character of the rural high schools because they are the earliest, the most peculiar and unusual feature in Danish rural life and education, and because, although conducted in the same spirit, they are different in form and methods from the industrial schools with which I have been mainly interested during the greater part of my life.

The high schools, however, are only one part of the Danish system of rural schools. In recent years there has grown up side by side with the rural high school another type of school for the technical training in agriculture and in the household arts. For example, not more than half a mile from the rural high school which I visited at Roskilde, there has recently been erected what we in America would call an industrial school, where scientific agriculture, as well as technical training in homekeeping are given. In this school, young men and women get much the same practical training that is given our students at Tuskegee, with the exception that this training is confined to agriculture and housekeeping. Besides, there is, in these agricultural schools, no attempt to give students a general education, as is the case with the industrial schools in the South. In fact, schools like Hampton and Tuskegee are trying to do for their students at one and the same time, what is done in Denmark through two distinct types of school.

I found this school, like its neighbor the high school, admirably situated, surrounded by beautiful gardens in which the students raised their own vegetables. In the kitchen, the young women learned to prepare the meals and to set the tables. I was interested to see also that, in the whole organization of the school, there was an attempt to preserve the simplicity of country life. In the furniture, for example, there was an attempt to preserve the solid simplicity and quaint artistic shapes with which the wealthier peasants of fifty or a hundred years ago furnished their homes. Dr. Robert E. Park, my companion on my trip through Europe, told me when I visited this school that he found one of the professors at work in the garden wearing the wooden shoes that used to be worn everywhere in the country by the peasant people. This man had traveled widely, had studied in Germany where he had taken a degree in his particular specialty at one of the agricultural colleges.

Perhaps the most interesting and instructive part of my visit was the time that I spent at what is called a husmand's or cotter's school, located at Ringsted and founded by N. J. Nielsen-Klodskov in 1902. At this school I saw such an exhibition of vegetables, grains, and especially of apples, as I think I had never seen before, certainly, not at any agricultural school.

I wish I had opportunity to describe in detail all that I saw and learned about education and the possibilities of country life in the course of my visit to this interesting school. What impressed me most with regard to it and to the others that I visited, was the way in which the different types of schools in Denmark have succeeded in working into practical harmony with one another; the way also, in which each in its separate way had united with the other to uplift, vivify, and inspire the life and work of the country people.

For example, the school at Ringsted, in addition to the winter course in farming for men and the summer school in household arts for women, offers, just as we do at Tuskegee, a short course to which the older people are invited. The courses are divided between the men and the women, the men's course coming in the winter and the women's course in the summer. During the period of instruction, which lasts eleven days, these older people live in the school, just as the younger students do and gain thus the benefit of an intimate association with each other and with their teachers. To illustrate to what extent this school and the others like it, have reached and touched the people, I will quote from a letter written to me by the founder. He says: "The Koerehave Husmandskole (cotter's school) is the first of its kind in Denmark. It is a private undertaking and the buildings erected since 1902 are worth about 400,000 crowns ($100,000). During the seven years in which it has been in operation 631 men and 603 women have had training for six months. In addition, 3,205 men and women have attended the eleven day courses."

In addition to the short courses in agriculture and housekeeping, offered by the school at Ringsted, some of the rural high schools hold, every fall, great public assemblies like our Chautauquas, which last from a few days to a week and are attended by men and women of the rural districts. At these meetings there are public lectures on historical, literary, and religious subjects. In the evening there is music, singing, and dancing, and other forms of amusement. These annual assemblies, held under the direction of the rural high schools, have largely taken the place of the former annual harvest home festivals in which there was much eating and drinking, as I understand, but very little that was educational or uplifting. In addition to these yearly meetings, which draw together people from a distance, there are monthly meetings which are held either in the high school buildings, or in the village assembly buildings, or in the halls connected with the village gymnasiums. In the cities these meetings are sometimes held in the "High School Homes," as they are called, which serve the double purpose of places for the meetings of young men and young women's societies and at the same time as cheap and home-like hotels for the traveling country people.

In this way the rural high schools have extended their influence to every part of the country, making the life on the farm attractive, and enabling Denmark to set before the world an example of what a simple, wholesome, and beautiful country life can be.

No doubt there are in the country life of Denmark, as of other countries, some things that cast a shadow here and there on the bright picture I have drawn. New problems always spring up out of the solution of the old ones. No matter how much has been accomplished those who know conditions best will inevitably feel that their work has just been begun. However that may be, I do not believe there will be found anywhere a better illustration of the possibilities of education than in the results achieved by the rural schools of Denmark.

One of the things that one hears a great deal of talk about in America is the relative value of cultural and vocational education. I do not think that I clearly understood until I went to Denmark what a "cultural" education was. I had gotten the idea, from what I had seen of the so-called "cultural" education in America, that culture was always associated with Greek and Latin, and that people who advocated it believed there was some mysterious, almost magical power which was to be gotten from the study of books, or from the study of something ancient and foreign, far from the common and ordinary experiences of men. I found, in Denmark, schools in which almost no text books are used, which were more exclusively cultural than any I had ever seen or heard of.

I had gotten the impression that what we ordinarily called culture was something for the few people who are able to go to college, and that it was somehow bottled up and sealed in abstract language and in phrases which it took long years of study to master. I found in Denmark real scholars engaged in teaching ordinary country people, making it their peculiar business to strip the learning of the colleges of all that was technical and abstract and giving it, through the medium of the common speech, to the common people.

Cultural education has usually been associated in my mind with the

learning of some foreign language, with learning the history and traditions of some other people. I found in Denmark a kind of education
which, although as far as it went, touched every subject and every land
that it was the business of the educated man to know about, sought
especially to inspire an interest and enthusiasm in the art, the traditions,
the language, and the history of Denmark and in the people by whom
the students were surrounded. I saw that a cultural education could
be and should be a kind of education that helps to awaken, enlighten,
and inspire interest, enthusiasm, and faith in one's self, in one's race,
and in mankind; that it need not be, as it sometimes has been in Denmark and elsewhere, a kind of education that robs its pupils of their
natural independence, makes them feel that something distant, foreign,
and mysterious is better and higher than what is familiar and close
at hand.

I have never been especially interested in discussing the question of
the particular label that should be attached to any form of education;
I have never taken much interest, for example, in discussing whether
the form of education which we have been giving our students at Tuskegee was cultural, vocational, or both. I have been only interested in
seeing that it was the kind that was needed by the masses of the people
we were trying to reach, and that the work was done as well as possible under the circumstances. From what I have learned in Denmark,
I have discovered that what has been done, for example, by Dr. R. H.
Boyd in teaching the Negro people to buy Negro instead of white dolls
for their children, "in order," as Dr. Boyd says, "to teach the children
to admire and respect their own type"; that what has been done at
Fisk University to inspire in the Negro a love of folk-songs; that what
has been done at Tuskegee in our annual Negro Conferences, and in
our National Business League, to awaken an interest and enthusiasm
in the masses of the people for the common life and progress of the
race has done more good, and, in the true sense of the word, been
more cultural than all the Greek and Latin that have ever been studied
by all Negroes in all the colleges in the country.

For culture of this kind spreads over more ground; it touches more
people and touches them more deeply. My study of the Danish rural
schools has not only taught me what may be done to inspire and foster
a national and racial spirit, but it has shown how closely interwoven
are the moral and material conditions of the people, so that each man

247

responds to and reflects the progress of every other man in a way to bring about a healthful, wholesome condition of national and racial life.

World's Work, 22 (June 1911), 14486–94.

1 Nikolai Frederik Severin Grundtvig (1783–1872).

An Article in *Outlook*

July 1, 1911

THE WOMEN WHO WORK IN EUROPE

Several times during my stay in London I observed, standing on a corner in one of the most crowded parts of the city, a young woman selling papers. There are a good many women, young and old, who sell papers in London, but any one could see at a glance that this girl was different. There was something in her voice and manner which impressed me, because it seemed to be at once timid, ingratiating, and a little insolent, if that is not too strong a word. This young woman was, as I soon learned, a Suffragette, and she was selling newspapers — "Votes for Women."

This was my first meeting with the women insurgents of England. A day or two later, however, I happened to fall in with a number of these Suffragette newspaper-sellers. One of them, in a lively and amusing fashion, was relating the story of the morning's happenings. I could hardly help hearing what she said, and soon became very much interested in the conversation. In fact, I soon found myself so entertained by the bright and witty accounts these young women gave of their adventures that it was not long before I began to enter with them into the spirit of their crusade and to realize for the first time in my life what a glorious and exciting thing it was to be a Suffragette, and, I might add, what a lot of fun these young women were having out of it.

It had not occurred to me, when I set out from America to make the acquaintance of the man farthest down, that I should find myself in any way concerned with the woman problem. I had not been in London more than a few days, however, before I discovered that the woman who is at the bottom in London life is just as interesting as the man in the same level of life, and perhaps a more deserving object of study and observation.

In a certain way all that I saw of the condition of women at the bottom connected itself in my mind with the agitation that is going on with regard to woman at the top.

Except in England, the women's movement has not, so far as I was able to learn, penetrated to any extent into the lower strata of life, and that strikes me as one of the interesting facts about the movement. It shows to what extent the interests, hopes, and ambitions of modern life have, or rather have not, entered into and become a force in the lives of the people at the bottom.

Thus it came about that my interest in all that I saw of working-women in Europe was tinged with the thought of what was going to happen when the present agitation for the emancipation and the wider freedom of women generally should reach and influence the women farthest down.

In my journey through Europe I was interested in each of the different countries I visited, in certain definite and characteristic things. In London, for example, it was some of the destructive effects of a highly organized and complicated city life, and the methods which the Government and organized philanthropy have employed to correct them, that attracted my attention. Elsewhere it was chiefly the condition of the agricultural populations that interested me. In all my observation and study, however, I found that the facts which I had learned about the condition of women tended to set themselves off and assume a special importance in my mind. It is for that reason that I propose to give, as well as I am able, a connected account of them at this point.

What impressed me particularly in London were the extent and effects of the drinking habit among women of the lower classes. Until I went to London I do not believe that I had more than once or twice in my life seen women standing side by side with the men in order to drink at a public bar. One of the first things I noticed in London was the number of drunken, loafing women that are passed in the streets of the poorer quarters. More than once I ran across these drunken and besotted creatures, with red, blotched faces, which told of years of steady excess — ragged, dirty, and disorderly in their clothing — leaning tipsily against the outside of a gin-parlor or sleeping peacefully on the pavement of an alleyway.

In certain parts of London the bar-room seems to be the general meeting-place of men and women alike. There, in the evening, neighbors gather and gossip while they drink their black, bitter beer. It is against the law for parents to take their children into the bar-rooms, but I have frequently observed women standing about the door of the tap-room with their babies in their arms, leisurely chatting while they sipped their beer. In such cases they frequently give the lees of their glass to the children to drink.

In America we usually think of a bar-room as a sort of men's club, and, if women go into such a place at all, they are let in surreptitiously at the "family entrance." Among the poorer classes in England the bar-room is quite as much the woman's club as it is the man's. The light, the warmth, and the free and friendly gossip of these places make them attractive, too, and I can understand that the people in these densely populated quarters of the city, many of them living in one or two crowded little rooms, should be drawn to these places by the desire for a little human comfort and social intercourse.

In this respect the bar-rooms in the poorer parts of London are like the beer halls that one meets on the Continent. There is, however, this difference — that the effect of drink upon the people of England seems to be more destructive than it is in the case of the people on the Continent. It is not that the English people as a whole consume more intoxicating drink than the people elsewhere, because the statistics show that Denmark leads the rest of Europe in the amount of spirits, just as Belgium leads in the amount of beer consumed per capita of the population. One trouble seems to be that, under the English industrial system, the people take greater chances, they are subject to greater stress and strain, and this leads to irregularities and to excessive drinking.

While I was in Vienna I went out one Sunday evening to the Prater, the great public park, which seems to be a sort of combination of Central Park in New York and Coney Island. In this park one may see all types of Austrian life, from the highest to the lowest. Sunday seems, however, to be the day of the common people, and the night I visited the place there were, in addition to the ordinary laboring people of the city, hundreds, perhaps thousands, of peasant people from the country there. They were mostly young men and women who had evidently come into the city for the Sunday holiday. Beside the sober, modern dress of the city crowds these peasant women, with their high boots, the bright-colored kerchiefs over their heads, and their wide, flaring, voluminous skirts (something like those of a female circus-rider, only a little longer and not so gauzy), made a strange and picturesque appearance.

Meanwhile there was a great flare of music of a certain sort; and a multitude of catchpenny shows, mountebanks, music halls, theaters, merry-go-rounds, and dancing pavilions gave the place the appearance of a stupendous county fair. I do not think that I ever saw anywhere, except at a picnic or a barbecue among the Negroes of the Southern States, people who gave themselves up so frankly and with such entire zest to the simple, physical sort of enjoyment. Everywhere there were eating, drinking, and dancing, but nevertheless I saw no disorder, very few people who seemed to be the worse for drinking, and in no instance did I see people who showed, in the disorder of their dress or in the blotched appearance of their faces, the effects of continued excesses, such as one sees in so many parts of London. The people were, for the most part, neatly and cleanly dressed, each class of people seemed to have its own place of amusement and its own code of manners, and every one seemed to keep easily and naturally within the restraints which custom prescribed.

I do not mean to say that I approve of this way of spending the Sabbath. I simply desire to point out the fact, which others have noticed, that the effect of the drinking habit seems to be quite different in England from what it is in countries on the Continent.

I had an opportunity to observe the evil effects of the drinking habit upon the Englishwomen of the lower classes when I visited some of the police courts in the poorer parts of London. When I remarked to a newspaper acquaintance in London that I wanted to see as much as I could, while I was in the city, of the life of the poorer people, he advised me to visit the Worship Street and Thames police stations. The Worship Street station is situated in one of the most crowded parts of London, in close proximity to Bethnal Green and Spitalfields, which have for many years been the homes of the poorer working classes, and especially of those poor people known as houseworkers and casuals, who live in garrets and make paper boxes, artificial flowers, etc., or pick up such odd jobs as they can find. The Thames station is situated

a little way from London Dock and not far from the notorious Rat-
cliffe Highway, which until a few years ago was the roughest and most
dangerous part of London.

Perhaps I ought to say, at the outset, that two things in regard to
the London police courts especially impressed me: first, the order and
dignity with which the court is conducted; second, the care with which
the judge inquires into all the facts of every case he tries, the anxiety
which he shows to secure the rights of the defendant, and the leniency
with which those found guilty are treated. In many cases, particularly
those in which men or women were charged with drunkenness, the
prisoners were allowed to go with little more than a mild and fatherly
reprimand.

After listening for several hours to the various cases that came up
for hearing, I could well understand that the police have sometimes
complained that their efforts to put down crime were not supported
by the magistrates, who, they say, always take the side of the culprits.

In this connection I might mention a statement which I ran across
recently of a man who had served at one time as a magistrate in both
the Worship Street and Thames police courts. He said that there was
a great deal of drunkenness among certain of the factory girls of East
London, although they were seldom arrested and brought into court
for that offense.

He added: "It must not be forgotten that the number of convictions
for drunkenness is not by any means a proper measure of insobriety.
If a policeman sees a drunken man conducting himself quietly or sleeping in a doorway, he passes on and takes no notice. Those who are
convicted belong, as a rule, to the disorderly classes, who, the moment
liquor rises to their heads, manifest their natural propensities by ob-
streperous and riotous conduct. For one drunkard of this order there
must be fifty who behave quietly and always manage to reach their
homes, however zigzag may be their journey thither."

That statement was made a number of years ago, but I am convinced that it holds good now, because I noticed that most of the
persons arrested and brought into court, especially women, were blood-
stained and badly battered.

In the majority of these cases, as I have said, the persons were allowed to go with a reprimand or a small fine. The only case in which,
it seemed to me, the judge showed a disposition to be severe was in

that of a poor woman who was accused of begging. She was a pale, emaciated, and entirely wretched appearing little woman, and the charge against her was that of going through the streets, leading one of her children by the hand, asking for alms because she and her children were starving. I learned from talking with the officer who investigated the case that the statement she made was very likely true. He had known her for some time, and she was in a very sad condition. But then, it seems, the law required that in such circumstances she should have gone to the workhouse.

I think that there were as many as fifteen or twenty women brought into court on each of the mornings I visited the court. Most of them were arrested for quarreling and fighting, and nearly all of them showed in their bloated faces and in their disorderly appearance that steady and besotted drunkenness was at the bottom of their trouble.

I have found since I returned from Europe that the extent of drunkenness among Englishwomen has frequently been a matter of observation and comment. Richard Grant White, in his volume "England Within and Without," says:

> I was struck with horror at the besotted condition of so many of the women — who were bearing children every year, and suckling them, and who seemed to me little better than foul human stills through which the accursed liquor with which they were soaked filtered drop by drop into the little drunkards at their breasts. To these children drunkenness comes unconsciously, like their mother tongue. They cannot remember a time when it was new to them. They come out of the cloudland of infancy with the impression that drunkenness is one of the normal conditions of man, like hunger and sleep.

This was written thirty years ago. It is said that conditions have greatly improved in recent years in respect to the amount of drunkenness among the poor of London. Nevertheless, I notice in the last volume of the "Annual Charities Register" for London the statement that inebriety seems to be increasing among women, and that it prevails to such an alarming extent among women in all ranks of society that "national action is becoming essential for the nation's very existence."

The statistics of London crime show that, while only about half as many women as men are arrested on the charges of "simple drunkenness" and "drunkenness with aggravations," more than three times as many women as men are arrested on the charge of "habitual" drunkenness. Another thing that impressed me was that the American police courts deal much more severely with women. This is certainly true in the Southern States, where almost all the women brought before the police courts are Negroes.

The class of people to whom I have referred represent, as a matter of course, the lowest and most degraded among the working classes. Nevertheless, they represent a very large element in the population, and the very existence of this hopeless class, which constitute the dregs of life in the large cities, is an indication of the hardship and bitterness of the struggle for existence in the classes above them.

I have attempted in what I have already said to indicate the situation of the women at the bottom in the complex life of the largest and, if I may say so, the most civilized city in the world, where women are just now clamoring for all the rights and privileges of men. But there are parts of Europe where, as far as I have been able to learn, women have as yet never heard that they had any rights or interests in life separate and distinct from those of their husbands and children. I have already referred to the increasing number of barefoot women I met as I journeyed southward from Berlin. At first these were for the most part women who worked in the fields. But by the time I reached Vienna I found that it was no uncommon thing to meet barefoot women in the most crowded and fashionable parts of the city.

Experience in traveling had taught me that the wearing of shoes is a pretty accurate indication of civilization. The fact that in a large part of Southern Europe women who come from the country districts have not yet reached the point where they feel comfortable in shoes is an indication of the backwardness of the people.

What interested and surprised me more than the increasing absence of shoes among the countrywomen was the increasing number of women whom I saw engaged in rough and unskilled labor of every kind. I had never seen Negro women doing the sort of work I saw the women of Southern Europe doing. When I reached Prague, for example, I noticed a load of coal going through the streets. A man was driving it, but women were standing up behind with shovels. I learned that it was the custom to employ women to load and unload the coal and carry it into the houses. The driving and the shoveling were done by the man, but the dirtiest and the hardest part of the work was performed by the women.

In Vienna I saw hundreds of women at work as helpers in the construction of buildings; they mixed the mortar, loaded it in tubs, placed it on their heads, and carried it up two or three stories to men at work on the walls. The women who engage in this sort of labor wear little round mats on their heads, which support the burdens which they carry. Some of these women are still young, simply grown girls, fresh from the country, but the majority of them looked like old women.

Not infrequently I ran across women hauling carts through the streets. Sometimes there would be a dog harnessed to the cart beside them. That, for example, is the way in which the countrywomen sometimes bring their garden truck to market. More often, however, they will be seen bringing their garden products to market in big baskets on their heads or swung over their shoulders. I remember, while I was in Budapest, that, in returning to my hotel rather late one night, I passed through an open square near the market, where there were hundreds of these market women asleep on the sidewalks or in the street. Some of them had thrown down a truss of straw on the pavement under their wagons and gone to sleep there. Others, who had brought their produce into town from the country on their backs, had in many cases merely put their baskets on the sidewalk, lain down, thrown a portion of their skirts up over their heads, and gone to sleep. At this hour the city was still wide awake. From a near-by beer hall there came the sounds of music and occasional shouts of laughter. Meanwhile people were passing and re-passing in the street and on the sidewalk, but they paid no more attention to these sleeping women than they would if they had been horses or cows.

In other parts of Austria-Hungary I ran across women engaged in various sorts of rough and unskilled labor. While I was in Cracow, in Austrian Poland, I saw women at work in the stone quarries. The men were blasting out the rock, but the women were assisting them in removing the earth and in loading the wagons. At the same time I saw women working in brick-yards. The men made the brick, the women acted as helpers. While I was in Cracow one of the most interesting places I visited in which women are employed was a cement factory. The man in charge was kind enough to permit me to go through the works, and explained the process of crushing and burning the stone used in the manufacture of cement. A large part of the rough work in this cement factory is done by girls. The work of loading the kilns is performed by them. Very stolid, heavy, and dirty looking creatures they were. They had none of the freshness and health that I noticed so frequently among the girls at work in the fields.

While I was studying the different kinds of work which women are doing in Austria-Hungary I was reminded of the complaint that I had heard sometimes from women in America, that they were denied their rights in respect to labor, that men in America wanted to keep women in the house, tied down to household duties.

In Southern Europe, at any rate, there does not seem to be any disposition to keep women tied up in the houses. Apparently they are permitted to do any kind of labor that men are permitted to do; and they do, in fact, perform a great many kinds of labor that we in America think fit only for men. I noticed, moreover, as a rule, that it was only the rough, unskilled labor which was allotted to them. If women worked in the stone quarries, men did the part of the work that required skill. Men used the tools, did the work of blasting the rock. If women worked on the buildings, they did only the roughest and cheapest kinds of work. I did not see any women laying brick, nor did I see anywhere women carpenters or stone-masons.

In America Negro women and children are employed very largely at harvest time in the cotton-fields, but I never saw in America, as I have seen in Austria, women employed as section hands on a railway, or digging sewers, hauling coal, carrying the hod, or doing the rough work in brick-yards, kilns, and cement factories.

In the Southern States of America the lowest form of unskilled labor is that of the men who are employed on what is known as public works; that is to say, the digging of sewers, building of railways, and so forth. I was greatly surprised, while I was in Vienna, to see women engaged side by side with men in digging a sewer. This was such a novel sight to me that I stopped to watch these women handle the pick and shovel. They were, for the most part, young women, of that heavy, stolid type I have referred to. I watched them for some time, and I could not see but that they did their work as rapidly and as easily as the men beside them. After this I came to the conclusion that there was not anything a man could do which a woman could not do also.

In Poland the women apparently do most of the work on the farms. Many of the men have gone to Vienna to seek their fortune. Many, also, have gone to the cities, and still others are in the army, because on the Continent every able-bodied man must serve in the army. The result is that more and more of the work that was formerly performed by men is now done by women.

One of the most interesting sights I met in Europe was the market in Cracow. This market is a large open square in the very center of the ancient city. In this square is situated the ancient Cloth Hall, a magnificent old building which dates back to the Middle Ages, when it was used as a place for the exhibition of merchandise, principally textiles of various kinds. On the four sides of this square are some of the principal buildings of the city, including the City Hall and the Church of the Virgin Mary, from the tall tower of which the hours are sounded by the melodious notes of a bugle.

On market days this whole square is crowded with hundreds, perhaps thousands, of market women who come in from the country in the early morning with their produce, remain until it is sold, and then return to their homes.

In this market one may see offered for sale anything and everything that the peasant people produce in their homes or on the farms. Among other things for sale I noted the following: geese, chickens, bread, cheese, potatoes, salads, fruits of various sorts, mushrooms, baskets, toys, milk, and butter.

What interested me as much as anything was to observe that nearly everything that was sold in this market was carried into the city on the backs of the women. Practically, I think, one may say that the whole city of Cracow, with a population of 90,000 persons, is fed on the provisions that the peasant women carry into the city, some of them traveling as far as ten or fifteen miles daily.

One day, while driving in the market of Cracow, our carriage came up with a vigorous young peasant woman who was tramping, barefoot, briskly along the highway with a bundle swung over her shoulder. In this bundle, I noticed, she carried a milk-can. We stopped, and the driver spoke to her in Polish and then translated to my companion, Dr. Park, in German. At first the woman seemed apprehensive and afraid. As soon as we told her we were from America, however, her face lighted up and she seemed very glad to answer all my questions.

I learned that she was a widow, the owner of a little farm with two cows. She lived something like fourteen kilometers (about ten miles) from the city, and every day she came into town to dispose of the milk she had from her two cows. She did not walk all the way, but rode half the distance in the train, and walked the other half. She owned a horse, she said, but the horse was at work on the farm, and she could not afford to use him to drive to town. In order to take care of and milk her cows and reach the city early enough to deliver her milk she had to get up very early in the morning, so that she generally got back home about ten or eleven o'clock. Then in the afternoon she took care of the house and worked in the garden. This is a pretty good example, I suspect, of the way some of these peasant women work.

All day long one sees these women, with their bright-colored peasant costumes, coming and going through the streets of Cracow with their baskets on their backs. Many of them are barefoot, but most of them wear very high leather boots, which differ from those I have seen worn by peasant women in other parts of Austria and Hungary in the fact that they have very small heels.

I had an opportunity to see a great many types of women in the course of my journey across Europe, but I saw none who looked so handsome, fresh, and vigorous as these Polish peasant women.

It is said of the Polish women, as it is said of the women of the Slavic races generally, that they are still living in the mental and physical slavery of former ages. Probably very few of them have ever heard of women's rights. But, if that is true, it simply shows how very little connection such abstract words have with the condition, welfare, and happiness of the people who enjoy the freedom and independence of country life. At any rate, I venture to say that there are very few women, even in the higher ranks of laboring women in England, whose condition in life compares with that of these vigorous, wholesome, and healthy peasant women.

How can work in the stifling atmosphere of a factory or in some crowded city garret compare with the life which these women lead, working in the fields and living in the free and open country?

The emigration to America has left an enormous surplus of women in Europe. In England, for instance, the women stand in the proportion of sixteen to fifteen to the men. In some parts of Italy there are cities, it is said, where all the able-bodied men have left the country and gone to America. The changes brought by emigration have not, on the whole, it seems to me, affected the life of women favorably. But the same thing is true with regard to the changes brought about by the growth of cities and the use of machinery. Men have profited by the use of machinery more than women. The machines have taken away from the women the occupations they had in the homes, and this has driven them to take up other forms of labor, of more or less temporary character, in which they are overworked and underpaid.

Everywhere we find the women in Europe either doing the obsolete things or performing some form of unskilled labor. For example, there are still one hundred thousand people, mostly women, in East London, it is said, who are engaged in home industries — in other words, sweating their lives away in crowded garrets trying to compete with machinery and organization in the making of clothes or artificial flowers, and in other kinds of work of this same general description.

The movement for women's suffrage in England, which began in the upper classes among the women of the West End, has got down, to some extent, to the lower levels among the women who work with the hands. Women's suffrage meetings have been held, I have learned, in Bethnal Green and Whitechapel. But I do not believe that voting alone will improve the condition of workingwomen.

There must be a new distribution of the occupations. Too many women in Europe are performing a kind of labor for which they are not naturally fitted and for which they have had no special training. There are too many women in the ranks of unskilled labor. My own conviction is that what the workingwomen of Europe need most is a kind of education that will lift a larger number of them into the ranks of skilled labor — that will teach them to do something, and to do that something well.

The Negro women in America have a great advantage in this respect. They are everywhere admitted to the same schools to which the men are admitted. All the Negro colleges are crowded with women. They are admitted to the industrial schools and to training in the different trades on the same terms as men. One of the chief practical results of the agitation for the suffrage in Europe will be, I imagine, to turn the attention of the women in the upper classes to the needs of the women in the lower classes. In Europe there is much work for women among their own sex, for, as I have said elsewhere, in Europe the man farthest down is woman.

Outlook, 98 (July 1, 1911), 493-99.

To Emmett Jay Scott

Fort Salonga, Long Island, N.Y. July 2d, 1911

My dear Mr. Scott: As soon as you can get to it, I wish you would send me the names of all the colored papers in the country. I want them for Mr. Hilles. I have told him there are about 200, all of them except about 6 favoring the administration. I wish you would indicate those that do not or are uncertain.

I had a very satisfactory interview with the President and Mr. Hilles Friday. I was with the President and Mr. Hilles together for an hour, and the President and Mr. Hilles were most cordial. I took care of the whole situation so far as the Age was concerned and cleared up matters fully to their satisfaction. There were many interesting elements in the interview which I will tell you about when I see you.

The President told me that he was having a hard time in trying to place Vernon somewhere, and asked my advice concerning Haiti. I told him frankly that unless he should have brought up the subject I should not have even ventured an opinion, but in my opinion Vernon was entirely too small a man for the place, and he said that now he thinks he would have made a mistake had he sent Vernon there. He is going to let Furniss remain. Yours very truly,

B. T. W.

TLI   Con. 607   BTW Papers   DLC.

To Ralph Waldo Tyler

Fort Salonga, Long Island, N.Y. July 2, 1911

Personal

My dear Mr. Tyler: I am writing you about two matters. First. As soon as Lewis returns to Washington I think you ought to have a frank talk with him, Napier, McKinlay and perhaps Gov. Pinchback and anybody else that you think well of, and put the matter up to them squarely of doing something regularly and systematically to support the Bee. It ought not to be necessary for you to carry that load. All of them ought to chip in something every month. Besides, by each one doing something the paper can be made a strong and helpful force. Chase just now is in great straits for money to pay his printer. I wish you would let him know that I have written you and that help will be forthcoming.

The other thing is this. If you think well of it, I wish you would see Mr. Bruce and find out if he can arrange to put Mr. Chase's son in the new Vocational School in charge of the printing. I have told Chase I have asked you to take it up with Mr. Bruce, but get a definite answer. You can tell Mr. Bruce it is my wish that Chase be given this position if he is competent. Certainly Mr. Bruce owes something to Chase's friends in this matter since Mr. Chase has let up in the matter of fighting him. Please let Chase know I have written you about his son. Yours very truly,

[Booker T. Washington]

TLc   Con. 442   BTW Papers   DLC.

To William Henry Lewis

Fort Salonga, Long Lsland, N.Y. July 5th, 1911

My dear Mr. Lewis: I have yours of July 3d with enclosure. To speak frankly, I should dislike very much to see you go to the Negro National Educational Congress. It is largely a fake affair. The people engaged in it for the most part are not interested in education, and they do not represent the real educators of the country. It is a kind of opposition movement to the National Negro Educational Association of which Mr. W. T. B. Williams, of the Hampton Institute, is President. It was started by a cheap politician in St. Louis two years ago. Really, the thing is not worth bothering with.

In order for you to carry out, however, the President's wish and enable you to accomplish a greater purpose, I can arrange for you to receive an invitation to speak at the National Negro Educational Association which meets in St. Louis the latter part of this month which will be an attractive, fine affair, one you ought to attend.

J. Silas Harris[1] is president of the so-called Congress which meets in Denver, and he has a very shady reputation.

If you want to attend the St. Louis meeting telegraph me and I will arrange matters. I am sure the President will be just as much pleased to have you attend the St. Louis meeting as the Denver meeting, especially in view of the fact that he does not know the difference in the two organizations.

Harris invited me to attend the Denver meeting, but I refused. Yours very truly,

[Booker T. Washington]

TLc   Con. 428   BTW Papers   DLC.

[1] J. Silas Harris was principal of the Sumner School in Kansas City, Mo., and president of the black state teachers association.

To William Henry Lewis

Fort Salonga, Long Island, N.Y. July 5, 1911

Dear Mr. Lewis: Referring again to the Denver meeting, you can easily see that in the nature of things it would be almost impossible for a colored educational congress to be made a success in that part of the country. We can only have a successful colored educational meeting where there are separate public schools. There are no separate public schools in that part of the country, consequently almost no colored teachers, and the distance is too far for teachers from the South and elsewhere to travel. You will accomplish three or four times as much good for the administration and the general cause in St. Louis as in Denver, besides you would have a dignified gathering and would receive a dignified hearing. Yours very truly,

[Booker T. Washington]

TLc   Con. 428   BTW Papers   DLC.

To Hollis Burke Frissell

Fort Salonga, Long Island, N.Y. July 5, 1911

My dear Dr. Frissell: Yours of June 27th regarding the Jeanes Fund spent in Macon County has been received. I am glad that you have approved the application.

I thank you very much for calling the matter of the amount of money spent in Macon County to my attention. I shall be very glad to follow your suggestion and talk the matter over with Dr. Buttrick at the first opportunity. I will let him know more definitely just what we have been driving at in Macon County. On the face of matters I am sure that there appears ground for criticism on account of the large amount of money spent in Macon County. It has been largely in the nature of an experiment, and all experiments of course are costly, but I believe in the end the result will justify what has been done.

I have had two central thoughts in mind in spending so much money in Macon County. First, to try the experiment of equipping one county pretty thoroughly with school buildings, good teachers, etc., in order to see if the people and the public school authorities together would not take care of the school system after help had been extended for a given time. It has been the plan all along to gradually withdraw from this county and take up another county. Already we are withdrawing from Macon County and are beginning to work in another county.

The second thought which I have had in mind is to find out through such an experiment if we could build up a school in a rural community that would concern itself with the actual life of white and colored people in the community, whether or not such a school would not win the approval of the average white man in the community.

Our experiment in Macon County has certainly thus far demonstrated that such a system will win the confidence of the white people. Whether or not the people will carry on the schools and keep them up to their present point of efficiency after we have largely withdrawn support is a question, but I believe the schools will be kept up to a reasonable high degree of efficiency with some supervision on our part.

When I first began using this money it was scattered over a pretty wide territory, but I soon found that much of it was practically thrown away because of lack of close supervision and I thought it wiser to concentrate on a small territory and supervise carefully.

As stated, we have already begun to close up matters in Macon County and are preparing now to undertake work somewhere else. I will inform you more about this in detail later. Yours very truly,

[Booker T. Washington]

TLc   Con. 617   BTW Papers   DLC.

To the Russell Sage Foundation

[Tuskegee, Ala.] July 11, 1911

Dear Gentlemen: Both races in the South are coming to realize that for the common good the health conditions of the Negro should be improved.

The attitude of the white people is shown by recent newspaper discussions of the danger to the general health arising from the unsanitary conditions of the Negro settlements in Southern cities. At the recent Virginia Child Welfare Conference applause was given several speakers who strongly condemned the custom of neglecting sanitary conditions in the streets and homes of the colored people. In some instances the white people are making some effort to improve such sanitary conditions.

The Negroes are likewise becoming aroused to the need of sanitary improvement. There is among them a general movement to improve health conditions. Women's clubs, secret societies, their insurance companies, in fact nearly every kind of Negro organization is giving some attention to improving the health of the people.

For a number of years the Tuskegee Institute in a limited way has been trying to improve the health conditions of the Negro. The attached statement and chart shows somewhat in detail the work that Tuskegee Institute has been doing along this line.

What is needed, however, is the organization of all the efforts now being made to improve Negro health conditions and also the initiating of other efforts for the same purpose. To accomplish this end three things should be done.

The first is to get together all the available information concerning what is being done through various agencies for the improvement of the health conditions of the Negro.

The second is to bring together in a cooperative way all the isolated efforts that are now being made to improve Negro health conditions.

The third thing needed is some central agency to comprehensively and systematically direct these efforts.

It is for the above purposes that the assistance and cooperation of the Russell Sage Foundation is solicited. The Tuskegee Institute would, to assist in improving the health conditions of the Negro, place at the disposal of the Russell Sage Foundation its numerous facilities for reaching and influencing the Negroes of the South, particularly its numerous extension activities and its Bureau of Research.

It is respectfully requested that financially and otherwise the Russell Sage Foundation cooperate with the Tuskegee Institute and other agencies:

1. To collect information about the health conditions of the Negroes, both in urban and rural communities.

2. In collecting information concerning what is being done by organizations and in other ways to improve the health conditions of the Negro. This to include:

   (a) What is being done by white organizations.
   (b) What is being done by Negro organizations.
   (c) What is being done by states and municipalities.

3. In the holding at Tuskegee Institute in 1913 in connection with the annual Tuskegee Negro Conference a conference on the "Improvement of Health Conditions Among Negroes."

4. To assistant in inaugurating in connection with this Conference on Health a comprehensive and systematic effort to improve generally the health of the American Negro. Sincerely yours,

[Booker T. Washington]

TLc   Con. 438   BTW Papers   DLC.

From Susan Helen Porter

Tuskegee Institute, Ala. July 11, 1911

Mr. B. T. Washington: I received the letter which you wrote to me from Fort Salonga, N.Y., in which you advised concerning the unwisdom of retaining *unpromising students* in the institution after they had been given a fair trial; and I heartily agree with your advice in this respect.

I shall interpret the term *unpromising* in its broadest sense and apply it with care; and it is my hope that future recommendations regarding such students will be approved, to some extent, by the Executive Council and General Faculty, especially. Very Sincerely,

S. Helen Porter

ALS   Con. 616   BTW Papers   DLC.

A Petition from Laundry Workers
at Tuskegee Institute

Tuskegee Insti., Ala. July 12, 1911

Dear Principal: We, the girls of the laundry division are writing to let you know that we are very much dissatisfied with the payment we are now receiving.

You know the laundry is the hardest work done by female hands on the grounds. And to receive an average of thirteen or fourteen dollars per month is insufficient pay for our labor. There are some among us who make even less.

We believe all honest laborers should receive fair payment for their labor, as long as they render conscientious services — regardless of sex.

Now to assure you that we have done this, we make mention of the double amount of work we have been doing for the last three weeks. We have the work of both students and teachers to carry on including that of the Summer teachers. On one occasion we remained until five o'clock on Saturday evening in order to supply the boys with their weeks laundry.

We hope you will not think of us as complainers, but, simply as children striving to perform their duty; and, at the same time receive some recompense in return. We are asking for higher wages.[1] May we have it? Very Respectfully,

Hopie J. Harville	Cora Williams
Evelena Baker	Florida J. Holmes
Lillie Scott	Georgia Alfred
Tempie Taylor	Daisy Bryant
Irene Syphax	Florence L. Harrison
Willie Hayes	Martha Robbins
Anna M. Holland	Alice Jackson
Willard Pinkston	Mamie H. King
Annie Lula Goodloe	Rosa H. French
Hilda Vavasseur	Mamie L. Morman
Lizzie Williams	Mary J. Bullard
Armenia Greene	Nettie Hardaway
Lillian Thompson	Carrie Thweatt
Marie Bowen	Carrie McIntyre

ALS Con. 611 BTW Papers DLC.

[1] A faculty committee recommended a 20 percent increase for boarding department and laundry workers up to a maximum of 72¢ per day. The average student worker was earning 50¢ per day. (John H. Palmer, Charles H. Gibson, and S. Helen Porter to the Executive Committee, July 15, 1911, Con. 611, BTW Papers, DLC.)

To Wilford H. Smith

[Tuskegee, Ala.] July 14, 1911

My dear Mr. Smith: I do not think that we should let up on the Ulrich matter simply because the Assistant District Attorney has advised that the matter can go over until fall.

If we can get Ulrich to the point where we want him, I think we could arrange to have the matter brought up in court at any time and settled. I think now is the time to continue to work on him as much as possible. If we cannot get him to go into open court and make confession, it might be wise to follow Mr. Cravath's way and have him go before the District Attorney and do this.

At any rate, we must keep at work. Yours truly,

B. T. W.

TLpI Con. 435 BTW Papers DLC.

To Addie L. Thornton[1]

[Tuskegee, Ala.] July 14, 1911

Miss Thornton: Judging by the number of complaints that come to this office from time to time I feel rather convinced that you lose your temper and speak too roughly to the girls in the dining room. There are frequent complaints to the effect that you call the girls "niggers" and otherwise speak to them improperly.

In a word, what I hear indicates that you too frequently lose your temper.

Nothing hurts a teacher more than to yield to the temptation of losing her temper. It is far more effective to always be calm, self-controlled and dignified when dealing with students. It is far better always to treat the girls as though they were women. Girls are much more likely to respond in a favorable way if they are put on their honor and treated as if they were women instead of as though they were children.

Booker T. Washington

TLpS Con. 610 BTW Papers DLC.

[1] Addie L. Thornton was a matron in the business agent's department from 1908 to 1913.

To Frederick Randolph Moore

[Tuskegee, Ala.] July 15, 1911

Personal

Dear Mr. Moore: Mr. Scott and I have been looking into the matter to some extent and we are both convinced that The Crisis is getting more of a hold and more of a circulation among the people of the country than you realize. One finds it largely circulated in nearly every portion of the South. The Age is the only paper that can compete with The Crisis and modify its opinion. For this reason, I urge upon you to leave no stone unturned to see that The Age gets and keeps a large national circulation.

We have it on pretty good authority that The Crisis people are now printing at least 15,000 copies a month. This is a remarkable growth for a periodical not six months old. This is nearly as many copies as The Age prints notwithstanding that it is twenty-five years old.

The Age ought to have by next fall a circulation of 25,000 copies. I believe you can get this number if you go straight after the people. In several of the barber shops I noticed that The Crisis people have bright, attractive signs up advertising The Crisis. You ought to send one of your men to every barber shop and colored business place in New York and have new signs put up advertising The Age.[1]

I am sure that your whole force will have to get a new move on them or The Age will find itself taking a second or third rate position.

Aside from what The Crisis is doing, one cannot shut his eyes to the fact that The Amsterdam News is fast coming to the front and is a publication that you will have to reckon with.

This week's issue of The Age I think is particularly good. Yours very truly,

[Booker T. Washington]

TLp   Con. 54   BTW Papers   DLC.

[1] BTW wrote again on the same subject after he saw attractive signs for *The Crisis* in a Seventh Avenue barbershop in New York City. (BTW to Moore, July 22, 1911, Con. 54, BTW Papers, DLC.)

To Hollis Burke Frissell

[Tuskegee, Ala.] July 15, 1911

Dear Dr. Frissell: Referring again to our correspondence as to the amount of Jeanes Fund money spent in Macon County, I have just been making some investigation in one direction.

When we began using the Jeanes Fund money in this county, such a thing as a school farm, so far as I know, had not been heard of in the South. At the present time, I find that in Macon County there are 117 acres of land being cultivated this year by parents and pupils for the purpose of producing cotton with which to extend the school term. At the usual price of cotton, this means that these people will raise on their farms $1500 worth of cotton with which to extend the school term.

But the main point is that the object lesson furnished by Macon County in this respect is now fast spreading to many portions of the South, and there are few counties in the Gulf States where the people are not beginning to have a school farm on the order of the school farms in Macon County. Yours very truly,

Booker T. Washington

TLpS Con. 617 BTW Papers DLC.

To Charles Dewey Hilles

[Tuskegee, Ala.] July 16, 1911

Personal

My dear Mr. Hilles: Enclosed I send you the list of practically all the colored newspapers in the United States. You will note first as I told you that there are about half a dozen which are opposed to the administration.

Those that are marked "critical" now and then criticise the President adversely but for the most part their tone is friendly.

Those marked "O.K." stand by the administration.

You will see that the situation is not bad by any means, but it is one that needs careful and constant attention.

You will note that there are only[1] 200 papers. Yours very truly,

Booker T. Washington

TLpS Con. 53 BTW Papers DLC. No enclosure found with letter.

[1] In Emmett J. Scott's hand the word "only" was circled and "about" was editorially inserted.

From Charles Dewey Hilles

The White House   Washington   July 17, 1911

Dear Dr. Washington: I am indebted to you for the list of colored newspapers in the United States. It is encouraging to find that five-sixths of the 187 papers are friendly to the President. I find that 21 of the 31 newspapers which are now hostile to the President are published in Southern States.

As I explained to you on the occasion of your recent visit, this list will be very useful to us. Sincerely yours,

Charles D. Hilles

I have secured the position for J. E. Johnson with the Postal Commission.

TLS   Con. 53   BTW Papers   DLC.

To Charles Dewey Hilles

Fort Salonga, Long Island, N.Y. July 22d, 1911

Personal

My dear Mr. Hilles: In your letter of July 17th you say, "I find that 21 of the 31 newspapers which are now hostile to the President are published in Southern States." This is hardly a fair statement of the case. I meant to have you understand that there were 31 that sometimes criticise the President adversely. They are not uniformly hostile. There are only about 6 or 7 that are uniformly hostile to the President.

In the case of the 31, I feel that with some special attention we can bring most of them around to the support of the President. I shall give that matter attention in the early fall.

I am glad to note that you have secured a place for J. E. Johnson. Yours very truly,

Booker T. Washington

TLS   William Howard Taft Papers   DLC.   A draft is in Con. 53, BTW Papers, DLC.

To Wilford H. Smith

[Fort Salonga, Long Island, N.Y.] July 22, 1911

My dear Sir: I notice that the case against Ulrich has been called again and that nothing has been done. Both my friends in New York and elsewhere as well as myself are now becoming impatient. I think you will agree with me that up to the present time I have not been unreasonable nor impatient in regard to seeing that Ulrich is properly dealt with. Up to the present time I have not cherished any ill will toward the man for I have felt all along that on the night that he assaulted me he was either intoxicated or was entirely mistaken as to the object for which I called. I have felt, however, that if he had known who I was that no assault would have been made. For all these reasons I have been inclined to be lenient and patient and have advised my friends to be lenient and patient, but this delay is disappointing and exasperating. It seems to me now that we ought to fight this case to the bitter end. My friends in New York ask me to say to you that if you want additional counsel they are willing to provide the means to supply additional counsel.

One other thing. Several of our strongest friends insist that the charge ought to be changed from simple assault to felonious assault. They are urging me to see to it that this change is made. My friends in New York say that they will be willing to go to the District Attorney and insist if necessary that the charge be changed from simple assault to felonious assault.

I do not want you to think that I am too impatient in urging you too strongly but I think you will agree with me that under all the circumstances that I have been lenient and patient.

All that I have insisted on in the past has been that Ulrich go into the courts and tell the straight truth in regard to the matter. No one could ask less than this. I do not ask that he misrepresent anything or cover up anything but to tell the truth. I have no feeling of vindictiveness against the man, but I want him to tell the truth.

Please let me hear from you as soon as possible so that I will know exactly what course of action is to be followed. Yours very truly,

[Booker T. Washington]

TLc   Con. 435   BTW Papers   DLC.

From Robert Russa Moton

London, W.C. July 23 [1911]

Dear Dr. Washington: We arrived here Tuesday from Holland. I have gone quite thoroughly into the situation with reference to the Congress. I have had a frank talk with Dr Du Bois & have read his address with care. While he refers to your program as an unsatisfactory one and failing to do what you & others honestly hoped it would accomplish, he says you were perfectly *honest & sincere* in your feelings — that you thought the acquiring of *property, education & character* were best method to get political and other rights. He says what he has said before that under your teachings things have gotten steadily worse. He puts you down as the *leading educator* of the *race* and of the *present generation*. It is on the whole a fine paper & strong & his reference to you is purely impersonal — & very dignified. I am down to lead the discussion of his address with a ten minute speach. There is quite a little interest in the congress in certain quarters. It ought to do some good. There is to be a preliminary meeting tomorrow a.m. to which I am invited.

I hope you are well. Remember Mrs. Moton and me in kindness to Mrs. Washington. We sail from Glasgow on Saturday 29th for Montreal via Donaldson Line. Yours Sincerely

R. R. Moton

ALS   Con. 54   BTW Papers   DLC.

From Isaiah Goda Sishuba[1]

Ethiopian Home   Queenstown   S. Africa   25. 7. 11

Dear Sir   Thank God to have given the Negro race man of your kind and stamp. A far seeing gentleman and up to date   I was more than pleased to read the Advertisement of the International Conference called by you to be convined at Tuskegee. I am the president of the Ethiopian Church in South Africa, our Annual Conferences sits in April every year. But now I have decided to have it earlier on account of the International Conference. Myself and Rev H. R. Ngcayiya[2] Secretary of the Ethiopian Church will attend the above Conference. The executive Board and a Special Conference of our Church has elected us to become delegates to represent them. As we have no friends to take care of us we shall come direct to your place according to the Advertisement. I shall be very glad to hear from you how much would it be from Cape Town to your place, and kindly let us know if you can arrange concessions so as to abate the expenses. I shall be very glad to hear about these particulars as soon as possible.

I also herewith most humbly beg you to be kind enough to accept our boys 8 in number who are unable to support themselves for a higher education. Should my humble application get favour to you I shall bring the boys along with me.[3] I close my letter wishing you success. I hope you will also be kind enough to fournish us by the programme of the Conference before we leave the shores of your ancestors.

I have the honour to be Sir, Your Obedient Servant

I. G. Sishuba

Full names of the Delegates
Rev. Isaiah Goda Sishuba
President Ethiopian Church
Queenstown, South Africa
&
Rev. Henry Reed Ngcayiya
Secretary of the Ethiopian Church
Johannesburg, South Africa

The above two names were also elecded Delegates to represent the Ethiopian Church in England on the Coronation day of King George the V.

I.

ALS BTW Papers ATT.

[1] Isaiah Goda Sishuba, born in Queenstown, Cape Colony, in 1865, was the son of a local Wesleyan Methodist preacher and reportedly of royal ancestry. After education at Lovedale and Zonnebloem College, he became a preacher in the Primitive Methodist Church in Orange Free State. Leaving that denomination because of its segregation policy, he conducted an independent church and school, but later joined the A.M.E. Church in the United States. He was presiding elder of the Johannesburg district until the Boer War forced him back to Cape Colony. With H. R. Ngcayiya he resisted the secessionist movement of the Ethiopian Church

from the A.M.E. Church in the United States. (Coan, "A.M.E. Church in South Africa," 475; Talbert, *Sons of Allen*, 190.)

[2] Henry Reed Ngcayiya (1860–1928), the son of a Wesleyan Methodist preacher in Cape Colony, attended Healdtown Institute and became a teacher and court interpreter. He was A.M.E. presiding elder of the Grahamstown district, organized more than a dozen churches, and persuaded some of the secessionist churches to return to the A.M.E. fold. (Coan, "A.M.E. Church in South Africa," 474; Talbert, *Sons of Allen*, 84.)

[3] BTW replied on Sept. 27, 1911, inviting the two men to attend the conference as guests of Tuskegee Institute, and agreeing to admit the students if they could meet the entrance requirements. (Con. 83, BTW Papers, DLC.)

Extracts from an Address before the Negro Methodist Quadruple Forward Movement in Atlanta[1]

Atlanta, Ga., July 27, 1911

I am glad to have the privilege of taking part in this forward movement of the Methodist Church. I congratulate Dr. Penn, Dr. Bowen and other leaders who are engineering this movement. It means a great deal not only to the colored people who are in the Methodist Church, but a great deal to our race as a whole. This effort means self-help on the part of our race. It means that the colored members of the Methodist Church have decided that they will not be burdens but that they will be burden lifters; that they do not mean to be carried by some one else, but they mean to help carry somebody.

. . . .

This meeting also means that the spirit of sectarianism is giving way to a feeling of unity and larger service among all religious denominations. This fact is indicated by the presence of representatives of prominent denominations on this platform and on the program.

. . . .

This meeting also indicates that the leaders of our race in Georgia as elsewhere, are beginning to learn the fundamental lesson that we must turn our minds away from our ills in the direction of our opportunities. No individual or race that contents itself by sitting down brooding over its troubles, its trials, its obstacles, can amount to much. Races, like individuals, that center their thought and activity upon their opportunities are races that are succeeding. There is no place in the world in a successful community for a pessimist. There are many places throughout the South for the optimist, for the man of our race who is determined to make the best of his surroundings.

As I see the condition of colored people in Georgia, and as I look over this magnificent audience, I cannot refrain from drawing a contrast between conditions here in Georgia among the colored people and conditions in Southern Europe where I recently spent some time. In Georgia every member of our race who wants to find work can get it; work seeks the man instead of the man having to seek the work. Wages paid to our people in Georgia are from five to ten times as high as wages paid for similar work in Southern Europe. The food eaten by the Negroes of Georgia is many per cent better, of a more varied and nourishing character than that eaten by the same class of people in Southern Europe.

Some are inclined to grow discouraged at times because of racial problems. In Austria-Hungary instead of having one race problem, they have seventeen race problems with seventeen different languages or dialects. Here we have only one race problem, and we speak the great world language — English.

. . . . .

Are the leaders of this forward movement justified in asking our people to put themselves into a position to make further progress in church extension? What is their foundation for their faith in the future of our race in Georgia? Let me indicate what the Negro is doing.

According to the statistics furnished by the State Comptroller of Georgia, the Negro last year added 71,000 acres to his holdings in Georgia. He added $4,000,000 to the taxable values of his property. The Negroes of Georgia own today, 1,607,000 acres of land valued at $10,000,000. Including land, furniture, tools, stock and what not, the Negroes of Georgia are paying taxes today upon $32,000,000 worth of property. In Fulton County, Georgia the Negroes pay taxes upon $1,665,000 worth of property, and they added to their wealth in Fulton County last year to the extent of $169,000.

The Negroes of Georgia are paying in the form of taxes toward the support of state, county and local government $[*blank*]² annually.

These figures indicate two things. First, that the colored people in Georgia are not burdens upon the state. They indicate, in the second place, that in the fundamental things of life in Georgia that the white people are our friends. It would be impossible for us to have secured $32,000,000 worth of property within forty-eight years unless we had in every community white friends who stood by us to guide, to help and to encourage us in the direction of bettering our condition.

I believe that the Negroes more and more should advertise their friends, and their enemies less. I will guarantee to say that there is scarcely a community in Georgia where a Negro who wants to purchase a home, improve his condition, educate his children, build churches, cannot find white friends who with money, advice and sympathy are willing to stand back of him.

Now what we want to do as a race is to turn in the state of Georgia as elsewhere, our material possessions, our material advancement into the higher and better things of life. Turn land values, house values, crop values into high, virtuous living; turn them in the direction of church extension, church building; turn them in the direction of Sunday schools, turn them in the direction of everything that this great forward movement on the part of the Methodist Church stands for.

· · · ·

There is little in our condition over which we need be discouraged. I am not overlooking difficulties, I am not overlooking wrongs, I am not overlooking injustices that crop out now and then in most every community where Negroes reside in this country, but I am bold enough to assert that my observation and study of the black races throughout the world convince me that the Negroes in the South own more land, live in better houses, wear better clothes, eat better food, secure more work, are better paid, are getting more education, are advancing morally and religiously to a larger degree than is true of a similar number of black people anywhere in the world.

Further, one cannot find, in my opinion, a spot anywhere in the civilized or uncivilized world where there are so many black people living side by side day by day of so many white people where there is such friendship and a spirit of helpfulness exhibited on the part of the white people to the black people as is true of the South.

Let us all then join hands and hearts with renewed effort to make this great Methodist Church forward movement a tremendous and lasting success for the redemption of our whole Southland.

TM   Con. 607   BTW Papers   DLC.

¹ This was the second in a series of conventions whose purpose was to relate religious teachings to the ethical and social questions faced by black Methodists. M. C. B. Mason presided. BTW spoke to a crowd of 10,000 persons of both races. (Atlanta *Constitution,* July 28, 1911, 2.)
² Figure omitted in original.

To Wilford H. Smith

[Tuskegee, Ala.] July 28, 1911

My dear Mr. Smith: I send you some more newspaper clippings which indicate how important it is that we not let up on that fellow.¹ You will notice that most of these dispatches, if not all of them, are sent out by "United Press." I wish you would put that on the list of the news associations to be served with the proceedings when the proper time comes. Yours very truly,

Booker T. Washington

TLpS   Con. 435   BTW Papers   DLC.
¹ Henry Albert Ulrich.

An Address before the
National Colored Teachers Association

St. Louis, Missouri, July 30, 1911

Mr. President, Ladies and Gentlemen: I congratulate this association upon the progress it has made during the few years of its existence. I congratulate especially your president, Mr. W. T. B. Williams, and your secretary, Mr. J. R. E. Lee. This association is one of the most potent agencies at work for the elevation of the black citizens of America. I am glad that this association is having its annual meeting in the city of St. Louis. With perhaps one exception, St. Louis has treated the Negro race more generously in providing school accommodations, in the way of buildings, good school terms, and intelligent teachers than is true of any other city in the United States. What I say of the city of St. Louis I can add with equal emphasis of the state of Missouri. The state of Missouri has not only been generous in supporting a good school system for our people in town and country, but it has been equally as generous in supporting the Lincoln Institute at Jefferson City. In return for this generosity I am sure that the colored people of St. Louis and of the state of Missouri feel resting upon them an especial obligation to make themselves good, useful, and law-abiding citizens so that they may not become a burden upon the city or upon the state or constitute an element of danger or irritation.

As to the kinds of education, I believe in all kinds of education — college, university, and industrial education — but I am most interested in industrial, combined with public school education for the great masses of our people; that is our salvation. There is a place, an important one, in our life for the college man, the university man, as well as the man with a trade or with skill in his fingers. To indicate what I think of college education, I would add that the Tuskegee Institute employs more colored graduates of colleges than any single institution in the world.

What is the function of education in our time? In past years it used to be considered that education was for the exceptional man, was for the classes rather than for the masses. It used to be considered that education was only to be used in connection with the extraordinary things of life rather than the ordinary things of life. All that is changing and will change in the future. The education of the future is to be that which will apply itself to the ordinary functions and activities of life, that which will link itself closely to every duty and responsibility of life. This means that education is to enter the kitchen, the dining room, the bed chamber, is to go upon the farm, into the garden, into the shop, and into every activity of life. This also means that the teacher of our race who would do his duty is to not content himself with being a mere salary-drawer but must consider it one of his highest duties to see that what is taught in the schoolroom is linked closely with the life of our people, in the home and in their work.

One of the functions of education is to help our race everywhere to become home owners, to own a little piece of soil somewhere either in town or city. This means that the colored teacher, more perhaps than any other class of teachers, should get among the people, get among the ordinary, hard-working people, study their needs, study their conditions, and enter into systematic and close coöperation with them.

Another important function of education is to see that every boy and girl, no matter what may be his or her condition in life, no matter what may be his or her ambitions, is taught the dignity of labor, is taught that all labor, either with the head or with the hand, is equally honorable. There is no hope for any race or for any group of people until they learn the fundamental lesson that labor with the hands is dignified, is something to be sought after, and something not to be shunned.

Another function of education, especially in a city like St. Louis, should be to get rid as fast as possible of that large loafing and idle element of our race who exhibit themselves on the corners of the streets, around barrooms and other places of disrepute. When racial outbreaks take place between white people and black people, in the majority of cases these difficulties can be traced to the idle, loafing, drinking, and gambling classes of both white and colored people. And then I sometimes fear that in many of our cities there is too large a class of our people who exist without steady, reliable employment, who float around from one community to another without any abiding place, who live upon the labor of somebody else and especially upon the labor of hard-working women. I repeat that it should be the function of education in a city like St. Louis to see to it that these loafers are reached and reformed, are gotten rid of.

For our race in its present condition, I believe in trade education as distinguished from mere manual training. Manual training is good so far as it goes in giving the principles of mechanics, but a hungry race cannot live upon "principles." Our people in their present condition need to be taught something that is definite in the way of a trade, something that will enable them to improve their economic condition. It is a dangerous thing in the case of any race of people, and it is especially dangerous in the condition of any race in the same relative stage of civilization which the masses of colored people find themselves in the United States today, to increase the wants of a race through mere book education without increasing the ability of that race to supply these increased wants along the lines in which they can find employment. There is no justification for my coming here to speak unless I am perfectly frank and straightforward in my remarks. In many parts of the country I hear complaints to the effect that Negro labor is not reliable, that the employer cannot depend upon the black workman for steady, constant work; that if the laborer is paid off on Saturday night there is no certainty as to when he will return to his place of employment. If in any degree this charge has a basis of truth in the community where any of you work as teachers, you should see to it that you make your influence felt in changing the reputation of our race. Everywhere we must see to it that the black race becomes just as reliable, just as progressive, just as intelligent in all matters of labor as is true of any other race. If we do not make progress in this direction, the time will soon come when in many parts of this country black labor will be replaced by white labor from European countries.

Another function of education should be to see to it that everywhere our race not only gets a proper idea of the dignity of labor, of proper methods of labor, but equally important, even more important, that they learn to save that which they earn. But many of our young people "scatter their earnings to the wind" as fast as the money comes into their hands. As teachers we should use our influence among the masses, and especially the present generation of young men and young women, in seeing to it that they form the habit of thrift, the habit of saving. As fast as possible we should see to it that every individual in the community whom we can influence has a bank account: a bank account is a great maker of character; a bank account is a great maker of useful citizens; a bank account teaches the lesson of saving today that we may have tomorrow; teaches the lesson of doing without today that we may possess tomorrow. If our present generation of young people are taught to save, are taught to invest their money in land or houses, are taught to put their money in the bank, the time will not be long before we shall be counted among the thrifty races of the earth. I have little patience with any man, white or black, with education, who goes through the country whining and crying because nobody will give him a job of work. A man with education should be able to create a job for himself, but in doing so he may have to begin at the very bottom.

But we should not be ashamed to perform the most ordinary things in order that we may lay a foundation for future growth and usefulness.

Another function of education in connection with our race should be to teach pride of race; to teach the Negro boy and the Negro girl that he or she should be just as proud of being a Negro as a German, as an Irishman, and as a Frenchman are proud of being members of their races. I have no patience with the man or woman of our race who is continually seeking to get away from the race; is continually seeking to belong to another race. There are some colored people, I am sorry to say, who would rather be classed as third-rate white people than to be classed as first-rate colored people. Personally, if you will excuse the reference, I am just as proud of being a Negro as any white man can be proud of being a member of the white race.

Another function of education should be to see that it is kept in the minds of the youths of our race that there are two races in this country and that each has a duty, that each has a responsibility, to the other; that in the case of our race no boy or girl grows up with a feeling of hatred or bitterness toward any other race. In the last analysis the race that hates will grow weaker, while the race that loves will grow stronger. No one race can harm another race, can inflict injustice upon another race, can strive to keep down another race without that race itself being permanently injured in all the fundamental virtues of life.

Do not misunderstand me: I do not fail for one moment to understand our present conditions. I am not deceived; I do not overlook the wrongs that often perplex and embarrass us in this country. I do not overlook injustice. I condemn with all the strength of my nature the barbarous habit of lynching a human being, whether black or white, without legal trial. I condemn any practice in any state that results in not enforcing the law with a certainty and justice, regardless of race or color.

Another function of education should be to emphasize in the minds and hearts of our youths the fact that in the United States we have great opportunities and tremendous opportunities. The millions of unoccupied and unused lands in the South are open to the black man as freely as to any white man; while the color line may be drawn in certain directions, nature draws no color line; an acre of land in the South will yield her riches as quickly to the touch of the blackest hand as to the touch of the whitest hand in America.

As one example of the progress our race has already made within forty-eight years in one of the states, I find that according to the statistics furnished by the State Comptroller of Georgia, the Negro last year added 71,000 acres to his holdings in Georgia. He added $4,000,000 to the taxable value of his property. The Negroes of Georgia own today 1,607,000 acres of land valued at $10,000,000. Including land, furniture, tools, stock, and what not, the Negroes of Georgia are paying taxes today upon $32,000,000 worth of property.

There is but one salvation for our country, and that is obedience to law, whether this law relates to human life, to property, or to our rights as citizens. For us, however, in our present condition, I believe that our greatest hope for salvation and uplift is for us to turn our attention mainly in the direction of progressive, constructive work. Let construction be our motto in every department of our lives North and South. Pursuing this policy, we will convince the world that we are worthy of the best treatment.

We should see to it too that we not only emphasize in our work as teachers the opportunities that are before our race, but should also emphasize the fact that we ought to become a hopeful, encouraged race. There is no hope for any man or woman, whatever his color, who is pessimistic; who is continually whining and crying about his condition. There is hope for any race of people, however handicapped by difficulties, that makes up its mind that it will succeed, that it will make success the stepping stone to a life of success and usefulness.

E. Davidson Washington, ed., *Selected Speeches of Booker T. Washington* (Garden City, N.Y., 1932), 200–207.

An Article in *The International*

July 1911

Sir: Instead of directly answering your questions, I have written a short article on race prejudice, which I think will answer your purpose.

One of the difficulties about prejudice is that it is hard to define. You do not know what you are dealing with. If prejudice, whether race prejudice or any other sort of prejudice were based on reason it would be possible to deal with it. It would then be possible to argue with a man who was prejudiced. But race prejudice is not based on reason. It is what is called an instinctive feeling or attitude. It grows up in the mind and is not something that is formulated there.

Race prejudice grows up and then spreads from one individual to another. It is like some noxious weed in a garden. You may drive it out one place and it will appear in another.

Another difficulty about race prejudice is that it turns up in very different forms. It is one thing in one place and another in another. An individual may be prejudiced against another individual in one direction or in one relation of life and not in another; for instance, there is a very great difference between the race prejudice which exists in the North and the race prejudice which exists in the South. There is practically no prejudice in the South against a colored man engaging in any kind of labor. Where prejudice does exist against the labor of the colored man it is in those forms of labor in which the South has not been accustomed to find him.

The Northerners are prejudiced against the Negro because they are not acquainted with him. He is a stranger to them. They have heard a great many curious stories about him. They don't know how to treat him. They don't know just where he stands. They don't know just what he is going to do.

My experience is that people are prejudiced against anything that is new and strange, and as the Negro type is a different type of man and has a different color from many people, a man who meets him for the first time does not know just what to expect of him and if he hears bad reports about him he is very willing to believe anything that he hears. At the bottom I am convinced that prejudice is based on some kind of fear. A man who has traveled a great deal in Africa told me once that he had given up the attempt of carrying a colored servant with him in different parts of Africa because as soon as he went into the interior with a strange type that man was likely to be poisoned.

The same prejudice seems to have been one of the reasons why the different African tribes were willing to sell each other into slavery. There was no fellow feeling between the men of one tribe and those of another. Fellow feeling is a product of civilization. Race prejudice is a relic of barbarism.

In the Middle Ages at a time when barbarism had overspread all

Europe and practically destroyed civilization race prejudice was based not on color but on religion. If one man was a Catholic and another man was a Protestant that was a reason for treating him cruelly, refusing to live with him, and perhaps murdering him. The War of the Crusades was very largely based upon this religious prejudice and it was at this time that there was the greatest outbreak of prejudice against the Jews. The first crusades were carried on largely by mobs of disorganized men moving over the country and wherever they came to the cities where there were Jews they felt it their duty to kill and murder and burn every Jew they could find. The Thirty Years War, during which millions of people perished, was a war based upon religious prejudices, which I suspect was very much akin to race prejudice.

But in both these cases race prejudice was to some extent overcome. For instance, when the crusaders reached Asia they found the Saracens a brave, courageous, intelligent people. The Saracens had preserved all the learning which the barbarian invasion had driven out of Europe. One of the secondary results of the Crusades was to make Europeans acquainted with the Greek and Latin literature. As soon as the Western people found that the Eastern people were their superiors in some respects; that they had something which was of value to them, namely the Greek and Latin learning, they began to take a very different attitude towards these people. I don't mean to say that prejudice entirely died out, but it was very greatly modified on both sides. It was modified because both the Western and the Eastern peoples found that each had something that the other wanted.

In the Thirty Years War religious prejudice was destroyed in a somewhat different way. The mass of the people who suffered most from these wars began to grow weary of bloodshed. They found that they did not reap any advantage from it. Not only were lives lost, but property was destroyed, homes broken up. Furthermore they began to find out that there were other motives than religious motives which led to these wars; they perceived that political leaders were taking advantage of the prejudice of the people to drive them to war for the personal advantage of the leaders and politicians. When the people began to find this out they refused to permit their religious prejudice to be used by private individuals for their own selfish ends.

There are some people who have said that the reason there is so little prejudice in labor matters in the South at the present time is due to the fact that the Negro has not yet come in competition with the white man and that as soon as competition develops that the white laboring man in the South will take advantage of the existing prejudice to drive the Negro out of the work he is now engaged in and that the final effect of this would be to greatly increase race prejudice.

I am quite confident that it will work out in the South as it worked out elsewhere when people have attempted to take advantage of religious or racial prejudice for selfish motives. If the Negro fits himself to perform a service it will not be to the interest of anyone in the South to prevent his performing that service and anyone who attempts to keep him from performing that service to the South as a whole cannot, I am convinced, understand either the South or the Southern people.

My observation convinces me that there is only one way of removing prejudice. You can not argue it away. You cannot drive it out of the man by injuring him or intimidating him. There is only [one] way in my mind to do away with prejudice and that is for people to get on a practical working basis with each other. Wherever two people of a different race or of groups find that they have some common interest or by working together they are benefited, there race prejudice disappears.

People talk about the Japanese having destroyed race prejudice by their war in Asia. I think we all did have a higher opinion of the Japanese after that war as far as the nation itself is concerned. The other nations were more disposed to accept the Japanese on a level with themselves. The English entered an alliance with the Japanese nation after that war; but England did that because she found that Japan was valuable to her; that they had a common interest. In Asia admiration for the Japanese nation increased. In America I do not think that prejudice against the individual Japanese man decreased, but only against the Japanese nation. On the contrary it increased. People were more afraid of the Japs after that war than they were before.

The greatest example of the overcoming of race prejudice is in my opinion in the Southern States. When the Southern people imported into America the wild African they brought among them a man more different, strange and mysterious than any they had ever seen. It took a very long time to accustom the Southern people to Negro slavery. For nearly a hundred years they tried to get along with the white bond servant from England; but in the competition between the two races the African at that particular time and in those particular circumstances proved the more valuable man and he remained. For the next hundred years the black man in America and the white man in America on the whole and considering the difference in their characters got on very well. Indeed, in many cases there grew up a very genuine affection between the master and the slave, particularly with those servants who lived with him in his home and became best acquainted with him. The white man found the Negro not only a valuable servant, but an affectionate, devoted and lovable companion and help, and the affection that grew up in some instances between the white people and the black people is something that it is very difficult for anyone anywhere outside the South to understand. I think that the white people and black people in America have proved more than anything else that people apparently the most different in their characteristics can live together and be on terms of friendship with each other and that is a very important lesson for the whole world because in the Twentieth Century the great problem of civilization, as I look upon it is to be in bringing the whole world together on terms of mutual helpfulness.

Now, I have said, that it seemed to me, considering the difference in their characteristics that there is actually less race prejudice in the South and the two races are getting on together better than any two such dissimilar races in any other part of the world. I don't mean to say that there is. But the peculiarity of that race prejudice is that it is prejudice against the Negro as a group, not as an individual. I think that prejudice goes back to the time before the war when the masses of the people who held slaves lived in fear of an insurrection. They did not fear their own slaves. Them they knew. But they did fear the slaves in the abstract. Part of it goes back to the time of the reconstruction and the prejudice against the Negro in politics. But in other directions there is very little prejudice in the South.

There are some people who are very active in their efforts to fight race prejudice — some people in the North and some people in the South. They are trying to fight it by argument. They are trying to fight it by retaliating in kind. If the white man curses the Negro, they believe that it will destroy prejudice to curse the white man in return. If the white man ill treats a Negro they think the best way to destroy prejudice is to injure the white man. If the white man tries to terrorize a certain class of Negroes these people think that the thing to do is to terrorize the white man in return.

Now, there are two things I would say in regard to this. First, that is the old vicious circle — if I injure my neighbor of course my neighbor is bound to injure me in return — and of course there is no end to that pursuit. No civilization was ever built up on that. On the contrary civilization, especially our civilization, has been built up on the principle of [not] retaliating, of not doing evil to other men as they do to you. On the other hand while I believe in imitating him, not in the evil things, but in the good, for the people who curse the Negro are not the best white people but the worst. The best white people are those who are seeking to educate the Negro, to build him up, to make him a Christian and they are the people who do not reply with retaliation but return good for evil rather than evil for evil.

The International, 4 (July 1911), 30-31. This was one of a series of replies to questions in "A Symposium on Race Prejudice." Among other participants were John Spargo and the sociologist Edward A. Ross.

Emmett Jay Scott to Wilford H. Smith

Tuskegee Institute, Alabama   August 2nd, 1911

Personal.

My dear Mr. Smith: I have [am?] becoming just a little bit troubled with reference to the Ulrich matter.[1]

You have seen how the Guardian has featured this matter in its issue of July 22nd and 29th. It has worked that United Press Special for all it was worth with distorted headlines and comments calculated to do us great harm. Some of the Negro newspapers are following the Guardian's lead, including of course Harry Smith's paper. You probably have also seen that paper.

I now find that a number of colored newspapers, including the Nashville Clarion, and others which have been more or less friendly to us, are carrying little editorial notes reading about as follows:

"When the case against Ulrich was called for trial, Dr. Washington failed to put in appearance; no action was taken and it may never be tried."

Now, the point of this letter is to ask if it is not possible for you to arrange to send out from New York to the colored newspapers an official statement regarding the status of this case, so that the un-thoughtful may not be misled. It is decidedly painful to have to stand such widespread publicity as Trotter and others are giving to what they call our failure to be represented when Ulrich was called for trial recently.

I believe that you are watchful of every interest in this matter, and yet I cannot fail to appreciate the harm likely to be occasioned by our failure to counteract the baneful prejudices now being propagated. Yours very truly,

[Emmett J. Scott]

TL Copy Con. 607 BTW Papers DLC. Enclosed in Scott to BTW, Aug. 2, 1911, Con. 607, BTW Papers, DLC. A press copy is in Con. 435, BTW Papers, DLC.

¹ When the Ulrich case came up in July and BTW failed to appear, thus caus-ing postponement until the fall term, black newspapers inclined to be censorious of BTW, including the Boston *Guardian* and the Cleveland *Gazette,* renewed earlier criticisms of his seeming reluctance to prosecute. Harry C. Smith wrote in the Cleveland *Gazette:* "He certainly had had plenty of time (many months) in which to arrange to be present if he intended to 'prosecute Ulrich to the full extent of the law,' as he promised many weeks ago." Smith suggested that BTW did not wish to have to explain what he was doing in that "free and easy" section of the city, "and on a Sunday, too." (Cleveland *Gazette,* July 22, 1911, 2.)

To Edgar Gardner Murphy

Fort Salonga, Long Island, N.Y. August 5, 1911

My dear Mr. Murphy: I have your letter of July 31st. I shall be very glad to call to see you sometime when I am in New York. I hope that you are reasonably well and are having a good summer.

I have just returned from Alabama, and am glad to say to you that conditions are very hopeful there. I have never seen a better feeling of good will and cooperation between the races in Alabama than there is now. All the Montgomery papers, especially the Advertiser, are more friendly and helpful than they have been before. The Journal, you will be glad to know, has turned over a new leaf, and it has been a good many months since I have seen anything in the Journal bitter against colored people.

Just before I left, I had a very good letter from Governor O'Neal stating that he meant to visit Tuskegee and inspect our work just as soon as his official duties would permit him to do so.

The only discouraging element in the whole situation is the putting of whiskey back into Montgomery, Mobile and possibly Birmingham and Huntsville. This I think is going to be distinctly hurtful to the colored people.

I have never seen the white planters of Alabama take so much interest in their colored tenants as they are doing now. You will be surprised to know the number of white planters who are giving barbecues during the month of August at which prizes are given out to the colored tenants who are the most successful. Our teaching force at Tuskegee is constantly called on to attend these barbecues and deliver addresses.

The boll weevil is playing a large part, in my opinion, in the uplift of the colored people. Certainly white people in Alabama who have never taken any interest in the education of the colored people are now trying to instruct the colored people in better methods of farming in order that they may be prepared to raise diversified crops when the boll weevil comes. Yours very truly,

[Booker T. Washington]

TLc   Con. 54   BTW Papers   DLC.

To Robert Russa Moton

Fort Salonga, Long Island, N.Y. August 5th, 1911

My dear Major Moton: I have received both of your letters. I did not reply because I was uncertain as to whether my letters would reach you before you sailed or not.

I thank you so much for writing me so fully about your European experiences. I shall hope to hear more at length when I see you.

I am anxious to hear about the Race Congress. Almost nothing appeared in the American papers regarding the Congress, so I am in the dark.

Would it not be possible for you and Mrs. Moton to come out and spend at least a day with us here before you go South? I shall be here until the morning of the 11th. My telephone number is 127-J Northport.

I hope both of you have had a good rest. Yours very truly,

[Booker T. Washington]

TLc   Con. 54   BTW Papers   DLC.

To George Washington Albert Johnston

Fort Salonga, Long Island, N.Y. August 5, 1911

Personal

Dear Albert: I have your letter of August 2d. In regard to the appointment of the postmaster in Montgomery I would say that if a convenient opportunity offers itself I will speak to the President or his secretary, but I hardly think it wise under the conditions that now exist for me to urge the matter at this time, unless I were in Washington and the President or his secretary spoke to me about the matter. The fact is, I fear that anything I might say in that direction would get to the public and would eventually do Mr. Thompson more harm than good.

In the last analysis, of course, Mr. Taft is going to look to Mr. Hitchcock for recommendations, and Mr. Hitchcock would try to defeat anybody in whom he thought Mr. Thompson was interested.

I think the best way to secure the appointment of Mr. Bowron[1] is for Mr. Thompson not to show his hand.

I am glad that your Aunt Susie[2] and Lilla[3] are visiting you. We are all well.

I hope that somebody will go from Birmingham to the Business League meeting in Little Rock. Your uncle,

[Booker T. Washington]

TLc   Con. 424   BTW Papers   DLC.

¹ G. W. A. Johnston had written at J. O. Thompson's instance to ask BTW to recommend Thomas Bowron, the young assistant cashier of the First National Bank, for postmaster of Birmingham, not Montgomery. BTW apparently confused the two cities because Johnston had mentioned J. H. Montgomery, the Birmingham postmaster who had just died. (Johnston to BTW, Aug. 2, 1911, Con. 424, BTW Papers, DLC.)

² Susie Miller Washington, wife of John Henry Washington.

³ Lilla D. Washington (b. 1895), daughter of Susie M. and John H. Washington.

To George Augustus Finch

Fort Salonga, Long Island, N.Y. August 8, 1911

My dear Mr. Finch: Yours of August 2d addressed to Mr. Scott has been received. Last night I sent you a telegram reading as follows:

Please telegraph Mr. Reed Paige Clark¹ that I shall be glad to see him here at my summer home on Thursday or Saturday of this week in case it is convenient for him to call. Other dates in August uncertain.

It is possible I shall be here on the 25th, 26th, and 27th of August. I shall be very glad to see Mr. Clark.

I think you will be interested to know that I have just received word from a generous friend in this country that she will be willing to give $15,000 for buildings and other equipment for starting an industrial school in Liberia, and she will also give a small amount annually for its maintenance. I shall be very glad to have any of your ideas on the subject. My own idea at present is to make it purely a farming school. Development in agriculture I think is the greatest need of the Liberian people. Yours very truly,

[Booker T. Washington]

TLc Con. 422 BTW Papers DLC.

¹ Reed Paige Clark (1878–1958), a graduate of George Washington University, taught at George Washington from 1898 to 1900 before becoming private secretary to Senator Henry E. Burnham of New Hampshire and clerk of various senate committees from 1901 to 1911. From 1911 to 1916 he was receiver of Liberian customs, and later entered the U.S. consular service, where he remained until his retirement in 1943, having served in Africa, Latin America, and Europe.

George A. Finch arranged for Clark to meet with BTW before Clark assumed his duties in Liberia. Finch had written to Emmett J. Scott that "Mr. Clark rightly believes that his prestige in Liberia will be greatly enhanced if he should make the acquaintance of Dr. Washington before he goes down...." (Aug. 2, 1911, Con. 422, BTW Papers, DLC.)

To Emmett Jay Scott

Fort Salonga, Long Island, N.Y. August 8, 1911

Dear Mr. Scott: Do not fail to remind me at Little Rock to have three fraternal delegates elected to attend the next meeting of the Association for the Advancement of Colored People. I want to get three strong men.

We ought to begin planning in advance for the overhauling and reorganization of our Executive Committee. There are several men on it that are of no value, among them Taylor[1] of Richmond. It is unfortunately true, also, that in many communities and states where we have officers the League is very weak.

I saw a good deal of Mr. Gordon[2] of St. Louis, and in my opinion he ought to go on the Executive Committee. He is a strong, progressive, liberal man, not afraid to spend money in right directions, and besides, he is able to spend money. He strikes me more favorably than anybody I have seen lately, as being a fit person for our Executive Committee. Yours truly,

Booker T. Washington

TLS BTW Papers ATT.

[1] William Lee Taylor of Richmond, Va., had been since 1897 the Grand Worthy Master and President of the United Order of True Reformers. Born in 1854 in Caroline County, Va., he was a farmer and railroad construction worker, secured an education, and became a Baptist preacher and public school teacher. He began active work in the True Reformers in 1888 and rose through its ranks. He was a member of the executive committee of the NNBL, and in addition to the business activities of his order, he was interested in a shoe-supply company in Richmond and an oil and gas company in Chicago.

[2] William Claud Gordon was a black undertaker in St. Louis, Mo. Born in Columbia, Tenn., in 1862, he moved to St. Louis as a youth, worked as a Pullman porter, and established one of the largest undertaking businesses west of the Mississippi River. He also invested in real estate, a steam laundry, and a fleet of motor hacks.

To Monroe Nathan Work

Fort Salonga, Long Island, N.Y. August 8, 1911

Dear Mr. Work: In preparing my Business League annual address,[1]
I have just had an opportunity to go carefully through the figures
covering Arkansas, Georgia and the South as a whole which you prepared for me, and I want to thank you most heartily for preparing
these figures for me and to let you know how very valuable I consider
them. It is impossible to go on placing these great truths before our
race without great good being accomplished. Yours very truly,

[Booker T. Washington]

TLc BTW Papers ATT.

[1] BTW delivered his annual presidential address before the NNBL on Aug. 16
in Little Rock, Ark. The speech cited statistics on property accumulation, agricultural production, and business opportunities for blacks in Arkansas and other
parts of the South. BTW's notes for the address are in Con. 957, BTW Papers,
DLC.

A News Item in the Los Angeles *Times*[1]

Austin (Tex.) Aug. 9 [1911]

CAPITOL NOT FOR NEGROES

TEXAN LAWMAKERS BOO-HOO
RESOLUTION TO LET BOOKER T.
WASHINGTON SPEAK

When Representative Schuleter of Travis county, formally presented
today a resolution intended to grant the use of the House chamber to
Booker T. Washington, the negro educator, the uproar of noise which
greeted the first reading was so decisive that no formal vote was taken.
The second reading was not reached and the matter was laid aside.

Members of the negro race had been hoping that Washington might
be permitted to speak in the Capitol on the occasion of his visit next
October.

From all parts of the House cries of "No" came when the resolution was read.

Los Angeles *Times,* Aug. 10, 1911, Clipping   Con. 446   BTW Papers   DLC.

[1] John H. Washington, Jr., sent this clipping to BTW and advised him to stay out of Texas. "The cities possibly may be alright," he wrote, "but those little towns where you must pass thru — are too fierce for you to go thru." (Aug. 10, 1911, Con. 446, BTW Papers, DLC.)

From Robert Russa Moton

Hampton, Virginia   Aug. 11, 1911

My dear Dr. Washington: I had a brief talk with Mr. Moore in New York on Tuesday and asked him to state the situation to you as he said he would see you the next day. The Congress on the whole was very good and was in my opinion worth while. So far as the American Negro is concerned his case was very well put. Dr. Du Bois, who by the by gave me every possible consideration. I spoke frankly with him and he did the same with me. His speech was really very good. He simply made a scientific statement of the case of the Negro in general and in America with relation to other races. There was, of course, no reference made to any particular thing in the United States. He did not read his paper as there was no time for it. He really put the case very well. Prof. Scarborough, who was very anxious to get on the program for three minutes was finally put on at my suggestion and I was very sorry that I did it. His remarks were exceedingly pessimistic but no one paid any attention to what he said. I think he meant to create a sensation but the papers only made a brief paragraph of what he said and fortunately quoted the best of what he said which was very good. But Milholland, to my great surprise, who spoke after Prof. Scarborough put things with as much emphasis and optimism as you would have put it. His address was very different from the letter he wrote regarding you a year ago. Indeed he took just the opposite view. He said that we did not come to England to air any grievances about America, but that the American people black and white would settle their problems, the Negro simply asked equal chances and in his opinion would get it. Indeed some of his sentences sounded as if you had written them out for him. I gave Mr. Moore a brief report for the "Age" and I think it is very fine that he is going to give both Milholland and Du Bois credit for having shown very good judgment and sanity so far as his public utterances were concerned. There are a number of things about the meeting which I wish to speak to you when I see you.

I am sorry that Mrs. Moton and I could not accept your kind invitation to Northport. I am, Yours as always,

R. R Moton

TLS   Con. 430   BTW Papers   DLC.

To Robert Russa Moton

Memphis, Tenn. August 21st, 1911

My dear Major Moton: I have your letter regarding the Texas trip. I really think you will make a great mistake for yourself and Hampton not to go on this trip. More and more I feel that such institutions as Hampton and Tuskegee ought to reach the race in a larger way every year. Our work in Arkansas in getting hold of the masses of the people from Oklahoma, Arkansas and surrounding states is tremendously telling. We can stir up the whole state of Texas in a way that will help do as much good as if you were working directly on the grounds at Hampton. I very much hope you will talk the matter over with Dr. Frissell and get his consent for you to go. Both Hampton and Tuskegee constantly ought to have a strong hold on such a state as Texas. We should have first hand knowledge at all times concerning such states as Texas, and such knowledge can only be gotten by actually seeing the people on the grounds. It hardly seems possible now to bring about a change of dates so far as the Texas trip is concerned.

Would it be possible for Mr. Aery[1] to go on this trip and write something for Northern papers?

The Business League meeting in Little Rock was by far the best we have ever held. You would have been surprised at the high type of the delegates and especially pleased with the many beautiful homes owned by our people in Little Rock.

We spent yesterday, Sunday, at the home of Scott Bond where I spoke to an audience of seven thousand white and black people. Old man Bond stands for much more than I had heretofore realized. He is in many ways a great man. Yours very truly,

[Booker T. Washington]

TLc   Con. 54   BTW Papers   DLC.

[1] William Anthony Aery (1882–1963) was editor of the *Southern Workman* and instructor in social science at Hampton Institute beginning in 1906. He graduated from Columbia College (B.A. 1904) and Teachers College, Columbia University (M.A. 1906). He was on the faculty of Hampton for thirty-three years. During World War I he lectured at army camps on war aims, and from 1942 to 1948 he was a personnel officer of the Langley Field Laboratory, National Advisory Committee for Aeronautics, in charge of securing draft exemptions for essential employees.

To William Demosthenes Crum

Fort Salonga, Long Island, N.Y. August 26, 1911

Personal and Confidential

My dear Dr. Crum: Mr. Reed Paige Clark, the new Receiver General and Customs Officer for Liberia, spent a day with me here yesterday at my summer home, and we talked about Liberia. Mr. Clark is a young man from Vermont,[1] but has had much experience in the State and other departments at Washington. In my opinion he is thoroughly equipped for his work, and I feel pretty sure that you will like him. He is thoroughly without race prejudice so far as I can discover. I hope you and our other friends in Liberia will give him a hearty reception. As I understand it, he plans to reach there sometime in October or November.

One other thing. One of the men that did some hard work on the American Commission to Liberia is Mr. George A. Finch. Mr. Finch is not now connected with the State Department but is with the Carnegie Peace Foundation in Washington. Notwithstanding he has severed his connection with the State Department, no man in Washington has done so much for Liberia since he came home as Mr. Finch. It has been largely through his reminding of the Department and constantly urging and advice that matters have been brought to their present point. Mr. Finch lets no opportunity slip by to manifest his deep interest in Liberia. I am sure that it would please Mr. Finch very much if the Liberian government could see its way clear to confer upon him some kind of decoration. This could be fittingly done now especially as he is out of the State Department. I hope in your own way you can make this suggestion to the government.

I hope that you and Mrs. Crum are well. Please remember us kindly to her. Yours very truly,

[Booker T. Washington]

TLc   Con. 420   BTW Papers   DLC.

¹ Actually New Hampshire.

To Daniel Edward Howard¹

Fort Salonga, Long Island, N.Y. Aug. 26, 1911

Personal and Confidential

My dear Sir: A sum of money has been placed at my disposal that can be used for the establishment of a school of some character in Liberia. I want to use this money to the very best advantage in a way to really help the people of Liberia.

Without asking you to make a definite statement or to commit yourself in any official way, I would like to know, however, if in your opinion the government of Liberia would be likely to donate a tract of land for this school, say 50 or 100 acres. This information would enable me to begin forming plans pretty soon.

I might add that before anything definite is done, it is my present idea to send a man to Liberia to look the ground over and consult with the people there who are most interested. I realize quite fully that local conditions which are quite different there from what they are in this country, have got to be taken fully into account.

Mr. Reed Paige Clark, the new Customs Advisor for Liberia, spent a day with me here yesterday at my summer home, and we went over some matters pretty carefully regarding Liberia. Mr. Clark is a young man, a native of the state of New Hampshire. He has had, however, much experience in the departments at Washington, beside during the last eight or nine months he has been making a thorough preparation for his work in Liberia. I think you will like Mr. Clark. He is certainly thoroughly in earnest, and is without race prejudice.

I am sorry that matters regarding Liberia have moved so slowly in this country, but you can easily understand that with all the work that is going on in Washington that everything moves slowly. A few of us, however, have kept the interests of Liberia constantly before the Department and it looks now as if matters are coming out all right.

Whenever I can be of service do not fail to command me. Yours very truly,

[Booker T. Washington]

TLc Con. 424 BTW Papers DLC.

[1] Daniel Edward Howard in 1911 was chairman of the True Whig party in Liberia, after earlier service as party secretary and governor of Montserrado County. He was president of Liberia from 1912 to 1920.

To Julius B. Ramsey

[Tuskegee, Ala.] Sept. 7, 1911

Major Ramsey: Please let me have the names of all married teachers who are occupying rooms in your Department that might be occupied by students.

In an increasing degree we shall have to enforce the policy of letting families provide rooms for themselves on the outside. It is not fair to our students to have some of our best rooms taken by families. We do not permit students to board on the outside and for this reason, we ought not to cramp them, when teachers might go a short distance from the school grounds and provide rooms or houses for themselves.

Besides we shall be helping the teachers in proportion as we teach them how to become independent in the way of providing a place to live. Young people especially ought to be taught that before they get married, they ought to think about some place to live that is owned by themselves, rather than by somebody else.

[Booker T. Washington]

TLp   Con. 614   BTW Papers   DLC.

Thornwell Fay[1] to Emmett Jay Scott

Houston, Texas, September 9, 1911

Dear Sir: Replying to your personal favor of September 7th, I beg to advise that there can be no objection to Dr. Washington engaging drawing-room over our lines from New Orleans to Maricopa. This is an interstate journey and the state laws would not apply. I would suggest that Dr. Washington purchase through ticket, which would include passage from New Orleans to Maricopa direct. Upon his return, he can purchase ticket from Maricopa or Phoenix to San Antonio and can then also use drawing room to destination.

I am sending copy of this letter to the ticket agent at New Orleans, in order that he may make drawing room reservation for Dr. Washington, whenever he is called upon to do so. Yours truly,

T. Fay

TLSr   Con. 458   BTW Papers   DLC.

[1] Vice-president and general manager of the Galveston, Harrisburg, and San Antonio Railroad.

From Charles William Anderson

New York, Sept 10/11

My dear Doctor: Do you remember Hubert H. Harrison?[1] He is the man who wrote two nasty articles against you in the New York "Sun." He is a clerk in the Postoffice. The Postmaster is my personal friend, as you probably know. Harrison has had charges preferred against him and I think he is liable to be dismissed from the service.[2] If not dismissed, he will get severe punishment. Can you see the hand? I think you can. Please destroy this, that it may not fall under another eye — unless it is Emmett's. I will attend to Harrison. If he escapes me, he is a dandy. Hastily Yours,

Charles W. Anderson

ALS   Con. 52   BTW Papers   DLC.

[1] Hubert H. Harrison was a prominent black radical of Harlem. Born in the Virgin Islands, he moved to New York in the early years of the twentieth century. A socialist, a student of African history, and a defender of the black racial heritage, he conducted formal lectures on what he called the "Harlem School of Social Science." The Hubert H. Harrison Memorial Church in Harlem honors his memory. (Osofsky, *Harlem*, 132–33.)

[2] Anderson reported the dismissal of Harrison with mock regret. (See Anderson to BTW, Oct. 30, 1911, below.)

To James F. Oyster[1]

[Tuskegee, Ala.] September 11, 1911

Dear Sir: I have been away from my mail considerably lately and this accounts for my failure to write you more promptly.

I can state unreservedly that the reference in my World's Work article was not at all to Mr. Bruce, who was Director of our Academic Department, and not the person in charge of the Division of Education as my article states. Mr. Bruce, I feel quite sure, well understands to whom reference is made in the particular article to which you refer.[2]

Mr. Bruce served this institution as Director of the Academic Department for three or four years and voluntarily resigned to take the position to which he had been elected as Supervising Principal of Colored Schools of Washington.

I very much hope that no harm may come to Mr. Bruce by reason of the article to which you refer and which has been cited as expressing my lack of confidence in him.

I still have the utmost confidence in Mr. Bruce, both as an educator and as a man, and believe that the interests of the colored schools of Washington could not be under the direction of a more competent or a more conscientious executive. I have watched his course there with much interest, and believe he is rendering a service that is in every way worthy of the encouragement and hearty support of the officials of the Board of Education.

Mr. Bruce, you may recall, went to Washington with my hearty endorsement, and I have in no way withdrawn it.

You are, of course, well acquainted with Mr. Bruce's earnest, consistent, and, I believe, sincere efforts to establish in connection with the public schools of Washington adequate provision for training Negro boys and girls in various trades and industries, and for training teachers of cooking, sewing and manual training. I consider no work more important. It is fundamental.

Trusting that my reply to your inquiry has not been too long delayed, I am: Yours very truly,

[Booker T. Washington]

TLc   Con. 418   BTW Papers   DLC.

¹ James F. Oyster, born in Washington in 1851, had been engaged in the butter, egg, and cheese business in that city since 1870. He was president of the board of education of the District of Columbia for many years beginning in 1907, and became a director of the Federal Reserve Bank of Richmond when it was established in 1914.

² G. David Houston, a Howard graduate, was head of the normal and preparatory department from 1905 to 1907. BTW discussed his failure as a teacher as an illustration of "the way in which too much learning will hamper a man who finds himself in the presence of a new problem — one not in the books." See excerpt from *My Larger Education* in *World's Work,* 20 (Dec. 1910), 1378–79.

To Jacob Henry Schiff

[Tuskegee, Ala.] Sept. 11, 1911

Dear Mr. Schiff: I received your kind letter of August 30 regarding the schools which you have under consideration for the present year. I have delayed answering your letter because it required a little time to look a little more closely into the work being done by some of these schools. It is very satisfactory to know that you will continue your generosity in this direction for another year.

After going carefully into the matter, I advise that you contribute as last year except in the following cases:

Take away $50 from the Utica Normal & Industrial Institute and add it to Fisk University, Nashville, Tenn.

Take away $25 from the extra $50 contributed to the Farmers Improvement Society, Ladonia, Texas, and give it to the Calhoun Colored School, Calhoun, Ala.

Most of the new schools applying to you are not very important.

I am glad to say that I have had a good vacation and am ready for a hard year's work.

I shall hope to see you sometime in October when I shall be in New York.

I hope that your trip abroad has been a great benefit to you. Yours very truly,

Booker T. Washington

TLpS Con. 55 BTW Papers DLC.

To Whitefield McKinlay

[Tuskegee, Ala., ca. Sept. 11, 1911]

Confidential

My dear Mr. McKinlay: I suppose you know through our friend, Mr. Tyler, that I am standing by Mr. Bruce in his present fight.[1] I take for granted that this course has your approval.

You ought to impress, however, upon Mr. Bruce upon every occasion that he must in the future try to stand by himself in a larger degree than he has in the past and above all things, he ought to cultivate a spirit of loyalty to those who assist him. I hear a good many people complaining of him in these two regards. This, of course, is very confidential.

If things get serious against Bruce, I should not object to going to the President, but I do not want to do it unless it is absolutely necessary. I hope you, Mr. Tyler and Mr. Cobb will keep a close eye on the situation. Of course since we have begun supporting Mr. Bruce, we shall not want to fail. Yours very truly,

Booker T. Washington

TLpS Con. 54 BTW Papers DLC.

¹ When William M. Davidson became superintendent of education of the District of Columbia in 1911, Richard R. Horner, a black member of the school board, questioned the legality of R. C. Bruce's continuing in office as assistant superintendent, but the attorney for the board gave the opinion that Bruce could remain until Davidson dismissed him. At a closed session of the board on Sept. 19, 1911, Horner, William V. Tunnell, and Mrs. Carrie Harris, the black members, failed to convince the superintendent and other board members that Bruce should be dismissed. After a long investigation, Superintendent Davidson found untrue the charges that Bruce had made several improper promotions and demotions. The board on Mar. 20, 1912, by a 5 to 3 vote, supported the superintendent's recommendation that Bruce be retained. Though the criticisms of Bruce by the black school board members centered on his appointments, and they were in turn accused of favoring their own relatives and protegés, another underlying cause of dissatisfaction with Bruce among many blacks was his support of industrial education and his endorsement by whites. (Washington *Bee,* Sept. 23, 1911, 1, Sept. 30, 1911, 4, Mar. 9, 1912, 1, Mar. 23, 1912, 1; Washington *Post,* Sept. 16, 1911, 1, Sept. 20, 1911, 1, Mar. 21, 1912, 2.)

From William T. McKinney¹

Washington, D.C. September 11, 1911

Dear Dr Washington; Since our talk in the Union Station, of this city some days ago, I have been making a few mental comparisons, some of which I have endeavored to put into this letter. It is needless for me to tell you how glad I was of the opportunity of spending a few minutes with you, and that opportunity made me think of the innumerable things that have fallen in between "Ruffner's Lane" and Tuskegee.

Old Dr DeGraffe used to define growth as being all that takes place in ones life from infancy to tottering old age. To see growth as applied to your life, one must travel from the old Ruffner homestead in Malden, with its familiar inmates; the Gen'l and Mrs Viola Ruffner, Miss Banks, "Uncle" Frank Randolph, "Uncle" Reeves, and "Miss Stella" to Tuskegee, with its fertile fields, commodious buildings, humming industries and large student body. I do not call you by name in this arrangement, for you and Tuskegee are one.

May we not enjoy a little mental retrospect just here, and return to Malden and listen to the whistle of the boiling salt pans on the old furnace and hear again the crack of the mule driver's whip as he brings the cars of furnace coal through the old "Ruffner gate," where sat "Uncle" Billy DeHaven, with his stiff leg and spear pointed walking stick? So many things come to me now; your practically penniless departure for Hampton, your graduation there from and early teaching in the little brick meeting house in Malden. When I recall those early school days, I think of how proud we boys were to have one of us, who had been to "college," come back and teach us. How our hearts swelled with the feeling that some day we would do likewise, and we went about our tasks with greater energy. Now comes to my mind those Friday afternoon speakings at school and "Gid" Randolph and his speech;

> "Junebug has a glossy wing,
> Lightningbug carries a flame;
> Bedbug has no wing at all,
> But he gits there jis' the same."

Also our school debates that we enjoyed so much. I recall one debate when the question was, "Which is the most benefit to man, the horse or cow?" Sam Courtney (Dr S. E. Courtney) was one of the disputants and he closed his discussion with these words, "Give me the horse or give me death." I distinctly remember this for you seemed to enjoy most extravagantly Sam's parody on a portion of Patrick Henry's famous Virginia speech. On another afternoon we were favored with an "original" poem by "Si" Randolph (S. H. Randolph, Atty.) subject, "No Hafway Doin's." It opened like this:

> "Belubed feller trablers, in holdin' forth de day,
> I dusent kwote no spushul vurse in what I has ter say.
> But its good ole gospul scriptur an' dis am de tex'
> Dat haf way doin's aint no count, in dis worl ner de nex'."

It ran for perhaps 40 or 50 lines. "Si" was a pretty spry fellow and always beat the most of us in "doing" things, and that poem made us hail him as our coming poet. (I read the same poem a number of years later in Harper's magazine, where the author had republished it by request.)

Can you remember those splendid school exhibitions we used to have at the close of each school year, which we later called "Closing Exercises" and now "Commencements"? At these annual feasts each girl would have a new frock and each boy new jeans trousers and round-about made by a devoted mother and "on her fingers." "Beadle's Dime Dialogues," "single" pieces and "singing" would make up the program. The pastor of the church or some "licentiate" preacher would open the exhibition with prayer and you would conduct the exercises. To these exhibitions came the old and the young. In fact Malden with the surrounding community would turn out on its good behavior. Each parent was filled with hopes of his boy or girl whom he was anxious to hear "say his piece." Then would come vacation days and those of us who were large enough would go to work, mostly in the mines. During the summer vacation we would have our annual picnics. On these occasions you would deliver an address, largely along the line of your speeches now. This brings us up to the meeting of the Mt Olivet Baptist Association. You were many times clerk of this organization, which always met in August after the watermelons had "dropped their blossoms" and the spring chickens were well "feathered." To these meetings came ministers from far and near, of every color and every grade of intelligence. These annual gatherings laid the foundation for much the race is now accomplishing. Coming nearer home, I am now reminded of the big meetings we used to have the third Sunday in each month, they were known as "communion Sunday." The housewives would vie with each other in seeing who could prepare the best dinner and which could be first in extending hospitality to those who came in from the outlying country. It was on one of these occasions that one Dr Baty appeared on the scene and preached at the morning service to a very large audience. I say *Doctor* Baty, for he was the first gentleman of color to come around our way wearing the title of "Doctor." After warming himself up to his subject, he proceeded to issue forth those peculiar sounds which always set the brethren and sisters to rocking and moaning and giving vent to their feelings in various ways. Dr Baty was so carried away by the spirit that he grabbed the Bible and threw it into space with the exclamation, "Here God, take the Bible." It struck your dear old mother, "Aunt" Jane, on the arm and it was feared for a time that it was broken, but fortunately it was only bruised. This outburst of "spiritual enthusiasm" on the part of the preacher was soon overlooked for he was "in the spirit" and was not responsible. Your mother always sat in the "amen" corner along with "Aunt" Violet Taylor, "Aunt" Mary Rice, my mother and others of the "old mothers in Israel," who have long since gone to a Saint's reward.

May we now peep in at one of the monthly business meetings of the church. On these occasions, "Father" Rice, grand old man and pioneer preacher, would be moderator and you church clerk. After devotional exercises and you had read the "minutes of the previous meeting," the routine business was taken up. These meetings furnished many occasions for the display of "eloquence" and references to "parliamentary practice." Often the members would get into a tangled web over some question as to whether it was debatable or not, or whether it was an amendment or substitute, and "Father" Rice would stroke his sparse growth of whiskers and lean over and whisper to you for instructions. After he had untangled the knot according to your coaching, business would proceed. I remember one night at one of these meetings a heated discussion arose over some question and things were pretty warm for a time. As I can now recall the disputants were Joe Pete Hughes and Musey Strawder. They were approaching each other in a very belligerent manner, and friends were intervening to keep them apart. The whole church appeared to be "on its feet." "Father" Rice, as he usually did on such occasions, struck up the hymn, "Blest be the tie that binds" &c. "Uncle" Wash Ferguson, your dear old step-father, who had been asleep from the beginning of the meeting, was suddenly awakened by the confusion and arose to his feet and exclaimed, "Put out them lights, put out them lights." This raised quite a laughter and made all forget about the threatened melee. "Uncle" Frank Randolph, the "head" deacon, said "Be quiet brothers, be quiet, brother Wash was 'sleep and when he 'woke he thought he was at one of them dances we used to have in slavery time when the lights would be put out to stop the 'niggers' from fightin'." All in good humor again, business proceeded.

Let me here mention those debating contests that Joe Pete Hughes and Gilbert Lovely used to arrange with nearby towns when you a mere boy, were the center of attraction. They would get a two horse wagon and fill it with debaters and "rooters" and go to the town where the debate was to be held. They would always take "Booker" along to make their closing argument, and you would always "clean up" for them. I believe those occasions had much to do with your great success as a public speaker years later.

There are many incidents that rush in on me to which I would like to refer if space permitted. I would like to discuss some of the peculiar characteristics of many of the old people around about Malden it was your good fortune to know, whose lives stand as a fitting background to the magnificent pictures you have painted in the foreground.

I cannot close this disconnected reminiscent letter without referring to those splendid lessons of life you taught us as boys and girls while you as teacher, were scarcely out of knee breeches and round-about. I can now recall with appreciation how strangely you always seemed and how different you were from the rest of the boys. As I can now remember it, you always appeared to be looking for something in the distant future. There was always seen a future look in your eyes. This look has been seen in the eyes of many of our great men. Robert Fulton looked into the future and saw the floating palaces that ply our streams; Thomas A. Edison looked into the future and saw the world illumined by a light a little below the brightness of the sun; you looked into the future and saw a struggling race that needed

> A directing word, and a chance to do,
> A hand to lead and a life anew,

and out of this future came Tuskegee. Now, a last word. You had sentiments and beliefs and you put them into words, and from words you made them into living things.

> A wheel here, a spindle there,
> And a work bench in between;
> A writing desk, a case of books,
> And fields of rolling green.

Yours very sincerely,

W T McKinney

TLS   Con. 429   BTW Papers   DLC.

¹ William T. McKinney, who had been BTW's student in the Malden, W.Va., black school, married the daughter of Rev. Lewis Rice. He was a government clerk in Washington, D.C.

Ralph Waldo Tyler to Emmett Jay Scott

Washington   Sept. 11/11

My dear Emmett: Am enclosing you copy of letter just mailed to Mr. Hilles.[1] Think this the best way to get at it. I know that they are, or was sometime back, anxious to have a colored man either break into the rank of a line officer of the army. If Hilles replies to me direct, will advise you at once.

Lewis and Cobb both got back today, and are on their jobs. I need a rest very, very much, but I cant leave for a minute. Dont want these anties to put anything over, and you know how awfully close they came to it with "the eloquent one."[2] The anties are working every moment in the day, and we have just got to outwork them; i.e., work both night and day. And Chase always needs watching. I cant even leave him to go out and urinate.

By-the-way, you ought to stir up The Age. The lack of Washington correspondence for several weeks, and the character of the editorials, as a whole, is being criticized here, and especially will the lack of good Washington correspondence injure the circulation here and everywhere, for people want news from Washington.

Tyler

You see by The Bee I am burning up that National Independent Political League.

TLS   Con. 442   BTW Papers   DLC.   Postcript in Tyler's hand.

[1] Tyler urged Charles D. Hilles to persuade President Taft to nominate a black man to take the examination for admission to West Point and another to take the examination for the rank of second lieutenant. (Tyler to Hilles, Sept. 11, 1911, Con. 442, BTW Papers, DLC.)
[2] William Tecumseh Vernon.

To Henry Hess

[Tuskegee, Ala.] September 14, 1911

Dear Sir: I have your kind favor of September 11th advising me that you had shipped me a box of your cigars.[1]

These have not come to hand as yet, but when they do so, I assure you I shall enjoy them.

I appreciate your kindness in sending these to me, and shall also thank Dr. Owens for his share in the matter. Yours very truly,

Booker T. Washington

The box has come and like the cigars very much. Shall hope to send you an order in the future.

B. T. W.

TLpS   Con. 424   BTW Papers   DLC.   Postcript in BTW's hand.

¹ Hess, a maker of handmade cigars in Mobile, Ala., wrote that he had learned from his friend A. F. Owens of the Tuskegee faculty that BTW was "fond of a good cigar." He shipped BTW a box of his Perfectos and asked him to pass judgment on them. (Con. 424, BTW Papers, DLC.)

To John Davison Rockefeller, Jr.

[Tuskegee, Ala.] September 14, 1911

Personal.

My dear Mr. Rockefeller: It has now been several years since we had the privilege of having a visit from yourself and Mrs. Rockefeller.

I am writing in the hope that both you and Mrs. Rockefeller may see your way clear to visit this institution sometime during the present fall or sometime during the winter or spring. I think you will find many evidences of progress since you were here.

I am especially anxious that you see at first hand some of the results of the work in the uplifting of our race. Your father has been of so much help to us in bringing about these results, that we want you to see just what has been accomplished, and how it is being done.

We shall extend both you and Mrs. Rockefeller a hearty welcome whenever you can come. Yours truly,

Booker T. Washington

TLpS   Con. 438   BTW Papers   DLC.

To Hollis Burke Frissell

[Tuskegee, Ala.] September 14, 1911

My dear Dr. Frissell: I do not think any of us can sufficiently thank you for your foresight and generosity in sparing Dr. Jones from Hampton for the purpose of letting him help in connection with the Census. The work he is doing is of untold value. Without his presence in the Census Bureau, I feel very sure that the Negro race and the cause of education would have received a "black eye." I am myself just beginning to see and understand something of the hard untiring work he has been engaged in. We must all stand by him. Yours very truly,

Booker T. Washington

TLpS Con. 617 BTW Papers DLC.

From Whitefield McKinlay

Washington, D.C., 9/14/11

Dr Doctor Washington: I am closely watching B's fight, but keeping in the background, but you can safely conclude that he will pull through mainly because the people who are fighting him are known to be activated by selfish motives. Horner[1] is doing him more good than harm, as the members of the Board are beginning to read him (Horner).

This fight will do Bruce a lot of good as he needs just such a lesson to teach that loyalty & truthfulness are valuable virtues.

You must *not* be known in this fight. Ever yrs

W McKinlay

ALS Con. 54 BTW Papers DLC.

[1] Richard R. Horner.

From George Washington Carver

[Tuskegee, Ala.] Sept. 14 — '11

Mr. B. T. Washington, I write to ask that you please arrange so that I can get the first installment of goods for my laboratory before you go away, otherwise according to past history nothing will be done.

Nearly eleven months ago, (See note of Nov. 23d) my work was arbitrarily changed. I was asked to sever my connection with a work that 15 years of my life's blood had gone into, pioneer years in which no one wanted it; this I reluctantly did, but accepted the promise.

Afterward it was modified to the extent that I must yet teach classes, this I did, with the understanding that my laboratory would be hurried along.

Feb. 20th (See note) another assurance was given, Sept. 14th has come and absolutely no equipment.

I am being annoyed by committees that sometimes say very unhandsome and unbecoming things; which causes me to indulge in the same spirit, with the result that the laboratory is yet empty.

My mind is not in condition to do good work, and if it was I could not do it because I have nothing to do with. I am attempting to teach the two higher classes in Agriculture.

Again I am trying to develop something that cannot help but mean much to the entire South, and of course primarily to Tuskegee Institute.

As I have said before I had hoped to make a big display of paints, stains, kalsomines, toilet powders ect. at the Montgomery and Macon Co. fairs but cannot do more than one half, which of course is a great disappointment. I have divided the total amount into three groups Viz. 1-2 & 3, which I trust you will allow to come sufficiently far apart so as not to press you for the means.

Kindly excuse me from meeting any more committees on it as my nerves will not stand it. Yours very truly

G. W. Carver

ALS   Con. 615   BTW Papers   DLC.

To Frederick Randolph Moore

[Tuskegee, Ala.] September 16, 1911

Dear Mr. Moore: A few days ago, I wrote you concerning the fine paper which you got out either last week or week before last.

I am sure you will not misunderstand me, because I am simply writing in your interest, when I say that the issue for this week is way down. It is a real slump. *The editorials, in my opinion, are especially unfortunate. They are about twice too long and then they deal for the most part with dead subjects, rather than with live subjects.* There is a great slump also in the local news. I have sent you about a half-dozen editorials recently which I notice have not appeared. I have tried to deal with live subjects, but for some reason, they did not seem to be fortunate enough to get printed. Yours very truly,

Booker T. Washington

TLpS   Con. 54   BTW Papers   DLC.

To Ralph Waldo Tyler

[Tuskegee, Ala.] Sept. 16, 1911

Dear Mr. Tyler: I see by the Age that Major Lynch has resigned. Is it not possible to put a colored man into his place? Look into the conditions surrounding it. If we cannot put a colored man in his place, it will mean that another position is lost to the race.

If there is any hope of our getting favorable action, I should be willing to take the matter up directly with the President. Please telegraph me. Yours very truly,

Booker T. Washington

TLpS   Con. 442   BTW Papers   DLC.

From Ralph Waldo Tyler

Washington, D.C. Sept 18/11

Dear Doctor: Yours of the 16th at hand. Impossible to land colored man in Lynch's place for the reason staff officers in the army are taken from the line, via regular promotion. Only in time of war, where an extra quota of paymasters, as well as line off[ic]ers must be provided, are civilians made paymasters with line officers' rank. Had it not been for the Spanish-American war, Lynch could not have become a paymaster.

Unfortunately his retirement means a loss of a position for the race with no chance to succeed him by another colored man. The fight here on Bruce by Horner and the other two colored board members, Tunnell & Mrs Harris,[1] has been fierce, but up to this hour we have them beat. This Washington life is wearisome — simply one scrap after another. Washington Negroes furnish the best possible argument for those whites who contend the Negro is incapable of self-goverment. I have been in the fight with my sleeves rolled up, because I know it is really aimed at you and your friends. I can beat this bunch of anties here seven days out of seven.

R. W. Tyler

ALS Con. 442 BTW Papers DLC.

[1] Carrie Harris.

From John Davison Rockefeller, Jr.

New York   September 18, 1911

Dear Mr. Washington: Your letter of September 14th, inviting Mrs. Rockefeller and me to visit Tuskegee during the fall or winter, is received. We remember with pleasure our former visit and shall be glad indeed when it is possible for us to come to Tuskegee again. With four little children Mrs. Rockefeller finds it difficult to go very far from home and I have not myself been in the South for some years. We shall

314

gladly remember the invitation and when next we are able to do so will take much pleasure in coming to Tuskegee. We keep in touch with your constantly growing work and are gratified with the development which is taking place.

With kind regards, I am, Very truly,

John D. Rockefeller, Jr.

TLS   Con. 438   BTW Papers   DLC.

Charles Norvell Love to Emmett Jay Scott

Houston, Texas, Sept 19, 1911

Dear Emmett: This is to advise that Mayor H. B. Rice has acquiesced and will personally welcome Dr. Booker T. Washington, that City Superintendent Horn[1] and County Superintendent Pugh[2] have accepted invitations to occupy seats on the platform, that the Cotton Exchange and Chamber of Commerce, through their secretaries, will be officially represented, that Editors R. M. Johnston[3] and M. E. Foster[4] have accepted invitations to be present and that Mayor Rice on his own motion will have appear with him other leading business men, such as bankers, merchants and others of that stripe at the City Auditorium Wednesday night, Sept 27th. The two superintendents are enthusiastic and are working like beavers getting up attendance. Mother and wife at present are doing fairly well. This may be all till I see you.

C. N. Love

ALS   Con. 828   BTW Papers   DLC.

[1] Paul Whitfield Horn.

[2] L. L. Pugh.

[3] Rienzi Melville Johnston (1850–1926), editor and large stockholder of the Houston *Post*.

[4] Marcellus Elliot Foster, owner and editor of the Houston *Chronicle* (1901–26) and editor of the Houston *Press* (1927–36).

An Introduction to Matthew Alexander Henson's
A Negro Explorer at the North Pole

[Sept. 20, 1911][1]

One of the first questions which Commander Peary was asked when he returned home from his long, patient, and finally successful struggle to reach the Pole was how it came about that, beside the four Esquimos, Matt Henson, a Negro, was the only man to whom was accorded the honor of accompanying him on the final dash to the goal.

The question was suggested no doubt by the thought that it was but natural that the positions of greatest responsibility and honor on such an expedition would as a matter of course fall to the white men of the party rather than to a Negro. To this question, however, Commander Peary replied, in substance:

"Matthew A. Henson, my Negro assistant, has been with me in one capacity or another since my second trip to Nicaragua in 1887. I have taken him on each and all of my expeditions, except the first, and also without exception on each of my farthest sledge trips. This position I have given him primarily because of his adaptability and fitness for the work and secondly on account of his loyalty. He is a better dog driver and can handle a sledge better than any man living, except some of the best Esquimo hunters themselves."

In short, Matthew Henson, next to Commander Peary, held and still holds the place of honor in the history of the expedition that finally located the position of the Pole, because he was the best man for the place. During twenty-three years of faithful service he had made himself indispensable. From the position of a servant he rose to that of companion and assistant in one of the most dangerous and difficult tasks that was ever undertaken by men. In extremity, when both the danger and the difficulty were greatest, the Commander wanted by his side the man upon whose skill and loyalty he could put the most absolute dependence and when that man turned out to be black instead of white, the Commander was not only willing to accept the service but was at the same time generous enough to acknowledge it.

There never seems to have been any doubt in Commander Peary's mind about Henson's part and place in the expedition.

Matt Henson, who was born in Charles County, Maryland, August

8, 1866, began life as a cabin-boy on an ocean steamship, and before he met Commander Peary had already made a voyage to China. He was eighteen years old when he made the acquaintance of Commander Peary which gave him his chance. During the twenty-three years in which he was the companion of the explorer he not only had time and opportunity to perfect himself in his knowledge of the books, but he acquired a good practical knowledge of everything that was a necessary part of the daily life in the ice-bound wilderness of polar exploration. He was at times a blacksmith, a carpenter, and a cook. He was thoroughly acquainted with the life, customs, and language of the Esquimos. He himself built the sledges with which the journey to the Pole was successfully completed. He could not merely drive a dog-team or skin a musk-ox with the skill of a native, but he was something of a navigator as well. In this way Mr. Henson made himself not only the most trusted but the most useful member of the expedition.

I am reminded in this connection that Matthew Henson is not the first colored man who by his fidelity and devotion has made himself the trusty companion of the men who have explored and opened up the western continent. Even in the days when the Negro had little or no opportunity to show his ability as a leader, he proved himself at least a splendid follower, and there are few great adventures in which the American white man has engaged where he has not been accompanied by a colored man.

Nearly all the early Spanish explorers were accompanied by Negroes. It is said that the first ship built in America was constructed by the slaves of Vasquez de Ayllon, who attempted to establish a Spanish settlement where Jamestown, Virginia, was later founded. Balboa had 30 Negroes with him, and they assisted him in constructing the first ship on the Pacific coast. Three hundred slaves were brought to this country by Cortez, the conqueror of Mexico, and it is said that the town of Santiago del Principe was founded by Negro slaves who later rebelled against their Spanish masters.

Of the story of those earlier Negro explorers we have, aside from the Negro Estevan or "little Steve," who was the guide and leader in the search for the fabulous seven cities, almost nothing more than a passing reference in the accounts which have come down to us. Now, a race which has come up from slavery; which is just now for the first time learning to build for itself homes, churches, schools; which is learning for the first time to start banks, organize insurance companies, erect manufacturing plants, establish hospitals; a race which is doing all the fundamental things for the first time; which has, in short, its history before it instead of behind; such a race in such conditions needs for its own encouragement, as well as to justify the hopes of its friends, the records of the members of the race who have been a part of any great and historic achievement.

For this reason, as well as for others; for the sake of my race as well as the truth of history; I am proud and glad to welcome this account of his adventure from a man who has not only honored the race of which he is a member, but has proven again that courage, fidelity, and ability are honored and rewarded under a black skin as well as under a white.

BOOKER T. WASHINGTON

Matthew A. Henson, *A Negro Exprorer at the North Pole* (New York, 1912), xv-xx. A press copy of BTW's typed manuscript is attached to E. J. Scott to Henson, Sept. 20, 1911, Con. 424, BTW Papers, DLC.

1 The date that E. J. Scott forwarded BTW's final draft of the introduction to Henson. (Scott to Henson, Sept. 20, 1911, Con. 424, BTW Papers, DLC.) On Feb. 19, 1912, BTW wrote to Henson that he had received the book, and congratulated him "upon the splendid way in which you have told your story." (Con. 456, BTW Papers, DLC.)

To William T. McKinney

[Tuskegee, Ala.] September 21, 1911

Dear Mr. McKinney: I have your letter of some days ago, with enclosure.[1]

Let me say with all candor, that nothing has given me greater pleasure in a long while than the reading of your letter of reminiscences. The scenes, figures and incidents described by you are all so vivid, that for a few moments I felt myself carried back once more to my boyhood days. That one particular period of my life will always stand out most prominently in my mind.

I shall hope to keep your letter at hand, and read it again when I have opportunity.

With regard to the matter of your securing a better position, I shall be very glad to keep this in mind, and if opportunity offers directly to serve you, I shall be more than pleased to embrace it.

With kindest regards always, I am, Yours very truly,

Booker T. Washington

P.S. I return Mr. Cabell's[2] letter, as requested.

TLpS Con. 429 BTW Papers DLC.

[1] Accompanying McKinney's letter of reminiscence dated Sept. 11, 1911, was a cover letter dated Sept. 12 in which McKinney solicited BTW's help in finding a better position within the government service than the one he held in the Treasury Department.

[2] Royal E. Cabell, U.S. Commissioner of Internal Revenue.

From Thomas Jesse Jones

Washington September 22, 1911

Dear Dr. Washington: Director Durand will probably announce the Negro population of the United States some time during the week beginning September 24. This announcement will show that the rate of increase of the colored people for the last ten years is a little over 11 per cent. As this increase is a decrease from 18 per cent in 1900, it is important that the facts be properly presented to the country, otherwise calamity howlers will take pleasure in growing eloquent over the disappearance of the race. As a matter of fact the rate of increase which is to be announced is, in the opinion of the best statisticians, a perfectly normal rate for a people increasing entirely by the excess of births over deaths. A similar rate for the English people, announced for the 1911 population is 12.4 per cent, only one per cent in excess of the rate for the Negro.

The high rate of increase announced by the 1900 Census is undoubtedly explained by the undercount in 1890. The Census Bureau, however, can not officially cast doubt upon a previous Census. For that reason I am exceedingly eager that you shall send out an interview which will have as wide a circulation as the Census announcement itself. In order to make this easy for you in case you consent to do it, I have prepared a statement discussing the situation in full.[1] This statement you will of course use in any form suitable to your own

319

ideas. I hope, however, that the statement or its contents may go before the country through the Associated Press and every other means that will give it wide publication. Your own statement, of course, must be held up until Director Durand has made his official announcement of the increase. I shall see that you receive Director Durand's announcement as soon as it is available.

Will you please let me know immediately what your address will be next week so that I may communicate with you either by special delivery letter or telegram.

We are eagerly awaiting your favorable reply with regard to presenting the claims of the colored Social Settlement of Washington to the people here.

With very kind regards I am   Sincerely yours,

Thomas Jesse Jones

TLS   Con. 426   BTW Papers   DLC.

¹ In the enclosed statement, "Negro Population in 1910," Jones explained in more detail the discrepancies in the census returns of blacks in 1890, 1900, and 1910. BTW used the statement almost verbatim. (See BTW to Edward Dana Durand, Oct. 25, 1911, below.)

From Ruth Standish Bowles Baldwin

Washington, Conn. Oct 2, 1911

My dear Mr. Washington: A rumor comes to me that you are far from well.

I am greatly distressed and I do hope you are trying to arrange to go a bit slow and to get & keep yourself in good condition.¹

I am going to be in N. Y. at 99 Madison Ave. (You know Washington Conn is now "home") from Oct 9 to 13th & if you are to be there then I wish you could spare me a little time as there are two or three matters about the local & national urban work on which I covet your advice. Yours very sincerely,

Ruth S. Baldwin

ALS   Con. 417   BTW Papers   DLC.

To Ruth Standish Bowles Baldwin

[Tuskegee, Ala.] October 7, 1911

My dear Mrs. Baldwin: Thank you for your letter of October 2nd.

I am glad to say that I am all right now. During the latter part of the summer I had considerable trouble.

I shall hope to see you in New York, and am very glad to have your new address.

I have just returned from a ten days tour through the state of Texas. It was a great trip. The meetings were most enthusiastic and largely attended by both white and colored people. My health was first rate during the whole trip although it was rather taxing from a physical point of view.

Will you be kind enough to let me know if you are keeping house. If you are we want to send you some Tuskegee sweet potatoes. Yours very truly,

Booker T. Washington

TLpS   Con. 417   BTW Papers   DLC.

To Joseph Oswalt Thompson

[Tuskegee, Ala.] October 7, 1911

Personal.

Dear Mr. Thompson: As you know, I am to speak in Birmingham on the night of the 13th. I shall hope to see you.

I am particularly anxious that a large and representative audience of white people from Birmingham be present. I express this wish especially because of the dirty fight that Manning and others have made upon me in that section.

I am glad to tell you that my meetings in Texas were overwhelmingly successful. The white people were just as enthusiastic as the colored people and turned out in as large numbers in many places. Yours very truly,

Booker T. Washington

TLpS Con. 442 BTW Papers DLC.

An Account of Washington's Tour of Texas

Tuskegee, Alabama, October 7, 1911

RECEIVE GREAT OVATION IN TEXAS

PRINCIPAL WASHINGTON AND PARTY WELCOMED BY THRONGS AT MANY POINTS

The El Paso Herald contains the following report of Principal Washington's visit to El Paso, which was the beginning point of his recent tour through Texas:[1]

The noted educator arrived at 5:30 o'clock yesterday afternoon from Arizona. He went immediately to the home of C. W. Bradley,[2] 1209 Wyoming Street. At 6:30 o'clock he attended a dinner given him by the colored women of El Paso at the home of the Perretts,[3] 507 S. Campbell Street. At 8 o'clock he addressed a large audience of both black and white races at the El Paso theatre.

After this lecture, he spoke at the Second Baptist church and the First Methodist church to colored people on special problems connected with the race.

TO VISIT JUAREZ

This morning at 9 o'clock, Dr. Washington will visit Juarez, where he will meet the mayor, councilmen and other officials. At 10:30 o'clock he will leave for San Antonio.

The Executive committee of colored men having in general charge the entertainment of the famous lecturer while in El Paso and who sat upon the platform at the theatre last night, included C. W. Bradley, E. D. Williams[4] of Las Cruces, LeRoy White,[5] Rev. H. R. Wilson,[6]

Rev. L. M. Saunders, Rev. E. L. Russell, Rev. L. J. Jacks, Amos Williams,[7] F. D. Clopton,[8] Jasper Williams[9] and William Sublette.

William Coleman,[10] principal of the Douglass School of this city, introduced Dr. Washington as the man who, when everything seemed dark for the future of the Negro race and progress seemed an idle dream, appeared upon the scene and by the power of his personality, the wisdom of his advice, and the light of his example, pointed the way to the happy condition in which now "both races are living under the same flag, side by side, in peace and harmony."

OVATION TO EDUCATOR

When Dr. Washington appeared upon the platform, he was given a great ovation by the crowd of both white and colored people, a crowd grown so large by this time as to preempt all standing room in the theatre and around the doors and windows. On responding to the introduction and welcome tendered him, Washington touched upon a number of incidents of his early life telling how he used to observe the eight-hour day faithfully — eight hours of work in the morning and eight hours in the evening — how he made the molasses doled out to him seem larger by spreading it over the surface of his plate by tipping it first one way and then another. He told of his labor on farm, in salt and coal mines, in hotels, and in other occupations of life. Abandoning his personal experiences, he launched into his general address.

From El Paso, the party moved on to San Antonio, and then on to Houston. The following account of the meeting at Houston is taken from the Houston Post of September 28th:

Over 7,000 people, about 2,000 of whom were white, thronged the City Auditorium last night and listened for two hours to Booker T. Washington, the well-known Negro educator, deliver one of the sanest and most helpful addresses on the relation of the white and black races in the South that has ever been heard in the city. White and black joined in vigorous applause throughout the address, showing perfect accord in their indorsement of the sentiments of the speaker, and at times the great audience was swayed by such enthusiasm as to make it difficult for Dr. Washington to proceed.

Dr. Washington spoke to his race frankly, and he spoke to the white people present frankly. He declared that the two races have to live together in peace, and that on the whole they are living together in peace. He advised his people to be good workmen. To make themselves good workmen in so many lines that they would become indispensable to the white man. He exhorted them to save their money, to accumulate property, to be good husbands and wives and fathers and mothers, and, above all, to be good citizens. And all of this was applauded to the echo by both white and black.

The meeting at the Auditorium was the climax of a most strenuous day spent by Dr. Washington in Houston. Arriving in the city seven hours late, his special train being delayed by a wreck, the program which was to have filled the day was curtailed somewhat, but the afternoon was filled with engagements which the committee insisted upon his filling. Most of these, however, were with institutions of his own race, and it was not until the evening meeting that the general public, both white and black, met the great educator face to face and listened to his eloquent and wholesome advice.

WAS GIVEN AN OVATION

As early as 6 o'clock in the evening before the lights were lit in the big Auditorium, Negro people began to file in and take possession of the most desirable seats. By the time that the place was lit up a large portion of the seats was already taken. Long before the opening of the meeting every available seat was occupied, and there were a large number standing.

When Dr. Washington stepped on the platform he received an ovation. To one side of the platform were a number of Tuskegee alumni, and they greated their former chief with the college yell. Dr. Washington acknowledged both gracefully and took his place on the platform. With him on the platform were a number of leading Negro professional men and the following white men: L. L. Pugh, county superintendent of schools; Adolph Boldt,[11] Rev. Peter Gray Sears,[12] Rev. Stephen F. Power, Rev. G. W. Strong, Prof. J. A. Brown,[13] Judge Lock McDaniel,[14] Judge T. W. Ford,[15] Lewis R. Bryan[16] and G. Van Ameringen.[17]

TRIBUTE TO TEXAS NEGROES

In opening Dr. Washington took occasion to pay tributes to three Texas Negroes whom he declared to be examples of what the Negro can become.

"You have here in Texas," he said, "two of the finest examples of what a colored man may become, what he may accomplish in helping his own race and winning the respect of the white race that I know of in the United States. I refer to J. B. Bell,[18] citizen of Houston, a black man, who, by reason of his ownership of property, his honest dealings with his fellow-men, and above all, by reason of his common sense, is a constant and shining example for colored people to pattern after throughout the country. What Mr. Bell has done others can do.

"Another example is that of R. L. Smith who, with his wife, is devoting himself most unselfishly, wisely and generously in the direction of helping the Negro in Texas to get homes, become farmers, save their money and lead useful lives. I know no one organization originated and carried [on] by a colored man that is accomplishing more good in laying a foundation for success among our people in the fundamental things of life than is true of the Farmers' Improvement Society, together with his barnyard auxiliary, carried on by R. L. Smith and his good wife. I hope that the Farmers' Improvement Society may be encouraged by every white citizen in Texas, and that every Negro farmer may become a member and supporter of this useful organization.

"I am always glad to come to Houston. The Tuskegee Institute in Alabama owes a debt of gratitude to Houston which it can never repay. Here it was some years ago when I was seeking throughout the country for a man of high character and common sense, combined with intelligence, who could serve as my right hand man in the capacity of a secretary, I found a man for the place in the person of Emmett J. Scott, who was reared in this city and trained in your public schools. From the first day that he came to Tuskegee in this capacity until the present he has not only performed his duty, but is always ready and anxious to do more than his duty, and in this has set a rare example to the rest of the young men of the country.

"Houston, unlike some other cities, sees the wisdom of treating the Negro fairly and justly in the public schools. There are few places in the country, if any, where the Negro has better provisions made for his public school education than is true of Houston. From year to year, I read with deepest interest the reports of your city superintendent, concerning what the colored people are accomplishing in this city, and these reports show that your public schools are teaching and influencing the life of the Negro in a remarkable degree.

"While speaking of Houston I can not forget to thank Mayor Rice and the city officials for their wise generosity in providing a public library for the colored people. If a library is necessary to save and keep the people of the white race, it is equally necessary for a race that is behind the other race in many respects."

Entering fully upon his address, Dr. Washington said:

"I have been surprised and delighted ever since I came into the state of Texas to note the evidences of progress on the part of my race. It is a matter of the greatest satisfaction to accept the invitation extended to me by the Texas State Negro Business League and other organizations and the citizens of the state of Texas to spend some days in making a journey through this state."

The travelers left Houston this morning for Prairie View State Normal and Industrial College (Negro). This college has an enrollment of six hundred students, and a faculty of forty men and women. Luncheon was served to the party and friends who had come in from the surrounding country; about a hundred white farmers with their families were there to hear the message of the educator. A Negro band was stationed on the campus.

Dr. Washington spoke in the afternoon from a portable reading stand invented and made by a Hampton Institute (Va.) student. A box of cut flowers was received from the white citizens of Houston. In his address Dr. Washington spoke of the aristocracy of schools as they had been held by the whites, and then explained the significance of the dawning of democracy in education, saying that the time would come when the ignorant man and not the learned man would be the curiosity of a community. He told the students to apply their education to home conditions, and added that he "regretted that all too often the educated boy or girl left for the city after graduation, being too proud to stay on the farm." This brought forth expressions of approval from both whites and blacks, and he followed it up with the assertion that the country communities and homes should be made attractive enough to hold the educated young person.

"The Negro race," he continued, "has made greater progress in the last twenty years than in all the previous history. The chance in Texas for the Negro is as good, if not better, than any other place in the South."

WONDERFUL PROGRESS IN STATE

Dr. Washington spoke in part as follows:

"According to the most accurate records that we can find, colored people in Texas own and pay taxes on $30,000,000 worth of property. In 1900 the colored people in this state owned and paid taxes on 70,000 farms; during the last ten years they have bought 4,000 additional farms. While this is not as great a gain as has been made in some other states, it indicates great progress in farm getting, and I urge upon all my people, with all the emphasis that I can command, the importance of their owning land, of their getting out of the city into the rural districts, on to the soil. As a rule, our people are better off in the country districts cultivating the soil than they are in large cities. If we do not get hold of farms now, the time will come when it will be impossible for us to do so.

"I find further, that last year the colored people raised in Texas about 465,000 bales of cotton, valued at about $32,000,000; that they raised 16,000,000 bushels of corn, valued at about $12,000,000. It is safe to say that the colored people in Texas got for their farm products of all kinds about $40,000,000. It is safe to say further, that colored people living by other forms of occupation than farming, earned about $10,000,000 more, making the total earnings in Texas for our race about $50,000,000.

SECRET OF RACE PROBLEM

"To a very large extent, the problem of the Negro in the Southern States is a labor problem. In order to secure effective and satisfactory labor from any race, two things have got to be borne in mind: First, people must be taught a love for labor, must be taught the dignity of labor, and at the same time given proper methods in direction of skill. Secondly, they must have their minds and ambitions awakened, so that their wants will be increased. No individual labors except as he has a motive for doing so. The ignorant, untrained Negro in South Africa works only one or two days in each week. He quits and returns to his little hut at the end of that time. The white man in South Africa wonders why this is true, grows impatient and angry for this kind of conduct.

"The white man in South Africa forgets that he ought to do the same thing with the Negro there, that has been done with the Negro in the Southern States — that he ought to educate the Negro so that he will want more. The Southern Negro wants land, wants a house with two or three rooms in it, wants some furniture, books, newspapers, education for his children; wants to support the minister and the Sunday school, and in proportion as those wants are increased, he is led to work an increasing number of days each week, in order to satisfy them.

"In all that concerns the welfare of the Negro in the South, there is no person in the world who can be so helpful to him as his white neighbor. The Negro wants education for his children. He has an ambition to improve the life of his family. If he finds in the city, as he usually does, a school well equipped with good teachers, either by missionary effort or by public school funds, that is in session eight or nine months in the year, and if he finds in his own community a public school taught in a broken-down log cabin, with a poor teacher and the school term not longer than three or four months in the year, the Negro is tempted to move into the city, where he can educate his children.

"Our white friends can help the Negro and help themselves at the same time by seeing to it that the Negro's family is provided with just as good school accommodations in the country as in the city. In my opinion, it would pay in the matter of dollars and cents for every white man who owns a large plantation in this state to see to it that on that plantation a good teacher and upright minister are encouraged in that community. This will mean that labor will come to that plantation, will be satisfied there; that the individual who owns such a plantation and makes provisions for school and church, will not have to seek labor, but labor will seek him.

"Wherever any race or group of people learn to do a common thing in an uncommon way, by putting brain, skill and conscience into labor, that race or group of people is likely to solve all the problems that surround them."

THE BEST IS LEFT UNSAID

"One embarrassment that confronts both races here in the South grows out of the fact that the world hears of the worst things that take place between the black man and the white man in the South. The outside world rarely hears of the best things that occur between the black man and the white man in the South. In nine-tenths of the cases the two races in Texas are living together in peace and harmony but the outside world does not hear of this. It hears of the lynchings, of the burnings, of the mob. In a large degree as a race we must learn to advertise our friends more and our enemies less. I have rarely found a case where a colored man who is industrious and law-abiding, was not encouraged and helped by his white neighbor to get more property and to educate his children. I have rarely heard of a case where a colored man who wanted to improve his condition, where there was not a white man in the community, who was not willing to lend his money to give him advice and encouragement in the direction of making himself a stronger and more useful citizen.

"In the last analysis, I find that the relations between the individual Negro and the individual white man are closer in the South than they are between the black man and the white man in any other part of the world. The Negro as an individual understands the white man better and the white man as an individual understands the Negro better. We must use this relationship as the basis for still further progress. There is no reason why we should not strive to enter upon a new era of life and make up our minds that we are going to settle down in some one community to get hold of property there, become a taxpayer there, make a reputation for virtuous living, for industry there, and work to remain a permanent part of some one community in Texas. In proportion as this shall be true, I repeat over and over again, that everywhere in an increasing degree, we shall find white men who will stand by us and encourage us to make out of ourselves all that is possible for any race to make of itself."

Tuskegee Student, 23 (Oct. 7, 1911), 1, 2, 4.

[1] BTW spoke in Phoenix, Ariz., on Sept. 22, 1911. (See extracts of his speech in Con. 825, BTW Papers, DLC.) The Texas tour began in El Paso on Sept. 25 and ended in Texarkana, Ark., on Oct. 5.

[2] Charles W. Bradley, a black barber.

[3] Exel T. Perrett was a black railroad switchman.

[4] E. D. Williams was a black barber in Las Cruces, N.Mex.

[5] A black barber.

[6] Henry R. Wilson, black pastor of the Second Baptist Church.

[7] A black janitor at the El Paso city hall.

[8] Frederick D. Clopton was a black teacher at the Douglass High School.

[9] Jasper B. Williams was a black messenger employed by the U.S. Immigration Service.

[10] William Coleman, born in Georgia in 1870, studied at Valdosta Academy for eight years and Howard University for five years before attending Brown University, where he received an A.B. degree in 1897. While assistant principal of the black high school in Ft. Worth about 1900, he was one of the organizers

of the first black bank in Texas, the Fraternal Bank and Trust Co. He had been principal of Douglass High School in El Paso since 1907.

11 Secretary of the Houston Business League.

12 Rector of Christ Church, Episcopal.

13 Possibly James A. Brown, employed by the Houston *Chronicle*.

14 Lodowick McDaniel (b. 1847), U.S. district attorney for the southern district of Texas since 1907.

15 Thomas W. Ford (b. 1847), an attorney in Houston since 1890 and a former judge and legislator.

16 Lewis Randolph Bryan (b. 1858), an attorney in Houston since 1901.

17 Garrett Van Ameringen was a driver for the American Express Co.

18 John Brown Bell (b. 1858) was a black grocer and real estate dealer in Houston. In 1915 he leased the former house of E. J. Scott in Houston and converted it into a black hospital and clinic.

To Wallace Buttrick

Tuskegee Institute, Alabama   Oct. 11, 1911

Dear Dr. Buttrick: I told you sometime ago that I would make you a written report regarding the use of the Jeanes Fund which I control in this county. As I stated to you verbally, I acknowledge that on the face of matters it seems as if we have spent a great deal of money, but it has not been without a definite plan in view.

First of all, we thought it worth while to thoroughly equip one county in school buildings, in teachers, etc., to see to what extent the people and county authorities would continue the work after we have given it up and moved on to another county.

Second, we wanted to see after the schools had gotten to the point where they did really first class work in their local communities, whether this would not win the support of the white people residing near these schools.

Third. We have tried to make an object lesson in the way of showing how rural schools might be partly supported through the use of school farms especially in communities where cotton is the main product.

In all this work we have cooperated with the Demonstration Agents, and the result is that there is a general improvement in agriculture throughout the county among both white and colored people.

The results so far seem to demonstrate the wisdom of our course. We are now planning to take up work elsewhere, not, however, abandoning entirely the supervision in Macon County. Our experience convinces us more and more that every dollar spent for supervision is money well spent, that the people can do a great deal to help themselves provided they are properly supervised. Yours very truly,

[Booker T. Washington]

TLd   Con. 53   BTW Papers   DLC.

An Account of Washington's Tour of Texas
by Horace D. Slatter

Tuskegee, Alabama   October 14, 1911

RESUME OF THE TRIP
THROUGH TEXAS

Texarkana, Ark., Oct. 5. — The tour of Dr. Booker T. Washington who was accompanied by a party of prominent and well known colored men from various portions of the country came to an end here today. Everywhere the distinguished educator received overwhelming demonstrations of regard and affection, mingled with exultant pride on the part of the Negro people. Equally cordial was the reception given him by representative white men in various places, notably, the conference with Mayor Callaghan in San Antonio, the presentation free of cost of the City Auditorium, a building seating more than 7,000 people by the mayor of Houston, the more than cordial address by Mayor T. P. Wooldridge of Austin, the address of welcome by City Superintendent J. C. Lattimore at Waco and the perfectly frank, yet friendly address of introduction by Hon. Chesley Adams, former county superintendent of public schools, at Marshall.

As on former occasions, Dr. Washington was accompanied by a party of distinguished Negroes. Among others with him were Emmett J. Scott, his secretary, his son Booker T. Washington, Jr., Dr. J. A. Kenney, resident physician, W. T. B. Williams, agent John F. Slater and Jeanes Fund Boards, Hampton, Va.; Bishop I. B. Scott, Bishop of Africa for the Methodist Episcopal Church; Dr. H. T. Kealing, president Western University, Quindaro, Kan.; Dr. E. C. Morris, president National Baptist Convention, Helena, Ark.; Charles S. Tator, representing the New York Evening Post, New York City; Dr. R. E. Park, magazine writer, Boston, Mass.; Horace D. Slatter, general newspaper correspondent, Hopkinsville, Ky.; A. P. Bedou, official photographer, New Orleans, La.; Walter L. Cohen, former register U.S. Land Office, New Orleans, La.; J. B. Bell, capitalist, Houston, Texas; R. L. Smith, president Texas Negro Business League, Waco; R. C. Houston, Jr., president Provident Savings Bank, Fort Worth; Dr. E. M. Griggs, president Farmers Bank and Trust Co., Palestine, Texas; Rev. L. L. Campbell,[1] president General Baptist Convention, Austin, Texas; Dr. M. W. Dogan,[2] president Wiley University, Marshall, Texas; Dr. E. L. Blackshear, principal Prairie View State Normal School; Prof. W. C. Rollins, treasurer Prairie View State Normal School and others. Others from Tuskegee were Capt. B. E. Ammons of the Tuskegee Institute Battalion, Mr. A. R. Stewart, and Mr. Nathan Hunt, Dr. Washington's stenographer.

Coming into the state from Arizona, the first address on Texas soil was made in El Paso, where Dr. Washington had an immense audience, two-thirds of whom were white people. On account of the comparatively small number of colored people in El Paso, the white people of the city made up 85 per cent. of the expenses necessary to hire the theatre in which Dr. Washington spoke.

The welcome and reception given the distinguished educator in San Antonio, where the party mobilized, in a very commendable way set the pace for all other cities, under the leadership of Dr. J. T. Walton.[3]

Fully three thousand people, about one thousand of whom were white, filled every available seat in Beethoven Hall, crowded in the windows and stood around the walls and aisles to hear the famous Tuskegee educator speak.

The big audience cheered the speaker at almost every utterance, and at his own request, the Negro members sang two old-time Negro plantation songs, "Lord, I'm Climbing Up Jacob's Ladder" and "The Old Time Religion."

On behalf of the choir of the Second Baptist Church, Dr. Washington was presented a sofa pillow with the picture of the Alamo on it by J. C. Boisseau,[4] "in the spirit of the heroes of the Alamo who thought so little of life as to die for a principle."

In the afternoon Dr. Washington spoke to the school children at the

Second Baptist Church, counseling them to make their education worth while in their every-day lives and to take their mothers and fathers in their training with them. "Don't let people discourage you," he said on this occasion. "Do not listen to such talk that will make you despondent or dissatisfied. People will tell you that you are poor, that you are black and members of a despised race. Take lessons after the foreigners who come here in the direct poverty, peddle bananas on the streets, then rise to owners of small stores and afterwards to directors in banks. Begin now to save your pennies and help your mothers and fathers in your own support."

Dr. Washington was met by a reception committee and taken immediately to the residence of Dr. J. T. Walton, where he was entertained during the day. At 11:35 o'clock he and his party went to the City Hall, where he paid his respects to Mayor Callaghan. "I am pleased to meet you," said the mayor. "Your name is known throughout the world and I have great respect for your great work at Tuskegee." He was greeted in a manner equally cordial by Aldermen Mauermann[5] and Wickeland.[6] He expressed great satisfaction over the friendly relations existing in San Antonio between the races, adding that when away from here San Antonio Negroes were loud in singing the praise of the city. "We are fair to our colored citizens," declared the Mayor, who was invited by Dr. Walton to attend the meeting at Beethoven Hall. The Mayor then greeted young Booker T. Washington, who was clothed in the uniform of an officer of the Tuskegee Institute battalion.

The welcome given Dr. Washington at the Douglass High School, where he was entertained at luncheon was unique and cordial, the luncheon was unique and prepared by the Domestic Science Class. The children of the high school [were] arranged in tiers on the steps and singing "Our Leader" as he approached the building. Just before being seated, they again sang, "We Welcome You," a song especially written for the occasion by Principal S. J. Sutton of the high school.

SPEAKS TO CHILDREN

All the Negro school children of the city were addressed by Dr. Washington for about fifteen minutes at Second Baptist Church, many of the parents crowding into the church to hear him. Some 2,000 people in all were crowded into the building.

A large number of white people were in the audience, and to them as well as to the Negroes did Dr. Washington address sane and safe counsel with reference to the color question in the South. His address was filled with sparkling gems of eloquence and many pungent witticisms, and at all times, he was able to hold his audience by some remarkable anecdote aptly told.

The meeting was presided over by Dr. J. T. Walton, a local Negro physician, who delivered an address of welcome. Dr. Walton paid a high tribute to Dr. Washington, and said in part:

"This great race question must be solved from within, where the white man and the black man live side by side. The Negro race, shot like a catapult into a civilization all new, and for which it was all too little prepared, has gone for half a century, misguided, buffeted about by designing politicians and over ambitious would-be Negro leaders, until Booker T. Washington arose to point the right way. Who is it among us of clear mind, unprejudiced heart and right habits will say that Booker T. Washington is not right, in counseling his people in the way of industry, enlightenment and morality, and in soliciting the aid and sympathy of the white man in his uplift movement?"

GETS AN OVATION

Declaring that few living Americans had made such an impression upon public opinion, removed so many prejudices and awakened greater helpfulness in relation to the solution of a problem, Dr. W. M. Drake introduced Dr. Washington to the audience, who rose to speak amongst deafening applause. He paid a high tribute to the Southern white man who had aided, counseled and encouraged the black people in their efforts to make progress, and called by name several prominent white citizens of San Antonio, among them George W. Brackenridge,[7] Albert Steves[8] and John T. Wilson.

A wreck on the Southern Pacific made the train seven hours late reaching Houston and much of the program mapped out by the local committee had to be curtailed. Here Emmett J. Scott received another ovation, this being his home place, and the point from which he joined Dr. Washington fourteen years ago to become his secretary.

Fully 2,000 white and colored people crowded to the station, and lined the sidewalks on the way from the Southern Pacific station to the home of the Orgen company, to which place Dr. Washington immediately repaired and made a short speech to the Negro business men of the city. In an informal way he told the Negro business men to cultivate friendly relations with the white business men, and congratulated them upon the remarkable showing made.

Visited School Children

From the office of the Orgen company, Dr. Washington and his party drove immediately to Trinity Methodist Episcopal church, where the colored school children had assembled to hear him. City Superintendent P. W. Horn and County Superintendent Pugh had made arrangements whereby the entire force of colored teachers and students could hear the distinguished Negro educator. Speaking for about ten minutes, Dr. Washington gave a whole lot of common sense advice to the children, encouching his remarks in such language as could be easily understood by the smallest child in the big assemblage.

The automobile ride that had been planned was abandoned owing to the lateness of the hour, and the Washington party was conducted to the home of J. B. Bell, 2121 German Street, where dinner was served the party. A feature of the dinner was disclosed in the fact that it had been prepared entirely by the female students of the Langston School in the domestic science department.

Guest of Library Trustees

Beside the men of the immediate party there were present at the reception: Y. U. Jones, Thompson, Texas; C. N. Love, editor of the Texas Freeman; Rev. G. A. Des Landes, Prof. David Abner,[9] R. W. Walker, Rev. F. L. Lights,[10] Prof. F. W. Gross,[11] George W. Jenkins,[12] J. Leon Jones[13] and Campbell A. Gilmore.

From the residence of J. B. Bell the party was entertained by the trustees of the Carnegie Library at the residence of Dr. J. B. Covington.[14] The reception was largely a tribute to Dr. Washington and his Secretary, Emmett J. Scott, who more than any other individuals, were responsible for securing the donation of a library for the colored people of Houston. The trustees entertaining the party were: E. O. Smith,[15] John Adkins,[16] J. B. Bell, W. E. Miller,[17] L. J. Spivey,[18] W. D. Johnson,[19] Andrew Parr,[20] Richard Locket,[21] Nat Q. Henderson.[22]

335

WAS GIVEN AN OVATION

As early as 6 o'clock in the evening, before the lights were lit in the big Auditorium, Negro people began to file in and take possession of the most desirable seats. By the time that the place was lit up a large portion of the seats were already taken. Long before the opening of the meeting every available seat was occupied, and there was a large number standing.

When Dr. Washington stepped on the platform he received an ovation. To one side of the platform were a number of Tuskegee alumni, and they greeted their former chief with the college yell. Dr. Washington acknowledged both gracefully and took his place on the platform. With him on the platform were a number of leading Negro professional men and the following white men: L. L. Pugh, county superintendent of schools; Adolph Boldt, Rev. Peter Gray Sears, Rev. Stephen F. Power, Rev. G. W. Strong, Prof. J. A. Brown, Judge Lock McDaniel, Judge T. W. Ford, Lewis R. Bryan and G. Van Ameringen.

One very interesting and pleasing feature of the Houston engagement was the address of Mr. Scott, who was repeatedly called upon by the people for a speech. With evident embarrassment, born of his modest and retiring disposition, he in a few short words accepted the greetings of his fellow townsmen, saying:

"It is the common-place, the trite, the quite bromidic thing to say that I am glad to be here tonight with Dr. Washington in this matchless city, the place of my birth, the Queen City of the Lone Star State. The years have not flown too fast to dim my memory of the greatness of Texas, nor have the duties and responsibilities of the advancing years served to make me forget the radiant glory of the golden crown which encircles her imperial brow. No matter where I find myself, I am first of all a Texan!

"These minutes, however, are too precious to be used except for the purpose which has brought you here; I must use but few of them. We have made educational pilgrimages similar to this one through the states of Oklahoma, Mississippi, Tennessee, North Carolina, South Carolina, Delaware and Virginia. I have constantly said to Dr. Washington, 'wait till we get to Texas; wait until you have seen something of the progress of the Negroes of Texas and of the more than friendly relations that here exist between the races.' I have said to him over and over again that in this state the Negroes and the whites have literally seized upon the pregnant passages of his epoch-making Atlanta address and are working out the destiny of both races, side by side, 'separate as the fingers,' as he has phrased it, 'in all matters purely social and yet one as the hand in all matters that concern the moral and material well being of this our common section.'

"In Texas we practically have no race problem for there can be no problem in any section where blacks and whites alike acknowledge and appreciate the fact that races and men not only have duties toward each other but responsibilities as well.

"And then quite naturally I have wanted you to know him better. I have wanted my old friends and neighbors to have full opportunity to see face to face the man whose life has been spent for a race, and whose work has everywhere won the unstinted plaudits of the fair-minded and the just. Do you recall those oft quoted words from Emerson: 'If a man write a better book, or preach a better sermon, or make a better basket than his neighbor tho' he build his house in a wilderness yet will the world make a beaten track to his door.' This truth has been proved in his own great unselfish life; it is the philosophy which underlies all of his teaching and all of his work; for to every Negro the message he brings is that if a man make a better basket than his neighbor, make his life permanently useful, he will not go unrecognized or long be denied those opportunities which are withheld from no man anxious and willing to prove himself worthy of good citizenship. And that is why I am glad to be here tonight, why I am glad that Dr. Washington is here, that you may hear him deliver his own message of hope and good cheer."

Singing an original song dedicated to Booker T. Washington, eight hundred Negro students of the Prairie View Normal and Industrial Institute lined up in two rows, gave the famous Negro educator a royal welcome here this morning, when he and his party approached the institute grounds.

The regard and affection with which Booker Washington is held by the young people of the county, many of whom have been inspired by his teachings and writings, was fully shown in the remarkable demonstration. "What's the matter with Washington," they sang. "He is our leader loved and true; he, large of heart and broad of view. Then Rah, Rah, Rah, for Booker T.; he is the man for me." College yells, one for Prairie View and the other for Tuskegee came in rapid succession, while prominent individuals making up the party were singled out for the attention of the students, those from Texas claiming the larger portion of their acclaim.

The venerable Bishop I. B. Scott, the only Negro bishop in the Methodist Episcopal Church, received a remarkable tribute, as did also R. L. Smith, the Negro farmers' friend in Texas. Mr. Scott, Dr. Washington's Secretary, here as at Houston received a remarkable ovation and was repeatedly called upon for a speech.

As soon as the party could break away from the frenzied young people, they were taken to the home of the members of the faculty, and later to luncheon at the mess hall.

The entire party led by Principal Blackshear and Dr. Booker T. Washington went on a round of inspection of the industrial divisions. Here he spoke to about 5,000 farmers of both races.

The address at Temple was made at midday Saturday, when hundreds of country folk, white and black were in town for their week end shopping and other business errands. The audience was composed of more white than colored, the speaking taking place in the open air on the public square.

That night at Austin, the following night Dr. Washington spoke in Wooldridge Park, in a natural amphitheatre formed by the rise of the hills on each side of the speaker's stand. Fully five thousand people heard his address here. He was welcomed to the city by Mayor Wooldridge, in whose honor the park had been named, and who said in the course of his remarks:

"I have very great pleasure in presenting to you a really great colored man, distinguished in learning and ability, distinguished in the great service which he has rendered our common country, and the great services he has rendered both races in the South in making them known to each other.

"To the white people here, I wish to say that I do not bestow too much praise in saying that his life is consecrated to making his race better understood by the white people and to bringing about more harmonious relations between the races. To my colored friends, I simply speak of him as your great leader, worthy of respect, worthy of your love, and worthy of your admiration.

"Dr. Washington, I would say to you, as speaking from Texas, the greatest democratic state in the United States, that our people are a liberal minded people, they want to see your race prosper, they want to see them become more contented and happy.

"As to the colored people, I have known them ever since my early manhood, and I am glad to bear testimony to their good character and their worth. I am glad to say that for the most part the colored people around here are a law-abiding and self-respecting class of citizens. They are not by any means a burden upon their white friends and neighbors.

"It is a pleasure to welcome Dr. Washington here, largely because of his personal worth and by reason of the great race which he represents. I have heard about him, I have talked about and I have read from him in many of the magazines. He is not only a man of learning and ability, but a man who is peculiarly devoted to the welfare of his race and to bringing about harmony and peace between the races in their contact here in the South. That is the one supreme passion of his life. He believes in teaching his people the simple truths and virtues of honesty, industry and dependableness, and I am glad to say that I know they are beginning to be very prevalent. He stands for the best interest of his race, and we are glad to have him here because he stands for those principles that make him worthy of the respect and admiration of white and black alike.

"He represents a constituency considerable in numbers, considerable in wealth. There are about 12,000,000 Negroes in the United States, fully one-tenth of the entire population. In our own community fully one-third of the population is colored. This number of colored people have property of which the assessed value will equal $1,000,000.

"I welcome him here because of his personal worth, his service to his race, and I also welcome him here because of that vast constituency, of which he is pre-eminently representative."

Here at Austin the whole party went through a round of festivities, having breakfast at the St. John Orphanage, dinner at Sam Houston College and luncheon at Tillotson College. At all places where there were institutions of learning, Dr. Washington was pressed into service for short addresses to the students.

Waco, the home of R. L. Smith, president of the Texas Negro Business League, gave the party the noisiest welcome and biggest relative crowd at the station that had been encountered up to this point. Many people surrounded the station when the train arrived several hours late. Young people, old people, people of all ages and conditions shouting themselves hoarse when Dr. Washington came into view. Every man, woman and child had an American flag which was being waved high in the air, while the band played "Dixie." One enthusiastic man, evidently returning from his work, pressed a new, shining, silver dollar into Dr. Washington's hand. With difficulty the party accompanying Dr. Washington wended its way to the waiting carriage. A woman grasped his hand, shouting, "Praise the Lord," while still another man, perfectly contented that he had seen his leader, went off declaring: "Now I's seed him and shuk his han'; I's satisfied." The students of Central Texas and Paul Quinn Colleges gave him a joyous reception, and at night in the baseball park, while he was being introduced by city superintendent of schools, the Prof. J. C. Lattimore, the entire student body, male and female of Baylor University, a well known Southern College for white youth took seats on the grand stand. Prof. Lattimore in his introduction surprised Dr. Washington by giving a detailed account of the sights he witnessed and the impressions made upon him in a recent trip to Tuskegee Institute. Dr. Washington was warmly greeted by Dr. S. P. Brooks,[23] president of Baylor University, Prof. Lattimore, Samuel Sanger,[24] a Texas merchant prince, and other well-known white men of Waco.

A belated train greatly inconvenienced the waiting throng at Fort Worth, which in many respects is one of the most important towns from a Negro standpoint in the state. While the party was scheduled to reach Fort Worth in the afternoon and Dr. Washington was to have spoken at three o'clock, the audience of about 5,000 persons, a large portion of which were white, kept their seats in the theatre until 9 o'clock, when the train finally reached the city. The reception by reason of the tardiness of the party was none the less vigorous, and was in many respects a great tribute to the remarkable esteem in which R. C. Houston, the Fort Worth leader is held by his fellow-townsmen. Despite this handicap and the fact that the Fort Worth engagement was on Sunday night, all the prominent Negro business houses were open for the inspection of the party, the most interesting features in Negro life in Fort Worth being the Masonic Temple, erected at a cost of $50,000 and the Negro High School, which is considered the best in the South, and the large number of business establishments of various kinds conducted by the colored people. A large number of people heard Dr. Washington at the State Fair grounds in Dallas on Monday.

In the matter of enthusiasm and spectacular display, the small town of Marshall outdid itself in the demonstration given Dr. Washington. The local Negro Business League had charge of the arrangements and with more than ordinary acumen, dispatched Dr. W. M. Dogan to accompany the party, within a few days of Dallas. Whatever Dr. Dogan saw at other places, he was able thereby to have Marshall surpass all other places. A parade, more than a mile in length, in which the various industrial divisions from Wiley University and Bishop College and the Central High School were represented on tastily decorated floats. Girls from sewing classes were at work on the floats, from the printing divisions, the domestic science departments, and so in all departments, emphasizing more than any other one thing that the Wizard's doctrine of industrial education had taken root firmly in Texas.

Small boys from the woodworking departments dressed in overalls, carrying their tools, mule driven teams drawing street cleaning and street building apparatus, followed, while the parade was headed by the Wiley University brass band and the local Business League.

As at the other points visited, the people who attended the meeting seemed to be of the very best element, well dressed, well-behaved. The singing by the Wiley University glee club here was a feature of the occasion. Dr. Washington was introduced by Hon. Chesley Adams, former county superintendent of public schools, who paid a high tribute to Dr. Washington and the Negroes of Harrison County. In the course of his remarks Mr. Adams said:

"You have made a remarkable demonstration in honor of the distinguished citizen who is your guest, and I am glad to welcome him to our city in the name of every citizen, white and black, whose love for humanity has been tested, whose broadminded conceptions have been proven to have been the best for the educational, moral and spiritual uplift of the people.

"I know of no great public leader whose advice to his people has been more helpful, more hopeful, and of greater influence than that of Dr. Booker T. Washington. I present him to you as one of the greatest men and most forceful educators of the day, and the one great leader of his people. The policies advocated by him, in their effectiveness mark him not only as a great teacher, but as a statesman. I present him as the greatest living character the Negro race has yet produced,

341

in this or any other clime. I would to God that every Negro in East Texas stood within the reach of his voice and listened while he reasoned to them out of his righteous judgment.

"In presenting you to Harrison County, I present to you the best element of Negroes in the world. They are intelligent, peaceful and law-abiding, largely because of the influence of these two schools. Harrison County rightfully claims the best Negro citizenship in the state of Texas.

"I have always believed that the education of the Negro would make him a better citizen. The South has been for a long time burdened by a great mass of brute ignorance. You make a brute out of yourself, when you continually carry a pistol to intimidate and dominate your neighbor."

Tuskegee Student, 23 (Oct. 14, 1911), 1–4.

[1] Lee Lewis Campbell (b. 1866) was the pastor of Ebenezer Baptist Church in Austin and a leader of the prohibition movement among blacks through his publication, the *Baptist Herald.*

[2] Matthew Winfred Dogan, born in 1863, a graduate of Rust University in 1886, had been president of Wiley University since 1896. He had the courage, not shown by every southern black college head, to allow his faculty to join the NAACP. (Barr, *Black Texans,* 163.)

[3] James Tart Walton (b. 1875), a graduate of Meharry Medical College, was a surgeon and obstetrician in San Antonio beginning in 1896. He was also a wealthy real estate developer whose firm built more than 400 houses for blacks on the easy-payment plan. He also had business investments in banking, printing, and a drugstore.

[4] J. C. Boisseau was a black schoolteacher.

[5] Possibly Bernard J. Mauermann, a realtor.

[6] John Wickeland, alderman-at-large.

[7] George W. Brackenridge, born in Indiana in 1832, a Harvard graduate, was president of the San Antonio National Bank.

[8] Albert Steves was head of a large lumber company founded by his father in 1866.

[9] David Abner, Jr., born in 1860 in Gilmer, Tex., was the son of a black legislator. After graduation from Bishop College and Virginia Theological Seminary and College, he was president of Guadalupe College, Seguin, Tex., for fifteen years, and since 1909 had been president of Conroe College in Houston. He was also a realtor and an active Republican, serving as delegate to several Republican national conventions.

[10] F. L. Lights was a black Baptist clergyman and president of the Orgen Banking Co. of Houston.

[11] Frederick William Gross, born in Marshall, Tex., in 1861, a graduate of Bishop College, had been president since 1907 of Houston College. He had also been grand secretary of the United Brothers of Friendship of Texas since 1889, and of its savings and loan adjunct.

¹² Cashier of the Orgen Banking Co.

¹³ A black realtor.

¹⁴ Benjamin J. Covington was a black surgeon in Houston.

¹⁵ Ernest O. Smith was principal of Booker T. Washington High School in Houston.

¹⁶ John M. Adkins was a black messenger for the U.S. courts in Houston.

¹⁷ William E. Miller was the black principal of Gregory Institute in Houston.

¹⁸ Leonard H. Spivey, a black mail carrier.

¹⁹ Walter L. D. Johnson, a black high school teacher.

²⁰ Andrew Parr, a black real estate operator.

²¹ Richard G. Lockett, a black high school teacher.

²² Nat Q. Henderson, a black man of Colorado County, Tex., in 1897 formed an "Anti-rape Association," which also denounced lynching. (Rice, *Negro in Texas*, 252.)

²³ Samuel Palmer Brooks (1863–1931), a Baptist, was president of Baylor University beginning in 1902, and president of the Southern Sociological Congress in 1915.

²⁴ Samuel Sanger, born in Bavaria, was one of four brothers in Sanger Bros., the leading wholesale and retail dry-goods and clothing firm in the Southwest. He was in charge of the firm's Waco store.

To the Editor of the Boston *American*

[Tuskegee, Ala.] October 16, 1911

Mr. Booker T. Washington Corrects a Wrong Impression

The enclosure referred to below by Mr. Washington and which gives the impression that the distinguished educator was told by the railroad officials on his recent trip through Texas that he must either ride in a negro compartment or charter a special car, was sent out by the Associated Press and printed throughout the country. The American gladly gives space to Mr. Washington's explanation of the circumstances.

Editor Boston AMERICAN:

My Dear Sir — Regarding the enclosed, which was published in your newspaper. I would state that it serves to create an entirely wrong impression.

For four years, at the request of colored people and white people in various Southern States, I have been making educational tours covering, during this time, Arkansas, Mississippi, Tennessee, Delaware, Virginia, North Carolina and South Carolina.

Recently, on the invitation of the Negro Business League of the State of Texas, composed of leading colored people of that State, I made a ten-days' tour of Texas. Everyone can well understand that [it] would be impossible from a physical point of view for any individual to endure ten days of constant travel, speaking three or four times a day without some provision for sleeping at night.

On the Texas trip I had to travel practically every night to reach the engagements which had been made for me, speaking two and three times a day at meetings composed of from one thousand to eight thousand persons, and shaking hands with hundreds of them after the meetings. Because of the physical strain the colored people of Texas themselves, at their own expense, provided a Pullman car for me and for the two dozen other colored people, most of whom lived in Texas, who accompanied me. So far from getting away from the colored people, I was with two or three dozen colored people all the time.

The white people and colored people throughout Texas understand the situation and registered no objection. I did not hear a single word of adverse criticism during the ten days I was in Texas. On the other hand, the newspapers in Texas were most cordial and generous. The theatres or halls where meetings were held were largely provided by the white people themselves. There was a most cordial feeling manifested at all of these meetings and I was thanked over and over again by Mayors, Judges and other public officials, as well as by hundreds of the leading white people of Texas, for my visit to their State.

The harm that such publications as the attached can do grows out of the fact that they give the impression that there is constant strife and misunderstanding between white people and black people in the South, which does not exist. When I came back, returning through the States of Louisiana and Mississippi, the railroad authorities, on their own motion, kindly put at my disposal a day coach, giving as their reason that they wanted to make me as comfortable as possible after my ten days' hard work.

So far from getting away from the colored people, my whole life has been spent in direct contact with them, except during the time when I am compelled to be in the North for business purposes, and this the colored people thoroughly understand. My purpose in using the Pullman car provided for me by the colored business men of Texas was not as it has been assumed to get away from my own race, because in the special Pullman car used I was really in contact with more colored people than I possibly could have been in the regular day coach set aside for the use of colored people. Yours very truly,

Booker T. Washington

Boston *American,* Oct. 16, 1911, Clipping   Con. 1058   BTW Papers   DLC.   A similar letter appeared in the London *Times,* Oct. 30, 1911, Con. 7, BTW Papers, DLC.

From Edward Lavoisier Blackshear

Prairie View, Texas   October the sixteenth, Ninteen hundred-eleven

Dear Dr. Washington: My wife, daughter and myself read with great interest and pleasure your kind letter relative to your trip to Prairie View and to Texas; and although such a letter does not really demand a reply, I cannot refrain from expressing a feeling of satisfaction with which all thoughtful colored people in Texas and thoughtful white people as well regard your recent visit. Its influence is unquestionably for great good among both races and all reports and comments are distinctively and positively favorable. I had fully expected that the trip through Texas would be a success judging from the reports of tours through other States; but I must say that the cordial reception given you and the remarkable effect of your words and personality upon all who heard you of both races surpassed my expectation and gave me a higher opinion of my own State, Texas, than I had before.[1] It was a novel thing for both races in Texas to have a distinguished colored man and his friends touring the State in a respectable manner in a Standard Pullman. It is true that it is a custom of those attending large gatherings out of the State to charter one or more pullmans and chair cars to carry large delegations to National religious and fraternal conventions; but never before did a party of colored people making a tour within the State enjoy first class accommodations. Yet I did not hear or see during the entire trip any expression of disrespect or antagonism on account of your occupying and traveling in a pullman car. This alone is, to quote one of your expressions, worth the price of admission; and has, I am sure, set a higher standard for respectable col-

345

ored people both in their own minds and in the minds of the public generally. I hope that you will make another visit and tour of Texas after the lapse of a reasonable length of time; although you would be well received in Texas at any time, I know business engagement will not permit of your early return. If it were practicable however, a splendid tour could be arranged for next summer going through entirely different country and reaching thousands of people both white and colored who are anxious to see you. The people of such towns as Brenham, Navasota, Bryan, Calvert, all centers of vast Negro populations are extremely anxious to see and hear you. I think I ought to say that I can see that your influence is steadily growing, gathering in momentum and in wisdom; and you are applying the leaven of hope and wide endeavor to the lump and by and by in God's providence and through his mercy the whole will be leavened. Yours sincerely,

E. L. Blackshear

TLS Con. 417 BTW Papers DLC.

1 BTW replied that he was pleased with the trip to Texas and experienced no disrespect or antagonism "during the whole of our trip." He did note, however, that a Judge Brashear had sounded "a somewhat discordant note" in the Houston *Chronicle.* (Oct. 25, 1911, Con. 417, BTW Papers, DLC.)

A Speech by William Howard Taft[1]

Los Angeles, California, October 16, 1911

My fellow-citizens: No friend of the negro race would or could minimize the obstacles against which you have to contend in building up yourselves individually, and in building up your race as a community in the United States. No one who deals with you truthfully would attempt to depreciate the difficulties or mental suffering that many of your race have to undergo in encountering cruel and unreasonable race prejudices, and no one either would do you any good who attempted to stir up in your minds that kind of a prejudice against those difficulties, against that prejudice, which would lead you to do something that your friends would regret. It is one of the facts that have to be overcome and one of the facts, which, when you have overcome them, will entitle you to the greater credit for the successful struggle that you have made.

I have taken a great interest in what is called the negro problem, and I believe it is to find its solution in the widespread industrial education of the race, especially in that part of the country where the race is most numerous, through the Southern states; and while there is a strong feeling at the South that presents a difficulty, those who have studied the question and those who live in the South know that there is a large element of the white men in the South who are the real true friends of the people of the South, and those who are his enemies are not of the best people of the South and do not have the true patriotism and the desire to solve the question presented by the races in the proper way. I know that there are differences among you. I know that your greatest leader, Booker Washington, finds those who do not agree with his method of uplifting your race. Personally, I think Booker Washington one of the greatest men of this and the last century, white or black, and I think so because he has had the courage, while he loves your race — his race, and would not be other than of that race — he has had the courage to tell you the truth, and to tell you the only way by which you can earn your place in the community and render it better and better and higher and higher. He has had the courage to tell you that it is work, attention, industry, that shall make you valuable to your community, that will cure the prejudices that you now have to struggle against, and that when you furnish a mercenary or a selfish motive to the white man, however low he may be, to respect you and to ask for your labor to assist in building up the community, then prejudices disappear and his interest yields and you get your rights.

Now, my friends, I thank you for your kindly testimonial. I want you to know, whether you do know it or not, that there are those of the white people in this country, and they number millions, that sympathize deeply with you in the struggle that you have to undergo and realize that those sufferings are not to be done away with by eloquence, not to be done away with by expressions of sympathy, that they are real, hard burdens to carry, but it may help you to carry them to know that you have friends in the white race, that you have men who have a sense of responsibility for this Government and this people — this Government and this people that in times past brought you here against your will and have necessitated the conditions that now exist. Therefore, the United States is responsible for you and for your betterment, but that responsibility cannot, in the nature of things, reach to a point where it will save you and elevate you unless you shall struggle on with bravery and courage and self-restraint and a determination to win.

TD Con. 442 BTW Papers DLC. Ralph W. Tyler forwarded this copy to E. J. Scott.

1 Taft spoke before an audience of about 1,000 blacks in Blanchard Hall in a meeting organized by the Los Angeles Afro-American League. One newspaper reported that the President was well received and that when he referred to BTW it "created a hurricane of applause." (Los Angeles *Times,* Oct. 17, 1911, 14.)

To Schiller Brothers Distilling Company

[Tuskegee, Ala.] Oct. 25, 1911

Gentlemen: My attention has just been called to the offer of my picture along with others to persons who will agree to order some of the products of your distillery.

I write to say that such an offer as this is entirely distasteful to me and I write to ask that you discontinue at once the use of my picture as a premium for such purposes.[1]

Hoping that you will give this matter your immediate and prompt attention, I am, Yours truly,

Booker T. Washington

TLpS Con. 439 BTW Papers DLC.

1 The distillery, with facilities in Cairo, Ill., and Kansas City, Mo., manufactured Sunny Times Whiskey and Schiller's Beer. The firm replied that it would gladly discontinue the use of BTW's picture as a premium. (Oct. 28, 1911, Con. 439, BTW Papers, DLC.)

To Edward Dana Durand

[Tuskegee, Ala.] Oct. 25, 1911

My dear Mr. Durand: Please accept my thanks for sending me the advance statements concerning the Negro population.[1]

This favor is very much appreciated. I have examined both exhibits carefully and find them very interesting. The exhibit concerning the Negro population by sex shows for the various states about what I had expected. Although I had expected the recent census to show a greater preponderance of mulattoes than was shown by the former census, I was surprised to see how decided during the past twenty years has been the tendency toward a mulatto type. I am especially interested in the general increase of the Negro population from 1900 to 1910 which, however, is considerably less than I had thought it would be. On this point I have prepared the accompanying statement. I hope you can find time to read it. Yours very truly,

Booker T. Washington

[*Enclosure*]

NEGRO POPULATION IN 1910

Dr. Booker T. Washington when interviewed concerning the fact that the rate of increase for the Negroes for the decade 1900-1910 is considerably less than for the decade 1890-1900 gave out the following statement. He said:

"I have examined very carefully the statement concerning the Negro population of the United States as announced October² [*blank*] by Director Durand of the Census Bureau. It appears that there are now in this country about 9,800,000 Negroes. This is an increase for the decade 1900-1910 of about 994,000 or 11 per cent. The increase for the decade 1890-1900 was 1,345,318 or 18 per cent. From 1880 to 1890 the increase was 889,247 or 13.5 per cent.

"I have studied very carefully the best authorities on increase of population and find, according to them, that for a people increasing entirely by excess of births over deaths an increase of 11 per cent is indicative of a normal growth. It is interesting to note that the 1911 Census of England has just announced for the period 1901-1911 an increase for the English people of 12.4 by excess of births over deaths. The similarity of the rate of increase of the American Negroes and the rate of increase of the English people is an indication of the accuracy of the 1910 Census as well as an evidence of the normal character of the increase for the Negroes during the last ten years.

"The best statisticians have for a long time doubted the increase of 18 per cent reported by the census of 1900. For the increase for the

349

whites in 1900 including all the additions by immigration was only 21.2 per cent. In 1905 Prof. Willcox of Cornell University, in an article in the Harvard Quarterly Journal of Economics on "The Probable Increase of the Negro Race," explained the unusual increase reported in 1900 as the result of an undercount in 1890. This explanation is quite probable for it was felt by many that the enumeration of the Negro in 1890 was quite defective. A rearrangement of the rates of increase computed by Prof. Willcox in the article mentioned above shows these rates to be about 17 per cent in 1890, 14 per cent in 1900 and 11 per cent in 1910. The decreases in these rates of increase are quite natural for a people increasing without the aid of immigration. Similar rates for the English people show similar decreases. I wish also to call attention to the fact that a decreasing rate of increase does not at all mean that there is danger of a people becoming extinct for suppose that the rate of increase for the Negroes during the next hundred years should decrease until the average rate for each decade should be 5 per cent. In the year 2,010 there would be in the United States about 16,000,000 Negroes.

"A comparison of the increase of Negro farmers with the increase of total Negro population brings out the striking contrast of a population increase of 11.3 per cent and an increase of farmers of 19.5 per cent. The same facts for the whites show that the white population increased 21 per cent while the white farmers increased only 9.1 per cent.

"It appears from this comparison that the Negroes of the United States with their smaller rate of increase are becoming farmers at more than twice the rate of the whites. In view of the increasing importance of checking the tide away from farming as an occupation, this strong movement into farming on the part of the Negroes is a most hopeful indication of the present condition of the race."

TLpS Con. 421 BTW Papers DLC.

[1] Durand sent BTW, on Oct. 21, 1911, statistics on the proportion of the sexes and of mulattoes in the black population for 1910, comparing them with earlier census returns. (Con. 421, BTW Papers, DLC.)
[2] Blank space left for insertion of exact date.

From Charles William Anderson

New York, N.Y. October 30, 1911

Confidential

My dear Doctor Washington: I am sure you will regret to learn that Mr. Hubert H. Harrison has been dismissed from his position as clerk in the New York Post Office. I am certain also that you will regret to hear that he is blaming me for his dismissal. As Postmaster Morgan[1] is a *particular personal friend* of mine of long years standing, and as the charge against Mr. Harrison was considered (by Harrison) trivial, that "brother" believes that some sinister influence was at work against him, and that influence was set in operation by me. Well, I can endure the charge with fortitude and good humor. Harrison had a dispute with the Superintendent of the Branch Post Office in which he was employed, and as he had had several of these disputes with this and other Superintendents before, I presume the Postmaster thought it high time to drop him and get a man who would talk less and work more. He is now stumping for the Socialist party, and will probably have plenty of time in the future to learn that God is not good to those who do not behave themselves. Yours very truly,

Charles W. Anderson

TLS Con. 52 BTW Papers DLC.

[1] Edward M. Morgan (1855–1925) was postmaster of New York City from 1907 to 1917.

A Statement on Prohibition[1]

[Tuskegee, Ala., ca. Oct. 31, 1911]

THE NEGRO AND PROHIBITION

Long years of observation have convinced me that strong drink is one of the worst evils that beset the Negro. If the money they spend annually for strong drink was invested in property their wealth would be increased each year by millions of dollars.

Ever since prohibition has been agitated in the South I have been

351

greatly interested in it and have watched closely its effect upon the Negro. My own observations and the best information that I can obtain convinces me that prohibition is a good thing for the Negro. Under prohibition he generally drinks less whiskey than he does when he has access to licensed saloons. I am reliably informed that since the restriction of the sale of liquor in South Carolina drinking has visibly decreased among the Negroes. In Alabama since prohibition went into effect the amount of liquor consumed by the colored people has been greatly reduced. This I have observed to be especially true in my own County.

Another thing that prohibition does is to enable the Negroes to save more of their money. In a single court in Atlanta since prohibition has gone into effect the fines imposed upon Negroes have decreased fifty per cent. annually. This means that these same Negroes will have that much more money to spend for food, for clothing and to invest in property.

Another thing that prohibition has done has been to reduce crime. I find that it is true that wherever there is prohibition crime among the colored people has decreased. Chief Justice Walter Clark[2] of the Supreme Court of North Carolina says that since the state wide prohibition law has gone into effect in that state crime has been reduced fifty per cent; murder in the first degree in North Carolina decreased thirty-two per cent; burglary twenty per cent; attacks with deadly weapons thirty per cent; larceny thirty-two per cent; manslaughter twenty-five per cent; murder in the second degree thirty-five per cent. In some instances according to Chief Justice Clark crimes have decreased more than sixty per cent since prohibition.

I find that in Columbus, Georgia, Negro arrests after prohibition went into effect decreased twenty-six per cent.

I recently made an investigation of the effects of prohibition upon crime in Alabama. I sent out inquiries to sheriffs, chiefs of police and recorders of police courts asking their opinion as to the chief causes of Negro crime and the effects of prohibition upon Negro crime. The majority of these replies show that strong drink is the chief cause of crime among the Negroes of the state. These statements were corroborated by the report of the State Attorney General which shows that fifty-three per cent of all murders in the state were due to strong drink.

The effects of prohibition upon crime among the people of my race has in many cases been remarkable. In my own county in Alabama crime has been reduced sixty per cent since prohibition went into effect in the county four years ago. In many other counties in the state there has been a like reduction in the amount of crime since the advent of prohibition. When everything, therefore, is considered it appears that prohibition is an excellent thing for the Negro.

TMp Con. 52 BTW Papers DLC. Enclosed in E. J. Scott to Charles Banks, Oct. 31, 1911.

[1] Prepared for Mrs. Eliza Paterson of Texarkana, Tex., a national organizer among blacks for the Women's Christian Temperance Union.

[2] Walter Clark (1846–1924), a Confederate veteran of planter background, was one of North Carolina's leading spokesmen for progressivism. He became a justice of the state supreme court in 1888 and was chief justice from 1903 until his death. He used his position on the bench to attack child labor and corporate power, and to support labor welfare and education. (Brooks, *Walter Clark;* Woodward, *Origins of the New South,* 469.)

To J. S. B. Seale[1]

[Tuskegee, Ala.] November Second 1911

Dear Sir: I have your letter of some days ago.

If anybody in your neighborhood is canvassing stock of a silver mine in Mexico and has connected my name with the scheme in any way, it is a gross misrepresentation.

I am in no way connected with any mining venture. It is simply a scheme on the part of a dishonest man to secure funds from the ignorant colored men and women. Yours very truly,

Booker T. Washington

TLpSr Con. 439 BTW Papers DLC. Signature initialed by Charles H. Fearing.

[1] Seale wrote from Philadelphia, Miss., on Oct. 30, 1911, that a white man was there trying to sell shares in a silver mine by stating that BTW was interested in it. He asked for BTW's advice. (Con. 439, BTW Papers, DLC.)

From Anson Phelps Stokes, Jr.

New Haven, Conn., November 2, 1911

My dear Mr. Washington: I enclose herewith for your confidential information a proposal which I expect to bring before the Phelps-Stokes Trustees at their next meeting. You will see that it is an attempt to help in the solution of the negro problem from a different side than has been emphasized in the past, namely by training at a great Southern university a group of Southern white students who will investigate the negro and his problems with the view to assisting in improving conditions. I have talked the matter over carefully with Dr. Dillard and Dr. Alderman who feel that the plan is a very important one. I would appreciate your estimate of it and any suggestions that you may make regarding it. If successful I hope we may be able to establish a similar fellowship at the University of Georgia, perhaps elsewhere. I feel that the fellowship will result in accomplishing three purposes:

First. The mere existence of the fellowship at a Southern white university under state auspices will be significant.

Second. The researches of these fellows should result in bringing together a body of facts regarding the negro that will be of material assistance in solving his problem.

Third. The fellows should form a body of men who would be of great assistance in the future in leading in various educational and sociological movements in the South. Very truly yours,

Anson Phelps Stokes

TLS Con. 439 BTW Papers DLC.

To Samuel Bratton Donnelly[1]

[Tuskegee, Ala.] November 6, 1911

My dear Sir: I want to thank you for the courageous stand which you have taken in relation to the colored employees of the Government Printing Office.[2] The two fundamental rights guaranteed to the Negro by emancipation was the right to own property and to freely sell his own labor. I am certain that no man who is in earnest in his desire for a free government in this country wants to see these rights abridged. In fact I am certain that the laboring unions themselves, unless the question at issue were confused in their minds, would be the first to stand by the right of the Negro to labor as a free man should.

You have performed a service not only to ten millions of my own race, but to the whole country in the firm stand for justice and for freedom which you have taken. I am, Very sincerely,

[Booker T. Washington]

TLp Con. 421 BTW Papers DLC. A copy was sent to Charles D. Hilles with the request that he call it to the attention of President Taft. (BTW to Hilles, Nov. 6, 1911, William Howard Taft Papers, DLC.)

[1] Samuel Bratton Donnelly (1866–1946), a former president of the New York Typographical Union No. 6 (1895–98), and commissioner of the New York Board of Education (1901–8). Donnelly was public printer in Washington, D.C., from 1908 to 1913. After 1913 he was secretary of the Building Trades Employers' Association in New York.

[2] Six bricklayers, members of the Central Labor Union, went on strike against the Government Printing Office when a black bricklayer was also hired. Donnelly publicly replied: "Colored persons work in the Government Printing Office side by side with other employes in harmony and with great efficiency. Any employe of this establishment who tries to precipitate the devilish stricture of race prejudice will be immediately dismissed and will not again be employed." Soon thereafter he hired three more black bricklayers. (Washington *Bee*, Oct. 28, 1911, 1.)

From Anna Karger[1]

Columbus, O. Nov. 6, 1911

Honored Sir: This is the first time in my life, that I feel ashamed of being a white woman. I am even ashamed of our Republic; but law and justice are — at present — not identical in our country.[2]

I live at a Hotel in this city and have sent to every colored employee, waiters, bell boy, porters, a red carnation in your honor. Most respectfully

Anna Karger (Miss)
Care of Board of Education,
Columbus, O.

ALS Con. 435 BTW Papers DLC.

A News Item in the New York *Age*

New York [ca. Nov. 6, 1911]

DR. WASHINGTON AGAIN FACES HIS
ASSAILANT

New York, Nov. 6, 1911 — Dr. Booker T. Washington, the Tuskegee educator, appeared in the Court of Special Sessions again to-day when the case against Henry A. Ulrich was called for trial. Ulrich is the German dog fancier who brutally assaulted Dr. Washington on a public street in New York eight months ago. Despite every effort of Ulrich's counsel to delay the trial, Dr. Washington has continued to press the prosecution; to-day he again appeared, although he had to cancel a series of engagements in Wisconsin and other Western States.

The story of the assault was told in detail by Officers Hagan and Tierney,[1] and a Wall Street bank clerk[2] who witnessed it, and by Dr. Washington himself. So complete and convincing was the testimony showing how Ulrich and another assailant had brutally beaten the educator that the spectators were astounded when, after Ulrich and the woman who was variously described in the testimony as "Mrs. Ulrich" and "Mrs. Alvarez" had testified, the judges by a divided decision of two to one decided to acquit the defendant, on the ground that the proof of assault had not been clearly proven. To prove his contention that he had nothing to conceal Dr. Washington fought the case to a finish, and is in no way cast down because the judges refused to convict the culprit, who, with his alleged paramour, swore most atrociously in their efforts to fasten odium upon him. He feels he has done his full duty to his race and to himself in coming to New York to prosecute his assailant, at great expense and loss of time and energy.

Immediately, following the trial, Ulrich was arrested by New Jersey officials on a warrant for desertion sworn out by his legitimate wife, who lives in Orange, New Jersey.

Assistant District Attorney James E. Smith, who conducted the prosecution, was most earnest in his efforts to secure the conviction of Ulrich; it was no fault of his that a conviction was not secured. He did his full and complete duty.

New York *Age*, ca. Nov. 6, 1911, Galley proof   Con. 435   BTW Papers   DLC.

[1] Benjamin S. Tierney.
[2] James Crowe.

From Charles Neale Field[1]

Washington D.C. November 7th [1911]

Dear Dr. Washington   My attention has been called this morning to the injustice which has been done to you in New York. I need not say how absolutely unfair your friends will consider such treatment & I am only glad that some of the judges did not concur. At the same time I feel that you have set us all a good example by the way in which you have acted. When our Lord was reviled, he reviled not again.

Permit me a poor white Priest of the Episcopal Church to express my sympathy with you & at the same time my admiration of your conduct. Few of us would have been as brave.

God Bless you & keep up your courage in the good work you are doing. Yours sincerely

C. N. Field

ALS   Con. 434   BTW Papers   DLC.

[1] Charles Neale Field (1849–1929), an Episcopal missionary who worked with black missions for many years, was provincial superior of the Society of St. John the Evangelist in America from 1904 to 1911, residing in Boston, Mass.

From Roscoe Conkling Bruce

Washington, D.C. 7 November '11

My dear Mr. Washington: I have read the newspaper reports of the decision in the trial of the man, Ulrich, with astonishment. Fortunately, everybody knows how the judges of the inferior courts in some of our cities are chosen and what they often are.

The ten million Americans of Negro descent may well be aroused at this decision. First of all, a Negro whose services to his country and to mankind have in his own lifetime become historical, has been beaten by a ruffian and the courts of the metropolis have granted no redress.

Secondly, if the courts accept the testimony of a dog-fancier and wife-deserter as conclusive against that of the greatest educator and publicist of our race, of what avail is the testimony of a black mechanic or farmer however industrious and honest as against the most worthless of white men?

Thirdly, if a man of Ulrich's stripe may in the North assault Booker T. Washington with impunity, pray what security of life and limb has any of us in this broad land?

In a word, this heart-breaking incident has no mere personal significance — it affects vitally every Negro in America. And you may be sure that all the people understand this thing and that they look upon you as a martyr to the disabilities which they every one suffer.

Whenever you come to Washington, please remember that my heart and home are yours. Faithfully yours

Roscoe C. Bruce

TLS Con. 434 BTW Papers DLC.

An Article in the New York *World*

[New York City] November 7, 1911

DR. WASHINGTON, NOTED NEGRO, FAILS TO PROVE ASSAULT

Court Sets Free Henry A. Ulrich, Who Declares He Found the Educator Peeping through a Keyhole

TUSKEGEE'S CHIEF DENIES HE INSULTED A WOMAN

But Mrs. Alvarez Swears He Said to Her "Hello, Sweetheart!" the Night of March 19

Henry A. Ulrich, carpenter and dog fancier, who was arrested the night of March 19 last on complaint of Dr. Booker T. Washington, the noted negro educator and friend of Theodore Roosevelt, was acquitted yesterday in Special Sessions of the charge of assault. Justices Moss and Zeller voted for acquittal, Justice O'Keefe dissenting.

Dr. Washington, who was in court with a large following, positively refused to make any comment after the decision had been announced.

Mrs. Laura Alvarez, who has also been referred to as Mrs. Ulrich, was jubilant when the verdict was announced. But only a short time before she had sworn that Dr. Washington greeted her with "Hello, sweetheart!" on the night in question, and that she had caught the colored educator peeping through a keyhole in the hallway of the house in which she lived.

Ulrich was defended by Lawyer James I. Moore, a Texan, with offices at No. 302 West Fifty-fourth street. Assistant District-Attorney James E. Smith had been especially assigned to prosecute Ulrich. He tried his very best to discredit the witnesses offered by the defense.

POLICEMEN'S ACCOUNT OF THE ARREST

Police Hagan and Tierney told practically the same story they had related in the Magistrates' Court shortly after the assault. They told how Dr. Washington had been arrested on complaint of Ulrich, who accused the educator of having been found peeping through keyholes in the hallway of No. 11½ West Sixty-third street. On the way to the station Ulrich said to the policemen:

"I think he (Dr. Washington) was after two young girls who live in the house, and, officer, if you hadn't come along I would have knocked his black head off."

Dr. Washington was called to the witness stand by Mr. Smith. He was standing in a dark blue sack suit, wore a standing collar and a black bow tie. He took the Bible in his right hand as the oath was being administered.

"This defendant," testified Dr. Washington, "ran into the hall where I was standing — I mean the vestibule — caught me around the neck and choked me. He was calling out, "You were trying to break into this house." He kept on striking me with his fists. In warding the blows I think I struck him once. I found he was getting too strong for me and pulled the street door open. He asked some one to hand him a stick and began to beat me again. I told him not to strike me; that if I was violating the law he should send for an officer. But he kept on striking me."

LOOKING AT THE DOOR PLATES

"What were you doing in that hallway?" asked Justice Zeller.

"I was looking at the door plates," was the reply.

"Whom were you looking for?" asked Justice Moss.

"I was looking for a friend."

"Colored or white?" asked Lawyer Moore.

"Such a question is an insult to this witness," Mr. Smith shouted.

The Justice overruled the Assistant District-Attorney, and the witness answered "white," — adding:

"I was looking for the auditor of my college. His name is D. C. Smith."

"Had you any reason to suppose that he lived there?"

"I did not expect to find his name on the door. I thought he was with a Mr. McClure or some one with a name like that. I could not find that name, but I found a name resembling it and I rang that bell. I thought Mr. Smith was staying there."

Thinks He Saw the Woman

Dr. Washington thought he recalled seeing a woman with a dog on the street, but was not quite positive. He said that at the West Sixty-eighth street station Lieut. Quinn, after receiving his card, dismissed the complaint Ulrich made and entertained a charge of assault against Ulrich.

Lieut. Quinn swore Ulrich told him: "Two days ago a colored man followed into the house two little girls who belong to the Rob Roy theatrical company."

Mrs. Alvarez was put on the stand.

"When I came out of my flat on the ground floor that night," she testified, "I ran into Dr. Washington. He was peeping into the keyhole."

She said that Dr. Washington followed her to the house later while she was returning with her French bulldog.

"He looked me right in the face," she testified, "and said: 'Hello, sweetheart.' I ran into the house and told Mr. Ulrich. He said: 'I will go out and see what the man is doing.' "

Ulrich told practically the same story he had related in the police court.

He denied having struck Dr. Washington with a stick.

"We will recall Dr. Washington," said Mr. Smith. The educator again went to the witness chair and denied he had been "peeping."

"Did you meet Mrs. Alvarez in the hall or call her sweetheart?"

"Oh, I never opened my mouth to a man, woman or child," protested Dr. Washington. "I have never spoken to a strange woman in all my life."

The three Justices consulted and five minutes later Justice Moss announced:

"The court acquits the defendant by a majority decision, Judge O'Keefe dissenting."

Ulrich, smiling, hurried out of the court room. In the hallway Detective Thomas of Mr. Whitman's office arrested him. Detective Sergt. Drabell of Orange, N.J., had brought to the court an indictment charging Ulrich with abandonment. Chief Magistrate McAdoo committed Ulrich to the Tombs, saying that only a Supreme Court Justice could fix bail in an extradition case. Mrs. Ulrich, who lives in Orange, had obtained the warrant for her husband's arrest.

New York *World*, Nov. 7, 1911, 20.

From James A. Cobb

Washington, D.C. November 8, 1911

Dear Dr. Washington: Shocked, but not surprised at the outcome of your case in New York. In my opinion it is true as has been said, that no one who successfully practices law in the Police Court, of New York, is not at any time more than two hours out of the penitentiary. In other words, in order to get a judgment, you have to buy all the petty officers including the alleged Judges.

The judgment of the Court was an outrage upon justice from any angle, and upon the showing made by the defense, judgment should have been in your favor. The assault was clearly established and in no wise justified, admitting for the purpose of the case, which no sane individual believed, that you called the woman in question "sweet heart," that would have been no justification for an assault, and if an assault was committed, alleging such a defense, it should not even [have] been admitted in evidence, for it was not only no justification for the assault but not even an excuse.

The decision was so unjust as was disclosed by the evidence, that it will be a boomerang, and, in my opinion, will do as much good as a verdict in your favor. I have talked with a number of the most prominent lawyers in this city and, without exception, they say that such a decision could not have been rendered in the District of Columbia, and that it was an outrage upon justice.

You will not lose one jot of your prestige among your real friends, for the reason as above stated that the decision was not based upon facts but upon prejudice. Sincerely yours,

James A. Cobb

TLS   Con. 434   BTW Papers   DLC.

From Addison Wimbs

Greensboro, Ala., 11th — 8th 1911

Dear Sir: The head lines in daily press "WASHINGTON FAILS TO OB-
TAIN REDRESS FROM THE COURTS" is very suggestive and illuminates
the actual conditions existing in this country so far as the same relates
to Colored People regardless of their standing as to wealth, education
and morality and puts to flight the opinion entertained in some quarters that the Negro who "behaves himself" is never lynched, assaulted
or unmercifully treated in and out of the Courts of the land.

An awakened white public sentiment is need[ed] in the country and
we need also to be potent factors at the polls. It is my opinion that we
will never obtain anything akin to our rights until we pursue the avenues to obtain them that the white man does. I believe we actually
concede too much and are too prone to allow or ask the "other fellow
to make the toe mark from taw" for us, instead of making it ourselves.

I was very much afraid you were going to let this matter drop as
was given out in the press but am grateful to you that you pushed the
matter so that the situation would be fully illuminated.

I think also if you would get the press clipping bureau to furnish
you with the comments on this matter by the press of the country,
especially the rural press it would further give true light on American
Sentiment and these clippings put into pamphlet form would be valuable to the student of conditions. Your Friend

Ad Wimbs

TLS Con. 435 BTW Papers DLC. On stationery of the Grand Lodge,
Colored United Knights and Ladies of Progress of Alabama and Affiliated Organization, the Colored Fraternal Model Farm Improvement Association.

From Reed Paige Clark

Washington, D.C. November 10, 1911

My dear Doctor: Yesterday Mr. Hale,[1] the Third Assistant Secretary
of State, Captain McCoy[2] of the War Department and I were discussing the matter of the appointment of a military attaché at Monrovia to

aid in the reorganization of the Liberian Constabulary, or Frontier Police. The military attaché would act in an advisory capacity only, but his advice, if the services of the right man can be secured, would have great weight and would be invaluable.

There seems to be one colored officer on the active list of the Army who is especially well fitted for the work and that is Captain Charles Young, Ninth Cavalry, U.S.A., (now at Fort D. A. Russell, Wyoming), who was recently attached to our legation at Port au Prince, Haiti. He has made an admirable record and is apparently just the man for a position where considerable tact and great executive ability are required. Captain Young is a graduate of West Point. He was highly recommended by Mr. Justice Stewart,[3] of the Liberian Supreme Court, who was in Washington last week.

If you care to write to Captain Young, whom you probably know, and to enlist his active interest in Liberia I shall be very grateful, as I am anxious to have the reorganization of the Constabulary proceed in an orderly manner and with the minimum of delay.

With best wishes, I am   Yours very sincerely,

Reed Paige Clark

TLS Con. 441 BTW Papers DLC.

[1] Chandler Hale (1873–1951), who had been secretary of American embassies at Rome and Vienna, was third assistant secretary of state from 1909 to 1913.

[2] Frank Ross McCoy (1874–1954) was on the general staff of the U.S. Army from 1911 to 1914. A West Point graduate, he served during the Spanish-American War and World War I, and eventually achieved the rank of major general.

[3] Thomas McCants Stewart.

A Statement on the Bible

[Tuskegee, Ala., ca. Nov. 10, 1911]

The first book I knew was the Bible, and it is the book from which I have received the greatest amount of instruction and inspiration.

The part of the Bible which interested me perhaps more than any other was that which told the story of the way in which Moses led the people out of the House of Bondage.

For many years the Bible was the only book the colored people knew. Even in slavery, when very few could read or write, the older people managed some how or other to gain a pretty good acquaintance with the Bible, and the younger generation have not yet forgotten what they learned on their mothers' knees.

TMc Con. 915 BTW Papers DLC. Enclosed in BTW to J. S. Dickerson, ca. Nov. 10, 1911. Dickerson was managing editor of *The Standard* in Chicago, Ill.

Kelly Miller to the
Editor of the Washington *Star*

[Washington, D.C.] November 11, 1911

THE ASSAULT ON BOOKER WASHINGTON

To the Editor of The Star: The decision of the court in New York setting free the assailant of Dr. Booker T. Washington, the foremost negro in the world, has caused the entire race to put on sackcloth and ashes. That this illustrious American, the blamelessness of whose life embodies the Christ-like spirit of meekness, humility and forgiveness of spirit, should be stricken down with impunity fills the just and righteous mind with indignation for the assailant and infinite pity for the victim.

President Taft, in his calm, judicial, patriotic spirit, proclaims that he reverences the process and personnel of the courts. Would to God that the courts were so true to their function that every American could share in this lofty sentiment. No negro in America feels that he can get justice in any court where the race feeling is involved. Even the President of the United States will, I am sure, forgive the negro for not sharing his feelings of reverence for courts and judges, whose august personality is so exalted that they must not be called into account for deeds done on the bench.

I take it for granted that every reasonable man will regard the allegation that the conduct of Mr. Washington was provocative of the assault as absurd in the last degree. That a man who for well nigh a generation has gone in and out among the American people, every feature of whose conduct has been under the white light of public observation, and who for so long has stood the test as being without moral spot or blemish, should, of a night, be transformed into an insane libertine is too impossible to be entertained for a moment. No candid-minded American believes that Booker T. Washington addressed any woman on the streets of New York in terms of lustful endearment. That he was peeking through a keyhole in a cheap apartment house with lascivious intent is so inherently silly that it would not even be repeated against any other American of like established character and renown.

The fact that Dr. Washington failed to prove the charge against his assailant to the satisfaction of the court before whom it was tried ought not to reflect upon his honor or prejudice his reputation. The fact that one judge out of three held the assailant to be worthy of punishment robs the decision of judicial conclusiveness. Dr. Washington was not on trial before that court; nor should he be before the American people.

Righteousness of practice, precept and principle is the negro's only hope. This is indeed the only salvation of the weak among the strong. Dr. Washington has preached and exemplified this in his life. That he should be stricken by lawless hands, declared innocent by law, as an alleged transgressor of the gospel, upon which hinges the mission of his life and the salvation of his race, is to me the most tragic occurrence in our annals since the assassination of Abraham Lincoln. And yet I feel sure that the high-minded American people will abate no whit of their respect, support and admiration for this gentle-spirited, pure-souled man because of the humiliation which even a blameless life may not enable the most illustrious negro to escape.

Kelly Miller

Washington *Star,* Nov. 11, 1911, 1.

An Editorial in the New York *Amsterdam News*

[New York City] Nov. 11, 1911

A MISCARRIAGE OF JUSTICE

The acquittal by Justices Moss and Zeller — with Justice O'Keefe vigorously dissenting — of Henry Ulrich, the brutal assailant of Booker T. Washington last March 19, was an outrageous miscarriage of justice. It is but another evidence of the uneven handed justice meted out to colored citizens by courts of law North as well as South. No man could have sat through the trial of the Eleventh avenue gang leader, accused dog thief and admitted wife and child deserter, have heard the record of the miserable wretch completely exposed in court, then have seen his word as to the act of assault taken against that of the Christian peer of any man now living — because the Christian happened to be colored and the felon with his judges white — and not felt that the tribunal of American law is reeking with rank race prejudice. No Fiji Islander could have been present, heard the culprit confess using his fists, pursuing his victim, heard a police officer sworn to uphold the law tell of the pursuit by the drunken dog dealer, and the bloody, battered condition of his victim, hear a disinterested citizen, of the same color as the defendant, tell of the repeated cowardly clubbing, even while his unarmed victim was upon the ground, and then have conscientiously or legally decided that the dastardly attack was not an assault. No Turk or cowboy could have been so cruel or conscienceless as not to have given the full penalty of his condemnation to so base a bully. No Congoese or Kaffir would have been so unpatriotic as not to have exacted extreme punishment from one of his race's rounders when that rounder had assaulted one of his nation's leading lights. Justice Zeller from the outset obviously determined against his colored complainant, was primarily responsible, we believe, for this great travesty on justice. It was his pugnacious, persistent domination that carried the vacillating Presiding Justice Moss to the side of grave error and injustice. Let the colored people always remember Justices Zeller and Moss whenever hereafter they would seek judicial or political preferment. With an equal eternal gratitude must the black man of America remember the fair and firm Justice O'Keefe, who alone of the three, had the courage of his convictions. Nor should colored citizens forget the courtesy of the present District Attorney's office, and especially the unprejudiced, unswerving Assistant District Attorney Smith, who blazed out in diamond light the guilt of the dog dealer and his putrid paramour.

Dr. Washington, however, has earned as never before the approval of every member of his race. White men and colored men of power and prominence had brought a tremendous pressure upon him to quit the case, to refuse to prosecute his assailant on the grounds of his position and race harmony. But, listening to the voices of the millions of his people, for the sake, not so much of his own good name as that of his race, he never faltered in the entire ordeal of the tedious prosecution. He did not have the case hushed up. Without malice he insisted upon the court of public knowledge seeing its every detail. He comes away with his Christian character unsullied, the courageous moral leader of his people. To-day as never before he has the love and confidence of his race. The acquittal of Ulrich was a monstrous injustice. The vindication of Dr. Washington through the complete publicity of the trial is a source of great satisfaction.

New York *Amsterdam News,* Nov. 11, 1911, 8.

From Kelly Miller

Washington, D.C. November 15, 1911

My dear Dr. Washington: Mr. McKinlay advises me that he has already sent you a clipping from the Star, containing my statement of the outcome of the fiasco of a trial in New York.[1] I read the proceedings before getting out of bed on Tuesday morning, and instantly reached the conclusion that the influential colored men in Washington, the Capital of the nation, who ought to understand and help influence right public sentiment, should formulate a strong statement of protest for the associated press. Pursuant to this judgment I called up several leading men, including Mr. McKinlay, who advised against the suggestion. I was naturally enough influenced by their advice, but felt so strong in the matter, that I could not refrain from an expression of my own feeling and judgment. I found that the local papers were very much averse to handling the matter, although they had given wide-spread publication to the trial under flaring head lines, not wholly complimentary. It was only after Mr. McKinlay and myself used personal influence with the Editor[2] of the Star that he was induced to print the matter, after cutting out certain important parts. If the Negro race does not cry out at this great outrage it will be constrained hereafter to forever hold its peace, when mobs and courts conspire against it. If there be any Negro (and I fear there are some) who can extract satisfaction or delight out of your predicament, I can only pray "Father forgive them for they know not what they do." The whole race expects you to preserve the same sane fortitude and calm heroism of spirit, which has characterized your life and conduct, in other situations almost as trying as this.

With best wishes. Yours truly,

Kelly Miller

TLS Con. 435 BTW Papers DLC.

[1] See Kelly Miller to the Editor of the Washington *Star*, Nov. 11, 1911, above.
[2] Theodore Williams Noyes.

To Bradley Gilman

[Tuskegee, Ala.] November 17, 1911

Dear Dr. Gilman: You do not know how cordially I appreciate your kind letter of November 11th.[1] Similar expressions have come to me from hundreds of the best people in America and none of them will ever know how much their confidence has meant to me. I fear there is no way of taking this case to a higher court, because it was one of assault and the claim would be that the man was being again placed in jeopardy.

I am very glad to learn that Mr. Harrison[2] is doing so well with his newspaper. He is, as you say, rather crude, but I think that in time this will wear away. Yours very truly,

Booker T. Washington

TLpS Con. 434 BTW Papers DLC.

¹ Gilman wrote that he was indignant over the outcome of the Ulrich case, and asked BTW if the matter could be appealed "and in some higher court a higher type of judge be found." (Gilman to BTW, Nov. 11, 1911, Con. 434, BTW Papers, DLC.)

² J. Thomas Harrison, editor of the Cambridge *Advocate,* a black weekly newspaper.

To Reed Paige Clark

[Tuskegee, Ala.] November Eighteen 1911

My dear Mr. Clark: I shall write Capt. Charles Young, as you suggest and hope to receive a letter from him favoring the suggestion outlined in your letter of November 10th.

If you could secure Captain Young for this service, I am quite sure that you would find him immensely valuable and helpful in the reorganization of the Liberian Constabulary.

With best wishes for your success, I am   Yours very truly,

Booker T. Washington

TLpS Con. 420 BTW Papers DLC.

To Charles Young

[Tuskegee, Ala.] November Eighteen 1911

Personal.

My dear Captain Young: The matter which I wish to bring to your attention is outlined in a communication just received from Mr. Reed Paige Clark, who has been designated by President Taft to serve as Receiver of Customs for Liberia and who is planning to go to Monrovia very soon to help the Liberian people re-organize and otherwise straighten out their difficulties. I enclose a copy of Mr. Clark's letter and also copy of my reply.

Will you kindly let me hear from you at your convenience. Yours very truly,

Booker T. Washington

TLpS Con. 446 BTW Papers DLC.

From William Taylor Burwell Williams

Hampton, Virginia   Nov. 18, 1911

My dear Dr. Washington: I am writing to thank you again for including me among those you invited to accompany you on your recent tour of Texas. The oftener I go the more convinced I am of the great good you are doing the colored people and the South by these visits. To get out the great crowds of white people in Texas to hear you was a great triumph, to say nothing of reaching them as effectively as you know so well how to do. A white man at Marshall bitterly opposed to Negroes was induced to come hear you. On leaving he said, "That man disarms criticism."

Maj. Moton has spoken to me regarding your invitation for your tour in Florida in March. I shall hold myself in readiness to join you.

Again thanking you for your consideration, I am, Yours most sincerely,

W. T. B. Williams

TLS   Con. 445   BTW Papers   DLC.

To Amanda Ferguson Johnston

[Tuskegee, Ala.] November 20, 1911

My dear Sister: Your letter of October 26th has been received, but I have not had time to answer it before now.

I am sorry to say that just now I am cramped so much in my finances that it would be impossible for me to take up the matter of the house. I may be able to do so sometime in the future.

I hope that all are well. Your Brother,

B. T. W.

TLpI   Con. 426   BTW Papers   DLC.

To Kelly Miller

[Tuskegee, Ala.] November 20, 1911

Personal.

My dear Professor Miller: My last letter to you was written rather hastily, and I did not have time to express to you fully all that was in my mind.

You do not know how grateful I am to you for what you have written.

I see that your statements have been widely published in the colored papers. Of course, I realized from the beginning that in bringing this case to a head, I was at a great disadvantage in having to face a number of people who did not scruple to perjure themselves. But I felt that I owed it to my race and to myself to bring things to a head, regardless of all that.

I wish also to say to you that there was not a word of truth in a single statement made on the witness stand by the woman, and many other statements were just as false. Yours very truly,

Booker T. Washington

TLpS Con. 435 BTW Papers DLC.

To Jennie E. Watson[1]

[Tuskegee, Ala.] November 20, 1911

Personal & Confidential.

Dear Madam: Your kind letter has been received, and I wish to assure you that I appreciate the interest which you manifest in my behalf.[2]

I wish to say that in the first place, I called at the house mentioned in the papers on a wholly legitimate mission. In the second place, the testimony given on the witness stand in court against me was almost wholly perjured testimony. I went on the witness stand and denied all of these falsehoods. Having denied them, I cannot see what would be gained by making any other statements at this time.

The question simply resolves itself into this: Shall my word be taken, or that of a loose and common woman, who is living as another man's paramour?

I believe that in the last analysis, when people have had time to sit down and think carefully about this matter, they will feel as most of them now feel — that I have been the victim of perjury and falsehood.

I shall be very glad to hear from you further whenever you have time to write.

By this mail, I send you a copy of my last annual report to the Board of Trustees. Yours very truly,

Booker T. Washington

TLpS Con. 435 BTW Papers DLC.

¹ A resident of Minneapolis, Minn.
² She urged BTW to make a public statement on the Ulrich case. (Nov. 14, 1911, Con. 435, BTW Papers, DLC.)

To Wilford H. Smith

[Tuskegee, Ala.] Nov. 20, 1911

Dear Mr. Smith: I want to make a gift to my daughter, Mrs. Portia M. Pittman, of the two lots which I own in New Jersey. Will you be kind enough to make out a deed for these two lots. Enclosed I send you the data. Yours very truly,

Booker T. Washington

TLpS Con. 439 BTW Papers DLC.

To Anson Phelps Stokes, Jr.

[Tuskegee, Ala.] November 21, 1911

My dear Mr. Stokes: I am sorry to be delayed in answering your recent letter in which you enclosed a proposed resolution regarding the endowment for a fellowship at the University of Virginia.

The plan proposed seems to me on the whole wise, and I think it will prove helpful.

373

I wish to add, however, that I very much hope that later the Trustees can see their way clear to endow a similar scholarship in the far South.[1] Such a fellowship at the University of Alabama, for example, will prove most helpful.

I am still hoping to see you for a few minutes before you go to Europe. Yours very truly,

Booker T. Washington

TLpS   Con. 439   BTW Papers   DLC.

[1] The Phelps-Stokes trustees decided to establish two initial fellowships, one at the University of Virginia and one at the University of Georgia. (Stokes to BTW, Nov. 27, 1911, Con. 440, BTW Papers, DLC.)

To Hightower T. Kealing

[Tuskegee, Ala.] Nov. 21, 1911

Dear Mr. Kealing: I hope you will plan to be in Washington December 14th for the meeting of the Jeanes Fund Board. There is just an element of risk in connection with the matter, but nevertheless it is practically settled that you will be elected to the vacancy occasioned by Bishop Grant's death. The committee is to meet in Washington at that time.

With kindest regards always, I am   Yours very truly,

Booker T. Washington

TLpS   Con. 427   BTW Papers   DLC.

To Frank Moore Wilmot[1]

[Tuskegee, Ala.] Nov. 21, 1911

My dear Sir: Replying to your letter of November 14th regarding the case of Boyce Lindsay, I would state that I have looked into the matter carefully. We tried in every way possible to get the boy satisfied and to have him remain here but we were not successful.

Regarding the board, I would state that no reasonable person could find fault with our food. Many persons who are in the habit of visiting educational institutions tell us that we have the best equipped and cleanest kitchen of any school in this part of the country. Our dining hall is large, airy and light and everything possible is done to make it cheerful. Students put flowers on their table so that the whole appearance of the dining room is very attractive. We try to supply the students with plenty of fresh, well cooked food. Of course the food is different from the kind that the students in many cases have been in the habit of getting before coming here. Many of the Southern colored people use various kinds of sweet breads, crackers, cheese, etc., in an irregular way. All that of course here is cut out. We confine them to a simple, healthy diet. It often occurs that it requires several months for a student to adjust himself to this new plan of living, but after adjustment is made they find themselves much stronger and more healthy than they were before coming here.

I have just talked with our Commandant regarding sleeping arrangements, and he tells me that it is true that the boys do sleep on pine straw. Two-thirds of our students sleep on ticks filled with pine straw. For the first two or three weeks it is a little trying for the students until they get the pine straw "broken in," but we have preferred to use the pine straw because it is healthy and the ticks can be often refreshed. We have decided to give the boy, however, another chance, and I have instructed Major Ramsey, our Commandant, in case he comes back to give him another kind of tick. We shall do everything within our power to carry out your wishes and to help the boy.

Insofar as you can, I advise that you impress upon the boy this fact that in some degree he is responsible for himself. I confess that we have not been very successful in dealing with students whose way is paid by somebody else. Our finest students and the most successful class of students are those who feel an individual responsibility for their expenses and for remaining here.

Enclosed I take the liberty of sending you a copy of my last annual report which I hope will interest you.

Let me add that it is a great satisfaction to us as a race of people to know from time to time your commission recognizes heroic services performed by the members of the colored race. All this is of great encouragement to our people. Yours very truly,

Booker T. Washington

TLpS Con. 445 BTW Papers DLC.

[1] Frank Moore Wilmot (1872–1930) of Pittsburgh, Pa., was manager of the Carnegie Hero Fund Commission, and director and secretary of several charitable organizations.

To Emmett Jay Scott

N. Y. [City], Nov. 23, 1911

Dear Mr. Scott: I do not know that I made myself very clear when talking with you over the telephone from Chehaw.

What I had in mind was this: For Dr. Park and Mr. Work together to prepare an article for The Outlook which I can sign on some such subject as this: "What the Late Census teaches regarding the Negro."[1] Show, for example, what has been accomplished in getting farms in various states — that the general movement of the Negro has been away from the cities to the farms, while in the case of the white people, the opposite has been true. Take up the birth rate and compare it with England, for example. In this connection, the statement sent out from Washington by Dr. Jones will be very helpful.

Anything else bearing upon the Negro from the Census that can be brought out, will be helpful.

Tell Mr. Work that I want him to begin preparing an article which I can use in the Independent, showing to what an extent the Negro is encouraged by the white people to take part in county and state fairs in the South. Show what he is doing cooperating with white people, making exhibits at their fairs, and also what he is doing in an independent way.

I suppose you saw in yesterday's Advertiser how your article on the Tuskegee baseball team was used rather effectively.

I am very anxious that this Census article be ready by the time I return.

B. T. W.

TLI   Con. 985   BTW Papers   DLC.

¹ Presumably this was the article in *The Independent,* Apr. 11, 1912, below. The census information on the black farmer was used in an article in the *North American Review,* Feb. 1912, below.

From Charles Young

Fort D. A. Russell, Wyo., November 24, 1911

My dear Dr. Washington: In reply to your communication of the 18th instant, relative to the Military Attaché detail to Liberia, I wish to state that I am always willing to aid in any work for the good of the country in general and our race in particular, whether that race be found in Africa or in the United States.

Mr. Oswald Garrison Villard of the New York Evening Post, wrote me sometime ago asking if I would undertake the organization of a Negro Regiment in connection with the New York National Guard, provided the War Department would consent to loaning me for such duty. I consented, not knowing that I would be wanted for the *"Homeland"* detail. Since then I have heard nothing of the progress of things in New York.

Now if you and the War Department think I can be of more good to the country and our people on the African detail with Mr. Clark, I am perfectly willing to go, and shall render him faithful and loyal service.

Always with the same esteem and friendship, Your sincere,

Chas. Young
(Capt. 9th Cavalry)

TLS   Con. 446   BTW Papers   DLC.

From Albert Ernest Jenks[1]

Minneapolis   November 27th, 1911

My dear Sir: I give a course of lectures in this University on the negro American, and in reading your numerous publications I have failed to find your belief as to the matter of amalgamation. Frankly, personally, I believe amalgamation between the white and the negro American unwise, and I so teach my students. I favor and teach desirability of universal and uniform laws against *all* forms of sexual intercourse between the two peoples in question. I do this in the face of the fact that several careful American students claim there is no indisputable evidence of the superiority or inferiority of either peoples.

If, with the above explanation, you care to write me, I shall greatly appreciate a quotable statement of your belief in the matter. Respectfully yours,

A. E. Jenks

TLS   Con. 915   BTW Papers   DLC.

[1] Albert Ernest Jenks (1869–1953), a University of Wisconsin Ph.D. (1899), was an anthropologist and ethnologist who taught at the University of Minnesota from 1907 to 1938.

To Elmer Kneale[1]

[Tuskegee, Ala.] November Twenty-nine 1911

Dear Sir: I am not a student of biology and cannot answer with any definiteness the questions you ask.

It seems to me that the question of evolution is very largely a question for experts and I am willing to leave it to them to settle.

As to the general ideas of the progress of mankind, which have been associated with the name of Darwin in most of our minds, I confess that I share them, though I have never taken much stock in the theories that people have advanced from time to time as to the way in which this progress has come about. As far as my experience goes, I have seen but very little progress either moral or material that was not pretty closely associated with work. It is the evolution brought about by human beings who work that I believe in. Yours very truly,

Booker T. Washington

TLpSr Con. 427 BTW Papers DLC. Signed and initialed in E. J. Scott's hand.

[1] Writing on stationery of the Springfield *Illinois State Register,* Kneale asked for BTW's opinion of Darwin's teachings and their present and future acceptance. (Oct. 20, 1911, Con. 427, BTW Papers, DLC.)

To Charles Young

[Tuskegee, Ala.] Dec. 1, 1911

My dear Captain Young: I have your kind letter of November 24th, and cordially and sincerely appreciate the generous sentiments you express with regard to accepting detail as Military Attaché to the American Minister of Liberia. You will have a splendid opportunity I think, to render service in a particular most needed in that important field. You will find Mr. Clark a splendid gentleman and one whom you can work with with real satisfaction and pleasure.

I enclose herewith a report of the American Commission to Liberia, and also Mr. Scott's paper before the Conference on Africa and the Near East at Worcester, Mass., which may give you some impressions of Liberian conditions. Yours very truly,

Booker T. Washington

TLpS Con. 446 BTW Papers DLC.

To Ralph Waldo Tyler

[Tuskegee, Ala.] December 1st, 1911

Personal and Confidential.

My dear Mr. Tyler: Before you go too far in seeking the promotion of our friend, Mr. Johnson, the United States Consul in South America, it might be well to inquire if his father-in-law is not a rabid, anti-Taft and pro–Du Bois man.

I am very fond of Mr. Johnson, and did what I could to get him his present job, but I think it just as well to know the facts.

Also, I think it would be well for you to take up the matter of seeing if some of our friends cannot be placed in that consular position in France, now occupied by the son-in-law of Judge Gibbs. Judge Gibbs, and his son-in-law, Napoleon Bonaparte Marshall, both spend their time in heaping abuse upon the administration and the friends of the administration. I think it might be just as well to have some of our friends in that post in France.

I think Mr. Anderson could throw some light on the first matter that I have mentioned.

Please do not use my name, but I think it is time for people to stand up and show their true colors, or be openly against us. Yours very truly,

Booker T. Washington

TLpS Con. 443 BTW Papers DLC.

To Anson Phelps Stokes, Jr.

[Tuskegee, Ala.] Dec. 1, 1911

My dear Mr. Stokes: I am writing in the hope that this will reach you before you start for Europe. I made several efforts to go to New Haven while I was in the North, but I found myself so much occupied in many directions that it was impossible. I will try to put in writing one of the things I had in mind.

Enclosed I send you some printed matter which will give you some idea of what I have been trying to accomplish during the last three or four years in making trips through various Southern states.

The most interesting and I think valuable part of these trips is in the fact that while I speak primarily to colored people that in every case these meetings are attended by large numbers of white people; in some cases the number of white people, both men and women, is equal to the number of colored people, and the whites are just as enthusiastic as the colored people.

Of course it is a lamentable fact that practically one-half of the Negro children in the South today are not in school for a single month in the year, and in other cases a large proportion are in school only three or four months. The public school money is in the hands of the white people, and unless we can convert the masses of the white people to the point where they will believe in Negro education we will not make much progress in the future. One of the points which I have in mind in making these trips is to win the Southern white people over thoroughly to Negro education.

These trips are costly because I have to cover a large amount of territory within a short while. A large part of the expense is borne by white people and colored people in the states themselves. Several friends in the North have been kind enough to help me, and the other portion has come out of my own pocket. I very much fear that I cannot call on the same individuals in the North to help me much longer, and my own funds are exhausted. I am wondering, under the circumstances, if the Stokes Fund Board of Trustees would not think it worth while to contribute a small amount of money for a period of say three years toward this kind of work? It would enable me to do much more effective work if it could be done.

I am sending you a copy of an address delivered before the Theological Department of Vanderbilt University some years ago, in which I advocated that the very same thing be done in Southern white universities which your Board has decided to do. Yours very truly,

Booker T. Washington

TLpS   Con. 440   BTW Papers   DLC.

To Joseph E. Wiley

[Tuskegee, Ala.] Dec. 2, 1911

My dear Mr. Wiley: I received your letter while I was in Boston, but I had no time to see you when I was in New York as I was there but a very short while.

I do not want to discourage you, but I think you had better consider very thoroughly the following matter: Is it possible for a cotton mill to succeed in any rich section of the South, that is where the lands are rich and producing cotton in great abundance? I know of practically no section of the South that a cotton mill has succeeded for any length of time where the land is rich as it is around Dallas. The difficulty seems to be that the people find that they can make more money in growing cotton than they can in spinning cotton and the result is that when the cotton mill needs labor the labor goes to the farm. You will find, I think, that the cotton mills that have succeeded are located in the Piedmont sections of the South on or near the poorer lands, where people cannot make so much money in growing cotton. I may not be right, but I think this is worth thinking about. Yours very truly,

Booker T. Washington

TLpS   Con. 445   BTW Papers   DLC.

To Harlan Page Amen[1]

[Tuskegee, Ala.] December 2, 1911

Personal.

My dear Mr. Amen: I have been thinking of writing you several times recently.

Disagreeable and unfortunate as it was, I feel that my son, Booker T. Washington, Jr., got a valuable lesson from his experience at Exeter.

I think you will be interested to know that ever since he left Exeter, he has been a student at Fisk University, Nashville, Tennessee. He entered the preparatory department, and has continued in that institution until he is now a member of the Junior Class in college. He is as settled and as thoughtful as a man many times his age. He does not give a single bit of trouble or cause us any anxiety whatever. He is a completely changed boy, and promises to make a strong, good, useful man. Yours very truly,

Booker T. Washington

TLpS   Con. 415   BTW Papers   DLC.

[1] Harlan Page Amen (1853–1913) was principal of Phillips Exeter Academy in Exeter, N.H.

To Walter Hines Page

[Tuskegee, Ala.] December 2, 1911

Dear Mr. Page: I have been reading with a great deal of interest the articles written by Professor Mims on recent developments in the new South.

One thing I notice in reading these articles is that one of the real difficulties in the advancement of the South is the lack of education and industrial training among all classes of the laboring people, but especially among the Negroes.

I believe there is a chance here for a series of articles that will show what Negroes are doing among themselves, directly and indirectly through Negro churches, Negro schools and Negro business enterprises, to improve the industrial efficiency in the masses of the race. During the last twenty years since the leaders of the race have turned from politics and given their attention to the material and educational development of the race they have learned by experience in business and other ways the needs of their own race. They are now prepared I believe to work in cooperation with the white man of the South to do a valuable service in training, disciplining and organizing the masses of the people in a way to fit them for higher and more efficient service.

My plan would be to make a close study of three or four banks, three or four of the smaller industrial schools, perhaps also three or four churches that are doing genuine service in disciplining the masses, teaching them habits of thrift and industry, etc. In this way I believe I could give the Southern white man a better understanding of the value of the work that Negroes are doing for themselves. At the same time such an article or series of articles would be a source of inspiration to the colored people themselves.

There are at least three counties in the South where the Negro owns at least 60,000 acres of land. It might be well to start with a study of these three counties.

Incidentally these articles would give me opportunity to call attention to more general facts illustrating the material and educational advancement of the race during the past ten years.

No one unacquainted with the facts of the inside can appreciate, for example, the progress the Negro has made in Mississippi in these directions. The Negroes in Mississippi, while Vardaman and others have been howling about their political rights have gone on quietly getting land, building houses, organizing banks and industrial schools and colleges. For example, within the last ten years the Negroes in Mississippi have bought 35,000 farms; in Georgia they have bought 49,000 farms.

I believe a series of articles, well written and well illustrated will not only attract a good deal of attention but will accomplish a lot of good just now in many directions.

In this connection I think it would be well to say in these articles what influences prohibition has had upon the development of the Negro. While prohibition may have failed in other sections, in the South it has helped the Negro immensely.

I think that many of your readers would be surprised to see what fine houses some of the colored farmers have built in different parts of the South. I do not mean city houses but houses way out in the country, in many cases miles from the railroad. Yours very truly,

[Booker T. Washington]

TLc   Con. 53   BTW Papers   DLC.

From Madame C. J. Walker[1]

Indianapolis, Indiana   12/2, 1911

My Dear Sir: I am desirous of attending the Farmers convention which will convene at your school Jan. 17th., 1912.

I am writing to ask if you will allow me to introduce my work and give me the privilege of selling my goods on the grounds.

Enclosed find my booklet which will give you an idea of the business in which I am engaged.

Thanking you in advance for an early reply, I am, Yours respectfully,

Mme C. J. Walker

TLS   Con. 917   BTW Papers   DLC.

[1] Madame C. J. Walker (1867?–1919), born Sarah Breedlove in Delta, La., into a family of poor black farmers, was married at the age of fourteen. When her husband died six years later, she supported herself and an infant daughter as

a washerwoman. In the 1890s she married Charles J. Walker and moved to St. Louis, where she invented in 1905 a hair-straightening formula and a metal comb for styling hair. Madame Walker peddled her preparation and acquired enough money to establish a black cosmetics factory in Indianapolis. She eventually became a millionaire, built a large mansion on the Hudson, supported many black welfare and civil rights activities, and left large sums to black educational institutions and other worthy causes. BTW at first opposed membership in the NNBL for her and other cosmetics manufacturers on the ground that they fostered imitation of white beauty standards, but he later relented.

A Review of *My Larger Education*
in the Atlanta *Constitution*

[Atlanta, Ga., Dec. 3, 1911]

This book, written by a well-known negro, perhaps the leader of his race, especially in an educational view, invites a few decided views to be gleaned therefrom.

The trouble with Washington, he is trying to do too much, with the help of the rich people of the north and east whom he has come in contact with. He goes about all over the country, flitting here and there like a butterfly, but what has he accomplished for the negro schools, except to raise money, some of which goes to the schools, and some does not? Has he not been a hindrance to the up-building of the negro race? The leaders of the negroes, as a whole, do not approve of his methods, and his only following, perhaps, is with the white people of the north, with whom he pours forth his woes, and the woes of his people; he interests them and creates a sympathy for his race. The negroes are flourishing and in a good condition, but what part, if any, in attaining that prosperity has been done by Washington?

He has traveled over the whole world, nearly; has been to England, Denmark, Germany, Hungary and Austria, and I expect he has been found in Turkey to interview the Mohammedans. Every place he goes he gathers in the shekels. What has he done with all the money? or for all his people of the south? He should stay at home and devote himself to the work he has here.

We have heard good people say, who live in the vicinity of Tuskegee, that that school has turned out more negroes to fill the chaingangs of the country than have ever gone from there as good citizens!

The place for Washington is at Tuskegee, where he should work that school. Let him put it on a systematic basis, and make it one large central school which will radiate to other sections, and establish good schools in every district where there are negroes. Leave off the higher branches till they become efficient in the lower ones, as well as have manual labor schools, where work is the motive power.

Washington cannot run a school and live in New York and write books, he will have to discontinue that to run Tuskegee.

There is no system in the negro schools, and neither is there any in many of the white schools; if a child don't want to learn, there is no incentive to make them. Let Washington build up Tuskegee in good morals and honesty, and efficiency by his example and presence there.

If he does this he will certainly not be found in New York, in the night time, "hunting keyholes," and attending police courts, with himself on the criminal side of the docket.

Take it as a whole, this is an interesting book, which will please many people, who fail to see its defects, as it appears to many others.

Atlanta *Constitution,* Dec. 3, 1911, 4G.

To Albert Ernest Jenks

[Tuskegee, Ala.] December Fourth 1911

My dear Sir: In reply to your letter of November 27th permit me to say that the only reason I have not said anything directly on the subject you mention is because I have not hitherto seen any particular advantage in doing so. I have never looked upon amalgamation as offering a solution of the so-called race problem and I know very few Negroes who favor it or even think of it, for that matter.

What those whom I have heard discuss the matter do object to are laws which enable the father to escape his responsibility, or prevent him from accepting and exercising it when he has children by colored women. I think this answers your question, but since there seems to be some misunderstanding as to how colored people feel about this subject, I might say this in explanation of what I have already said:

The Negroes in America are, as you know, a mixed race. If that is an advantage we have it; if it is a disadvantage it is still ours, and for the simple reason that the product of every sort of racial mixture between the black man and any other race is always a Negro and never a white man, Indian or any other sort of man.

The Negro in America is defined by the Census as a person who is classed as such in the community in which he or she resides. In other words the Negro in this country is not so much a man of a particular color or particular racial stock as one who shares a particular condition. It is the fact that they all share in this condition which creates a cause of common sympathy and binds the members of the race together in spite of all differences.

There are a good many persons in the Negro race who are perfectly able to pass muster as white people if they choose to do so, but, as a matter of fact, I believe there are very few who really want to escape. Some of them have tried it and have found it unsatisfactory.

They have learned that no man can amount to much who is ashamed of his mother, or can have much respect for himself, and that no class or race can hope for the respect of the world that does not respect itself. Besides that, Negroes have resources for enjoyment and satisfaction among themselves that white people do not, perhaps, fully understand. I know there are some colored people who have complained about ostracisms, but it is pretty hard to ostracise a whole race of 10,000,000 people. For this reason, amalgamation has become a subject of merely academic importance for most colored people.

Those who are fighting race distinctions are doing so, I think you will find, not because they want amalgamation or because they want to intermingle socially with white people, but because they have been led to believe that where race distinctions exist they pave the way for discriminations which are needlessly humiliating and injurious to the weaker race.

Let me add that I do not wholly share this view myself. While there may be some serious disadvantage in racial distinctions, there are certainly real advantages to my race at least. Yours very truly,

[Booker T. Washington]

TLc   Con. 915   BTW Papers   DLC.

Pinckney Benton Stewart Pinchback
to Emmett Jay Scott

Brooklyn N.Y. Dec. 4./11

My dear Emmett: I ordered shipped to you a case of the best Scotch whiskey to be found on the market. It is 5 Star Haig & Haig (12 bottles). It should reach you not later than Saturday. Six (6) bottles are for Mrs. Washington, four (4) bottles are for your good self and two (2) bottles for J. H. Washington. These are my Christmas gifts to you all. I trust they will be accepted as they were the best I could think of and afford.

I will send the Doctor some cigars later. I dare say he would like them better.

I am just back from a visit to Mrs. Pinchback at Washington. Very, very sorry to inform you she is not well. Poor dear soul, she is making a game struggle to live and is entitled to and should succeed. May the good Lord be her guide & shield and enable her to regain her health.

I did not see many of the friends while in W. My time was given to Mrs. P. Of course I cant have any news from this end of the line.

Remember me very kindly to all the members of your family, and accept for yourself assurances of my highest regard & lasting friendship. Yours very truly & sincerely

Pinchback

P.S. I hope it will not put you to too much trouble to deliver my presents to parties named.

P.

ALS   Con. 441   BTW Papers   DLC.

From George Augustus Gates

Nashville, Tennessee   Dec. 4, 1911

My dear Dr. Washington: A Japanese student wants to come to us. Is the Japanese student a colored man or a white man?

I just put that question up to our City Attorney and he admitted that that was a new one for him and laid him low until he could look the matter up. Have you ever had any cases which would test the matter?

While writing let me ask another question. I was talking with a very prominent citizen of America yesterday whose home is in Nashville and he raised a question or two which I am going to put up to you, both for his sake and for the reason that I am also interested in it. He said, "What do the graduates of Tuskegee do after they graduate?"

I presume you have a plenty of printed matter which will answer the question. I can answer it only in a general way but I am sure you have had to answer it a few hundred times.

You may be interested to know how the matter came up. He told me that he owns a large plantation in a neighboring state. A few years ago he took it into his head that it would be a good idea to get an educated and trained Negro to superintend the plantation. He thought by getting a man of both education and character he could do a good turn for himself as well as for all concerned.

But when he raised the question with the Negroes on the plantation they smiled and looked embarrassed but finally said: "You know we Negroes do not like to work for Negroes, we prefer working for white men. The fact is your plan won't work, it is sure to break down." The result was that the matter was dropped.

I am likely to meet the man again and I should like to know what I am to tell him in this general matter. Sincerely yours,

George A. Gates

P.S. I notice that you inquire particularly about the last meeting of the Board of Trustees. I am having a copy of the minutes made for you. I was under the impression that a copy had been sent by Dr. Ryder to all the trustees. G.

TLS   Con. 423   BTW Papers   DLC.

To Charles Allmond Wickersham

[Tuskegee, Ala.] December 5, 1911

Dear Sir: I am sure that you will agree with me that it has been a long while since I bothered you regarding stopping Train No. 38 at Chehaw in the morning.

But I am compelled to be in Washington early on the morning of December 14th, to attend a meeting of the Jeanes Fund Board at the White House. I am also compelled to be here on the night of the 12th.

Under all the circumstances, I wish very much that you might see your way clear to give an order to stop Train No. 38, the morning of the 13th.

Please let me hear from you. If not asking too much, will you please telegraph answer at my expense so that I may make arrangements regarding reservations.

We are planning to have a good many Northern visitors here during the winter and early spring. Yours truly,

Booker T. Washington

TLpS Con. 445 BTW Papers DLC.

A Manuscript of an Article

[Tuskegee, Ala.] Dec. 5, 1911

RACE PREJUDICE IN EUROPE

Ever since I can remember I have had a special and peculiar interest in the history and progress of the Jewish race. The first book that I knew, the Bible, was a history of the Jews, and to my childish mind the most fascinating portion of that book was the story of the manner in which Moses led the children of Israel out of the house of bondage, through the wilderness, into the promised land. I first heard that story from the lips of my mother, when both she and I were slaves on a plantation in Virginia. I have heard it repeated and referred to many times since. In fact, I am certain that hardly a day or week goes by that I do not meet, among my people, some reference to this same Bible story.

The Negro slaves were always looking forward to the time when a Moses should arise from somewhere, who would lead them, as he led the ancient Hebrews, out of the house of bondage. And after freedom, the masses of Negro people have still continued to look to some great leader, some man inspired of God, who would lead them out of their difficulties into the promised land, which, somehow, they never seem able to reach.

I learned in slavery to compare the condition of the Negro with that of the Jews in bondage in Egypt, so I have frequently, since freedom, been compelled to compare the prejudice even persecution which the Jewish people have had to face and overcome in different parts of the world, with the disadvantages of the Negro in the United States and elsewhere.

I had seen considerable of the poorer classes of the Jews in New York City before going to Europe, and when I visited Whitechapel, London, I had an opportunity to learn something of the condition of the Polish and Russian Jews who are driven from their native land to find refuge in England. It was not however, until I reached Cracow, in Austrian Poland, or Galicia, that I really began to understand what life in the Ghetto, of which I had heard so much, was really like. It was not until then, that I began to comprehend what the wear and tear of centuries of persecution, poverty and suffering had meant in the life of the Jews.

One of the first things I observed in regard to the Jews abroad was the very different forms which racial prejudice takes in the different countries which I visited. For example, in East London, which has long been the refuge for the poor and oppressed of other countries, the Jew is tolerated, although he is not liked. It is not clear just what is the source of the English prejudice. Complaint is sometimes made that the Jewish immigrant has driven out the native Briton, from certain parts of East London, but it is admitted at the same time that [in] such cases it is because the Jew has proven a better tenant. He does not drink, he is law-abiding and he pays rent regularly. It seems to be true in London, also, as it is in New York, that as soon as the Jewish immigrant has made a little success he does not remain in the same quarters of the city. He moves out and his place is taken by some new and half starved fugitive from Russia or Roumania, so that there is a constant stream of "greeners," as they are called, coming in, and another, perhaps, somewhat smaller stream of those who have been successful moving out. In spite of this fact, it is generally admitted that general conditions have improved under the influence of the Jews. English prejudice where it exists, seems to be due, therefore, partly to economic causes and partly to the general distrust of the alien that seems to be gaining in England with the influx of immigration from Southern Europe.

In Denmark, on the contrary, where the Jews seem to be very largely represented among the educated and well-to-do classes, I discovered a great deal of prejudice against the Germans but almost none against the Jews. In fact, one of the most distinguished men in Denmark, outside of the King, a man who has been a leader in the intellectual life of that country during the past thirty years, Prof. George Brandes, is a Jew.

In Germany I learned that, while the Jews are prominent not only in business but in the professions, it is still difficult for them to rise in the army or to advance to the position of a professor in the universities, unless they have first been baptized.

In speaking about this matter to a German whom I met at one of the hotels in Vienna, I called to mind the name of a distinguished professor whose name I had heard, as an instance of a Jew gaining a high position in a German university.

"Oh, well," he replied, "he has been baptized."

That recalls to my mind a conundrum which an acquaintance propounded, while we were discussing some of the peculiarities of race prejudice in Europe.

"When is a Jew not a Jew," he asked. The answer is, of course, "When he is a Christian." In other words, prejudice in Germany seems to be directed only against the Jew who clings to his religion.

When I reached Prague in Bohemia I learned that among the masses of the people there is little distinction made between Jews and Germans, since both speak the same language and the Czechs, confusing one with the other, hate both with a double hatred, first for what they are and then for what they seem to be.

In Vienna and Buda-Pest the Jews, through the newspapers which they control, seem to exercise a powerful influence on politics. I remember hearing repeated references while I was there to the "Jewish press." In Prague it is said that every German paper but one is controlled by Jews. Jews are represented, however, not only in the press in Austria-Hungary, but in the army and in all the other professions. They are not only financiers and business men, but doctors, lawyers, artists and actors as elsewhere in Europe where they have gained their freedom. Nevertheless it is still against the law for Jews and Christians to intermarry in Austria-Hungary.

Some notion of the conditions under which the Jews lived, in almost every part of Europe a hundred years ago, may be gathered from the restrictions which are imposed upon them today in Russia and Roumania. In Roumania a Jew can neither vote nor hold office in the civil service. He is excluded from the professions. He is not permitted, for example, to become a physician or even open a pharmacy. He is not permitted to live in the rural districts. He can neither own land outside of the town nor work as an agricultural laborer. In the mills and factories not more than twenty-five per cent of the employees may be Jews. Although they are practically restricted to business enterprises, Jews may not become members of chambers of commerce. Jews are bound to serve in the army; they pay heavier taxes, proportionately, than other portions of the community, but they are classed under the laws as "aliens" not subject to alien protection.

In Russia, Jews are not allowed to live outside of what is called the "Pale of Settlement," which includes twelve provinces on the western and southwestern borders which Russia has annexed during the past two hundred years. Only merchants who pay a special license of 1,000 rubles, or about $500, university graduates and a few others may live outside the Pale. A Jew is not even permitted to live in Siberia unless he has been sent there as a punishment for crime.

Inside the Pale, Jews are not allowed to live outside the cities and incorporated towns. Although Jews are allowed to vote in Russia and send representatives to the Duma, they are not permitted to hold office or be employed in the public service. They are compelled to pay in addition to the ordinary taxes, which are heavy enough, taxes on the rents they receive from property owned by them, on inheritances, on the meat killed according to the Jewish law, on candles used in some of their religious observances, and on the skull caps they wear during religious services. In spite of this they are excluded from hospitals, schools and public functions which, in the Pale, are mainly paid for out of the extra taxes imposed upon them.

The most singular thing about it all is that the disabilities under which the Russian Jew now labors are at once removed by baptism. Not only that, but every Jew who allows himself to be sprinkled with holy water, in sign of the renunciation of his religion and his people, receives thirty rubles "thirty pieces of silver," as a reward.

Nothing was more forcibly impressed upon me during my study of conditions in Europe than this, namely, that we can tell very little from the mere fact that this or that political institution exists in a country, just what privileges or disadvantages these institutions bring to the masses of the people. In fact, it seems to be just as true in Europe as it is in America, that mere legislative enactments can of themselves, no more produce industry and thrift than they can produce justice and freedom. After the physical bondage has been destroyed there still remains the bondage of superstition, of ignorance and of religious class and racial prejudice.

During my stay in Prague, I took a walk one day through an ancient quarter of the city which had been formerly inhabited by Jews. The Ghetto of Prague is said to have been the largest and most famous in Europe. It was, in fact, a city in itself, for it contained not merely the oldest synagogue in Europe, with a famous old Jewish burial ground attached to it, but also a Rathouse or a city hall and a market in which, according to tradition, Jewish traders at one time sold Christian slaves. So thoroughly were the Jews at one time established in this quarter of the city that it went under the name of Judenstadt or Jewtown. There they maintained, in a small way, just as they do, to a lesser extent, in Russia today.

After Prague, the city which has the oldest and most interesting Ghetto in Europe, is Cracow, and the most interesting thing about it is the fact that it is still inhabited by Jews. They live there today very much, I suppose, as they did a hundred years ago, a race separate and apart, more removed apparently, from the manners, the customs and comprehension of the rest of the world than any people this side of China.

I have known Jews nearly all my life. I have done business with them and have more than once talked to them in their synagogues and have always found sympathy and support among them for the work I have had to do for my own people. I have frequently visited and studied, to some extent, the poor classes in the Jewish quarters on the

East Side in New York. In spite of this, however, when certain strange figures in long black coats, soft felt hats, with pale faces, lighted by dark glittering eyes and framed by glossy curls which hung down on either side in front of their ears, were pointed out to me in Vienna, I had not the slightest notion to what nationality or people these belonged. Later on when I reached Cracow, these same slender figures and pale delicate faces, became very familiar to me and I learned to recognize in them the higher type of Polish Jew.

I have been through the Jewish Quarter in New York, with its confusion of push carts; its swarms of black-eyed children, and its strange old men, with gray-brown beards wandering, care-worn and absorbed, through the crowded streets, each anxiously intent on some thought or purpose of his own. The Jewish Quarter on the East Side in New York is, however, a pale reflection of the Ghetto in Cracow. For one thing the Jew in New York, though he retains many of the habits and customs of the country from which he came, seems, in most cases, to be making an earnest effort to make an American of himself; to learn the language, and adopt the dress and, as far as possible, the manners of the new country of which he is soon to become, if he is not already, a citizen.

The masses of the Polish Jew, however, still cling tenaciously to the customs of their religion and of the Ghetto in which for a thousand years or more they have lived as exiles and, more or less, like prisoners. Instead of seeking to make themselves look like the rest of the people, among whom they live, they seem to be making every effort to preserve and emphasize the characters in which they are different from the people about them.

Although I met in Cracow Jews in all the various stages of transition — as far as their dress is concerned — from the traditional Ghetto Jew to the modern literary, professional or business man, nevertheless, the majority of the Jews still cling to the long black coat which they were compelled to wear in the middle ages. Certain ones have discarded this symbol of exclusiveness, but still wear the long beard, and the side curls in front of their ears, which seem to be especially dear to them, perhaps, because, for some reason I could not understand, they are forbidden to wear them in Russia.

Perhaps it was the effect of the costume, which gave them a strange and alien appearance, but it seems to me, at first, as if every Jew in

Cracow had exactly the same features, the same manner of walking and the same expression of countenance. As I watched the different figures in the crowded streets more closely, however, I discovered that beneath the peculiar dress and manner many different types of human beings were concealed. There were the pale-browed students, who move through the crowd with a hurried and abstracted air. There were slender and elegant aristocrats, who, while still wearing the uniform of their race, dressed with a scrupulous correctness and looked at you with an expression which seemed a curious mingling of the traditional humility of the Jew and the scorn of a Pharisee.

I was interested in all that I saw of the life of the Jew in Cracow because it gave me an idea of the poverty, degradation and squalor in which more than half of the Jewish race is living today, in different parts of Europe. Of the twelve million Jews in the world, about nine million live in Europe. Of this number more than one million live in Russia and about a million and a half in Austria, Roumania and the other parts of southeastern Europe. I have given some idea of the poverty of the Jews in Galicia, where they are politically free. From all that I can learn the Jews in Russia and Roumania are very much worse off than they are in the Austrian province of Galicia. Most of us, who are acquainted with the Jews only in America or in Western Europe, have been made to believe, in spite of the evident poverty of many of the Jews who live on the East Side in New York and in the Whitechapel district in London, that, as a race, the Jews are extremely wealthy. I was surprised, therefore, to read recently the statement, made by Jews who have investigated the condition of their own people, to the effect that, while, during the past hundred years, they have been granted their freedom, taking the Jews as a whole, they are poorer than any other civilized nation in the world. In short, one writer has said, "If we were to capitalize their wealth and distribute it among the twelve million of Jews, they would dispute with any poor nation for the lowest place in the scale of wealth."

The direction in which the Jews seem to be superior to all the rest of the world is apparently not in wealth but in education. Even in Russia, where they do not have the same educational advantages that are given to the rest of the population, it is found that, while 79 per cent. of the total population can neither read nor write, the percentage of illiteracy among the Jews is 61 per cent. less than that of the rest of the population.

There are many points of similarity in the conditions of the Jew and the Negro in the prejudice that is manifested toward each one of them. For these reasons, therefore, the Negro should be especially interested in the story of the Jew. The history of his struggles and persecutions and how he has risen in spite of them should be carefully studied by my people.

If there were no other reason why the story of the Jew should be studied, it would be interesting and inspiring as showing what education can do and has done for a people, who, in the face of prejudice and persecution, have patiently struggled up to a position of power and pre-eminence in the life and civilization, in which all races are now beginning to share.

The Jew has won and is winning his way to success largely through constructive, progressive effort. The Negro has much to learn from the Jew.

Booker T. Washington

TMS   Con. 957   BTW Papers   DLC.

Charles William Anderson to Emmett Jay Scott

New York, N.Y., December 5, 1911

Confidential

My dear Emmett: Enclosed please find clipping from the New York Sun of this morning (Dec. 5th) which will explain itself.[1] I have been following this man up pretty closely, and when I discovered that the New Jersey authorities had applied to Governor Dix[2] for a requisition, I immediately got on the job. I saw to it that my friend Mason,[3] now Secretary to Governor Dix, but the Collector of Internal Revenue in this district during the last administration of President Cleveland, and therefore one of my predecessors, was made fully aware of the antecedents of this scoundrel and of his villainous private character. He will now have to stand trial in New Jersey. I mean to see if something cannot be done to let the proper authorities over there know all about him, to the end that he may be given what he deserves. Just where he will be tried and before whom, and whether or not we have friends in the tribunal, I am not now prepared to say, but if we have, I will do my best to see that there is not another miscarriage of justice in his favor.

Phil[4] sent the yams around to me last Thursday. On Sunday we looked them over before starting our dinner and found that six out of the seven sent were bad. We were therefore only able to save one from the wreckage. I am sure "our friend" did not deliberately send me all the bad ones, but sotto voce, you know that self-sacrifice is not one of his strong characteristics. That is to say, it is not his habit to give his friends the cream and retain the skim-milk for himself.

Hoping you and yours are very well, and with kind regards to the friends, I remain, Faithfully yours,

Charles

[1] The clipping reported that Governor Dix of New York had approved extradition of Henry A. Ulrich to face charges of abandonment in New Jersey.

[2] John Alden Dix (1860–1928), a lumber company head, was Democratic governor of New York from 1910 to 1912.

[3] John A. Mason.

[4] Philip A. Payton.

To Madame C. J. Walker

[Tuskegee, Ala.] December 6, 1911

My dear Mme Walker: I have your kind letter of some days ago.

I fear you misunderstand the kind of meeting our Tuskegee Negro Conference will be. It is a meeting of poor farmers who come here for instruction and guidance, and who have very little or no money.

I am well acquainted with the business in which you are engaged, but somehow I do not feel that a visit to our Conference would offer the opportunity which you seem to desire.

With kind regards, I am, Yours very truly,

Booker T. Washington

TLpS   Con. 917   BTW Papers   DLC.

From James Carroll Napier

Washington, Dec. 6th, 1911

Dear Mr. Washington: I have looked anxiously for your letter yesterday and today. I am somewhat disappointed that it did not follow your telegram.

I felt exactly as you expressed yourself with regard to the place of holding the banquet. My original purpose was to have a dinner at my house and invite twelve or fifteen gentlemen to feast with you. But when the brethren got wind of it they wanted to take it to some first class hotel. I told them how I felt about the matter and showed them your telegram. They, however, seemed wed[d]ed to the hotel idea and selected the Arlington Annex, the old Charles Sumner residence. I think that you will be pleased with this arrangement although I regret that it was not arranged to accord with your idea.

Let me know the hour of your arrival that I may meet you. Very truly yours,

J. C. Napier

ALS   Con. 431   BTW Papers   DLC.

Ralph Waldo Tyler to Emmett Jay Scott

Washington, D.C. Dec. 6th., 1911

My dear Emmett: Are you coming up to the Jeanes Fund Board meeting? Let us know so we can make arrangements for you at the dinner we are arranging to give the Doctor on the 14th. The dinner, quite select, will be served in the Charles Sumner suite of the Arlington Hotel. Bit of sentiment here, ah? And a breaking of the ice to get the Arlington. There was not a bit of hesitation about serving the dinner there — question of color never raised when told it was to be in the Doctor's honor. Hastily,

Tyler

TLS   Con. 441   BTW Papers   DLC.

From Theodore Roosevelt

New York   December 6th, 1911

Dear Mr. Washington: I am very much afraid that I cannot get down to Tuskegee. Any moving about through the country at this time results in more trouble to me than you can imagine, and incidentally is always regarded as being made with some sinister purpose on my part. I want to talk with you over what I regard as the foul injustice done you in connection with that trial. I see that your assailant is now called upon to answer charges by his wife. Sincerely yours,

Theodore Roosevelt

TLS   Con. 365   BTW Papers   DLC.

To George Augustus Gates

[Tuskegee, Ala.] Dec. 7, 1911

My dear Dr. Gates: I see no objection on earth to your taking the Japanese student. We have had both Japanese and Chinese students and no adverse criticism has been made; in fact, a Japanese student graduated a few years ago.

In answer to the question, what do the graduates of Tuskegee do after they have graduated, I send you two printed pamphlets which I hope will answer that question in some degree. I shall be glad to send more copies if they would be useful.

The trouble with many white men in the South is that they own land and they feel that without giving it any personal attention or without living on it that in some way colored people ought to bring them in a large profit from that land; in other words, in many cases it is an effort to get something for nothing, which cannot be done.

There is nothing whatever in the charge that Negroes will not work for other Negroes. We have many examples proving the contrary; in fact, a great many of the large land owners in this county have recently dispensed with their white managers and have put colored managers in their places because they find that the colored managers can get more labor with less trouble than is true of the white managers.

I am very anxious to know if any special action was taken at the recent meeting of the Board of Fisk Trustees. Yours very truly,

Booker T. Washington

TLpS Con. 423 BTW Papers DLC.

To James Carroll Napier

[Tuskegee, Ala.] Dec. 8, 1911

Dear Mr. Napier: I have just caused Mr. Scott to send you a telegram, copy of which I am enclosing. The more I think of it the more I feel it is entirely needless for us to run the risk of sensational newspaper criticism just now, in the face of all that has taken place in the recent past. Our friends must bear in mind that Washington is full just now of newspaper correspondents from all over the country, who are constantly looking out for a sensation. All they want is the basis for a sensation, and they do not care about the facts.

As you know, there are not a few colored people in Washington who would help the white papers on in the direction of making a cock and bull story out of this matter.

We would have to stand criticism from a certain element of the white press. On the other hand we would be criticised by our own people. They would naturally ask the question why in a city like Washington would the president of the National Negro Business League and the president of the Executive Committee, both of whom stand for the inculcation of business ideas among our own people, leave aside our own race and go to a white hotel.

Besides, in my opinion, there would be a want of freedom of action and speech in such a place that would not obtain in a place owned and controlled by colored people. I think I have gone through enough to convince our people in Washington and elsewhere that I am not afraid of criticism and willing to do anything that I feel it is my duty to do whether I am criticised or not, but when nothing is to be gained by incurring criticism I think it is rather a mistake to go forward and incur it without some compensation being in sight. Yours very truly,

Booker T. Washington

TLpS   Con. 431   BTW Papers   DLC.

From William Sidney Pittman

Washington, D.C. Dec 8 1911

My dear Mr Washington   I very much fear this idea of having your banquet at the *Arlington Hotel* under the auspices of *those in charge* and at *such rates* will in no wise lend itself to the high purpose you have in view. Criticisms are already afloat & of a serious nature. . . .[1] Also an affair of greater importance in point of demonstration is also booked for the same evening — under Odd Fellow auspices, is or would be at your disposal & would serve well — if left to me. Am fearful of the other thing.

Though I may be wrong I am still conscious of my interest in your continued success.

Pittman

ALS   Con. 436   BTW Papers   DLC.

[1] Ellipses in original.

From Joseph E. Wiley

Brooklyn, N.Y., Dec. 8, 1911

My dear Dr. Washington: Your letter of the 2nd in which you call attention to the fact that Cotton Mills have not heretofore been built in the richer farming sections of our country and that where they have been so built, they have not as a rule been successful, is before me.

For the sake of argument, let us assume this statement to be true; then I have to answer that the Mills in question have been manned by white labor exclusively and the conditions which call them from the Mill in the rich growing sections are far different from those surrounding the colored man in the same sections.

The surplus white labor of these sections is drafted and fully absorbed in commercial pursuits, while the surplus colored labor remains only partially employed and on the lowest wage basis.

There is, however, one season, namely the cotton picking season, that is quite different — the months of September and October constitute the outing season for the average colored citizen of all Southern towns and cities — this period is to them, what the months of July and August are to the Northern and Eastern man — they spend their outing industriously in the cotton fields, getting their amusement and recreation incidentally and in connection with their work, their earnings are large for this period and the Mill owner will do well to shape the business of his plant giving these facts full credit and consideration.

We are meeting this two months short labor period, by having our business year end September 1st — then in the first two months of our new business year all such work as (over hauling machines) and (general preparations for the years run) are taken up. This I find of good advantage as at this time, the prices of cotton which will control for the new crop year are being settled and the mill man can intelligently map out and lay his course for the year, with time for mature thought and deliberation.

I have given much thought to this proposition also to the other phase of it — to wit: "The unfavorable influence of a large city" upon the mill operative — I have attempted to meet both these objections by creating an environment suited to our needs by the development of our Mill City settlement. The central idea being the assembling and associating together of individuals, seeking the study of, and training in the Textile Arts coupled with the opportunity to find full employment and individual advancement as their skill increases.

Our Mill is designed rather along the lines of artistic development followed in the factories in and around Philadelphia rather than the "Piece goods" Mills of New England and the South. Making useful articles ready for family use — to be marketed directly to the consumer. This will appeal directly and intelligently to the race pride of our people and assure to us a definite appreciative market.

The cotton Mill must soon be generally appreciated by our people as the means of getting the highest market values out of the cotton they grow — and they will be able and ready investors in Mills — when the industry has been established among them on a sound, reliable working basis.

Looking upon this industry from the stand point of the real position of [that] our people occupy in this country; I am bound to conclude that the industry is aptly suited to our needs and the richness of the section in which it is located will rather add to its opportunities, both for business success, and the practical scope and advantage of its usefulness to us.

The Mill will double the value of the farmers cotton — it will double the earning value of colored labor — it will form the nucleus around which the highest types of social settlement and home life will be grouped and developed.

To me the manufacture of cotton by our people appears as an economic necessity, a duty the neglect of which must invite the scorn of our more energetic and thrifty neighbors, and to them appear as an opportunity lost by us because we have not the courage and initiative necessary to accept and utilize an open opportunity.

Let me thank you for the opportunity you afford me to discuss these matters with you and I should like to know what conclusion you finally reached. With highest regard, believe me, Sincerely yours,

Joseph E. Wiley

TLS   Con. 445   BTW Papers   DLC.   On stationery of the Mill City Cotton Mills, Dallas, Tex., New York office.

To Pinckney Benton Stewart Pinchback

[Tuskegee, Ala.] Dec. 9, 1911

My dear Governor Pinchback: At last I have found what I have been looking for for several days, and that is a good fat opossum for your Christmas dinner. I am also sending you in the same box express prepaid, some potatoes to go with the opossum. I am sending this to Brooklyn not knowing whether you will be in Washington or New York, but I take for granted it will reach you.

I am sorry to learn through Mr. Scott of the illness of your wife, and I hope she will grow better speedily. Yours very truly,

Booker T. Washington

TLpS   Con. 436   BTW Papers   DLC.

To Charles William Anderson

[Tuskegee, Ala.] Dec. 9, 1911

My dear Mr. Anderson: For several days I have been trying to get hold of a good fat opossum for you, and have at last succeeded, and am by today's express sending it to you with the necessary amount of potatoes grown on our own farm to go with it. I hope that you and Mrs. Anderson will enjoy it, and that it will reach you in time for Christmas.

Enclosed I send you some copies of correspondence that have passed between me and some of our Washington friends. They have a great idea just now of breaking the ice by jumping into a white hotel, but I do not intend that they shall break the ice with me just at present. Please keep this confidential.[1] Yours very truly,

Booker T. Washington

TLpS   Con. 52   BTW Papers   DLC.

[1] BTW telegraphed Anderson on Dec. 10: "Be very sure not to reveal contents of letter dated December ninth regarding Washington matter to any one as I shall be embarrassed if it should get out that I had given this information to you or any one else." (Con. 52, BTW Papers, DLC.)

From Ralph Waldo Tyler

Washington, D.C. Dec 9/11

Dear Doctor: The Odd Fellows give a banquet on the evening of the 14th. An invitation has been sent you. They desire that you come straight from the dinner we have arranged at the Arlington to the Odd Fellows hall, and will give you unlimited time to speak. I think you ought to accept. The dinner at the Arlington is a small affair, and is in no sense a banquet. We have had hard work keeping the list down. If you are afraid of criticism, by attending a dinner at the Arlington, and we have to call it off, there is only one way we can possibly save our face, and that is to receive wire from you that you find you will have to leave for the East immediately after the close of the Jean[e]s Fund Board meeting.

The hotel has never raised a question. They know the dinner is in your honor. Now why should we ourselves raise a question? No subterfuge has been practiced on the hotel people. They were told in the onset who the dinner was to be given for, and they offered us any banquet room in the hotel in which to hold the dinner. Respectfully

R W Tyler

ALS   Con. 466   BTW Papers   DLC.

To William Sidney Pittman

[Tuskegee, Ala.] Dec. 10, 1911

Without using my name wish you would see Mr. Napier and put view which you have expressed in your letter before him.

B. T. W.

TWIr   Con. 436   BTW Papers   DLC.

From William Henry Lewis

Washington, D.C. December 10, 1911

I appreciate your anxiety. We are not taking any long chances. Letters and telegrams have been shown to Johnson.[1] Reason for calling it off will be public property for criticism. We are between the devil and

the deep sea. I prefer the devil. Tyler, Cobb and myself feel strongly
that you should stand by us. Please wire answer.

William H. Lewis

TWSr   Con. 428   BTW Papers   DLC.

[1] A White House staff member, "M. K. Y.," reported to Charles D. Hilles on
Dec. 8, 1911, that Recorder of Deeds Henry Lincoln Johnson had come to the
White House that afternoon expressing fear that the newspapers would criticize the
dinner to honor Booker T. Washington at the Arlington Hotel. Johnson said that
J. C. Napier agreed with him as to the inadvisability of selecting the Arlington for
the dinner, and that he believed Whitefield McKinlay would also agree. Johnson was
quoted as saying that he did not intend to lose out with blacks by "wearing a swallow-tail coat at a five-dollar dinner at the Arlington," and sent his regrets with his
check subscribing to the dinner. On Dec. 11, 1911, the same staff member reported
to Hilles that that afternoon the choice of the Arlington was put to a final vote by
the seven black presidential appointees, and it was decided four to three to meet
at the Arlington, Johnson, Napier, and McKinlay opposing. Johnson reiterated that
the dinner might do incalculable damage. (William Howard Taft Papers, DLC.)

A Sunday Evening Talk

[Tuskegee, Ala.] December 10, 1911

OUR DEATH RATE

No one can study the Census figures which have recently come from
the Census Bureau in Washington without being convinced that the
death-rate among our people, while not alarming, is very great —
greater than it should be. It is through the influence of such men and
women as we are training here that the death-rate in the future is to
be decreased. More and more throughout the civilized world, people
are not paying so much attention to the healing of disease as they are
to trying to prevent disease through various measures, and you are
to be among the leaders in this matter of preventing disease among
our people in city and in country.

When we first came out of slavery, I think we just as well face the
fact, the death-rate was not so large as it is now. There were certain
restrictions, with all the disadvantages of slavery, that gave us perhaps
more healthy bodies than some of us have now, and we, like many other
races, have got to learn what freedom means, have got to learn to

exercise a certain degree of control in freedom that is true of all races of people.

I think the death-rate is due to several causes; first among them, I should put improper houses. A large number of our people in the North and in the South have recently moved from the country and come into cities, meeting a life, a condition that they are not accustomed to. One of these conditions is that of being congested in small rooms. Many of them come from country districts, where they have had plenty of room. Certainly they have been out in the free, open air. They go to the large cities in the North and in the South and they find themselves, instead of having plenty of room, congested in one or two small, poorly ventilated rooms. Poor housing means, in many cases, bad air and then it means, as I shall mention later, poor food and insufficient clothing. It is lamentably true that in many of the large cities, especially in the North, our people have to pay such high rent for the small apartments they occupy, that they have, after paying rent, very little left with which to supply themselves with either proper food or proper clothing. It is a great change going into a city life from the country life. In the country, in many cases, or in the small cities, they have been paying $4.00 or $5.00 per month for rent. When they go to a large city, they find themselves confronted with a rent bill of $25.00 or $30.00 per month. That means they have got to do without many of the necessities of life in the way of food and clothing in order to meet the rent bill.

As I have stated, insufficient clothing in many of the large cities is largely the cause of a large death-rate among our people. The bad air to which I have referred, is not confined to the houses; you will find our people suffer by reason of poorly ventilated bed-rooms, poorly ventilated churches, poorly ventilated lodge rooms. I think you will find, if you examine into it carefully, that many of our people, most of them, in many cities, belong to some kind of lodge. They go into these lodge rooms and feel that every window must be down, every curtain must be down, no air permitted to come in; and the same is true of the church houses, filled with people, breathing foul air for hours and hours, and I am sorry to say that the same thing is often true of school rooms — school rooms under the control of seemingly intelligent people.

Another cause of the high death-rate especially in cities North and

South, is the kind of food our people live on. In many cases, it is the cheapest food; in many cases, it is not only the cheapest food, but stale food, unwholesome food, composed of knickknacks — cheese, crackers, a few cakes thrown in here and there, and as you know, it takes some of the students a good while to get accustomed to the kind of food they get here. They do not get the cheese, they do not get the crackers, the cakes, the cheap pie they have been living on before they came here. It takes you some time to get accustomed to our food, but it is borne out by the health records here after students come here and get into the habit of eating our food — well-prepared, fresh food. You will find that in body you are five times more healthy and stronger by eating this clean, fresh beef, many times more healthy by eating good, fresh corn bread, much better than cheese, crackers and cakes that many of you have been in the habit, perhaps, of picking up or living on, in too many cases in large cities. Take students who come here, with a pale, weak appearance and go through our routine, getting this food regularly three times a day at a certain hour, very soon you will find their bodies straightening up; their eyes grow brighter, and they grow strong, healthy and vigorous.

Many of our people suffer, not only in cities, and it adds to the high death-rate also, because they do not have any regular eating time. There is irregularity in eating. They have no special time for breakfast, no special time for dinner, no special time for supper. A little food taken at a regular time on the minute each day is many times better than much food taken at irregular times. That is one of the lessons we are trying to teach you here and we hope you will go out and spread that lesson. Practice it first, then spread it among your fellows — the lesson of regular eating at regular times. Even though the food is very plain, if it is well cooked, well prepared and taken at regular hours, it will result in adding immensely to the health of the bodies of our people.

Again in cities and towns, more in the cities than in the rural districts, a large death-rate is caused by reason of the fact that so many of our people are given to strong drink, to the use of the poorest kind of liquors, the poorest kind of wines — the cheapest and the poorest kind of strong drink of every kind.

In many cases, this high death-rate is due too because of the uncleanliness by which too many of our people are surrounded. This does not apply, I am glad to say, in any large degree, to the people who live in the country districts, because it is a delightful thing to say that no matter how poor or how ignorant our people are who live in the country, you will usually find them clean in the house and outside of the house. When they come into the city and get in these filthy crowded alleys, you will find filth on the inside of the house and filth on the outside of the house, and this adds every time to the high death-rate.

There are two lessons which I want to impress upon you: first, that the salvation of our race in its present condition largely rests upon its willingness to live, for the most part, in the small towns and country districts. The city is a dangerous place for poor people of any race to go to and wherever you have a choice, wherever you can exert an influence, urge our people in the immediate present and in the near future, to live either in the country or in a small town, where conditions are more inviting, more healthy than they are in the average large city, either North or South; and then in connection with this, of course, the final remedy is education — education not only in books, education of the larger and broader sense, the education of our people in right methods of living, in healthy rational living to prevent disease, on the part of the teacher, on the part of the minister, on the part of everybody who can exert the slightest influence upon the masses.

Tuskegee Student, 23 (Dec. 23, 1911), 1-3. Stenographically reported.

To William Sidney Pittman

[Tuskegee, Ala.] Dec. 11, 1911

Find affair to be small and private therefore think no harm will be done. Not necessary to see Mr. Napier.

B. T. W.

TWpIr Con. 436 BTW Papers DLC.

To William Sidney Pittman

[Tuskegee, Ala.] Dec. 11, 1911

Have accepted invitation to be at Odd Fellows banquet after other dinner is over.

B. T. W.

TWpIr   Con. 436   BTW Papers   DLC.

To William Henry Lewis

[Tuskegee, Ala.] Dec. 11, 1911

Your telegram places matters in different light. Since is to be small affair and private think no harm will be done. Hope, however, no undue publicity will be given matter. When matter was mentioned in my presence took for granted Mr. Napier had already perfected his plans to have affair at his house and other places were mentioned only in incidental way.

B. T. W.

TWpIr   Con. 428   BTW Papers   DLC.

Ralph Waldo Tyler, James A. Cobb, and William Henry Lewis to Emmett Jay Scott

Washington, Dec. 11, 1911

W. must attend dinner. Thirty acceptances. leading friends. Fierce criticism awaits failure.

Tyler.   Cobb.   Lewis.

TWSr   Con. 428   BTW Papers   DLC.

From Charles William Anderson

New York, N.Y. December 11, 1911

(Personal)

My dear Doctor: I have read the enclosed with interest. Like you, I fear it was a mistake to have secured the place. I know the new proprietor of the house very well. I stopped with him on my last visit to that city. He comes from New York, and is himself all right, but the unusual spectacle of such a group holding a function in such a place, is very apt to arouse unpleasant comment among the newspaper men. They are always looking out for just such things. I have subscribed, as has also the Governor, Jim Johnson and Counsellor Curtis. The trouble is, that even if the place is changed now, the black kickers may send out a report that it was cancelled by the proprietor, or that those in charge of it did not have the moral courage to accept an opportunity when offered to them. Thus you see, our tactless friends have bungled it in such a way as to expose us to criticism which ever horn of the dilemma we may take. I shall keep the contents of your letter of the 9th strictly under my vest.

I want to thank you for the gift which you have ordered shipped to me, and know I will enjoy it. Yours very truly,

Charles W. Anderson

P.S. Your second letter puts a new face on the matter.

C. W. A.

TLS   Con. 52   BTW Papers   DLC.   No enclosures found with letter.

To William P. Blake[1]

[Tuskegee, Ala.] December 12, 1911

My dear Sir: Replying to your kind favor of December 9th I would state that I appreciate thoroughly the difficulties and embarrassments outlined in your letter. It is a matter that has been cal' 'd to my attention and also to the attention of Dr. Frissell, the Principal of Hampton Institute, a good many times.

One of the difficulties grows out of the fact that there are so many people throughout the country who give a few dollars to irresponsible people without taking the time to make inquiries and this, of course, keeps these people on the road, enabling them to pay travelling expenses and board bills, but even where they are honest, they do not get enough to help the institution, in many cases, that they are representing. As soon as I get an opportunity, I will talk the whole matter over with Dr. Frissell and see if we cannot devise some such plan as you suggest. In the meantime, I shall be very glad to serve as a medium for passing out to small institutions any sum of money which you may care to place in my hands. I might add that for several years before he died, the late Mr. H. H. Rogers of New York placed in my hands a sum of money which I used in this way. At the present time, Mr. Jacob Schiff, of Kuhn, Loeb and Company, New York City, asks me at the beginning of each year to make up a list of institutions which ought to be helped.

In regard to helping orphan asylums in the South, I will state that you will make no mistake if you go on the principle that there is no need that any orphan asylum should make an appeal to people in the North. In the first place, colored people are different from most races, in that they support either through individual help or through their churches, or some organization, individuals who are unfortunate, whether they are children or grown people. In all my experience in the South, I do not think I have ever seen a little child suffering by reason of the fact that no one would take him into his family. There is always some relative or acquaintance in that community who is at once willing to adopt an orphan child and in nine cases out of ten, when a child gets into a family, he is better off than he is in an orphan asylum.

In the next place, wherever an orphan asylum is actually needed, the people in that community are pretty likely to take care of it. In the county in which The Tuskegee Institute is located, there are some twenty-five or twenty-six thousand colored people. The public authorities support a poor-house, but the Superintendent of this poor-house tells me that he has never had, in all of his experience, more than two or three colored children there at one time and that they rarely remain more than a week or two before some colored family will come and take them away for adoption.

As I stated in the beginning, however, I shall be glad to consider

413

this whole matter with Dr. Frissell and see if some plan cannot be devised that will improve present conditions. Yours very truly,

Booker T. Washington

TLpS   Con. 418   BTW Papers   DLC.

¹ A lawyer in Boston.

To Theodore Roosevelt

[Tuskegee, Ala.] December 12, 1911

My dear Colonel Roosevelt: Your kind letter of December 6th has been received, and I thank you for writing me.

I am very sorry that the prospects for your attending the Trustee meeting February 22nd and 23rd seem so slight. I can readily understand, however, the embarrassment under which you are laboring at the present time. All of us, I am sure, appreciate your point of view, and if you finally decide that it is not wise for you to do so, we shall have to abide by your decision, hoping that at some time in the near future you will be able to attend the meeting here. The use of your name on our board, however, I wish to assure you, is accomplishing good.

In regard to that assault case, I wish to say in the first place, that personally I felt assured almost from the beginning that the man was not going to be convicted. Nevertheless, both my friends and I thought that I owed it as a duty to my race and to myself to go into court and make the attempt to convict him. It was a tremendously unpleasant duty. Of course, we could not control the action of the court. I think I hardly need tell you that practically all the evidence given on Ulrich's side was pure fabrication. I never realized before that it was possible for persons to tell so many untruths in so short a time.

In the second place, I have learned on what I deem good authority that the whole matter as to the decision was prearranged by one of the Tammany Hall leaders. I am glad to say that so far as I can discover, the decision has had no bad effect upon me personally or upon our work, either North or South. Of course, I presume a different verdict might have been possible if I could have had a lawyer of my own to conduct the case, instead of entrusting it to the Assistant District Attorney, and then a different impression would have been made. Or, if I had yielded to the suggestion to spend money in getting witnesses to testify; that, I absolutely refused to do, or permit my friends to do. I was determined from the beginning not to spend or permit to be spent a single dollar that I could not absolutely justify in the open. In the midst of much that is conflicting, however, and even somewhat discouraging, it is a great consolation to feel that in our country, in the last analysis, the common sense of the average man asserts itself in the right direction.

I think you will be glad to know that Mr. Julius Rosenwald, head of the firm of Sears, Roebuck and Company, Chicago, the Jew who has recently given so much money for Y.M.C.A. work among colored people in the cities, has consented to become a member of our Board of Trustees. I think he is one of the strongest men we have ever gotten on our Board. Mr. Rosenwald, his wife, and several of his Chicago friends came here recently and spent several days inspecting the work of the school. He was so pleased, that he readily consented afterwards to become a member of the Trustee Board. Yours very truly,

Booker T. Washington

TLpS   Con. 365   BTW Papers   DLC.

Ralph Waldo Tyler to Charles Dewey Hilles

Washington   December 12, 1911

Dear Mr. Hilles: Mr. Johnson is far too apprehensive and needlessly alarmed. The dinner to Dr. Washington is but a very small affair, and as a matter of sentiment, and reverence for the past and present, it is to be served in the old Charles Sumner House, which is an annex to the Arlington, in the private suite of that annex.

The Arlington has never drawn the color line, accommodating Colored men of standing without discrimination. Only last year a delegation of Liberians stopped there and it did not cause a ripple. When it was proposed, Mr. Johnson was as enthusiastic as any one, and insisted that no money or pains be spared to make it a success. I cannot account for his sudden change, unless it is due to his desire not to wish the rights and privileges of an American citizen. The dinner is given on the occasion of the meeting of the Jeanes Fund Board, of which the President is a member, and it was decided to invite all the members. I am ill at home — flat on my back and so was unable to attend the last two meetings — Sunday and today, to perfect the final arrangements, but I do know that Mr. Johnson as late as yesterday afternoon had assured Mr. Napier he would be present, "swallow-tail etc."

The arrangements have all been perfected. Mr. Johnson states he would not get in bad with his constituents by wearing a swallow-tail to a banquet. A Constituency that has not evoluted to the point where it will permit a presidential appointee to appear modern in the society of his equals, can be set down as an ignorant, voteless constituency, and Colored Georgians do not vote — not even those like Mr. Johnson who can if they would. The dinner will be but a small assemblage of the best and leading Colored men in the country, and has not the remotest political significance attached to it.

I cannot see what wrong there is in giving the dinner at the Arlington especially since that hotel does not draw the color line. It is a small affair and not [of] sufficient importance to even attract attention. I am surprised that Mr. Johnson would bother you with so small and so foreign an affair. Respectfully,

Ralph W Tyler

TLS   William Howard Taft Papers   DLC.

From Theodore Roosevelt

New York   December 15th, 1911

Dear Mr. Washington: I am delighted to hear that about Mr. Rosenwald. Do give him my warm regards when you see him. I wish you could get into The Outlook office when next you come to New York. If there is anything we can do about that case, of course we want to do it. Sincerely yours,

Theodore Roosevelt

TLS   Con. 438   BTW Papers   DLC.

From Arthur Wergs Mitchell[1]

New York City   December 15, 1911

My dear Dr. Washington: I was very regretful when I heard today that you would not come to New York while on this trip. I have been up in New England for several days working in the interest of our school at Panola, and chanced to meet many of your old friends. I was very much surprised to find out the prevailing sentiment among these people, who heretofore have spoken so highly of you and the work at Tuskegee. I find very much to my regret that the New York affair, coupled with your trip through Texas and your owning a summer home on Long Island, is being used as capital with which to fight you and the work at Tuskegee. Almost every leading minister with whom I have conversed and in whose churches I have spoken has had something to say about these three things, and the sentiment among them is indeed hurtful, for some of them go so far as to say that they are sick of Tuskegee and Booker Washington's leadership. Perhaps you remember Dr. Lewis,[2] Minister of St. Johns Episcopal Church of Waterbury. He is the most radical that I have met. He told me in the presence of Mr. Holmes, a congregationalist minister, from Watertown, that he would never again speak for Tuskegee nor for anything with which Tuskegee is directly connected nor will he give or permit his church to give aid, for the reasons just stated. He said that this was the sentiment among a large number of the white people of the State of Connecticut. He further said that he would be glad to see you and would tell you all that he said to us and more. Mr. Brown[3] another very prominent minister, who now has the First Congregational Church at Waterbury, is certainly your friend, but is beginning to waver in his opinion. He thinks that some grave mistake has been made by you. I had a long and confidential talk with Mr. Taft,[4] of the Taft School, Watertown. Mr. Taft is inclined to take a far more liberal view of all the matters mentioned, but thinks there may be danger of these things being used to the detriment of Tuskegee. He said he would not like to see anything happen what would in any way hinder Tuskegee from being placed on self supporting basis. You can rely upon Mr. Taft as your friend, yet he says that there must have been something crooked about the New York affair, and that he also has been informed that at times you drank excessively.[5] All of these things were recited to me by more

people than the ones named, but I have tried to quote the most prominent. I also find that the Negro ministers of the North, that is a large
number of them, are using this as capital. This, however, I do not
take with any degree of seriousness. Mr. Brown urged me to talk this
matter over with you and say to you that he thought it would help
you and the cause which you represent very materially, if some of
your friends would come out and speak in your behalf. He said he
would not dare tell you just what method to pursue in order to set
aside these criticisms, but he would like for you to know about them
and that you could use your own method in setting aside same.

I am planning to return to the South and will be at home for a few
days in the early part of the month of January and if you are going
to be at Tuskegee, I shall be glad to come that way and can explain
to you perhaps more fully what I have tried to say in this letter. All of
this is spoken to you in the strictest of confidence for you know how I
love Tuskegee and there is no man living that I esteem so highly as
I do you. If my life means anything at all in the way of helping our
people I owe that impetus of feeling and inspiration to you, and I count
it a great pleasure to do or say anything that will in even the remotest
way help Mother Tuskegee and help you, whom I esteem as a father.

Hoping that you are well and wishing you the greatest possible success, I am, Sincerely yours,

Arthur W. Mitchell

TLS   Con. 425   BTW Papers   DLC.

1 Arthur Wergs Mitchell (1883–1968) was a member of the Tuskegee Institute
B middle class in 1901–2. He later attended Columbia University and Harvard
University. For many years Mitchell taught in the rural schools of Alabama. In
1927 he began a law practice in Washington, D.C., and then moved to Chicago in
1929, where he continued his law practice and established a real estate business.
An active Democrat in Chicago, he was elected to Congress, serving from 1935
to 1943.

2 John Neher Lewis (b. 1869).

3 Robert Elliott Brown (b. 1873) was pastor of the Second Congregational
Church, not the First, from 1911 to 1924.

4 Horace Dutton Taft (1861–1943), brother of W. H. Taft, founded the Taft
School and served as its headmaster from 1890 to 1936.

5 Mitchell was more explicit in conversation with Fred R. Moore, who wrote
a memorandum attached to this letter: "Mr. Horace Taft principal of Taft School,
Watertown, states that since your trouble in New York that it has been generally
circulated through the North that you are a hard drinker, and that at times you
would come to the Manhattan Hotel and get broiling drunk." (Con. 425, BTW
Papers, DLC.)

A News Item in the Washington *Star*

[Washington, D.C.] December 15, 1911

DISTRICT COLORED MEN
HONOR LEADERS OF RACE

BOOKER T. WASHINGTON AND OTHER
TRUSTEES OF EDUCATION FUND
GUESTS AT BANQUET

In the annex of the Arlington Hotel, the historic old Charles Sumner house, at Vermont avenue and H street — Booker T. Washington and forty other colored men were dined last night. The dinner was given by colored men of the District in honor of Booker Washington and other trustees of the Anna T. Jeanes fund of $1,000,000 for the education of the rural negro population of the south.

PRESIDENT TAFT SENDS LETTER

Assistant Attorney General W. H. Lewis arranged the dinner. Letters from President Taft and Andrew Carnegie were read. There were no set speeches, the guests discussing their affairs while the dinner was in progress. Judge Terrell of the Municipal Court gave a few reminiscences of the Sumner house.

Preceding the banquet the trustees of the Jeanes fund held a meeting at the White House, at which President Taft presided. Andrew Carnegie and Booker T. Washington attended the meeting, at which Dr. H. T. Kealing, president of Western University, was elected to the vacancy on the board created by the death of Bishop Abraham Grant of Kansas City.

LIST OF THOSE PRESENT

Those present at the banquet were: Dr. Washington, Maj. R. R. Moton, Robert L. Smith, Prof. H. T. Kealing, E. C. Williams, Dr. M. O. Dumas, Dr. J. R. Wilder, Dr. W. A. Warfield, John W. Johnson, Charles W. Anderson, Wilford Smith, Dr. C. Sumner Wormley, Robert J. Harlan, W. Calvin Chase, Dr. Samuel G. Elbert, Dr. John R. Francis, Prof. Kelly Miller, R. C. Bruce, P. B. S. Pinchback, Wyatt Archer, Dr. A. S. Gray, Henry Lincoln Johnson, Cyrus Field Adams, Lieut. T. R. Clark, Dr. George W. Cabaniss, Prof. George W. Cook,

Dr. W. C. McNeill, John C. Dancy, Dr. E. D. Williston, Dr. A. M. Curtis, Whitefield McKinlay, Prof. L. B. Moore, Ocea Taylor, George Harris, James A. Cobb, Capt. Walter Cohen, Robert H. Terrell, Ralph W. Tyler, Prof. W. Bruce Evans, H. C. Tyson, William H. Lewis, Prof. W. J. Hale, Fred R. Moore, Prof. A. T. Glenn and Prof. Ernest Just.

Washington *Star,* Dec. 15, 1911, 2.

To Frederick Randolph Moore

[Tuskegee, Ala.] December 18, 1911

My dear Mr. Moore: Only because I "view with alarm" the present tendency of The Age do I call to your attention the matters which follow:

First: Considerable amount of your advertising is of that character which subjects us to the ridicule of even our best white friends — I refer to such advertisements as "Hair Straightening" and "Fortune Telling."

Second: I think The Age is being cheapened by using matter from that man who calls himself a Bishop of the Church of Christ and God, whatever that is.

The Age reaches too intelligent a class of people to carry such cheap, meaningless stuff as this man Evans' advertisements.

I do wish you could put a first class advertising man to work to get advertisements to take the place of this particular kind of advertising. These clairvoyant advertising, mineral company advertising, hair straightening advertising, and fake religious advertising do not add, I assure you, to the prestige of your newspaper.

You ought to very seriously consider this matter and I hope you will. The Age owes something to its past history and something to the intelligence of its readers. Yours very truly,

Booker T. Washington

P.S. Since writing the above I have thought also that I would call attention to the present character of your editorials. They are not at all in keeping with the reputation which The Age has achieved throughout the country.

B. T. W.

TLpS Con. 54 BTW Papers DLC.

From Charles William Anderson

New York, N.Y. December 18, 1911

(Personal)

My dear Doctor: I regretted very much that you were compelled to leave the dinner the other evening before I got a chance to have my little say. I took occasion to talk "brass tacks" to the brethren because I thought I detected some timidity on the part of the speakers that preceded me, as they seemed to have forgotten that the dinner was given in your honor, and apparently had concluded that it was a Charles Sumner celebration. It was not until the old Governer got loose that the guest of honor came in for any mention whatever. When my turn came, I concluded that it was about time somebody frankly acknowledged the obligation that he and the entire race were under to you, and to state plainly and unreservedly his loyalty and affection for you, and his gratitude for the great work you have done and are doing. In my weak way, I tried to do this, and if you had been present to witness the manner in which it was received by those of the diners who were not on the toast list, you could not have been otherwise than highly gratified.

I did not see the Washington papers the following day, but the New York papers did not attempt to make any sensation of the holding of this dinner at the Arlington. Thus you see, those who were trying to stir up trouble failed signally. It curiously happens that whenever you try to have the white papers make a sensation of a thing, they invariably decline to do so. It is only when you try to prevent them from it that they are able to see snakes. Please let me know when you will again be in this neck of the woods, as I have some matters to talk over with you. By the by, did you know that Chief Lee had taken in his sign and closed up his colored democratic club. He is permanently down and out, and has retired from the contest. Of course, I am not a prophet nor the son of a prophet, but I predicted over a year ago that he would be knocked out and Woods[1] would win.

With kind regards to all the friends at Tuskegee, I remain, Yours very truly,

Charles W. Anderson

TLS   Con. 52   BTW Papers   DLC.

[1] Robert N. Wood, leader of one faction of the United Colored Democracy in New York City, controlled the organization from 1912 until his death in 1915.

Emmett Jay Scott to James A. Cobb

[Tuskegee, Ala.] December 18, 1911

Dear Cobb: You have received by now a telegram from me. The only point of the telegram is to emphasize the fact that you and our friends have simply overwhelmed the Doctor and our other friends with your great and signal kindness.

He is particularly anxious that no feeling shall follow, and that nothing shall creep into the newspapers that will even halfway indicate anything other than fine feeling between all the forces. He is of the opinion that Mr. Johnson and Mr. Napier, in their own way were simply trying to carry out the wishes expressed by him in his various telegrams. This does not mean, of course, that he endorses the methods employed by Johnson, but he is willing to be magnanimous and charitable in his opinion. Yours very truly,

Emmett

Write me — *often!*

TLpS   Con. 441   BTW Papers   DLC.   Postscript in Scott's hand.

From Walter Hines Page

Garden City, N.Y. December 19, 1911

My dear Dr. Washington: I notice that the *Atlanta Constitution* has had a very ugly review of "My Larger Education."[1] I don't know what is the matter, but this displeases me very much indeed. My first impulse was to sit down and write to Mr. Clark Howell, but I don't believe that that would be wise, for this reason: An editor resents, instinctively and even bitterly, any word from a publisher about a book. He immediately thinks that the publisher is trying to dictate to him, and it is likely to make him worse in the future than better. On reflection, therefore, I think I had better not say anything; but I am going to try to get word, in a roundabout way, verbally to Mr. Howell, which may, I hope, suggest to his mind the possibility of his having the wrong sort of reviewer.

A very Merry Christmas to you. Always heartily yours,

Walter H. Page

TLS Con. 61 BTW Papers DLC.

[1] See A Review of *My Larger Education* in the Atlanta *Constitution*, Dec. 3, 1911, above.

To Charles William Anderson

[Tuskegee, Ala.] December 20, 1911

My dear Mr. Anderson: Thank you for your letter of December 18th.

I am very sorry, indeed, that it was not possible for me to remain longer at the Arlington dinner. It certainly was a very fine affair and everything went off spendidly.

I especially thank you for writing me with reference to what you had to say to the brethren when you came to speak. It is, as a rule, slightly amusing to notice such affairs diverted from their intention, but I know that everyone felt all right and I am not disposed to quarrel. What you had to say upon this occasion simply puts me under renewed obligations to you.

Just now my plans for visiting New York are somewhat indefinite as we have a number of very important gatherings here early in January, and I am bending every effort to make these a success.

I had not heard that your rival political club had been dismantled. From what I have been reading in the newspapers, I was in a way prepared for your statement that Woods had won out in his contest with Chief Lee.

With kindest regards to Mrs. Anderson, and wishing you both the compliments of the season, I am: Yours very truly,

Booker T. Washington

P.S. One reason why I got away from the banquet a little earlier than I otherwise would have done so, was because several of the brethren, as you doubtless observed, were losing control of themselves because the wine in which they were indulging was evidently new to them in type, and I felt quite sure if we stayed there for an hour longer some fellow might say or do some "fool thing" which might spoil everything that had been accomplished.

It was very noticeable that several of our friends in Washington cannot stand the taste of much real good wine.

B. T. W.

TLpS   Con. 52   BTW Papers   DLC.

To William Henry Lewis

[Tuskegee, Ala.] December 20, 1911

My dear Mr. Lewis: Through you, I want to express the deep gratitude which is in my heart to all who had a part in tendering me the magnificent banquet on the 14th. It was indeed a unique and most satisfactory function. I have never attended a banquet which was more tastefully and beautifully conceived and executed than was true of this one.

Of course words would fail me if I were to try to let each subscriber to the banquet know in any slight degree just how much obligated I am for this expression of their good will. Some things one had better not try to express. They stir emotions that are too deep and tender for expression. Yours very truly,

Booker T. Washington

TLpS   Con. 428   BTW Papers   DLC.

Julius Rosenwald to the
Tuskegee Institute Executive Council

Chicago, Dec. 20, 1911

Gentlemen: If I am not mistaken, when I was in Tuskegee I spoke to the gentleman who has charge of the shoemaking and told him that we have from time to time a certain amount of returned shoes partly worn, and some of them very much worn, but all of which would give more or less wear.

I have sent by prepaid freight 1260 pair of these shoes in various states of preservation and usefulness.

It has been the custom for Sears, Roebuck & Co. to sell these to outside people to repair and resell, so I thought best to buy them and send them to you, thinking you might get a good deal of service out of them.

If they serve your purpose, I shall be very glad to send them once or twice a year hereafter. Yours very truly,

Julius Rosenwald

TLS Con. 747 BTW Papers DLC. Letter addressed to Tuskegee Institute. Docketed in E. J. Scott's hand: "Council."

To Walter Hines Page

[Tuskegee, Ala.] December 22, 1911

My dear Mr. Page: Thank you for your letter of December 19th concerning the review of "My Larger Education" in the Atlanta Constitution. I saw this the next day after it was published.

My own feeling is that it is far better to pay no direct attention to the review. It was evidently written, as one can easily see, by not only a very prejudiced man, but by a very ignorant man. The Sunday before, this same man had a review of Dr. Du Bois recent book, "The Quest of the Silver Fleece" and he was so ignorant, that he referred to Dr. Du Bois as being a Frenchman and living in Paris, notwithstanding the fact that Dr. Du Bois has lived many years right in the city of Atlanta. I am taking indirect ways to overcome the influence of this review. I think that is better than taking the matter up directly with Mr. Howell. So far as this particular review is concerned, if you could work on Mr. Howell indirectly, without referring directly to this particular review, I am sure it would accomplish good. Yours very truly,

Booker T. Washington

TLpS   Con. 61   BTW Papers   DLC.

To Theodore Roosevelt

[Tuskegee, Ala.] December 26, 1911

My dear Colonel Roosevelt: This is a brief reply to your last letter.

When I am in New York again, I shall certainly look into the Outlook Office, as you suggest. I have been kept here lately more than I have for sometime, on account of several pressing matters.

You ask if The Outlook can do anything with reference to the recent case. Perhaps you have seen, according to a recent account in the papers, that Ulrich my assailant, is now in the penitentiary in New Jersey. I might say that if The Outlook can see its way clear to make any editorial reference to the matter in the enclosed circular, it will help us very much.

I thought you might care to see an extract from a letter which came to me today from Mr. Charles Wake,[1] Shickley, Nebraska. This is written on the attached sheet.[2] The contribution Mr. Wake sends is one of the few we have received from the state of Nebraska. Yours very truly,

Booker T. Washington

TLpS   Con. 438   BTW Papers   DLC.

[1] Charles Wake of Shickley, Neb., a dealer in lumber, coal, and cement blocks, sent BTW $25 as his annual contribution to Tuskegee on Dec. 18, 1911. Wake complimented BTW on securing Theodore Roosevelt as a trustee. "I am sorry you did not get justice in that assault case in New York," he remarked, "truly you and your race have much to endure." (Con. 748, BTW Papers, DLC.)

[2] Not attached to the press copy, and the letter is not in the Theodore Roosevelt Papers, DLC.

From James Carroll Napier

Washington   December 26, 1911

Dear Mr. Washington; I have not before this had time to give you a detailed account of our visit to Mr. Carnegie. There is very little more of it however, than that which I sent you signed by the Committee; as I have already said on account of Mr. Carnegie's absence we failed to see him on the 19th, but made an engagement on that day to see him at 11:30 A.M. on the 20th.

At that hour we made our appearance promptly at his door. We were admitted by a young man who seemed to think we might have accomplished as much by the use of a two-cent stamp as by a visit of this Committee, but this was merely the opinion of an underling. He soon disappeared taking with him a copy of your letter to Mr. Bertram, which you had sent me. Shortly thereafter, Mr. Carnegie and Mr. Bertram appeared.

The old gentleman seemed to be in high feather, and received us very cordially making some pleasant reference to each one as he shook hands, but, though both Mr. Smith and I had been meeting him for a number of years, I think he had no personal recollection of any of us except Mr. Banks.

Upon our making known to him the mission upon which we had come he said; "I have a friend to whom I entrust all matters of this sort — his name is Booker T. Washington. You gentlemen tell Mr. Washington to write me what is needed and whatever request he makes in connection with the League I will grant."

This he repeated more than once. He also said that he was highly pleased with what he had learned of the League.

Nothing was said to him about the three-year limit, or the reduction of the amount which he has been giving so that, from what he said, and the way I think he feels, I am quite confident if asked, he will continue to donate as much as he has heretofore given.

Mr. Banks stopped over in Washington a day on his return home. He seemed much gratified with audiences which I secured for him with the President and Mr. Hilles.

I have reserved ticket and sleeping accommodation for the 29th. as per your request. Pleasant references to your recent visit to Washington are still heard on every hand and I hope we shall soon have the pleasure of seeing you again. Very truly yours,

J. C. Napier

TLS   Con. 431   BTW Papers   DLC.

To the Editor of the New York *Times*

[Tuskegee, Ala.] December 27, 1911

In my opinion the five greatest achievements in the year Nineteen Hundred Eleven are:

1. Carnegie Endowment for the Peace Movement, and Carnegie gift of 25 million dollars to capitalize his benefactions to schools, libraries, and other philanthropic bodies.
2. The organization of the Men and Religious Forward Movement.[1]
3. Establishment of Postal Savings Bank.
4. Abrogation of the treaty of 1832 with Russia on account of racial prejudice.
5. Discovery by Dr. Simon Flexner[2] of serum for the cure of spinal meningitis.

Booker T. Washington

TWpSr   Con. 431   BTW Papers   DLC.

[1] The Men and Religion Forward Movement, with headquarters in New York City, was an interdenominational movement for the promotion of Christian living among men and boys. In July of 1911 about 300 delegates held a founding conference in Silver Bay, N.Y. BTW spoke before the organization in Carnegie Hall. (See Extracts of an Address before the Men and Religion Forward Movement, Apr. 21, 1912, below.)

[2] Simon Flexner (1863–1946), a pathologist, was director of the laboratories of the Rockefeller Institute for Medical Research from 1903 to 1920, and director of the entire institute from 1920 to 1935.

To Julius Rosenwald

[Tuskegee, Ala.] December 27, 1911

My dear Mr. Rosenwald: Yours of December 20th regarding the 1260 pair of shoes which you have been kind enough to send, has been received, and you do not know how very grateful we are to you for this very fine and rare gift. It will help us more than you can realize.

A little later I shall write you in detail about the use we shall make of this gift, but in the meantime you can be assured that we can make all the shoes serve a good purpose in helping out our students. Yours very truly,

Booker T. Washington

Dictated by Mr. Washington but not signed by him.

TLpSr Con. 647 BTW Papers DLC. Signed in E. J. Scott's hand.

From George Richards Lyman[1]

Pasadena, California, Dec. 27. 1911

My dear Dr. Washington: I take pleasure in enclosing herewith, from Mrs. Lyman, our daughter Alice and myself, check for $150.00 to cover the three one-year scholarships of which I spoke to you. Please accept this gift as a little souvenir of our delightful visit among you, and of our warm appreciation of the uniformly tactful, intelligent and courteous attention shown us on every hand, and of the magnificent work the Institute is doing under the leadership and control of yourself and Mrs. Washington.

In going to Tuskegee we expected much, but we found more. You have built up in material equipment, and in the consecrated lives of enthusiastic and efficient co-workers, an instrumentality wisely conceived and admirably administered for the uplift and development of your race, and thus for the solving of a great national problem. Not often has it been given to a man to dream such a dream, and less often yet to live to see his dream come true. God has been very good to you, for he has wonderfully helped you to realize great possibilities of service.

429

Now may I venture to repeat and to carry a point further what I took the liberty of saying to you on the football field that victorious afternoon:

Don't end your work with a mistake! Don't cut short, as General Armstrong cut short, in the case of Hampton, your unique personal contribution to the applied solution of these problems to which your life stands dedicated. Don't do it of your own volition, and don't be persuaded to do it. Confess to your Trustees and other advisors and benefactors that even your endurance has its limit: learn to yourself recognize that limit: and then steadfastly refuse to permit yourself to be pushed or constrained beyond it.

Boards of direction and conditional givers are forever sacrificing to a Cause devoted and heroic men, and thus, unwittingly, sacrificing the Cause itself. They do this, sometimes through sheer inability, or careless failure, to sense a breaking load; and sometimes through criminal neglect to ease that load, or to ease it in time. You have no moral right to permit to be thus cut short by a single day the influence of your own living personality, and your priceless personal service to Tuskegee and the Negro race, and to the Nation.

I know you will pardon this freedom of speech, because I know that you will recognize its friendliness and utter sincerity. And I believe that, in your heart of hearts, you will also recognize that the suggestions offered are sane and timely: — this entirely apart from any resulting benefit to yourself, but solely in the interest of the Cause itself, a cause which you represent and embody as no other man represents and embodies it.

We wish you all a Happy New Year, and many happy New Years, and may God long keep you in health and vigor, and continue to bless you and bless your work.

In our united behalf, Sincerely yours,

Geo. R. Lyman

ALS Con. 754 BTW Papers DLC.

[1] George Richards Lyman (b. 1844), a Minneapolis merchant in the wholesale drug business for many years, and president of Corporate Investment Co. beginning in 1892. Lyman and his wife and daughter visited Tuskegee Institute, where he addressed the students in the chapel and at several smaller gatherings. (*Tuskegee Student*, 23 [Nov. 25, 1911], 2.)

Emmett Jay Scott to Wilford H. Smith

[Tuskegee, Ala.] December 27, 1911

Personal:

Dear Mr. Smith: Can you find out absolutely and definitely in some official way what has become of Ulrich. Mr. Abbott's letter of December 9th to you[1] indicated that he was unable to secure a proper bondsman. Has he yet been able to secure one? Write me at your convenience. Yours very truly,

Emmett J. Scott

TLpS Con. 439 BTW Papers DLC.

[1] A. W. Abbott of the Children's Aid and Protective Society of the Oranges reported that Ulrich was sentenced on Dec. 3, 1911. He was placed on three-year probation and ordered to furnish a bond of $1,000 and to pay $10 a week for the support of his wife and children. In default of the bond, he was committed to the Essex County penitentiary at Caldwell, N.J., for one year or until he could furnish bond. (Abbott to Smith, Dec. 9, 1911, Copy, Con. 439, BTW Papers, DLC.)

To W. A. Conner

[Tuskegee, Ala.] December 29, 1911

Dear Sir: Answering your letter of a recent date[1] permit me to send you the following replies.

Your question as to whether graduates of industrial schools for Negroes are contented to enter the ordinary vocations without aspiring to political and social equality has never been considered by me in just the way that you put it. The graduates of Tuskegee and other Negroes, as far as I know, do not generally associate together economic and political questions, hence when the subject of taking up a vocation is considered the question of political and social equality, so far as I know does not enter in.

We have sent out from Tuskegee a large number of persons to work in the trades. Instead of being kept out of the trades by the objections of white men we are unable to fill the demands made upon us by white persons for our graduates to work in the trades. Since the American Federation of Labor voted last year to unionize the Negroes in trades, there has of course been much less tendency for white persons to object to Negroes working in the industries. Recently in Tampa, Florida, white workmen struck because a Negro had been discharged and the matter was referred to arbitration, and settled by the Negro being. . . .[2]

Replying to your third question I do not know of any dormant discontent among the colored people because of political or social inequality. On the contrary everywhere I go I find the Negro very optimistic.

I send you under another cover a pamphlet showing somewhat in detail what the graduates and former students of Tuskegee Institute are doing industrially. I also refer you to my recent book, "The Story of the Negro," published by Doubleday, Page and Company, New York. Several of the chapters which deal with the economic conditions of the Negro will, I am sure, interest you.

I suppose you are acquainted with the rapid advances that the Negroes are making industrially. Recent Census bulletins show that Negroes are becoming farmers about twice as rapidly as white persons are. Negroes are also working in about all the trades and occupations that white people are working in; and the fact that the American Federation of Labor is seeking to unionize Negro labor indicates that the Negroes have become an important factor in the labor world.

You are no doubt aware of the rapid manner in which the Negroes are accumulating property. Starting forty years ago with $15,000,000 or $20,000,000 worth of property they have now some $600,000,000 worth of property. They are each year adding to their wealth from $12,000,000 to $15,000,000. In some states, as you know, separate records are kept of land and other property owned by whites and Negroes. In Virginia during the past year the Negroes added over 50,000 acres to their land holdings and increased the amount of their property holdings about $1,000,000. The Negroes of Georgia during the past year bought over 47,000 acres of land. They invested $560,000 in city and town property. Altogether the Negroes of Georgia in one year added $1,450,000 to their taxable property.

Trusting that your interest in this subject will continue, I am, Very truly yours,

Booker T. Washington

TLpSr Con. 419 BTW Papers DLC.

[1] W. A. Conner, describing himself as a "student of political economy," wrote to BTW on Dec. 16, 1911, from Stillwater, Okla., where he may have been a

college student. After reading *The Future of the American Negro,* he asked whether graduates of industrial schools were content to enter trades without seeking political and social equality, whether whites allowed them to enter these trades, and whether there was not discontent among blacks denied equality, and if so, what was the remedy. (Con. 419, BTW Papers, DLC.)

2 Remainder of sentence obliterated in press copy.

From James Bertram

New York, December 29, 1911

Dear Mr. Washington, Mr. Carnegie has received yours of December 26th and will be glad to subscribe Fifteen Hundred Dollars a year for the next three years to the National Negro Business League. Very truly yours,

Jas Bertram

TLS   Con. 49   BTW Papers   DLC.

A News Item in the Springfield *Republican*

[Springfield, Mass.] December 31, 1911

NEGRO DINED WITH KING

MR WASHINGTON IN DENMARK

COMMENTS ON RULER AND PEOPLE

Translating His Public Address — The Courtesy of the King and the Customs at Dinner

In the New York Age, Booker T. Washington, principal of the Tuskegee normal and agricultural institute in Alabama, tells the interesting story of his visit to the king and queen of Denmark, as follows:

I have had, in the course of my experiences, a good many surprises, but, next to receiving an invitation from the president of Harvard university to be at that seat of learning for the purpose of receiving an honorary degree, I think that the following letter which was placed in

433

my hands just as I entered my hotel in Copenhagen gave me my greatest surprise:

AMERICAN LEGATION.

COPENHAGEN.   October 2, 1910

My Dear Sir: His majesty, the king of Denmark, has through his master of ceremonies, commanded you to be at the Amalienborg palace at 10 o'clock on Monday (tomorrow). You will be received on your giving your name to the marshal of the court.

I am delighted to inform you that the king and the queen are greatly interested in your work and very sympathetic with it. They show this by granting you, on their own initiative, the honor of a private audience.

The legation will be glad to be of any possible use to you. I want especially to call your attention to my friend, Pastor Strom's invitation to you. I am yours sincerely

(Signed)   MAURICE FRANCIS EGAN

If anything further were necessary to make my welcome to Copenhagen complete it was the unexpected arrival of this friendly letter from the American ambassador, in which he expressed the interest of the king in my work and his desire to honor me, as the letter stated, with a "private audience."

Of all the places that I planned to visit during my brief sojourn in Europe I think I can safely say that Denmark was the country from which I hoped to learn most, the one in which, therefore, I felt the most lively interest. In order not to miss anything that was worth seeing I was out of bed early in the morning.

Of course, the first thing that I encountered was another change of language. During the past few weeks, however, languages had changed so frequently that I had grown accustomed to that. Besides, the difference between Danish and German is not so great as that between German and Hungarian, for instance, and both are more like English than any of the strange tongues to which my ears had been accustomed.

The first thing that attracted my attention, after crossing into Denmark, was the appearance of the children. They seemed to have a sparkle in their eyes and a rich color in their faces that indicated vigor and health; they had, too, an alertness and activity in their bodies which was in marked contrast with the appearance of the children which I had seen in many other parts of Europe. The Danish children, in a word, seemed to be enjoying life.

And then, too, I soon began to note that the women of all classes were better and more sensibly dressed than in most places I had visited. They seemed happier, they talked more, laughed more, and, apparently, read more than any women I had seen in Europe. I confess, however, that I was a little startled when I saw women in a first-class restaurant sitting at a table with gentlemen smoking and apparently enjoying it.

The change that I have indicated in the appearance of the children and the women was equally marked in the case of the men. I have referred particularly to the changed appearance of the children and women, however, because my observation has taught me that the appearance of children and women is a pretty good indication of the civilization of a people.

As the train journeyed onward toward Copenhagen I soon noticed the fine farms and stock which were in evidence on every hand. I had recently been in portions of Hungary, where the government is spending large sums of money in teaching the people better methods of farming, but it did not seem to me that the Hungarian government was succeeding to the same extent as Denmark in getting results from the money spent on the education of its farming population. The difference, it seemed to me, consisted in this: Hungary was forcing her methods on the people from the outside: Denmark was bringing about a change in the methods of farming from the inside, that is, by making each individual man and woman more intelligent, more skilled and more patriotic.

A CORDIAL RECEPTION

As my train approached nearer to Copenhagen it seemed to become pretty generally known that I was on the train, and long before I reached Copenhagen many sorts of people approached me and bade me welcome to Denmark. This welcome was not the usual formal, stereotyped greeting. There was something in the words and the manner of the people that convinced me that, much to my surprise, they knew about my work in America. In fact, several of the persons I met told me they had read my books. So numerous and hearty were the greetings that I received that I found myself holding a sort of informal reception all the way to Copenhagen station. There I was met by a reception committee composed of journalists, educators and other distinguished persons.

I was immediately conveyed to my hotel, where I found a suite of rooms had been placed at my disposal. I spent a tremendously busy day. All kinds of invitations, from all kinds of people, poured in upon me. They were invitations to speak at various functions and to see this

435

and that interesting object. As my sojourn in Denmark was limited, I determined to follow the plan which I had previously found advisable elsewhere, namely, of letting myself be guided during my stay in Denmark wholly by the committee of gentlemen in charge. This meant that I had to disappoint a great many people, but I found that the committee was well informed as to who and what I ought to see and what not to see and had my program mapped out. The chairman of committee was Veggo Cavling, editor of the Politiken, the leading paper in Denmark, to whom I am indebted for many courtesies.

AT A FAMOUS RESTAURANT

Soon after I had finished brushing the dust from my garments and had gotten myself into some sort of presentable condition, I was taken by the committee to a famous restaurant on the water for breakfast. From this restaurant I had a fine view of the harbor. Among other things, my attention was attracted by the English man-of-war which was occupied, I was told, by the queen mother of England,[1] who was then on a visit to her royal relatives in Denmark.

Soon after breakfast we called upon the American minister, Maurice Francis Egan, to whose kindness and consideration I am indebted for much of the pleasure and success of my visit to Denmark. I might add that lest he should be absent from Denmark during my visit, Mr. Egan had previously sent a cablegram to Mr. Carnegie at Skibo castle in order to learn the exact date of my arrival in Copenhagen. Then having informed himself on that point, he shortened his vacation and returned to Denmark for the express purpose of being of what service he could to me during my stay in that country.

After calling upon the American minister we spent a good part of the day viewing the many points of interest about the city, and that evening, in accordance with the program which had been arranged for me, I spoke in one of the large auditoriums of the city.

If I had not been prepared for the hearty welcome which I had already received, I was still less prepared, upon entering the hall, to see the audience, which filled every part of the building, rise to its feet and cheer as I came upon the platform. I had been uneasy all day for fear that my speech would not be understood, but I was positively frightened when I saw this large audience and, from the enthusiasm with which I was greeted, got some idea of what was expected of me.

A Speech with Interpreters

I had already had some experience with translators. While, at the beginning it was not so bad to have to be compelled to stop at the end of every few paragraphs, to have my words translated, I found that when I was fairly launched on my address, and reached the point where I began to feel my speech in my blood and bones, it was very trying to stop, with my mouth open, so to speak, until the audience, by the aid of an interpreter, caught up with me.

I had not been talking more than a few minutes, however, until I found that the majority of my audience were able to follow me almost as well as if I had been speaking in their own tongue. Even the anecdotes I told, which were based very largely upon local conditions in the South, were for the most part understood, and so I went right on to the end of my address without stopping. I think I must have spoken for at least an hour and a half. One of the professors in the Royal college of agriculture, whose name unfortunately I cannot now recall, followed me. This gentleman took notes during my address and, after it was over, translated the substance of my remarks to the audience. As near as I could judge, he performed his part of the program with great success. At least it was better than the halting method with which I had previously had experience. At the close of this meeting I was entertained at supper at one of the hotels by a committee of representative people of Copenhagen.

The main thing which led me to go to Denmark, however, was that I might get a clear and definite idea of agricultural conditions, especially the dairy industry. I wanted not only to see the condition of farming and dairying, but to learn, if possible, how the Danish farmer had been educated to the point which made it possible for Denmark to lead the world in the dairy industry. Much as I should have been inclined to accept some of the numerous invitations that would have kept me in the city, I determined that on the following day I would cut everything possible and get right out into the heart of the country, where I could meet the farmers, study their methods and observe the results. I wanted to see, also, some of the high schools, agricultural schools and common public schools. All this, however, the committee, headed by Mr. Cavling, had carefully thought out and planned for in advance.

The only thing that disturbed me and led me to hesitate in carrying out this decision was the command for me to appear at the king's palace the next day at 10 o'clock. No one seemed to know just what further commands the king might have in store, but everyone was certain, at the same time, that it would be an unforgivable thing for anybody to fail to accept an invitation from the king.

So it was decided that, Monday morning everything else must wait until I had been to the palace to see the king. On the previous day I had been carefully instructed by Minister Egan as to the exact time to appear at the palace and as to the kind of dress that I was to wear. Fifteen minutes before the hour of my reception, the American minister's carriage drove up to my hotel, and I was conveyed in quite a ceremonious manner to the entrance to the king's residence. Before reaching the entrance of the palace we encountered a rather formidable array of soldiers and bayonets. Reaching there, however, thanks to the good offices of Minister Egan, there seemed to be plain sailing.

A VISIT TO THE KING

I was met at the entrance by some official, clad in imposing uniform, and by him I was conveyed through several rooms or halls until finally I reached the reception-room of the king's chamberlain. The chamberlain, as soon as I entered the room, greeted me warmly and asked me to take a seat. In the meantime he himself stood through the whole proceedings. In fact he did all of his writing standing, with his sword by his side, and I did not see him sit during the whole time I was in the room.

Soon after I entered, the chamberlain went in and presently returned to tell me the king would be ready to see me in about five minutes. At the end of the five minutes exactly, the door was opened and I found myself in the king's chamber. I had expected to see a gorgeously fitted apartment, something to compare with what I had seen elsewhere in the palace. Imagine my surprise when I found practically nothing in the room except the king himself. There was not a chair, a sofa, or, so far as I can recall, a single thing in the way of furniture — nothing except the king and his sword. I was surprised again, considering the formality by which the king received me, and by his excellent English. Both of us remained standing during the whole interview, which must have lasted 20 minutes. I say we remained standing, because, even had etiquet[te] permitted it, we could not have done anything else because there was nothing in the room for either of us to sit upon.

I had been warned by the American minister and Mr. Cavling, however, as to what might be the result of this interview. Among other things in regard to which I had been carefully instructed by the American minister was I must never turn my back upon the king, that I must not lead off in any conversation, that I must let the king suggest the subjects to be discussed and not take the initiative in raising any question for discussion. I tried to follow Minister Egan's instructions in this regard as well as I could, but I fear I was not wholly successful.

KNEW ABOUT TUSKEGEE

I had not been talking with the king many minutes, before I found that he was perfectly familiar with the work of the Tuskegee school, that he had read much that I had written and was well acquainted with all that I was trying to do for the negroes in the South. He referred to the fact that Denmark was interested in the colored people in their own colony in the Danish West Indies, and that both he and the queen were anxious that something be done for the colored people in the Danish possessions similar to what we were doing at Tuskegee. He added that he hoped at some time I would find it possible to visit the Danish West Indian islands.

As I have said, I had been warned as to what might be the result of this visit to the king and that I had best be careful how I made my plans for the evening. As the interview was closing, the king took me by the hand and said, "The queen would be pleased to have you dine at the palace to-night," at the same time naming the hour.

The minister had told me that this was his way of commanding persons to dine, and that an invitation given must be obeyed. Of course, I was delighted to accept the invitation, though I feared it would wreck my plans for seeing the country people. The king was so kind and put me so at my ease in his presence that I fear I forgot Minister Egan's warnings not to turn my back upon him, and I must confess that I got out of the room in about the same way I usually go out of the room when I have had an audience with President Taft.

Leaving the king and the palace, I found out on the street quite a group of newspaper people, most of them representing American papers, who were very anxious to know, in the usual American fashion, just what took place during the interview, how long I was with the king, what we talked about, and what not. They were especially anxious to know if I had been invited to the palace for dinner.

439

As soon as the audience with the king was over, our automobile was ready and we went straight to the country. The automobile had been provided by Mr. Cavling because he was anxious that I cover just as much territory during the day as possible. We drove through magnificent farming districts, saw some of the finest cattle that one can find anywhere in the world.

A TYPICAL DANISH HIGH SCHOOL

Our first stop was at a typical Danish high school, at Roeskilde, the former capital of Denmark, one of the unique institutions which has made education in Denmark famous. The usual term "high schools," however, has little meaning in connection with the Danish high school. A Danish high school is an institution that has for its object the instruction of the masses of the people regarding Danish history and Danish traditions; in a word, its object is to inspire the people. These high schools are not only attended by the youths of this country, but during certain seasons of the year they are attended by men and women. For a given number of weeks the wives attend these schools, living in the institution. At the end of their time the wives go home and their husbands come and remain several weeks.

The first high school at which we stopped was, I think, about 40 miles from Copenhagen. Though it was during the vacation season, much to my surprise, when reaching this school I found a large audience of people from the surrounding country gathered for the purpose of giving me a reception and listening to me speak. After being introduced to the members of the faculty and inspecting the surroundings of the high school and partaking of a well-prepared lunch, a large audience assembled in the chapel and I spoke for 20 or 30 minutes, telling them about our work at Tuskegee and elsewhere in the South. But as I mingled with the people, men and women, I was surprised to find that they already knew almost as much about Tuskegee and its work as any similar audience in America.

From this high school we went into another farming district to visit a typical Danish agricultural school, and this school was one of the most interesting sights that I saw in Denmark. It was located right out in the country. The buildings were not costly nor showy, but everything indicated that it was a real farmers' school. Here again I found a still larger audience of people from the surrounding country gathered, and I had scarcely gotten within sight of the school buildings when I saw a large American flag hanging across the roadway. Not only that, but American flags were flying in all parts of the school grounds, as well as on many of the buildings. The people received me with many cheers. They sang Danish patriotic songs and American patriotic songs. In fact the heartiness and warmth of their reception nearly took me off my feet. What interested me as much as anything else was to note that the women, the wives of the farmers, were just as intelligent concerning Tuskegee and its methods as the men.

TEACHING ADAPTED TO CONDITIONS

What interested me especially about this school was to see that all the teaching was adapted to meeting the condition and needs of the people in that district, that any farmer could come there and see, for example, the best breed of pigs, and within a few days learn how to care for and grow them on his own farm. Any woman could come there and see the best garden, the best fowls, and be taught how to improve her own garden and her own fowls. Here, again, I found that it was the custom during certain weeks in the year for the farmers' wives to come and live in the institution and be taught the best methods of cooking, the best methods of table serving, the best methods of doing everything that a farmer's wife is called upon to do. At the end of two or three weeks these wives go home and the husbands come and are given instruction in the same way. The farm surrounding this agricultural high school I noticed, while not large, was a model of perfection. The people who came to these two meetings, to which I have referred, were happy, joyous and prosperous people. It was evident that they took pride in their country and in their part in its success.

As at my former stopping place, the people assembled in the chapel. In this case the audience was so large that it could not get on the inside of the room, and I spoke to the people standing in an automobile. As I drove away at the close of my address, American and Danish flags were waved and a familiar American song was sung with great heartiness. All this warmed my heart, taught me to love Denmark and made me feel that it was and is one of the happiest countries in the world.

After making further inspection of farm life and farm conditions, we turned our way toward Copenhagen. We had to hasten on in our journey because of the dinner at the palace, and I confess that, notwithstanding I was seeing so much that was new and instructive, all through the day I was trembling a little in anticipation of the ordeal that was awaiting me at night. I had never taken a formal dinner with a king and queen, and I did not know exactly what to expect or exactly what to do. Here again Minister Egan came to my rescue. He had carefully instructed me as to what time to appear at the palace for dinner and exactly how I was expected to conduct myself.

"THE POLITIKEN" GARDENS

Before speaking more at length concerning the dinner, I must mention that, notwithstanding the fact that it was getting dangerously near the hour when I had to start for the king's summer residence, we stopped to inspect one of the gardens maintained through the generosity of the Politiken some few miles out of Copenhagen. These gardens or farms, so far as I know, have no counterpart in America. They are small bits of land which the people are encouraged to cultivate. On Sunday and at other times when the city people care to do so, they can go out into these gardens and cultivate their little patch of land and live for the day if they wish to in a tiny house constructed on this land. Thus from the crowded city they are permitted to get a touch of real Nature.

The dinner was not at the palace where I was received in the morning, but at the summer palace several miles out of Copenhagen. When I reached the hotel from the country, it soon dawned upon me that I was in great danger of being late. To keep a king and queen and their guests waiting on one for dinner would of course be an outrageous offense. I dressed as hastily as I was able, but just as I was putting on the finishing touches to my costume my white tie burst. I was in a predicament from which for a moment I saw no means of rescuing myself. I did not have time to get another tie, and of course I could not wear a black one. As well as I could, however, I put the white tie about my neck, fastened it with a pin, and earnestly prayed that it might remain in decent position until the dinner was over. Nevertheless I trembled all through the dinner for fear that my tie might go back on me.

I succeeded in reaching the summer palace about 10 minutes before the time to go into the dining-room. Here again I was met by the king's chamberlain by whom I was conveyed through a series of rooms and, finally into the presence of the king, who, after some conversation, led me where the queen was standing and presented me to her. The queen received me graciously and even cordially. She spoke English perfectly, and seemed perfectly familiar with my work. I had, however, a sneaking idea that Minister Egan was responsible for a good deal of the familiarity which both the king and queen seemed to exhibit regarding Tuskegee.

Food out of Gold Dishes

As I entered the reception-room there were about 20 or 25 people who were to be entertained at dinner. I will not attempt to describe the elegance, not to say splendor, of everything in connection with the dinner. As I ate food for the first time in my life out of gold dishes, I could not but recall the time when as a slave boy I ate my sirup from a tin plate.

I think I got through the dinner pretty well by following my usual custom, namely, of watching other people to see just what they did and what they did not do. There was one place, however, where I confess I made a failure. It is customary at the king's table, as is true at other functions in many portions of Europe, I understand, to drink a silent toast to the king. This was so new and strange to me that I decided that, since I did not understand the custom, the best thing was to frankly confess my ignorance. I reassured myself with the reflection that people will easier pardon ignorance than pretense.

At a certain point during the dinner each guest is expected, it seems, to get the eye of the king and then rise and drink to the health of the king. When he rises he makes a bow to the king and the king returns the bow. Nothing is said by either the king or the guest. I think practically all the invited guests except myself went through this performance. It seemed to me a very fitting way of expressing respect for the king as the head of a nation and as a man, and now that I know something about it, I think if I had another chance I could do myself credit in that regard.

During the dinner I had the privilege of meeting a very interesting old gentleman, now some 80 years of age, the uncle of the king, Prince ————, who spoke good English. I had a very interesting conversation with him, and since returning to America I have had some correspondence with him.

In Two Royal Autograph Books

As I have already said, the queen mother of England was at this time in Copenhagen, and, as I afterward learned, her sister, the queen mother of Russia,[2] was also there. As both of these were in mourning on account of the recent death of King Edward, they did not appear at this dinner. I was reminded of their presence, however, when as I was leaving the king's palace after my interview in the morning one of the marshals presented me with two autograph books, with the request that I inscribe my name in them. One of the books, as I afterward learned, belonged to the queen mother of England. The other belonged to the queen mother of Russia.

After the dinner was over, my next problem was to get away in time to catch the night train for London, where I had a very important engagement to speak before the Liberal club. At the time of my audience with the king in the morning I had told him that I was compelled to take a night train for London. I very much feared that he had forgotten this, and I knew, of course, that it would have been entirely out of place for me to have left the king's palace without his command. At a convenient hour after the dinner, the king very kindly and graciously came up to me, shook my hand, and gently and tactfully reminded me that the queen would be glad to bid me good night, as I had to catch my train. In this way I got away in ample time for my train.

I went straight from the king's palace to Minister Egan's residence. I told him all about my adventures and he seemed quite as much pleased as I was that I had gotten through with it so successfully as I did. I was accompanied to the station by a committee of Danish gentlemen, who looked after every possible comfort. Thus ended one of the most pleasant and eventful days of my life.

Springfield *Republican,* Dec. 31, 1911, 22.

¹ Alexandra (1844–1925), widow of Edward VII, was the daughter of Christian IX of Denmark.

² Maria Fëderovna (1847–1928), daughter of Christian IX of Denmark, was the widow of Alexander III of Russia.

A Manuscript of an Article

[1911]¹

A Southern City Solving Its Race Problem

Five years ago when the two races clashed in the city of Atlanta the general public supposed that this city was rushing into the state of

Sodom and Gomorrah. And maybe it was. If so the check and turning about, the enlightening of one race as to the genuine feeling of the other, have made this riot a blessed visitation.

During the riot the best men of each race, all unknown to the general public, met together each night to deliberate on the best methods to restore peace and good will. They had not assembled two nights before these picked men from both sides began to open their eyes. "I did not know we had such intelligent conservative colored people anywhere in the country" exclaimed the white men again and again. "Why these white people are friendly, they are not afraid of contamination, they are really interested in the general welfare of us all," reported the colored men.

And so they began to understand. Order came, and Atlanta since then has been steadily laboring for the uplift of its colored citizens.

Startling as it may seem, it was at this period that religion as far as the South goes, broad human religion, for the first time actually took a hand in adjusting the relationship of the two races. The chief of police soon afterwards saw the cruelty of consigning Negro boys to the chain gang[,] making of petty offenders thru contact with hardened criminals life long jail birds. The leading men too began to be concerned about the church life and school life of the Negro. The Atlanta Constitution took up the fight and presumed to preach a sermon to the churches, preaching to the text that the church was going to India, Africa, and other foreign countries and neglecting the heathen at its door. Two significant points here came to light. The white people did not know the Negroes, did not go among them to see what they were doing, to touch the better side of the Negro's life. The other was that the several white men whose business took them among the Negro published abroad that the Negroes were, the better Negroes, law-abiding and standing for all that was good.

Evidently the sermon hit the mark; for day after day for more than two months letters came from the people all over the state acknowledging the timeliness of the sermon and expressing surprise that attention had not been before called to this method of solving the so-called race problem.

In so far as the sermon touched the conscience of the white men just so far it benefited the Negroes. Better accommodations were offered on many of the cars. Negroes had much better seats at the theatres and operas, and were treated with great civility everywhere, so

445

that now when white people hold their mid winter operas Negroes are given respectable seats and when Negroes give their entertainments in the same building white people in turn are given respectable seats. Thus now for five years a better understanding, a better feeling, a feeling on the part of all for the common good has been more and more asserting itself in this most complex of southern cities.

But the most significant instance of this better feeling and of religion taking a hand in this problem of the South, occurred a few months ago when the leading men of the city left their offices to raise $600,000 for several Y.M.C.A. buildings. There was a crying need for a large central building, for a boys' building, a building for the Georgia Institute of Technology and a Negro building. With committees in a perfectly organized system, with an appeal based upon an unassailable foundation — the saving and development of young men — these men were about to set forth in what the Atlanta Constitution called a "Whirlwind Campaign" to raise this amount in ten days.

But right in the face of all their enthusiasm and confidence one vexatious question suddenly sprang up: "will the public subscribe if we include the Negroes?" The Y.M.C.A. Executive committee consisting of some of the best men of the city was for the time checked. It was the unanimous consent that the Negro building should be included, that here was just the place where the two races could work together for the good of all, and yet would the public see this? This was the question. The chairman of the committee an ardent Southerner for at least three generations declared that in his opinion the measure was right, and that he would stand by it believing that since it was right the scheme could not fail. In this he was not supported, the remainder of the executive committee taking the ground that while the scheme was right it would be discreet to keep the Negroes' share of the funds in the background.

Meantime the Negroes of the city had already in a way taken hold of their situation. The Negroes already owned their lot, valued at $10,000 with a wooden structure which they had been using for an Association building. But they had no secretary, and the business of the association was going to ruin. J. B. Watson[2] one of the Negro international secretaries, living in Atlanta, seeing this condition, secured permission from headquarters to cease his travels for a time and undertake to lift the Negro Y.M.C.A. from the rut. This he did, getting some coal from one friend, and wood from another, and other necessaries from others, he soon had the association in running order. Then he set about to raise funds when the white people called upon him to assume a share of the responsibility of raising the funds among the Negroes for a new building. J. E. Moorland another International secretary was summoned and placed in charge of the Negro wing of the campaign. The Negroes' share of the $600,000 was $100,000. Of this sum the Negro wing was to raise $10,000 among the colored people.

As the Negro association would receive $25,000 from Mr. Ben Rosewald [Julius Rosenwald], this left the white people to be responsible for $35,000. Thus organized the committees set out to raise $600,000 the Negroes to work among their people, the white people among theirs, but keeping the Negroes' part well in the background. They had a central meeting place at noon where accounts were taken and reports bulletined. As I have said, the Negroes' share in the campaign was embarrassing. But day after day as the figures of the black men were read out at headquarters, applause grew louder and louder from the white committees. Pretty soon they were put on the bulletin board. Then the whole story got into the papers. Even the names of the Negro contributors were published with the amount given. The black man soon transcended so far the expectations of his white friends, that his report became a feature and an inspiration. What they actually accomplished is best told by an editorial in the Atlanta Constitution of March 9th. Speaking of the $100,000 the Constitution says:

"Of this $100,000 the Negroes were assigned to raise $40,000 in ten days.

"They did that and more! At the expiration of the ten-day period, they had raised $57,000 in addition to the equity in their present building. That did not satisfy them. They hammered and fine-tooth combed and persisted until when finis was written to the campaign, they had pledged the sum of $67,000 or $27,000 in excess of the amount required of them! And they are still subscribing!

"The details of their campaign are nothing short of marvelous. The total number of Negroes subscribing is placed at 5,500. In proportion to the givers among the white people and in ratio white and Negro population of Atlanta — the ratio between the white and Negro subscribers in proportion to population is about 3 to 1 with the predominance in favor of the Negroes."

The conclusions of this editorial are even more significant. "The result stands for itself" it goes on; "It disproves the misgiving, first entertained by the committees in charge of the campaign that the Negroes would need help from the whites to complete their quota."

"Astute students of the Negro" says this same paper, "have emphasized his lack of race consciousness and cohesion as the main premises for misgiving. Both indictments were sweepingly dismissed by the Atlanta campaign. The explanation is simple but portentous. The Negro was assigned a task that assumed citizenship, manhood and the possession of possibilities inherent in both."

In the same strain the Constitution points out in this conduct of the Negroes and whites a lesson for Atlanta and for the whole South.

"It has done away with a great deal of our race problem here," said Mr. Marion M. Jackson, chairman of the executive committee, and the man who dared to base his hope on the justice of the scheme. "I was surprised" he said, "am still surprised as I think of it" at the ability to organize in these colored men.

That it has meant much to the colored people I can speak with even greater assurance. At one of these mixed gatherings during the campaign, one Negro speaker said to the white men present: "we thank you not for help, but for the opportunity to show you what we can do for ourselves." "We felt we were on trial["] said one of the leading colored men later, ["]and the money had to be raised. It was the educated Negroes that were on trial and we responded.["]

This response was another thrilling example of the coming efficiency and good service of the educated Negro to his own people. They gave every cent they could personally afford to give, and then they left their business, the college president's chair, their class rooms, their offices and went into the streets and begged the rest.

Untold good has already come to both races. The Negro Y.M.C.A. is now a regular branch of the central association, just as is the boys' building, the railroad branch and Georgia [Institute of] Technology. All the funds collected from Negroes go like the rest to the central committees and are receipted. The Negro secretary is on the regular pay roll of the central association, and the Negro executive committees like those of the other branches co-operate with the executive committee at the central building. This saves time. It saves money. It teaches organization. It brings together in constant contact the best of each race, instead, as is too often true, the best on one side the worst on the other in each race.

And why should there not be this kind of co-operation? There is no social contamination, no friction, but a holy effort to help all and be helped. "I believe," said Mr. Marion M. Jackson "that the solution of this whole thing is thru religion. When we all get so we can carry our religion into our business and everywhere among both races, why there will be no race problem."

Surely this is progress. Twenty years ago there could have been no such common meeting ground as that reached by these two races. The wounds of slavery were still sensitive and the social and political bugbear was driving the two races daily farther apart. In the words of the Constitution once more:

"Is it not well for Atlanta[,] for Georgia, for the South to analyze the lesson of the achievement of the Negroes in the Y.M.C.A. campaign? It shows that it pays to help make decent law-abiding citizens of the Negro, instead of taking it for granted that the whites must be taxed to treat them as criminals.["]

TM Con. 607 BTW Papers DLC.

¹ Though the manuscript is undated, the first sentence refers to the Atlanta Riot five years earlier in 1906.

² John Brown Watson, a black man born in Smith County, Tex., in 1872, was a graduate of Brown University. After teaching at Morehouse College for four years, he became secretary of the International Committee of the Y.M.C.A. in 1908. Later, he was president of Leland College in Alexandria, La.

Frederick Randolph Moore to Emmett Jay Scott

New York City Jany 5, 1912

My dear Emmett: I phoned over to Orange (County jail).¹ They informed me that Ulrich preferred remaining to giving up $15.00 weekly which his wife demanded. If he agreed to this he could secure the bail. The bail required is $1000.00. His trial has not yet been set. So you see it is stubborn[n]ess on his part.

I am going to D.C. tomorrow Saturday night to try to get some money from agents. Will be there until Tuesday afternoon. Can be reach[ed] at my sisters 938 T. St N.W. if anything needed. Back here Wednesday. Yours,

Moore

Didn't telegraph. Didnt see Church, wasn't necessary.

F.

ALS   Con. 60   BTW Papers   DLC.

   [1] Moore was responding to a telegram from Scott, who was anxious to learn whether Henry A. Ulrich was in jail because he could not raise bail or because he refused to pay child support. (Dec. [Jan.] 4, 1912, Con. 60, BTW Papers, DLC.)

From Chester A. Hagan

[New York City] Jan. 7, 1912

My Dear Sir; Your very welcome letter has been received; and it is o.k. beyond a very small change.

   Your steneographer has my first name as Charles instead of Chester; I also think it advisible to leave out my house address; and put in its place "attached to Central office."

   I am sending back your letter with corrections so that you will understand me better.

   Of course it is only natural that I should thank you; which I certainly do; but besides this I can read[i]ly understand now why they say you are such a powerful man; your letter is beyond a doubt one of the finest worded documents I have ever read; and if it was not a Confidential Matter I would show it to my Cousin "John C Freund"[1] a friend of yours. Thanking you again and hoping for the desired[?] results I Remain   Yours Faithfully

Chester A Hagan

ALS   Con. 918   BTW Papers   DLC.

   [1] John C. Freund (1848–1924), born in London of German parentage, emigrated from England in 1871 after three years' attendance at Oxford. While a student he had edited a literary journal, the *Dark Blue Magazine*. In New York beginning in 1873 he published a series of musical trade journals, the *American Musician, Music Trades, Musical America,* and *Musical and Dramatic Times.* He produced several Broadway plays and wrote articles on a variety of subjects. In

1904 he contributed $1,000 to the support of the *Colored American Magazine* and $150 to the Boston *Colored Citizen,* apparently because of sympathy with BTW. (Fred R. Moore to BTW, Apr. 25, 1904, Con. 23, BTW Papers, DLC.)

To the Editor of the Atlanta *Constitution*[1]

Tuskegee, Ala. January 10, 1912

Editor Constitution: Through your paper I wish to call the attention of the men of my own race to the frightful loss of life and serious wounding and maiming of human beings that grows out of the habit of carrying concealed weapons. No one can read the daily papers, giving account of the crimes and accidents growing out of shootings during the Christmas holidays, without being impressed with the fearful and useless loss of life and limb resulting from the habit of carrying concealed weapons.

During Christmas week a rough calculation shows that in Alabama there were twenty-eight persons killed and about the same number of persons seriously or fatally wounded.

Taking for granted that an equal number were killed and wounded in the remaining twelve southern states, and I think this is a conservative estimate, we have a total of about 300 persons killed and an equal number wounded during Christmas week.

Of course I realize that all of this shooting was not done by colored people, but the majority of the crimes or accidents relate to the members of my own race.

My object in writing is to appeal to the masses of our people through ministers, teachers and other leaders to give up once for all the habit of carrying concealed weapons. It is a subject that should be taken up in the pulpit, in the Sunday school, in the home and continually agitated until every member of our race who is now in the habit of carrying concealed weapons will feel ashamed to do so. During all the years that I have lived in Alabama I have never carried a concealed weapon, I have never kept one in my house and have never felt the need of one. I have traveled through all parts of the south by night and by day and have never felt that I have been in the least danger, and if I had I am quite sure I would not have been protected by reason of carrying a pistol. Where a pistol or gun keeps a person out of trouble one time, nine times it gets him in trouble. Besides, carrying concealed weapons

451

not only does not protect life, but carrying concealed weapons is a barbarous, coarse and vulgar habit. There is no reason why a person in a civilized country like the United States should get into the habit of going around in the community loaded and burdened with a piece of iron in the form of a pistol or gun.

If this subject is taken up at once and discussed and agitated throughout the south by our people I am sure that within a few weeks at least the colored people will cease carrying weapons and there will not be so great a loss of life and limb as is now true.

Booker T. Washington

Atlanta *Constitution,* Jan. 10, 1912, 6.

[1] An editorial on the same page pronounced BTW's appeal "strong and timely" and urged the conservative black leaders to bring an end to black "gun-toting." BTW sent the letter also to the Mobile *Register,* Memphis *Commercial Appeal,* New Orleans *Picayune,* and Houston *Post.* The press copy of the letter, dated Jan. 6, 1912, is in Con. 920, BTW Papers, DLC.

From Robert Ezra Park

Wollaston, Mass. Jan 11, 1912

My dear Mr Washington: I have sketched out the article on Negro Rural Communities for the Annals of the American Academy[1] as well as it is possible to do here. It will take but a few hours to complete it and get it copied when I reach Tuskegee.

The article upon the Carnegie Hero Fund Commission[2] has been written. I suggest to you that you send it out to the colored papers in the same manner as the The Man Farthest Down articles. I think they will find this even more interesting than those articles. It is well to give the colored papers material which their readers will be glad to read and which will give dignity to their pages in order to establish confidence in the papers and the public so that you can use their columns to say to the people some things that they otherwise would not be so willing to hear.

After it had been printed in the Student I would send marked copies to the Outlook, Independent and the prominent daily papers. In this way I believe you create interest and excite comment on the matters you are trying to bring before the public in a way that you could not do if the article were merely printed in a magazine. In other words I think the interest in this article will be more the fact that you are saying this sort of thing to the colored people than in the contents of the article itself.

If the articles on the Census are sent to the North American Review they should be thoroughly recast.[3] Dr Jesse Jones is very greatly concerned about your article on the population. I met him at Hampton and promised I would drop into the Census office on my way down to Tuskegee to look at their records and convince myself that the present figures are as near right as they have ever been. After I have done that it may be best to modify the article to some extent to indicate you intend no reflection on the Census Office at Washington.

I am sending today the last chapter of The Man Farthest Down to the Publishers. In some way or other, it appears, they lost the last six pages of the manuscript.

I think the best time for the articles referred to in Mr Page's letter would be next year, the year of the 50th anniversary of Emancipation. I think it would be well to start as soon as possible to get material for this series and perhaps for other articles along the same line. If you think well to suggest to Mr Work to study up the statistical material along these lines, when I get to Tuskegee I can go over his plans with him and aid him in getting hold of the significant things in the matter.

I think the suggestion you [made] in regard to a series of articles on the personal struggles and successes of Tuskegee students is a good one. My notion has been to get up single biographies in miniature which would serve the purpose so mention[ed]. While I was at Hampton I looked over all their material and took specimens of all of it home with me. I d[id] not find the tract you refer to among them. I will write and get it. I would like to do these little biographies so well that they would be real literature.

I have read the review of My Larger Education in the Outlook.[4] Considering the way in which that book was thrown together I confess I am surprised that it has made as good an impression as it did. It is not as good as I hoped it would be when you started out. But then.

I saw the article describing your meeting the King and Queen of Denmark in the Age and am glad to learn that it has been reprinted in the Springfield Republican.[5]

I am now working on book Tuskegee and its Problem.[6] At the rate

I am moving it does not look to me as if I should ever get it finished. Perhaps in the end I shall have to give up my work at Tuskegee in order to complete it.

I am still turning over in my mind the question of what, if anything, I should say at the International Conference in April. It seems to me the best thing I can do will be to say something that will indicate in detail just what the relation of Tuskegee Institute and its methods is to the African problem and suggest some things in which this school might cooperate with workers in Africa.

I shall expect to be going South again in a very few days. I have had a good time here but it is mighty hard to do much work here. very truly

Robert E. Park

TLS Con. 61 BTW Papers DLC.

[1] Robert E. Park, "Negro Home Life and Standards of Living," *Annals of the American Academy of Political and Social Science,* 49 (Sept. 1913), 147–63.

[2] Booker T. Washington, "Carnegie Heroes and the Race Problem," *Tuskegee Student,* 24 (May 18, 1912), 1, 3.

[3] See An Article in the *North American Review,* Feb. 1912, below.

[4] *Outlook,* 99 (Dec. 30, 1911), 1070. The favorable review praised BTW as the most "widely influential" individual on the race question and declared that "this remarkable book, replete with telling facts, possesses a distinct pedagogical value for all professional teachers."

[5] See A News Item in the Springfield *Republican,* Dec. 31, 1911, above.

[6] Park did not complete this project.

From William Watson Thompson

Liverpool, Ala. Jan. 13th 1912

Dear Sir: I gave my tenants last year about $150.00 in prizes.[1] About $80.00 of this was distributed by a committee from your school to the farmers, who had the best cultivated farms, the best gardens, and to those who had their ditches in the best shape and to the women who kept their homes in the neatest condition. I gave $20.00 in gold to the farmer making the largest number of bales of cotton on a one-horse farm. The man who received this $20.00 prize, raised seventeen bales weighing 500 pounds and 786 pounds of seed cotton.

As to just how the money was distributed by your committee, I have forgotten. In fact they never furnished me with a list of those to whom they had awarded the prizes.

This year I am offering the following prizes: $5.00 to the man raising the best garden; a nice dress to each of ten women who keep their houses in the best condition during the year; $20.00 to the man making the largest crop on a one horse farm, of cotton, corn, peas and potatoes. I am offering $10.00 to the man who raises the best acre of corn; $5.00 to the one who has the best acre of cotton and to those who pay their debts and save $50.00 towards building a home, I am going to give free of charge, an acre of land on which to build a home, and will secure for them a loan of enough money to put up a house, after their paying the $50.00.

I believe that every man or woman who is a property owner, is a better citizen for any country than one who does not own anything, be they white or black. They at least take more interest in the development of their country.

I think that you are doing a great work with your Farmers' Conferences each year. Sorry I could not accept your invitation to be present yesterday but had an engagement with Mr. W. M. Blount, President of the Birmingham & Southeastern R. R. on some business matters that prevented my doing so. Very respectfully yours,

Wm Watson Thompson

P.S. It might be interesting to you to know that our 65 houses here raised 736 bales of cotton, 375 tons of cotton seed 4500 bushels of oats, 6,000 bushels of corn. We saved 20,000 bundles of fodder, 2,000 bales of hay, and raised 200 hogs, about 50 head of cattle, enough syrup to supply most of the families and all of my tenants raised some peas and potatoes.

TLS Con. 625 BTW Papers DLC.

[1] J. W. McLeod, another Macon County landlord, offered $200 annually in prizes to his tenants south of Warrior Stand, Ala. He wrote to Clinton J. Calloway: "Contesting for the prizes advances my own interest, at least, to the amount of prizes besides the satisfaction of helping the unfortunate child race which is dependent on us." A handbill announcing McLeod's prizes stated that "Any man or woman getting drunk or abusing his or her family or children will be barred from this contest." (McLeod to Calloway, Jan. 12, 1912, with handbill enclosed, Con. 625, BTW Papers, DLC.)

W. W. Campbell, president of the Macon County Bank, wrote that during 1911 he had given three ten-dollar gold pieces to tenants on one group of his plantations, and planned to give $50 in prizes during 1912 for general improvement of stock and home improvement, and to encourage "their spirit of saving." He also planned to build a schoolhouse on one of his plantations. (Campbell to Calloway, Jan. 12, 1912, Con. 985, BTW Papers, DLC.)

From William Jay Gaynor

City of New York   January 15, 1912

Dear Mr. Washington: I am very glad to receive your letter recommending officer Hagan. I do not know that he can be promoted, as you know all appointments and promotions in this city are by competitive examinations. But I will see what I can do for him.

I was most glad to see you vindicated. I took a personal interest in the matter at once, as I saw that some people would be glad to do you an injury. We have such people here in the north, I am sorry to say. Sincerely yours,

W. J. Gaynor
Mayor

TLS   Con. 918   BTW Papers   DLC.

From Madame C. J. Walker

[Tuskegee, Ala.] Jan. 17, 1912

Mr. Washington: I am writing you this note to ask if you will be kind enough to introduce me to this Conference.[1] I do not want to explain my work, but I do want them to know that I am in the business world, not for myself alone, but to do all the good I can for the uplift of my race, which you well know by the great sacrifice I made in the interest of the Y.M.C.A. of Indianapolis. I believe that if others knew of my great struggle from the age of seven years without any parents to assist me up to six years ago, when I entered the business arena at that time and having succeeded in building it up to where my income is now more than $1,000 per month, it would be a great inspiration to them to do likewise.

Trusting you will not deny me this one opportunity, I am: Obediently yours,

(Mme) C. J. Walker

TLS Con. 917 BTW Papers DLC.

¹ BTW arranged for her to speak for ten minutes at the Tuskegee chapel on the evening of Jan. 17. He thought this a more proper occasion than at the regular meetings of the Tuskegee Negro Conference. (E. J. Scott to Madame C. J. Walker, Jan. 17, 1912, Con. 917, BTW Papers, DLC.) An undated clipping from the Indianapolis *World* reported that while at Tuskegee she gave treatments to eighty-four persons, including BTW and members of his family. (Ca. Jan. 27, 1912, Clipping, Con. 919, BTW Papers, DLC.)

To Charles Dewey Hilles

[Tuskegee, Ala.] Jan. 19, 1912

Personal

My dear Mr. Hilles: The name of the lady whom the business men of Tuskegee want appointed postmistress is Miss Mattie Moulton Lane.¹

For a number of years she has served as first assistant in the office and in a way has been largely responsible for the conduct of the office. She is perfectly competent and satisfactory.

I have just learned through Mr. Scott that the papers in her case were sent to the Post Office Department rather than to the White House.

I think I need not tell you that I knew absolutely nothing about the intended action of Mr. Joseph O. Thompson. I had not had the least inkling that he had any such thing in his head. In a letter received after he had issued his letter the following quotation occurs:

"I did not consult you in any way regarding my Roosevelt letter because I wanted to be absolutely free to say that you knew nothing of it, and besides, I wanted to save both yourself and myself embarrassment after I decided upon the action I intended to take." Yours very truly,

Booker T. Washington

TLpSr Con. 58 BTW Papers DLC.

¹ She was not appointed. James A. Grimmett became postmaster on Feb. 19, 1912.

From Emmett Jay Scott

[Tuskegee, Ala.] 1/19/12

Dear Mr. Washington: Called on Mr Hilles by appointment today. He tells me he is left high & dry in the air by Mr. J O Thompson. He has just received a three page letter telling him Thompson is for Roosevelt: & scoring the President as weak & as not being the kind of President he wants to support. We have gone over the whole situation — all of the Barker[1]-Thompson controversy. He took up Mr Thompson, he says, at your *request* & has stood by him on your account. He says H.[2] told the President in his presence that *J O T* was erratic & opposed to the President & that this action complicates him in every way in handling the *P. O.* matter @ Tuskegee. He took from his desk all the papers in the case where he has kept them, so as to continue G C Thompson[3] — & much else of a private nature he told me, of which I will speak when I return. To be short however on his personal responsibility he has written to the *Referee* & told him to get in touch with *you* for a Recommendation &c. I used some plain talk as [to] your help & as to this recognition & he agreed with *me*. Did not know that Business men there were interested. Had not heard of it & wishes papers sent to him. I gave him Miss Lane's name & he says he will call for her papers if they have been filed. In short he is *all right*. I will go over everything soon as I return. He wants me here next week for a Conference to plan some things but I have told him I am due home by early next *week*. Was glad to have the Roosevelt word regarding H. Have pushed everything much as possible & leave tonight for New York. Yours truly,

Emmett J Scott

He (H.)[4] says the *J O T* letter read like a letter from a *crazy man* & said among other things "I will spend no more time away from my office *fighting* the President than *Barker* will fighting for him" — *&c &c!* He is quite *sore* & thinks *Mr J O T* might have thought of where he has been placed. He spoke openly of the break with Hitchcock & privately told me all about it.

E J S

ALS Con. 620 BTW Papers DLC.

[1] Prelate Demick Barker (b. 1835) was postmaster of Mobile, Ala., from 1890

to 1913. He was a member of the Republican National Committee from 1908 to 1916.

[2] Frank Harris Hitchcock.

[3] Grover Cleveland Thompson was the postmaster of the town of Tuskegee, Ala., from 1907 to 1912. He also owned an undertaking business in Tuskegee.

[4] Charles Dewey Hilles.

Ralph Waldo Tyler to Emmett Jay Scott

Washington, Jan. 19, 1912

My dear Emmett: We were with the President, in his library, again last evening, from 6 to 8 o'clock. We went thoroughly over the ground, and talked very frankly to him — told him that the Negroes could not defend his Southern policy as now carried out; could never defend it, and that in the South, with their elective franchise taken away, it made mere serfs of the Negro. We urged him to make a few Negro appointments in the South, and urged him to restate his Southern policy at the earliest opportunity so as to make it clear to subordinates that it did not mean positive exclusion of Negroes from office everywhere in the South, and positive action, on the part of subordinates, to preclude the advancement of Negroes in offices in the South. We told him that Judge Hook's[1] appointment, in view of his two decisions upholding the jim-crow car law of Oklahoma, would be very distasteful to the race, and even plainly said that the Negroes were complaining that he had appointed two ex-confederates to the Supreme Court, and elevated a third to chief justice. We cited the dismissal of Negro postmasters in the South, told him of discriminations against the race in Civil Service appointments, and in governmental promotions. Called his attention to lynchings, and to the fact that if he expected the Negro vote he must give us something to go before our people upon which to base an appeal for their support. We talked right out in meeting, as it were — was perfectly frank and plain. Every man of us, even Link Johnson, stood up manfully, and were a unit in our protestations and requests for bettering conditions. He listened to us most patiently and most interestedly. He gave us assurance that he would demand investigation of every case we brought before him as to discrimination because of color; requested us to present him specific cases; expressed his willingness to restate his Southern policy so as to leave no room for doubt that he does not mean to close the door against the Negro holding office everywhere in the South; expressed his decided opposition to court decisions upholding jim-crow car laws, and to denial of suffrage, and his willingness to strongly pronounce against lynching. Sitting around him, smoking his Havana cigars, which he passed to us, we remained at the White House from 6:30 to 8 o'clock Wednesday evening, and from 6 to 8 on Thursday evening — a record-breaker for conferences between a president and Negro officials. In every way it was a most satisfactory interview. He seemed deeply interested, and equally interested in hoping for an opportunity to shelve his Southern policy without stultifying himself. I certainly wish you might have been here and with us. The understanding was that the conference was to be sort of confidential, but I requested that he remove any restriction as to secrecy, and permit me to see that the colored press received the news of the conference having been held, and he readily gave permission, and I shall therefore send a number of colored papers an account of it. I told the President that although his other cabinet held but two sessions a week, the "black cabinet" held daily sessions, whereupon he said our cabinet was the most industrious. Nothing came up to mar the meeting, and he appeared to recognize that we were primed with facts and figures. We hardly left anything untouched that deeply concerns the race. I told him that you had only arrived home when the message was received to be present, and could not make the journey in time. Frequently we referred to the Doctor to give him the impression, which he has, that we regard the Doctor as the real leader, and that our protestations against unjust policies is but a backing him up or carrying out his known wishes. He was in splendid humor both evenings, and the conference was enlivened by a story by him, and one by Lewis. We early — immediately, got down to brass tacks, and without hesitation or interruption kept hitting that tack squarely on the head. Sincerely yours, though hastily,

Tyler

TLS Con. 466 BTW Papers DLC.

1 William Cather Hook (1857–1921) served as a judge of the eighth U.S. judicial circuit from 1903 until his death. In 1912 Hook was considered for elevation to the Supreme Court, but failed to receive the appointment. BTW's opposition to Hook was expressed in his letter to Blanche Kelso Bruce, Feb. 17, 1912, below.

To James Crowe[1]

[Tuskegee, Ala.] Feb. 3d, 1912

My dear Sir: Mr. Smith has shown me a copy of your letter of January 22d, and I wish to assure you that I have not forgotten you, and neither do I in any way under-value the service which you rendered.[2] I am most grateful to you for it. I am not going to say more, but when I go to New York I want to see you and will try in some way to do something that will be entirely satisfactory to you.

I hope that something has been done for our mutual friend.[3] Tell him to write me. If I can serve him in any way further at any time tell him to not hesitate to call upon me. Yours truly,

Booker T. Washington

TLpS Con. 917 BTW Papers DLC.

[1] James Crowe, a Wall Street bank clerk, testified at the trial of Henry A. Ulrich that he was on the corner of Sixty-third Street and Central Park West on the night of the assault on BTW. He saw BTW running with Ulrich in pursuit and remarked to his companion, Chester A. Hagan: "Here's a thief." He witnessed Hagan's arrest of BTW and Ulrich's charge of theft. (New York *Evening Post,* Nov. 6, 1911, 16.)

[2] Wilford H. Smith wrote to James Crowe that BTW was under the impression that Crowe's expenses as a witness in the Ulrich case were to be paid by the state of New York. Smith said that BTW was grateful to Crowe, "and it was no doubt owing to the effect of the adverse decision that he overlooked writing you a letter of thanks." (Jan. 25, 1912, Con. 921, BTW Papers, DLC.)

[3] Chester A. Hagan.

To John Mitchell[1]

Tuskegee Institute, Alabama   February 13, 1912

Dear Sir: We are each year endeavoring to turn out from Tuskegee Institute a number of persons to work in trades, such as carpentry, bricklaying, etc. This fact, in connection with the reports which I receive from time to time from our graduates who are working in the trades, has caused me to become deeply interested in the subject of Negro Trade Unionism. I have endeavored to ascertain the extent that Negroes have become members of Trades Unions, what kind of Trade

Unionists they make, etc. The information I have received, however, is conflicting and contradictory. I am taking this occasion to write to you and a number of other well informed persons to see if I cannot get at the truth. I will be very grateful if you will kindly answer for me the follow questions:

(1)   What are the rules of your Union concerning the admittance of Negroes?

(2)   Do Negroes in your opinion make good union men?

(3)   If they do not, what in your opinion is the cause?

(4)   What do you advise concerning the Negro and Trades Unions?

Thanking you in advance for this information, I am, Very sincerely yours,

Booker T. Washington

TLSr   John Mitchell Collection   DCU.

[1] John Mitchell (1870–1919) entered the coal mines of Braidwood, Ill., at the age of twelve. He joined the Knights of Labor in 1885, but three years later the long, unsuccessful strike at a nearby mining town convinced him of the need for a separate miners' union. When members of the Knights and the National Federation of Miners formed the United Mine Workers in 1890, Mitchell joined. He advanced in the union hierarchy to become president in 1898. He led the Pennsylvania anthracite strike in 1902, when his skill at bringing together miners of many ethnic origins brought about victory over the recalcitrant operators. He lost his presidency in 1908 after unsuccessful strikes in the bituminous coal fields. Later, he headed the trade-agreement department of the National Civic Federation and chaired the New York state industrial commission. Mitchell was a conservative business unionist but supported the solidarity of miners across racial and ethnic lines.

Robert Ezra Park to James Bertram

[Tuskegee, Ala.] February 13, 1912

Dear Sir: I am writing to you at the suggestion of Mr. Emmett J. Scott, Dr. Washington's Secretary, in regard to a project which he presented to you some weeks ago, for the organization of a Bureau of Research to be devoted to the study of problems connected with the Negro, particularly in the Southern States. As you no doubt gathered, the rather imperfect notes which he left with you, offer a mere sketch. My purpose in writing to you is not to complete that sketch, because to write out all the specifications of the plan would take too much of your time. I should like, however, to emphasize certain points which seem to me unusual and do not connect themselves with the notion of "research," as it is ordinarily understood.

My own observation, during the years that I have been at Tuskegee as one of Dr. Washington's helpers, has convinced me that the thing which is most needed is:

1. Complete and accurate information in regard to what is actually being done by Negroes for themselves, through the medium of their churches, schools and business enterprises.

2. An institution which, through the medium of this information, will direct these forces in such a way as to get the best results.

Let me give an example of what I mean. Some twenty years ago, or more, a Negro preacher by the name of W. W. Brown,[1] of Richmond, Virginia, organized a secret . . .[2] organization prospered. In order to have a repository for the funds it collected, the True Reformers established a bank. In the course of time, it collected a considerable capital. The possession of the capital led to the organization going into a number of different kinds of enterprises, some of them benevolent and others of a business character. In addition to the bank, the Order established an "Old Folks" Home, conducted a hotel, acquired real estate and erected buildings in different parts of the country. It loaned money to local branches to build halls and then started stores for selling merchandise. Finally it failed. The fundamental reason for this failure was the fact that it was not properly organized and that the men who were at the head of the organization did not fully understand what they were doing. This organization is typical of many similar enterprises started by energetic colored men without experience.

Now, one of the unfortunate things about this failure is that, as far as the masses of the people are concerned, the causes of the disaster are still involved in mystery. The race, on a whole, has not been able to profit by the experience because there has been no one to study into the sources of the failure and give the benefit of what was learned to the whole people. This will suggest one of the functions of such a Bureau of Research as outlined in the notes Mr. Scott handed you. Without attempting to report on the credit of such enterprises in a way to affect the individual concerns, and without attempting to interfere directly in their business operations, the Bureau of Research would be able to gather and disseminate information that would enable the younger generation to avoid the pitfalls which the older organizations have fallen into. Gradually, Negro business could be put on a solid basis. Such a Bureau might, for instance, not only make the studies of Negro business institutions as I have suggested, but it might also prepare text books especially adapted to the needs of colored schools and, by working first in cooperation with such institutions as Hampton and Tuskegee and second with such other agencies as the Jeanes Fund, the missionary boards that have schools in the South, it might be possible to get these books adopted generally throughout the South . . .³ of students in colleges and it might, at the same time, make use of the Negro papers and the Press associations to give wide circulation, through the colored press, to information of this character and so make these newspapers a means of popular education.

What I have said about the case of the True Reformers and Negro business is merely an illustration of what could be done in much the same way for the churches, the schools and the benevolent organizations. Such an organization could turn to new and wider public uses not merely the existing colleges, industrial schools, etc., but the fraternal insurance companies, the Negro medical organizations and the hospitals.

In connection with the sort of work I have suggested, this Bureau could be made a means, for example, of turning the attention of the Negro colleges to more practical subjects and giving them a wider outlook than they now have. These colleges, or certain of them, could be used as centers at which information might be gathered and from which it would be distributed. Gradually a class of men would be trained through this work who would go from these institutions with a preparation which fitted them to take hold of and direct the churches, the schools, fraternal organizations, etc., in such a way as to get vastly better results from them than at present. I have in mind, for one thing, the money that is being wasted by Negroes in some of their miserable little colleges, simply because the men who conduct them do not know how. They have never had a decent education themselves and are generally without intelligent direction in what they are doing.

I believe that such a Bureau by merely collecting accurate information on the subjects referred to and by getting at the people in the way I have outlined, could, in the course of time, build up an adequate system of common schools for Negroes in the South out of existing materials and resources.

The reason why I believe that this research work could be done in the way I have suggested is because it has already been done in a small way at Tuskegee and Hampton.

My hope is that the suggestions contained in the matter Mr. Scott submitted and in what I have written may lead to a very thorough investigation of the project. I believe if it were possible to obtain money enough to make a sort of preliminary survey it would not be difficult to convince you and Mr. Carnegie of the wisdom of establishing such an endowment. I say this although I realize that the amount of money necessary to do so compared with what is ordinarily given for Negro education would be very large.

I very much hope you will read this memorandum along with the one submitted to you by Mr. Scott. Yours truly,

Robert E. Park

TLpS Con. 18 BTW Papers DLC.

[1] William Washington Browne (1849–97), born a slave in Alabama, ran away during the Civil War and enlisted in the Union Navy and later in the infantry. After attending school in Wisconsin, he taught until 1874 in Georgia and Alabama, where he became an organizer among blacks of the interracial Independent Order of Good Templars. Two years later he led a separation from the parent body that formed the all-black Grand Fountain of the United Order of True Reformers, with headquarters in Richmond, Va., and branches in twenty states by 1893–94. Its mutual benefit plan allowed the heirs to receive support payments for a considerable time after the death of a member. The True Reformers also established a savings bank in 1889 that survived the panic of 1893. After Browne's death, less careful banking practices and lax supervision caused the failure of the bank in 1910. (Burrell and Johnson, *United Order of True Reformers.*)

[2] First page of press copy ends here; presumably a line or two was obliterated.

[3] Obliterated passage at bottom of second page of press copy.

From Joel Elias Spingarn

New York February 14, 1912

My dear Dr. Washington: I enclose my usual little contribution for the running expenses of Tuskegee Institute. I have mislaid the name of your Treasurer, and I am therefore sending the cheque direct to you.

I hope you will believe that no difference of opinion as to the ideals and ambitions of the American negro can diminish my sense of the value of the actual achievement of Tuskegee. Cordially yours,

J. E. Spingarn

TLS Con. 756 BTW Papers DLC. A notation on the letter indicated that the contribution was $25.

To Blanche Kelso Bruce[1]

[Tuskegee, Ala.] Feb. 17, 1912

Personal

My dear Mr. Bruce: On my arrival home I received your telegram regarding Judge Hook. I feel rather sure that you have not read Judge Hook's decision. I do not see how any colored man after reading this decision could advocate the cause of Judge Hook. It is a deliberate insult to a whole race of people. He goes further in trying to humiliate us than any Southern judge has ever done. I am sure Judge Hook would respect any colored man more who would tell him outright that he does not agree with him and opposes him than he would a colored man who tries to have him rewarded for this infamous decision.

I am telling you practically what I told the President of the United States, that any man who would render such a decision is certainly unfit for the Supreme Court bench in my opinion.

I mean to say that the decision shows upon its face that the Judge is so prejudiced against our race that he is not fit to sit on the highest court in the United States.

I am sorry that I cannot comply with your request, and I am sure that Judge Hook at the bottom of his heart would not respect me if I did so. Yours very truly,

Booker T. Washington

TLpS Con. 916 BTW Papers DLC.

[1] A nephew and namesake of the Mississippi senator Blanche Kelso Bruce (1841–97), and principal of a Kansas black public school. He urged BTW to support Judge Hook, despite his decisions regarding the separation of the races in railroad coaches in Oklahoma. (Bruce to BTW, Feb. 7, 1912, Telegram, Con. 916, BTW Papers, DLC.)

From John Mitchell

[New York City] February 17, 1912

My dear Dr. Washington: Your favor dated February 13th received just as I am leaving on a lecture trip.

Replying, I beg to say that the United Mine Workers of America, of which I am a member, discriminates in no way between white and colored men. While I have no exact statistics as to the number of negro members of the United Mine Workers of America, it is safe to say that not less than 30,000 of the 300,000 members are negroes. Many important offices are filled by colored members.

The negroes who are mining coal in the northern states make first class union men. In the southern states where negroes are employed in large numbers in the mining industry, unionism is not so strong. This, however, is in part accounted for by the fact that the mine owners oppose strongly the organization of their workmen, and the miners are so poor that they cannot contend successfully against the corporations unless they are supported financially by the organized men in other states.

My judgment is that the negro workingmen should be encouraged to become members of the trade unions and to strive for a higher standard of living.

I am obliged to hurry to get a train, and must therefore ask you to excuse this brief reply. Yours very truly,

[John Mitchell]

TLc John Mitchell Collection DCU.

To Charles Dewey Hilles

[Tuskegee, Ala.] Feb. 19, 1912

Personal

Dear Mr. Hilles: Mr. Scott and I during the past few months have been devoting ourselves to the Louisiana situation, counseling in every way possible our friends there to avoid anything that would resemble a contest.

The enclosed letter from Mr. Walter L. Cohen explains itself and

467

shows how all our well meant efforts have gone for nothing because of the perverse attitude of the Lily Whites in that state.

Four years ago about this time I had occasion to call to Mr. Taft's attention the high-handed attitude of those men who represent the Lily White wing of the party in Louisiana. What they are now doing is not helping Mr. Taft in the slightest way. They are only helping themselves and are hurting the administration throughout the country by having it understood that the administration stands back of the Lily White movement in that state.

The newspaper clippings which are attached show that after the Lily Whites were forced into the primaries that fourteen representatives from the old line Republican Party were selected for a place on this committee. Of these fourteen, eleven were colored. The Lily Whites have seated the three white men and have absolutely excluded the black men stating, so it is reported, that they will not serve on any committee with Niggers, and those men call themselves Republicans. I do not believe that the President would be disposed to countenance their un-Republican conduct, and it is a pity that after all the work that has been done to save a contesting delegation that the Lily Whites would be the ones to make such contest necessary.

The enclosed letter has just been received by Mr. Scott who has written urging that anything that can possibly be done to save a contest be done.

I hope that favorable action will follow. Yours very truly,

Booker T. Washington

TLpS Con. 58 BTW Papers DLC.

From Chester A. Hagan

N. Y. City. Feb. 21, 1912

My Dear Sir; Relative to the last letter that you sent me I beg to inform you that up to the present time I have heard nothing; and as you stated in your letter you wanted to be kept informed as to what was going on, so, I thought I would write and let you know.

I also wish to again thank you for whatever action you may have taken in my behalf. I personally think you have done everything that was possible for you to do; and as I do not wish to put you to any more trouble I will not feel offended if you let the matter drop hoping that I may have the pleas[ur]e of meeting you again, in a different manner than the last. I Remain   Very Respectfully

Chester A Hagan

ALS   Con. 921   BTW Papers   DLC.

From George A. Myers

Cleveland, Feb 26–1912

Personal & Confidential

Dear Dr Washington — Press dispatches to-day carry the announcement that Theodore Roosevelt is a candidate for the nomination of President of the United States, subject to the Republican National Convention which convenes at Chicago in June and furthermore that he is in the race to stay. Knowing that Mr Taft and Mr Roosevelt are both personal friends and your interests are indissolubly linked to each, as a friend I am writing to suggest that you consider well before expressing a preference for either. Loyalty is a trait admired by all, no one condemns a man for being loyal to his friends. You have been and are still loyal to each. Mr Taft your loyal friend was among the first to publically express his confidence in you and to extend his sympathy. Mr Roosevelt is one of your Trustee's, but so far as I know, I have never read of or heard any expression from Mr Roosevelt over your late unpleasantness, deeply deplored by all of your friends everywhere. (The incident and Mr Roosevelts silence). Mr Taft has made a very acceptable President. He has done things and while perhaps he has not done enough to please every "brother" — nevertheless he has done much. The "brother" in Ohio with few exceptions are for him and with him to stay. Aside from our loyalty, its easy for us to say that he is the candidate of our home State. With you as our representative, mediator and friend at "Court" it is quite different, furthermore you are not a politician or skilled in the ways of one, neither would you endeavor to deceive or mislead either Mr Taft or Mr Roosevelt. It is my personal belief that neither of them would seek to put you on record. Go ahead just as you have been doing and let us your friends fight the battle for Mr Taft. It should be an easy matter to line up the negroes of the North for him, While the brother is "quick to forget and easy to forgive" — The Brownsville affair like Banq[u]o's ghost will not down and is sufficient to cement his opposition to Mr Roosevelt. With best wishes for continued health and prosperity for you and Mrs Washington in which I am joined by Mrs Myers, I am — Your Friend.

George A. Myers

ALS Con. 919 BTW Papers DLC. Docketed in Scott's hand: "Said you're car[ry]ing out plan he suggests 2/29."

An Excerpt from an Article in *The Nautilus*

February 1912

WHY I MADE TUSKEGEE AN INDUSTRIAL SCHOOL

Tuskegee Institute was started, in a small way in the summer of 1881. At that time the negro had lost practically all political control in the South. As early as 1885 there were scarcely any members of my race in the National Congress or state legislatures, and long before this date they had ceased to hold state offices. This was true, notwithstanding the protests and fervent oratory of such strong race leaders as Frederick Douglass, B. K. Bruce, P. B. S. Pinchback, and John M. Langston, with a host of others. When Frederick Douglass, the greatest man that the negro has produced, died in 1895, it is safe to say that the negro in the Southern States, with here and there a few exceptions, had practically no political control or political influence, except in sending delegates to national conventions, or in holding a few Federal positions by appointment.

It became evident to many thoughtful negroes that the members of the race could no longer look to political agitation and the opportunity of holding office as a means of gaining a reputation or winning success. In short they must look to something more tangible and substantial upon which to base their future. It was at this period in the negro's development, when the distance between the races was greatest and the spirit and ambition of the colored people most depressed, that the idea of industrial or business development was introduced and began to be made prominent.

It did not take the more level-headed members of the race long to see that while the negro in the South was surrounded by many difficulties, there was practically no line drawn and little discrimination in the world of commerce, banking, storekeeping, manufacturing, the skilled trades, and in agriculture; and in this lay his great opportunity. They understood that, while the whites might object to a negro's being postmaster, they would not object to his being president of a bank, and in the latter occupation they would give him assistance and encouragement. The colored people were quick to see that while the negro would not be invited to attend the white man's prayer meeting, he would be invited every time to attend the stockholders' meetings of a business concern in which he had an interest, and that he could buy property in practically any portion of the South where the white man could buy it.

The white citizens were all the more willing to encourage the negro in this economic or industrial development, because they saw that the prosperity of the negro meant also the prosperity of the white man. They saw, too, that when a negro became the owner of a home and was a taxpayer having a regular trade or other occupation, he at once became a conservative and safe citizen and voter; one who would consider the interests of his whole community before casting his ballot; and, further, one whose ballot could not be purchased.

It was at this time that I set out to start an industrial school for the members of my race at the little town of Tuskegee, in what is known as the Black Belt of Alabama.

The first thing I did, as soon as I arrived at the place for establishing the new college, as it was called, was to study the actual needs of the people around it. For this purpose I spent several weeks traveling about in different parts of the county, visiting the colored people in their homes and talking to them in their churches. At the same time I felt compelled to take account of the attitude and disposition of the white people in regard to the new school. I did this because the legislature was furnishing the funds for starting the school and because I saw clearly that there was no hope of putting negro education on a firm basis in the South, unless it was possible to secure the interest and sympathy of the white people. I saw that, if the school I proposed to establish was to be successful, it must find a common ground some-where between the races. Thus it was that I set out at the very start to secure the support and interest of both white people and black people.

Many people, especially in the North, have a wrong conception of the attitude of the Southern white people towards negro education. It has been very generally thought that what is termed "higher edu-cation" of the negro has from the first been opposed by the white South. This opinion is far from correct. I remember that, when I be-gan work at Tuskegee, practically all of the white people who talked to me on the subject took it for granted that instruction in Greek, Latin and modern languages, would make up the greater part of the curriculum. No one opposed this course of study. In fact, there are many white people in the South today who do not know that instruc-tion in the dead languages is not given at Tuskegee Institute.

The truth is that a large part of the people in the South had little faith in any kind of education for the negro. They were indifferent, but not openly opposed to it. On the other hand, there has always been an influential group of white people in the Southern States who have stood out prominently and courageously for the education of all the people, regardless of race. This group of people has thus far been suc-cessful in shaping and directing public opinion, and I think that it will continue to do so more and more. This statement must not be taken to mean that there is as yet an equitable division of the school funds between the two races in all sections of the South, although the South-ern States deserve much credit for what has been done.

I wish, however, to emphasize the fact that, while there was open antagonism or indifference in certain directions it was the introduction of industrial training in the negro's education that furnished the first basis for anything like a common interest and united action between the two races in the South, and between the whites in the North and those in the South. Aside from its direct benefit to the black race, in-dustrial education has furnished a basis for mutual confidence and co-operation. And this has meant more to the South, and to the work of education, than has been realized.

From its inception the white people of the South were favorable to industrial education for the negro because they had noted, what was not unnatural, that a large portion of the colored people were disposed immediately after emancipation to interpret freedom to mean freedom from work with the hands. The white people saw in the setting up of schools to teach the negro youth that labor with the hands was honorable, something that would lead the negro into his new life of freedom gradually and prevent him from flying from one extreme of life to the other.

Besides that industrial education appealed directly to the interest of the individual white man and to the community. They saw at once that intelligence, coupled with skill, would add wealth to the community and to the state. Crude labor, in the days of slavery, had been made profitable to a certain extent. The ignorant and unskilled labor, in a state of freedom, could not be made so. Practically every white man in the South was interested directly or indirectly in agriculture or in some other business or trade which employed manual labor. Every white man was interested in all that related to the home life, the cooking and serving of food, laundrying, dairying, poultry raising and housekeeping generally, so there was a general recognition of the fact that the education of the black people, who had hitherto performed this kind of work, was of vital interest to every white man in the South.

If the black man became a lawyer, a doctor, a minister or a teacher his professional duty did not under ordinary circumstances bring him into contact, in any direct and vital way, with the life of the white people of the community. The result was that as long as the education of the negro was of a purely literary or professional character it had little interest or significance to the average white man. There was a confused idea that such kind of education might bring about a higher and better type of negro manhood, but that seemed remote and doubtful.

The minute, however, it appeared that as a result of industrial education the negro would not only, for example, study chemistry but apply that chemistry to the enrichment of the soil and the production of crops; apply it to cooking, to dairying and to other practical matters; the minute it was seen that in the new industrial school the negro was not only learning geometry and physics but applying his knowledge to blacksmithing, brickmaking, house building and what not; at that moment there began for the first time to be a common bond between the

473

two races and an opportunity for co-operation between the North and the South in the matter of negro education.

It was not so easy to convince the masses of the colored people that there was any virtue in a school that taught their children to work with their hands. They argued, not unnaturally, that they and their people had been worked for 250 years in slavery and now they thought they ought to have a little rest. At any rate, it seemed to them, that a school was the last place on earth where work ought to be so much as mentioned.

I said to them, in reply to these arguments, that it was true that they *had been worked* in slavery; but that now I proposed to teach them *to work*. I said to them that there was a great deal of difference between working and being worked. I said that a man who was worked was a slave but that a man who worked was a free man. I tried to make clear to them that as long as it was necessary to have some one over them to direct, superintend and follow them up in everything which they did they would remain slaves, but as soon as they learned to work independently, to put skill and intelligence and conscience into their labor then, and not till then, would they become free. It was not easy at first, because of the prejudice that had grown up in slavery against working with the hands, to make the mass of the people see and believe that there was any advantage in having their sons taught to plow and their daughters to cook. They said these things they had done at home and now they wanted them to go to school and learn something new and different.

Nevertheless, the Tuskegee Institute has gone forward year after year, preaching the gospel of the beauty and the dignity of labor and putting it in practice in the shops, in the kitchen and on the farm. Year by year the number of students has grown as the facilities of the school have increased. Still hundreds of students are turned away every year because we have not room for them in the school grounds. In the meantime, I am glad to say the sentiment with regard to work has completely changed inside the school. Today our students are just as eager to perform the work allotted to them on the farm or in the shop as they are ready to go to a lesson in history, geography or arithmetic.

At the same time the sentiment towards work has changed among the masses of the colored people outside of the school. In fact I have always believed that the most important service which the Tuskegee Institute has performed, during its thirty years of existence, has been in the direction of changing the sentiment of the masses of the negro people in the South towards the subject of labor with the hands.

The Nautilus, 14 (Feb. 1912), 49–51. Excerpted from "The Story of Tuskegee Institute," 44–51.

An Article in the *North American Review*

February 1912

THE NEGRO AS A FARMER

One of the most striking facts that I have learned from a study of the bulletins of the 1910 census thus far issued has been the rapid and continued increase in the number of negro farmers in the Southern States. For example: there has been an increase of 469,061, or 17.9 per cent., in the total number of farms and farmers, white and colored, in the Southern States, which shows that the South is far in advance of the rest of the country, as far as concerns the increase in the number of farms. In fact, fully three-fourths of all the total increase in the number of farms in the United States during the past ten years is in the Southern States. In the North Atlantic, what we used to call in the old geographies the New England and Middle Atlantic States, there has been a decrease of almost four per cent. in the number of farms during this period. In the North Central or States of the Middle West, the increase amounts to only one per cent. There has been an increase of fifty-two per cent. in the number of farms in the Western States, but while the percentage of increase in this part of the country is large, the absolute increase in farms and farmers was only 126,336, as against an increase of 469,061 in the Southern States.

The point, however, which I wish to emphasize is that, rapid as has been the increase in total number of farms of both races in the South, the number of negro farmers has increased proportionately more rapidly than the number of white farmers. While the white farmers in fifteen Southern States increased from 1,870,600 in 1900 to 2,191,805 in 1910, the negro farmers increased from 739,835 in 1900 to 887,691 in 1910, making an increase of 17.0 per cent. for the whites and 19.9 per cent. for the blacks.

No figures have yet been published showing the relative increase, as between the white and colored people, in the number of landowners, and it does not follow, of course, that the number of negro landowners has increased in the same ratio as the number of negro farmers. In fact, the statistics of land ownership in the Southern States show that, not taking account of the different races, the total number of land-owners has increased only about half as rapidly as the total number of farmers. In what proportion the 170,032 new landowners in the South are distributed between the races, has not, so far as I know, been definitely ascertained.

While the census figures show that, taking the Southern States as a whole, the negro farmers have increased more rapidly than the white farmers, they also show that this increase has not been evenly distrib-uted throughout the South. In some States, notably in Louisiana, there has not only been no increase in the number of negro farmers, but there has been a very marked absolute decrease, a decrease of not less than 3,350 negro farmers, during the ten years.

The following table shows the actual numbers of negro farmers, to-gether with the changes and fluctuation in the numbers and proportion of the white and colored farmers in fifteen Southern States. The figures do not include Delaware or the District of Columbia, although these are usually classed in the census figures with the Southern States.

TABLE SHOWING NUMBER OF NEGRO AND WHITE FARMERS FOR
FIFTEEN SOUTHERN STATES, SHOWING INCREASE FOR EACH RACE

	1900		1910		Increase	
State	White	Colored	White	Colored	White	Colored
Alabama	129,137	94,083	152,347	110,373	23,210	16,290
Arkansas	131,711	46,983	150,920	63,355	19,209	16,372
Florida	27,288	13,526	35,125	14,709	7,837	1,183
Georgia	141,865	82,826	168,158	122,341	26,293	39,515
Kentucky	223,429	11,238	247,036	11,706	23,607	468
Louisiana	57,809	58,160	65,460	54,810	7,651	*3,350
Maryland	40,169	5,843	42,402	6,367	2,233	524
Mississippi	92,124	128,679	109,390	164,430	17,266	35,751
North Carolina	169,773	54,864	187,831	65,594	18,058	10,730
Oklahoma	94,775	13,225	168,910	20,528	74,135	7,303
South Carolina	69,954	85,401	79,484	96,696	9,530	11,295
Tennessee	190,728	33,895	207,260	38,249	16,532	4,354
Texas	286,654	65,536	346,565	69,812	59,911	4,276
Virginia	123,052	44,834	135,743	48,019	12,691	3,185
West Virginia	92,132	742	95,174	702	3,042	*40
Total	1,870,600	739,835	2,191,805	887,691	321,205	147,856

* Decrease

One of the interesting things brought out by the comparison of the different States in this table is the fact that, in the five States of Oklahoma, Texas, Virginia, Louisiana, and Florida, the number of white farmers has increased at a more rapid rate than the number of negro farmers. Five other States, West Virginia, Kentucky, Maryland, South Carolina, and Alabama show the same rate of increase for both races. In the five States, Tennessee, North Carolina, Mississippi, Georgia, and Arkansas, in which nearly half of the total negro population in the South live, negro farmers have increased during the past ten years more rapidly than the white farmers, in proportion to population of the respective races of these states.

In Georgia and Mississippi the number of negro farmers has increased both absolutely and relatively more rapidly than the same class of whites. In Georgia the number of negro farmers has grown from 82,826 in 1900 to 122,341 in 1910, a gain of 39,515 in ten years. In the same period the number of white farmers in Georgia increased from 141,865 in 1900 to 168,158 in 1910, a gain of 26,293 in ten years.

In Mississippi, where negroes now represent fifty-six per cent. of the total population and sixty per cent. of the farmers, the number of negro farmers increased from 128,679 in 1900 to 164,430 in 1910, an increase of 35,751. During the same period the number of white farmers increased from 92,124 in 1900 to 109,390 in 1910, an increase of 17,266.

Whatever else this increase of negro farmers may mean, it certainly indicates that, in proportion to their numbers, and in spite of a certain amount of negro emigration to the North and a considerable immigration of the white population to the South, negroes are entering in proportionately larger numbers into farming in the South, and becoming more and more responsible, either as owners or as tenants, for the success or failure of agriculture.

I can, perhaps, give a better idea of the part which negro farmers, as compared with white farmers, are actually taking in the agriculture of the South by comparing the statistics of farmers with the statistics of population. The following table shows the relative percentage of the white and colored in the total population of fifteen Southern States in 1900 and 1910, together with the percentage of white and colored farmers for the same periods.

TABLE SHOWING PERCENTAGE OF NEGRO AND WHITE FARMERS COMPARED WITH POPULATION OF EACH RACE

	1900				1910			
	Per Cent. of Total				Per Cent. of Total			
	Population		Farmers		Population		Farmers	
State	White	Colored	White	Colored	White	Colored	White	Colored
Alabama	54.8	45.2	58.0	42.0	57.5	42.5	58.0	42.0
Arkansas	72.0	28.0	74.0	26.0	71.8	28.2	70.0	30.0
Florida	56.3	43.7	67.0	33.0	58.9	41.1	70.0	30.0
Georgia	53.3	46.7	63.0	37.0	54.9	45.1	58.0	42.0
Kentucky	86.7	13.3	95.0	5.0	88.6	11.4	96.0	4.0
Louisiana	52.8	47.2	50.0	50.0	56.8	43.2	54.0	46.0
Maryland	80.2	19.8	87.0	13.0	82.1	17.9	87.0	13.0
Mississippi	41.3	58.7	42.0	58.0	43.7	56.3	40.0	60.0
North Carolina	66.7	33.3	76.0	24.0	68.4	31.6	74.0	26.0
Oklahoma	84.8	15.2	88.0	12.0	87.2	12.8	89.0	11.0
South Carolina	41.6	58.4	45.0	55.0	44.8	55.2	45.0	55.0
Tennessee	76.2	23.8	85.0	15.0	78.3	21.7	84.0	16.0
Texas	79.6	20.4	81.0	19.0	82.3	17.7	83.0	17.0
Virginia	64.3	35.7	73.0	27.0	67.4	32.6	74.0	26.0
West Virginia	95.5	4.5	99.0	1.0	94.7	5.3	99.0	1.0

This table shows that while the white population has grown more rapidly than the colored population in all but two of the fifteen Southern States mentioned, namely West Virginia and Arkansas, the number of white farmers has grown more rapidly than the negro farmers in only five, namely: Oklahoma, Texas, Virginia, Louisiana, and Florida. In the States of Oklahoma, Texas, and Florida, there has been a very considerable immigration of farmers from the Northern States. In Virginia there has been a very considerable decrease in the negro, as compared with the white, population. At the same time, the decrease in the number of negroes as compared with the white farmers has been only one per cent.

In Louisiana, where there seems to have been an absolute loss of 3,550 of negro farmers, conditions are not so easily explained. The white population of Louisiana has grown to some extent by immigration, and there has been a very considerable emigration from Louisiana to Arkansas and Oklahoma, and this has tended to alter the ratio of the white and colored population, but does not wholly account for the decrease in farmers, as there has been no corresponding decrease in the rate of increase in the negro population. The figures seem to indicate, therefore, that negro emigration from Louisiana westward has come almost wholly from the country districts. An explanation suggested is that the coming of the boll weevil has discouraged negro farmers in that part of the country. The boll weevil has not had the same effect elsewhere, however, so that I am disposed to attribute the decrease to local causes which are not yet wholly explained.

The census for 1910 shows, then, that there has been a proportionately larger increase in the negro than in the white farmers in the Southern States. I do not intend to suggest that this fact by itself is of any great importance. The real significance of this increase in the number and proportion of negro farmers is that it has gone along with an enormous development of Southern agriculture as a whole.

There has been, for example, an increase of $4,034,483,000 in the total values of farm lands and buildings during the last ten years, and an increase of $112,284,000 in the value of farm machinery. The South is spending $74,324,000 more for farm labor and $46,145,000 more for fertilizers in 1910 than it did in 1900. While there has been a very large decrease in the farm acreage in the South, due principally to the fact that hundreds of thousands of acres of mountain, timber, and swamp land, reported as farms in 1900 and used to some extent for grazing purposes, were not reported as farms in 1910. At the same time there has been an increase of 24,058,000 acres in the amount of improved land, and an average decrease of from fifteen to thirty acres in the size of farms. The decrease has been fifteen acres for farms in the South Atlantic, and thirty acres for farms in the South-Central States. Both these facts indicate a more intensive and higher type of farming; indicate, in short, that farmers were putting more labor and more intelligence into the cultivation of the soil in 1910 than they did in 1900.

There has been a larger increase in value of farm lands and a larger increase in expenditures for labor and for fertilizers in the Southern States than in any other part of the country, except the Western States. If one compares the different geographical divisions, as to the increase in land values, it appears that in the North Atlantic States there has been an increase of 27 per cent. in the value of farming lands and buildings; in the North Central States this increase has been 114 per cent.; in the South Atlantic the increase has been 105 per cent.; in the South Central, 133 per cent.; and in the West 193 per cent.

The value of an acre of farm land has increased 32 per cent. in the North Atlantic; 99 per cent. in the North Central; 110 per cent. in the South Atlantic; 152 per cent. in the South Central; 157 per cent. in the Western States.

Not only has this great advance been made in the South, where the Negro has a proportionately larger share in agriculture than he had a decade ago, but if we compare the Southern States in which the number of negroes is proportionately large with those States in which it is proportionately small, it will be seen that there has been on the whole just as much progress, if not more, where the proportion of negro farmers was large as where it was small. The following table shows the percentage of negro and white farmers, and the percentages of increase in the average value per acre of land in the different Southern States. In these tables, the first seven States are arranged in the order of the percentage of negro farmers, and the last eight in the order of the percentage of white farmers.

PERCENTAGE OF NEGRO AND WHITE FARMERS IN SEVEN STATES
HAVING HIGHEST PERCENTAGE OF NEGRO FARMERS WITH
AVERAGE INCREASE IN LAND PER ACRE IN EACH STATE

State	Per Cent. Negro Farmers	Per Cent. White Farmers	Per Cent. Increase In Value of Land Per Acre
Mississippi	60	40	115
South Carolina	55	45	172
Louisiana	46	54	78
Georgia	42	58	156
Alabama	42	58	113
Arkansas	30	70	118
Florida	30	70	141

PERCENTAGE OF NEGRO AND WHITE FARMERS IN EIGHT STATES
HAVING HIGHEST PERCENTAGE OF WHITE FARMERS WITH
AVERAGE INCREASE IN LAND PER ACRE IN EACH STATE

State	Per Cent. Negro Farmers	Per Cent. White Farmers	Per Cent. Increase In Value of Land Per Acre
West Virginia	01	99	67
Kentucky	05	95	65
Oklahoma	11	89	245
Maryland	13	87	41
Tennessee	16	84	84
Texas	17	83	204
Virginia	26	74	100
North Carolina	26	74	138

From all these figures, it would seem to be apparent that, in spite of all that is said to the contrary, the negro in the South is beginning to heed the advice of those who have told him to stick to the farm. It does not follow from this, however, that negro farmers are sticking fast on the land on which they were planted years ago. On the contrary, the census figures show that there is a very considerable movement of the negro population to the new territory, where there is opportunity to better their condition, as in the case of the negro population in Oklahoma, which has grown 147 per cent. in the past ten years. But, on the whole, the negro is sticking to the soil.

At the same time these figures prove, it would appear, that the negro is able and willing to improve in his methods of farming. It is evident that all this advance in land values would not have taken place in spite of the negro. He must have had, as he has always had, his share during this time, in the work of building up the farming industry in the South, and, considering the little education he has had in agriculture and the limitations owing to his lack of general education that prevented his taking advantage of the opportunities for improvement that are offered to farmers in other parts of the country, it must be admitted that he has done well.

Booker T. Washington

North American Review, 195 (Feb. 1912), 175–81.

To Henry Lee Higginson

Lakeland, Fla. March 5th, 1912

My dear Major Higginson: I have sent you some papers this week giving some account of an educational campaign which I have been making through the state of Florida. I have been reaching large numbers of both white and colored people and arousing them on the subject of education and speaking against lynching and other crimes, and trying to bring about better relations between black people and white people, and I am glad to say that the trip is a great success.

I have been spending considerable time trying to increase our endowment fund and have had some success, but in the meantime we have run considerably behind in our current expenses.

I shall hope to see you when I am again in Boston. Yours very truly,

Booker T. Washington

TLS   Henry Lee Higginson Collection   MH.

A Press Release on Washington's Tour of Florida

Jacksonville, Fla., March 8. [1912]

Dr. Booker T. Washington concluded his tour of Florida here last night, speaking before an audience of about 2,500 white and colored persons in Duval Theatre. In order to make the engagement in Jacksonville, it was necessary for the party to come to Jacksonville by special train from Daytona, the preceding stop, and reached the city about 5 p.m. An elaborate program had been arranged by the Jacksonville Negro Business League, including a drive about the city, a banquet in Odd Fellows Hall, and a drive the next day to the various colored schools of the city, and seeing the various points of interest. Dr. Washington left the city Friday night for Chicago, where he has important engagements connected with his Tuskegee interests.

At Jacksonville, an original song was sung by a chorus from the Clinton Graded School, and he was introduced by Hon. G. C. Bedell,[1] member of the School Board.

Throughout the state, from Pensacola to the Southern points and up the East Coast to Jacksonville, Dr. Washington received one ovation, by white and colored people alike, as if the whole populace was responsive to his efforts to promote the progress of the negro people in the South and to bring about more friendly relations between the races.

Leaving Pensacola Friday morning, March 2nd, his car attracted attention along the route for 250 miles, and in many instances he was compelled to come to the rear platform in order that the waiting throngs might see the distinguished negro. Many an old woman or man, who had seen slavery, shouted for joy on beholding what time had brought forth in the person of the distinguished leader of the race. At Quincy, where a twenty-minute stop was made, the entire student body of the Quincy Graded School met Dr. Washington, the children waving flags and singing America. Little Altia Hart, a young miss of about ten years presented Dr. Washington a beautiful bouquet of flowers in very choice sentiments, to which he responded gracefully and appropriately. W. A. King, principal of the Quincy Dunbar School, led the delegation that greeted the Doctor.

Fully 5,000 people gathered at the station to meet Dr. Washington when the train reached Tallahassee. A parade made up of negro farmers, artisans and professional men, headed by the brass band from the Florida State Normal School was quickly formed, Dr. Washington speaking to the audience in the open air in the Public Square. An informal reception was given in honor of the visitors at the chapel of the State Normal School, presided over by Prof. N. B. Young, principal, at which short addresses were made by Hon. J. C. Napier, register of the treasury; Dr. M. W. Gilbert, president of Selma University; Dr. George C. Hall, of Chicago, and Alain LeRoy Locke, of Philadelphia.

It was at Lake City, only a few weeks previous that six negro men were quietly and silently hung on a Sunday morning, who had been brought there for safe keeping. The town otherwise bears a notorious reputation, noteworthy for keeping its negroes in their place. Practically all of Sunday was spent in that town. The beautiful lakes from which it derives its name were inspected and an excellent dinner served at the residence of Prof. L. A. Jones, principal of the colored schools. A crowd that completely filled the Court House heard Dr. Washington['s] speech, but at the beginning, there could be plainly seen disapproval on the faces of many of the white people in the audience. Gri[m-]visaged, stoic-looking, they were a hard set to move, and of course had a corresponding effect upon the colored people in the audience. That he completely mastered that set of men, who were there determined to disapprove of the teachings of Dr. Washington, and wrought from some of them hearty handshakes and the highest endorsement of his position, goes a long way in proving the fact that his position on racial matters is the most tenable and far reaching.

At Ocala, the situation was entirely different. Here one found the utmost freedom of movement, found two negroes on the board of aldermen, found negroes owning drug stores, grocery stores, big farms, and owning fine carriages, automobiles and well appointed homes without number. Here Dr. Washington was introduced by Judge W. S. Bullock,[2] in an address that for sincerity and the highest praise can have no equal.

"In presenting this distinguished citizen to you, my friends," said Judge Bullock, "I feel that I speak with prophetic vision when I say that the evidences point that God has again rambled amongst the hills and dales of the old dominion and produced a leader for this benighted and unfortunate race of people according to his own choosing. Dr. Washington needs no introduction to you. His fame has far preceded his coming in our midst. The few paltry words of commendation that I might utter would be a poor tribute to his worth. His great work in the interest of the negro erects a monument to the negro race that is more lasting than tablets of stone. His precept and example to the negro race stands as a beacon light whose lustre can not be dimmed, shunning the bogs and sandbars, logs and snags, across the channel of their advancement. We must esteem ourselves most favored to have such a man to come in our midst. He is an inspiration to every negro in this land and a benefactor to this nation.

"Dr. Washington, you are engaged in a great work. We sympathise with you in the delicate and arduous undertaking. The intelligent patriotism of this country is sustaining you. My countrymen and my friends, I commend to you our distinguished guest on this occasion. He comes upon a mission that we welcome. He is the leader of the negro race in America. In our fair lands he destroys the idols that have been erected by demagogue[s] and unworthy politicians, and is erecting in their stead schools of industry and intelligence. He is taking the benighted, vicious, ignorant and superstitious negro from their [his] condition and clothing him in the garments of industry, intelligence and morality. In short, he is qualifying the negro for citizenship. His work entitles him to our aid and co-operation. I commend him to your intelligent consideration, and ask that you extend to him in this work the hand and heart of encouragement."

From Ocala to Tampa, the party went, where Dr. Washington spoke in the Tampa Bay Casino,[3] and where he was heard by a large number of colored people, as well as Northern tourists who were stopping at the Tampa Bay and other leading hotels of the city. A Spanish supper after the program was given by the Local Business League.

At Lakeland, Dr. Washington was introduced by Gen. J. A. Cox, an ex-Confederate soldier, who represented the County School Board. Dr. Washington here received the most remarkable tribute of his life. General Cox is a typical Southerner of the old School, and referred in a feeling manner to his experiences with the slaves on his father's plantation when a boy, and to the fidelity of his own slaves when he went to war. The General declared that when he set forth to the war there was a fight between six of his men slaves as to which should accompany him, and that to the herculean efforts of his aide, he now owed his life. This boy, he declared bore him off the field wounded when the Federal soldiers were within fifty yards of his body, and that while no white person save his wife, aged father and child were left on the plantation, they were tenderly cared for and protected by the thirty odd slaves remaining. "God forbid that I should now say one word or do one thing against the negro," he said in closing his address.

A special train was secured to conduct the party from Lakeland to Eatonville, the seat of the Robert Hungerford Normal and Industrial School. The Hungerford school was begun several years ago by R. C. Calhoun, a graduate of the Tuskegee Institute, and in many respects has grown to be one of the most useful schools that have come out of Tuskegee. Since the death of Mr. Calhoun, the principal and founder, the work has been carried on by Mrs. Calhoun[4] and an able corps of assistants. Some misunderstanding in the itinerary led the people of Eatonville and surrounding territory to expect Dr. Washington at ten o'clock in the morning, and several thousand colored people as well [as] a number of the tourists who make their winter homes in the community had gathered to hear him. The crowd had not in the least abated at five o'clock when Dr. Washington and his party reached the grounds. Some old time plantation singing was done by the students in a creditable manner, and after Dr. Washington had concluded, several other members of the party delivered short addresses.

Palatka and Daytona were visited the next day. The speaking occurred in Howell Theatre at Palatka, after the party had visited the colored schools and had otherwise received marked courtesy at the hands of the colored citizens. At Daytona, the entire party were the guests of the Girls Industrial School, of which Mrs. Mary Bethune is principal. Dr. Washington made one address in the evening at the First Presbyterian Church to a large audience of colored people, and the next morning at the Theatre, to an audience, composed, for the most part of white people, winter tourists and natives of the community. The audience was responsive to a high degree and frequently applauded the remarks of the noted educator.

Throughout the trip Register of the Treasury J. C. Napier received marked attention, as did also Dr. George C. Hall, Major R. R. Moton and Alain LeRoy Locke. Judging from the large crowds that heard Dr. Washington during the seven days, the applause that greeted nearly every utterance, and the sympathetic and encouraging editorials in most of the newspapers, his trip through Florida will prove most helpful to the people of both races.

TMc Con. 826 BTW Papers DLC.

[1] George C. Bedell practiced law in Jacksonville, Fla., from 1897 to 1949. In 1911–12 he was a member of the Jacksonville Board of Public Instruction.

[2] William S. Bullock was a circuit court judge in Florida's fifth judicial district for many years beginning in 1908.

[3] A printed version of BTW's speech of Mar. 4, 1912, and an account of the ceremonies and those in attendance is in Con. 457, BTW Papers, DLC.

[4] Mary Clinton attended Tuskegee Institute from 1885 to 1890 but did not graduate. After teaching at Voorhees Normal and Industrial School in South Carolina, she married Russell C. Calhoun, a Tuskegee graduate of 1896, and both began work at what became Robert Hungerford Normal and Industrial School. When R. C. Calhoun died in 1910, she succeeded him as principal.

To Emmett Jay Scott

Boston, March 20, 1912

Dear Mr. Scott: Du Bois and his aggregation are going to meet in Chicago the latter part of April. I wish you would ask Mr. Hosmer[1] in his own way to get into close touch with what is going on in Chicago in connection with this organization, and keep us informed.[2]

B. T. W.

TLI Con. 456 BTW Papers DLC. Docketing indicates that the letter was sent to Cornelius B. Hosmer, who returned it with thanks.

[1] Cornelius Bailey Hosmer of Covington, La., graduated from Tuskegee Institute in 1906. For three years he worked as a midwestern agent of Tuskegee, soliciting funds and managing the summer tours of the student quartet. BTW reprimanded Hosmer in 1911 for a letter he had written to a married woman but allowed him to continue working for the school. (BTW to Hosmer, Nov. 21, 1911, Con. 424, BTW Papers, DLC.) In the fall of 1912 he resigned to take a position at the Robert Hungerford Normal and Industrial School in Eatonville, Fla., but a year later he returned to his old position as field agent. In 1914 he moved to the Tuskegee campus as rural school field agent and manager of the school's publication, *The Negro Farmer*.

[2] Hosmer in two letters reported details of the local sponsors, speakers, and topics of the NAACP convention. "Du Bois and Villard are expected to be very bitter; and radical in their speeches," he informed Scott, but he had heard that the resolutions "will be mild, tame, and generally conservative." (Apr. 6, 1912, Con. 456, BTW Papers, DLC.) Two days later, he reported that O. G. Villard had said at a banquet in his honor that Tuskegee was doing good work but that it was only a "very small part of what *must* be done in order to *free* the Negro in America." (Apr. 8, 1912, Con. 456, BTW Papers, DLC.)

To Charles Dewey Hilles

Boston, March 20, 1912

Personal and Confidential

My dear Mr. Hilles: I understand on pretty good authority that there is to be a change made soon in the office of Assistant Register of the Treasury.

I very much hope that in case Mr. Cyrus F. Adams gets out of this position, Mr. Phil Waters, of Charleston, West Virginia will be appointed. President Taft already knows about Mr. Waters. Senator Scott, and other prominent Republicans in West Virginia, have urged his appointment.

Just now, the appointment of Waters would strengthen the President in West Virginia for the nomination, and would also be of great value to him during the campaign, after the President's nomination.

I understand that there are two other candidates for the position —

one a clerk by the name of Harlan,[1] who is now connected with the Treasury Department. The appointment of Harlan will not only be of no service to the President, but will really hurt, for the reason that he is nothing but a clerk and has no influence. Besides, he has the reputation of trying to pass for white whenever he can.

I also understand that certain people are urging the appointment of Mr. Alain LeRoy Locke, the young colored Rhodes scholar. While he is an excellent young fellow, his appointment will bring no strength to the President, as he is wholly unknown as a public factor. Yours very truly,

Booker T. Washington

TLS   William Howard Taft Papers   DLC.   Docketed: "Did not we promise this to an Arkansas man   W H T."

[1] Robert J. Harlan, Jr., son of the nineteenth-century black Republican leader Robert J. Harlan of Cincinnati, was a clerk in the office of the Surgeon General from 1899 to 1902 and a clerk in the office of Register of the Treasury from 1903 to 1914 and 1917 to 1924. (Gerber, *Black Ohio*, 117–18, 123, 325–26.)

An Article in *The Continent*

Mar. 21, 1912

IN DARKER LONDON WITH JOHN BURNS

I had heard a good deal, from time to time, about John Burns before I went to Europe, and when I reached London, a year or more ago, I took advantage of the first opportunity that offered to make my acquaintance with him a personal one. This meeting was a special good fortune to me at the time because, as I already knew, there is in all probability no one in England who better understands the hopes, ambitions and the prospects of the laboring classes than the Right Honorable John Burns, president of the local government board, himself the first laboring man to become a member of the British cabinet.

John Burns was born in poverty and went to work at the age of 10. He has known what it is to wander the streets of London for weeks and months looking for work. He had an experience of this kind once after he had lost his job because he made a socialistic speech. Having learned by experience the life of that industrial outcast, the casual laborer, he organized in 1889 the great dock laborers' strike, which brought together into the labor unions 100,000 starving and disorganized laborers who had previously been shut out from the protection of organized labor. Besides that he has been an agitator; he was for years a marked man, and at one time gained the name of "the man with the red flag." He has several times been arrested for making speeches and was once imprisoned for three months on the charge of rioting.

Meanwhile he had become the idol of the working masses and even won the admiration and respect of the leaders of public opinion. He was elected in 1889 to the first London county council, where he worked side by side with such distinguished men as Frederic Harrison[1] and Lord Rosebery.[2] He was chosen a member of parliament in 1890, where he became distinguished for the store of practical information which he had accumulated during his experience in the London county council.

BURNS ONCE AN ENGINEER IN AFRICA

When he was 21 years of age Mr. Burns went as an engineer to Africa, where he spent a year among the swamps of the Lower Niger, occasionally fighting alligators and devoting his leisure to the study of political economy. When he returned he spent the money he had saved in Africa in six months of travel and study in Europe.

Speaking of what he learned in Africa, Burns once said: "You talk of savagery and misery and slavery in heathen lands, but from my own experience I can tell you that there is more of these, and more degradation of women, in the slums of London than you will see on the west coast of Africa."

He has had a wider experience than most men with mobs, for he has not only led them but in 1900 he defended himself with a cricket bat for two days in his home in Lavender Hill, Battersea, against a mob said to number 10,000, which hurled stones through the windows and tried to batter down the door of his house because he had denounced the Boer war in parliament.

In 1906, after he had been successful in writing something like a hundred labor laws into the acts of parliament, he accepted the position of president of the local government board and then became, as I have said, the first laboring man to accept a place in the British cabinet.

HIS CHOICE BETWEEN OFFICE AND "AGITATION"

In reply to the criticisms which were offered when he accepted this high and responsible position in the government, Burns said: "I had to choose whether, for the next ten years, I should indulge, perhaps in the futility of faction, possibly in the impotence of intrigue, or whether I should accept an office which in our day and generation I can make useful of good works." I have noted this statement because I suspect this choice is one that most reformers and agitators have to face sooner or later.

He recognized, as he said, that "the day of the agitator was declining and that of the administrator had begun," and he did not shrink from accepting a position where he became responsible for administering laws he had helped to make. In his present position as the head of the local government board, Mr. Burns is probably doing more than any other single man to improve the situation of the poor man in London and in the other large cities of England.

It is a rare thing for a man who began life in poverty to find himself in middle life in a position of such power and usefulness as the head of one great branch of the British government occupies. It is still more remarkable, however, that a man who began life as an agitator, the representative of the unemployed, the most helpless and unfortunate class in the community, should find himself a comparatively few years later charged with the task of carrying into effect the reforms which he had preached from the prisoner's dock in a police court. It is all the more fortunate for England that the government has found a man with these qualifications, who has at the same time the training and qualities of a statesman, to carry the reforms into effect. As Mr. Burns himself once said, "Depend upon it, there are no such places for making a public man as Pentonville prison and the London county council."

To me, however, the most surprising thing about it all is that a man with this history and qualifications should have found his way, by the ordinary methods of politics, into a position he is so well fitted to fill. It suggests to me that, in spite of all the misery that one still may see in London, in England, at least, there is hope for the man farthest down.

It is not my purpose to write a biography of John Burns but rather to describe what I saw, under his direction, of what has already been done in London in the work of what I have called "reconstruction."

It seemed to me, however, that it would not be out of place to say something, by way of introduction, in regard to the man who is, perhaps, as much if not more than anyone else, responsible for the work of rebuilding London now going on, and whose life is connected in a peculiar way with that part of the city. I had opportunity to visit with him the improvements that have been made there.

What the Boy Promised His Mother

John Burns was born and still lives in Battersea, a quarter of the city inhabited for the most part by artisans, mechanics and laborers of various kinds, with a sprinkling of gipsy peddlers and the very poor. Battersea is directly across the river from and in plain sight of the parliament buildings, and there is a story to the effect that as Burns was coming home one winter night, helping his mother carry home the washing by which she supported herself and family, the two stopped within the shadow of those buildings to rest. Turning to his mother the boy said: "Mother, if ever I have health and strength no mother shall have to work as you do." He has health and strength and is now making a brave effort to keep that promise to his mother. Aside from Colonel Roosevelt, I do not think I ever saw a man who seemed his equal in vigor of mind and body; who seemed able to compress so much into a short space of time; or one who goes at the task before him with a greater zest. In all England I do not believe there is a man who works harder, accomplishes more for the good of his country and the world, or one who is happier in the work he is doing.

I found him late in August, when everyone else connected with the government had left London on vacations, buried deep in the details and concerns of his office, but chock full of energy, enthusiasm and high spirits.

What Burns is doing, and the spirit in which he is doing it, will perhaps appear in the course of my description of a trip which I took with him through his own district of Battersea and the region adjoining it, to see what the London county council is doing there to make the life of the poor man better. I am sorry I shall not be able to describe all I saw on the trip, because we covered in a short time so much ground, and saw so many different things, that it was not until I had returned to my hotel and had an opportunity to study out the route of that journey that I was able to get any definite idea of the direction in which we went or of the connection and general plan which under-lay the whole scheme of improvement.

I think it was about 2 o'clock in the afternoon when we left the offices of the local government board. Mr. Burns insisted before we started that I see something of the parliamentary buildings, and he promised to act as my guide. This hasty trip through the buildings served to show me that John Burns, although he entered political high life as a socialist, had a profound reverence for all the historic traditions, and a very intimate knowledge of English history. I shall not soon forget the eloquent and vivid manner in which he summoned up for me, as we passed through Westminster hall on the way to the house of commons, some of the great historic scenes and events which had taken place in the ancient and splendid room. I was not only impressed by the familiarity which he showed with all the associations of the place, but I was thrilled by the enthusiasm with which he spoke of and described them. It struck me as very strange that the same John Burns once known as "the man with the red flag," who had once been imprisoned for leading a mob of workingmen against the police, should be quoting history with all the enthusiasm of a student and a scholar.

In the course of our journey we passed through a small strip of Chelsea. I remember that among the other places we passed he pointed out the home of Thomas Carlyle. I found he was just as familiar with names and deeds of all the great literary persons who had lived in that quarter of London as he was with the political history.

When he afterwards told me he had had very little education in school, because he had been compelled to go to work when he was 10 years of age, I asked him how he had since found time, in the course of his busy life, to gain the wide knowledge of history and literature which he evidently possessed.

"You see," he replied, with a quiet smile, "I earned my living for a time as a candle maker, and I have burned a good many candles at night ever since."

PROVIDING DECENT HOMES FOR WORKERS

Mr. Burns had promised to show me, within the space of a few hours, examples of the sort of work which is now going on in every part of London. A few years ago, on the site of an ancient prison, the London county council erected several blocks of workingmen's tene-ments. These were, I believe, the first, or nearly the first, of the tenements erected by the city in the work of clearing away unsanitary areas and providing decent homes for the working classes.

It was to these buildings, in which a population of about 4,000 persons live, that we went first. The buildings are handsome brick structures, well lighted, with wide, open brick-paved courts between the rows of houses, so that each block looked like a gigantic letter "H" with the horizontal connecting line left out.

Of course these buildings were, as someone said, little more than barracks compared with the houses that are now being erected for laboring people in some of the London suburbs, but they were clean and wholesome, and to anyone familiar with the narrow, grimy streets in the east end of London it was hard to believe that they stood in the midst of a region which a few years ago had been a typical London slum.

Just below here we crossed the river, into what Mr. Burns referred to as "my own district," Battersea, where he was born and where he has lived and worked all his life, except for the year spent as an engineer in Africa.

The great breathing place for the people of this region is Battersea park, and as we sped along the edge of the beautiful green space, stopping to look for a moment at the refreshment booths or the cricket grounds, or to speak to a group of well-dressed boys going from school to the playgrounds, Mr. Burns interspersed his information about workmen's wages, the price of rents and the general improvement of the laboring classes, with comment on the historic associations of the places we passed. Where Battersea park now stands there was formerly a foul and unwholesome swamp. Near here the Duke of Wellington had fought a duel with the Earl of Winchilsea, and a little farther up Julius Caesar, nearly 2,000 years ago, forded the river with one of his legions.

FRIENDLY GREETINGS FROM BATTERSEA FOLK

It was a happy and novel experience to observe the pleasure which Mr. Burns took in pointing out improvement in the people, in the dwellings and in the life of the people generally, and to note in turn the familiar and cheerful way with which all sorts of people we met on the streets greeted him as we passed.

"Hello, Johnny Burns!" a group of school boys would call as we passed. Once we passed by a group of some fifteen or twenty workingwomen sitting in one of the refreshment booths drinking their afternoon tea, apparently holding a neighborhood meeting of some kind or other. As they recognized the man who, as a member of the London county council, had been responsible for most of the improvements that had been made in the homes and surroundings in which they lived, they stood up and waved their handkerchiefs and even attempted a faint and feminine "Hurrah for Johnny Burns!" the member from Battersea.

There are 150,000 people in Battersea, but Mr. Burns seemed to be acquainted with every one of them, and when he wanted to show me the inside of some new "county council houses," as they are called, did not hesitate to knock at the nearest doors, where we were gladly welcomed. The people seemed to be just as proud of their new houses and of Mr. Burns as he was of them.

The houses which we visited were, some of them, no more than three or four rooms, but every one of them was as sweet and wholesome as if they had been palaces. They were very compactly built but provided with every sort of modern convenience, including electric lights and baths.

There were houses of five and six rooms, which were intended for clerks and small business men and rented for a pound a week, and there were cheaper houses for ordinary laboring people, which rented for $2 per week. These houses are built directly under the direction of the London county council and are expected to pay 3 per cent upon the investment after completion.

The London county council was not the first to make the experiment of building decent and substantial houses for the laboring classes. Some thirty years before, on what is known as the Shaftesbury Park estate, 1,200 houses, which provide homes for 11,000 people, were erected and the investment had been made to pay.

I looked down the long lanes of little vine-covered buildings which make up this estate. It seemed as if some great army had settled on the land and built permanent quarters.

These labor colonies were interesting, not merely for the improvement they had made in the lives of a large section of the people living in this part of the city but as the forerunner of those garden cities which private enterprise has erected at places like Port Sunlight, near Liverpool; Bourneville, in the outskirts of Birmingham, and at Letchworth, thirty-four miles from London.

PUBLIC BATHS, WASHHOUSE AND GYMNASIUM

Not far from Battersea park, and in a part of the city which was formerly inhabited almost wholly by the very poor, we visited the public baths and a public washhouse where, during the course of a year, 42,000 women come to wash their clothes, paying at the rate of 3 cents an hour for the use of the municipal tubs and hot water. Children pay a penny, or 2 cents, for the use of the public baths. The building is provided with a gymnasium for the use of the children in winter, and also contains a hall which is rented to workingmen's clubs at a nominal price.

What pleased me most was to see the orderly way in which the children had learned to conduct themselves in these places, which, as was evident, had become not merely places for recreation but, at the same time, a school of good manners.

We passed on the streets groups of neatly dressed, well-bred looking boys, with their books slung over their arms, going home from school or making their way to the park. Mr. Burns was delighted at the sight of these clean-cut, manly looking fellows. "Look at those boys, Mr. Washington," he would exclaim, as he pointed proudly to one or another of these groups. "Isn't that doing pretty well for the proletariat?"

Then he would leap out of the automobile, before the driver could stop, put his arm around the boy nearest him and in a moment come back triumphant with the confirmation of his statement that the boy's father was, as he had said, only a small clerk or a letter carrier, or, perhaps, the son of a common laborer, a navvy.

When I contrasted the appearance of these well-dressed and well-behaved boys with some of those I had seen elsewhere, with the children who attend the so-called "ragged" schools, for example, I understood and shared his enthusiasm.

From Battersea park we went to Clapham common, and as we were speeding along through what appeared to be a quarter of well-to-do artisans' homes Mr. Burns nodded casually in the direction of a little vine-clad cottage and said:

"That is where I live."

Although Mr. Burns now occupies one of the highest positions in the British government, in which he has a salary of $10,000 a year, he has not yet assumed the high hat and the long-tailed coat which is the recognized uniform in London of a gentleman. On the contrary, he wears the same blue reefer coat and felt hat, speaks the same language, lives in the same style and is apparently in every respect the same man that he was when he was living on the $25 a week guaranteed him by the Battersea labor league when he entered parliament. He is still a laboring man and proud of the class to which he belongs.

It was at Clapham common, although Mr. Burns did not mention this fact, that he was arrested for the first time away back in 1878 for making a public speech. It was somewhere in this region, if I remember rightly, that he pointed out to us a private estate on which 3,000 houses of the cheaper class had been erected.

A COMPETITOR OF THE SALOONS

"And, mind you, there is no public house," said Mr. Burns. Instead he showed us a brand new temperance billiard hall which had been erected to compete with, and take the place of, the barrooms which had disappeared.

At Lower Tooting, an estate of some thirty-eight acres, the London county council is building outright a city of something like 5,000 inhabitants, laying out the streets, building the houses, even putting a tidy little flower garden in each separate front door yard. It was as if the county council had gone to playing dolls, so completely planned and perfectly carried out in every detail is this little garden city.

Mr. Burns, who has all his life been an advocate of temperance, although he had once served as pot boy in a public house, pointed out here as he did elsewhere that there was no public house.

In the building of this little paradise all the architectural and engineering problems had indeed been solved. There remained, however, the problem of human nature, and the question that I asked myself was, Will these people be able to live up to their surroundings?

It is fortunate, in this connection, that in John Burns the inhabitants have a leader who dares to speak plainly to them of their faults as well as of their virtues and who is able at the same time to inspire them with an ambition and enthusiasm for the better life which is opened to them. Engineering and architecture cannot do everything, but education — leadership of the right sort — may complete what they have begun.

At Warden street and Lydden road, on our way back to the city, we stopped to look for a moment at what Mr. Burns said was the most wretched part of the population in that quarter of the city. The houses were two-story dwellings, with the sills flush with the pavement, in front of which groups of lounging idle men and women stood or squatted on the pavement. A portion of the street was given up to gipsy vans and the whole population was made up, as I learned, of peddlers and pushcart venders, a class of people who, in the very center of civilization, manage somehow to maintain a nomadic and half barbarous existence, wandering from one place to another with the seasons, living from hand to mouth, working irregularly and not more than half the time.

A little farther on we passed by the Price candy factory, "where I began work at a dollar a week," said Mr. Burns in passing. A group of workmen were just coming from the factory as we passed and the men recognized Mr. Burns and shouted to him as he passed. Then we drove on back across the Chelsea bridge and along the river to the parliament buildings again.

"Now," said Mr. Burns at the end of our journey, "you have seen a sample of what London is doing for its laboring population. If you went farther you would see much, but little that is new or different."

The Continent, 43 (Mar. 21, 1912), 389–91.

[1] Frederic Harrison (1831–1923), English positivist philosopher, was an alderman on the London County Council in 1889.

[2] Archibald Philip Primrose, fifth Earl of Rosebery, was Liberal foreign secretary (1886, 1892–94) and prime minister (1894–95).

Charles William Anderson to Emmett Jay Scott

New York, N.Y. March 27, 1912

Personal

My dear Emmett: As you will see by the papers, the Taft forces swept the city at the Primaries yesterday. The Colonel did not win a single delegate in Greater New York. He will get one, however, as Comptroller Prendergast,[1] who is for him, was elected without contest. It was a sad sight to see this great man in the hands of a lot of little grafters of both colors. His tardiness in getting into the ring was responsible for this, as every influential man of both races had already been committed to President Taft. The following colored men handled the black end of the Roosevelt movement: Isaac B. Allen, late of

Boston; W. T. R. Richardson; Roscoe Simmons; George Harris[2] of the Amsterdam News; Charles E. Conick[3] and a few other little fellows, with James C. Thomas as president of the Roosevelt Colored County Committee, Harris secretary, and Henry Parker,[4] treasurer. None of these men knew whether they were afoot or horse-back, but the black election districts of Harlem went overwhelmingly for Roosevelt, but not through the leadership of any of these gentlemen. The colored troops simply would not vote for Mr. Taft. The white districts, however, went for Taft all over the city. Hence, the colored brethren were unable to help their friend. I caused Wilford H. Smith to be named as alternate on the regular ticket, and when the Roosevelt people put up their ticket they named E. A. Johnson, formerly of North Carolina, against Smith. Of course, Smith won by a handsome plurality. I was elected a delegate to the State Convention; a member of the County Committee of this County and a member of the Congressional Committee. But so much for politics.

After my three weeks serious illness, I am feeling something like my old self again. I have, however, to be a little careful with myself from now on.

With kind regards to the friends and family, I remain, Yours truly,

Charles W. Anderson

P.S. It provokingly happens that I am spitting blood again today.

C. A.

TLS Con. 447 BTW Papers DLC. Postscript in Anderson's hand.

[1] William Ambrose Prendergast (1867–1954), comptroller of New York City from 1910 to 1917, nominated Theodore Roosevelt at the Progressive convention in 1912 and headed his campaign in Brooklyn. Returning to the Republican party, he was chairman of the state public service commission from 1921 to 1930.

[2] George Wesley Harris (1884–1948) graduated from Harvard in 1907, attended Harvard Law School for a year, was briefly associate editor of the New York *Age,* and edited the New York *Amsterdam News* from 1910 to 1913. For several years thereafter he published the New York *News.* He was a New York City alderman (1920–24) and remained active in local Republican politics. He was at one time an organizer of local chapters for the NNBL, and at the time of his death was president of the Harlem Association of Trade and Commerce.

[3] Charles E. Conick, a black resident of Yonkers, N.Y., was stenographer or clerk at various times for Theodore Roosevelt, his nephew Douglas Robinson, the surrogate court at White Plains, N.Y., and the homicide bureau of the King's County district attorney's office.

[4] Possibly Henry C. Parker, of John E. Nail's black real estate firm.

To Mary Caroline Moore

[Tuskegee, Ala.] March 28, 1912

My dear Miss Moore: I regret very much to be so tardy in answering your letter,[1] but the fact is, I have been on the train in the South and in the North almost continuously for the last month.

It is a matter of deep concern to me to hear that there is any plan that will result in the dissolution of the Framingham Normal School. While I do not live in the state of Massachusetts, I have been in such close touch with the school at Framingham that I almost feel that it is a part of my life and, therefore, I hope I may be excused as an outsider, for expressing an opinion.

From the very first, Framingham has had a warm place in the heart of the colored people of this country. Some of the very first colored teachers who were sent out immediately after the freedom of the Negro race were graduates of Framingham. Miss Olivia Davidson, who afterwards became Mrs. Washington, as you know, was a graduate of Framingham and we have had several graduates in our employment. Few influences, if any, were more vital and important in the establishment of Tuskegee than the helpful ideas and influences which Miss Davidson got at Framingham. We have always felt that Framingham had an important part in the founding of this institution. Further than that, many of the ideas and methods used in education here have been gotten from Framingham.

I am sure that I speak not only for this institution, but for a wide circle of colored people throughout the country when I say that it would be a matter of deep regret to have the school at Framingham dissolved.

Though it may seem rather personal, I might add, also, that I am greatly indebted to Framingham for the helpful training which my daughter received there. Yours very truly,

[Booker T. Washington]

TLp Con. 919 BTW Papers DLC. Enclosed with a personal letter of the same date.

[1] Mary C. Moore to BTW, Mar. 2, 1912, Con. 919, BTW Papers, DLC. Moore appealed to BTW for aid in the campaign to save the Framingham Normal School from dissolution or from being converted into a school only for the training of teachers in "household arts."

To Charles Dewey Hilles

Tuskegee Institute, Alabama
March Twenty-ninth, Nineteen Hundred Twelve

Personal.

My dear Mr. Hilles: I do not believe that either you or President Taft have any accurate knowledge of what the lily white Republicans are doing in such states as Virginia, North Carolina and Texas to completely eliminate colored people from all party councils.

Aside from the inherent wrong of this action, it is going to prove exceedingly hurtful and dangerous to the President, after he is nominated, in the canvass for the election.

These lily white Republicans are not going to contribute a single electoral vote for the President in November, but their action, I fear, is going to alienate from the President hundreds and thousands of Negro votes in the North and West, where the Negroes' votes are counted.

I am wondering if some definite, plain word could not be said to these lily white Republicans that would make them reasonable.

The Republican party is about as effective in Alabama, Georgia and Florida as it is in most of the Southern states, and in these latter states there is no appreciable attempt made to eliminate the Negro.

Enclosed I send you two editorials taken from colored papers, bearing upon the action of the lily whites. Yours very truly,

Booker T. Washington

TLS   William Howard Taft Papers   DLC.

An Article in the *Annals of the American Academy of Political and Social Science*

March 1912

THE RURAL NEGRO COMMUNITY

The first rural Negro communities were started in slavery times. They were established by free Negroes, who emigrated from the

South, in order to escape the hardships of the "Black Laws" which, particularly in the latter days of slavery, bore with unusual severity upon the class known as "free persons of color." The establishment of the American colony of Liberia, Africa, was a result of this desire on the part of free colored people to find a place where they might escape some of the indirect burdens of slavery. Liberia, however, merely represented a widespread movement among Negroes, who had escaped slavery, to establish homes and communities of their own, not only in Africa but wherever freedom was assured them.

For a number of years before emancipation little colonies of free Negroes were established in several parts of Canada, and in states of the Middle West, especially Ohio, Indiana and Illinois, the region which, by the Ordinance of 1787, was dedicated forever to freedom. There were colonies of free Negroes established at this time in several other states — New Jersey and Michigan, for example. After the Civil War was over and Negroes were granted the same rights and the same freedom as other citizens these little rural communities tended to break up and disperse, but the remnants of them still exist in many parts of the country.

The Negro rural communities which have grown up since emancipation have had other and different motives for their existence. They have generally sprung up as a result of the efforts of Negro farmers to become landowners.

For the first twenty years of freedom there was no great disposition, so far as I can learn, on the part of Negro farmers to become landowners. During this period the Negro people and particularly the Negro leaders, were absorbed either in politics or in religion, and constructive efforts of the race were chiefly absorbed in organizing their religious life and building churches.

After the masses of the Negroes lost the influence in politics, which they had exercised directly after the war, there was a period of some years of great discouragement. Gradually, however, it began to dawn upon the more thoughtful members of the race that there was hope for them in other directions.

They found, for example, that in communities where there was very little encouragement for a Negro to vote there was nothing which prevented him from owning property. They learned, also, that where their white neighbors were opposed to a Negro postmaster they had not the slightest objection to a Negro banker. The result was that the leaders of the race began to turn their attention to business enterprises, while the masses of the people were learning to save their money and buy land.

The first Negro bank was established in the latter part of the eighties. At the present time there are something over sixty Negro banks in different parts of the United States. In the meantime the Negro farmers, particularly in recent years, have been getting hold of the land on which they work. There are, for example, at least three counties in the South in each of which Negroes own and pay taxes on something like fifty or sixty thousand acres. In Louisa County, Virginia, Negroes own 53,268 acres; in Liberty County, Georgia, they own 55,048 and in Macon County, Alabama, Negroes pay taxes on 61,689 acres of land.

Some years ago I wrote a series of magazine articles on the subject of the Negro Town.[1] In each of these articles I attempted to describe a distinctive type of Negro rural community. One of these was a town that had grown up around a Negro college in Ohio, two others were towns that has been settled and built up by Negro farmers and had become the centers of Negro farming communities. One of these was Mound Bayou, Mississippi; the other was Boley, Oklahoma.

I shall not attempt to repeat here the descriptions which I gave at that time of these Negro towns and the communities surrounding them; I only refer to them as illustrating a more general movement which has been going on, for a number of years past, on a smaller scale in other parts of the country.

It is this more general movement and the smaller and more remote farming communities it has produced that I desire to describe here.

The first rural Negro communities that were established after the war grew up almost invariably around a little country church. The church was at this time the center around which everything revolved. It was in fact the only distinctively Negro institution that existed. It was in the church or, perhaps, in the grove surrounding it, that the political meetings were held in the days when the masses of the people were still engaged in politics. After politics had ceased, to some extent, to be a live interest the church still remained the center of the intellectual, as well as of the religious life of the people.

When I first went to Alabama I spent a large part of my time going about the country speaking to the people in the churches about the

kind of education we are trying to establish at Tuskegee. Not infrequently I found that, in connection with the church, there would be
a debating society which met at some time during the week to discuss
questions of various kinds. After country people had ceased to discuss
political questions these clubs, when they found nothing of more burning interest to talk about, sometimes got into lively debates over some
good old-fashioned questions such as, "Which is better, the town or
the country," or "Which is more useful, the mule or the horse." I
found that in these churches anyone who had any new question to
present was always sure of a large and interested audience.

In more recent years, in many parts of the country, the school has,
to a large extent, taken the place of the church as the center of life in
the rural districts. In the early years of freedom the place of every
individual was fixed in the community by the fact that he supported
either the Baptist or the Methodist denomination. At present, however,
the management and welfare of the school occupies, in many parts of
the country at least, as large a part of the interest and attention of the
community as the church.

In many cases the people have united to tax themselves, in order
to build schoolhouses and to lengthen the school terms. Most of the
efforts made by outside agencies, like the Anna T. Jeanes Fund, to
improve the rural public schools have been directed to bringing the
work of the school into closer relations with the practical interests of
the rural communities.

Although in the Southern States the school officials are invariably
white men, the Negro communities frequently elect trustees of their
own. These colored trustees have no legal standing, but the conduct
of the school is very largely in their hands and in the hands of the
"patrons," that is to say those individuals in the community who contribute something to the support of the schools.

On the whole, I believe that the control which, in this indirect way,
Negroes have come to exercise over their own schools has had a good
influence not only on the people, but also upon the schools. It has
introduced a new interest into the life of the community. There is
more to do and to think about than there used to be, and I believe I
can safely say that there is a greater disposition among the people,
in spite of the attraction of the city, to settle down upon the land and
make themselves at home in the country districts.

Perhaps I can best illustrate the results of the changes by describing the progress which has been made, during the past eight years, in the country directly around Tuskegee Institute. Macon County, Alabama, in which the institute is situated, has a population, according to the last Census of 26,049, of which 22,039 are Negroes. The county is situated in the edge of the great prairie or Black Belt of Alabama, on which the great plantations are located. The result is that there are very striking differences in the character of the population in the different parts of the county. When, after emancipation, the colored people first began to get hold of the land, they settled as the class of poor whites before them had done, upon the light soil and cheap lands in the northern half of the county. As these settlers grew more numerous they generally formed little communities made up, for the most part, of men who owned their own lands. The majority of the Negroes, who were not willing or able to acquire lands of their own, remained as tenants on the large plantations in the southern part of the county. As might be expected there is a good deal of moving about of tenants on these big plantations. In the early days a Negro tenant felt he must move about more or less, merely in order to assure himself that he was actually free. This disposition has not yet, I am sorry to say, entirely disappeared. The result is that except in those cases where tenants have become attached to the plantation on which they work and made to feel at home there, Negro communities of tenant farmers have not been very permanent. There are, however, in Macon County several model plantation communities.

There are altogether about fifty distinct Negro farming communities in the county. Each one of these has a church and a schoolhouse, little stores, or a cotton gin belonging to some of the larger Negro landowners or to the white planter on whose land the community is located. There are about sixty business enterprises of various kinds carried on by Negroes in the county. Forty-eight of these are in the town of Tuskegee and the village of Greenwood adjoining the Tuskegee Institute and the remainder are little country stores in the country districts.

As concerns the Negro landowning communities I ought, perhaps, to say that it was not until about ten years ago that Negroes began to buy land to any very large extent in this part of the country. Down to 1900 there were not, according to the Census, more than 157 Negro farmers in Macon County who owned their own farms. At present they number 503. Negroes pay taxes on property of the assessed value of $419,821. The figures in the county tax assessor's office show that within a period of two years from 1908 to 1910 the tax value of lands owned by Negroes increased $94,347.

Directly and indirectly this growth in the number of Negro land-owners has been, to a very large extent, brought about by the improvement of the colored public schools throughout the county. About six or seven years ago the Tuskegee Institute was given a sum of money, in order to determine by experiment to what extent the Negro farming communities in the surrounding county could be improved, materially and otherwise, if serious effort was made to improve the rural schools. It was not intended to use this money for the purpose of giving colored people schoolhouses and providing them with teachers. It was to be used rather to encourage them to help themselves. The money thus secured was called the Rural School Improvement Fund and in order to carry out the plan proposed a man was employed as agent, who, with the consent of the county superintendent, acted as a sort of supervisor or assistant superintendent of Negro schools. His real work consisted less, however, in supervising the work of the rural teachers than in carrying on an educational campaign throughout the county in order to stimulate the colored people to raise funds among themselves to rebuild their schoolhouses and lengthen their school terms. As a result of the campaign begun in this way colored people raised during the next five years something like $20,000 which was used in building schoolhouses and lengthening school terms.

As soon as a certain number of these schools were established advertisements were inserted in the colored newspapers throughout the South advertising the fact that land could be purchased in small tracts near an eight months' school. Very soon the advertisements began to attract attention. Colored farmers began to move in from the adjoining counties. Many of them came to obtain the advantages of a good country school for their children. Others came not merely for this purpose but to buy land. The effect was to bring in a more enterprising class of Negro farmers and to increase the price of land.

Meanwhile a little farmers' newspaper, *The Messenger,* as it was called, had been started for the purpose of organizing the county, stirring up interest in the improvement of the schools and stimulating the efforts of the farmers to improve their methods of farming. The preachers and teachers of the county organized an association for the purpose of pushing forward the movement. Demonstration plots were established in the neighborhood of the schools and, under the direction of the United States Demonstration Agent, the teachers began teaching farming in the schools. The preachers encouraged the movement from the pulpit and *The Messenger,* the farmers' newspaper I have referred to, made an effort to report every step that was taken, in any part of the county, looking to the education and general improvement of the people.

Through this paper the farmers of the county were brought into closer touch with the work of the Institute and the influence of the school upon the community was strengthened and deepened. In fact, it would not be far from the truth to say that the Negro communities in Macon County have made more progress during the last five years than they did during the previous twenty-five.

The work which was attempted on a small scale in Macon County, Alabama, has been undertaken in a larger way in Virginia where the state has created a state supervisor or superintendent of Negro schools, whose task has been to co-operate with and to encourage and direct the Negro people of the state in their efforts to improve the conditions of the rural schools. More than this, under the leadership of Major R. R. Moton of Hampton, what is called an "organization society" has been formed for the purpose of bringing about co-operation between the various Negro organizations of the state religious and secular, to improve the school system and bring the work of the schools into closer touch with the life and practical daily interests of the people.

In what I have written I have sketched the conditions and the progress of a type of rural communities in which Negroes own, to a very considerable extent, the lands they work. A large part of the lands in Macon County are held, however, in the form of big plantations and worked by tenants. As I have already said tenants on large plantations do not, as a rule, permanently settle on the land, and, as a result, community life is not as well established. There are, however, several plantations in Macon County where something like a permanent tenant community exists. In order that I may give a definite notion of the way landlord and tenants get on together on such a plantation as I have referred to, it will not, perhaps, be out of place to repeat here the substance of a letter which I wrote to the editor of the *Montgom-*

ery Advertiser,[2] concerning the manner in which one of our most successful while planters, Mr. J. W. McLeod, controls the little Negro community on his plantation.

The greater part of Mr. McLeod's plantation of 1,800 acres is located in Macon County, but it extends over the line a half mile into Bullock County. At Hannon's Station, which is about the center of the plantation, there is a colored settlement of about seventy-five or eighty families. This community has a good schoolhouse, with attendance of 110 pupils. The building alone cost, I understand, about $800, and last year the people raised $127 to put in regular factory-made seats and desks.

For several years Mr. McLeod has followed the plan of giving an annual barbecue dinner to the tenants, making that dinner the occasion for distributing prizes among those who had made the most progress during the year, and for giving them good, wholesome advice, that would help them and encourage them to do better in the future. This year Mr. McLeod celebrated the close of the farming season by distributing $200 in prizes among his tenants. A number of teachers from the Tuskegee Agricultural School were invited to inspect the homes and the general conditions and act as committee to assist in awarding the prizes. The committee spent two days on the place, visiting and inspecting the farms and homes of forty-one tenants.

Prizes were given to those who showed the most progress in the preparation and cultivation of the crops; to those whose stock showed the most intelligent care and treatment; to those who kept the best homes. Then there were several prizes to certain individuals for special interest in the care of stock; for making good upon a steer farm, and for making a success at rough land farming. The prizes ranged all the way from $12 to $25. Any man or woman guilty of drunkenness or of abusing his or her family was debarred from the contest.

The program this year was a long one. There was first an evening meeting at the schoolhouse on the day of the arrival of the committee. At this meeting there were reports on the Farmers' Improvement Club of Hannon, interspersed with singing of good old-fashioned plantation melodies. Then there was a debate in which all the farmers and their wives took part. The subject was: "Resolved, That Woman Is of More Service Upon the Farm Than a Man." The women won, "not because," as one man explained it to me, "they were really of more use than the man, but because they were better in an argument." Meanwhile the animals had been slaughtered for the barbecue and, while a crowd of laughing, happy people gathered around the pit where the two whole beeves, two hogs and four young goats were already sizzling over the glowing coals, they were entertained with coffee and buttered biscuits, spiced with much good humor and lively conversations. The next day a crowd of at least a thousand people gathered to share in the barbecue and see the prizes distributed. There were speeches by several white planters and business men, and then by several colored farmers and, finally, by the committee of teachers from Tuskegee.

I can perhaps give a better notion of the relations of Mr. McLeod to his tenants and the conditions which prevailed in the community if I quote from his letter to the judges who were to award the prizes for the year. This letter was as follows:

To the Judges:

I am glad to be able to report that there has been a decided improvement in conditions over 1910, as seen by me and reported by Mr. Colvard,[3] in efforts on the farm and in the care of work stock, with the exception of three tenants.

There has been general improvement in conduct, no broils, all peaceable amongst themselves, and all seem to have regard for each other, and are ready and willing to receive advice from Mr. Colvard.

There is one case especially. This tenant had gone to the bad from the use of whiskey, but is now making a man of himself and is treating his family as a husband and father should.

I am sorry to report there is one who has not fully reformed, but I am sure that he will profit by the experience of others and during the year 1912 will stand in line with others who are trying to live sober and correct lives.

Of the women, they are keeping cleaner houses and taking better care of the children, which is a decided advance with them.

To improve the conditions of the black man along the lines I have mentioned I have given prizes during the last two years, and feel sure it has been worth while to them and paid me pecuniarily; besides it is quite a satisfaction to see them advance in all of their interests.

(Signed) J. W. McLeod

I might add, in conclusion, that the committee of teachers from Tuskegee who acted as judges were greatly impressed with the results that have been obtained by these methods, not only in the way of improvement upon the farms, but also in the homes. As one committee who inspected the different homes on the plantation said to me: "One woman kept her house so clean and so attractive inside and out that we were ashamed to go in it." What I have said concerning this and other Negro rural communities, both on and off the large plantations, is an indication of what can and is being made of farming life by Negroes under favorable conditions; that is to say, where they have had a chance.

Annals of the American Academy of Political and Social Science, 40 (Mar. 1912), 81–89.

[1] "A Town Owned by Negroes: Mound Bayou, Miss., An Example of Thrift and Self-Government," *World's Work,* 14 (July 1907), 9125–34; "A Negro College Town: The Uplifting Influence of Fifty Years' Growth of Wilberforce, O.," *World's Work,* 14 (Sept. 1907), 9361–67; "Boley, a Negro Town in the West," *Outlook,* 88 (Jan. 4, 1908), 28–31. (See above, vol. 9.)

[2] BTW's letter to the editor appeared in the Montgomery *Advertiser,* Jan. 15, 1912, 4.

[3] William J. Colvard (b. 1872) was reported as a Macon County farmer in the 1900 census.

From Charles Dewey Hilles

Washington, D.C. April 2, 1912

Personal

Dear Dr. Washington: I have received your letter of March 29, and agree with all you say.

I believe our real friends in North Carolina are not responsible for the situation there; and I shall speak to Mr. Cabell in reference to Virginia.

In Texas and Louisiana it is our action that has made it possible for the colored people to have representation and recognition. Cecil Lyon[s] had eliminated the colored people from the Republican party in Texas, and we are making a strong appeal to them. Pearl Wight had eliminated them from the party in Louisiana, and it is because of the action of our friends in giving them proportionate recognition on the State committee that we are having opposition in that State. Sincerely yours,

Charles D. Hilles

TLS Con. 58 BTW Papers DLC.

To John Harvey Kellogg[1]

[Tuskegee, Ala.] April 3, 1912

My dear Dr. Kellogg: When I was in Battle Creek a little over a year ago, you were generous enough to give us $500.00 toward our operating expenses for the year. Of course, I understand fully that that gift did not imply any promise to continue to help us from year to year.

During the past year, however, I have been devoting a good deal of my time and strength to an effort to increase our Endowment Fund, and have had some success in that direction. In the meantime we have gotten behind in our operating expenses, and if you could see your way clear to help us again this year, it would be very much appreciated, I assure you.

I shall long remember my visit to Battle Creek. I am glad to say that Mr. Crayton[2] is rendering fine service in many directions here. He is fast opening people's eyes to what your methods mean.

The marked portion of the enclosed circular I hope will interest you. If you do not care, however, to give on the plan outlined here, you can give in any way that you deem wise. Yours very truly,

Booker T. Washington

TLps Con. 754 BTW Papers DLC.

[1] John Harvey Kellogg (1852–1943), a surgeon who graduated from Bellevue Hospital Medical College, established the Battle Creek (Mich.) Sanitarium in 1876. His activities expanded from medical practice to include public health, nutrition, and massage. His diet foods were the basis for the development of the Kellogg breakfast food business.

[2] William P. Crayton was a nurse at the Battle Creek Sanitarium from 1901 through 1911. BTW said of him in an address at Battle Creek in 1914: "Some three years ago I found myself almost out of commission physically. Without my knowledge or consent, my wife in some way got hold of a colored man trained here under Doctor Kellogg, by the name of Mr. Crayton. He came to Tuskegee, was installed in my home by my wife and for six months he had charge of me. At the end of that six months I was a new man, and not only a new man, but I knew more about living and enjoying life than I had ever known before. And so I want to express to you, Doctor Kellogg, my deep personal gratitude." (See An Address on the Negro Race at the First National Conference on Race Betterment, Jan. 8–12, 1914, below, vol. 12.)

To Thomas Jesse Jones

[Tuskegee, Ala.] April 5, 1912

My dear Dr. Jones: Major Moton told me sometime ago that you were now with the Bureau of Education and I am glad to hear this.

One thing which I very much hope can be accomplished through you while you are in the Bureau of Education is this: The money which has been going to the Negro schools from the Government in the various states to promote agricultural and mechanical education, in a large measure, has been wasted and is being wasted simply because there seems to be no one whose duty it is to look after the expenditure of this money.

I very much hope that in some way you can exercise an influence in the direction of seeing that this money is spent for the purpose for which Congress appropriated it.

One other thing: Will you not be kind enough to send me copies of all the bills which have been passed by Congress appropriating money to the various states for agricultural and mechanical education, as well as for experiment station work? Yours very truly,

Booker T. Washington

TLpS   Con. 457   BTW Papers   DLC.

To Charles Dewey Hilles

[Tuskegee, Ala.] April 6, 1912

Personal

My dear Mr. Hilles: Thank you for yours of April 2d concerning the Lily White movement in various Southern States. The facts you have given me will enable me to place this whole matter before the colored people through the colored press in a helpful manner, and I shall begin doing so at once. Yours very truly,

Booker T. Washington

TLpS   Con. 58   BTW Papers   DLC.

From Alain LeRoy Locke

Camden [N.J.] April 7th 1912

My dear Dr. Washington, I thank you very much for your kind letter of endorsement for the Kahn Fellowship,[1] and for your personal note as well. I go to New York this week to present my credentials and endorsements — (a duplicate copy of the former I shall send you) — and to interview President Butler if the procedure seems best. Should you receive any intimation or comment from Dr. Butler in the matter that might be of assistance to me, I hope you will be good enough to let me have word of it. I shall keep you informed of significant developments, and hope to report ultimately success.

With thanks for your interest and support,[2] Very truly yours,

Alain LeRoy Locke

P.S. Did you notice in the reports of the South African Native National Congress that the initiative of suggestion and organization was taken by Mr. Isaka Seme? Rev. Mr. Dube, the President, is his cousin.

A LeR L.

ALS Con. 458 BTW Papers DLC.

[1] The Kahn Foundation for the Foreign Travel of American Teachers, established by Albert Kahn of Paris, France, in 1911. Locke did not receive the fellowship.

[2] Locke, who had accompanied BTW on a week's tour of Florida, wrote to E. J. Scott of BTW's "statesmanlike proportions and dimensions." (Mar. 22, 1912, Con. 458, BTW Papers, DLC.) He wrote to BTW endorsing Tuskegee and particularly its extension work, and said that his eyes had been opened to the possibilities of race work at such an institution. (Mar. 23, 1912, Con. 458, BTW Papers, DLC.)

An Article in *The Independent*

April 11, 1912

THE CENSUS AND THE NEGRO

When the census figures of 1900 were published they revealed the fact that in the forty years since slavery the negro population had doubled. It was 4,441,830 in 1860 and 8,833,994 in 1900. Now that we are beginning to get returns from the 1910 census, we learn that during the past ten years the race has added almost another million (994,300) to its stature, so that according to the thirteenth census the negro population was 9,828,294, and if it has increased at the same rate since 1910 that it did before, namely, 11.30 per cent. for the decade, or about 100,000 per year, it is now considerably more than ten millions.

The importance of these facts is that it assures the physical existence of the race. The negro is not dying out. The rate of increase among negroes is not as great as it was some years ago, but that is true of every civilized country in the world in which the population is not increased by immigration. The census of 1911 shows, for example, that the rate of increase for the English people, measured by the excess of births over deaths, is 12.4 per cent. The natural rate of increase of the white population, excluding increase by immigration, was estimated at twenty per cent. in the period 1880 to 1890, and is not quite fifteen per cent. for the period 1900 to 1910. The census shows that the white population is increasing more rapidly than the negro in the Southern States. This is due in part to the fact that, while there is a movement of the black population northward from the border States like Kentucky, Tennessee and Maryland, there is at the same time a movement of the white population southward, particularly in the direction of Florida, Louisiana, Oklahoma and Texas. The statistics show, for example, that while the negro population has actually decreased in the border States I have mentioned, and the increase in Virginia and Delaware was no more than 1.6 per cent., the increase of the negro population in the Northern States was 18.4 per cent.

This does not mean, as some persons have said, that the negro population is shifting from the Southern to the Northern States. The fact is that the total increase of negro population in the North, during the decade from 1900 to 1910, amounted to no more than 167,879. During the same period negro population in the South has grown from 7,922,969 to 8,749,390, an increase of 826,421. As a matter of fact, the increase in the North over the South has been no more than one half of one per cent. of the whole negro population.

The truth is, that negro emigration from the border States has not been directed exclusively toward the North. On the contrary there has been, perhaps, an even larger movement of the negro population South and West. For example, in Arkansas, Oklahoma and West Virginia the negro population has not only increased in numbers more rapidly than in most other Southern States, but this increase has been more rapid than that of the white population in the same States. In Oklahoma the white population increased 115.5 per cent. from 1900 to 1910. In the same period the negro population increased 147.1 per cent. In West Virginia the percentage of increase for whites was 26.4 per cent.; for negroes, 47.5 per cent. In Arkansas the percentage of increase for whites was 19.7 per cent.; for negroes, 20.7. In Florida, where there has been a large immigration from the North during the past decade, the negro population increased less rapidly than the white. In spite of this fact, the percentage of increase was 33.8, showing that there has been a very considerable negro immigration into Florida from other parts of the South. The average increase of negro population in the Southwestern States — Kansas, Louisiana, Texas and Oklahoma — has been 17.1 per cent.

Another striking fact which the census figures have disclosed is that in the readjustment which is now taking place in the South between the city and the rural population, the negro on the whole remains in the country, while the white man goes to town. This is shown, for one thing, by the relative decrease of the negro population in all the larger cities in the South. The four cities which had a larger negro population than white in 1900 will serve as an illustration. These cities were Charleston, S.C., Savannah, Ga., Montgomery, Ala., and Jacksonville, Fla. In 1900 the population of Jacksonville was 28,429. In 1910 it had grown to 37,699. In 1900 there were 57 negroes in the population to 43 whites; in 1910 the ratio was 51 negroes to 49 whites. Montgomery, Ala., increased its population in the same period from 30,346 to 38,136. In 1900 the ratio of negroes to whites was 56 to 44; in 1910 the ratio was 50.6 negroes to 49.4 whites.

In the case of Charleston, S.C., while the population as a whole increased from 55,807 in 1900 to 58,833 in 1910, the negro population of the city actually declined. In 1900 the proportion of negroes to whites was 56.5 to 45.5;[1] in 1910 it was 53 to 47.

Another fact which indicates that the negro is gaining in the rural districts, as compared with his white neighbor, is the rapid increase in the number of negro farmers. In every Southern State except Florida the census shows that the number of negro farmers has increased more rapidly than the negro population as a whole. In spite of the fact that the white population has grown more rapidly than the colored population in all but two of the fifteen Southern States, in only five of these States has the number of white farmers grown more rapidly than the negro farmers.

In conclusion, I do not believe I can do better than quote a statement of President E. C. Branson, of the State Normal School at Athens, Ga., who, in a very interesting paper on farm life conditions in the South, sums up his own observation in regard to the negro as follows:

"Another significant economic tendency in the Southern farm life is the fact that negroes are resisting the lure of city life and sticking to the farm better than the whites. In every Southern State, except Kentucky, the white farmers are a lessening ratio. On the contrary, the negro farmers in the South, except in Florida, Louisiana and Texas are a growing ratio. In South Carolina and Alabama the negro population on the farm grew in the last census decade nearly twice as fast as the negro population in general in these two States; more than twice as fast in Mississippi, and nearly three times as fast in Georgia.

"On the other hand, there is the steady drift of white farm owners and white tenants cityward; the first for business opportunities and social advantages, and the last for work in the mills and factories. Thus the growth of urban population in Georgia was three and a half times, and in Mississippi, five times, the growth of rural population. Negroes rent the vacated farms and remain in the country, and oftentimes they move back into the country from the towns — a thing seldom true of the whites.

"Thus there are fourteen Mississippi counties in which the negro farmers outnumber the white farmers five to one; in four of these more than twenty-five to one; in one of them nearly thirty to one.

"And I may add, that the negro is fast rising out of tenancy into ownership. In ten counties of Mississippi the farms cultivated by negro owners outnumber the farms cultivated by white owners. But the increasing ownership of farms by negroes thruout the South is a conspicuous fact, even when they are thinly scattered in white communities. The fact appears so uniformly upon the county tax digests that it has ceased to be surprising.

"It means, of course, that the negro is working out his own salvation upon an economic basis. It may be that he is traveling along a hard, difficult road; but in simple truth there seems to be no other way."

The Independent, 72 (Apr. 11, 1912), 785–86.

¹ Thus in original.

Ralph Waldo Tyler to Emmett Jay Scott

Washington, D.C. April 12/12

My dear Emmett: Your note to hand, an[d] Liberia's flag went forward today, via express to you. Regret that it took me so long to return it.

Well old man things are certainly at white heat, and in the language of a Confucian, "hell's to play." To all colored newspapers, I gave instructions not to attack the Colonel. I was sorry to see Moore attack him in The Age. It seems to me it would be the best policy to speak well of the President without speaking ill of the Colonel. There is no use in putting ourselves in a position to eat crow, if we can help it. If the Colonel plays even in Pennsylvania; that is gets half of the delegates from that state tomorrow, its my confidential opinion that he will come damn close to getting the nomination. He's like the proverbial cat — nine lives. And he cant tell when he's whipped. I see my state, Ohio, did the mean dirty thing by Lewis — invited him to address the Constitutional Convention, and then withdrew it. Singular, but significant, it was a Democrat who introduced and spoke on, and forced the adoption of the resolution to invite him, and the same Democrat fought the withdrawal. The Convention is non-partizan, or supposed to be. I cant learn who the men were who voted to withdraw, for the motion to recommit it to the committee was adopted by a viva voce vote — nobody going on record.

We have got Wm C Mathew's appointment favored by both the White House and Attorney General, but we are solicitous about the District Attorney at Boston, who may or may not block it. Lewis had a talk with him yesterday.

The Doctor's meeting here — some weeks ago, for attendence, beat the President's meeting two to one. There were many vacant seats last Tuesday evening. The committee managed it poorly, in the way of advertising. However, the enthusiasm made up for lack of attendence. The President spoke out strong against lynching but side-stepped the Southern policy which we so strongly urged him to restate.

I am just worked to a frazzle, and am fast getting to a point where I will be but a bundle of nervous nerves. The pace is hot, never saw so many Negro grafters in my life, and the preachers lead the graft procession. Regards to family

Tyler

ALS Con. 466 BTW Papers DLC.

To the Editor of the Indianapolis *Star*

[Tuskegee, Ala.] April 15, 1912

Personal and Confidential

My dear Sir: I have read with interest your recent editorial upon Dr. Du Bois' lecture in Indianapolis, also the letter which he wrote in answer to your editorial, and also your brief comment on his letter.[1]

I would state in the beginning that I have no personal animosity toward Dr. Du Bois, in fact, rather than disliking him I rather pity the man. He is puffed up with insane vanity and jealousy, and this deprives him, it seems, of common sense. He misrepresents my position on most occasions. He knows perfectly well I am not seeking to confine the Negro race to industrial education nor make them hewers of wood and drawers of water, but I am trying to do the same thing for the Negro which is done for all races of the world, and that is to make the masses of them first of all industrious, skillful, and frugal, to enable them to combine brains with hand work to the extent that their services will be wanted in the communities where they live, and thus prevent them from becoming a burden and a menace.

Dr. Du Bois is in the position of a doctor offering a sick child candy or medicine. The average child will take the candy because it pleases him for the minute and refuse the medicine which will permanently cure his ills. I am glad to say, however, that the great masses of colored people are not deceived by Dr. Du Bois' sophistry and are seeing more and more the wisdom of what I am trying to teach them. For the first

517

time this year I am making an effort to get colored people to manifest their faith in our work by money contributions, and I have been surprised as I have never been in my life by the liberality manifested by the colored people in all parts of the country by their small contributions to this institution.

So far from industrial education being applied to the Negro alone, for example in the state of Georgia today there are being spent on the industrial and technical education of the white boys and girls $324,000 and $8,000 annually for the industrial and technical education of the black boys and girls.

I shall hope to see you sometime when I am in Indianapolis. We are constantly grateful to you for your many acts of kindness and generosity. Yours very truly,

[Booker T. Washington]

TLpS Con. 465 BTW Papers DLC.

1 W. E. B. Du Bois spoke at the Bethel A.M.E. Church in Indianapolis on higher education as more essential than industrial or technical training. "The boys of brain are the wealth of a community," he said. "We can only come forward through the mind, not by digging or washing. There is no culture or uplift in washing clothes." (Indianapolis *Star,* Mar. 30, 1912, 16.) The Indianapolis *Star* called this "a dangerously misleading doctrine," particularly for blacks, "for the reason that by nature a large proportion of them are self-indulgent, easy-going, and disinclined to unnecessary exertion of mind or body." It contrasted Du Bois's views with the efforts of BTW to inculcate among blacks "the habit of industry." (Indianapolis *Star,* Mar. 31, 1912, 16.) Du Bois replied to the editorial by saying that he had not decried common labor but had simply asserted that the aim of education was "not the output of goods but the training of men." Persons who opposed this perfectly rational program, said Du Bois, were those who wanted to keep blacks forever subordinated. The *Star* replied: "The Star is not a Negro hater; but it looks upon the teaching of Dr. Du Bois as false and mischievous for the children of any race. Booker Washington is right and Dr. Du Bois is wrong." (Indianapolis *Star,* Apr. 8, 1912, 6.)

To Ralph Waldo Tyler

Tuskegee Ala   April 17–12

Please call personally at white house and explain to the President the nature and object of the international Conference on the negro which is now in session. We have delegates from twenty one foreign countries and colonies. Get him to send a telegram of greetings. Signed by himself. Should like to read this telegram to the conference today or tomorrow.

B. T. W.

From William Calvin Chase

Washington, D.C. April 17, 1912

PERSONAL.

My dear Dr. Washington: Some months ago, I suggested to you the importance of your friends in office, in this city, assisting "The Bee" financially. You stated that you would see Mr. Tyler, and have them to make such contributions that would keep the paper from being embarrassed financially. This has been about two years ago. Mr. Tyler himself had been contributing twenty-dollars per month, out of his own pocket, and the paper was being used for the defense of everybody connected with you, as well as your self. Mr. Cobb, however informed me, that seven persons including himself, were contributing a prorato share of the twenty dollars which was not a drop in the bucket, considerating their salaries, and the expense I have to under go to run "The Bee."

About a month ago Mr. Tyler informed me that the twenty-dollars, which he was contributing had to be discontinued.

Now while I appreciate what you have endeavored to do for me, and what your friends, have done, I want to be frank, by informing you that I, cannot allow "The Bee" to be used any longer for their personal use without receiving some benefits. When I informed Mr. Tyler what I thought of it, he stated: "Well you know they have to live," as if to say it makes no difference whether I live or not. You will remember that I asked for a place for my son in school or elsewhere, and a small place for the manager of "The Bee" both have been promised a year ago. With assistance in this direction, I could have been of great benefit to you and your friends. Places can be made for every-body else except your loyal friend, and those who could be serviceable to you. Mr. Tyler is about the only person that has made any kind of disposition to help you or me. Cobb would do if he could.

I thought it best to inform you, because you are no doubt of the opinion, or have been of the opinion that your friends were contributing liberally to the paper. I cannot continue to be used for the benefit of others, and receive no consideration. With but "ONE EXCEPTION" you have the weakest set of supporters in office that I would want to meet. All they think about is SELF and dont give a continental whether others sink or swim.

I know you will appreciate this frank and honest statement because, you know I have been loyal and true to you, but under the circumstances, I shall be constrained to seek assistance from other sources. Gratefully yours,

Wm. Calvin Chase

TLS   Con. 450   BTW Papers   DLC.

The Opening Address of the
International Conference on the Negro[1]

[Tuskegee, Ala.] April 17th, 1912

I need not say how glad we are to welcome each and all of you to the grounds and property of the Tuskegee Institute. We have an old saying here in this part of the world which carries with it a wealth of meaning: "Make yourselves at home." That means that you are to be one of the household while you are with us and I am sure that every teacher and student and resident of Tuskegee will do their part in making each one of you feel at home while you are in this part of the world.

First, it seems necessary to say a word as to what this Conference is not expected to be. We did not expect to have a large gathering. We expected to have a small group of interesting and valuable people who have something to contribute toward the purposes of this Conference and in the second place, we do not intend that this Conference shall be formal or complex in its nature. We hope that it will be a simple Conference. I note from time to time as I have had experience with the world that there [are] a great many people who if you can get them around a fireside with two or three present, they exhibit a great deal of common sense, of good sense. Take those same individuals and put them into a large audience and tell them to make a speech and all their common sense and good sense seems to leave them at once. So we shall hope not to have any formality in connection with this Conference. Very few speeches, but a simple direct, heart-to-heart talk concerning the conditions and concerning the problems that are nearest to the hearts of teachers.

For a number of years, we have received here at Tuskegee letters from various parts of the world, letters from missionaries in foreign fields, letters from Governmental officials, especially in Europe, asking for some information that would put them into touch with the methods of education employed here at Tuskegee and it occurred to us after receiving a number of these communications, that it would be perhaps a wise thing and a natural development for us to ask these persons representing Missionary Organizations, representing Governments that have to do with the darker races of the world to come here and spend a few days, first of all in observing the methods that we are trying to employ at Tuskegee and then, in so far as it is possible, in informal discussion based upon their observations to see to what extent the methods employed here can be applied to the problems concerning the people in the countries that are peopled by the darker races.

I do not mean to suggest that we have anything at Tuskegee that is very superior, or that this Conference is to be confined in any degree to a discussion of methods employed at Tuskegee. Incidentally, I hope that you will look through our plant, go through all the departments here and if you find anything which will be of value in your own communities, in your own homes, why we shall count ourselves most happy to have made a small contribution toward the uplift of the people that you represent.

For a number of years, we have had on our grounds a number of students from countries outside of the United States. From year to year we have from 100 to 150 students representing foreign countries and we are anxious that these students be fitted to go back to their homes and render the highest and best service. We shall hope, therefore, that during the discussion, we shall get much valuable information as to the actual needs in the countries from which these students come, so that they will be trained to some definite point of usefulness in their home communities. We want these students to go back home after they get their education and we want them to prove of service there as a result of what they have learned. I am perfectly aware of the fact, as I am sure many of you are, that with all of our faults — we damn the United States a good deal — but as a rule when a fellow once gets into this country, it is pretty hard to get him out. We hope most of you will get out. I notice, however, that a good many young men and women come from Africa, and from South American countries, from Porto Rico and Cuba and Jamaica and when they first arrive they praise their own country pretty highly, nothing like it. They stay here one month, then two months, then a year in studying at some institution and the first thing you know they have forgotten their old country and they never go back home any more. We do not want that to be true of the men and women we train at Tuskegee and I am sure in helping us to give these students that which will serve them best and serve you best, in the communities from which they have come, you can help us immensely during these meetings.

TM   Con. 450   BTW Papers   DLC.

¹ For a detailed account of the conference from a white South African perspective, see Maurice S. Evans, "International Conference on the Negro," *Journal of the African Society,* 11 (July 1912), 416–29.

To William Howard Taft

Tuskegee, Ala., April 19, 1912

THE PRESIDENT. International Conference on the Negro with twenty one foreign countries or colonies of foreign countries and thirty six different missionary organizations now assembled at Tuskegee appreciates your kindly greeting. I am directed by the conference to say that together with the faculty and students of the Institute hereby beg to tender to the President of the United States to the relatives of those on the Titanic who lost their lives in terrible calamity which has taken away so many distinguished citizens of the United States. Our deep and sincere sympathy   this resolution passed by rising vote of those people assembled.

Booker T. Washington

TWSr   William Howard Taft Papers   DLC.

From Willis Duke Weatherford

Nashville, Tenn. April 20, 1912

Dear Dr. Washington: We are just opening up our splendid new Blue Ridge buildings for Christian conferences and training, near Black Mountain, N.C., on the first of June. We have put one hundred and twenty-five thousand dollars into these training grounds and equipment, and we think it is equal to, if not better, than anything else of this kind in the country.

The buildings will be open for three months, June 1st to Sept 1st. During the first two months we shall have a series of conferences, missionary, biblical and otherwise, which will draw the very choicest of the college men and the college women of the entire South together. Knowing that many of your girls have to work during the summer in order that they may put themselves through the winter, I thought that we might be able to use a number as waitresses and chambermaids in these buildings. I am very anxious to have a group of very high grade, industrially trained negro girls for two reasons. First, they will enable some two thousand of the most open-minded and best trained white people in the South to come into contact with the high grade of work which these girls, who have had genuine training, do. This, in my judgment, will be worth a tremendous amount, inasmuch as practically every college in the entire South will be represented in this Conference this summer.

In the second place, I believe it will be a great blessing to these girls to find how open-minded a group of college men and women can be and are. This would help on the other side in giving confidence to your girls in the best type of Southern white men.

We, of course, cannot pay them princely wages, but will be glad to pay a little more than is generally paid in that section.

I shall be on hand the first month of this Conference, and if your girls would like to have a series of lectures on some practical, religious or intellectual themes, I would be glad to undertake to give these myself. I think you can trust us to give to your girls the kind of treatment they ought to have.

I have taken this matter up with the Virginia teachers and also with Hampton, and it may be possible that I can secure a number of these girls from that field. We shall need thirty waitresses for the first two months, and twenty from that date on. We shall need eight housemaids for the entire three months.

Kindly let me hear from you if you agree with me that this is a good thing, indicating whether I could secure such help from your institution. Yours sincerely,

W. D. Weatherford

TLS Con. 692 BTW Papers DLC. Written on stationery of the International Committee of Young Men's Christian Associations, office of Southern Student Secretaries.

Cornelius Bailey Hosmer to Emmett Jay Scott

Milwaukee, Wis. April 20 — 1912

Dear Mr. Scott — In addition to what I have said elsewhere concerning the agitation carried on in Chicago preparatory to the holding of "the Conference of the Association for the Advancement of Colored People" — April 28th. to 30th. — the following may be of some interest. I learn that enemies of our cause and Dr. Washington followed him at his various meetings recently in Chicago for the purpose of criticism in the immediate future. Some of this is shown by the recent appearance of editorials in three Chicago newspapers. The white paper (the "Evening Post") lead off, and then the two Negro papers: "Fellowship-Herald," and "Broad-Axe" have followed. I have heard Mrs. Ida-Wells-Barnette speak to her followers lately. Her talks bespeak jealousy at the influence of Dr. Washington, at the growth and importance of the Local and National Negro Business League, as well as at the success of the Chicago Negro Y.M.C.A. And so it goes.

Prof. Richard T. Greener, late Consul to Russia is about on the fence. He is just a little irritated at Dr. Booker T. Washington because he didn't take him up and give him a job in or since 1906, during which year Mr. Greener lost his political post. Mr. Greener says he is 60 years of age.

Much talk centers about Chicago now concerning Prof. W. E. B. Dubois' recent address in Indianapolis, Ind., in which he denounced "the teaching of too much industrial work" in the schools of Indianapolis. I havent been able to secure a report of his speech from the papers.

Is it desired that I attend some of the sessions of this Dubois meeting in Chicago the 29th. of April? It is impossible for me to find out just what kind of resolutions are going to be adopted now. Very Sincerely yours,

C. B. Hosmer

ALS   Con. 456   BTW Papers   DLC.

Extracts of an Address before
the Men and Religion Forward Movement[1]

Carnegie Hall, New York City, April 21, 1912

What can the church do to strengthen and conserve the ten millions of black Americans, 82 percent of whom live in the country districts and small villages? In the rural districts, the Negro, all things considered, is at his best in body, mind and soul. In the city he is usually at his worst. Plainly one of the duties of the church is to help keep the Negro where he has the best chance. In a marked degree the Negro is a social being. The Negro more largely than is true of any other race, uses the church as the rallying point for his social life. Whether it is a meeting relating to farming, business, education, politics, or a secret society, the Negro church house is used.

Negro population follows the church building. Few things delight the soul of the Negro so much as to erect a church building, even [if] it be so crude and small as to be almost ridiculous in its appearance. Even though individuals may own no home, and are without proper food, clothes or shelter, they will part with their last nickel to assist in building a church. This is all commendable. Christian civilization does not have to force the church upon the Negro.

Here then is the opportunity for us to use this great Forward Movement to improve the church life of the country Negro and thus help to keep him on the land where he has a chance to grow a strong, healthy body, and be away from the temptations and complexities of large city life.

How can this be done? Make church life for the Negro in the rural districts as attractive as it is in the city. The Negro problem is to a very considerable extent the problem of rural life everywhere. So long as the Negro finds a poor, uncomfortable, unattractive church house in the country, and a good church house in the city, or finds a weak ignorant minister in the country, and a strong, intelligent minister in the city, or finds in the country church service held once a month and in the city church services held twice each Sunday, so long will the Negro be tempted to leave the country and migrate to the city.

So long, too, as the Negro in the rural districts is fed upon the old worn-out theological dogmas, instead of getting from the pulpit inspiration and direction in practical work of community building, connecting religion with every practical and progressive movement for the improvement of the home and community life, so long will he forsake the land and flee to the city. If we would save the Negro, 82 per cent. of whom, as I have said, live in the country, he must be taught that when the Bible says, "The earth is full of thy riches," it means that the earth is full of corn, potatoes, peas, cotton, chickens and cows, that these riches should be gotten out of the earth by the hand of man and turned into beautiful church buildings and righteous, useful living.

In dealing with the millions of the Negroes, let us in America learn a lesson from what has taken place in England where agriculture and the farm have been neglected by church and state, with the result that the cities of England are filled with millions of unfortunate misfits who are in the gutters instead of being on the soil and out in the free, bracing air where God meant that man should live.

When I was in London, England, recently, I found that the churches and other philanthropic agencies of that vicinity alone were spending $50,000,000 annually, not to keep people on their feet and help them to make greater progress in positive, constructive directions but to save the drunkard, the gambler, the loafer, the pauper and the destitute after they had fallen into the ditch. Happily, the Negroes of America have not as yet fallen into the ditch; and I pray that, as a result of the great Forward Movement, a way may be provided, through the Negro church and Sunday school that the Negro, while it is a new, fresh and vigorous race, may, as the old plantation hymn puts it — be kept from "sinking down." From a money point of view it is much cheaper to keep men from falling than to lift them after they are down.

No class of people should be interested in this Forward Movement so far as it concerns the Negro than the capitalists, the captains of industry, those who directly, or indirectly, employ Negro labor. Nothing pays so well in producing efficient labor as Christianity. Religion increases the wants of the laborer. The man without religion is too often satisfied when he has worked long enough to provide himself with a little coarse food, a chew of tobacco and a bottle of whiskey. The Negro workman with the spirit of Christ in his head and heart wants land, wants a good house, wants another house, wants decent furniture, wants a newspaper or magazine. He wants to provide himself with the means with which to maintain his church and his Sunday school, and his family with a Bible and hymn book. Some Negro laborers have already reached the point where they want a prayer book.

Through the medium of religion let us continue to multiply the wants of the Negro, and they will render six days of honest labor in order to supply these increased wants, and thus become one of the most efficient class of laborers that the world has seen.

Another thing which I hope this Conservation Congress will do for the white man in the South and in the North is to convince them and convert them to the duty which they owe to the millions of Negroes in the South, in providing them with education.

Today, as we stand here and deliberate as to methods of Christian regeneration, in the Southland there are about one million black children who entered no school room this year, and another million who have been in school only three or four months in the year.

Putting the ignorant Negro under arrest will not give him Christianity. Putting him in the jail or the penitentiary will not give him Christianity.

So far as the Negro is concerned, there is supreme need for this Forward Movement. Do you realize, my Christian friends, that within

527

this civilized land, during the year 1911, there were in the United States alone 8,272 persons including both races — lynched and murdered. In contrast to this there were only 74 legal executions as against 71 lynched. This includes both races.

We do not know just how many Negroes were included in this eight thousand who died by personal violence: it is very probable, however, that that number amounted to two thousand or more, which is several times larger than the number of persons killed by personal violence in the whole of Great Britain and Germany. Cursing and damning the Negro on the part of the white man will not work a reformation. Cursing and damning the white man on the part of the Negro will not do it. Nothing but the spirit of religion and education vitalized in every community, North and South, will do it.

No more negative and neglected policy, which would push the Negro outside as a thing not to be considered, will help either the Negro or the white man.

It is well that you have given the Negro a part in this Forward Movement; for in the most vital things in American life, despite all the laws that can be passed, the life of the black citizen touches the life of the white citizen, and we rise or fall together. In a large section of our country, a large portion of the food consumed by the white man is produced by the hand of the Negro. A large part of the raw material used in clothing the nation is produced by black hands. When food is prepared and served in a large portion of our country, the life of the Negro touches that of the white man. When clothes are laundered, the life of the Negro touches that of the white man. When sickness and death comes to the white man's house, the life of the Negro touches his. Crime draws no color line. Filth draws no color line. Contagious diseases draw no color line.

Another result of this movement, I hope, will cause each one of you as he returns to his home or community, to make an effort to know the Negro better in your own town, in your own street. Unfortunately, in this country many of the best white Christians do not know about the best type of Negroes by first hand information. The white man in many sections knows more about the criminal Negro than about the law-abiding Negro. When you return home, without the cost of money or sacrifice of social prestige, you can get into helpful contact with the best Negroes. To do this you will not have to cross the ocean; in many cases it will be only to merely cross the street.

I want the white man in every part of America to see more of the struggles and the progress that the Negro is making in the direction of better homes, Young Men's Christian Associations, better Sunday schools, better churches, better schools and colleges as well as in commercial growth. In a large degree in the future the white man must try to judge the Negro by his best types, not by his worst. In all these things the church furnishes a potent and practical agency through which the two races can know each other better and cooperate with each other more sympathetically.

Mine is not a selfish plea to the church. I want to see the Negro saved for his own sake, and I want to see the Negro saved in order that the white race which surrounds him may be saved. All history teaches that wherever the white race has been surrounded by a weaker race and a neglected race of any color, that there the white man has yielded to the temptation to degrade himself because of injustice perpetrated upon the weak race.

It is a glorious thing to be permitted to live in this country. Changes are taking place in human civilization such as were never witnessed before.

I count it a rare privilege to belong to a race whose ancestors were brought here only a few years ago as savages. You of the white race should count it a glorious thing to have had a part in transforming twenty slaves into ten millions of aspiring, hopeful Christian citizens. We are yet a new race. Our best is before us. Already we speak the tongue that you speak, wear the same clothes, eat the same food, profess the same religion, and love the Stars and Stripes as dearly as you do, and in traveling still further toward a more perfect religious life, gladly will be helped and guided by you.

TMc Con. 957 BTW Papers DLC.

¹ Ten copies of this speech were forwarded to Roy Bergen Guild, executive secretary of the Men and Religion Forward Movement. BTW wrote: "I ought to add that I do not write out my addresses in full and the other portion of it will have to be taken in shorthand, if you wish the whole of it." (Apr. 15, 1912, Con. 831, BTW Papers, DLC.)

To Woodrow Wilson

[Tuskegee, Ala.] April 23, 1912

My dear Sir: I hesitate very much to seem to interfere in a matter that does not directly concern me.

I understand that there is a bill before the Legislature of New Jersey, which is likely to pass, providing for special juvenile courts in the large cities. If the bill passes, I wish to call to your attention Mr. Algernon T. Sweeney,[1] of Newark, New Jersey, as being a man fit to be the judge of one of these courts.

I have known Mr. Sweeney for a number of years in connection with educational and social work, and I know of few men in the country who, in my opinion, possess better qualifications for such a judgeship than is true of Mr. Sweeney.

My race in Newark and vicinity owes Mr. Sweeney a special debt of gratitude for his deep interest in their uplift. Yours very truly,

[Booker T. Washington]

TLc. Con. 467 BTW Papers DLC.

[1] Algernon T. Sweeney (1823–1912) practiced law in Newark, N.J., from 1896 until his death. He had been judge of the criminal court in Newark.

To Willis Duke Weatherford

[Tuskegee, Ala.] April Twenty-seventh, Nineteen Hundred Twelve

Dear Dr. Weatherford: I telegraphed you this morning as follows:

Am canvassing girls. Will wire Monday what can be done.

As soon as your letter was received I promptly took it up with Mrs. Washington to see what could be done in the way of providing you with the help you need at your conference. Mrs. Washington feels that she can provide you with as many as fifteen or twenty girls, and that she can provide all of the chambermaids during the vacation period.

We are compelled to keep here at Tuskegee one hundred or more girls to carry on the summer work because of our summer school for teachers and other activities which go on during these three summer months.

I thank you sincerely for giving us the opportunity of supplying girls for this work and I am sure it will be helpful to them and to the persons with whom they come in contact. I should think the lectures which you mention as willing to give to these girls would be a most helpful thing and I very much hope you can see your way clear to do this.

I hope that from Hampton Institute you may be able to get the remaining number of girls you desire. Yours very truly,

Booker T. Washington

TLpS   Con. 692   BTW Papers   DLC.

From Duse Mohamed Ali[1]

London, E.C. [England] 1st. May 1912

Dear Dr Washington   Thanks so much for your kind replies to the questions which I consider a most valuable contribution to the journal. I beg to enclose herewith the proof foreword which will convey some idea of our policy.[2] I would like you to send us a short up-to-date "write-up" of your institution with photos of the premises and the principal tutors.[3]

I must tell you that I have received most encouraging letters from, among others, Mons Finot[4] of the Paris Review, (copy enclosed) Sir Harry H Johnston, the Countess of Warwick,[5] Prof Scarborough, H. G. Wells, the novelist, and a host of other prominent persons.

I would like to have a condensed but lucid report of the Negro Conference; *with photos* of the most prominent participants for our second number. (July) We *go to press* on the *Third Tuesday in each month*. With every good wish   Yours very sincerely

Duse Mohamed

P.S. We are wanting agents and correspondents in every part of the United States. Can you aid us in this matter? Kindly state whether you would like copies for free distribution and how many.

D M

ALS   Con. 459   BTW Papers   DLC.

¹ Duse Mohamed, later Duse Mohamed Ali (1866–1945), was a transitional figure between the Pan-Islamic movement in the nineteenth century and the Pan-Africanism of the twentieth century. Born in Alexandria the son of an Egyptian army officer and his Sudanese wife, he went to England at the age of nine for his education. After studying at King's College, University of London, he spent several years as an actor and playwright in England and the United States.

Inspired by the Universal Races Congress in London in 1911 and concerned about growing race prejudice in England, Mohamed founded and edited the *African Times and Orient Review,* from 1912 to 1915 and 1917 to 1920. This journal espoused Egyptian home rule, a theme also of his short history of modern Egypt, *In the Land of the Pharaohs* (1911). He encouraged persons of African descent in Europe and the Americas to identify themselves with the cultural heritage of Africa. Marcus Garvey worked for the journal in 1912–13, and Duse Mohamed Ali, as he called himself after 1917, influenced the early Garvey movement.

From 1921 to 1931, Duse Mohamed Ali lived in the United States as a lecturer, a writer for the *Negro World,* and an advocate of black unity. In 1926 he founded the Universal Islamic Society in Detroit, and in 1927 the American-Asian Association. In 1931 he migrated to Nigeria, where he took part in the struggle for independence as editor of the weekly *Comet,* which advocated nationalism both as home rule and as opposed to tribal particularism. An admirer of BTW, he never succeeded in founding the industrial institute which he considered ideal for the developing agricultural society of Nigeria. (Khalil Mahmud, introduction to Mohamed, *In the Land of the Pharaohs* [2nd ed.], ix-xxxiii.)

² Enclosed was a proof of the first issue of the *African Times and Orient Review,* June 1, 1912.

³ When Mohamed repeated the request, BTW replied that the trustees and the public might object if Tuskegee made a bid for foreign students, though it accepted foreign students who came voluntarily. (ca. Nov. 1, 1912, handwritten draft, Con. 460, BTW Papers, DLC.)

⁴ Jean Finot (1858–1922), born Jean Finckelhaus in Warsaw, was a French journalist and student of social movements. He founded in 1890 the *Revue des revues* and was the author of many books, including *Le préjugé des races* (1905), which expressed approval of Tuskegee and other black industrial schools.

⁵ Frances Evelyn Maynard Breville, Countess of Warwick (1861–1938), a Socialist, founded on one of her estates a technical institute for rural children and on another a home for crippled children. She was involved in many social reform movements, and wrote a life of William Morris.

To James Hardy Dillard

[Tuskegee, Ala.] May 3, 1912

Dear Dr. Dillard: I have held the within letter longer than I intended.

I beg to hand you herewith a copy of one of Mr. Coon's articles on "Public Taxation and Negro Schools," which you may be inclined to send to Mr. Swearingen[1] as an answer to his third question. Mr. Swearingen's attention might also be called to the fact that Negro education is not primarily for the benefit of the Negro, but is for the benefit of the South, in order that it may have the fullest development. When this view is taken of Negro education, it does not become then, in a way, a matter relating only to him personally, and for his special benefit, but it relates to the South as a whole and is for its larger benefit. I submit this memorandum for whatever use it may be to you.

I am sorry to see a State Superintendent of Education raising the question as to the appropriation of taxes paid by each race. When a Negro is hanged for committing a crime, in order that society may be protected, one does not go around seeking to find out how much of the expense of hanging was contributed by white people and how much by Negroes. Both races pay for the hanging in order that society may be protected, and both races pay for the education of all the people so that society may be protected.

I have had an analysis made of the expenditure of money for Negro education in South Carolina. I send you a copy herewith. You will see by it that it is questionable whether the Negro is getting back in South Carolina what he pays in direct taxes. Aside from this, certainly some proportion of the taxes coming from public franchises such as railroads, saloons and what not, ought to go to the Negro.

I shall hope to talk with you on these points when I see you. Yours very truly,

Booker T. Washington

TLpS Con. 57 BTW Papers DLC.

[1] John Eldred Swearingen (b. 1879), though blinded at the age of nine, taught in public schools from 1899 to 1908 and was South Carolina state superintendent of education from 1909 through 1922.

From Arthur Copeland

Auburn, N.Y. May 9 1912

Dear Sir: Your quintette, accompanied by Mr. Wood, gave two entertainments in our prison last Sunday: in the men's and women's prisons, and were a great source of enjoyment and help to our 1400 men and 130 women. They were enthusiastic[al]ly received, and I hope they will come again. I also placed them here in the city at two of the Churches, where they were most kindly received.

I have just had an interview with Mr. Harry Prince, one of our inmates, who has been here four years, and has two years more to serve on a charge of grand larceny. He was an inmate here some seventeen years ago for a short term. He is thirty-five years of age, and unmarried. He is very much interested in poultry raising, and it is the ambition of his life to run a poultry farm. He complains of a trouble in his side and his kidneys, and his coming here has not helped it, but rather made it worse. He is one of what are called our "trusties," and is sent outside the walls by the authorities and trusted to many things which they could not confide to others. He has never been punished for any offense since coming here the last time.

He wants me to write and ask you if you cannot use your influence with Governor John A. Dix to commute his sentence, if possible. He says that you may remember him as being a first cousin to the Honorable Clarence Matthews of Boston, an Assistant United States Attorney; also from the fact that he was with you at the time of that great accident in Birmingham, about 1898, at the Baptist Conference held at Rev Walker's Church; when a large number of people were trampled to death in a panic, at which time he opened a trap door in the platform and let you down through, and out to safety. He thinks that perhaps you would be willing to open a door for him out to liberty.

He would like to interview your able speaker and manager, Mr. Wood, and if you can direct Mr. Wood, when next in this vicinity, to call and see him, if possible, he would be greatly pleased. (We were all delighted with Mr. Wood. He is a rare man with a magnificent voice for public speaking, modest, and a delightful representative of your institution.) I trust you may be able to write Mr. Prince soon, some good word that will show your interest in him. Yours respectfully,

Arthur Copeland
Chaplain

TLS Con. 463 BTW Papers DLC. Written on stationery of Auburn Prison.

From Charles William Anderson

New York, N.Y. May 10th, 1912

Private & confidential

My dear Doctor: Only a line to say that a few days ago the New York "Times" published a Washington despatch headed "Booker Washington working for Roosevelt," in which it stated that Banks and Howard[1] of the Mississippi delegation would support Roosevelt, and that they were both your personal friends and members of the "Business League," etc. etc. I took occasion to touch on the matter in conversation with the President's brother[2] here, and told him that I happened to know where your sympathies were, and that I knew the "Times" article to be wrong.

The fact that this story emanated from Washington inclines me to the belief that some of our "own crowd" have been talking this sort of stuff around Washington. You will recall that I told you about a certain person who said they believed you were for the Colonel, and stated that it was very strange that Bishop Clinton came straight from you in Florida and signed the Roosevelt circular in Washington. This is in confidence.

With warm regards, I remain, Yours faithfully,

Charles W. Anderson

TLS   Con. 550   BTW Papers   DLC.

[1] Perry Wilbon Howard, born in Ebenezer, Miss., in 1877, was for many years a lawyer in Jackson and leader of the black faction of Republicans in Mississippi. He graduated from Rust University (1898) and Illinois College of Law (1906). He was president of Campbell College in Jackson (1899–1900), and taught mathematics at Alcorn A & M University (1900–1905). From 1921 to 1927 he was a special assistant to the U.S. Attorney General.

[2] Henry Wallace Taft (1859–1945), a New York corporation lawyer, raised presidential campaign funds for his brother in 1912.

From Frederick Randolph Moore

New York City May 13, 1912

Confidential,

My dear Mr. Washington: I went down to Washington Monday of last week to talk over the matter of the paper and was afterwards asked to wait over to see the President and Mr. Hilles. I could not wait over, so they asked me to come back again last Friday, so I went down Friday and saw the President and Mr. Hilles and then the members of the President's campaign committee. I found out that some colored men, they would not give me the names, had written them saying that you were writing letters to the colored delegates in the South urging them to stand for the nomination of Mr. Roosevelt. I emphatically denied this and told them that I knew of your interest and friendship for the President. While we had never conversed about the matter yet the fact that The New York Age was giving the President so loyal support, it was largely done through my friendship for you and your friendship for the President. There is someone somewhere who is trying to misrepresent you. I find also that some of our friends are doing great harm in having been elected as delegates and pledged to Taft, are now making overtures or allowing overtures to be made to them for their support of Roosevelt. Andrews[1] of South Carolina was particularly mentioned and Charles Banks of Mound Bayou. I gave them the highest recommendation possible for character and stability and told Mr. McKinley[2] that I knew them to be men that would not break faith or who were men susceptible to be bought. They then asked me if I would not do what I could to help keep Southern delegates in line. Cohen and S. W. Green[3] were also spoken of and I promised to do what I could to help them. While the committee is without funds they promised me that The Age would be given first consideration in the event of Taft's nomination, immediately after the nomination. I was back and forth with them until Sunday night, remaining over Saturday and Sunday at their request to have them consult with Mr. Hilles about the matter which appears in this week's Age on the President's treatment of Negroes. This matter was prepared by W. H. Lewis and is in my opinion a straightforward exposition of the President's attitude. I did not want you to be misrepresented by anyone and I hope that the position I took is approved by you. I am writing to Charles Banks today,[4] for it would be almost suicidal for him to go otherwise than for Taft in as much as the President told me that he was interested in Mound Bayou, and was trying to help them out in every way possible in their efforts to establish Mound Bayou. I consider my trip to have been a very favorable one for I got a chance to learn what was going on, and what was their feeling and I am frank to say that I believe that I allayed the suspicions felt by them through someone in the South who is undoubtedly trying to do you injury. Sincerely yours,

Fred. R. Moore

TLS   Con. 60   BTW Papers   DLC.

[1] William Trent Andrews, born in 1864, graduated from Fisk University in 1890 and from Howard University Law School in 1892. He combined a law practice in his home town, Sumter, S.C., with extensive investments in real estate. Active in Republican affairs in South Carolina, he attended the national conventions of 1908 and 1912 as a delegate. He was a close friend and frequent correspondent of Whitefield McKinlay.

[2] William Brown McKinley (1856–1926) was a Taft leader in Illinois in 1912. He was a Republican congressman (1905–13, 1915–21) and U.S. senator (1921–26).

[3] Smith W. Green of New Orleans was Supreme Chancellor of the black Knights of Pythias for about twenty years beginning in 1909. Born near Waterproof, La., he owned and operated a store in Lake Providence, La., and first became a member of the Knights in 1883.

[4] Moore wrote Banks: "It is very necessary that our leading men stand out strong in support of Taft and not allow any suspicions to attach to them." (May 13, 1912, Con. 60, BTW Papers, DLC.)

To Henry Smith Pritchett

[Tuskegee, Ala.] May 20 [1912][1]

My dear Dr. Pritchett: The enclosed letter[2] relates to Miss Mary F. Mackie, a former Principal of the Academic Department of the Hampton Institute. If you have ever read my book, "Up from Slavery" you will see that I described how I got into Hampton by sweeping the floor. Miss Mackie is the woman who gave me this opportunity. She is now old and in great need.

I am wondering if it would be possible for the Carnegie Foundation to make an exception in her case. I hesitate to write you because I know how easy it is for one to make a bore of himself in asking for exceptions, but while I have asked your Board to make several exceptions, you do not know in how many cases I have absolutely refused to sign papers or have anything to do with those who were applying to your Board.

Miss Mackie is one of the finest characters in the whole country and there are hundreds of fine men and women educated at Hampton who owe their usefulness to her. Dr. Frissell would endorse, I am sure, all I am saying to you about Miss Mackie. Yours very truly,

[Booker T. Washington]

TLp   Con. 462   BTW Papers   DLC.

¹ Year established by BTW's letter to Lucy Gillett, May 20, 1912, Con. 454, BTW Papers, DLC., agreeing to write to the Carnegie Foundation on behalf of Mary Mackie.

² Lucy Gillett to BTW, May 13, [1912], Con. 454, BTW Papers, DLC.

To Monroe Nathan Work

[Tuskegee, Ala.] May 20, 1912

Mr. Work: Please let me know by Thursday of this week what the colored population of Macon County is, and how many colored people have been in jail in this county within the last 12 months. I wish also you would let me know later on what the colored population of Fulton County, Georgia is and how many colored people have been in prison from that county within the last 12 months; and the same thing regarding Montgomery County, Alabama.

B. T. W.

TLI   Con. 985   BTW Papers   DLC.

To Charles Banks

[Tuskegee, Ala.] May 20, 1912

Personal and Confidential

My dear Mr. Banks: You will see that the public press has linked your name up with mine in connection with Mr. Roosevelt and Mr. Taft. You can easily see that if you should shift from Mr. Taft, it would be very embarrassing to me. Of course, this is highly confidential. I presume you have seen the various newspaper dispatches on this subject. I am quite sure that these dispatches are fakes, hatched up in Washington, but they were purported to be sent out from Montgomery, which I am quite sure is false and not true. Nevertheless they are having their effect. Yours very truly,

[Booker T. Washington]

TLp   Con. 56   BTW Papers   DLC.

Margaret James Murray Washington
to Lucy Brown Johnston[1]

[Tuskegee, Ala.] May 21, 1912

Dear Madam: Your letter to Mr. Washington has been received and since he is not now at the school, his Secretary has sent the letter to him for reply.

I am happy to be able to go on record with you for the absolute freedom of women in all things pertaining to the life she lives. The colored women of the country, thus far, have done little or nothing, however, for the suffrage movement. There have been and are still other questions of vital importance to us as a race of women and it is with these questions and problems that we have been engaged. We are trying hard to fit ourselves to take our stand with the women of your race when the country reaches the point of giving the women equal rights with all other citizens.

Colored men generally have thus far taken no stand either for or against woman suffrage to any large extent because they, too, have

539

been working in [the] direction already traversed by your race. I am sure, however, that our men will be found to be just as broad upon this question of the independence of money [women?] as many of the men of your race are today, realizing that the exercise of one's will even though it be that of a woman, cannot help but strengthen and dignify that person and so strengthen and dignify the entire race. I believe with you that this question of suffrage for women is one that must affect not only women but the entire human race. Yours very truly,

Mrs. Booker T. Washington

TLpS Con. 457 BTW Papers DLC.

1 Lucy Brown Johnston (b. 1847) was a white clubwoman. Born in Camden, Ohio, she attended Western College for Women in Oxford, Ohio. Moving to Kansas as the wife of William Agnew Johnston, she wrote to BTW in 1901 as president of the Kansas Social Science Federation asking whether BTW did not agree with her that black women's clubs should maintain their separate identity rather than seek admission to the General Federation of Women's Clubs. (Dec. 16, 1901, Con. 201, BTW Papers, DLC.) She served two years as president of the Kansas Federation of Women's Clubs and two years as state regent of the Daughters of the American Revolution. While president of the Kansas Equal Suffrage Association, she asked BTW to endorse woman suffrage. (May 11, 1912, Con. 457, BTW Papers, DLC.)

From W. C. Daniel

Tuskegee, Ala. May 21 1912

Sir Yours received and contents noted will say that my Jail Register shows that there was (226) two Hundred & twenty six Negros committed to Jail in the past twelve months Ending May 1st 1912 would like to say that I think that is a small number out of about twenty thousand Population.

Most of this number was for some small offence such as Card playing on Sunday & Fals Pretence that did not amount to much
any time I can do any thing to help you let me no Resp

W C Daniel
Sheriff

ALS Con. 985 BTW Papers DLC.

From William E. Reynolds[1]

Milledgeville, Georgia   May 22, 1912

Sir: In an address delivered before an immense audience in the Milledgeville Opera House, Hon. Thos. E. Watson, of this state, is quoted by a gentleman present as making the unqualified statement that Governor Woodrow Wilson, of New Jersey, sent to you a message of sympathy, either by letter or telegraph, following the trouble with Ulrich in New York City.

I am personally acquainted with Mr. Watson. Was in college with him, belonged to the same secret fraternity, and have been his personal friend for more than thirty years.

On yesterday, I received a letter from Hon. Wm. F. McCombs,[2] Mgr. Governor Wilson's campaign, carrying an emphatic denial of the statement made by Mr. Watson and by others, with reference to sending you any message by Mr. Wilson. Later in the day, I received a letter from Governor Wilson himself, in which the denial was made in the most emphatic terms.

I addressed two letters on yesterday to Mr. Watson, enclosing copies of the letters received from Mr. McCombs and Mr. Wilson, and asking him as his friend, if he would not furnish me with the authority upon which he based the statement made in the address referred to. I am seeking this information simply to satisfy myself personally as to the truth or falsity of this charge that has been brought against Mr. Wilson, with the evident intent and purpose to injure his chances for the Democratic nomination.[3] I intend to make no political use of the information, but mean simply to defend the character of a Christian gentleman, against what I consider an unrighteous assault.

Will you do me the kindness to state, over your signature, whether Mr. Wilson did or did not send such message of sympathy to you after your trouble in New York? I shall be glad to have your prompt reply to this letter, and I have no doubt that you will be absolutely frank and sincere in whatever statement you may make to me on the subject. Respectfully,

Wm. E. Reynolds

TLS   Con. 463   BTW Papers   DLC.

1 President of Georgia Military College.

2 William Frank McCombs (1875–1921), an Arkansas-born graduate of Princeton (1898) and of Harvard Law School (1901), managed the campaigns for Wilson's nomination and election in 1912 and 1916. He was chairman of the Democratic National Committee from 1912 to 1916.

3 Luke Clancy of New York City also wrote asking whether Woodrow Wilson had telegraphed or written to BTW deploring the Ulrich incident and offering support. (Clancy to E. J. Scott, May 16, 1912, Con. 450, BTW Papers, DLC.)

To Charles B. Purvis

[Tuskegee, Ala.] May 27, 1912

Confidential.

My dear Dr. Purvis: Please do not let anyone see this letter.

Of course, at the next meeting of the Howard University Trustee Board, June 1st, the matter of the next president will come up. I very much fear it will not be possible for me to be present.

I really think that the best and wisest thing to do would be to postpone the matter until we can have time to consider it thoroughly, and call a special meeting for the purpose of taking up the matter of the presidency. I hope you will urge this view upon the Trustees. Yours very truly,

Booker T. Washington

TLpS   Con. 455   BTW Papers   DLC.

To James Hardy Dillard

[Tuskegee, Ala.] May 27, 1912

My dear Dr. Dillard: I am very glad to receive your letter of May 22d written from Hotel Warwick.

I have heard directly and indirectly something about the success of the Conference to which you refer and you know I am deeply gratified.[1] Our future salvation as a race depends largely upon working the white people of the South up to a conscientious and intelligent interest in our welfare. This I am more and more convinced of each day.

I should be very glad to see you here at any time. According to my present plan, I shall be here until the 20th of June, though I may be called away for a few days.

You will be glad to know that Bishop Strange of North Carolina preached our Commencement Sermon yesterday. Yours very truly,

Booker T. Washington

TLpS   Con. 57   BTW Papers   DLC.

[1] At the first meeting of the Southern Sociological Congress in 1912, Dillard led in the formation of the University Commission on Southern Race Questions. Representatives of eleven state universities agreed to encourage southern college men to approach the race question "with intelligent information and sympathetic interest." The commission drew black educators into its ranks and promoted the study of race problems in white universities. (Tindall, *Emergence of the New South,* 175–76.) In a letter to BTW, Dillard called the sessions "the best I have ever attended," with "good talks by white and colored men." (May 22, 1912, Con. 57, BTW Papers, DLC.)

From Kelly Miller

Washington, D.C. May 27, 1912

Personal & Confidential.

My dear Dr. Washington: As I telegraphed you, I had hoped that en route either to or from Savannah, I might make it possible to come by Tuskegee but the Railroad connections are so uncertain in the south that I find it is impossible for me to do so and reach here by Friday morning when the President will return.

President Thirkield will, of course, resign in order to assume his duties as Bishop in the Methodist Church. The fundamental question is whether a white man or a colored man should be chosen for the vacancy. This is, of course, a serious question and should be given full consideration. I am decidedly of the opinion that the time has now arrived for colored men to be put in control of activities intimately connected with the racial life and uplift. We still need and shall for a long time need the support and encouragement of rightly disposed white men to encourage and uphold our cause. The Tuskegee plan strikes me as representing the best working relationship between the races. The managing board is made up chiefly of white men of the highest standing and connection, while the intimate handling of the affairs of the institution is placed in charge of colored men. At Howard University the situation is somewhat complicated, because we have white men on the Faculty in various places who are doing the work with great acceptability. Under a change of policy these would of course gradually withdraw. There would be some disadvantages in making the re-adjustment; but there is no reason to suppose that colored men might not be found or developed to carry on the activities of this great institution.

The next question is one of candidates for the position. Of course many colored men feel that they are qualified for any task which any other colored man may be expected to perform. In my judgment the University should select a colored man who embodies the spirit and the aim and ideal of the University and who is able to impress this influence inside of the University circle and upon the outside world at large. My name has been used in this connection. I want to say, that I regard Howard University as infinitely larger than the claims and aspirations of any individual. My supreme desire is that the best man be secured for the place. If in the general judgment I am found to be such a person I shall, of course, regard it as a call to duty and devote all of my character, intelligence and energy towards promoting the welfare of the Institution. If on the other hand some other clearly proves to be a better man for the function, then I am perfectly willing to fall in behind him in promoting the same task.

I believe that the one selected should be able to work in harmony with the general educational and philanthropic movements of the time, while of course, emphasizing the specialty for which his work stands. In this regard I think I can appeal to a long standing consistency, as I have already deprecated any controversy among those who are co-laborers in the same vineyard of racial uplift. I have thus written freely and frankly because I am sure that you appreciate this spirit and disposition.

If you are to attend the meeting on Saturday I shall be glad to see you in the city at any time or place suitable to your convenience. Yours truly,

Kelly Miller

TLS Con. 460 BTW Papers DLC.

From Charles William Anderson

New York, N.Y. May 27, 1912

PERSONAL. Private & confidential.

My dear Doctor: The situation is still peculiar. The most regrettable thing in connection with it is that "our big friend"[1] or his advisors seem to be suspicious of everybody. The false and malicious report that you had gone to Mississippi to sway Banks is only one of the many which have been made to the headquarters at Washington. Gilchrist Stewart tells me that he was told by Congressman Olcott[2] that our "big friend" on being requested to appoint a certain colored man in Cincinnati to help out the Ohio fight, replied, that he would do nothing of the kind, as the brethren were ungrateful and were all against him, notwithstanding, all he had done for them, and added that only one negro office-holder in the country was really loyal to him. He said, so the report goes, that he had had private reports on all of them, and with the exception of this one man, they were all shouting for the Colonel. Whether there is anything in the story or not, I am not prepared to say. I pass it on to you with the name of the man who passed it to me. Sometime ago two or three different persons informed me that The Gov. and Moore[3] were in a deal to discover which way I was leaning and report the same to headquarters. Mr. Moore called on each of these gentlemen and asked him to engage me in conversation and find out how I talked, and put him in early possession of a report which he said he intended to send to Washington. This is such scurrilous conduct, that it was difficult for me to believe him capable of it, and yet the three men are men of truthfulness and incapable of lying, and are also men who could have no possible motive in bringing the story. Just think of it! You know what I have done in the past for both of these men. I appointed one of them to office, and the other one I fought for for many years, against great odds. Whether this story is true or false, both men are very bitter against every man whom they suspect of being for the Colonel. Their threats of punishment to be visited on all office holders who do not agree with them, is the talk of the town. They are constant companions, and in fact, the elder man is now living at the home of the other man's daughter. They have made several trips of late to Washington, and it was while on one of these trips that Dr. Elbert was visited, and the gentleman's suspicion that you were working the other way, was confirmed. I pass this on in strictest confidence.

As I told you in a previous letter, I wrote a strong letter to Mr. H. assuring him that the rumor about your trip was false. Enclosed is the reply to my letter. In my opinion, if our friends at Washington had played fair, these rumors would have been killed at headquarters. The "powers" did me the honor of classing me as the man closest to you, now that the air is full of false rumors. Formerly, when you were supposed to be closest at court and your loyalty was unquestioned, the colored friends at Washington were very busy convincing the President and his friends that they were the closest people on earth to you. It now appears that they are not especially close. You and I seem to be the only occupants of that room in which the hidden wires of political intrigue are being manipulated. As for me, I wish no higher compliment than to have people know that I am the loyal friend of the leader of my race, and the man who has done more for me than any other living man. I know that you, and I think you know that I, never play false with any one, high or low, and never betray a friend, or depreciate another that we might gain strength or influence for ourselves. By and by when this storm passes over, we will both be able to distinguish between the real and the pretended friends. In the meantime, we can afford to say nothing and "saw wood." No man need fear the future when his purposes are high and his motives pure.

Hoping to see or hear from you soon, I remain, Yours truly,

C. W. A.

TLI   Con. 56   BTW Papers   DLC.   No enclosure found.

¹ William Howard Taft.

² Jacob Van Vechten Olcott (1856–1940), a Republican lawyer, served in Congress from 1905 to 1911. His New York City district included the black neighborhood known as San Juan Hill, where BTW spoke in his favor in 1906. (BTW to E. E. Olcott, Nov. 9, 1906, Con. 329, BTW Papers, DLC.)

³ The names of "The Gov." (P. B. S. Pinchback) and Fred R. Moore were left blank in the typed letter and were filled in by Anderson in his own hand.

To Kelly Miller

[Tuskegee, Ala.] May 29, 1912

Personal and Confidential

My dear Professor Miller: I do not mind saying to you through my pen what I intended to say in person, had we had an opportunity to meet. Of course, this is highly confidential and is not to pass from your hands.

I very much hope that the Board will not attempt to select a President at the meeting next Saturday. I think it will be a mistake to do this and I have so written one or two of the Trustees. I think the whole matter ought to be postponed for a special meeting and give us time to deliberate carefully. I am very sorry on account of our own Commencement it is a physical impossibility for me to be present at the June meeting.

There are two questions to be decided:

First: has the time come when a colored man should be at the head of Howard University? Without committing myself on this point, I would say I believe it has, still I confess I am open to argument.

Second, if a colored man is to be put in charge, I have thoroughly made up my mind that you are the person. You are the logical man and I find the country practically unanimous on this point. If the main question as to the advisability of putting in a colored man is decided in the affirmative, I do not believe there would be any opposition to amount to anything to your being appointed and I would do whatever I could to further that end.

If a white man is to be chosen, I am very anxious to have a conference with you before I enter into any meeting looking toward the choosing of a white man. Yours very truly,

Booker T. Washington

TLpS   Con. 460   BTW Papers   DLC.

To Charles B. Purvis

[Tuskegee, Ala.] June Fifth, Nineteen Hundred Twelve

Dear Dr. Purvis: Thank you for your letter from Washington.[1] I shall follow your instructions and plan to be present at the next trustees meeting.

You and I agree thoroughly regarding the new Bishop.[2] We want to get somebody who is not in any way under his control or influence personally. I have practically no faith in him.

I hope to talk with you before the meeting of the board. Yours very truly,

Booker T. Washington

TLpS   Con. 462   BTW Papers   DLC.

[1] Purvis wrote on June 1, 1912, urging BTW to attend the next Howard University board meeting and to nominate a strong candidate. He opposed any candidate that W. P. Thirkield would propose "upon general principles," and opposed "creating a place for some hungry Methodist minister." He urged BTW out of his wide experience to name a candidate of broad outlook, saying: "A *business man* is needed, a man of moral courage, & who has connections." (Con. 462, BTW Papers, DLC.)

[2] Wilbur Patterson Thirkield.

From Monroe Nathan Work

[Tuskegee, Ala.] June 6, 1912

Mr. B. T. Washington: I have carefully examined Sheriff Daniel's letter of May 31 concerning the commitments to the Macon County Jail.[1] I have also had an interview with him. I find that the 226 commitments to jail are all the persons that were "Committed for offences that are liable in Circuit and County Courts." This does not, however, include all who had been arrested by the sheriff and his deputies. I do not believe that by taking jail commitments you can get a clear convincing statement concerning the orderliness of Macon County as contrasted with other counties.

The United States Census reports that in 1904 875 Colored persons were committed to all jails, workhouses, and penitentiaries in the state.

You will observe that the commitments to the Macon County Jail for the past year, 226, were almost one-fourth of what was reported as committed to all prisons in the state for 1904. The commitments of Negroes to all Georgia prisons for 1904 were 958.

The use of the word "commitments" by the United States Census does not mean the same as it does when used by Sheriff Daniel. The difficulty comes, however, in trying to distinguish between the two uses of the word.

Permit me to suggest what I believe is a better and a convincing way of contrasting the orderliness of Macon County with other counties and cities. This can be done by comparing the number of criminal cases tried in Macon County with the number of criminal cases tried in other counties and cities.

We can easily secure from the clerk of the Macon County Court the number of criminal cases tried in this county. The biennial report of the attorney general of the state furnishes the data for other counties and cities. The comparison would be thus: for each thousand persons in Macon County there was probably about five criminal cases; the number of criminal cases for each thousand persons in Jefferson County was 27; in Walker County, 39; in the City of Montgomery, 20; in Bessemer, 60; Talladega City, 83. This appears to indicate that there is from two to ten times more disorderliness in some other parts of Alabama than there is in Macon County.

The number of murder cases tried in the Macon County Court can also be contrasted with the number of murder cases tried in the courts of other counties and cities; for example, the three or four murder cases in the Macon County Court can be contrasted with the 13 murder cases in the Anniston City Court, or the 35 murder cases in Montgomery, the 13 murder cases in the Gadsden City Court, the 25 murder cases in the Mobile City Court, the 17 murder cases in the Jackson County Court, the 20 murder cases in the Tuscaloosa County Court, the 27 murder cases in the Walker County Court, and the 92 murder cases in the Jefferson County Court.

If this suggestion meets your approval, I will frame a letter to the clerk of the Macon County Court, and will also try to interview him.

[Monroe N. Work]

TL   Con. 985   BTW Papers   DLC.

From Clara J. Johnston

Malden, West. Va. June 9th 1912

Dear Uncle Booker: Mamma ask me to write you for her and thank you for the check. Mamma is sick with neuralgia of the body. She has been sick nearly two weeks. I have the doctor to come to see her.

We are glad you are going to be at Institute a day this summer and hope you will get to come to Malden while you are in West Virginia. Dr. Gamblin[1] called to see if any of us were going to Tuskegee.

Homecoming is on the nineteenth. We wish you and Uncle John could be with us. Mr Lovely is here and send his best regards to the Washingtons.

Mr Lovely is up every morning   he works by four o'clock and goes to the head of Campbell Creek, fourteen miles. He loads coal. From three to five cars a day. Mr Straughter[2] rides the labor train due at Malden five forty five A.M and back to Malden six fifty two P.M. He works on the coke yard.

Several who have not respond to your letter will do so a little later. We are wearing our heavy coats of mornings and evenings.

Mamma, Miss Mary, and Ben[3] join me in best regards to you Aunt Jacobum and the children.

Hope all are well. With best wishes for you in your work   Your neice

Clara

ALS   Con. 457   BTW Papers   DLC.

[1] Henry Floyd Gamble.
[2] D. Musey Strawder.
[3] Her brother, Benjamin H. Johnston, attended Tuskegee in 1904–5.

From William Henry Lewis

Washington. June 19, 1912

Dear Dr. Washington: I have received the enclosed[1] suggesting that I become a member of the Association for the Advancement of Colored People. I am inclined to do so if you see no objection. It may be that I can be of service by being on the inside.

Please write me what you think about it at your earliest convenience. Sincerely yours,

William H. Lewis

TLS   Con. 458   BTW Papers   DLC.

[1] May Childs Nerney, secretary of the NAACP, wrote to Lewis inviting his membership, which she said would strengthen the NAACP's support of him in his efforts to gain membership in the American Bar Association. (Copy, June 17, 1912, Con. 458, BTW Papers, DLC.) Lewis wrote to W. E. B. Du Bois that he planned to join the NAACP. (June 21, 1912, W. E. B. Du Bois Papers, MU.)

To George Washington Carver

[Tuskegee, Ala.] June Twentieth, Nineteen Hundred Twelve

Mr. Carver: I think, unconscious to yourself, that there is growing within you a disposition to take in an unkind way the orders or requests which are made in the Council and elsewhere in reference to the Experiment Station work.

I fear that you, like some other members of the Council, are inclined to misinterpret my suggestions which in many cases, in fact most cases, are but a polite way of giving orders.

I do not want the Council to become a debating club, where every member feels that he must either object to or debate every order or suggestions given by the Principal. I have reasons for every order I give and suggestions that I make in reference to any department, and it is not necessary for any head to feel that when I do make suggestions that it is because he is not doing his duty or trying to do it. We can all make improvements and changes by hearing suggestions from other people, and I should dislike very much to see you get to the point where you feel that it is a personal affront for suggestions to be made to you in reference to the improvement of your work.

Booker T. Washington

TLpS   Con. 630   BTW Papers   DLC.

To Julius Rosenwald

[Tuskegee, Ala.] June 21, 1912

Dear Mr. Rosenwald: I have considered carefully the suggestion which you made regarding the method of helping the colored schools of the South, and after looking into the matter with some care, I am convinced, as I suggested to you, that it would hardly be possible to help through the medium of the state, as the states, as states, do not recognize the matter of race with reference to dealing with the public schools. The only provision made in the constitutions of the Southern states is that the schools must be separate as to race, and that the money must be divided equitably between the races. This means that the money given by the state is sent out into the various counties of the state and that the county board of education divides the money between the races as it sees fit, in most cases, the colored schools receiving a very very small share.

In addition to the appropriations made by the states, there is a plan in many of the states, and it is growing in favor, whereby the counties can impose extra taxes upon themselves for the purposes of education. The amount raised in this way, however, is small, and only a few of the counties have as yet attempted this plan. I am convinced that it would be a wise plan to begin with one or more states, letting the matter develop gradually and learning by experience.

I would suggest, however, that a good, strong man be employed to overlook the expenditure of the fund, and that this man work through and with the state and county authorities. There are some dangers to be guarded against — one to have the counties understand thoroughly that you would give a certain amount provided they would give a certain amount in the way of an increase over what is now being done. The temptation in some places would be for the counties to lean on you, and do even less than they are now doing instead of more. The wisest plan would be for the man in charge of the fund to get in thorough touch with, say, a half dozen county superintendents and county boards who are in thorough sympathy with the plan, get them to work in their county, and in this way it would soon attract the attention of other county officials, and they would make application to have the same thing done in their counties. Beginning in this way with a few counties at first, I believe the plan would attract attention and gradually spread throughout the South. If the right kind of man is employed to take charge of the matter, he could not only accomplish a great deal of good in connection with the county officials, but equally as much good could be accomplished by him in going through the South, talking to the Southern white people and convincing them that it is to their interest to help educate the Negro. There is no work that I do in the South that I get more satisfaction out of than going through different states and talking directly to Southern white audiences about the interest they should take in the education of the Negro. I have been surprised at the responses I have gotten. The Southern white man likes to be talked to, but does not like to be talked about. Great care should be exercised to let the county officials feel as far as possible that they are doing the work — in a word, to place the responsibility upon them.

As a basis for you to reckon from, the state of Alabama appropriates from its treasury $2,865,254 each year for public school education. I should say that in the rough, $357,585 of this amount goes to the Negro schools. I think this is a fair sample of what other states are doing.

To begin with, I think the publication of the general scheme in the newspapers of the South, as you suggested, would create a good deal of discussion pro and con. This in itself would do good in the direction of helping the Southern people and Northern people as well to look into the facts as to what is actually being done for Negro education.

Enclosed I send you a memorandum describing conditions in Willcox County, Alabama.[1] I am sorry to say that there are many counties in the South that are going in the same way toward Negro education. I should be glad to talk with you, however, regarding the scheme, when I see you.

I have enclosed somewhat in tabulated form my ideas. I would add that I have gone over this matter thoroughly with a number of our workers, and the plan suggested has their approval. I should hope that the scheme would carry with it a plan for building school houses as well as extending the school terms. Many of the places in the South where the schools are now taught are as bad as stables, and it is impossible for the teacher to do efficient work in such places. Yours very truly,

Booker T. Washington

[*Enclosure*]

SCHEME FOR HELPING COLORED SCHOOLS

1. Begin with one or more states.
2. Make the county rather than the state the unit for operation.
3. Put a man in charge of the fund who would work with and through the county officials.
4. A few of the most favorable counties to be selected to begin with.
5. Plan should embrace building of schoolhouses, extention of school terms, and increase of teachers' salaries.
6. Care should be taken to see that the county is not permitted to fall back on this fund and do less than it is now doing, but more in each case.
7. Some of the time, the person in charge of the fund should talk in public and in private to Southern white people in the direction of convincing them of the value of Negro education.

TLSr Copy   Con. 62   BTW Papers   DLC.

¹ This enclosure not found.

Emmett Jay Scott to William Henry Lewis

[Tuskegee, Ala.] June Twenty-Second Nineteen Hundred and Twelve

Personal

Dear Lewis: In re: your letter to Dr. Washington just received:

Please pardon a word of temerity from an old friend. If that association should succeed in annexing you, I think you are likely to find yourself in association with that entire group of malcontents who opposed your appointment and at the same time, or afterward, did every-thing they could to bring about the failure of your confirmation.

Their first movement always seems to be to go about "annexing" those friends of ours that they can, so as to put themselves in position to continue their underhanded, and as we are able to definitely state, malicious attacks upon the Doctor and his work, and at the same time, say they have our friends as members of their association, and therefore, are not opposing him.

I feel quite sure that the Doctor will be writing you himself at the first convenient opportunity. I hope I may see you soon. I leave here for New York within the next day or two. Yours truly,

E J Scott

TLSr Copy   Con. 458   BTW Papers   DLC.

From Emmett Jay Scott

New York, July 4, 1912

Mr. Washington: Mr. Trumbull,[1] Mr. Wiley informs me, has re-quested the latter to talk over the mill proposition with you, and yes-terday, so I am also informed by Mr. Wiley, suggested that he would like to talk with you and Mr. Wiley together before you leave town about the matter. I suggested to Mr. Wiley that it would be best not to trouble you about the matter today as I feel quite sure you would want to rest up from your engagements.

I have taken the time during your absence to examine very care-fully all of Mr. Wiley's papers, etc. I find that he has within $4,000 of securing all the money to accomplish what he is trying to do. Two thousand of this amount will be forthcoming almost immediately upon the expression of an opinion on your part — not in specific approval of the Wiley enterprise, but in general approval of the idea of encour-aging black people to go into such movements; in other words, what Mr. Trumbull has written is in the direction of giving the colored people a chance, and he is willing to sign this letter from what he has written you, if you view his letter, which is very conservative, from a favorable angle.

I have looked at Mr. Wiley's original papers, and find that Col.

Higginson, Mr. Endicott,[2] of Kidder, Peabody & Co., Mrs. R. P. Hallowell,[3] Mr. Kelsey,[4] Mr. V. Everit Macy, Mr. Bowdelet,[5] Sanger Bros.[6] of Dallas, Texas, and others, all subscribe to his plan for amounts of $500, 1000 and $1200, and others are to follow soon thereafter.

Under all the circumstances, I have brought myself to feel that you would not care to have the whole enterprise go astray because of what might look like an unfavorable attitude on your part. These white business men, including Mr. Kelsey as you will remember, have examined the prospectus and have endorsed it more favorably than one could reasonably expect.

One good thing in Mr. Wiley's favor, as I understand it, is he has not sought to impress you in this matter at all. Your connection with the matter comes about because of Mr. Trumbull's desire to have a favorable word from you since he wishes, as I understand it, to feel that since he is a trustee of Tuskegee that he is doing something for others if not in the same direction, then in the same general direction. I beg to make a plea in Mr. Wiley's behalf.

I think well to keep in mind that an advisory board at Mr. Trumbull's suggestion, composed of some of the wealthiest citizens of Dallas, who are to serve as a finance committee, has been organized and will represent Mr. Trumbull and other subscribers, thereby becoming responsible for the safe and sane conduct of the mill. Yours very truly,

Emmett J. Scott

TLSr Con. 620 BTW Papers DLC.

[1] Frank Trumbull (1858–1920), chairman of the board of the C & O Railroad, was a trustee of Tuskegee Institute beginning in 1910.

[2] William Endicott, an 1887 Harvard graduate, was employed by the Boston banking firm of Kidder, Peabody and Co. from 1887 to 1897, when he became a partner of the firm, a relationship he continued for more than thirty years.

[3] Anna Davis, born into a Quaker family in Philadelphia in 1838, married Richard Price Hallowell in 1859 and moved to West Medford, Mass.

[4] Clarence H. Kelsey (1856–1930), a Yale graduate (1878) and lawyer, was president of the Title Guarantee and Trust Co., which he had helped to found in 1882. He took a lifelong interest in Hampton and Tuskegee, raised a $5 million endowment for the two schools in 1925, and was chairman of the Hampton board of trustees.

[5] Charles Pickering Bowditch of Boston (b. 1842) was president of the Pepperell Manufacturing Co. and a student of Mayan archaeology.

[6] Isaac, Alexander, Philip, Samuel, and Cornelia Sanger were directors of Sanger Bros., a wholesale and retail dry-goods and clothing firm in Dallas. Alexander Sanger was also vice-president of the Dallas Trust and Savings Bank.

To Edward Page Gaston[1]

[Tuskegee, Ala.] July 5, 1912

Dear Sir: I take pleasure in sending you some information on Prohibition of Drink Traffic as affecting the Negro population in America. The Negro is made an issue in the agitation of the Prohibition question in practically all the Southern states. It is now, however, on the same grounds that he is being made an issue in South Africa. That is, that the agitation of Prohibition will tend to decrease the assaults upon women. The contention here is that Prohibition will make the Negro more reliable, a better workman, and reduce his general crime rate.

I am sending you a manuscript copy of a little pamphlet published under the auspices of the Colored Women's Christian Temperance Union.

Judge William Holcombe Thomas, who has had long years of experience as judge in the courts of Montgomery, Alabama, in a recent address before the Southern Sociological Congress at Nashville, Tennessee in May, 1912, on the Negro and Crime said:

> If I were asked to give two chief causes of crime, out of an experience of ten years as a trial judge, I should answer, "ignorance and drunkenness." Yet this is difficult to prove.
>
> Of drunkenness as a cause, two examples will suffice for this discussion. Contrast the decrease in crime to Alabama for the "dry" year of 1908 with the "wet" year 1907. In the cities of seventeen counties with 201,900 population, in 1907, there were 6,637 arrests for drunks and in 1908 there was a decrease of 5,131. The arrests for all offenses for 1907 were 24,345 and in 1908 there was a decrease of 11,742. For example, in Tennessee, I am informed, that in the year 1905–6 your prison record showed 1,350 prisoners committed. The "wet" counties, with a population of 601,622 furnished 851, or one for every 707 of population; the other eighty-four counties with a population of 1,418,993 furnished 499, or one for every 2,844 of their population.
>
> No argument is necessary as to the effect of strong drink on the ignorant and on those not having learned the lesson of self-control.

Wishing you every success in your efforts, I am   Very truly yours,

Booker T. Washington

TLpSr Con. 465 BTW Papers DLC.

[1] Edward Page Gaston of London, honorary secretary of the International Prohibition Confederation, had asked for information on the effects of prohibition on blacks in the United States. (Gaston to BTW, June 19, 1912, Con. 465, BTW Papers, DLC.)

To Frank Trumbull

New York City, July 5, 1912

Dear Sir: I have just had a talk with Mr. Jos. L. Wiley regarding his cotton mill proposition, and I am writing to say that in my opinion if a cotton mill of the kind that he describes can be properly organized and financed it will be of great benefit to our race, and I very much hope that Mr. Wiley through the aid of friends as well as his own efforts can succeed in putting his undertaking on a good foundation and that it will be so conducted that it will be a first-class paying investment as well as an object lesson in the direction of showing what the Negro can do in manufacturing enterprises. Yours truly,

[Booker T. Washington]

TLc   Con. 466   BTW Papers   DLC.

To Sophie Rosenwald Adler[1]

Boston, Mass. July 9th, 1912

My dear Mrs. Adler: I have just finished reading "The Promised Land,"[2] and I want to thank you again for putting it into my hands. It is a wonderful book, inspiring and helpful.

I was just a little sorry, when the author referred to the Negro race on two occasions in the book, that she didn't exhibit a little more kindly and sympathetic spirit. I was a little disappointed that she referred to the Negro in about the same careless and rather indifferent way that the average white American refers to my race. I was especially interested to see how she would refer to the Negro, in view of her own suffering. But there is so much that is good in the book that I ought not to call attention to any little defect.

I have just sent the book to my oldest son with the request that he read it during the summer. Yours very truly,

[Booker T. Washington]

TLc   Con. 447   BTW Papers   DLC.

¹ Sister of Julius Rosenwald and wife of Max Adler.
² *The Promised Land* (Boston, 1912), by Mary Antin, was a popular account of the immigrant experience in America.

To Ernest Ten Eyck Attwell

Boston, Mass. July 15, 1912

Dear Mr. Attwell: You have already seen from Mr. Carter's report how the Boarding Department is running behind, largely owing to the fact, I fear, that we are giving the students a class of board that is too costly. I want you to bring about a change at once. I have the feeling that we can get various kinds of food stuffs in Chicago at a low cost that will answer the purposes of our students very well. The large packing houses there have an output of a large quantity of all kinds of side lines in the way of pigs feet, ears, and so on. These can be gotten cheap. They would make a good and palatable change for the students. It might pay you to make a trip to Chicago for this special purpose of seeing what could be gotten.

I want you to keep right up with the Boarding Department every day and see that it ceases to come out in debt. I want to see a better showing made for the month of July than has been true for June. Yours very truly,

[Booker T. Washington]

TLc   Con. 623   BTW Papers   DLC.

To the Editor of *The Independent*

Parker House, Boston, Mass. July 17, 1912

Personal

My dear Sir: I have meant before now to send a line to thank you most heartily in behalf of my race for the courageous position which you take regarding the Negro in the editorial in your issue of July 11th regarding the Negro and the present campaign.[1] I am going to try to get the New York Age to copy a large part of this editorial.

My race will never cease to thank you for what you are always doing in its behalf. Yours very truly,

[Booker T. Washington]

TLc Con. 457 BTW Papers DLC.

[1] The editorial endorsed Taft over Wilson for president, and claimed that the disfranchisement of black voters in the states controlled by the Democratic party was a great injustice. *The Independent* declared it would be "a rare negro, a white blackbird, that will vote the Democratic ticket." (*The Independent,* 73 [July 11, 1912], 99–101.)

From Robert Ezra Park

Wollaston [Mass.], July 17, 1912

My dear Mr Washington: I am sending enclosed the article for the Outlook.

Mr Scott has sent me an article by Clarence Poe to be published in the Progressive Farmer in Birmingham. The editor wants a reply. I am working on one which I will show you in a few days.

In this connection it occurs to me that you might make a point that would get under the skins of Southern White people by referring to the way in which stronger races have treated weaker races.

First They used to Kill them: then they kept them and ate them: then they enslaved them and taught the world incidentally in this way to work: then they imposed tribute on them or made them pay taxes which were used for the benefit of the stronger race or the stronger classes in the community; then freed them but left them in ignorance

and in proverty, uncared for and neglected. Then nations began to
see that they could not maintain their superiority if they allowed the
masses of the people to go uncared for; if they allowed them to live
in ignorance; then they began to educate them. They began to see
that the welfare of the highest was bound up with that of the lowest.

This is not to say that sentimental motives did not contribute to the
changes referred to but at any rate it was discovered that in the long
run these changes paid. very truly

Robert E. Park

TLS Con. 65 BTW Papers DLC.

From Washington Gladden

Columbus, Ohio July 19, 1912

Dear Dr Washington: Some of your friends here are anxious to know
your attitude on woman suffrage. I do not know that I have ever read
anything you have written about it; and I make bold to write to ask
you how it looks to you.

I expect, myself, to vote for the suffrage amendment to our constitution, but I am not a very strenuous suffragist. My hesitation arises
from the unwillingness of many good women to accept the responsibility. On the whole, however, I think that I shall vote to impose that
burden on them.

If you have any delicacy about committing yourself on this question,
I shall respect your wishes; but if your mind is clear and you are ready
to express it, I think your words would be useful.

I hope that all is going prosperously with you.

Remember me kindly to Mrs Washington   Yours truly

Washington Gladden

ALS Con. 454 BTW Papers DLC.

To Julius Rosenwald

Parker House, Boston, Mass. July 20, 1912

Dear Mr. Rosenwald: Your letter of July 15th marked "Personal" has been received. I want to say that since I wrote you regarding the Bartlett Normal and Industrial School in Missouri, I have received three very strong letters from white professors at the University of Missouri endorsing that school in high terms. I want to, however, look into the matter further. I have learned by experience that very often Southern white people endorse schools when they know little or nothing about the real work being done, and little about the character of the individual conducting the school. I am going to try to have somebody visit this school, and then I will be in a position to make you a report on it.

Regarding the letter from Mr. Houston,[1] of Huntsville, Texas, which I return, I would state that I have the very strongest evidence that he is doing good work and is worthy of help.

I think it well to bear in mind that both in regard to Missouri and Texas, our people as a rule receive more money from public school funds for their education and have better public schools than is true of most of the Southern States.

I shall be very glad to send you my recommendation and opinion regarding the use of $25,000 in helping institutions which are offshoots of Tuskegee or are doing similar work. Such a sum of money will prove a Godsend to these institutions and can be made to accomplish more good just now than any one realizes. I think I am not stating it too strongly when I say that a wise expenditure of such a sum of money will enable these schools to do fifty or one hundred per cent better work than they are now doing. Just as soon as I return to Tuskegee, which will be within a few days, I shall take up your suggestion carefully with some of our heads of departments, and shall write you fully regarding the whole subject. It is most generous and kind of you to think of these schools in this way.

I have no objection to your referring to me in any way you want to whenever you think it wise to do so.

I am glad to say that the receipts from various sources for Tuskegee

are very encouraging this summer, better than for a good many summers. While I am making a pretty strenuous and active campaign, I
am glad to say that my health keeps very good.

I want to cut out about two weeks in September to devote wholly
to the matter of securing the remaining portion of the fifty thousand
dollars on the five year plan. Every one that I present the matter to
seems greatly pleased with the idea, and I think two weeks of active
and constant work will close the matter up. I do hope that Mr. Byllesby[2]
will do something generous. Yours very truly,

[Booker T. Washington]

TLc   Con. 56   BTW Papers   DLC.

[1] Samuel Walker Houston, a black man born in 1871, founded in 1907 the
Houstonian Normal and Industrial Institute in Huntsville, Tex. He studied at
Atlanta University (1888–91) and Howard University (1891–94), was a govern-
ment clerk in Washington for five years, and was a school principal and editor in
Huntsville (1902–7).

[2] Henry Morison Byllesby (1859–1924) was an electrical engineer educated at
Lehigh University, an early associate of Thomas A. Edison, the president of a
large engineering firm, and director of many utility companies. He was on the
executive committee of the National Civic Federation.

To William Howard Taft

Parker House, Boston, Mass. July 20, 1912

Personal and Confidential

My dear Mr. President: You may have already covered the points
outlined in the enclosed memorandum, but I feel rather sure that if
you could get the substance of what I have written on the enclosed
memorandum into your address of acceptance that it will accomplish
a great deal of good. Yours very truly,

Booker T. Washington

[*Enclosure*]

Memorandum for President Taft in connection with address of
acceptance.

From its very inception as a party, the Republican Party has taken an especial interest in the elevation and encouragement of the Negro race in America. It was largely through the work of the party that the Negro was made free and started on the road to citizenship, and therefore it is seen that our party has a special duty as well as a special privilege in the matter of encouraging the advancement of this race in every way possible.

The present administration has always been alive to the interest of the Negro. It has sought in every way possible to encourage him in his education and progress in other directions. History will show that the efforts of this administration have not been without tangible results.

Further than this, this administration has sought from time to time to place colored men of distinguished ability and character in important positions, not only in recognition of the worth of these individuals but that they might be held up as an object lesson to other members of their race. Without undue self-praise, I think I can safely say that this administration has gone further in placing colored men in distinguished and high positions than is true of any administration in the past.

The central government is hampered and circumscribed in its efforts to protect the lives of citizens against mobs and against the lynchers. From time to time in our various states, mob violence directed especially against the Negro, both in our Northern and Southern states, has been of frequent occurrence. Such outbreaks are a disgrace to any civilized country, and our whole people North and South should be called upon to use their influence to blot out for all time the practice of using the mob to accomplish that which should be accomplished through the medium of our courts. Wherever and whenever this administration could use its influence by word or deed to discourage and prevent mob violence it has always acted. I am glad to call attention to the fact that the number of lynchings in the country is gradually decreasing, and there are many evidences to the fact that the Negro race is making steady and substantial progress. And I think I can say further, that at the present time there are more friendly relations existing between the black and white races in this country than has been true of any period since the days of reconstruction.

In 1913 the Negro will have been free in this country fifty years, and the National Negro Business League and other organizations are preparing to celebrate that occasion, and the colored people ought to be encouraged and helped in every way possible to have a celebration that will call the attention of the world to the progress that the Negro race of ten millions now in this country has made.

TLS and typed enclosure   William Howard Taft Papers   DLC.

From G. Lake Imes[1]

Detroit, Mich. July 20/12

Dear Sir: I wish to report an incident that occurred this morning of which I think you should have knowledge. On visiting the secretary of the Y.M.C.A. where we have a meeting tomorrow, he asked me to accompany him to a meeting at a school for stammerers and address the students. I consented to do so. Upon my introduction I expressed my pleasure in meeting a group of young people engaged in overcoming a serious obstacle to their progress in the way that they were doing. Having been a Negro for so long and so long engaged in mastering the difficulties, obstacles and disadvantages that went along with that, I felt a sense of fellowship with any one who was likewise engaged in overcoming any handicap in the way of their progress. Indeed, said I, in this very work you can know a little of what it means to be a Negro and in that sense (that you are working with all your might, all your energies and powers to overcome this obstacle — in your speech) you are just like the Negro who ———.

At this point I was interrupted by the President who excitedly protested against having his students likened in any way to Negroes. The President is a Canadian but at some time in his career has lived in the South. He protested that there were students in the audience from the South who counted it an affront to be likened in any way to the Negro. At the first opportunity I hastened to withdraw any statement that would give offense, the Secretary apologized after attempting my defense and we withdrew at the Secretary's suggestion.

I make this report to you lest developments arise in which case you should have a first hand knowledge of the incident. I had not been speaking a minute when this developed. Yours

G. L. Imes

ALS Con. 468 BTW Papers DLC.

¹ G. Lake Imes in 1911 became a teacher and in 1912 dean of the Phelps Hall Bible Training School of Tuskegee Institute.

To Washington Gladden

[Tuskegee, Ala.] July 30, 1912

My dear Dr. Gladden: Thank you very much for your kind letter of July 19th regarding woman suffrage. I regret exceedingly I have been so tardy in replying to it.

I think you have expressed my own attitude very fully in your own letter. I have moved rather slowly in this matter, but I think if you care to make any statement regarding my own position, it should be to the effect that I am in favor of woman suffrage. I do not believe that any harm can be done, and I think on the other hand that much good might be accomplished. While I take this position I also feel that there are many other questions of far greater importance before the country for immediate attention than this, but perhaps when we can get this question settled we will then be in a position to move on in the direction of settling some others which are more fundamental. I thank you for writing me.

Mrs. Washington desires to be remembered to you. I hope at some time you can come to see us. Yours very truly,

Booker T. Washington

TLpS Con. 454 BTW Papers DLC.

To Ernest Ten Eyck Attwell

[Tuskegee, Ala.] July Thirty-first, Nineteen Hundred Twelve

Mr. Attwell: In addition to what I wrote you this morning about closing the club house hereafter not later than 10 o'clock,[1] I wish to state that when this house was erected it was my thought that the teachers would use it as a kind of center for recreation and literary improvement as well as for games, but I find that the club house seems to have degenerated into practically a pool room or billiard room. This was not my idea when the building was constructed. I had hoped and expected that books, magazines and papers would be kept in the club house of a character that would prove elevating to all who visited the club.

Booker T. Washington

TLSr Copy   Con. 623   BTW Papers   DLC.

[1] BTW wrote to Attwell, actually on July 30, 1912, that the late closing of the club house was "having a demoralizing and hurtful effect on the community," and urged a strict rule closing it at 10 P.M. (Con. 623, BTW Papers, DLC.)

To Robert Ezra Park

[Tuskegee, Ala.] July 31, 1912

Dear Dr. Park: I have been considering pretty carefully the suggestion made by you some months ago as to your future work.

I find that our financial condition will not permit us to employ a special additional man to do the magazine and newspaper work which we had in view when you were employed, and until the school is in better financial shape I do not see but what we shall have to ask you to devote the major portion of your time to the same kind of work you have been doing, of course not giving up or laying aside the work which you outlined in your letter to me. The plain English of this is that we cannot just now employ an additional man to do the kind of work which you have heretofore been doing. I have not overlooked or forgotten the suggestions which you made in regard to the reorganization and strengthening of certain departments. Yours very truly,

Booker T. Washington

TLpS   Con. 61   BTW Papers   DLC.

From Handy Eugene Fant[1]

Seneca S.C. July 31st 1912

Dear Sir: The negro of the Southern states engaged in agriculture is so I am told by U.S. Demonstration Agts. (white) *very anxious to take up farm demonstration work* under cooperation of the Bureau of Plant Industry. I am a white man but nevertheless I am anxious to see the *industrious negro* succeed and the Ag. Dept. should be made to increase appropriations along this line. Cant you bring proper pressure to bear upon Pres. Taft and lets see what can be done. I wrote the B. P. I. that the *"Field was black unto the harvest"* and they agreed with me as per letter enclosed, but I cannot agree with them that this would incite race prejudice as my line of proceedure to reach the ambitious negro farmer would be to employ Demonstration agents from their own race & I wish to see them installed in both Oconee and Anderson Counties. I am a friend of your friend David Dooley the honest negro blacksmith of Anderson S.C. a natural local leader among the better class of negroes in upper S.C. I have long been a patron of his shop and admire him for his frugality and energy. I made all my negro renters make the trip to Anderson S.C. 20 miles to hear your address. Furnished them a team & every one of them said you *stuck to the truth* no matter which race it favored or disfavored. And that you showed the good & weak points of each side. Your influence on my hands was good and really afforded them inspiration that I could notice. I am a Southern man my ancestors owned slaves, doctered them and fed them & treated them in every way humane. It amused me to find boot blacks and older ones among your race jealous of you & your fame this I found out by asking them if they were going to hear you speak at Anderson. This is human nature I suppose with all races according to degree of intelligence. If you mail me some of your college literature I

568

will turn it over to Paul Singleton a mulatto deacon in Shiloh Baptist Church near me & have him distribute it for you. He has good judgement & is an ideal Demonstration Agent if I could get Ag. Dept. to serve the negroes here as they serve the whites. I am a friend to your race wherever they merit it and am not one of those "white vultures" who stir up strife among the races. I stand for cooperation & unity am a farmer & seed breeder of long staple cotton. Yours Respc

H. Eugene Fant

ALS   Con. 453   BTW Papers   DLC.

¹ Handy Eugene Fant (1873–1961), born in Anderson, S.C., was the owner and operator of the Valley View Seed and Stock Farm near Townville, S.C. In 1913 he and a cousin started a hide concern in Athens, Ga., where he resided from 1919 until his death.

An Account of a Speech
in Newport News, Virginia

Newport News, Va., August 1 [1912]

PRINCIPAL AT NEWPORT NEWS

With rare tact and force Dr. Booker T. Washington, who is a master in handling men and solving difficult problems, recently spoke to a large group of colored men and boys who are employed at good wages by the Newport News Shipbuilding and Dry Dock Company. Dr. Washington spoke very plainly on the subject of colored men and boys attending more strictly to their work. There is a distinct need of having the 2,250 colored men and boys co-operate with the general manager, Mr. Homer L. Ferguson, and other officers of the great shipbuilding plant who have clearly shown, even under the most trying conditions, their desire to give the colored workers a square deal.

The question to be settled has not been one of hours and wages but one of getting colored men and boys to work regularly. It has been customary for many of the colored employees to spend much of their time in idleness when their services were needed not only by the shipyard management but by their fellow-workers. For a time the introduction of foreigners was almost certain. An increase in pay of colored workers seemed to make matters worse instead of better. Idleness and irregularity were increased.

Finally, a group of colored men from Newport News, headed by Walter K. Jones, who has the respect and confidence of white and colored people alike, brought the matter before Major R. R. Moton, of Hampton Institute, and he in turn secured the good offices of Dr. Washington in bringing the problem fairly and squarely before the colored workers in the shipyard and those who can bring unusual influence to bear upon them — mothers, wives, ministers, doctors, lawyers, teachers, and business men.[1]

Dr. Washington outlined the condition of working men in Southern Europe. He told graphically the story of his trip through Europe and his experience with men and women who were poorly fed, poorly clothed, poorly housed, and poorly paid for their laborious service. He showed by contrasts how much better off are the Negroes of America who do not have to seek work and who with thrift can improve their economic condition. The Newport News shipyard pays weekly to colored workers twenty-five thousand dollars. This fact shows the important economic reason for Dr. Washington encouraging the colored workers to stick to their jobs and, instead of recklessly and foolishly spending their good wages, build better homes and churches.

An eloquent appeal was made by Dr. Washington, who, through actual experience, knows the hardships of an uphill struggle, and his audience, both white and black, followed him closely. He urged the colored people to do their full duty and more than they were being paid for, to keep their word, to put heart and conscience into their work, to co-operate heartily with those in authority, and to cultivate civic pride.

He called upon the white people to exercise more patience with the colored people with whom they deal, for, after all, the American Negro is a loyal, Christian, American citizen. He asked that the colored men and boys of the shipyard be given the opportunity of making a new start. The eyes of the colored people throughout the United States are turned upon the men and boys who have in their grasp the success or failure of many many Negroes in industry.

The Newport News Shipbuilding Company will open a Young Men's Christian Association with a paid secretary, a night school, and will do all that it can to keep its colored workers off the streets and give them an opportunity of becoming more efficient and reliable.

Tuskegee Student, 24 (Aug. 17, 1912), 1. Written by William A. Aery. Another account, also written by Aery, appeared in the *Southern Workman,* 41 (Aug. 1912), 452–53.

[1] Moton wrote to E. J. Scott that as much as he hated to burden BTW with the task of speaking to the black shipyard workers, "Dr. Washington is the only man who can do it." (June 19, 1912, Con. 60, BTW Papers, DLC.)

From Isaiah Benjamin Scott

[New York City] August 2, 1912

My dear Dr. Washington: I have considered the communications from Miss Stokes touching the establishment of an industrial school for Liberia. I am gratified to know that she is thinking of such a benefaction; for I am confident that there is nothing more urgently needed in that line than to emphasize the importance of labor and to teach the people how to do it intelligently. Commerce is advancing because the capital which flows into the continent from Europe is used to push its interests along all lines; but I do not put it too strongly when I say that, industrially, the republic is at a standstill, and its only hope in this particular is to have it quickened by the instruction imparted by the Missionary forces at work in Liberia.

As delighted as I am with the thought that Miss Stokes proposes to take hold of this feature of Missionary endeavor, I must say I fear the amount of money proposed is not sufficient to accomplish what she has in mind. In the first place, building in that part of Africa is very expensive, not only because accomplished mechanics are scarce, but because much of the building material must be imported. Then too, it is always necessary in building in Africa to use such material as cannot be destroyed by the bug-a-bug or white ant. There are certain woods in the forest of Africa that this insect cannot burrow into; but as there are no sawmills operating in the republic at present, these woods are not available when building is to be done on a large scale; and so far as foreign woods are concerned, I know of nothing that stands the test except the American pitch pine. To import this to Africa is quite an expensive undertaking, and yet we are compelled to do so. As a rule, all our roofs are made of the corrugated iron, not only because it is proof against the white ant, but because it is difficult to get anything else.

Again, Miss Stokes suggests a willingness to provide as much as a thousand dollars a year for a stated period to be used for current expenses. But right here I feel that I ought to mention an item of necessary expense which we have in Africa that may not be met with in some other Missionary fields. In addition to paying the salaries of workers, purchasing machinery, and the upkeep of buildings, etc., we have also to calculate on feeding and clothing our students, providing books, and whatever is necessary in the school room. This, I regret to admit, must be done by the management of the school. This condition is without doubt due to the indulgence of the colonization societies in the early years of the republic, and it must be admitted has been kept up, and to some extent, by Missionary organizations now at work on the field. We are trying to rectify this abuse by having the pupils perform the labor necessary to the upkeep of the farms or gardens conducted by the Missions. Having made this general statement as to the conditions that must be met with in establishing and conducting an industrial school in Africa, I shall now proceed to present two plans on which the proposed school may be inaugurated and run, and these will give Miss Stokes an opportunity to decide which is the most feasible.

Should you proceed to secure lands and begin an industrial school on such lands, it is well to consider that everything necessary must be provided. This, of course, includes buildings for dormitories, the academic school, shops, etc. Knowing the cost of building, I calculate that would require from $25,000 to $30,000 to inaugurate such an institution in a permanent way; and because of the trying climate in the tropics, it is useless to provide anything that is not thoroughly substantial. The foregoing statement includes the machinery and other implements necessary to an industrial plant. At the same time, it is only fair to say that if a good location on the river is secured and you are fortunate enough to get the right kind of man as principal, the necessary buildings may be erected from brick prepared on the grounds, and student labor can be utilized in their erection. This, of course, would tend to reduce the cost already referred to. It is evident that this plan would also delay the active life of the institution, but nevertheless the young people would be acquiring useful knowledge while the work is being done.

The other plan which I have in mind to suggest is the following; and I feel free to present it, because of the suggestion found in Miss Stokes' letter that she would desire to have such an industrial school conducted in harmony with all the other Missionary forces on the ground. The Board of Foreign Missions of the Methodist Episcopal Church which I represent has the beginning of an industrial school including more than 700 acres of land on that most beautiful Liberian river, known as the St. Paul River. We have been trying to conduct an industrial school here for a number of years, but find it quite an expensive undertaking to do so in connection with the regular Mission work of the Board. About 20 miles from Monrovia, we have a substantial brick building on one side of the river that is already in use by the party now in charge of the work. In addition, there are several smaller buildings now used for store houses, sleeping places for the boys and the carpenter shop. There is also a second brick building which could be put in proper repair for much less than a new one can be erected and in a shorter time. This could be used for such purpose as may be thought best. The land is on both sides of the river and gives a large river frontage, which is difficult to secure at this time unless the property is purchased from private individuals. While I have not consulted the authorities of my Board in New York, I am confident that such terms can be arranged with that body as will be entirely satisfactory to Miss Stokes, and will work no hardship or injustice to the Board. I am more confident of this because of the fact that our Board is simply seeking to christianize and uplift the people of this region of Africa, and it is evident to me that Miss Stokes has the same purpose in view.

It might be necessary to have a Board of Trustees composed of prominent citizens of the republic chosen from the various church organizations represented in Liberia. This plan would give us one strong industrial school instead of the attempt to run two where one would seem to be all that is necessary at this time. It might not be out of place to say to you that our Board has already inaugurated a training school for Mission workers with funds provided from the estate

573

of a lady whom I understand to be a sister of Miss Stokes whose bene-faction we are now considering. I am confident there would be nothing inappropriate in having what she now desires to do for Liberia carried forward in the same region of the country where the Stokes Bible Training School has recently been established. The fact is I doubt not that she would be pleased with the idea.

I need only to say in conclusion that it is my purpose to return to Liberia in the fall, and no matter on what line Miss Stokes may prefer to have the work proceed, I shall be only too glad to be of any service I may in carrying it forward. I am: Yours sincerely,

I. B. Scott

TLSr Copy   Con. 63   BTW Papers   DLC.

From Julius B. Ramsey

[Tuskegee, Ala.] August 3, 1912

My dear Mr. Washington: This is to inform you that John Thomp-son[1] and David Shackleford[2] are guilty of drinking whiskey Tuesday evening July 30, and the effects of the whiskey made them sick. Both of these young men told me that Mr. Elbert one of the cooks offered them the whiskey and that they partook of it several times. Mr. Elbert lives in the cottage by Mr. Scott's residence.

My sympathy goes out for these two young graduates but I wish that it were possible for us to control this situation among the young teachers, and impress upon them the effect that such an example has upon the students.

Drinking whiskey, playing cards, and smoking in the dormitories is strictly against the school's rules, but it is very hard to enforce these rules. Yours very truly,

J. B. Ramsey

TLS   Con. 629   BTW Papers   DLC.

[1] John Nicholas Thompson of Boston, Mass., graduated from Tuskegee in 1911 and was enrolled as a postgraduate student in 1911–12.

[2] David Devon Shackleford, Jr., of Gulfport, Miss., graduated from Tuskegee in 1911.

From Clara Johnston

Malden, West. Va. Aug 4th 1912

Dear Uncle Booker; Mamma ask me to write and thank you for sending the box with the coffee in it She did not get the boxe for two days after you had gone. many thanks to you Uncle Booker, I did not know you have so many friends in Malden til since you spoke here two and three White people have been to see us every day since you left talking about the speech you made. I think the speech will still live when there is no more Uncle Booker I dont know what will become of poor Mr Lovely. His talk is about Tuskegee and the Washington boys.

We have had fair days right cool weather Having fires and wearing winter wraps Mamma, Mr Lovely, and Ben join me in best regards to you and family

Always wishing you success Your neice

Clara

ALS Con. 457 BTW Papers DLC.

From Oswald Garrison Villard

New York August 5, 1912

Dear Dr. Washington: Have you given your name to the National Emancipation Memorial Society whose elaborate programme I enclose? They wish the use of my name and I do not wish to give it unless I can find out that it will be a really worthy undertaking. It looks pretty top-heavy to me.

I cannot refrain from a little "I told you so" in connection with Roosevelt's kicking the Southern negro delegates out of the Progressive Party. I do hope now that the bulk of the colored people who have still clung to this man will realize the falsity of his nature, and will no longer follow his leadership. Faithfully yours,

Oswald Garrison Villard

TLS Con. 63 BTW Papers DLC. A carbon is in the Oswald Garrison Villard Papers, MH.

575

From Julius Rosenwald

Chicago   August 5, 1912

Dear Mr. Washington: I am in receipt of yours of the 3rd, enclosing information concerning the distribution of funds for institutions that have grown out of Tuskegee Institute, or where officered largely by Tuskegee men and women, and are doing the same kind of work as Tuskegee branch schools, and want to thank you very much for the trouble you and your assistants have taken in this matter.

The plan that I believe I would favor most, provided you concurred in it, would be the following: You select such schools as in your judgment should participate, naming the amount for each and the purpose for which the money is to be used, if you so desire, and, as soon as any school which you have named has raised an equal amount, I will pay to it such an amount as you have designated. I will agree to pay a total of twenty-five thousand dollars (25,000) to such schools as soon as they furnish a list of bonafide subscriptions equal to the amount you have designated.

I expect to celebrate my 50th birthday on the 12th of this month, and would like to announce this gift, together with some others that I am contemplating. My idea would be to make the announcement as concerns this gift in this manner: "$25,000 for colored schools that have grown out of Tuskegee Institute, or are doing the same kind of work as Tuskegee branch schools, the funds to be distributed by Dr. Booker T. Washington, or Tuskegee Institute, under certain conditions and for certain purposes."

I would kindly request that you frame this to suit yourself and write me (special delivery) immediately so that I shall have the letter not later than Friday. It might be advisable to send a night letter, charges collect, instead of writing, and make the telegram as full and complete as though it were a letter. It does not matter if it costs $5.00, or even more if necessary. Please express your opinion freely as to the advisability of the conditions and the method of announcement. If you, for any reason, prefer that the name "Trustees of Tuskegee" be substituted for your name, or the burden not put upon Tuskegee for the distribution, please do not hesitate to so state. I believe it is wise to make the condition as to the raising of an equal amount, because the incentive will be great for others to give and the trustees of the various institutions will put forth work under such conditions that they would not be likely to do other-wise. Yours very truly,

Julius Rosenwald

Reply to letter of Aug. 2.

In regard to the engaging of a man to work with Mr. B.[1] while he is working at Tuskegee would say I heartily approve of the plan — but would want to know the salary and if reasonable will gladly pay same.

Julius Rosenwald

TLSr Copy   Con. 62   BTW Papers   DLC.   Another copy is in Con. 56, BTW Papers, DLC.

[1] Joseph A. Bebbington (d. 1915), born and trained as an accountant in England, was auditor for the trustees of Hampton Institute, Tuskegee Institute, and a number of other educational institutions.

From Robert Russa Moton

Hampton, Virginia   Aug. 6, 1912

My dear Dr. Washington: I have talked with Mr. Aery regarding the Chicago trip and I think he will go. Mrs. Aery's condition leaves an element of doubt. He will, however, write to you. I hope I can be present also.

I think with you that the Business League in Virginia isn't accomplishing as much as it ought to and I hope we can get it re-established on a little different and perhaps better basis so far as the individual men are concerned than it was before. I have been personally somewhat unactive so far as the state work is concerned because primarily of the character of the men who were the natural leaders of the movement in Virginia, but there are men who can make it go; men with clean and honorable reputations and who are successful business men. I am writing to Mr. E. C. Brown[1] to-day suggesting that he take up the matter with some men in Richmond and Suffolk to see if we can't stir up the matter.

The Women's Meeting[2] went off nicely. Mrs. Washington left Wednesday night to fill her engagement with Dr. Blake[3] Thursday. We were sorry to have her leave for I think her stay here after the Convention was restful. Mrs. Napier and Mrs. Bruce left Saturday.

Your talk at the Shipyard stirred up things tremendously and the people colored and white feel that it was a splendid thing to do and that your address hit the mark.[4] They have already seen the results of it. I am very glad you could come and I hesitated in urging you to do it because I know so well what a tremendous strain you are constantly under, but I felt that a trip of that kind would be so very unique and interesting to you that it would in the long run be restful. We were all very happy here over Mrs. Washington's election. She gave a splendid talk to the students Sunday evening and spoke beautifully to the boys out at the farm, Shellbanks the same afternoon. Yours always sincerely,

R. R. Moton

TLS   Con. 60   BTW Papers   DLC.

[1] Possibly Edward C. Brown, a black businessman of tidewater Virginia and Philadelphia. Born in Philadelphia in 1877, he was president of the Crown Savings Bank of Newport News, Va., the Brown Savings and Banking Co. of Norfolk, and the Beneficial Insurance Co. of Norfolk. He also dealt in real estate in Philadelphia.

[2] The eighth biennial convention of the National Association of Colored Women met at Hampton Institute on July 23–27, 1912. Margaret Murray Washington was elected president.

[3] Possibly John Bapst Blake (b. 1866), surgeon-in-chief of Boston City Hospital beginning in 1911.

[4] See An Account of a Speech in Newport News, Virginia, Aug. 1, 1912, above.

An Address before the
National Negro Business League in Chicago

Chicago, Ill. August 21, 1912

Mr. Chairman, Gentlemen and Ladies of the League, Friends: This organization does not use either the steam roller or the stone presser. (Laughter.) It does use, however (in cases of emergency) — a chloroform bag in the shape of an Executive Committee who jointly "boss" and solve most of our troublesome questions. (Applause.)

I am glad, as the President of this organization, to give voice to the sentiment which is in the hearts of all the members, to the effect that we are grateful to the local business league of Chicago, we are grateful to all the citizens of Chicago, for what they have done for us thus far and we hope that we shall have our feeling of gratitude constantly increased until the end of the present session.

It is a matter of great encouragement to have gathered here, hundreds of men and women from various sections of our country and from countries outside of the United States, not for the purpose of promoting their own selfish ambitions but with the central end in view of bettering the condition of their fellow men. It has been my privilege to be with, and to work with men and women of various types and characters in different parts of the country who are interested in this or that subject, but it has never been my privilege to be or labor with any group of people, white or black, who have exhibited a more unselfish spirit than is true of the men and women who comprise the membership of this League. And the same assertion, in an especial degree, is true of the members of the Executive Committee who travel long distances, at their own expense, who spend their money, who spend their time, their energy and their influence with the single end in view of furthering the objects of this organization. These men, for weeks in some cases, have laid aside their business affairs to promote the interests of this League.

"There is a tide in the affairs of men, which taken at the flood leads on to fortune. Omitted, all the rest of their lives is bound in shallows and miseries." These words from Shakespeare have an especial application to our race at the present time. The men and women of our race of this generation hold in their hands the future of the generations that are to follow. This is in an especial sense true of the Negro business man and woman. If we do not do our duty now in laying proper foundation for economic and commercial growth, our children, and our children's children will suffer because of our inactivity or shortness of vision.

I want to say while I am on this subject that I have been surprised and delighted at the progress which has been made by colored business men in Chicago. As I drove down State street the other day for a mile and a half I am sure that two-thirds of the places of business I saw were conducted by colored men. If they were not owned by colored people they were at least patronized by them. I was equally surprised and delighted when I drove down Wabash avenue and through some of the adjoining streets to discover what handsome houses many of our people are living in. As I have had a chance to visit these houses I have been pleased to find how handsomely, even artistically, they were furnished and carefully and neatly they were maintained. It would be a revelation, almost a miracle, to our people of forty years ago to see the kind of homes in which their children and grandchildren were beginning to live. In fact, it would astonish a good many of our people in other parts of the country even to-day to see the progress of the colored people in Chicago. I do not think there is a large city in this country, where there is a community of colored people living together in such numbers as you do here, which has made so rapid progress in so short a time, or where the opportunities are so good.

All this imposes a heavy responsibility upon you who live here and enjoy these opportunities. In a section of the city where the colored people are in the majority, it is the colored people who are responsible for conditions in that portion of the city. If there is drunkenness, if there is gambling, if there is crime, the colored people will be held responsible, because this is a recognized colored community. You will not escape this responsibility by saying that the person who maintains the saloon is a white man, or that the man who runs the gambling place is a white man. You might say this in some place down South, but you cannot say [it] in Chicago.

Now, I do not know anything about your local political conditions and I do not mean to say anything about them. What I do wish to emphasize particularly to members of my race who have come here from the South, where they have had little or no share in the government by which they were controlled, that here in Chicago a new and grave responsibility rests upon them in that respect. And this responsibility extends not merely to your own people here in Chicago, but it extends to the race everywhere. It rests upon the Negroes of Chicago, with the magnificent opportunities before you, to demonstrate to the rest of the world to what extent a Negro community like this, amid all the temptations of a great city, can make itself a united, progressive, law-abiding community, one that will be looked up to and respected, one which the world can point to as a model.

In order to accomplish this we must unite ourselves with all the forces in this city that are striving for better things. We must unite all the best elements among ourselves. The local Business League can exercise a wide influence in this direction. It can do this by putting its influence behind the man or the business which is really trying to do a good thing.

Our great Creator has ordained that races and nations shall prosper in proportion as they find, develop and use the natural resorces of the earth in promoting wealth, intelligence, happiness and justice.

If I can, I want to sound a note of warning to the ten millions of Negroes throughout our country. We are now ten millions strong. This means a population nearly twice as large as the population of the Dominion of Canada. It is a population three million greater than that of Belgium. It is greater than that of Holland and Switzerland combined, or the combined populations of Norway, Sweden and Denmark.

We have the advantage of many of the races of the old world in that we are citizens of a comparatively new country, whose natural resources are just beginning, as it were, to be discovered and developed. Our country is new and our race is new so far as freedom is concerned. Now is the time — not in some far-off future, but now is the time — for us as a race to prove to the world that in a state of freedom we have the ability and the inclination to do our part in owning, developing, manufacturing and trading in the natural resources of our country. If we let these golden opportunities slip from us in this generation, I fear they will never come to us in a like degree again.

At the present time there are over 270,000,000 acres [of] unused and unoccupied land in the South and West. In fact, one-half of the land in the South and two-thirds of the land in the West is still unused. Now is the time for us to become the owners and users of our share before it is too late. From ownership of the soil comes independence, self-support, happiness and real manhood rights. Land that can be gotten at ten dollars an acre now, a few years hence cannot be gotten for two and three times as much. If the white man from America and Europe can establish and operate a saw mill and gain wealth and independence from the use of our millions of acres of forest land, why not more Negroes do the same thing?

If the white man can secure wealth and happiness by owning and operating a coal mine, brick yard, or lime kiln, why not more Negroes do the same thing?

If other races can attain prosperity by securing riches on a large scale from our seas, lakes and rivers in the form of fish and other sea foods, thousands of Negroes can do the same thing. Activity in all these directions finds no race or color line.

This year our country will probably produce 3,125,000[000][1] bushels of corn, 695,443,000 bushels of wheat, 1,136,700,000 bushels of oats, 338,800,000 bushels of potatoes and 16,000,000 bales of cotton. In this tremendous production here again is no color line. We want to see to it that as a race we not only produce our share, but that we hold on to our share of the wealth that grows out of the manufacturing of, trading in, and transporting these commodities. Activity in these directions will bring to us influence and usefulness that no political party can give us or take from us. Before it is too late, I want my race to lay hold on the primary sources of wealth and civilization.

Our country produces and uses annually about one billion dollars' worth of live stock in the way of cattle, pigs, sheep, and $500,000,000 worth of dairy products and $150,000,000 worth of fowls and eggs. Here again there is no color or race line.

I do not want members of our race to be content with merely skimming around over the outer edges in the form of securing odd and uncertain jobs, but I want them to get in at the bottom of these fundamental industries and stand among the leading producers. There is no law in this country to prevent Negroes from owning and operating iron foundries, cotton mills, oil mills, shoe factories. Our race uses a large number of coffins every year. There is no reason why more of these coffins should not be manufactured by us. There is no reason why more of the bedsteads, bureaus and chairs used in our homes should not be manufactured by us.

In the South, especially, just now, millions of dollars are being earned every year by white people operating large peach orchards. In the far West other millions are being earned by growing apples on a large scale. The white man is as willing to buy peaches and apples grown by black hands as by white hands. If the Italians and Greeks can come into this country strangers to our language and civilization and within a few years gain wealth and independence by trading in fruits, the Negro can do the same thing.

Throughout our country we consume millions of dollars' worth of buggies and wagons. Why not more of our young men who are graduating at colleges and universities enter this field?

The whole West and South are dotted with flourishing towns and cities that have been founded in places where twenty-five or fifty years ago there was the primeval forest or naked prairie. These new communities in many cases have been started by Germans; in other cases by Hollanders, or Danes, or by Swedes, or Norwegians, Poles or Hungarians who came to this country in comparative poverty. In not a few cases the little settlement had for its beginning or foundation a little saw mill, grist mill, blacksmith shop, cotton factory, coal mine, cooperative creamery, or country store. With one of these simple industries for its beginning the little community grows and expands year by year. Soon the railroad comes, then the depot, then the postoffice comes, then follow the telegraph and telephone. Stores are established, then more stores. Schoolhouses are built, churches are erected. A bank is opened. The industries are established. Business is diversified. There is a call for more and better residences, for the architect and skilled mechanic. There is a demand for organization, for a governing body, a mayor, board of aldermen, school committee, school principals and school teachers. Soon the doctor and lawyer are needed. There is a demand for a commercial club, for a literary society, a woman's club, a musical society, and all this comes and grows in a natural, logical way.

If the settlement is started by the Poles, a Polander becomes the depot agent, a Polander becomes a telegraph operator. The first mayor is a Polander. The president of the school board is a Pole. The president of the first bank is a Pole. There is no segregation of the Poles in that city. There is no discrimination against the Poles here. There is freedom and a chance for unfettered and unlimited growth.

What foreign races coming to this country are doing in building towns and cities, there is a chance for Negroes to do in any number of places in the South and in the West, as the founders and builders of Mound Bayou in Mississippi, and Boley in Oklahoma, have proven.

But to do things we cannot start at the top, but must begin at the bottom. I call upon the men and women from our colleges and universities to lead the way in these fundamental directions.

It was natural and right that in the beginning of our freedom the work of the teacher and minister should receive the greatest attention. There is still an emphatic need for more teachers and ministers, but we have now reached, as a race, a new era, almost a crisis, in our growth. Along by the side of the teacher and minister is [are] needed leaders in economic and agricultural and commercial growth. By the side of the teacher and minister we must have in increasing numbers the independent farmer, the real estate owner, the mechanic, the manufacturer, the merchant, the banker, and other kinds of business men and women. These will strengthen the teacher and minister, and they in turn will help the business man.

This is an era of specialization and organization. Our race should take heed of this and act. We shall be a potent force in all directions in proportion as we organize and work together North and South. In racial unity, racial peace and coadhesiveness and organization will be our strength and life. We should put behind us the day of childish things.

Besides our advantage in numbers, we have the advantage of living by the side of and in the midst of the most progressive and highest type of white man that the world has seen. Let us, then, use our strength in concentrated, organized directions, and in proportion as we do it the white man will respect us.

I repeat that this is an era of specialization and organization. White men who deal in land are organized. White men who grow grain are organized. Those who grow peaches are organized. Those who grow apples are organized. Those who mine coal and iron are organized. Those who manufacture furniture are organized. Those who manufacture shoes are organized. Those who make dresses are organized. Those who make hats are organized. Those who sell groceries are organized. Those who bury the dead are organized. Those who are bankers are organized. Those who work in tin, lead, copper and wood are organized. If we as Negroes would increase our business strength and influence, we must organize. Organize, organize, locally in the state and nation. Work together and stick together.

The local League should be the chamber of commerce for the Negro. Every community should have its local League, and wherever possible and practicable there should be a State League, all working in harmony with the National Negro Business League.

Let us act in all these matters before it is too late, before others come from foreign lands and rob us of our birthright.

Development and activity in all these directions does not mean that we are to be commercialized as a race, does not mean that we are to be merely breadwinners or hewers of wood and drawers of water, but it means that we shall be producers of bread, owners of bread, manufacturers of bread, dealers in bread, and that we shall gather wealth from it which can be turned into the highest and best things of life. All this does not mean that we are to be hewers of wood and drawers of water, but that we are to be the owners and users of wood in a way that will bring to us happiness, usefulness and prosperity. All this does not mean that we are to be merely drawers of water, but it does mean that we are to be the owners of water and help turn it into the promotion of agriculture, into steam and electric power, so that it will add to our independence and influence.

To be more specific. There are places in the South for 5,000 additional dry goods stores, and there are colored people enough to support them. In the South the Negro merchant is not dependent upon the trade of his own race alone, but throughout the South, while there is prejudice in other directions, in business the Negro has little prejudice to contend with along this line. Not only the colored man trades at the colored man's dry goods store, but the best white people are not afraid to patronize a first-class Negro store, and the same thing is true of other business enterprises owned and controlled by colored people.

There are openings in the South for at least 8,000 additional grocery stores, for 3,500 drug stores. There are openings in the South for 2,000 shoe stores, 1,500 millinery stores, and there are communities in the South where 2,000 Negro banks can be operated and supported. Further than this, there are places in the South where at least 25 self-governing, self-supporting, self-directing towns or cities may be established, where the colored people can have their own mayor, their board of aldermen, their own self-government from every point of view. In the last analysis, local self-government is the most precious kind of government.

All that I am here advocating and emphasizing does not mean the limitation or circumscribing of our race mentally, morally, civilly or in other directions, but it does mean real growth and real independence in all these directions. Growth in these economic directions will help the teacher, the minister, will help the school, the college, the university, the Sunday School and church, will help the lawyer, the doctor, the dentist, and add to our political independence. (Prolonged applause and great cheering.)

Report of the Thirteenth Annual Convention of the National Negro Business League, 1912 (Washington, 1912?), 49–54. A typescript is in BTW Papers, ATT.

¹ The typescript version contains this figure as a handwritten correction.

To Julius Rosenwald

[Tuskegee, Ala.] August 29, 1912

Confidential.

Dear Mr. Rosenwald: Referring to the enclosed correspondence from Mr. William H. Ferris, I would state that I have not seen Mr. Ferris' manuscript, and, of course, am not in position to judge of its value.

Mr. Ferris represents a very pathetic case. He is a graduate of Yale and has done post graduate work in several departments of Harvard University. He has tried to do several kinds of work since he graduated, but has proved a failure in everything.

I have great sympathy for the man, but I really do not believe that he can write a book that anybody would care to buy and read. I have tried several times to find a place that he could fill, but have not been successful. Yours very truly,

Booker T. Washington

TLpS Con. 62 BTW Papers DLC.

To Oswald Garrison Villard

Tuskegee Institute, Alabama August 29, 1912

Dear Mr. Villard: Mr. Scott has already replied to your letter of August 5th referring to the National Emancipation Memorial Society. I feel, however, that I ought to send you a personal word.

I have done my best to urge Jesse Lawson and the other leaders of the Washington movement to make their celebration local — that is, show the progress of the colored people in the District of Columbia.

In this they could succeed. In attempting to spread out as they are now doing, however, without any money, I fear that the whole thing is going to prove a fiasco. In spite of repeated refusals on my part to consent to be one of the members of the committee, Mr. Lawson has used my name.

The enclosed slip shows the plan for the celebration which the Executive Committee of the National Negro Business League decided upon sometime ago.[1] This, I think, is the only practicable thing that can be done now, since Congress refused to make any appropriation.

I think I shall have to talk with you about the "Colonel"[2] when I see you, as there is the deepest disappointment among the colored people. Yours very truly,

Booker T. Washington

TLS   Oswald Garrison Villard Papers   MH.   A press copy is in Con. 63, BTW Papers, DLC.

[1] The enclosure suggested a local rather than a national celebration of the fiftieth anniversary of emancipation. (Con. 63, BTW Papers, DLC.)
[2] Theodore Roosevelt.

To George Woodward Wickersham

[Tuskegee, Ala.] August 30, 1912

My dear Mr. Wickersham: I cannot find words with which to sufficiently thank you for the brave and statesmanlike manner in which you have stood by our friend, Mr. William H. Lewis.

I am sure that all right thinking people in the United States honor you for what you have done. But for your efforts I feel sure that Mr. Lewis and the other colored men would have been turned out of the association.[1]

Our race shall never cease to thank you. Yours very truly,

Booker T. Washington

TLpS   Con. 458   BTW Papers   DLC.

[1] American Bar Association.

BIBLIOGRAPHY

THIS BIBLIOGRAPHY gives fuller information on works cited in the annotations and endnotes. It is not intended to be comprehensive of works on the subjects dealt with in the volume or of works consulted in the process of annotation.

Antin, Mary. *The Promised Land.* Boston and New York: Houghton Mifflin Co., 1912.

Barr, Alwyn. *Black Texans: A History of Negroes in Texas, 1528–1971.* Austin, Tex.: Jenkins Publishing Co., 1973.

Brooks, Aubrey Lee. *Walter Clark, Fighting Judge.* Chapel Hill: University of North Carolina Press, 1944.

Burrell, W. P., and D. E. Johnson. *Twenty-five Years History of the Grand Fountain of the United Order of True Reformers, 1881–1905.* Richmond, Va.: privately printed, 1909; reprint: Negro Universities Press, 1970.

Coan, Josephus Roosevelt. "The Expansion of Missions of the African Methodist Episcopal Church in South Africa, 1896–1908." Ph.D. dissertation, Hartford Seminary Foundation, 1961.

Edmonds, Helen G. *The Negro and Fusion Politics in North Carolina, 1894–1901.* Chapel Hill: University of North Carolina Press, 1951.

Gerber, David A. *Black Ohio and the Color Line, 1860–1915.* Urbana: University of Illinois Press, 1976.

Henson, Matthew A. *A Negro Explorer at the North Pole.* New York: Frederick A. Stokes Co., 1912.

Kellogg, Charles Flint. *NAACP: A History of the National Associa-*

tion for the Advancement of Colored People, 1909–1920. Baltimore: Johns Hopkins University Press, 1967.

Mohamed, Duse. *In the Land of the Pharaohs, a Short History of Egypt from the Fall of Ismail to the Assassination of Boutros Pasha.* New York: D. Appleton and Co., 1911; 2nd ed., London: Frank Cass and Co., Ltd., 1968.

Murray, Pauli. *Proud Shoes, the Story of an American Family.* New York: Harper and Brothers, 1956.

Osofsky, Gilbert. *Harlem, the Making of a Ghetto: Negro New York, 1890–1910.* New York: Harper and Row, 1966.

Rice, Lawrence D. *The Negro in Texas, 1874–1900.* Baton Rouge: Louisiana State University Press, 1971.

Talbert, Horace. *The Sons of Allen.* Zenia, Ohio: Aldine Press, 1906.

Tindall, George Brown. *The Emergence of the New South, 1913–1945.* Baton Rouge: Louisiana State University Press, 1967.

Washington, Ernest Davidson, ed. *Selected Speeches of Booker T. Washington.* Garden City, N.Y.: Doubleday, Doran and Co., 1932.

Weare, Walter B. *Black Business in the New South: A Social History of the North Carolina Mutual Life Insurance Company.* Urbana: University of Illinois Press, 1973.

Woodward, C. Vann. *Origins of the New South, 1877–1913.* Baton Rouge: Louisiana State University Press, 1951.

INDEX

591

intoxicated, 117-18, 119; attorneys offer services, 44-45, 159; believes he will be vindicated, 36; blames Tammany Hall politics for decision in trial, 414; certificate from doctor requested, 112-13; claims innocence of wrongdoing in Ulrich case, 47; claims to be victim of perjury, 372, 373, 414; congratulated for bringing assailant before court, 22; critics softened by Ulrich incident, 46; defended by Seth Low, 25; defended in newspaper editorials, 365-66, 367-68; denies addressing indecent remarks to woman, 85; denies attack was justified, 42; denies exonerating assailant, 108; evasive when questioned, 115; excessive drinking rumored, 417, 418; expresses gratitude to W. H. Taft for support, 64-65; expressions of confidence appreciated, 369; expressions of sympathy received upon acquittal of assailant, 355-56, 357, 358, 362, 368-69; eyewitness describes BTW's demeanor after being assaulted, 8; growing impatient with case, 272, 278; handling of case criticized in newspaper editorial, 34-35; has support of W. H. Taft, 25; loyalty of C. W. Anderson, 65-66; notoriety causes trouble at New York hotel, 92-93; offered lessons in self-defense, 13; orders search for letter explaining his presence in New York City, 3, 4; payment of witnesses, 40, 87-88; physical condition after assault, 26, 75, 107; physician certifies no intoxication, 96-97, 114-15; plans strategy with lawyer, 40-41, 267-68; police officer seeks promotion, 124-25, 128, 160, 176, 190, 468-69; receives advice from former student, 50-51; receives advice from T. Roosevelt, 50; receives letter of support from W. H. Taft, 10; receives poem from well-wisher, 44; receives report on press coverage, 36; receives sympathetic letters, 4, 5, 6-7, 10, 11, 12, 13, 14, 15, 18, 19, 20, 22, 23, 30; reportedly exonerates assailant,

102; resolution of NAACP, 69; results in criticism from northern whites, 417-18; seeks statement from police department, 127; sees good resulting from, 80; sees no change in support, 110-11; sentiment in New York City favorable, 82; strategy in case, 42, 43, 104-5, 156, 170-71; supported by mayor of New York, 76; supported by Methodist Episcopal Church, 33; supported by whites in Tuskegee, 94, 96; supported in southern newspapers, 52; thanks NAACP for resolution, 109; thanks W. H. Taft for support, 16; treatment at hospital, 98; unfavorable publicity, 288-89; version of incident questioned, 100-102; views of wife, 24; W. H. Taft criticized for supporting, 35; wants to publicize incarceration of assailant, 426; whereabouts of D. C. Smith questioned, 54; writes letter of recommendation for police officer, 450, 456; writes letter of thanks to witness, 461

Washington, Booker Taliaferro, Jr., *2:361-62; 331, 559; father sees developing maturity, 382; letter to, 10; named in BTW's will, 212

Washington, Charles Dean, *8:323, *215; letter to, 214-15

Washington, Ernest Davidson, *2:518-19; 36; named in BTW's will, 212

Washington, John Henry, *2:5-6; 120, 550; letter to, 89-90; named in BTW's will, 212; receives whiskey as Christmas present, 388

Washington, John Henry, Jr., *8:323; 295

Washington, Lilla D., 291, *292

Washington, Margaret James Murray, *2:514-15; 194, 195, 429, 577; believes good will result from Ulrich incident, 24; elected president of National Association of Colored Women, 578; letter to, 168; letter to Lucy B. Johnston, 539-40; letter to Lugenia B. Hope, 24; named in BTW's will, 212; receives whiskey as